Encyclopedia of Energy

Encyclopedia of Energy

Morris A. Pierce
University of Rochester
GENERAL EDITOR

Volume III

Jamaica – Rwanda

Salem Press

A Division of EBSCO Publishing
Ipswich, Massachusetts

The paper used in these volumes conforms to the American National Standard for Permanence of Paper for Printed Library Materials, X39.48-1992 (R1997).

LIBRARY OF CONGRESS CATALOGING-IN-PUBLICATION DATA

Encyclopedia of energy / Morris A. Pierce, University of Rochester, general editor.
    pages cm
 Includes bibliographical references and index.
  ISBN 978-1-58765-849-5 (set) -- ISBN 978-1-58765-850-1 (volume 1) -- ISBN 978-1-58765-851-8 (volume 2) -- ISBN 978-1-58765-852-5 (volume 3) -- ISBN 978-1-58765-853-2 (volume 4) -- ISBN 978-1-58765-854-9 (ebook set) (print) 1. Power resources--Encyclopedias. I. Pierce, Morris A.
 TJ163.16.E47 2013
 333.7903--dc23
                        2012020281

First Printing

PRINTED IN THE UNITED STATES OF AMERICA

Produced by Golson Media

Contents

Jamaica

Official Name: Jamaica.
Category: Geography of Energy.
Summary: Jamaica relies heavily on imported petroleum to meet the energy needs of its transportation sector and its bauxite/alumina industry, the high and volatile price of which threatens the island nation's economic development.

Jamaica's heavy reliance on fossil fuels for energy has placed its economy at a disadvantage. The high and volatile cost of imported petroleum, which is the source of 95 percent of the island nation's energy matrix, has hampered its development. The transportation sector uses the largest share of imported petroleum, followed by the bauxite and alumina industry and finally by electric power generation.

The economic downturn that has affected the global economy since 2008 has exacerbated these conditions by hampering tourism and the bauxite/alumina industry. As a result, unemployment in Jamaica has remained in the double digits. As Jamaica's foreign debt continues to rise, the country is in need of alternatives to imported petroleum to power its future. Petroleum as a primary energy source also raises environmental and climate change concerns to which Jamaica, as a signer of the Kyoto Protocol, is sensitive.

In response, Jamaica has sought to diversify its energy portfolio. Government policy explicitly seeks to expand alternative and renewable fuel use with the aims of mitigating harmful environmental impacts, controlling spiraling energy costs, and creating local jobs. These goals exist within the context of the need to foster economic and human development and to adapt to natural hazards because of environmental change. Although Jamaica's geography has not lent itself to significant oil and natural gas discoveries, the island nation has other resources at its disposal.

Jamaica is one of a few Caribbean nations that have demonstrated an interest in nuclear energy. While it has no commercial nuclear reactors operational, it has a small reactor at the University of the West Indies' Mona Campus.

More notable is the expansion and development of indigenous renewable resources. Since Jamaica was a successful sugar-producing colony before its independence in 1962, the use of bagasse, an energy-intensive by-product of sugar production, has contributed to Jamaica's energy mix. About 3 percent of Jamaica's electricity production capacity can run on bagasse, but most of that is used in the sugar processing itself, and only a small percentage is sold back to the national electric grid.

Other biofuels, such as ethanol, are more significant to Jamaica's economy than to its energy mix. For example, an ethanol production plant uses feedstock from Brazil to create ethanol to be sold to the United States, while using little of it locally. However, Jamaica's recent mandate that all gasoline contain at least 10 percent ethanol has expanded the local market.

Currently, about 3 percent of Jamaica's electric production capacity is in the form of small hydroelectric dams. Interest in tapping much more of the island's hydroelectric potential is mitigated by difficulties in financing, because the current high debt level makes funding capital-intensive projects, such as dams, difficult.

Jamaica's location and topography also show promise for the use of wind to generate electricity. Only 1 percent of Jamaica's electricity, however, is currently generated by wind. Although wind power capacity has been and is expected to continue to expand, growth in overall energy demand has outpaced this capacity. Thus, while real wind capacity has been growing, the percentage of Jamaica's energy that comes from the wind has been shrinking.

Energy Efficiency

Energy efficiency is a tool that Jamaica has embraced in meeting its energy needs. Simple and cost-effective energy efficiency solutions are being supported by the government, such as the use of more efficient lighting. One pilot program showed a reduction of 25 percent of peak energy demand. Other programs are being tested and expanded around the country.

Human development is an important part of Jamaica's energy future. Currently approximately 90 percent of households have access to electricity. There have been small efforts to provide the remaining 10 percent of unelectrified population with solar energy. With more than 15 percent of the population living below the poverty line and

unemployment exceeding 10 percent, the affordability of energy is as important as its availability in meeting the country's human development goals.

Debora Ley

Further Reading
Central Intelligence Agency. "Jamaica." In *The World Factbook*. https://www.cia.gov/library/publications/the-world-factbook/geos/jm.html.
Jamaica Ministry of Energy and Mining. "About MEM." http://www.mem.gov.jm/men.htm.
United Nations, Economic Commission for Latin America and the Caribbean. "A Study on Energy Issues in the Caribbean: Potential For Mitigating Climate Change." LC/CAR/L.233, December 3, 2009. http://www.eclac.org/portofspain/publicaciones/xml/8/38238/lcarl233.pdf.
U.S. Energy Information Administration. "Country Analysis Brief: Jamaica." http://205.254.135.7/countries/country-data.cfm?fips=JM.

See Also: Biodiesel; Ethanol: Corn; Natural Gas; Parsons, Charles; Solar Thermal Systems.

Japan

Official Name: State of Japan.
Category: Geography of Energy.
Summary: Japan's energy production is focused on fossil fuels, and its consumption of energy is concentrated in the commercial and public services sectors.

The country of Japan is a highly developed, technologically advanced Asian country located to the east of the Korean Peninsula and off mainland China. Japan is surrounded by the North Pacific Ocean and the Sea of Japan, along with the East China Sea and the Philippine Sea to its south.

With the world's third-largest economy after those of the United States and China, Japan had an estimated $5.4 trillion gross domestic product (GDP), based on official exchange rates, as of 2010.

Furthermore, based on July 2011 estimates, Japan had the 10th-largest population in the world, with an estimated 126.5 million people.

Japan has relatively few domestic resources for energy production and consequently is heavily reliant on the importation of energy resources, including coal, natural gas, and petroleum. Japanese firms, however, are widely involved in global, upstream energy operations.

While most of the following is based on 2008, 2009, and 2010 data, it is important to note that Japan suffered from a severe earthquake registering 9.0 on the Richter scale on March 11, 2011. The ensuing tsunami and consequent loss of life and property, which included severe damage to the country's electricity generation and specifically its Fukushima Daiichi nuclear power plants, dealt the country a major blow and could hinder the future development of nuclear power plants not only in Japan but also around the world.

Energy Production

In 2008, Japan had slightly more than 280 gigawatts of total installed electricity-generating capacity. Like its global economic ranking, this installed electricity-generating capacity was also ranked third globally, after the United States and China. (There is often a correlation between the size of a country's economy and the overall amount of electricity that it produces.)

Throughout 2008, Japan generated about 1 petawatt-hours of electricity. In 2009, which was comparable to the years 1990 through 2008, approximately 63 percent of Japan's electricity was generated with conventional thermal resources, while 27 percent of its electricity came from nuclear power plants and 8 percent of its electricity came from hydroelectric power.

It is important to note that the largest power company in Japan is the Tokyo Electric Power Company, and the company generates more than a quarter (approximately 27 percent) of Japan's electricity. This concentration in the national electricity sector is unusual compared to the United States, but other countries, such as Mexico, have greater concentrations of domestic energy resources due to state ownership.

Thermal Resources

Japan, like many countries around the world, largely depends on conventional thermal resources for its electricity generation. The country's coal and natural gas resources combine to generate about 54 percent of the country's electricity, or the equivalent of about 86 percent of Japan's total conventional thermal resources (54 percent divided by 63 percent).

Among all of the available energy resources and specifically within the conventional thermal resources category, coal accounts for the largest share of Japan's electricity generation, at approximately 28 percent. This is comparable to other large economies, such as the United States, China, Germany, and Australia.

However, as previously mentioned, Japan has relatively few domestic energy resources. As opposed to the United States and China, which both have extensive domestic coal supplies, Japan's coal production ended in 2002. In 2009, Japan imported 182 million short tons of coal, supplied mainly by Australia.

Ranked a close second place behind coal in the conventional thermal resources category and steadily increasing over the last several years in its importance for Japan's electricity generation is natural gas, which accounts for about 26 percent of the country's electricity.

Japan does have some domestic sources of natural gas. According to the *Oil and Gas Journal*, "Japan had 738 billion cubic feet of proven natural gas reserves as of January 2011. Natural gas proven reserves have declined since 2007, when they measured 1.4 trillion cubic feet."

Geographically speaking, such natural gas fields are primarily located along Japan's western coast in the Sea of Japan. Nearly 50 percent of Japan's domestic natural gas is produced at the natural gas field of Minami-Nagaoka, also located on the western coast.

Japan has a large nuclear power industry, and its significance to Japan cannot be overstated; in fact, Japan is the third-largest producer of nuclear energy, after France and the United States.

Japan is reported to have a total of 54 operating nuclear reactors with a total installed generating capacity of nearly 50 gigawatts. In 2009, Japan produced an estimated 266 terawatt-hours of electricity from nuclear power plants, which represented approximately 24 percent of the country's total in 2008. Nuclear power plants can be found throughout Japan, including near the northern city of Sapporo, the southern city of Nagasaki, and on both the east and west coasts. Japan's surface area is much smaller than that of the United States, and its nuclear power plants are much closer together than are those in the United States.

As previously mentioned, Japan experienced a severe earthquake in March 2011 which has had a severe and ongoing effect on the country's total number of operating nuclear power plants and consequently its total installed generating capacity. Prior to this incident and according to the U.S. Energy Information Administration, "the government [of Japan had] stated plans to increase nuclear's share of total electricity generation from 24 percent in 2008 to 40 percent by 2017 and to 50 percent by 2030, according to the Ministry of Economy, Trade and Industry."

In the months and years following the Fukushima nuclear accident, caused by a seismic event that was not that unusual in a zone vulnerable to seismic events, Japan will face challenges dealing with its nuclear polices and both international or domestic investment in nuclear energy. In the

Wikimedia

An aerial view of the damage in Japan in March 2011 after a 9.0 magnitude earthquake and subsequent tsunami devasted the area. This disaster has had a severe and ongoing effect on the country's total number of operating nuclear power plants and consequently its total installed generating capacity.

short term, it is expected that natural gas and coal imports will supplement the loss of nuclear power.

From 1990 to 2009, approximately 8 percent of Japan's annual electricity generation was via hydropower. Like Japan's nuclear power plants, Japan's hydroelectric power facilities are also spread throughout the country. The top two hydroelectric projects in Japan, Niikappu and Takami, are owned by the Hokkaido Electric Power Company, while other top hydroelectric plants are owned by the Tokyo Electric Power Company. All of the top ten hydroelectric projects, listed below, are of the pumped storage design:

1. Niikappu
2. Takami
3. Daini Numazawa
4. Shin Takasegawa
5. Tamahara
6. Imaichi
7. Shiobara
8. Kazunogawa
9. Azumi
10. Kannagawa

As a highly developed, technologically advanced country, Japan has several domestic firms involved in the solar photovoltaic industry, including Honda, Kyocera, Mitsubishi, Panasonic-Sanyo, Sharp, and Toshiba. While solar contributes only a minor fraction of Japan's overall electricity generation, such firms are having a global impact on the solar industry.

Located in the volcanic Ring of Fire region, Japan also has significant geothermal resources. In fact, Japan is currently ranked sixth in the world among the largest geothermal energy producing countries, after the United States, the Philippines, Italy, Mexico, and Indonesia.

Such geothermal energy resources are located throughout Japan but primarily in the northern and southern parts of the country, with little representation in central Japan.

Energy Consumption

Although Japan does not rely very much on petroleum for electricity generation, approximately 46 percent of the nation's total energy consumption in 2008 was from oil. Thus, the transportation sector and particularly gasoline consumption contribute to this energy usage.

Comparable to Japan's domestic coal resources, which stopped producing in 2002, Japan has very limited domestic oil reserves. According to the *Oil and Gas Journal* (*OGJ*), Japan's oil reserves were "44 million barrels as of January 2011, ... down from the 58 million barrels reported by *OGJ* in 2007." Similar to Japan's natural gas fields, the country's domestic oil fields are primarily located on its western coastline.

The U.S. Energy Information Administration explains that "the government's 2006 energy strategy plan encourages Japanese companies to increase energy exploration and development projects around the world to secure a stable supply of oil and natural gas. The Japan Bank for International Cooperation supports upstream companies by offering loans at favorable rates, thereby allowing Japanese companies to bid effectively for projects in key producing countries. ... The government's goal is to import 40 percent of the country's total crude oil imports from Japanese-owned concessions by 2030, up from the current estimated 19 percent."

International petroleum projects in which Japanese firms are participating involve several nations, including Algeria, Azerbaijan, Brazil, Canada, Egypt, Kuwait, Indonesia, Norway, Russia, and Vietnam. Japan has diversified the nations with which it does business, including both developing and developed countries along with those of the Organization of Petroleum Exporting Countries (OPEC). It has assisted non-OPEC countries in various oil development projects.

Japan is the world's third-largest oil consumer (after the United States and China), the world's third-largest net importer of crude oil, the world's largest importer of liquefied natural gas (LNG), and the world's largest importer of coal.

As previously mentioned, Japan imports a significant amount of coal from Australia. It is important to note that other large regional sources of coal, although not necessarily exporters to Japan, include China, Indonesia, and the United States.

In terms of crude oil consumption, Japan is largely dependent on Saudi Arabia, the United Arab Emirates (UAE), and Qatar, which collectively account for approximately 59 percent of Japan's supply. In fact, more than 75 percent of Japan's crude oil imports are from OPEC nations.

In contrast, Japan's LNG imports are mainly from countries other than those from which it imports its crude oil, although Japan's LNG suppliers are similarly concentrated among only a few countries. The top three are Malaysia, Australia, and Indonesia, which collectively account for approximately 57.2 percent of Japan's LNG imports.

In 2008, Japan consumed approximately 964 terawatt-hours of electricity. Slightly more than one-third of this electricity (351 terawatt-hours) was consumed in the commercial and public services sector, with the industry (304 terawatt-hours) and residential (288 terawatt-hours) sectors coming in second and third, respectively. Within this residential sector and its energy consumption, it is important to note that Japan's largest cities are Tokyo (the capital), with 36.507 million people; Osaka-Kobe, at 11.325 million; Nagoya, at 3.257 million; Fukuoka-Kitakyushu, at 2.809 million; and Sapporo, 2.673 million. (Population estimates are for 2009.) Although Sapporo is located in northern Japan and Fukuoka-Kitakyushu is located in southern Japan, Japan's largest three cities are concentrated in its central region.

According to the U.S. Central Intelligence Agency's *World Factbook*, Japan's industry is mainly concentrated in motor vehicles (with companies such as Honda and Toyota), electronic equipment (Kyocera, Mitsubishi, Panasonic-Sanyo, Sharp, and Toshiba), machine tools, steel and nonferrous metals, ships, chemicals, textiles, and processed foods. Many of these are energy-intensive industries, accounting for the key role of industry in Japan's overall energy consumption.

BRIAN MCFARLAND

Further Reading

Central Intelligence Agency. "World Factbook: Japan." https://www.cia.gov/library/publications/the-world-factbook/geos/ja.html.

Federation of Electric Power Companies of Japan. "Location of Power Plants." http://www.fepc.or.jp/english/energy_electricity/location/index.html.

Institute of Energy Economics, Japan. "About IEEJ." http://eneken.ieej.or.jp/en/about/index.html.

Japan Agency for Natural Resources and Energy. "What's New!" http://www.enecho.meti.go.jp/english/index.htm.

Japan Atomic Power Company. "Corporate Overview." http://www.japc.co.jp/english/company/index.html.

Japan Coal Energy Center. "Outline of JCOAL." http://www.jcoal.or.jp/overview_en/overview.html.

Japan Oil, Gas and Metals National Corporation. "About Us: Overview." http://www.jogmec.go.jp/english/aboutus/index.html.

New Energy Foundation. "Geothermal Power Plants in Japan." http://www.nef.or.jp/english/new/pre_geo.html.

Nuclear Safety Commission of Japan. "About NSC: Overview." http://www.nsc.go.jp/NSCenglish/aboutus/overview/overview.htm.

U.S. Energy Information Administration. "Country Analyis Brief: Japan." http://205.254.135.7/countries/country-data.cfm?fips=JA.

See Also: Australia; Natural Gas; Nuclear Power; Oil and Petroleum; Organization of Petroleum Exporting Countries.

Jordan

Official Name: Hashemite Kingdom of Jordan.
Category: Geography of Energy.
Summary: This Middle Eastern country relies on imports for its oil and natural gas consumption. The government is actively seeking alternative sources of energy to support the growing demand for electricity that has accompanied the country's economic diversification and population growth.

The Hashemite Kingdom of Jordan is small country located in the Levant region of western Asia. Jordan is landlocked with the exception of 16 miles (26 kilometers) of coast on the Gulf of Aqaba. With few naturally occurring sources of energy and a semidry climate, Jordan's municipal demand for energy has pushed the state to investigate alternative energy sources to meet both energy and water consumption needs. Attempts by the government to encourage the adoption of renewable energy sources such as biofuel, solar energy, and wind power have not been widely implemented.

Lack of Natural Resources

Jordan's lack of natural resources is reflected in the relatively small size of its economy in comparison with those of other countries in the Middle East. Domestic energy requirements in Jordan are met using imported oil, petroleum, and natural gas products. According to the Central Intelligence Agency's *World Factbook*, Jordan imports an estimated 108,200 barrels of oil per day and consumes 108,000 barrels per day. In 2008, Jordan produced only 820 million cubic feet (250 million cubic meters) of natural gas and consumed 9.5 billion cubic feet (2.97 billion cubic meters).

Jordan is connected to the Arab Gas Pipeline, which carries exported oil from Egypt to Jordan. The first section of the pipeline is divided into three segments. The first segment consists of an overland pipeline and compression station and connects Al Arish, Egypt, with Taba, Egypt, on the Red Sea coast. The second segment runs undersea from Taba, Egypt, to Aqaba, Jordan. The third segment links the pipeline to a metering station and the Aqaba Thermal Power Station. Another section runs from Aqaba, Jordan, to El Rehab, near the Jordan-Syrian border. Still another section was completed in 2008 and connects El Rehab to Homs, Syria. In 2006, Jordan, Egypt, Syria, Lebanon, Turkey, and Romania agreed to extend the pipeline to the Turkish border, opening up the possibility of delivering gas to European nations.

Although a lack of oil and natural gas deposits has posed a significant energy problem, Jordan does possess measurable quantities of oil shale and uranium that could be used as future sources of energy. Oil shale deposits have been found in 60 percent of Jordanian territory, the equivalent of about 40 to 70 billion tons. The most significant oil shale deposits are all located within 46 miles (75 kilometers) of the Dead Sea, namely, Juref ed Darawish, Sultani, Wadi Maghar, El Lajjun, Attarat Umm Ghudran, Khan ez Zabib, Siwaga, and Wadi Thamad. Jordanian oil shale was mined by the Ottomans before and during World War I. Jordanian deposits are high in sulfur content and will require additional processing to yield usable petroleum products. In 2008, Jordan's Ministries of Energy and Natural Resources, the National Electricity Power Company, and Eesti Energia signed an agreement granting Eesti Energia the exclusive right to build an oil shale power station by 2015.

In addition to oil shale, Jordan is exploring the use of its uranium deposits as a potential source of energy. Jordan's uranium reserves amount to 2 percent of the world's total, or about 180,000 tons of uranium derived from uranic ore and phosphate deposits. Although neither of these resources has been incorporated into Jordan's current energy supply, various studies and negotiations are under way to establish uranium and oil shale as sustainable domestic energy resources.

Jordan is exploring the possibility of using its uranium deposits to create nuclear power. In 2007, the Jordanian government unveiled the National Nuclear Energy Strategy, a long-term plan aimed at mitigating the expense of importing oil from neighboring countries by introducing nuclear power stations for the generation of electricity. The government hopes to establish a nuclear program that can supply 30 percent of Jordan's electricity by 2030 or 2040. While no power reactors are currently under construction, the Jordanian government has cultivated a regulatory infrastructure to implement its nuclear energy plans.

Jordan is embarking on several research and development initiatives concerning alternative energy sources. In 1987, the government spearheaded a program to popularize the use of wind energy, but as of 2009 there were only eight wind energy stations in Jordan. Through institutions such as the National Energy Research Center, the Jordanian government is researching the possibility of incorporating biofuel, wind, solar, and photovoltaic power into its energy resources.

ALLISON HARTNETT

Further Reading

Ababneh, Mohammad, et al. "Investigation of Wind Energy in Jordan." International Conference and Exhibition on Green Energy and Sustainability for Arid Regions and Mediterranean Countries, June 15–17, 2009. http://www.eis.hu.edu.jo/Deanshipfiles/conf10462326.pdf.

Araj, Kamal. "Case Study: Programme for Nuclear Energy Development in Jordan." Interregional Workshop on Long-Range Nuclear Energy Programme Planning and Strategy Development. Jordan Atomic Energy Commission, June 14–17, 2010. http://www.iaea.org/ NuclearPower/Downloads/INPRO/Files/2010-June-IR-WS/Jordan_Energy_Workshop June2010_Vienna _rev2.pdf.

Central Intelligence Agency. "Jordan." In *The World Factbook*. https://www.cia.gov/library/publications/the-world-factbook/geos/jo.html.

Kabariti, Malek. "Identification of National Energy Policies and Access in Jordan." Paper presented at the Energy Research Group at the American University of Beirut, Lebanon, January 25, 2005. http://webfea.fea.aub.edu.lb/fea/research/erg/web/Policy%20Paper%20Jordan.pdf.

U.S. Energy Information Administration. "Country Analysis Brief: Jordan." http://tonto.eia.doe.gov/country/country_energy_data.cfm?fips=JO.

World Nuclear Association. "Emerging Nuclear Energy Countries." http://www.world-nuclear.org/info/inf102.html.

See Also: Aramco; Egypt; History of Energy: Ancient Rome; Iraq; Nuclear Power; Oil Shales; Saudi Arabia; Syria.

Joule, James

Dates: 1818–1889.
Category: Biographies.
Summary: James Joule made major contributions to the fields of heat, electricity, and thermodynamics, and was the first scientist to grasp the connection between heat and other forms of energy. He is best known for his articulation of the second law of thermodynamics, Joule's law, and the Joule-Thomson effect.

One of the most important physicists of the 19th century, James Prescott Joule was born on Christmas Eve 1818, in Salford, Lancashire, near Manchester, England. Joule's father was a wealthy brewer. Because he was ill as a young child, Joule was tutored at home until the age of 16 when he began studying mathematics and natural philosophy with eminent chemist John Dalton (1766–1844), who taught at the scientific academy of the Manchester Literary and Philosophical Society (later Manchester University). Under Dalton's tutelage, Joule examined current hot topics in science such as the caloric theory of heat, mechanics of the steam engine, and complexity of electric motors. He had a personal interest in such issues because the brewery was considering replacing its steam engine with the newer electric motor. That interest led Joule to conduct experiments in electrolysis, magnetic attraction, and electric motors. While still a teenager, Joule attempted to build a

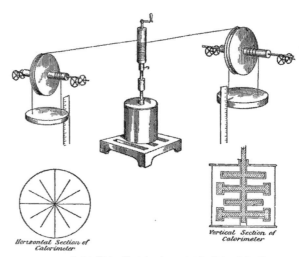

Joule's Water-Churning Apparatus for Determining the Mechanical Equivalent of Heat.

To obtain the mechanical equivalent of heat, Joule's apparatus churned water in a cylinder with paddles using a measured amount of mechanical energy. The rise in temperature was recorded and the heat generated calculated.

▷ *The Joule Effect*

Joule also developed the Joule effect, which states that when gas is allowed to freely expand into a vacuum, there is no apparent change in temperature. Joule's findings on the mechanical equivalent of heat became an essential element in teaching basic physics classes. Joule developed this theory as a result of his "paddle experiment" in which he used an insulated container holding liquid and paddle wheels. The system was controlled by a system of pulleys and weights. As the weights fell, they caused the paddles to agitate the liquid inside the container, resulting in a rise in temperature. The experiment allowed Joule to estimate the mechanical equivalent of heat, which became known as the Joule, referred to as "J" or "kJ."

Joule's law of conservation of energy became accepted as the first law of thermodynamics and has major implications for chemistry. The law states that changes in energy that occur within a system are equivalent to the heat in the system, plus the system itself, minus the labor produced by the system. Joule also conducted experiments on magnetostriction, determining that the shape of materials such as nickel, iron, and cobalt changes slightly in response to magnetization. That process is still referred to as Joule magnetostriction because he was the first to identify it.

perpetual motion machine, but eventually gave it up.

Because Joule continued to work at the brewery, most of his experiments were done in the early morning before the brewery opened, or late at night after it closed. Joule and his elder brother Benjamin took over the brewery when their father's health began to fail, and his passion for science was often viewed by family and friends as only an interesting hobby. In 1847, Joule married Amelia Grimes of Liverpool. She died in 1854, leaving him with a son and a daughter. His experimentations with heat led him to reject the popular caloric theory and replace it with a new mechanical theory of heat. Eventually, the success of his experiments and his conviction that he had viable contributions to make to the field won him respect from his peers.

Brought on by the Industrial Revolution, major changes were occurring in the understanding of scientific phenomenon during Joule's lifetime. He was the first scientist to recognize the relationship between heat and mechanical energy. Joule's early work was influenced by that of German physician and physicist Julius Robert von Mayer (1814–78), who is considered the founder of the principle of the conservation of energy. By 1840, Joule had articulated Joule's law, which states that heat produced within a wire by a constant direct current is always equal to the resistance of the current times the square of the current.

Joule met Scottish mathematician and physicist William Thomson, Lord Kelvin (1824–1907), at the British Association for the Advancement of Science in 1847. Thomson's interest in the result of Joule's paddle-wheel experiments also generated interest among other scientists at the meeting. The two men subsequently developed a prolonged and collaborative professional relationship. In 1854, they identified the cooling effect that became known as the Joule-Thomson effect as a result of the "porous-plug experiments," which allowed them to ascertain that temperatures of gases decrease when they are expanded through a porous plug under external pressure.

Joule's contributions were officially recognized by his peers in 1850 when he was elected as a fellow of the Royal Society. In 1870, he was awarded the Copley Medal by the society. Joule lost much of his fortune in 1875, and his health began to decline in subsequent years. He died in Sale, England, in 1889. His legacy continues to have major implications for modern electrical and refrigeration systems. Designers and manufacturers of contemporary refrigerators, freezers, air conditioners, heat pumps, and dehumidifiers all regularly employ his findings when creating their products. Utility companies also use his theories to determine supplies of voltage to their customers.

ELIZABETH RHOLETTER PURDY

Further Reading

Cardwell, Donald S. L. *James Joule: A Biography.* New York: Manchester University Press, 1989.

Cropper, William H. *Great Physicists: The Life and Times of Leading Physicists From Galileo to Hawking.* New York: Oxford University Press, 2001.

North, John, ed. *Mid-Nineteenth Century Scientists.* New York: Pergamon Press, 1969.

Segrè, Emilio. *From Falling Bodies to Radio Waves: Classical Physicists and Their Discoveries.* New York: W. H. Freeman, 1984.

Steffens, Henry John. *James Prescott Joule and the Concept of Energy.* Dawson, NY: Science History Publications, 1979.

See Also: Clausius, Rudolf; History of Energy: 1800–1850; Thermodynamics; Thompson, Benjamin (Count Rumford); Thomson, William (Lord Kelvin).

Kansas

Category: Energy in the United States.
Summary: A landlocked U.S. state bordered by Colorado, Nebraska, Missouri, and Oklahoma, Kansas has substantial fossil fuel resources, including natural gas, crude oil, and coal-bed methane, as well as excellent potential for developing wind power.

Kansas is a landlocked midwestern state that contains both the geographic center of the 48 contiguous U.S. states and the geodetic center of North America. It is the 15th-largest state (52.6 million acres) and has the third most cropland (26.5 million acres) of any U.S. state. It is relatively sparsely populated: Kansas's population of 2,744,687 ranks 34th in the United States, and the population density of 32.9 people per square mile places it at 40th. The state has a continental climate with cold winters and hot summers, and average precipitation between 1971 and 2000 was 28.8 inches annually. Major crops include corn, wheat, sorghum, soybeans, and sunflowers, and the primary livestock raised are cattle, hogs, and sheep.

Kansas has substantial fossil fuel resources, including the Hugoton Natural Gas Area, the fifth-largest natural gas field in the United States, which is located in southwestern Kansas. The state has a crude oil reserve of 258 million barrels (1.3 percent of the U.S. total), dry natural gas reserves of 3,279 billion cubic feet (1.2 percent of the U.S. total), and natural gas plant liquids reserves of 162 million barrels (1.9 percent of the U.S. total). It is one of the top 10 oil-producing states in the United States and also conducts substantial oil refining. Crude oil production takes place throughout the state; in 2009, there were 56,009 crude oil-producing wells and 20 rotary rigs. The oil is delivered through a network of pipelines to three refineries, which jointly account for 2 percent of the crude-oil-refining capacity in the United States.

Kansas also produces ethanol at 11 production plants with a capacity of 432.5 million gallons per year and consumes 2.532 million barrels of ethanol annually, although state law does not require that gasoline be blended with ethanol. Kansas uses a higher-than-average amount of liquefied petroleum gas (LPG) compared to other U.S. states, but overall its petroleum consumption is in line with the size of its population.

Kansas produces substantial natural gas (with 21,243 wells as of 2009) and also serves as a transportation hub for natural gas being transported across the country. The Mid-Continent Center in Wichita merges natural gas production from several midwestern states and pipes it toward consumption markets in the eastern United States. Most of the natural gas wells and pipelines in the state are in the southwest, in the Anadarko Basin. Kansas consumes about 85 percent of the natural gas it produces, and most of the remainder is shipped to Missouri and Nebraska. Kansas also imports some natural gas from Colorado and Oklahoma.

Untapped Reserves

Kansas has untapped reserves of coal-bed methane, and exploitation of this resource is rapidly increasing in the Cherokee Platform, in the southeastern part of the state. Kansas has small bituminous coal reserves in the southeast as well, and two small coal mines, but most coal used in the state is imported, more than 80 percent from Wyoming. Of the total electricity used in the state, 75 percent is produced from coal-fired power plants. In January 2011, Kansas paid less, on average, for electricity than the United States as a whole: Average prices were 9.35 cents per kilowatt-hour for residential customers (versus the U.S. average of 10.99 cents), 7.94 cents per kilowatt-hour for commercial customers (versus the U.S. average of 9.88 cents), and 6.33 cents per kilowatt-hour for industrial customers (versus the U.S. average of 6.73 cents).

Total energy production in Kansas in 2008 was 843 trillion British thermal units (Btu), 1.2 percent of the U.S. total. This included 3.94 million barrels of crude oil (2.0 percent of the U.S. total), 354.44 billion cubic feet of natural gas (1.6 percent of the U.S. total), and 185,000 short tons of coal (less than 0.1 percent of the U.S. total). Total net electricity generated in January 2011 was 3.8 terawatt-hours, with the primary sources being coal-fired (2.57 terawatt-hours), nuclear (884 gigawatt-hours), renewable sources other than hydropower (278 gigawatt-hours), and natural-gas-fired (115 gigawatt-hours). Total energy consumption in 2008 was 1,136 trillion Btu (1.1 percent of the U.S. total), or 406 million Btu per capita. Total petroleum consumption was 76.8 million barrels, including 31.5 million barrels of motor gasoline, 17.9 million barrels of distil-

late fuel, 16.3 million barrels of liquefied petroleum gases, and 2.4 million barrels of jet fuel. The industrial sector was the largest consumer of energy in the state (420.006 trillion Btu), followed by the transportation sector (277.578 trillion Btu), the residential sector (232.903 trillion Btu), and the commercial sector (205.130 trillion Btu). Most home heating (72 percent) in Kansas is done by natural gas, followed by electricity (17 percent) and liquefied petroleum gas (10 percent). Emissions from the electric power industry in 2009 included 36,207,066 metric tons of carbon dioxide, 46,772 metric tons of sulfur dioxide, and 45,814 metric tons of nitrogen oxide.

Wind Power

Kansas has excellent potential for wind power development and is already one of the top 10 wind power producers in the United States. In 2008, Kansas produced 1.759 terawatt-hours of electric through wind power, 3.8 percent of the state total. Wind was the only substantial renewable source of energy in the state; hydropower produced 11 gigawatt-hours of electricity in 2008.

Kansas has one operating nuclear power plant, Wolf Creek in Coffey County in east-central Kansas, 55 miles south of Topeka and 90 miles southwest of Kansas City. The Wolf Creek plant, which began operation in 1985, is run by the Wolf Creek Nuclear Operating Corporation, a subsidiary of Kansas City Power and Light (which has 47 percent ownership), Kansas Gas and Electric (47 percent ownership), and Kansas Electric Power Cooperative (6 percent ownership). The Wolf Creek plant represents 9.7 percent of the state's total capacity but produces 18.2 percent of its power; it also exports power to Missouri. In 1985, its first year of operation, the Wolf Creek plant generated 3.856 terawatt-hours; in 2007, it generated 8.497 terawatt-hours.

Sarah Boslaugh

Further Reading

Evans, Catherine S. *Geothermal Energy and Heat Pump Potential in Kansas.* Lawrence: Kansas Geological Survey, 2011.

Kansas Energy Council. *Kansas Energy Report 2009.* January 7, 2009. kec.kansas.gov/energy_plan/energy_plan_09.pdf.

Kansas Energy Information Network. "Energy Information for Kansas and Beyond." http://www.kansasenergy.org/.

U.S. Energy Information Administration. "Kansas Renewable Energy Profile." http://www.eia.doe.gov/cneaf/solar.renewables/page/state_profiles/kansas.html.

Wolf Creek Nuclear Operating Corporation. "About Wolf Creek." http://www.wcnoc.com/aboutwolfcreek.htm.

See Also: Ethanol: Corn; Missouri; Natural Gas; Nuclear Power; Oil and Petroleum; United States; Wind Technology.

Kazakhstan

Official Name: Republic of Kazakhstan.
Category: Geography of Energy.
Summary: After the collapse of the Soviet Union in 1991, Kazakhstan required foreign investment and technology to develop its oil and gas reserves. Kazakhstan also exports uranium and the country is becoming an important alternative source of energy to the Middle East and Russia.

Kazakhstan is a former Soviet country that spans the region between the Caspian Sea to the west, Russia to the north, and China to the southeast. The country is not only vast in land area but also rich in natural resources.

Prior to 1991, Kazakhstan was part of the Soviet Union and accounted for only 6 percent of the empire's total oil production and 1 percent of its total gas production. After the collapse of the Soviet Union, Kazakhstan did not possess the technological or financial ability to explore and develop its immense oil and gas reserves independently. In order to do so, Kazakhstan required significant foreign investment and technological expertise from international oil and gas companies (IOCs). IOCs perceived Kazakhstan to be a key source of energy and, in that capacity, an alternative to Russia and the Middle East. Throughout the 1990s, IOCs signed contracts with the Kazakh government to develop and profit from the country's resources. Since 1993, Kazakhstan's extractive industries have attracted $30.7 billion in foreign investments, which constitutes 76 percent of the total foreign investment in the country.

Kazakhstan has experienced tremendous economic growth since it declared independence in 1991, but much of that growth has been resource-dependent. Minerals, oil, and gas made up 73 percent of the country's exports and 39 percent of its total gross domestic product (GDP) in 2008. The Kazakh government is trying to diversify its economy, but sectors such as manufacturing and agriculture are still lagging, and the country remains vulnerable to oil and resource price volatility.

In 2009, Kazakhstan produced 1.54 million barrels of oil per day, and the full development of the country's oil fields could make it one of the world's top five oil producers. Kazakhstan's proven natural gas reserves in 2010 were estimated at 85 trillion cubic feet, as the country shifted from being a net importer to a net exporter of gas. Moreover, Kazakhstan holds 15 percent of the world's uranium reserves and therefore is a key actor in the future of nuclear energy.

Kazakhstan's total energy consumption in 2007 was 2.3 quadrillion British thermal units (Btu), of which 57 percent was coal, 20 percent natural gas, 19 percent oil, and 3 percent hydroelectricity, and the remainder other sources.

Major Oil and Gas Investments

The Kazakh government and the IOCs signed a number of contracts in the 1990s that were typically 40 years in duration. These contracts vary in the level of control the IOC has over the resource, as well as the compensation agreement between the company and the Kazakh government.

In 2002, the government established KazMunaiGaz, a national oil company, in order to enhance its role in the development of the country's resources and represent its direct interest in oil and gas contracts. As of 2011, the majority of the oil contracts either were joint ventures with KazMunaiGaz or were production-sharing agreements (PSAs). In both types of contracts, the IOC bears the cost and risk of the exploration phase.

Some of the major IOCs to sign contracts include Chevron, the Italian state-owned company Eni, and the UK-based British Petroleum and the British Gas Group (BG). IOCs have targeted the three major oil and gas fields: the Tengiz field, the Karachaganak field, and the Kashagan field. Tengizchevroil, an operating company in which Chevron is the majority stakeholder, has developed the Tengiz field since 1993. The field is located on the Caspian Sea and is currently Kazakhstan's largest oil-producing field.

The Karachaganak field is located in northwestern Kazakhstan and has reserves of around 8 billion to 9 billion barrels of oil and 47 trillion cubic feet of natural gas. BG Group and the Eni have the two largest stakes in Karachaganak Petroleum Operating, the field's operating company.

The Kashagan field is located offshore in the northern Caspian Sea and is believed to be the largest oil field outside the Middle East and the fifth-largest in the world. The field's recoverable reserves are estimated at 11 billion barrels of oil. Although the field was expected to start producing in 2005, in 2010 production had not yet begun. The delays in oil production have caused tension between the Kazakh government and Agip KCO, the field's former operator, which in 2009 passed on its responsibilities to the North Caspian Operating Company.

Changing Energy Policy

As a result of the scale of foreign investment in energy resources, IOCs and the Kazakh government have become mutually dependent, although this relationship can be tense. Kazakhstan has come to rely on IOCs for a number of social services. The contracts require IOCs to spend approximately 1 percent of their capital expenditures—typically amounting to between $10 million and $20 million per year—on social projects. The money for social projects is used for building schools, hospitals, and water supply systems, as well as supporting community education programs. These programs have greatly assisted the Kazakh government to continue to provide citizens with social services previously provided by the Soviet system.

Kazakhstan signed agreements with IOCs at a time of financial distress and when significant foreign investment and technology were required to develop its resources. Managing relationships with IOCs has been a key feature of Kazakhstan's energy policy, and it is likely to continue to be so in the future. Now that the energy sector has had more than a decade since independence to develop,

Wikimedia

Three major oil and gas fields have been targeted by some of the major companies in Kazakhstan, one of which is located on the Caspian Sea (above) and is currently Kazakhsan's largest oil-producing field.

the government has pursued a strategy of reclaiming control over its resources.

In 2007, the government passed a law that allows the state to renegotiate existing oil contracts with IOCs where they are deemed to threaten Kazakhstan's security. There is a risk that the Kazakh government can use this legislation as a negotiating tool to maximize its share of oil revenues and minimize unwanted interference from IOCs. KazMunaiGaz, the state entity, typically plays an increasing role in the oil and gas sector. In early 2008, the government announced that all new contracts would be joint ventures with KazMunaiGaz as a majority owner. In 2010, the government established legislation requiring the majority of work to produce the oil to be carried out by Kazakh companies and employees.

Kazakhstan is also seeking to develop closer relations with China and Russia to reduce the country's reliance on Western IOCs. KazMunaiGaz has developed strong ties with China National Petroleum Corporation (CNPC); together, they co-own a pipeline that allows oil to be imported directly from Kazakhstan's Caspian shore and transported to western China. CNPC also operates five oil field development projects in Kazakhstan. Despite this trend, the European Union (EU) and the United States continue to engage with the region in order to secure their energy needs. In 2007, the EU signed a strategic partnership agreement with central Asia, a key component of which involved Kazakhstan.

Coal and Nuclear Energy

In 2008, Kazakhstan ranked 10th in the world in coal production. Of Kazakhstan's total energy consumption, 57 percent comes from coal, and it is used to generate 80 percent of the country's electricity. Kazakhstan also exports coal, primarily to Russia and Ukraine.

In the mid-1990s, Kazakhstan's coal mining was restructured and privatized; coal production has declined by about 35 percent since the 1991 dissolution of the Soviet Union. The decline is attributed to the restructuring of the sector and the lack of sufficient foreign investment to upgrade existing coal-production infrastructure.

Kazakhstan has large reserves of uranium, and in 2009 it became the number-one uranium producer, with almost 28 percent of world production. Kazatomprom, the state-owned atomic energy company (established in 1997), controls all uranium exploration and mining as well as other activities relating to nuclear power. Uranium exports represent an increasing strategic interest for the Kazakh government.

Kazakhstan had a single nuclear power reactor that operated from 1972 until 1999. The reactor generated electricity and provided power for desalination. A second reactor, destined to be installed in the southeast near Lake Balkash, has been stalled as a result of safety concerns.

LIVIA ALEXANDRA PAGGI

Further Reading

Cohen, Ariel, and Kevin Rosner. *Kazakhstan: Energy Cooperation With Russia; Oil, Gas, and Beyond.* London: GMB Publishing, 2006.

Jones, Luong Pauline, and Erika Weinthal. "Prelude to the Resource Curse: Explaining Oil and Development Strategies in the Soviet Successor States and Beyond." *Comparative Political Studies* 34 (2001).

Kaiser, Mark J., and Allan G. Pulsipher. "A Review of the Oil and Gas Sector in Kazakhstan." *Energy Policy* 35 (2007).

Øverland, Indra, Heidi Kjærnet, and Andrea Kendall-Taylor. *Caspian Energy Politics: Azerbaijan, Kazakhstan, and Turkmenistan.* New York: Routledge, 2010.

United Nations, Economic Commission for Europe. *Experience of International Organizations in Promoting Energy Efficiency: Kazakhstan.* New York: United Nations, 2005.

U.S. Energy Information Association. "Country Profile: Kazakhstan." http://www.eia.doe.gov/cabs/Kazakhstan/Full.html.

World Nuclear Association. "Kazakhstan." http://www.world-nuclear.org/info/inf89.html.

See Also: Caspian Sea; China; Energy Policy; ExxonMobil; Flaring Gas; Oil and Petroleum; Russia; Uranium.

Kentucky

Category: Energy in the United States.
Summary: Of the United States' total energy in 2010, 24 percent depended on Kentucky, originating in either the coal exported from the state's two coalfields or the enriched uranium rods produced at the country's only low-grade uranium enrichment facility.

The Commonwealth of Kentucky is located in the central-southern United States and is the nation's third-largest producer of coal. Historically an agricultural economy, the state has come to rely more heavily on automobile manufacturing, medical facilities, and the energy sector. In 2010, 24 percent of the nation's total energy depended on Kentucky's coal and the enriched uranium rods produced at the Paducah Gaseous Diffusion Plant, the country's only low-grade uranium enrichment facility.

Located in McCracken County, near Paducah, the Paducah Gaseous Diffusion Plant was opened in 1952 as a government-owned facility to produce enriched uranium for military reactors and nuclear weapons. Beginning in the 1960s, the facility and its now shuttered sister plant in Tennessee began producing fuel for commercial nuclear power plants. The facility is now operated by the United States Enrichment Corporation (USEC), a publicly traded company created by the 1992 Energy Policy Act to privatize the enrichment of uranium for civilian use. The facility uses about 3,000 megawatts of electricity in its operations, supplied by the Tennessee Valley Authority. About 1,700 people are employed to run the facility, 1,100 employees of USEC operate it, and the Department of Energy (DOE) contracts an additional 600 as maintainers of the grounds and infrastructure. The DOE also provides for the water needs of residents in the area, who would otherwise rely on wells that have become contaminated by trichloroethylene as a result of the facility's operations.

Natural Gas

Natural gas production in Kentucky is fairly low, limited to the Big Sandy field in the east. Most

> ## Kentucky Coal Mining

More than 90 percent of Kentucky's energy comes from its coal-burning plants. Kentucky produces 10 percent of the country's coal supply and about a quarter of the production east of the Mississippi, with one-third of the country's coal mines. All Kentucky coal is bituminous, with sulfur content that varies depending on where it is mined; it is higher in the Illinois Basin and lower in the central Appalachian Basin.

of the natural gas used in Kentucky is imported, via a pipeline from the Gulf Coast, and is used by industry. A little more than 40 percent of Kentucky households use natural gas as their home heating fuel.

What little crude oil Kentucky produces is refined at the Somerset refinery, along with crude from Tennessee and West Virginia. The larger Catlettsburg refinery processes crude oil imported via the Capline Pipeline from the Gulf Coast. Kentucky also has two ethanol plants, which supply the Louisville metropolitan area and the Kentucky suburbs of Cincinnati; these are the only two parts of the state to require reformulated motor gasoline blended with ethanol.

Despite the state's uranium resources, Kentucky has no nuclear plants, but advocates have supported building one to help meet Kentucky's consumption needs and create jobs. The biomass energy potential of Kentucky is quite high, given the prevalence of agricultural land and waste, but the strength of the coal lobby has made other forms of energy difficult to pursue.

Per capita electricity consumption in Kentucky is the seventh-highest in the country. Industry accounts for much of the consumption: The energy-intensive aluminum industry is prominent in the state, and coal mining and automobile manufacture consume a good deal of energy as well. Even ignoring the industrial sector, though, per capita residential consumption is one of the highest in the country.

BILL KTE'PI

Further Reading

Kentucky Energy and Environment Cabinet, Department for Energy Development and Independence. "About Us." http://energy.ky.gov/Pages/AboutUs.aspx.

Kentucky Geological Survey. "Kentucky Energy Infrastructure." http://kgs.uky.edu/kgsmap/kycoal/viewer.asp.

U.S. Energy Information Administration. "Kentucky." http://www.eia.doe.gov/state/state-energy-profiles.cfm?sid=KY.

See Also: Investor-Owned Utilities; Mountaintop Removal Mining; Oil and Petroleum; South Carolina; Tennessee; Tennessee Valley Authority; United States; West Virginia.

Kenya

Official Name: Republic of Kenya.
Category: Geography of Energy.
Summary: Fuelwood, petroleum, and electricity are the three major sources of energy for the Republic of Kenya. Renewable energy sources, such as solar energy, windmills, power alcohol, and biogas, are becoming more important, yet still play a minor role.

Energy Production and Consumption

In 1922, through a merger of two companies (the Mombasa Electric Power and Lighting Company and Nairobi Power and Lighting Syndicate, both established in 1908), the East African Power and Lighting Company (EAPL) was established. In 1954, the Kenya Power Company (KPC) was formed as a subsidiary of the EAPL with the mandate to construct electricity transmission lines between Nairobi and Tororo in Uganda. With operations confined within Kenya, the company finally changed its name to Kenya Power and Lighting Company Limited (KPLC) in 1983.

As of 2008, Kenya had a total installed electric capacity of 1,480 megawatts and a peak demand of 1,050 megawatts, of which 57 percent was supplied by hydropower. As of the stated base year, Kenya's peak demand averaged 1,050 megawatts. The remaining major energy sources constitute thermal (31.7 percent), geothermal (11 percent), and wind (0.3 percent). Burning of wood and waste materials, along with some other renewables-based power generation, was the dominant energy source for Kenya in 2009, accounting for an estimated 78 percent of primary energy demand (PED); biomass was followed by oil, at 20 percent, and hydropower, at about 2 percent of PED.

With the population of Kenya expected to expand from 40 million to 46.6 million between 2010 and 2014, electricity consumption is also expected to increase, by more than 13 percent. Power consumption is expected to increase from an estimated 5.8 terawatt-hours in 2009 to 7.6 terawatt-hours by 2014, provided market coverage at an average annual growth rate of 5.9 percent in electricity generation occurs. Energy loss is more than 1 terawatt-hour during power transmission and distribution. Kenya heavily relies on imported petroleum. For example, in 2007, the country imported 57,000 barrels of crude oil per day. To reverse its energy crisis, Kenya has increased imports of electricity from Ethiopia.

Major Sources of Energy

The primary sources of energy are electricity from hydropower, geothermal power, and thermal power, as well as petroleum and biomass in the form of fuelwood.

Kenya generates electricity from hydropower, geothermal power, and thermal power. The installed power capacity, as of June 2005, was 1,155.0 megawatts: 679.3 megawatts from hydropower, 347.3 megawatts from oil-based thermal power, 128 megawatts from geothermal power, and 0.4 megawatt from wind power. The key players in the power sector are Kenya Power and Lighting Company (KPLC), Kenya Electricity

Generating Company Limited (KENGEN), the Electricity Regulatory Board (ERB), the Ministry of Energy (MOE), and independent power producers (IPPs). KPLC is 48.4 percent government-owned and is the only licensed public electricity transmitter and distributor.

Petroleum is the most significant source of commercial energy in Kenya. Imports of petroleum accounted for about 16 percent of the total import bill following 2002, consuming 31 percent of Kenya's foreign exchange earnings from the export of merchandise. Petroleum product consumption has been 2.4 million metric tons, with per capita consumption of 76.2 kilograms.

More than 70 percent of the country's energy consumption depends on fuelwood, which has remained the leading source of energy for the majority of households in Kenya. Of the country's total population, 80 percent depend on biomass fuels, which supply 90 percent of rural households' energy requirements and 85 percent of urban and semiurban households.

Renewable Energy Sources

With approximately 350 installed wind pumps, Kenya has an estimated 0.55 megawatt of wind power. In 2009, the government announced that about 365 wind turbines would be installed in northern Kenya, around Lake Turkana. After its completion in 2012, with a £533 million project cost, supported by the African Development Bank, it is expected to generate 300 megawatts. Kenya receives between 4 and 6 kilowatt-hours per square meter per day of solar energy (insolation). A Nairobi-based company called Kenital Solar has developed systems that can pump water using 2 solar modules of 80 watts each. It is known that standard street lighting poles already produce light with one 75-watt solar module. Biomass constitutes up to 70 percent of Kenya's final energy demand and fulfills 90 percent of rural household energy needs. About 80 percent of urban households' fuelwood demand is met by charcoal. There is also a potential for generating fuels from the sugar industries. In 2006, for example, bagasse production was estimated to be 1,878,153 metric tons, with a generating potential of 120 megawatts of electricity.

With a potential of 7,000 megawatts, geothermal energy from the Kenyan Great Rift Valley is the cornerstone of a government scheme to double national energy production by 2018. Kenya generates 130 megawatts of energy from three geothermal sources located in the Rift Valley. A new geothermal plant is under construction close to Hell's Gate National Park to increase capacity by 35 megawatts. With an installed capacity of 737.3 megawatts, hydropower is the leading source of energy in Kenya. The Gitaru hydroelectric dam, with 225 megawatts, is Kenya's leading power plant. Although a large proportion of potential hydropower is attached to smaller rivers, 6,000 megawatts of hydroelectric potential exists in Kenya; the economic feasibility of harnessing that power is, however, uncertain. Generally, about 1,120 megawatts of the hydroelectric potential has been shown to be technically feasible.

DEREJE TEKLEMARIAM GEBREMESKEL

Further Reading

Afrepren/Fwd.org. "Country Energy Profile: Kenya." http://www.afrepren.org/cogen/documents/country_info/Kenya%20Energy%20Profile.pdf.

Central Intelligence Agency. "Kenya." In *The World Factbook*. https://www.cia.gov/library/publications/the-world-factbook/geos/ke.html.

Disenyana, Tsidiso. *China in the African Solar Energy Sector: Kenya Case Study*. Johannesburg: South African Institute of International Affairs, 2009.

Kenya Energy Regulatory Commission. "About ERC." http://www.erc.go.ke/erc/index.php.

Kenya Ministry of Energy. "About Us." http://www.energy.go.ke/.

Kenya Power and Lighting Company. "About Kenya Power." http://www.kplc.co.ke/.

Kituyi, E. "Application of Life Cycle Management Approach in Sustainable Charcoal Production and Use in Kenya." *Journal of Cleaner Production* 12 (2004).

United Nations Environment Programme. *Kenya, Integrated Assessment of the Energy Policy: With Focus on the Transport and Household Energy Sectors*. Geneva, Switzerland: United Nations Environment Programme, 2006.

See Also: Carbon Trading and Offsetting; Djibouti; Geothermal Energy; Hydropower; Renewable Energy Resources; Utilities; Wind Resources; World Commission on Environment and Development.

Kinetic Energy

Category: Fundamentals of Energy.
Summary: Kinetic energy occurs from motion and the object in motion's ability to do work. For example, rivers contain kinetic energy in currents, which can do work by turning a turbine in a dam.

The word *kinetic* is derived from the Greek word for motion (*kinesis*), and the word *energy* is the ability to do something (*energia*). Kinetic energy, then, occurs from motion and the object in motion's ability to do work. Kinetic energy can take three forms: rotational, translational, and vibrational. Rotational kinetic energy comes from its rotational motion, such as that produced from the spinning of the Earth on its axis. Translational kinetic energy is generated when an object moves from one position to another, such as water flowing in a river or from a train traveling. Vibrational kinetic energy comes from vibration, such as the oscillation of a loudspeaker's cone.

History

From a historical perspective, Gottfried Leibniz (1646–1716) and Johann Bernoulli (1667–1748) depicted kinetic energy as a living force that was equal to mass times velocity squared. Gaspard-Gustave de Coriolis (1792–1843) first coined the term *work* and described the concept of kinetic energy in its contemporary form, equal to the expression $\frac{1}{2}mv^2$. William Thomson (Lord Kelvin) (1824–1917) coined the term *kinetic energy* in 1856.

The total kinetic energy of an object is the sum of its translational and rotational forms. In classical physics, the amount of translational kinetic energy can generally be determined by the equation $KE = \frac{1}{2}mv^2$, with m as the mass of the object and v its speed at the center of the object. (This equation is for an object that is not also rotating, and when v is less than the speed of light.) As with work and potential energy, the quantity of kinetic energy is expressed in joules, with a joule expressed as $kg*m^2/s2$, where kg is a kilogram, m is a meter, and s is a second. Kinetic energy is a scalar quantity, having magnitude but directionless. Rotational kinetic energy is equal to one-half the product of the moment of inertia around the axis of rotation times the square of the angular velocity. In relativistic physics, kinetic energy is equal to the increase in mass caused by motion multiplied by the square of the speed of light. The kinetic energy of a system is the total kinetic energy of the objects within the system, and is also the capacity to do work on other systems or objects.

From a point of zero kinetic energy when an object is at rest, the level increases as work is done on it and the object accelerates, while the kinetic energy level decreases with deceleration. According to the Work-Energy Principle, the amount of work can be determined by subtracting the initial quantity of kinetic energy from its current quantity. The amount of kinetic energy is relational, subject to the frame of reference. For example, a car being observed by a person moving at the same speed would have zero kinetic energy.

Kinetic energy can be transferred to another object(s) or forms. For example, soccer players can supply kinetic energy from their swinging legs to move a ball a distance on the field or in the air, while the brakes of automobiles dissipate kinetic energy into heat as they slow the vehicle. In the case of the soccer players' kicks, the energy is conserved in what is known as an elastic collision. In inelastic collisions, the total kinetic energy is not conserved as some is turned into other forms, such as the vibrating atoms in heat.

KIRK S. LAWRENCE

Further Reading

Firk, Frank W. K. "Essential Physics I." http://www . http://www.physicsforfree.com/essential.html.
George State University. "Kinetic Energy." http:// hyperphysics.phy-astr.gsu.edu/hbase/ke.html.

Young, Hugh D. *College Physics*. Upper Saddle River, NJ: Addison-Wesley, 2012.

See Also: Energy Transmission: Electricity; Energy Transmission: Liquid Fluids; Energy Transmission: Mechanical Energy; Fundamentals of Energy; Heat Transfer; Natural Energy Flows; Potential Energy; Work and Energy.

Kiribati

Official Name: Republic of Kiribati.
Category: Geography of Energy.
Summary: Kiribati is a country of scattered atolls in the Pacific Ocean that depends heavily on imported diesel for electricity generation but is promoting and building solar power units in outlying atolls that lack centralized modern energy services.

Kiribati comprises 33 coral atolls located in the Pacific Ocean straddling the equator, positioned about halfway between Australia and Hawaii. These atolls are arranged into three island groups: the Gilbert Islands, Phoenix Islands, and Line Islands. The scattered atolls rise a few meters above sea level, creating a total landmass of 811 square kilometers spread over 2.1 million square miles (3.5 million square kilometers) of ocean. Of the 33 atolls, 21 are inhabited, with 43 percent of the nation's estimated 100,000 population living in the capital of Tarawa. Generators fueled by imported diesel dominate the energy sector on the heavily populated Tarawa atoll. Energy on the outlying atolls depends on locally sourced biomass and increasingly on solar power generation. There is an as yet undeveloped potential for wind energy. Kiribati's national energy policy, adopted in 2009, seeks to address the country's energy needs through renewable and sustainable options. Kiribati's greenhouse gas emissions from energy usage are minimal, but the country could be severely impacted if global climate change causes sea levels to rise.

Approximately 43 percent of Kiribati's population lives in the capital Tarawa. Tarawa's electricity comes from diesel generators powered by imported fossil fuels. Kiribati has minimal industrial activity; the diesel power generation is for everyday household and business energy needs. The rising cost of gas and kerosene makes these fuels inaccessible to low-income families, who then for their cooking needs turn to local biomass, a limited resource on the heavily populated Tarawa. Kiribati's remoteness makes the transportation costs of imported fossil fuels high and leaves Kiribati more vulnerable to fluctuating high oil prices. Importing fossil fuels in bulk would help reduce cost, but Kiribati lacks adequate long-term storage.

Biomass Resources

The use of biomass for energy has been fairly stable and accounts for approximately 25 percent of the total national energy production. Biomass in the form of coconut husks, shells, and fuelwood is commonly used, and abundant, in outer islands. Such biomass resources are limited on the heavily populated Tarawa. The Kiribati Copra Mill Company is developing coconut into a clean biofuel with the intent to augment or replace imported fossil fuels. It is estimated that up to 30 percent of the diesel fuel dependence could be replaced with a sustainably harvested and processed coconut biofuel.

In May 2009, the government of Kiribati adopted a national energy policy that focuses on

In Kiribati, coconuts are being developed as a clean biofuel to augment or replace fossil fuels.

Wikimedia

▷ *Solar Energy Since 1984*

For a sparse and scattered population and excellent solar conditions, solar energy is a cost-effective solution to energy demand in Kiribati. About 30 percent of the outer islands' population have access to electricity, much of it provided by solar home systems. Since 1984, the government of Kiribati has promoted photovoltaic (PV) systems for rural electrification through the Kiribati Solar Electric Company (KSEC). At first, PV systems proved unpopular because of both their maintenance needs and their inability to meet performance expectations. To reverse growing antisolar sentiment, in 1992 KSEC shifted from selling PV systems to servicing them.

KSEC owns and maintains the home solar systems, and households pay for the service rather than purchasing a high-maintenance system outright. KSEC now manages more than 2,000 PV systems. Despite the growth in home solar systems, it is estimated that solar provides only about 1 percent of Kiribati's total energy.

long-term sustainable energy strategies to ensure energy security, economic growth, and livelihood improvements. This policy calls for affordable and reliable renewable energy to achieve sustainable development in Kiribati. However, Kiribati is dependent on foreign donor assistance to improve and expand its energy sector, whether that be improving diesel generators or expanding access to photovoltaic (PV) home systems.

Kiribati produces minimal carbon dioxide (CO_2) emissions from its energy usage; it was fourth from last among all countries in 2008. However, the nation is also among the most vulnerable to the effects of climate change: The projected sea-level rise (fueled by industrial countries) could flood much of Kiribati and cause salinization of already limited soils. In November 2010, Kiribati hosted the Tarawa Climate Change Conference and released the Ambo Declaration, expressing the concerns of vulnerable countries regarding the expected negative impacts of climate change in their territories. The declaration calls on the United Nations Framework Convention on Climate Change (UNFCCC) to enact prompt, immediate, and measurable action to curb the onset of climate change and provide mitigation, adaption, and relocation assistance to the most vulnerable states.

SHAUNNA BARNHART

Further Reading

Central Intelligence Agency. "Kirabati." In *The World Factbook*. https://www.cia.gov/library/publications/the-world-factbook/geos/kr.html.

Gay, D., ed. *Kiribati Diagnostic Trade Integration Study 2010 Report*. Suva, Fiji: United Nations Development Programme, Multi Country Office, 2011.

Global Energy Network Institute. "People Want Light, Not Photovoltaics: Islands of Kiribati." http://www.geni.org/globalenergy/research/rural electrification/casestudies/kiribati/index.shtml.

Renewable Energy and Energy Efficiency Partnership. "Energy Profile Kiribati." http://www.reegle.info/countries/KI.

U.S. Energy Information Administration. "Country Analysis Brief: Kirabati." http://205.254.135.7/countries/country-data.cfm?fips=KR.

See Also: Biomass Energy; Climate Change; Fossil Fuels; Photovoltaics; Solar Energy.

Korea, North

Official Name: Democratic People's Republic of Korea.
Category: Geography of Energy.
Summary: North Korea has obtained its energy mainly from coal and hydroelectric power. Currently, North Korea has severe energy shortages.

North Korea occupies the northern part of the Korean Peninsula, which has remained divided since the Korean War (1950–53) ended with an armistice agreement. Since the end of the war, North Korea has pursued autarky under the *juche* (self-reliance) ideology. This policy has caused its isolation from the rest of the world and has stalled the development of its energy sector. North Korea has been facing challenges in meeting its energy needs and developing its industries, especially since the mid-1990s.

For much of the 20th century and to the present time, North Korea has obtained its energy mainly from coal and hydroelectric power. Its lack of investment in new technology and innovation, however, has led these sectors to become obsolete and inefficient. Although North Korea's nuclear ambition is directly related to its program to develop nuclear weapons for security purposes, its nuclear power has been pursued as an alternative energy source to deal with these challenges as well. Since the country declared its nuclear development programs, the energy issue has been a key element for the resolution of the nuclear crisis.

History of North Korea's Energy Sector

The northern part of the Korean Peninsula has relatively abundant coal and hydropower resources. During the Japanese colonial rule over the Korean peninsula (1919–45), these resources were heavily exploited for energy generation. As a result, the northern part of the peninsula supplied most of the electricity used in the peninsula before its division.

Since North Korea was founded in 1948, the country has industrialized itself rapidly by using the energy and industrial infrastructure built during the colonial period. To feed its industrialization, North Korea established the national power grid by the late 1950s. Also starting in the 1950s, North Korea began to pay attention to nuclear power as the country sought more advanced energy generation techniques and nuclear weapons. Moreover, its abundant coal resources were widely used for modernization. Coal power plants were built near the country's industrial centers

throughout the 1970s and helped North Korea's fast industrialization until the early 1970s.

In the early 1990s, many power plants were under construction, including hydroelectric plants and thermal power plants. Four large hydroelectric power plants were built during this time. Several of them were built, with the assistance of China, near the Yalu River, which is on the border with China. Nevertheless, since the 1990s, North Korea has been suffering from a chronic energy shortage. Several factors explain this shortfall. First, the 1991 collapse of the Soviet Union and its communist bloc countries led to a transition to capitalist economies and thus has affected those countries' trading relationships with North Korea.

When it comes to the exchange in the energy sector, this meant that North Korea could no longer import oil at a reduced price from its former allies. Research and technological exchanges also came to a standstill. Second, in East Asia, China adopted a policy of economic reform in the late 1970s and accelerated the reform in the early 1990s. This transition of its former communist allies to market economies has caused the isolation of North Korea, which refused to undertake such changes. Finally, North Korea suffered a series of massive floods in the mid-1990s, which caused problems in coal and hydroelectric energy generation. These factors together have dealt a serious blow to North Korea's economic growth and development.

Status of Energy Sources

North Korea has abundant coal resources, with 10 times more coal reserves than South Korea. Even though the quality of coal is poor, its abundance has allowed the country to be mostly self-sufficient. Coal takes up more than 80 percent of the country's energy production, which is the highest ratio in the world. Most of the energy produced by coal is consumed by the industrial sector. The production of coal has rapidly decreased since the early 1990s, however, and North Korea now produces less than half of the amount of coal it produced then. The dramatic decline in coal production has dealt a serious blow to the country's economic recovery. In addition, existing mines

▷ *Shrinking Economy and Decreased Energy Production*

Since the 1990s, North Korea's economy has continued to shrink. This economic degradation has caused further decreases in energy production. North Korea has not had enough hard currency to pay for oil imports and cannot afford to maintain and improve the existing facilities. Therefore, the country's supply of energy has dropped by about one-half to two-thirds its level during the 1990s, and it has not grown back. Transmission facilities have deteriorated without infrastructure investment and maintenance. As a result, the national grid system remains dysfunctional, causing an enormous amount of waste during transmission. Under this vicious cycle of economic degradation that aggravates energy shortages that in turn hinder the economy, North Korea's leaders have emphasized energy savings at a household level. Instead of electricity, most of the houses in North Korea use wood or biomass. The use of wood for energy, however, has caused environmental repercussions such as deforestation and soil erosion.

More recently, the North Korean government has been trying to reconstruct its steel, chemical, and mineral industries, but the rehabilitation of these heavy industries requires energy. Given the decreasing production of energy and worsening transmission system, this ambitious goal looks difficult to achieve.

are not yielding as much coal as before. Moreover, most of the coal-fired power plants and coal mines are old, and their final products are of low quality, not to mention environmentally harmful. Management failures and mine-related accidents are also common.

Hydroelectric Power

North Korea's mountainous terrain creates suitable conditions for dam construction. Dams have been built since the colonial period and provided a substantial amount of energy by the 1960s. However, hydroelectric power has been subject to seasonal fluctuations, and a poorly connected national grid system has caused transmission problems. Thousands of midsize and small dams have been built to meet the energy needs of small factories in local areas and households. However, as with other types of energy sources, the amount of hydroelectric energy generation has dramatically decreased since the mid-1990s.

Oil is consumed mainly by the transport sector. Without domestic oil reserves, the country has relied on imported oil. There are two refineries in North Korea, one built with assistance from the Soviet Union and the other with assistance from China in the late 1970s. However, these refineries are becoming antiquated, and they often do not run at all because of oil shortages. North Korea's importation of oil from Russia came to a halt with the collapse of the Soviet Union. Since the early 1990s, therefore, North Korea has imported its oil from China's Daqing oil field through a pipe built in 1976. North Korea's lack of hard currency and its self-reliance ideology, however, make oil less desirable than coal and hydropower. The decrease in oil imports has meant that the transportation sector does not get an enough fuel, which in turn results in economic breakdown. To overcome this, North Korea has been exploring its offshore oil with assistance from China and advanced countries including Japan and Britain.

Nuclear Power

Nuclear power serves dual functions for North Korea. One is to provide an alternative to its aging and inefficient coal and hydropower energy generation. Nuclear power will help the country reduce its dependence on fossil fuels, including oil imports. Moreover, North Korea's nuclear program will serve as a deterrent to potential threats from the United States or South Korea. The country started to develop nuclear power in the 1950s. In the mid-1950s, North Korea signed a deal with the Soviet Union for research and collaboration. Its nuclear experts were sent to the Soviet Union for exchange and training programs.

This period set a foundation for North Korea's technological development. From the 1960s through 1970s, North Korea's research was in full swing. It built the first nuclear power research complex in Young Byun. In the mid-1960s, North Korea started exploring uranium mines with China.

Since the 1970s, the country has continued to expand its nuclear development programs and test its technology. In 1993, North Korea announced its withdrawal from the Nuclear Non-Proliferation Treaty. To resolve this crisis, the United States struck a Geneva Agreement with the regime in late 1994. This agreement's main elements included the provision of two light-water reactors (1,000 megawatts each) in return for North Korea's suspension of its nuclear weapons program. Interim energy alternatives such as heavy oil were to be provided, while the two light-water reactors for energy generation were built. However, North Korea has failed to comply with the agreement and has resumed its nuclear program.

North Korea first established a center for the development of renewable energy in the mid-1990s, and in 1998 it built about 200 units of small wind power generators. In 2001, the government also enacted a five-year plan to develop renewable energy. However, most of the renewable energy projects are still in their experimental stages. Without investment and technology transfer from advanced countries, development is not likely to be successful.

Energy Cooperation and Reunification

South Korea has been promoting energy cooperation with North Korea in preparation for future reunification. By improving North Korea's energy infrastructure and boosting the North Korean economy through energy supply, South Korea expects that it can lift the North Korean economy from its current dismal status and reduce the cost of reunification in the future. In negotiating with North Korea over its nuclear weapons program, South Korea has suggested assistance in energy development. For example, in 2005 South Korea proposed the provision of 2 gigawatts of power through the construction of power plants and extension of its grid networks.

Although such a program has been interrupted by North Korea's brinkmanship, South Korea considers energy cooperation with North Korea an essential step toward reunification. North Korea has also included the energy issue in its negotiations with South Korea and the other countries in the six-party talks, including the United States. Using its advanced technology, South Korea can provide technical expertise and financial investment to North Korea while the latter contributes its cheap labor and its own home-grown technology.

With the death of President Kim Jong-il on December 17, 2011, and his replacement as supreme leader by his son Kim Jong-un, barely 28 years old, the future of North Korea's energy situation, as well as the nation's overall world standing, has gained renewed international attention.

HEE-JIN HAN

Further Reading

Calder, Kent E. *Korea's Energy Insecurities: Comparative and Regional Perspectives.* Washington, DC: Korean Economic Institute, 2005.

Choe, Yoon-Young Angela. *Energy Assistance to North Korea: Options to Be Considered Immediately by the Six Parties and Beyond.* Stuttgart, Germany: Ibidem-Verlag, 2007.

Kim, Kyu-ryun, Minjok T'ongil, and Yon'guwon. *Energy Cooperation With North Korea: Issues and Suggestions.* Seoul: Korea Institute for National Unification, 2005.

Korean Peninsula Energy Development Organization. "Annual Report, 2005." http://www.kedo.org/pdfs/KEDO_AR_2005.pdf.

U.S. Energy Information Administration. "Country Analysis Brief: Korea, North." http://www.eia.gov/countries/country-data.cfm?fips=KN.

See Also: China; Coal; Japan; Korea, South; Nuclear Power.

Korea, South

Official Name: Republic of Korea.
Category: Geography of Energy.
Summary: South Korea is a major economic power in East Asia. In 2010, South Korea announced a plan to turn its capital city, Seoul, into a Green Growth city, with plans to reduce greenhouse gases and create jobs and profits from a new, sustainable energy economy.

The peninsula of Korea has been occupied since the Paleolithic period, and the current civilization began around the 24th century B.C.E. The modern nation of South Korea was formed in 1948 after the liberation of Korea from Japanese rule resulted in the division of the country between the democratic South Korea and the communist North Korea. After the subsequent war between the two Koreas, the South Korean economy gradually grew until the country became a major power in East Asia. Today a member of the G-20 major economies, its economy is the fourth-largest in Asia and 15th-largest in the world (12th when ranked by purchasing power parity). South Korea's economy is driven largely by exports, especially of electronics, automobiles, heavy machinery, robotics, and petrochemicals. In 2010, South Korea underscored its significance on the global stage with the announcement of its intention to turn Seoul into a Green Growth city, representing a new paradigm in sustainability and energy economics. Under South Korea's plan, Seoul not only will reduce its greenhouse gases but also will create jobs and generate profits in the process.

Energy Consumption

Seoul is the political, economic, and cultural capital of South Korea, and with 24.5 million people, it is the second-largest metropolitan area in the world. It has the highest per capita energy consumption in Asia, which has risen steadily and rapidly since the 1970s as South Korea's economy expanded. Its designation as a Green Growth city is thus all the more significant, because of the challenges presented by large or dense populations and the widely varying needs of the citizenry in large cities, which tend to be culturally and economically diverse. Even before the Green Growth designation, Seoul was known as one of the more technologically sophisticated cities in the world, an early adopter of wireless high-speed mobile Internet and a citywide fiber-optic broadband network.

The size of the metropolitan area has historically affected transportation issues in Seoul, which has the world's third-largest subway system and the Korean Train Express (KTX), a high-speed rail system that regularly travels at 190 miles per hour and serves about 150,000 passengers. Although major manufacturers like Samsung and Hyundai-Kia are based in Seoul, most of the area's air pollution comes from vehicular exhaust, and converting public transportation to green vehicles is a cornerstone of the Green Growth plan. The Master Plan for Low Carbon Green Growth sets out numerous goals from 2010 to 2030, including the reduction of greenhouse gases by 40 percent and a 20 percent increase in new or renewable energy sources, goals that naturally complement each other.

The plan also calls for the creation of 1 million new green jobs, which is really the crux of the Green Growth initiative: the state's vigorous promotion of the green technologies sector as the keystone of a new approach to urban planning. South Korea plans to spend $45 billion, with costs including the redesign not only of Seoul's buildings but also of its layout and transportation systems, with an end goal of a "human-oriented city" consuming less energy, employing more people, and making more money. Less than half of 1 percent of Seoul's energy is generated in the city, a figure the plan intends to change. Major investment is planned in hydrogen fuel cells and local solar power.

All new construction in Seoul will consist of green buildings, and 10,000 buildings larger than 6,561 square feet (2,000 square meters) will be converted to green buildings as well. New bus lines, rider incentives, bicycle lanes along all major roads, and public relations campaigns will increase public transportation ridership to 70 percent and bike ridership to 10 percent, and all public transportation will be converted to green vehicles, which will go far in achieving greenhouse gas reduction goals. Interestingly, the Green Growth

A view of an oil refinery in Seoul, South Korea, at night. According to the U.S. Energy Information Administration, South Korea has a large refining sector, but relies on crude imports for all of its oil needs. Seoul is the capital of South Korea and is known as one of the more technologically sophisticated cities in the world.

plan does not rely on carbon offsets; rather, it envisions actual emissions reductions.

The Hollywood of Sustainability

Seoul has essentially positioned itself as the Hollywood of sustainability—a city that can found its wealth on sustainable growth. The green jobs will take advantage of Seoul's experience in advanced technologies and will specifically focus on 10 areas: solar cells, hydrogen fuel cells, light-emitting diode (LED) lighting, green information technology (IT), IT electricity, green building, green cars, urban environment recovery, climate change adaptation technology, and recovering waste for repurposing into resources.

Like Seoul, South Korea is dependent on imported energy. In 1964, before the rapid expansion of the economy, energy imports were at only about 10 percent; by 1991, imports were 90 percent, and in the 21st century South Korea became the second-largest importer of coal and liquefied natural gas and the fifth-largest importer of crude oil. Dependence on Middle Eastern sources of oil has tied Korea's fortunes to volatile fuel prices, exactly the sort of morass the Green Growth plan hopes to plot a course away from, and in 2011 it announced plans to diversify its energy sources by importing liquefied natural gas from Australia, Russia, and North America. Furthermore, its industries are energy-intensive ones: It takes South Korea's manufacturing sector nearly twice as much energy to produce $1 million of outputs as it does Japan's manufacturing sector (also a heavy importer of fossil fuels), because of the high energy costs of industries such as petrochemicals, automobiles, and shipbuilding. The country has no oil reserves, and the domestic coal supply is scant and of low quality. The Korea District Heating Corporation supplies combined heat and power to Seoul and Daegu and is the world's largest distributed heat company. Hydroelectric power has been explored, and Korea Hydro and Nuclear Power, a subsidiary of the state-run Korea Electric Power Corporation, operates nine hydroelectric power plants in the country, although hydroelectric is generally considered difficult in Korea because of the disproportionate concentration of rainfall in the summer months. Renetec and Voith Hydro have jointly developed the Seaturtle Tidal Park, one of the world's largest tidal current power plants, which is expected to produce about 150 megawatts (enough for 100,000 homes) of renewable energy. The Seaturtle project, if it proves successful, is hoped to lead to more tidal power plants in Korea and elsewhere—another green technology from which Korea could profit.

Increasing Nuclear Power

For the time being, South Korea is heavily dependent on imported electricity, imported fuels, and nuclear power. After the Green Growth Master Plan was announced, South Korea announced its intention to cut its dependence on fossil fuels and imports by building 14 nuclear reactors by 2024. The goal is to increase nuclear power's contribution to the nation's electricity to about 50 percent. Furthermore, by 2030 South Korea hopes to export 80 nuclear reactors and to position itself as a significant force in nuclear power technology. Agreements have been signed to produce reactors for Jordan and the United Arab Emirates, a first for South Korea, and negotiations with Turkey are ongoing. Currently, nuclear power contributes about 28.5 percent of South Korea's electricity. The nuclear industry is actively exploring numerous advanced reactors, including high-temperature hydrogen generation and small modular reactors, as well as better modes of waste handling and fuel production.

The building of nuclear reactors in the Middle East is interesting, because both parties are in the same position of having to rely on imported energy. In South Korea's case, it is dependent on imported Middle Eastern fossil fuels because of a lack of domestic sources; in the case of the Middle Eastern countries with which it has contracted, they depend on imported energy because of rapidly rising domestic consumption. In the long term, both parties seek energy security. Key to South Korea's plan is the emergence of new energy customers such the emerging BRIC nations (Brazil, Russia, India, and China) and the Middle East—economies that will prove fertile markets for the sustainable technologies the Green Growth plan will help to develop.

Although many hope for an eventual unification of the two Koreas, South Korea's energy situation in the 21st century has made it clear what the energy costs of unification would be. The International Energy Agency predicted that South Korea's energy demand will increase by 37 percent between 2006 and 2020, and the country is on track to prove that prediction correct. Adding North Korea to the mix would add significantly to that increase, because of the number of new energy consumers whose consumption is currently constrained by the centrally planned economy of North Korea and the many limitations placed on its citizenry. Unification would include not only greater freedoms for current North Korean citizens but also an expansion of North Korean industry. North Korea lacks domestic oil and gas, just as South Korea does, although it does possess some mineral natural resources. Part of North Korea's current economic trouble is caused by the energy shortage that has been ongoing for two decades and forces North Korean industry to function well below capacity; unification could cut off the one supply of energy it does have, crude oil imports from its ally China.

BILL KTE'PI

Further Reading

Cho, Lee-Jay, Yoon Hyung Kim, and Chung H. Lee, eds. *Industrial Globalization in the Twenty-First Century: Impact and Consequences for East Asia and Korea.* Honolulu: University of Hawaii Press, 2002.

Choi, Y. H. "South Korea's Economic Development and the Evolving Role of the Government: Energy and Water." *Journal of East Asian Affairs* 25, Part 1 (2011).

Denmark, Abraham, and Zachary M. Hosford. *Securing South Korea: A Strategic Alliance for the 21st Century*. Washington, DC: Center for a New American Security, 2010.

Hong, S. "Where Is the Nuclear Nation Going? Hopes and Fears Over Nuclear Energy in South Korea After the Fukushima Disaster." *East Asian Science, Technology and Society* 5, no. 3 (September 1, 2011).

U.S. Energy Information Administration. "Country Analysis Brief: Korea, South." http://205.254.135.7/countries/country-data.cfm?fips=KS.

Xu, Yi-Chong. *Nuclear Energy Development in Asia: Problems and Prospects*. New York: Palgrave Macmillan, 2011.

See Also: International Energy Agency; Korea, North; Laos; Malaysia; Thailand; Vietnam.

Kuwait

Official Name: State of Kuwait.
Category: Geography of Energy.
Summary: Kuwait is a country that is a major oil producer. This energy sector represents the main source of Kuwait's gross domestic product. Oil and gas production has historically been dominated by local companies.

The emirate of Kuwait is situated at the head of the Persian Gulf and borders with Iraq, with which it has a long history of conflicts and tensions, and Saudi Arabia. Kuwaiti soil is extremely rich in oil, and it is calculated that the country has 8 percent of the world's total reserves: 104 billion barrels of proven oil reserves. Although this figure has been challenged as inaccurate and overly optimistic, new discoveries made in the 21st century have boosted the country's reserves by about 10 percent. There are more than 1,600 producing oil wells in the country, which since 2000 have been producing up to 2.55 million barrels per day and are expected to increase production to 3.5 million barrels by 2015 and to 4 million by 2020. These figures would represent a return to the level of production of the 1970s, when the country was the world's fourth-largest oil producer.

Oil and Gas Resources

During the 1980s and 1990s, the aging fields as well as violent conflicts with neighboring countries and a consequent lack of investments had a negative effect on the oil industry. After the progress made at the beginning of the new century, the Kuwaiti oil industry now ranks as the fifth most productive within the Organization of Petroleum Exporting Countries (OPEC), after Saudi Arabia, Iran, Iraq, and the United Arab Emirates. The majority of the country's oil exports are sold to Asian Pacific countries. Kuwait also has 63 trillion cubic feet of natural gas, found mainly in conjunction with oil. Nonassociated gas fields were first discovered in the northern areas of Sabriya and Umm Niqa in 2006.

The Greater Burgan Area includes the majority of the country's oil reserves, and the Greater Burgan field is the world's second-largest oil field after the Ghawar field in Saudi Arabia. Oil fields in the north of the country, such as those in the Sabriya and Umm Niqa areas, have been the focus of new discoveries since 2000. They have attracted the attention of international firms, which have repeatedly expressed interest in taking a more active role in the oil industry and in developing the full potential of these northern reserves. The Kuwaiti government also considers new discoveries in northern fields essential to reaching its target production levels. Therefore, a new and important terminal for oil export has been built on Bubiyan Island. About two-thirds of the country's oil production is from the southeast of the country, while northern and western areas of Kuwait contribute respectively about one-fifth and one-tenth of oil production. In addition to oil fields on its national soil, Kuwait shares with Saudi Arabia the resources in the Saudi-Kuwaiti Neutral Zone (also known as the Divided Zone).

Oil and Conflict

Against the expansionist ambitions of the Ottoman Empire, Kuwait signed an agreement with Great Britain in 1899 to become a British protectorate. Independent since 1961, the small country was repeatedly claimed by Iraq, which considered the emirate part of its land. Because of its position and its historic ties to Iraq, the country could not avoid being involved in the Iran-Iraq War in the 1980s. In this conflict, Kuwait supported Iraq. In August 1990, however, only a few years after the conclusion of the Iran-Iraq War, Kuwait was invaded by Iraq, which justified its action by arguing that the emirate was in Iraqi territory. However, what motivated Iraq to invade were economic considerations, such as Kuwait's refusal to forgive a large Iraqi debt and its decision to exceed its oil production quota as set by OPEC. This overproduction caused a decline in oil prices that had a negative impact on Iraq's already precarious economic situation. The annexation of Kuwait as Iraq's 19th province was prevented by a multinational force assembled through U.S. efforts. The ensuing brief Gulf War successfully drove the occupants from Kuwait and captured a large area of southern Iraq by early March 1991.

Although Operation Desert Storm, as the coalition's military operation was known, was successful in its aim to fight back the Iraqi troops of Saddam Hussein, the Gulf War left a disastrous legacy for the Kuwaiti environment and had a particularly negative impact on infrastructures. For example, the main Kuwaiti port for the export of crude oil, Mina al Ahmadi, was completely destroyed during the conflict and had to be completely rebuilt. During their retreat back to Baghdad, Iraqi forces blew up hundreds of oil wells, resulting in the burning of more than 1 billion barrels, which blackened and poisoned the air in the Gulf region. Moreover, 10 million barrels were poured into the sea, leading to the deaths of birds and sea life. This short war, therefore, represented a tragic environmental disaster, which, predictably, also had a negative effect on the lives of Kuwaitis, increasing the number of lung diseases and cancer.

Oil was central not only in Hussein's motivation to invade but also to the coalition's military oper-

ation. Critics of the Gulf War pointed out that the coalition's prime reason to enter the conflict was not its official concern for Kuwaiti democracy and the self-determination of nations but instead its economic interest in the region's vast oil supplies. Antiwar militants pointed out that Kuwaiti citizens did not live in a democracy before the Iraqi invasion. On the contrary, the country, like many other Arab nations that were members of the international coalition against Hussein, had a repressive regime. What motivated the United States and its allies to take action was the Kuwaiti energy industry and the fear that it would fall into the hands of a dictator who had proved impossible to control.

In addition to the environmental disaster, the war left a legacy of hatred between the two countries and relations remained tense until the fall of Hussein's regime. Since then, the two countries have started to explore new business and trade possibilities, and the energy sector may be an important focus for future collaborations. Given the damages suffered by Iraqi infrastructures and its vast, but underdeveloped, oil reserves, Kuwait could play a key role in helping the development of the Iraqi oil sector, providing the necessary technology and know-how. In return, Iraq could provide Kuwait with significant natural gas volumes, as it did before the Gulf War, through the pipeline connecting the southern Iraqi field of Rumaila to Ahmadi. Security in Iraq, however, continues to be a major obstacle in the process of restarting supply through the pipeline.

Oil as the Key Factor in Kuwaiti Economy

Throughout the decades, the performance of Kuwait's economy has been inextricably linked to the oil market. In the 1970s, the country gained considerable wealth from the significant rise in oil prices. The state-owned Kuwait Petroleum Corporation, which handles all local and international oil investments, became known as the "eighth sister," a nickname that put it on par with the seven largest international oil companies, often referred to as the Seven Sisters. In the mid-1980s and early 1990s, the country experienced a recession because of the slump in oil prices and

Iraqi aggression. The international influence of its oil industry went through a parallel decline. However, since 2000, the Kuwaiti oil industry has been making steady progress and is reestablishing itself as a leading force in the oil market.

Significantly, the hydrocarbon sector grew at an impressive average annual rate of approximately 33 percent between 2003 and 2008, and, together with the refining industry, as of 2010 it represented almost two-thirds of the country's gross domestic product (GDP). Kuwait gets more than 90 percent of its revenues from the hydrocarbon sector, and 90 percent of its export earnings come from oil, making Kuwait the oil-dependent country among those in the Cooperation Council for the Arab States of the Gulf (also known as the Gulf Cooperation Council, consisting of those Arab states bordering the Persian Gulf). Although the government is planning to increase oil production, it is also aware that such economic dependency has

to come to terms with the fact that oil reserves are nonrenewable. Thus, approximately 10 percent of oil revenues are invested in the Future Generations Fund.

Because the country is heavily dependent on oil, this resource is widely regarded as a national treasure, and foreign involvement in the sector has therefore traditionally been regarded with suspicion. Initially proposed in the 1990s, Project Kuwait (PK) aims to introduce foreign firms into the management of local natural resources, including oil and natural gas, to increase the country's production levels of hydrocarbons. PK focuses particularly on the northern oil fields of Abdali, Bahra, Ratqa, Raudhatain, and Sabriya, which is Kuwait's third-biggest field. The project has run up against fierce opposition and has been repeatedly deemed unconstitutional. Because production sharing and concessions to foreign firms are banned by the constitution, PK assigns

Wikimedia

The Burgan oil field is the world's second-largest oil field after the Ghawar field in Saudi Arabia. The Greater Burgan Area in Kuwait includes the majority of the country's oil reserves, but the oil fields in the north of the country have been the focus of new discoveries since 2000.

a per-barrel fee to be paid to international companies together with capital recovery costs and incentives to explore new reserves. Under this plan, Kuwait's government would retain full ownership of the reserves and full authority to decide production levels. The history of the Kuwaiti petrochemical industry shows that, after its nationalization in 1974, it has firmly remained in local hands, with the Supreme Petroleum Council devising the policies for the Kuwait Petroleum Corporation, responsible for refining, and the Kuwait Oil Company, in charge of producing, developing, and exploring for new oil and gas fields. While foreign firms have been present in the country since the beginning of oil production in the late 1930s, their role has so far been limited to that of technical advisers. Royal Dutch Shell and Kuwait Oil Company signed an important technical agreement for the development of the Jurassic Gas Field in 2010. This agreement is considered a first step toward an energy sector that is more open to foreign firms.

Gas and Electricity

Although Kuwait's natural gas reserves are not comparable to its crude oil fields, the country hopes to increase its gas production to meet constantly increasing electricity and water desalinization costs. The first phase toward a wider use of natural gas in electricity generation was the construction of the Mina al-Ahmadi–Subiya natural gas-oil pipeline project, awarded to the Australian company Worley Parsons in 2006. The pipeline joins natural gas and oil fields with the Subiya power station.

The extensive use of air-conditioning, the heavy dependency on desalinization to obtain drinkable water, and high government subsidies linked to the electricity costs make Kuwait's per capita consumption one of the largest in the world, exceeding 14,000 kilowatt-hours. Estimates calculate that power demand in the emirate rises between 7 and 9 percent every year. Because of this growing demand, Kuwait may suffer from power cuts, especially in the summer, when temperatures can go beyond 50 degrees Celsius and it is not uncommon to leave air-conditioning on

in houses even when people are out. The installed generation capacity of 9,775 megawatts, obtained by the country's five power plants, is below the required 11,730 megawatts to cover the demand. Since the new century, the government has been promoting campaigns to encourage a more sensible use of electricity and persuade citizens that, in spite of its artificially low prices, electricity is a valuable commodity.

The Electricity and Water Ministry, which became independent from the Oil Ministry in 2007, has planned massive investments to update Kuwait's infrastructure and build at least four more power plants by 2012. Even this expansion, however, is not deemed sufficient by scientists, who calculate that three more plants will be needed. Kuwait entered the Gulf Cooperation Council power grid in 2008 and is therefore linked to Bahrain and Saudi Arabia. This measure too, however, cannot be considered as a definite solution to Kuwait's electricity problems, as these two countries also suffer from shortages.

LUCA PRONO

Further Reading
Clough, Langdon D. "Energy Profile of Kuwait." In *The Encyclopedia of Earth*, edited by Cutler J. Cleveland. Washington, DC: National Council for Science and the Environment. http://www.eoearth.org/article/Energy_profile_of_Kuwait.
Cordesman, Anthony H. *Kuwait: Recovery and Security After the Gulf War*. Boulder, CO: Westview Press, 1997.
Cordesman, Anthony H., and Khalid R. al-Rodhan. *The Changing Dynamics of Energy in the Middle East*. Westport, CT: Praeger, 2006.
Singer, Clifford E. *Energy and International War: From Babylon to Baghdad and Beyond*. Hackensack, NJ: World Scientific Publishing Company, 2008.
U.S. Energy Information Administration. "Country Analysis Brief: Kuwait." http://www.eia.gov/countries/cab.cfm?fips=KU.

See Also: Bahrain; International Energy Forum; Oil and Petroleum; Organization of Petroleum Exporting Countries; Qatar; Saudi Arabia; War.

Kyoto Protocol

Category: Environmentalism.

Summary: The Kyoto Protocol is an international agreement to reduce greenhouse gas emissions through both national measures and alternative global market-based strategies of emissions trading, the clean development mechanism, and joint implementation.

The Kyoto Protocol is an international agreement that creates binding greenhouse gas (GHG) emission reduction targets of 5.2 percent below 1990 levels of emissions for 37 industrialized countries and the European community by 2012. To achieve this goal, countries must institute national measures to reduce their overall GHG emissions. Additionally, the Kyoto Protocol provides market-based mechanisms as alternative pathways to meeting national emission reduction targets: emissions trading, the clean development mechanism, and joint implementation. Supporters argue that the Kyoto Protocol's targets and mechanisms are necessary and equitable measures to combat global climate change. Critics argue that the Kyoto Protocol creates a new colonialism that allows industrialized countries to continue polluting while displacing emission reduction burdens onto developing countries through carbon markets.

Agreement to Reduce GHG Emissions

In 1992, the United Nations established the United Nations Framework Convention on Climate Change (UNFCCC) in recognition that adverse affects of climate change are a common concern for all humanity and that human activity is a prime driver for increasing GHGs in the atmosphere that are leading to climate change. The Kyoto Protocol is a greenhouse gas reduction agreement pursuant to the UNFCCC. The Kyoto Protocol was signed December 11, 1997, in Kyoto, Japan, but did not enter into force until February 16, 2005. A total of 191 states plus the European Union have ratified the Kyoto Protocol. The United States, which produces around 20 percent of the world's greenhouse gas emissions, has not ratified the Kyoto Protocol.

This international treaty commits 37 industrialized countries and the European Union to mandatory emission reductions, primarily through national measures, with the further option of three different market-based mechanisms, explained below. The protocol identifies possible national measures that can be taken to reduce GHG emissions, including improvements in energy efficiency, developing and promoting new and renewable energies, improving carbon sequestration (such as through sustainable forestry and afforestation), promoting sustainable agriculture, developing and utilizing environmentally sound technologies, and ending government subsidies to GHG-producing sectors. These industrialized countries are also expected to assist developing countries in clean development efforts through technology transfer and trade, which can occur through market-based mechanisms.

Market-Based Mechanisms

Industrialized countries that have committed to the Kyoto Protocol are expected to meet their emission reduction objectives largely through national measures. However, the Kyoto Protocol also established three market-based mechanisms—emissions trading, the clean development mechanism, and joint implementation—as additional emission reduction strategies. These three mechanisms jointly create what is now commonly referred to as the carbon market. The purpose of creating these market mechanisms is threefold. First, it is believed that these mechanisms will create market incentives to transfer technology and encourage sustainable development. Second, these are cost-effective mechanisms whereby a country can meet its emission reduction target by reducing emissions or sequestering carbon in another country. Third, the mechanisms provide incentive to both the private sector and developing countries, which are not bound by emission reduction targets, to participate in emission reduction activities.

Clean Development Mechanisms

A clean development mechanism (CDM) allows a country with binding emission reduction targets

▷ *Emissions Trading*

Under the Kyoto Protocol, industrialized countries are allowed a certain amount of greenhouse gas (GHG) emissions. Countries are to develop national mechanisms for measuring these emissions. If a country is emitting less than its allowance, it can "trade" its unused emissions to another country that has exceeded its emissions allowance. This allows the selling country to profit for successfully reducing emissions below the target and allows the buying country to continue current practices until it is able to implement improved practices that lower emissions. Globally, the amount of emissions remains the same, but the location of those emissions is shifted. Carbon dioxide is the principal greenhouse gas, and therefore emissions trading created a new global commodity in the form of "carbon credits" for a newly created "carbon market."

Wikimedia

to benefit from implementing an emission reduction project in a developing country. The developing country benefits from the development activity itself, and because that activity creates a new globally traded commodity known as certified emission reduction (CER) credits. Industrialized countries can buy these CER credits to offset their own emissions without actually reducing their own emissions. The CDM framework thus encourages developing countries to engage in sustainable development strategies that qualify for CER credits, creating a revenue stream to continue funding national development projects. The CDM framework has been operating since 2006 with more than 1,650 projects registered through 2010. CDM projects are regulated nationally by designated national authorities and internationally by the CDM Executive Board. To be approved, the CDM activity must reduce emissions below what would have been emitted without the implementation of the project, resulting in a net reduction of emissions. One example is switching to hydroelectricity from coal-powered electricity. Another example is installing household biogas plants that trap and use methane from cow manure for cooking to replace firewood, which releases carbon dioxide when burned.

Joint Implementation

A joint implementation (JI) project allows for cooperation between two countries that both have binding emission reduction targets. Like a CDM, a JI project must result in a reduction of emissions compared to the emissions that would have been produced in the project's absence. This can take the form of reduced emissions from sources or increased removal of emissions through sequestration. Also like a CDM, a JI project is subject to oversight to ensure compliance and actual emission reduction; the Joint Implementation Supervisory Committee oversees the program for the UNFCCC. Joint implementation is beneficial to both parties: The host country receives foreign investment and possibly technology transfer, and the sponsoring country has flexibility in meeting emission reduction targets.

License to Pollute?

Supporters of the Kyoto Protocol believe that the market mechanisms allow flexibility for countries to meet their targets while benefiting countries that pursue clean and sustainable development. It commits industrialized nations—the drivers of global climate change with their generations of GHG-emitting development—to be the pioneers in corrective behavior while not penalizing developing countries or restricting their development and industrialization opportunities.

Critics of the Kyoto Protocol argue that emissions trading leads to both environmental and social injustices by creating systems whereby major polluters are permitted, through the protocol's market mechanisms, to continue polluting. Connected to this argument is the claim that the market-based mechanisms constitute a new kind of colonialism imposed on developing countries, with negative consequences for local environments and peoples. Critics also argue that the reduction targets are not sufficient to prevent potential climate catastrophe.

SHAUNNA BARNHART

Further Reading

Aldy, Joseph E., R. N. Stavins, and Timothy E. Wirth. *Post-Kyoto International Climate Policy: Implementing Architectures for Agreement; Research From the Harvard Project on International Climate Agreements.* New York: Cambridge University Press, 2010.

Bachram, H. "Climate Fraud and Carbon Colonialism: The New Trade in Greenhouse Gases." *Capitalism, Nature, Socialism* 15, no. 4 (2004).

Faure, Michael, Joyeeta Gupta, and A. Nentjes. *Climate Change and the Kyoto Protocol: The Role of Institutions and Instruments to Control Global Change.* Northampton, MA: Edward Elgar, 2003.

Koh, Kheng Lian, Lin Heng Lye, and Jolene Lin. *Crucial Issues in Climate Change and the Kyoto Protocol: Asia and the World.* Hackensack, NJ: World Scientific, 2010.

Massai, L. *The Kyoto Protocol in the EU: European Community and Member States Under International and European Law.* Heidelberg, Germany: Springer, 2011.

Oberthür, Sebastian, and Hermann Ott. *The Kyoto Protocol: International Climate Policy for the 21st Century.* London: Springer, 2011.

United Nations Framework Convention on Climate Change. *Kyoto Protocol.* http://unfccc.int/kyoto_protocol/items/2830.php.

Victor, David G. *The Collapse of the Kyoto Protocol.* Princeton, NJ: Princeton University Press, 2001.

See Also: Berlin Mandate; Carbon Emissions Factors; Emissions Inventories; Global Warming; Greenhouse Gases; Intergovernmental Panel on Climate Change; Methane; Radiative Forcing.

Kyrgyzstan

Official Name: Kyrgyz Republic.
Category: Geography of Energy.
Summary: Kyrgyzstan has numerous natural resources, including hydropower, coal, oil, natural gas, and uranium. Potential renewables include wind and solar power, but these have not yet been developed.

Kyrgyzstan is a landlocked country in central Asia that was annexed to Russia in 1876, became a Soviet Republic in 1936, and became independent in 1991 when the Soviet Union dissolved. It has an area of 124,243 square miles (199,951 square kilometers), 5,064 of which is covered by water, including Issyk Kul (or Ysyk Köl) in the northeastern Tian Shan mountains, the second-largest saline lake in the world. The country has numerous natural resources, including hydropower, coal, oil, and natural gas, as well as deposits of gold, rare earth metals, and other minerals.

The population was estimated at 5,587,443 in July 2011, and the country has a negative net migration of minus 2.26 per 1,000 population. Measures of well-being are moderate to high, with 98.7 percent literacy, life expectancy at birth of 70.04 years, and a moderate infant mortality rate of 29.3 deaths per 1,000 live births (71st in the world). However, ethnic clashes and political unrest have damaged infrastructure and economic development. Real gross domestic product (GDP) declined by 3.5 percent in 2010 (whereas it grew 8.4 percent in 2008 and 2.3 percent in 2009), and per capita GDP in 2010 was $2,200 (185th in the world), with a 2007 Gini Index rating of 30.3 (0 representing perfect equality of income distribution and 100 indicating complete inequality) and 40 percent of the population living below the poverty line.

Oil Production

Total oil production in Kyrgyzstan is substantially lower than it was in the early 1990s and in 2008 was 950 barrels per day. Oil consumption in the same year was 15,000 barrels per day, making a negative balance (amount of required imports) of 14,050 barrels per day, although petroleum refinery capacity increased sharply in the mid-1990s and is currently 10,000 barrels per day. Proven oil reserves in 2008 were 0.04 billion barrels. In 2008, Kyrgyzstan produced 1 billion cubic feet of natural gas, a substantial reduction from the more than 2.5 billion cubic feet produced in 1992. Natural gas consumption in 2008 was 26 billion cubic feet, producing a negative balance of 25 billion cubic feet. Coal production in 2008 was 542 million short tons, a substantial drop from production levels during the Soviet era, while coal consumption was 1.443 billion short tons, for a negative balance of 901 million short tons. In 2007, Kyrgyzstan generated 15.96 terawatt-hours of electricity and consumed 9.00 terawatt-hours. Total energy production was 0.145 quadrillion British thermal units (Btu), and total consumption was 0.208 quadrillion Btu. Energy intensity (Btu per 2005 U.S. dollar) was 21,006 in 2006. Carbon dioxide emissions from consumption of fossil fuels was 5.68 million metric tons in 2008.

Hydroelectric Power

Most of Kyrgyzstan's electricity (80 percent) is produced by hydroelectric power, but low reservoir levels in 2008 caused a significant drop in production. The transmission system is also inefficient, with more than 50 percent of the power lost during transmission, due in part to technical losses (the electrical grid was created during the Soviet era and is outdated) and in part to theft, faulty meters, inaccurate billing, and other problems. Thermal power production provides most of the remainder; despite being a primary source of uranium, Kyrgyzstan has no nuclear power. Kyrgyzstan has fair potential for the development of wind energy, but development of this resource is primarily in the planning stages. The country also offers excellent opportunities for the production and use of biomass; biogas facilities produce about 6.5 million cubic feet (2 million cubic meters) of biogas and 70,000 tons of fertilizer, but the potential exists to produce 6.5 billion cubic feet (2 billion cubic meters) of biogas and 5 million tons of fertilizer. Kyrgyzstan has high potential for the development of solar power, particularly in Bishkek and Tien Shan, but this has not been developed; geothermal resources could also be used for heating and power generation.

Uranium Mining

During the years of the Soviet Union, the Mailuu-Suu district in southern Kyrgyzstan was a significant area for uranium mining, with more than 10,000 tons of uranium produced from this area in the years 1946–67; in fact, uranium from this area was used to create the Soviet Union's first atomic bomb. In 1997, the Kara Balta Mining Combine, created in the 1930s to mine and treat this ore, became a joint stock company, and in 2007 the Renova Group purchased the state equity in this company. Several companies from China, Canada, and Australia hold exploration licenses allowing them to prospect for uranium in Kyrgyzstan. The Kara Balta mill near Bishkek resumed operations in 2007 and produced 800 tons of uranium, increasing production to 2,574 tons by 2009. These uranium-mining activities have left the area extremely contaminated, with more than 6.43 million cubic feet (1.96 million cubic meters) of unsecured radioactive waste in the area—a problem exacerbated by the area's seismic activity, as earthquakes and landslides have already displaced some of the radioactive material into the Mailuu-Suu River. A 1999 study indicated that the cancer rate in this area was twice the national average.

Sarah Boslaugh

Further Reading

Blacksmith Institute. "Mailuu-Suu Legacy Uranium Dumps." http://www.blacksmithinstitute.org/projects/display/129.

European Bank for Reconstruction and Development, Renewable Development Initiative. "Kyrgyzstan Country Profile." http://www.ebrdrenewables.com/sites/renew/countries/Kyrgyzstan/default.aspx.

European Bank for Reconstruction and Development. "Strategy for the Kyrgyz Republic." June 12, 2007. http://www.ebrd.com/downloads/country/strategy/kyrgyz.pdf.

World Nuclear Association. "Uranium in Central Asia." http://www.world-nuclear.org/info/default.aspx?id=11492&terms=kyrgyzstan.

See Also: Afghanistan; Coal; Russia; Uranium; Uzbekistan.

Landfill Gas

Category: Energy Resources.

Summary: Landfill gas, a combination of methane and other products produced through the breakdown of garbage by bacteria and other organisms in dumps, can be captured, stored, and reused by businesses and even the landfill operator itself to generate electricity.

While it is common to think of trash as being dead, once deposited in a landfill it is anything but that. Bacteria, microbes, and other microscopic organisms work in conjunction with materials in the water, soil, air, and even garbage itself to decompose our trash. As those organisms do their work, they produce significant quantities of landfill gas, which is a mixture of methane (or natural gas), carbon dioxide, water vapor, and toxic organic compounds—although principally methane and carbon dioxide. In the past, landfill gas was allowed simply to seep upward from landfills and be released into the atmosphere, causing unpleasant smells for nearby residents. Because of its natural gas components, however, landfill gas has also been responsible for a number of explosions at landfills, as well as the contamination of groundwater resources around landfill sites.

In the mid-1990s, however, the U.S. Environmental Protection Agency ordered that all landfills meeting certain requirements monitor, collect, and manage landfill gas emissions. Monitoring can take place with equipment both near and inside the landfill itself, while collection typically takes the form of a "well" that is drilled down into the landfill, inside of which is created a slight vacuum to extract landfill gas from the site. Newer landfills might have a network of similar collection pipes built into them from the start, allowing the collection system to grow as the amount of solid waste grows.

The management of landfill gas is arguably the most important part of the process, however. It is thought that landfill gas contributes directly to climate change because of its heavy methane and carbon dioxide content. Preventing the release of landfill gas into the atmosphere might help slow climate change. There are a few ways in which landfill gas can be managed. The first is to flare the gas (simply burn it) upon extraction from the landfill. This mitigates the release of methane into the atmosphere but still releases considerable amounts of carbon dioxide as well as the potentially toxic organic materials that make up landfill gas.

The second major landfill gas management technique is to use the gas directly for another purpose. The methane content can be separated from the other material and fed through pipes to factories or other industrial operations that need natural gas to operate.

Equally promising are landfill gas management systems connected to electricity generators, whereby the methane can be combusted to produce electricity in a similar fashion to newer, combined-cycle gas turbines. Using landfill gas to generate electricity presents a number of benefits, because it prevents the release of toxic materials and gases that contribute to climate change while reducing demand for less clean sources of electricity such as coal.

Wikimedia

The waste gases (methane) given off by the landfill can be collected through pipes and compressed so it can be stored in reusable form, as a fuel gas.

Advantages

Generating electricity using landfill gas has a number of advantages over other means of producing power. The first is that, although it uses a fossil fuel (natural gas), this fossil fuel is continually being produced and is not being extracted from sensitive ecosystems such as wetlands or from deep under the ocean floor. Because the fuel is being produced in the landfill itself, there are no real costs for the fuel, as would be encountered at a typical power plant. Furthermore, because the distance the fuel must travel is fairly short (sometimes only a few hundred yards from the collection system to the gas-powered turbines), there is much less potential for disasters associated with burst pipelines and spills. Finally, because landfill gas is continually produced, the source for methane is quite reliable and the generating turbines can be operational almost 100 percent of the time, making landfill gas systems one of the most reliable and efficient means of producing electricity.

Landfill gas systems can be installed, in theory, on any landfill. In practice, however, they are typically installed either on those landfills that require landfill gas monitoring and management by state or federal regulators or on those landfills deemed large enough to produce sufficient landfill gas at least to offset the costs of installing the system. This means that some landfills, which would not necessarily come under the requirements of environmental regulations, have voluntarily installed landfill gas management systems because it has been profitable for them to do so, either by selling a clarified landfill gas to industrial users or by selling the electricity they produce to a utility company.

Using landfill gas for energy projects is becoming much more common in the United States as landfill operators come to realize that they can profit from selling methane or electricity. In 2011, more than 550 landfill gas facilities were operating in the United States, and more than 500 more landfills had been identified as candidates for such operations by the Environmental Protection Agency.

JORDAN P. HOWELL

Further Reading

Rajaram, Vasudevan, Faisal Zia Siddiqui, and M. Emran Khan. *From Landfill Gas to Energy: Technologies and Challenges.* Boca Raton, FL: CRC Press, 2011.

U.S. Energy Information Administration. "Landfill Gas." http://www.eia.doe.gov/cneaf/solar.renewables/page/landfillgas/landfillgas.html.

U.S. Environmental Protection Agency. "Converting Landfill Gas to Energy." http://www.epa.gov/lmop/basic-info/index.html#a03.

U.S. Environmental Protection Agency. "Landfill Methane Outreach Program." http://www.epa.gov/lmop.

U.S. Environmental Protection Agency. "National and
    State Lists of Landfills and Energy Projects." http://
    www.epa.gov/lmop/projects-candidates/index.html
    #map-area.

See Also: Agricultural Wastes; Carbon Footprint
and Neutrality; Cogeneration; Net Metering; Refuse;
Tennessee; Waste Incineration.

Laos

Official Name: Laos People's Democratic
Republic.
Category: Geography of Energy.
Summary: Laos relies heavily on hydropower
for energy production, although the population
still uses wood as its main source of energy for
cooking. The nation exports most of its surplus
energy to Thailand and Vietnam.

Energy coverage in Laos is very limited. Prior to
1996, only 19 percent of Laos's population had
access to mains energy (the general-purpose
electric power supply). By 2005, mains electricity access had increased to 50 percent; however,
more than 80 percent of the population still uses
wood as the main source of energy for cooking.
Electricity is reserved primarily for light and
entertainment. The government of Laos maintains that access to electricity is one of the main
indicators of development, and it is determined
to provide 90 percent of the country with mains
access by 2020.

Hydropower

Electricity production in Laos has made a rapid
transition to hydropower since the 1990s. The
country currently receives the majority of its electricity from dozens of hydropower dams located
on various tributaries of the Mekong River. Prior
to the 1990s, electricity was provided mainly
through diesel generators and coal. The electricity generated was consumed mostly in the capital,
Vientiane. For petroleum to supply its generators,

Laos was heavily dependent on imported fuel from
the Soviet Union. To ensure an uninterrupted supply of fuel, a pipeline was laid from Laos to the
coast of Vietnam in 1989.

Laos began to develop its coal industry in 1996,
and coal production increased 4.9 times between
1996 and 2006. Coal is produced from a number of
small mines scattered across the country. The coal
produced is heavily used by the cement industry
and represents approximately 30 percent of the
domestic power production. A small amount of
coal is exported to Thailand. The limited supply of
coal and the cost of fuel imports have contributed
to the development of the hydropower industry.

Laos's hydropower potential was first explored
in the 1960s. The first large-scale dam, the Nam
Ngum 1 Dam (now producing 155 megawatts),
began operation in 1971 with 30 megawatts of
electricity. Because of war, the mountainous
geography of the region, and a lack of financing,
only three hydropower dams had been developed
and brought into operation by 1993. In 1993, the
power sector was opened up to foreign investment. Shortly after the shift to the independent
power producer (IPP) model, the government of
Laos signed a memorandum of understanding
(MOU) with Thailand to supply 1,500 megawatts
of electricity from hydropower. In 1999, the government of Laos signed an MOU with Vietnam
to supply 2,000 megawatts. However, the Asian
financial crisis in 1990s caused the demand for
electricity in the region to stagnate. The development of the hydropower sector in Laos was further slowed by a shift away from large-scale dam
development by key financiers such as the World
Bank and the Asian Development Bank. This shift
was due to a growing concern for the environmental and the social costs of large-scale dams.

With the resurgence of the Asian economies,
the IPP model has allowed the government of Laos
to raise the financial capital required to develop
its hydropower potential and meet the energy
demands of its wealthier neighbors. As of 2010,
the MOUs with Thailand and Vietnam had been
expanded to 7,000 megawatts and 5,000 megawatts, respectively, and a new MOU had been
signed with Cambodia to supply 1,500 megawatts.

The shift to the IPP model and subsequent hydropower development has brought much criticism of Laos's hydropower industry. Laos has been accused of neglecting environmental and social concerns when constructing hydropower dams. The main focus of this criticism has been the lack of comprehensive environmental impact assessments (EIAs). For example, the Theun-Hinboun Dam (which produces 210 megawatts) displaced approximately 30,000 people, damaged fisheries, flooded farmland, and affected drinking water.

Despite these criticisms, the government of Laos has continued to encourage hydropower development. Laos's largest hydropower dam, the Nam Theun 2 (with a capacity of 1,088 megawatts), began operation in March 2010. There are now 11 dams operating in Laos with a total capacity of 1,914 megawatts. Seven projects are under construction, 24 are in the planning stage, and 42 are in the feasibility stage. There are also plans to build the first Mekong mainstream hydropower dams; however, these plans are proceeding slowly because of regional and international concerns regarding the dams' potential environmental and social impacts. The hydropower expansion in Laos is part of the government's plan to become the battery of Southeast Asia. The hydropower sector is the main driver of the economy, representing $4.1 billion since 2001.

NATHANIAL MATTHEWS

Further Reading

Central Intelligence Agency. "Laos." In *The World Factbook*. https://www.cia.gov/library/publications/the-world-factbook/geos/la.html.

Électricité du Laos. "Power Development Plan 2007–16." Vientiane: Électricité du Laos, System Planning Office, 2008.

Ewart, D. "South East Asian Coal Developments." http://www.marston.com/Portals/0/MARSTON_Southeast_Asian_Coal_Developments.pdf.

Laos Ministry of Energy and Mines. "Electricity Statistics of Lao PDR 2005." Vientiane: Department of Electricity, Ministry of Energy and Mines, 2005.

Powering Progress, Department of Energy Promotion and Development, Laos Ministry of Energy and Mines. "History of Hydropower in Lao PDR." http://www.poweringprogress.org/index.php?option=com_content&view=article&id=88&Itemid=126.

U.S. Energy Information Administration. "Country Analysis Brief: Laos." http://www.eia.gov/countries/country-data.cfm?fips=LA.

See Also: Coal; Hydropower; Vietnam; Wood Energy.

Latvia

Official Name: Republic of Latvia.
Category: Geography of Energy.
Summary: Latvia has attempted to escape its energy dependence on Russia by developing energy relations with the neighboring European Union states and implementing renewable energy projects.

Latvia does not have a nuclear power station. The country's energy system is connected with the Russian energy system. In Salaspils (near Riga), a small nuclear reactor operated, which was intended for scientific purposes. The reactor had neither an economic nor a sociopolitical effect on the Latvian energy sector. In 2009, in Ignalina, Lithuania, the second reactor of the nuclear power plant was closed. Therefore, Latvia's dependence on the Russian energy system and gas imports increased. As a result, the Lithuanian government invited the governments of Latvia, Estonia, and Poland to participate in building a new nuclear power plant in Lithuania.

In 2008, the Baltic Energy Market Interconnection Plan was prepared. It was initiated by the European Commission (EC), managed by J. Barosso. It was designed to integrate the three Baltic states into the European energy market by connecting their energy systems with those of neighboring European Union (EU) states. Latvia implemented Directive 2003/54/EC of the EC and opened the nation's electric power market. On July 1, 2007, restrictions on entering the market were abolished and it was allowed to offer lower prices for electric power to electricity-selling companies. Electricity consumers can freely choose their electricity supplier.

Gas Resources

Latvia has no natural gas resources. In the 19th century, when Latvia was incorporated into czarist Russia, the first geological studies started. After World War II, when Latvia belonged to the Soviet Union, that research was renewed. In 1962, gasification of Soviet Latvia started. The first gas main reached the republic. In 1991, after the reestablishment of an independent Latvia, the new government took control of all gas enterprises, and the national company Latvijas Gāze was established. From 1990 to 1993, usage of gas decreased 53 percent in the country. Most of the gas mains were built 20 or 30 years ago. Individual and corporate users did not have gas meters; therefore, it was difficult to measure the amount of gas used.

Latvia is dependent on gas imports from Russia. The country still does not have alternative gas sources. In 1997, Latvijas Gāze was privatized, and shares were sold to the Russian gas provider Gazprom and the strategic German investor Ruhrgas AG. In 1999, shares were also sold to the Latvian enterprise Itera Latvia.

The Inčukalns Underground Gas Storage facility belongs to Latvias Gāze. The storage facility was built in 1968 and is between 765 and 874 yards (700 and 800 meters) underground. The storage facility is filled with gas in summertime, when Latvia receives gas from Russia. In winter, therefore, Latvia cannot depend on the gas main. A part of the gas stored in the storage facility is provided to Russia (Pskov and other areas near the border), Estonia, and Lithuania. It is estimated that in 2009, Latvia imported 5.1 billion cubic feet (1.56 billion cubic meters) of natural gas, primarily from Russia. In 2010, Latvia started to consider building a regional liquid gas terminal in the seaport in Riga.

Oil Resources and Imports

In 1964, in the small Latvian town Adze, not far from the village Gudenieki, oil was extracted. Later, the search for oil was continued in the shelf of the Baltic Sea, where several prospective places for oil extraction were found. During the rule of the Soviet Union, 93 borings for research were made. Oil borings were not exploited because oil resources were inexpensively obtained from Russia. Oil borings received more attention when Latvia regained independence from the Soviet Union in 1991. A diplomatic "war" for the oil resources in the Baltic Sea started between Latvia and its closest neighbor and partner, Lithuania. According to various estimates, oil reserves in Latvia range from 250 to 730 million barrels. Several foreign business companies have obtained licenses for oil extraction.

Latvia has become an important part in the Russian oil transit and energy policy. Oil pipelines play an important role in Latvian oil transit. The system of oil pipelines is governed by a Latvian-Russian company, LatRosTrans. Of total company shares, 66 percent belong to the joint-stock company Ventspils Nafta (the biggest oil product transshipment company in the Baltic states), and 34 percent of the shares are governed by a Russian joint-stock company, Transnefteprodukt. The oil pipeline system comprises the oil pipelines in the territories of Latvia, Lithuania, and Belarus. The length of the oil pipelines is 435 miles (700 kilometers); they connect the oil refinery plant Orlen Lietuva in Mažeikiai, Lithuania, with the terminals in Ventspils, Latvia, and Būtingė, Lithuania. Three oil pipelines come from Polotsk (Belarus): one to Mažeikiai and two to Ventspils. The capacity of the pipelines to Ventspils is 8 million tons of oil and oil products per year. The dependence of the Latvian oil sector on Russia is evident in the decrease of oil transshipments, which has had a negative impact on the Latvian economy. The company Transneft, governed by Russia, transfers oil exports to the port at Primorsk in Russia in order to affect the position of the Latvian government in respect of Russia.

Renewable Energy Sources

Almost half of the electric power used in the country is provided by renewable energy sources. The main renewable resource is hydroelectric power. Latvia has laws that regulate the building of power plants and plans to sell electricity at higher prices. This is a stimulus for investment, especially taking into consideration the fact that Latvia cannot offer big subsidies in order to attract investment. A production quota is approved for each renewable energy source every year.

Jaroslav Dvorak

Further Reading

Baltic Environmental Forum. "Renewable Energy Sources in Estonia, Latvia, and Lithuania: Strategy and Policy Targets, Current Experiences, and Future Perspectives." http://www.bef.lv/data/file/RES.pdf.

Central Intelligence Agency. "Latvia." In *The World Factbook*. https://www.cia.gov/library/publications/the-world-factbook/geos/lg.html.

European Commision. "Baltic Energy Market Interconnection Plan (BEMIP)." http://ec.europa.eu/energy/infrastructure/bemip_en.htm.

U.S. Energy Information Administration. "Country Analysis Brief: Latvia." http://205.254.135.7/countries/country-data.cfm?fips=LG.

See Also: Air Pollution; European Union; Lithuania; Natural Gas; Oil and Petroleum; Russia.

Leadership in Energy and Environmental Design

Category: Energy Consumption.
Summary: Leadership in Energy and Environmental Design (LEED) certification has emerged as an internationally recognized symbol of environmentally sustainable buildings. LEED certification provides energy, as well as environmental and financial benefits.

The U.S. Green Building Council (USGBC), a not-for-profit organization based in Washington, D.C., developed Leadership in Energy and Environmental Design (LEED) in 2000. Voluntary LEED certification is achieved through meeting various energy and environmentally sustainable standards and is available to projects ranging from individual residences to commercial and professional buildings and neighborhoods. The Green Building Certification Institute (GBCI), a not-for-profit organization founded in 2008, oversees the LEED certification process to ensure consistency. The USGBC is comprised of approximately 15,000 organizations and companies, while the GBCI consists of various international certification organizations.

The USGBC developed LEED to encourage green building design and construction practices and to demonstrate their compatibility with lowered project and long-term building maintenance costs. LEED also demonstrates that green-building practices can reduce negative energy and other environmental impacts and can benefit the health of the building's occupants. LEED committees developed the voluntary LEED rating system and certification process through consensus. LEED emerged first as the national standard for environmentally sustainable or green buildings in the United States. The program has since spread globally through agencies such as the Canada Green Building Council and the World Green Building Council.

LEED offers a variety of project types, certification levels, and ratings categories to provide flexibility and allow individual project managers to suit their site, goals, scope, and budget. Guidelines help projects in all phases, from planning to daily operations, to identify and utilize suitable green building practices. The USGBC also provides a variety of LEED and other green building resources, including listings of LEED-certified projects, a directory of LEED-accredited professionals, reference guides, workshops, online training opportunities, a calendar of industry conferences related to green building, and references to relevant publications from other industry and environmental groups.

Project Types

The USGBC and GBCI recommend that potential green building projects identify their interest in LEED certification and implement LEED assessment as early in the project development cycle as possible. Considerations include project goals and desired certification level. LEED is designed to ensure environmental sustainability throughout the building's life, from design and construction to operations and maintenance. LEED even covers the energy and environmental education of the building's future tenants.

LEED developed different ratings systems for a variety of new buildings and projects, including residential homes, neighborhood development, and commercial, school, retail, and healthcare buildings. LEED also has rating systems for major renovations and existing building operations and maintenance. Areas covered within each rating system include sustainable site location and development, water savings, energy efficiency, indoor air quality, materials and resource selection, and indoor environmental quality.

LEED provides an independent, third-party certification of a building's environmental sustainability. The USGBC developed the original LEED certification process and is responsible for its ongoing development. The newest LEED rating system is known as LEED 2012. LEED rating systems are categorized based on building or project type. The categories are: New Construction and Major Renovations (LEED-NC); Schools New Construction and Major Renovations, Core and Shell (LEED-CS); Commercial Interiors (LEED-CI); Healthcare (HC); Retail New Construction (LEED-Retail-NC); Retail Commercial Interiors (LEED-Retail-CI); Neighborhood Development (LEED-ND); Existing Buildings Operations and Maintenance (LEED-EB); and Homes (LEED-H).

Certification Levels

LEED offers four possible certification levels within each project category: Certified, Silver, Gold, and Platinum, with Certified the lowest level and Platinum the highest level. LEED Rating System Checklists are available for all eligible building types. The LEED certification process considers a variety of areas, awarding points in each category. The maximum number of points is 100, with an additional 10 bonus points also possible. The point totals for each category are weighted to reflect their environmental and

human health priorities. The certification level earned by each project reflects the number of points awarded.

Sustainable Sites and Locations and Linkages evaluate site selection and development for environmental impact issues such as current land-use status, regional and environmental suitability and priority, proximity to local infrastructure and resources, ecosystem impact, and pollution potential. Materials and Resources promote sustainability throughout a material or resource's life cycle, as well as waste reduction, reuse, and recycling. Water Efficiency, Energy and Atmosphere, and Indoor Environmental Quality encompass factors such as interior and exterior water usage; landscaping; appliances, fixtures, and lighting; energy efficiency design, practices, and monitoring; the use of renewable or clean energy sources; and indoor air quality.

Awareness and Education encourages building and real estate professionals to educate future building tenants on the building's environmental features and their uses, as well as general sustainable living practices. Innovation in Design allows projects to earn up to 10 bonus points toward certification for innovation in areas not addressed elsewhere in the LEED certification process, for hiring LEED-Accredited Professionals, and through choosing projects that meet Regional Priority. Buildings that ultimately achieve LEED certification receive a plaque. An eligible project must complete all prerequisites and earn at least the minimum number of points required in order to achieve certification at any of the LEED rating levels.

Ratings Systems

A variety of professions use LEED ratings systems, certification processes, and educational resources, including architecture, real estate, engineering, interior design, landscape architecture, facilities maintenance, and construction. Governments and governmental agencies at the local, state, national, and international levels also use LEED in a variety of ways. Some require new government-owned or -funded buildings to meet LEED standards, have begun LEED initiatives, or offer incentives for LEED certification. According to statistics maintained by the USGBC and the GBCI, over 120 countries across the globe are home to building projects seeking LEED certification, led by the United States, Canada, Brazil, Mexico, and India. The statistics also show a global LEED participation rate of nearly 9 billion square feet of building space.

LEED also offers various levels of accreditation to a variety of individual building industry professionals who have studied LEED standards and environmentally sustainable building best practices and have completed LEED examinations. Levels include LEED Fellow, LEED Green Associate, and LEED Accredited Professional (LEED AP). Accredited individuals must undergo continuing education to maintain their accreditation.

LEED certification provides related energy, environmental, and financial benefits. Emphasis on energy efficiency and clean energy use reduces waste and greenhouse gas emissions while lowering operational costs. Utilization of LEED standards from a project's outset results in a better functioning, more cost-conscious integrated approach to environmental sustainability of the building or neighborhood development project. LEED certification can be used as a hallmark of a company's energy and environmental responsibility. Projects can also benefit from the tax rebates and other incentives offered for geen buildings at local and national levels.

MARCELLA BUSH TREVINO

Further Reading

Green Building Certification Institute. "Building Certification" (2011). http://www.gbci.org/main-nav/building-certification/leed-certification.aspx.

Green Building Certification Institute. "LEED Certification Policy Manual" (June 17, 2011). https://www.leedonline.com/irj/go/km/docs/documents/usgbc/leed/config/terms/Legal_Documents_Download/rating_system_doc_june_20_2011/June2011_Cert_Policy_Manual.pdf.

Ingersoll Rand. "LEED Background Information." http://company.ingersollrand.com/sustainability/GreenBuildingCertification/LEEDCertification/LEEDBackgroundInformation/Pages/default.aspx.

Malin, Nadav. "LEED Through the Years." *Environmental Building News*, 2008.

U.S. Green Building Council. "LEED" (2011). http://www.usgbc.org/DisplayPage.aspx?CategoryID=19.

See Also: Building Envelope; Conservation; Department of Energy, U.S.; Energy Intensity; Environmental Stewardship; Heat Island Effect; Mississippi.

Lebanon

Official Name: Republic of Lebanon.
Category: Geography of Energy.
Summary: Lebanon is located in the eastern Mediterranean Sea region. The country has no known fossil fuel, but does have hydropower. In 2009, a survey discovered more than 120 trillion cubic feet of recoverable natural gas in the Levant Basin Province in the eastern Mediterranean.

So far, Lebanon has not been able to exploit any kind of fossil fuel reserves. The nation's supply of energy is achieved through petroleum imports, which account for about half of the country's total fuel imports. Estimates dating back to 2005 calculate that the country imports 108,000 barrels of oil per day in the form of refined products. These are mostly supplied by the Kuwait Petroleum Corporation.

Although Lebanon has always been forced to import all the oil it consumes, before the outburst of inner religious tensions that led to a civil war that lasted for 15 years (1975–1990) the country was an important crude oil refining center. Because of its geographical position, Lebanon was a convenient place for Iraqi and Saudi oil exports to be refined. The oil was taken through pipelines to the two most important Lebanese refineries, Zahrani and Tripoli, in the south and north of the country, respectively. However, these refineries have not been in operation since the beginning of the civil war. In 2006, a joint agreement between the government and Qatar Petroleum

International seemed to pave the way for building a refinery that could operate between 150,000 and 200,000 barrels per day. The conflict with Israel, however, halted this important project, which could diminish by a third the country's expenses to import refined oil products.

Changing Oil-Power Plants to Gas-Power

The conflict had the same negative impact on the construction of a second natural gas pipeline from Syria to the Zahrani power station. This project was part of the conversion scheme that Lebanon undertook to change its oil-power-generating plants into gas-power-generating plants. In March 2005, a first pipeline running for 26 miles from the Baniyas plant in Syria to the Deir al-Ammar-Beddawi power plant in northern Lebanon had been completed. Because of the resulting higher demand for natural gas, Syria had also agreed to provide Lebanon with 1.5 million cubic feet per day from 2007 for a period of 10 years. However, as Syria's own gas production is declining, it is expected that Lebanon will have to import natural gas from Egypt too. In addition to oil and natural gas, Lebanon has thermal electricity-generating plants that have a total installed capacity of 2,259 megawatts. Électricité du Liban (EDL), an autonomous state-owned entity, also operates six hydropower plants with a capacity of more than 200 megawatts.

Lebanese electricity is almost entirely generated and distributed by EDL. Attempts to reform and privatize the company have so far run up against trade union opposition, although the agency is a considerable economic burden that greatly contributes to the public deficit. In the first half of 2006, prior to the war with Israel, EDL was already losing $1 billion. The conflict had a devastating impact on the electricity infrastructure, destroying fuel depots and power plants. A particularly tragic event was an Israeli air strike that destroyed the Jieh power plant, which provoked the spilling of 110,000 barrels of fuel oil into the Mediterranean and the contamination of more than 90 miles of Lebanese shoreline. It was calculated that the conflict caused $100 million in losses to the distribution network. The Lebanese environment had already suffered from damages

to and mismanagement of the energy sector during the civil war, when oil import terminals run by enemy groups exhibited little consideration for environmental regulations.

Negative Factors

The increasing energy demand, the devastating effects of local and regional conflicts, the surge in oil and gas prices, and the absence of a clear and shared central energy policy have all been negative factors that have shaped the Lebanese energy sector in past decades. The Lebanese government is trying to join with private partners to locate potential domestic energy sources. In particular, companies such as Shell, Occidental, TotalFinaElf, and Petro-Canada have expressed interest in conducting studies to find hydrocarbon reserves along the Lebanese coast. However, these international companies are still waiting for a definite legal framework within which to operate, as well as much needed political stability.

In 2009, the U.S. Geological Survey found a large natural gas reserve in the Levant Basin in an area whose waters are claimed to be within Lebanese borders. The Levant Basin is also reported to contain 1.7 billion barrels of recoverable oil. The discovery caused renewed tensions between Israel, Lebanon, and Syria as each of these three countries claims a share of the reserves. For the Lebanese government, this discovery could mean a new source of energy and a revitalized economy after years of conflict.

Luca Prono

Further Reading

Central Intelligence Agency. "Lebanon." In *The World Factbook*. https://www.cia.gov/library/publications/the-world-factbook/geos/le.html.

Dowding, Heather. "Energy Profile Eastern Mediterranean." In *The Encyclopedia of Earth*, edited by Cutler J. Cleveland. Washington, DC: National Council for Science and the Environment. http://www.eoearth.org/article/Energy_profile_of_Eastern_Mediterranean.

Nusca, Andrew. "USGS: Israel, Lebanon and Syria Harbor 122 Trillion Cubic Feet of Natural Gas."

April 9, 2010. http://www.smartplanet.com/blog/
smart-takes/usgs-israel-lebanon-syria-harbor-122
-trillion-cubic-feet-of-natural-gas/5825.

Oxford Business Group. *The Report: Lebanon 2006.*
London: Oxford Business Group, 2007.

U.S. Energy Information Administration. "Country
Analysis Brief: Lebanon." http://www.eia.gov/
countries/country-data.cfm?fips=LE.

See Also: Aramco; History of Energy: Ancient
Sumer and Babylon; History of Energy: Ancient Rome;
Jordan; Offshore Drilling; Saudi Arabia; Syria; Wind
Resources.

Lesotho

Official Name: Kingdom of Lesotho.
Category: Geography of Energy.
Summary: An impoverished sub-Saharan African
nation, Lesotho depends on South Africa for
electricity, to which less than 15 percent of the
population has access.

Formerly Basutoland, Lesotho became independent from Britain in 1966. South Africa surrounds Lesotho, and the country has an average
elevation of 8,268 feet (2,520 meters). The population, at 1.8 million, is generally impoverished,
with a high prevalence (23.2 percent) of population carrying the human immunodeficiency virus
(HIV), 180,000 orphans, and unemployment of
more than 45 percent. Political instability since
independence has included one-party rule for
more than two decades, the exile and return of
King Moshoeshoe II as well as military rule in the
1990s, and election turmoil that led to intervention by Botswana and South Africa in 1998. Since
then, relative stability has prevailed, with Letsie
III as king, although party disputes persist. Lesotho's principal industries include textiles, assembly of clothing, handicrafts, food and beverage
manufacture, tourism, and construction. Growth
of 3 percent ranked the nation at 116th in the
world as of 2010.

Lesotho relies for its energy on South Africa,
which produced 502 gigawatt-hours of electricity for Lesotho as of 2007, ranking it at 159th in
the world. (Another estimate is that Lesotho used
516.9 gigawatt-hours in 2007, placing it 161st.)
Lesotho imported an additional 50 gigawatt-
hours from South Africa in 2008. Lesotho has no
proven reserves of oil or natural gas. It imports
between 1,500 and 2,000 barrels of oil per day but
uses no natural gas. Only 10–15 percent of the
people have access to electricity, so the current
energy sources are imported paraffin, bottled gas,
coal, and petroleum. In 2007–08, the South African Power Pool, including Lesotho, had an electrification rate of 11 percent. Lesotho received
$16 million from the African Development Bank
in 2009 for electrification. Minihydropower, conservation, and demand management have been
measures taken to alleviate shortages. Also, restoration of a 2-megawatt minihydro plant was
expected to help cover Lesotho's shortfall of 17
megawatts.

The Environment and Energy program, under
the auspices of the United Nations Development
Programme (UNDP), offers tools for sustainable
management of natural resources, which could help
reverse land degradation through conservation of
biodiversity. High dependence on biomass energy
will continue or accelerate soil erosion and aggra-
vate the smoke-generated respiratory problems to
which HIV sufferers are especially susceptible.

Government Needing Assistance

Lesotho has ample sunshine and hydropower, and
most of the population use pit latrines (which
require no water access). Pit latrines and water-
less washing facilities could, if properly developed,
serve as a source of methane suitable for cooking
and heating. The country needs help in incorpora-
tion of biogas and solar power for household and
village use. The Ministry of Local Government is
working on development of these energy sources
but needs help.

Solar power is a government-recognized and
-supported source for heating water, providing light,
cooking, and pumping underground water. UNDP
began the Lesotho Renewable Energy-Based Rural

Electrification project in 2006. This program seeks to replace fossil fuels (including diesel and paraffin) for those rural dwellers not tied to the national grid in order to reduce carbon dioxide (CO_2) emissions. The Global Environment Facility (GEF) has been funding environmental programs for several years. GEF aids in resource conservation and use of alternative energy to halt land degradation. The program for promotion of renewable energy at household and community levels runs through 2012. The program has used qualifying local solar installers to give test districts the opportunity to purchase 65-watt solar photovoltaic (PV) systems with a government subsidy at 84 percent. The installers were helped to set up their offices, deal with credit programs, and identify 15 entrepreneurs in each district. Aside from informing the public, it was necessary to revive the Lesotho Solar Energy Society and to train the selectees in not only technical but also entrepreneurial skills. Solar was added to the National Rural Electrification Master Plan in 2008.

In another experimental program, Peace Corps volunteers and engineers from the Massachusetts Institute of Technology saw a solar bread cooker in Lesotho and, impressed, developed solar turbines to produce electricity, refrigeration, and hot water for off-grid residents. The turbines were made from used-car parts and run on the energy from the sun rather than photovoltaics. The system generates a kilowatt, enough for household use and enough to save some trees from being burned for fuel. The effort is especially significant because 90 percent of Lesotho is off the grid; it received funding of $130,000 from the World Bank.

Wind Power

Wind is ample all year round, thanks to the nation's altitude. Traditionally, Lesotho has used wind to create electricity and to pump water from boreholes, but the country shifted to manual pumping of water. Return to wind energy would reduce fuel costs. Lesotho has enough potential hydropower to export water to South Africa and still produce its own electricity, but the resource is significantly underdeveloped. The Muela hydropower station has the potential to generate additional electricity. The United Nations Children's Fund (UNICEF) recommends that the Group of Eight (G8) countries help upgrade the Muela station to provide electricity for the entire country and thereby help Lesotho incorporate power-generating capacity as it expands the number of dams for water collection.

Widespread use of photovoltaic, wind, and minihydro energy for household, community, and small business electricity needs is the goal of three pilot districts in the Renewable Energy-Based Rural Electrification project, which if successful would serve as the basis for a national alternative energy project. Subsidizing or offering free solar technology should be on the G8 agenda too. Finally, Lesotho needs

Wikimedia

The economy of Lesotho is based on agriculture, livestock, manufacturing, and mining. The majority of households subsist on farming, with nearly two-thirds of the country's income coming from the agriculture sector.

researchers to develop sunflower oil and other bio-fuels as alternative fuels.

JOHN H. BARNHILL

Further Reading

Central Intelligence Agency. "Lesotho." In *The World Factbook*. https://www.cia.gov/library/publications/the-world-factbook/geos/lt.html.

Greeneconomyinitiative. "Lesotho Gets US$ 16M for Energy Project." February 11, 2009. http://www.greeneconomyinitiative.com/news/181/ARTICLE/1441/2009-02-11.html.

Solarpanelspower.net. "Solar Energy for Lesotho." http://solarpanelspower.net/solar-power/solar-energy-lesotho.

United Nations Children's Fund. "Lesotho: Energy Use and Utilisation in Southern Africa." http://www.unicef.org/southafrica/SAF_youngvoices_g8lesotho.doc.

United Nations Development Programme. "Renewable Energy-Based Rural Electrification in Lesotho." January 25, 2011. http://www.undp.org.ls/energy/default.php.

U.S. Energy Information Administration. "Country Analysis Brief: Lesotho." http://www.eia.gov/countries/country-data.cfm?fips=LT.

See Also: Hydropower; Microhydropower; Photovoltaics; Utilities; Wind Resources.

Levitation

Category: Energy Technology.
Summary: *Levitation* refers to the elevated, stable floating of an object without any physical interference from gravity. Different technologies have been developed to produce the stable levitation of matter.

To overcome gravity, a vertically upward, vectored force equal to the gravitational force is presupposed. The related idea of antigravity refers to a place or object that is free from the force of gravity.

At present, there is no technological demonstration of antigravity. However, the idea has led to several technological innovations.

Technological Methods

At the beginning of the 20th century, Sir Isaac Newton's law of universal gravitation was superseded by the general theory of relativity, which describes gravity not as a force (as in Newton's mechanics) anymore but as the result of alterations in the geometry of space itself. In this model, antigravity is considered very unlikely.

In 1923, O. Muck obtained a patent for electromagnetic levitation (EML). Magnetic materials and systems are able to attract or repel each other, depending on whether they carry the same charge (repulsion) or different charges (attraction). Samuel Earnshaw's theorem demonstrates that by means of static ferromagnetism it is not possible to stabilize levitated objects, because the magnetic attraction decreases with cumulative distance, and the obverse is true. For a stable system with enabled movement of the levitated object, the opposite is necessary. Minimal movements should be pushed back to the equilibrium position, obtaining dynamic stability, as applied in servomechanisms, diamagnetic materials, superconductors, or systems involving eddy currents. Levitation techniques are useful tools in high-temperature, containerless melt property studies.

Diamagnetic substances repel magnetic fields, working in a fashion opposite to that of normal magnets. This is called electromagnetic suspension (EMS), which is caused by interaction with the screening currents. Earnshaw's theorem does not apply. In practice, the position and speed of the levitated object are measured, and the electromagnets are continuously adjusted to stabilize the object's motion, thus forming a servomechanism. Servo control keeps EMS maglev (from *magnetic levitation*) trains at a constant distance from the track. In very strong magnetic fields of about 16 teslas, even small live animals have been levitated, possibly because of the diamagnetic property of water in organisms.

Two physical phenomena related to conductors can be used to create magnetic repulsion. First is

Lenz's law: Upon bringing an electrical conductor, such as copper, aluminum, or silver, and a magnet close together, an induced current occurs in the conductor, creating an opposite field that repels the magnet. This is applied as electrodynamic suspension (EDS). Second is the Meissner effect, discovered by Walther Meissner and Robert Ochsenfeld in 1933: A normal conductor transmits a nearby electric magnetic field. In case the conductor is cooled below a so-called transition temperature for becoming a superconductor, any magnetic field will be blocked out.

EDS also occurs when an electromagnet is driven by an alternating-current (AC) electrical source, inducing a changing magnetic field. Magnetic levitation can be multiplied by means of Halbach arrays, instead of using single-pole permanent magnets.

In addition to using the methods discussed above, levitation can be simulated with pressurized gases. At high pressure, the density of gases, preferably noble gases (which have greatest stability because of their low reaction rates), can exceed that of some solids, thus providing the buoyancy to levitate objects.

In 1933, a method of acoustic levitation based on fixed ultrasound fields was discovered. This method is used for qualitative analyses in outer space under the influence of microgravity, allowing the precise placement of small assays contact-free in analytical tests. Forces due to the alternating pressure field of the fixed ultrasound waves act on the assay, placed at nodes of axial and radial forces.

Another example is gyroscopically stabilized levitation of a magnet by spinning it in a toroidal field created by a base ring of magnets. Although stable, this method is very unpractical, because it works only in a narrow region regarding space and the required rate of precession.

Applications and Research

Magnetic levitation is considered a promising propulsion technique, based on many super-conducting electromagnets using either EMS or EDS for lifting and propulsion. Maglev trains are much faster and quieter than wheeled trains, because the levitation of about 3.9 inches above the guideway avoids friction on guide rails. EDS allows larger gaps than EMS but requires support wheels for relatively low speeds (below 93 miles per hour), when levitation force is low.

In the late 1920s, Thomas Townsend Brown worked on high-voltage devices and obtained a British patent for a symmetric, parallel plate capacitor. Brown claimed his "gravitator" would produce a net thrust in the direction of the anode.

Between 1948 and 1967, the Gravity Research Foundation, formed by Roger Babson, was involved in research on gravity shielding, and it is still running an annual essay award. In 1956, the Institute for Field Physics was established by Bryce DeWitt at the University of North Carolina. The same year, the (later) Aerospace Research Laboratories (ARL) at Wright-Patterson Air Force Base in Dayton, Ohio, started research on gravitational and unified field theories. Also in the late 1950s, the Research Institute for Advanced Study (RIAS, founded by George S. Trimble of the Glenn L. Martin Company) developed nonlinear differential equations, providing the mathematical tools to understand general relativity. The Lefschez Center for Dynamical Systems began as a spin-off from RIAS.

Between 1996 and 2002, the National Aeronautics and Space Administration (NASA) funded the Breakthrough Propulsion Physics Program (BPP), studying antigravity-like designs for long-distance space propulsion, called diametric drive. The BPP program continues in the independent Tau Zero Foundation.

MANJA LEYK

Further Reading

DeWitt, Bryce. *Bryce DeWitt's Lectures on Gravitation*. New York: Springer, 2011.

Hathaway, George, B. Cleveland, and Y. Bao. "Gravity Modification Experiment Using a Rotating Superconducting Disk and Radio Frequency Fields." *Physica C* 4 (2003).

Moon, Francis C. *Superconducting Levitation: Applications to Bearings and Magnetic Transportation*. New York: Wiley, 1994.

Valoe, Thomas, ed. *Electrogravitics Systems: Reports on a New Propulsion Methodology*. Washington, DC: Integrity Research Institute, 2001.

See Also: Alternative Energy; Tesla, Nikola; Trains.

Liberia

Official Name: Republic of Liberia.
Category: Geography of Energy.
Summary: Liberia's impoverished population have no access to publicly provided electricity. Most power comes from privately owned gas-burning generators, the burning of biomass, or hydroelectric power. Liberia has the lowest level of electricity access in the world.

The Republic of Liberia is on the west coast of Africa and is one of the only sub-Saharan nations without political roots in the European-driven "scramble for Africa," a period of rampant European colonization during the late 19th and early 20th centuries. Liberia was established in 1847 by freed American slaves; the capital city, Monrovia, is named for President James Monroe, a supporter of the effort to establish a country for former slaves where they could govern themselves. Instability since a 1980 military coup has led to two civil wars and prolonged violence and economic despair, from which the country has not yet recovered. Liberia's nominal per capita gross domestic product (GDP) is only $226. Liberia also ranks low (162nd in the world) on the Human Development Index (a measure of human well-being, based on data from the United Nations Development Programme, that takes into account such factors as life expectancy, literacy, education, and standard of living).

Natural Resources

The Liberian economy has long depended on natural resources—timber, iron ore, and rubber—and foreign direct investment. The wartime economy exported the area's diamond resources, and for several years Liberian diamond exports were sanctioned by the United Nations because of the government's role in exporting "blood diamonds" from Liberia to Sierra Leone and Angola in exchange for weapons. War profiteering ruined the country's infrastructure: Monrovia was without water or power when the first postwar government was elected. Although the diamond ban was lifted in 2007 and contracts for the export of iron ore have been signed, the country remains deeply dependent on foreign humanitarian aid and annually imports nearly $5 billion in goods while exporting less than $1 billion. Inflation has fallen since the civil wars, but interest rates remain high.

Electricity

Most Liberians have no access to publicly provided electricity, and if they have power at all (most do not), obtain it from a gas-burning generator of their own. This is the lowest level of electricity access in the known world. Most publicly provided energy in Liberia is provided by wood-burning plants or hydroelectric power. A 1963 World Bank loan funded the construction of the Mount Coffee Hydropower Project on the Saint Paul River, which was completed in 1966. For years, it provided 64 megawatts of power, until it was extensively damaged in 1990 during the First Liberian Civil War. War prevented the possibility of repairing the plant until the 21st century, when the U.S. Trade and Development Agency funded a 2007 study of the facility's damage. Although the dam itself had suffered no structural damage, the bulk of the power generation facilities needed repairs estimated to cost close to $400 million. To date, the plant has not been repaired, and Liberia has floated the possibility of privatization, if foreign investors can be attracted.

The Firestone Hydroelectric Power Station, the first hydroelectric facility built in the country, has been in operation since 1942 and was built to supply power to the American military during World War II. Although it was the only hydroelectric plant to survive Liberia's civil wars, it has a generating capacity of only 4.8 megawatts.

The United States Agency for International Development (USAID) sponsored the Liberia

Energy Assistance Program, which ran from late 2006 to early 2009 and helped do some of the initial work in repairing Liberia's electricity infrastructure. Prepaid metering was installed in low-income networks, the number of working streetlights was tripled, solar systems were installed at critical places such as schools and clinics, and electricity access was expanded to include 25,000 new rural customers. The Norwegian government entered into an agreement with Liberia in 2007, expanded in 2010, to help Liberia restore its electricity capacity. A thorough evaluation of the country's situation was made, and cooperation agreements were drafted, covering electricity generation, distribution, and transmission, as well as institutional development. The support is expected to continue over the long term, as the situation in Liberia is dire enough that there is no quick solution to its problems—even if the worldwide depression that started in 2008 had not occurred.

BILL KTE'PI

Further Reading

Central Intelligence Agency. "Liberia." In *The World Factbook.* https://www.cia.gov/library/publications/the-world-factbook/geos/li.html.

Hetherington, Tim. *Long Story Bit by Bit: Liberia Retold.* New York: Umbrage Editions, 2009.

Olukoju, Ayodeji. *Culture and Customs of Liberia.* Westport, CT: Greenwood, 2006.

U.S. Energy Information Administration. "Country Analysis Brief: Liberia." http://www.eia.gov/countries/country-data.cfm?fips=LI.

See Also: Côte d'Ivoire; Guinea; Sierra Leone.

Libya

Category: Geography of Energy.
Summary: The north African country of Libya has an abundance of energy resources and is a net exporter of oil and natural gas. Significant oil reserves were discovered in Libya in 1959.

Using funds generated from oil exports, Muammar Qadhafi's government lent monetary support to international paramilitary organizations. These activities led to sanctions on Libya, most notably those from the United Nations (UN) and the United States in 1996 for Libya's alleged involvement in the bombing of a civilian aircraft over Lockerbie, Scotland. These sanctions led to a decrease in foreign direct investment in Libya's energy sector and limited its ability to export energy to certain countries. The UN lifted sanctions in 1999, but the United States continued to place sanctions on Libya until 2006. Since the suspension of sanctions, international oil companies have increased their foreign direct investment in hydrocarbon production and exploration in Libya. In 2011, Libyan politics experienced what has been termed a *revolution* by Middle East analysts: a civil war and an uprising during which fighting occurred between forces loyal to the Qadhafi regime and those seeking to depose his government. The conflict resulted in Qadhafi's death and the recognition of the National Transitional Council as the representative government of Libya. An interim government was officially inaugurated on October 24, 2011, with Abdel Rahim el Kib as heading the government. The constituent assembly was due to be elected in the first half of 2012.

Oil and Natural Gas Resources

Libya has substantial oil and natural gas resources and is a member of the Organization of Petroleum Exporting Countries (OPEC). The Libyan economy is heavily dependent on hydrocarbon exports. According to the International Monetary Fund (IMF), hydrocarbons comprised over 95 percent of export earnings in 2010. Additionally, earnings from the oil sector comprise 25 percent of gross domestic product (GDP) and 60 percent of public sector wages. Libyan oil production peaked at over 3 million barrels per day in the late 1960s. In 2010, crude oil production was estimated to be 1.65 million barrels per day. Libya maintains the largest oil reserves in Africa, estimated in January 2011 to be about 46.4 billion barrels, as well as approximately 55 trillion cubic feet of natural gas reserves. Most

Libya has substantial oil and natural gas resources. Earnings from the oil sector comprise 25 percent of gross domestic product and 60 percent of public sector wages. Libya maintains the largest oil reserves in Africa, estimated to be about 46.4 billion barrels. This is the El Saharara oil field in Libya.

of Libya's proven oil reserves are found in the Sirte Basin. In 2010, total oil production reached around 1.8 million barrels per day. Libya's natural gas production has increased dramatically in the last decade. Much of this increase in Libyan natural gas production and exports has occurred since the opening of the Greenstream pipeline to Europe in late 2004. Libya produced over 1 trillion cubic feet of natural gas in 2009.

Libya is a net exporter of oil and natural gas. According to the International Energy Agency, around 85 percent of Libyan oil exports are sold to European countries. Libya's domestic oil consumption was estimated to be approximately 270,000 barrels per day in 2010. Libya's net exports of oil were about 1.5 million barrels per day. In 2009, Libya consumed 212 billion cubic feet (Bcf) of natural gas and exported 349 Bcf to Europe. The primary method of exporting natural gas is via pipeline; a small amount is exported as liquefied natural gas. In 1971, Libya became the second nation to export liquid natural gas, but due to infrastructural and technological shortcomings and the effects of international sanctions, liquid natural gas exports have been consistently low. Natural gas exports to Europe have grown considerably since 2004 with the opening of the 370-mile Greenstream underwater natural gas pipeline from Libya to Sicily. The Greenstream pipeline is operated by Eni, in partnership with National Oil Company.

Rising Energy Demand

Libya's energy demand has been met through a consumption mix of 72 percent by oil and 28 percent by natural gas over last decade. Due to an increasing electricity demand, the government plans to expand domestic natural gas usage while also exploring solar and wind potential for rural electricity consumption. Natural gas comprises about 45 percent of generated electricity. According to the *Oil & Gas Journal*, Libya has five domestic refineries, with a combined capacity of 378,000 barrels per day (bpd). Libya's refineries include the Ras Lanuf export refinery, with a refining capacity of 220,000 bpd; the Az Zawiya refinery, with refining capacity of 120,000 bpd; the Tobruk refinery, with refining capacity of 20,000 bpd; Sarir, a topping facility with 10,000 bpd of capacity; and Brega, with refining capacity of 8,000 bpd. UN Resolution 883 of November 11, 1993, which banned Libya from importing refinery equipment, reduced Libya's capacity for refining oil until sanctions were lifted in the early 2000s.

The ongoing conflict in Libya and transition to National Transitional Council governance has impacted the Libyan energy sector significantly. Fighting between Qadhafi and rebel forces disrupted Libyan oil production such that it dipped below 100,000 bpd, and exports ceased completely in August 2011. According to the National Oil Company, production rebounded to approximately 430,000 bpd and exports were approximately 400,000 bpd as of October 2011. Analysts estimated that the Libyan oil sector would require between 18 and 36 months to resume production at prewar levels, because of infrastructural damage incurred during the conflict: The National Oil Company estimated that full recovery would require 14 months, and projected that oil exports would exceed prewar deliveries by April 2012, climbing to almost 1.4 million bpd.

Libya's capacity for nuclear power has been curbed by technical limitations as well as international opinion and policy. Libya has pursued bilateral negotiations to augment its ability to construct nuclear research facilities and power plants, but the nuclear program's progress has been mitigated by lack of oversight, technology, and foreign supplies and support.

ALLISON HARTNETT

Further Reading
African Energy. "Libya's Energy Future." http://www.africa-energy.com/html /Public/Libya_Report/Libya.html.

Hallett, Don. *Petroleum Geology of Libya*. Amsterdam: Elsevier Science, 2002.

International Energy Agency. *World Energy Outlook 2011*. Paris: International Energy Agency, 2011.

See Also: Algeria; Egypt; Liberia; Natural Gas; Oil and Petroleum; Organization of Petroleum Exporting Countries; Saudi Arabia; Tunisia.

Liechtenstein

Official Name: Principality of Liechtenstein.
Category: Geography of Energy.
Summary: The small principality of Liechtenstein is dependent mainly on imported energy, with an import share of 91.2 percent of total energy use.

Located between Austria and Switzerland, Liechtenstein has an area of only 62 square miles (160 square kilometers) and is considered the sixth-smallest independent nation in the world. In 2009, its overall energy consumption declined slightly to 1.3 terawatt-hours per year, which translates to an average per capita use of 37.7 megawatt-hours. Per capita use has remained about the same since 1990, varying with demand for heating. The overall amount of energy produced was only 118,785 megawatt-hours in 2009. Energy is used for heating (50 percent), transport (30 percent), and commercial and industrial production (20 percent).

Electricity
Electricity is the most important energy carrier, with a share of 27.9 percent of whole energy. Liechtenstein is dependent mainly on imported electricity. However, electricity production was 71,000 megawatt-hours in 2009, which means a share of self-supply of 17.9 percent of an overall electricity use of 378 gigawatt-hours. Nearly all produced electricity comes from two of nine hydropower plants, which provide 61,062 megawatt-hours. Five block-heating power plants produced 795 megawatt-hours, and 288 photovoltaic (PV) plants provide 927 megawatt-hours. A large part (54 percent) of the imported electricity from

France and Switzerland is from nuclear energy; other energy resources are mainly hydropower. The structure of electricity resources is the reason for the country's low carbon dioxide (CO_2) emissions in comparison to other nations.

Fossil Fuels

In 2009, fossil fuels were estimated to account for about two-thirds of energy consumption, with a total import rate of 100 percent. Gasoline use was estimated to decrease by about 32 percent between 2000 and 2009. Diesel use, however, increased by nearly 60 percent from 2000 to 2009, supplying 131 gigawatt-hours in 2009. For heating purposes, the demand for oil varies depending on the wintertime conditions: In 2009, for example, demand was for 242 gigawatt-hours, whereas in 2007 it was only 173. Heating gas is used more often than oil, and its consumption was 317 gigawatt-hours in 2009, accounting for 23.4 percent of total energy use. Coal has played a diminishing role in energy use: Consumption of 1 gigawatt-hours in 1985 decreased to 12 megawatt-hours in 2009.

Renewable Energy

Domestic energy production from renewable sources is significant. For example, hydropower for electricity production constitutes about 75 percent of domestic energy production, or about 66 gigawatt-hours. Apart from hydropower, the most important renewable energy source is solid biomass. Liechtenstein is located in a mountainous area in the Alps, so wood has traditionally been used for heating. In 2009, energy from wood (including wood pellets) accounted for 49 gigawatt-hours, or 3.6 percent of overall energy consumption. Energy consumption from thermal solar collectors increased from 194 megawatt-hours in 1997 to 7 gigawatt-hours (0.5 percent of overall energy use) in 2009.

Hydropower could be enhanced, through improvements in existing power plants, to an estimated 78 gigawatt-hours. Geothermal power has barely been used but has an estimated potential of 2 gigawatt-hours. Because of monetary subsidies for solar collectors, it is expected that use of solar power will steadily increase. A wind farm could be built in a natural reserve, although that possibility is regarded as unrealistic.

Challenges

Liechtenstein's major energy challenges concern traffic (tranport issues) and its settlement structure. Around 95 percent of current traffic is of domestic origin; only 5 percent is "through traffic." This is surprising, insofar as one of Liechtenstein's neighboring countries, Switzerland, has one of the best developed railway systems and most of the flows of trade are made with Switzerland. The reasons for Liechtenstein's dense traffic lie in its comparatively high number of workplaces, which leads to high rates of commuting traffic (13,000 persons daily among a resident population of 36,000). Moreover, urban sprawl makes it necessary to traverse large distances between workplaces and homes, a condition that favors individual automobile traffic as opposed to public transport.

Liechtenstein's settlement patterns also pose challenges: The country is characterized by a decomposition of traditional rural structures, leading to dispersed settlements and a loss of areas that are not built out. These structures entail an increased energy demand due to traffic and the building of infrastructures (such as canal systems and streets) to support that traffic, and a rise in the demand for heating. A referendum for a reform of the law for spatial planning was rejected in 2002, and it remains difficult to implement the necessary changes to implement more sustainable settlement structures.

PETRA WÄCHTER

Further Reading

Eccardt, Thomas M. *Secrets of the Seven Smallest States of Europe: Andorra, Liechtenstein, Luxembourg, Malta, Monaco, San Marino, and Vatican City.* New York: Hippocrene Books, 2005.

Encyclopedia of the Nations. "Liechtenstein." http://www.nationsencyclopedia.com/Europe/Liechtenstein-ENERGY-AND-POWER.html.

"Liechtenstein." In *The Stateman's Yearbook.* http://www.statesmansyearbook.com/

entry?entry=countries_li.ENERGY_AND_
NATURAL_RESOURCES.

Open Energy Information. "Liechtenstein." http://
en.openei.org/wiki/Liechtenstein.

Renewable Energy and Energy Efficiency Partnership.
"Energy Profile Liechtenstein." http://reegle.info/
countries/LI.

See Also: Austria; France; Hydropower; Switzerland.

Life-Cycle Analysis

Category: Environmentalism.
Summary: Life-cycle analysis provides a
framework and methodology to identify and
evaluate environmental impacts associated with a
lifetime of a product from "cradle to grave. "

Life-cycle analysis (LCA) is a methodology to identify and evaluate environmental impacts coupled
with the whole life cycles of materials and services.
The concept of LCA originated in the 1960s. In 1963,
Harold Smith, an engineer at the Douglas Point
Nuclear Generating Station in Canada, first presented his calculation of cumulative energy requirements for the production of chemical intermedi-
ates and products at the World Energy Conference.
Later, in 1969, the Coca-Cola Company conducted
research comparing different beverage containers
to determine the one with the lowest environmental
impact. This research built the foundation for modern methods of life-cycle inventory analysis.

Analyzing Environmental Problems
Many companies throughout the Western world
then followed the Coca-Cola Company and performed LCA on their products. The green movement in Europe, especially because of the increasing concern on solid waste in the late 1980s,
significantly boosted LCA as a tool for analyzing
environmental problems. However, in the 1990s,
many industries complained about the improper
use of LCA, and a variety of its standards, leading
to the standardization of LCA methodology in the

International Standards Organization (ISO) 14000
series. The birth of the ISO 14000 environmental
management standards offered a system for examination of environmental management including
labeling, performance evaluations, life-cycle analyses, communication, and auditing.

Three Basic Components
LCA is composed of three basic components:
inventory analysis, impact analysis, and improvement analysis. A general process of LCA moves
from goal and scope definition to life-cycle inventory, life-cycle impact assessment, and finally
interpretation. First, researchers must define the
goal and boundaries, or scope, of an LCA study
according to research questions. For example,
will the study analyze a full life cycle, a partial life
cycle, or individual stages? Sometimes, the need
for an LCA might apply only to the transportation
or distribution elements of a project. Then, what
is included and excluded from each step in the
process must be considered carefully. Certainly,
researchers need a good understanding of the
life cycles of their products before decision making. For example, the life cycle of a product often
includes raw materials acquisition, energy requirements, manufacturing, formulation, processing,
transportation and distribution, use, reuse, maintenance, recycling, and waste management.

At this point, many researchers create a conceptual model of an LCA analysis. Researchers
design process trees or flowcharts classifying the
activities in the conceptual model. The model may
also count the interrelations of different phases
and components. Gathering data from inside and
outside the company should be carried out in the
next step. Data accuracy is vital for an LCA analysis; therefore, peer reviews are sometimes adopted
to ensure data validity. Besides the data acquisition from inside the company, public information
for use in the life-cycle inventory is also available.
For example, the U.S. Department of Energy databases of energy uses by industry aggregate, the
U.S. Environmental Protection Agency databases,
and the U.S. Department of Commerce databases
provide excellent public information that can be
used for LCA.

▷ *Examining Various Dimensions of Sustainability*

Despite the fact that LCA is now a well-established tool to examine environmental burdens of materials and services, there are some recognized problems with it. A quantitative LCA is highly complex and costly. First, a lack of consistent data about all aspects of a product's life cycle is always an issue. Second, considering the massive data collection and conversion need to conduct an LCA, researchers must continuously make assumptions during an LCA analysis. Third, it is impossible to quantify every factor that a conceptual model needs. Fourth, interpretation of final reports is also challenging, because there is the lack of a standard evaluation scheme. Moreover, LCA usually ignores social implications: for instance, those regarding consumer behavior and policy regulations.

Nevertheless, LCA is on its way to becoming a standard tool for many applications. For example, LCA is now used to examine many dimensions of sustainability, such as people, ecosystems, and energy consumption. Moreover, social implications and economic behavior are increasingly taken into account in LCA. As the sophistication of LCA expands, the scope of an LCA is extending from predominantly product-related questions to sector- and even economy-wide levels.

When data are ready, researchers operate inventory analyses, involving the inputs and outputs of all life-cycle processes. Next, researchers need to interpret results by writing an assessment report. Usually, the report consists of the methodology used, the purpose of the study, the boundary conditions set, all assumptions used, and the audience of the study. Most LCA studies are for the internal use of a company or organization. Comparing different LCA studies must be presented cautiously because of different boundaries and conditions. Making suggestions for improvement is the last step of a LCA study and should aim to identify all areas for potential improvement.

Because all analyses have to be calculated in terms of materials and energy, unit conversion is often necessary. Inventory analysis establishes material and energy balances for each process step and event by looking at all the nitty-gritty details. Thus, this analysis is time-consuming. At present, there are many software programs designed to carry out inventory analyses, such as GaBi (by PE International) and SimaPro (by PRé Consultants).

One excellent LCA study was started by researchers at Chalmers University of Technology in Sweden in 2003: a life-cycle assessment of wood-based ethanol-diesel blends. The study was to evaluate the use of low-ethanol-content diesel blends (E-diesel) as automotive fuel. The project produced ethanol from lignocellulosic raw materials. The full-scale life cycle consisted of the production of diesel, ethanol, and additives; the mixing of different components; and the final use of the chosen fuel. The researchers studied two different E-diesel compositions used in heavy-duty diesel engines by conducting two case studies: one on a bus fleet driven under urban traffic conditions and one on a truck fleet run mainly on highways. The final report found that, as an experimental fuel, E-diesel was currently undergoing a very active demonstration stage toward acceptance by governmental and engine manufactures. Therefore, E-diesel still had a long way to go for commercialization in 2003. On the other hand, there were many advantages regarding the environmental performance of E-diesel. As far as climate change was concerned, E-diesel emitted about carbon dioxide (CO_2) emissions that were about 10 percent less than those of ordinary diesel. By replacing traditional fossil fuels with E-diesel, the research found, 20 percent and 10 percent reductions in particulate matter and sulfur dioxide (SO_2) emissions, respectively, could help improve local air quality.

Xiaoliang Yang

Further Reading

Ciambrone, David F. *Environmental Life Cycle Analysis*. Boca Raton, FL: Lewis, 1997.

Guinee, Jeroen B., et al. "Life Cycle Assessment: Past, Present, and Future." *Environmental Science and Technology* 45, no. 1 (2011).

Rodríguez, José Canga. "Life Cycle Assessment of Wood-Based Ethanol-Diesel Blends (Executive Summary)." February 2003. http://www.dantes.info/Publications/Publication-doc/LCA%20-%20E-diesel%20Summary.PDF.

U.S. Environmental Protection Agency. "Life Cycle Analysis." http://www.epa.gov/nrmrl/lcaccess/lca101.html.

See Also: Best Management Practices; Energy Payback; Environmental Stewardship; Gasohol; Industrial Ecology; Sustainability.

Lighting

Category: Energy Consumption.

Summary: Demand for artificial, indoor light comprises a significant portion of energy consumption globally. Electric lighting technologies have become more efficient over the past 150 years, providing more light while using less energy.

Electric lighting is the most common form of artificial lighting used today, although gas, candle, and oil lighting have all been used in the past and still continue to be used in some forms today. Early lamps were burned with whale oil, which drove a large whaling industry during the 1800s. Today, electric lighting constitutes 19 percent of energy consumption worldwide, with over 33 billion lamps in operation.

In lighting design, the term lamp refers to the replaceable component used to generate light that is more commonly known as a lightbulb. The components that house the lamp are known as the light fixture or fitting. There are a number of different lamp technologies currently in use.

Lamp performance is measured according to its light output (in lumens), power (in watts), efficacy (in lumens per watt), lifetime (in hours), lamp lumen depreciation (which is depicted as a percentage), correlated color temperature (CCT), color rendering index (CRI), dimmability, voltage, and temperature considerations.

Luminous Efficacy

An important metric for evaluating a lamp's performance is luminous efficacy, which is a measure of how effective a lamp is in converting electrical energy into light. Luminous efficacy is measured in lumens per watt. This is analogous to measuring a vehicle's efficiency in terms of miles per gallon. The typical incandescent lamp has a luminous efficacy of about 15 lumens per watt. In contrast, a metal halide lamp provides about 90 lumens per watt, a linear fluorescent lamp about 95, and a high-pressure sodium lamp about 110.

As lighting technology becomes more energy efficient, it also has greater luminous efficacy. However, it is impossible to tell by comparing the efficacy of two lamps whether one will be brighter than the other or if it would use less energy. The quantity of light emitted by a light source is measured in lumens per square foot, or foot-candles (in the United States), or in lumens per square meter, or lux, in nations that use the metric system. One foot-candle is equivalent to 10 lux. Illumination levels decrease further away from a lighting source according to the inverse square law. The Illuminating Engineering Society of North America (IESNA) develops and promotes standards and guidelines for good lighting design and practice. IESNA typically recommends foot-candle levels of 25–30 for homes and classrooms, and 50–100 for more intensive visual uses.

The appearance of the color of a white light source is described as its chromaticity and measured using CCT, which uses Kelvin (K) degree units of measure. Qualitatively, white light is described as being either "warmer" or "cooler." This can be misleading, as a light that appears "cooler" in color actually has a higher chromaticity, based on the observation that metal when heated first glows red, then white-hot, then appears almost blue as the temperature increases. Light sources generally range in chromaticity between 2,500 and 10,000 degrees K. Daylight typically ranges from 5,000 to 10,000 degrees K. Electric lamps are rated according to a CRI, which is a 100-point scale that measures how well the human eye can perceive colors when viewed under their light, relative to a reference source of the same CCT. Incandescent lamps are the most effective at rendering color, and have a CRI of 100.

Incandescent Lamps

Incandescent lamps use electrical current to heat a thin metal filament until it emits radiation in the visible spectrum, causing it to become white-hot or incandescent. Thomas Alva Edison's early models were made with carbon filaments; today, most filaments are composed of tungsten. A vacuum pump is generally used to evacuate the glass lightbulb that protects the heated filament from air. In halogen lamps, the bulb is filled with inert halogen gas, which makes it possible to increase the temperature at which the filament is heated without reducing the life of the lamp, thus resulting in a brighter light source. Most of the electricity used to power incandescent lamps is emitted as infrared radiation, or heat, making them a relatively inefficient source of light. This heat puts stress on the lamp in general, and incandescent bulbs are characterized by short lamp life (750–2,000 hours).

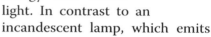

Since incandescent lamps emit radiation continuously across the visible spectrum, they make it possible for the human eye to perceive the full spectrum of visible light, which results in better color performance. They are often preferred as a lighting choice due to their ability to turn on to full brightness immediately, and their dimmability, which are both characteristics that early fluorescent technologies lacked. However, incandescents are being replaced in many applications by fluorescent lamps and light-emitting diodes (LEDs).

Fluorescent Lamps

All photos: Photos.com

Fluorescent lamps operate by running an electrical current through a tube filled with mercury vapor, which emits ultraviolet (UV) radiation. A phosphor coating on the inside of the tube converts the UV energy into visible light. In contrast to an incandescent lamp, which emits radiation continuously along the visible spectrum, a fluorescent lamp emits radiation along a discontinuous curve, emitting light at a few different peaks in the spectrum based on the type of phosphors used to coat the lamp. Fluorescent lights require an additional piece of equipment, the ballast, to start and regulate the flow of electricity through the lamp. The ballast can be either magnetic or electronic. Electronic ballasts operate at higher frequencies, and are more efficient than magnetic ballasts.

Although fluorescent lamps are available in a wide array of technologies, most fall into two categories: linear fluorescent (or fluorescent tube) lamps and compact fluorescent lamps. Linear fluorescent or fluorescent tube lamps are most commonly used in office buildings and other institutional settings for general lighting purposes. Compact fluorescent lamps (CFLs) are used principally as an energy-efficient alternative to incandescent bulbs. In contrast to linear fluorescents, they can be placed in the same decorative fixtures typically used to showcase incandescent light. Special ballasts must also be installed in order to use CFLs with a dimmer switch. The design of a CFL is essentially a curved glass tube that operates along the same principles as a linear fluorescent.

Fluorescent lighting is characterized by high efficacy, long life, and a high CRI. Early fluorescent technologies suffered from problems such as poor light color and flicker at start-up, but new fluorescent lamps without those challenges are now widely available at low cost. Energy efficiency incentive programs in the late 2000s were used to drive down the price of CFL bulbs, as they consume significantly less energy than equivalent incandescent lighting sources. Fluorescent lamps also have a much longer life span than incandescent lamps and therefore need to be replaced less frequently. However, the mercury contained in fluorescent lamps poses an environmental concern, and fluorescent lamps must be disposed of correctly.

High Intensity Discharge Lamps

High intensity discharge lamps produce light by creating an electrical arc between two electrodes using a gas as a conductor. They have a higher efficacy and longer life than fluorescent lamps, but their poor color quality and long warm-up time limit their useful applications.

The three most common types of high intensity discharge lamps are mercury vapor, metal halide, and high-pressure sodium. Mercury vapor lamps are the oldest of the three types. They cast a blue-white light and are used primarily for street lighting. Mercury vapor lamps are beginning to be replaced by metal halide lamps, which are brighter, render colors better, and are more efficient, but have a shorter lamp life. Metal halide lighting is also commonly used to illuminate indoor and outdoor stadiums. High-pressure sodium lamps, like mercury vapor lamps, have longer lifetimes but render colors poorly. They are generally used in outdoor applications where color is not important.

Light Emitting Diodes (LEDs)

LEDs directly convert electrical energy to light by forcing an electrical current to run through a semiconductor. Since LEDs do not produce infrared radiation, they are cool to the touch and use as little as one-tenth as much energy as an incandescent lamp to produce an equivalent light output. They also last much longer: their estimated useful lifetime ranges between 35,000 and 100,000 hours.

The light generated by an LED results when an electrical current is run through the semiconductor component. As the name suggests, semiconductors are not very good at conducting electrical current, and require sufficient voltage to allow electrons to pass from one end to another. Semiconductors are divided into two regions, the positively charged p region and the negatively charged (i.e., electron-dominated) n region, which are separated by a junction. When an electrical current is applied to the leads of the LED, electrons in the n region are pushed through the junction into the p region, where they are immediately attracted to positively charged particles. When the negative and positive charges recombine and settle into a lower-energy state, the negative particle emits the energy it acquired in the electrical current in the form of a photon, which gives off visible light.

The color of the light emitted by an LED is dependent on the type of semiconductor used in its construction. Early LEDs were only capable of producing low-intensity red light and were commonly used as indicator lights in household electronics. Modern LEDs are available in a wide variety of color combinations. Due to their long life and high efficiency, LEDs are increasingly being used in a wide variety of applications, including streetlights and traffic signals.

In the United States, new standards for lighting efficiency are driving the market for more efficient lighting products. The Energy Security and Independence Act of 2007 required many inefficient lightbulbs to be phased out of production by 2014, as has already occurred in several other countries. Despite political opposition, the phase-out began in early 2012.

Helen Aki

Further Reading

Brox, Jane. *Brilliant: The Evolution of Artificial Light.* New York: Houghton Mifflin, 2011.

Halonen, Liisa, Eino Tetri, and Promod Bhusal. *Guidebook on Energy Efficient Electric Lighting for*

▷ *The Cycle of Lighting in the U.S. Workplace*

Office buildings in the early 20th century relied heavily on natural light, as electricity was still in its early stages and inadequate for workplace use. High ceilings and large windows, as well as a domestic aesthetic, had characterized professional spaces of the Victorian era. As incandescent lights became available, individual desks might utilize a single down light to help illuminate documents.

As rapid industrialization led growth in the white-collar workforce after the turn of the 20th century and the spheres of home and work began to become differentiated, improved lighting technology made it possible to artificially illuminate a uniform workplace. Individual task lighting ceded to ambient reflected light; higher overall lighting levels were thought to improve productivity. It was not uncommon to observe lighting levels in excess of 100 foot-candles.

By the 1950s, fluorescent lamps were the predominant source of lighting in the workplace. However, the sterility of a bright, ambient fluorescent-lit environment began to go out of fashion in the 1960s. When energy prices spiked in the 1970s due to oil shortages in the Middle East, task lighting regained popularity, as it reduced the amount of ambient light needed in office spaces. Today, new statistics about worker health and productivity have begun to inform green building design requirements that encourage natural lighting and ventilation in the workplace.

Buildings: Summary Report. Aalto, Finland: Aalto University School of Science and Technology, 2010.

Mesh, Steve. "Lecture on Lighting Fundamentals." Pacific Energy Center (2009). http://www.pge.com/energyclasses.

U.S. Department of Energy. "High-Intensity Discharge Lamps." http://www.energysavers.gov/your_home/lighting_daylighting/index.cfm/mytopic=12080.

U.S. Department of Energy. "Lifetime of White LEDs." http://apps1.eere.energy.gov/buildings/publications/pdfs/ssl/lifetime_white_leds.pdf.

See Also: Compact Fluorescent Lightbulbs; Daylighting; Edison, Thomas Alva; Industrial Revolution; Municipal Utilities; Photovoltaics; Solar Energy; Westinghouse, George.

Lithuania

Official Name: Republic of Lithuania.
Category: Geography of Energy.
Summary: The Baltic nation of Lithuania's current goal as a member of the European Union is to increase its use of renewables and reduce its dependence on fossil fuels. Nuclear energy has played a significant role in providing electricity in the past but is problematic from an environmental perspective.

Lithuania was the largest state in Europe at the end of the 14th century. By 1800 it no longer existed, partitioned with Poland among its neighbors. A new, independent Lithuanian state emerged after World War I, but the Soviet Union annexed it in 1940. It was the first of the Soviet republics to declare independence, doing so in March 1990, even before the official dissolution of the Soviet Union in 1991. Russian troops finally withdrew in 1993, after which Lithuania reorganized its economy along Western European lines. In 2004, with a population of 3.5 million and an area of 25,000 square miles, Lithuania became a member of the North Atlantic Treaty Organization, the World Trade Organization, and the European Union (EU).

Lithuanian industry produces a range of products, from small appliances, furniture, and textiles to ships, refined petroleum products, computers, and other electronics. While important, at 28 percent of the economy, this sector is less than half the scope of the services sector, which accounts for about two-thirds of Lithuania's gross domestic product (GDP). Agriculture makes up about 3 percent. The GDP growth rate of 5.8 percent in 2011 ranked Lithuania 49th among world nations.

Electricity Challenge

In the area of electricity consumption and production, Lithuania is still feeling the aftereffects of its 50 years as an annexed republic of the Soviet Union. The impacts are threefold. First, Lithuania is the site of two Russian nuclear power reactors at the Ignalina station, its only such reactors and both now permanently shut down. Second, its electricity transmission grid was heavily oriented to Russian priorities. Third, much as it has for decades, Lithuania still buys nearly all its natural gas from Russia.

The government's electricity energy policy is focused on strengthening infrastructure that will reduce its dependence on Russia and increase its ties to its Baltic neighbors—Estonia and Latvia—as well as Poland and western Europe in general. Among the ongoing initiatives are construction of Lithuania's first nuclear power station, Visaginas, planned to start in 2015; construction of the Baltic Energy Market Interconnector, a land and undersea electric transmission network that will link the country with Poland, Finland, and Sweden, and by extension to Germany; and technological upgrades to the key Elektrenal power plant, in order to bring it up to EU environmental standards.

Dalia Grybauskaite, president of Lithuania, said upon her election in 2009 that she was committed to moving Lithuanian power off the Soviet-era grid and creating an open internal energy market in place of the national monopoly. She also planned to separate production and distribution oversight, at the time handled by the same government agency. Like other European nations, Lithuania's industrial development plans have been somewhat stalled by the world economic downturn. Still, in October 2010, Lithuania adopted a formal energy strategy to guarantee energy independence by 2020. The goal for renewables was 23 percent by 2020. Also included were plans to reduce emissions and enhance energy efficiency across the industrial, residential, and transportation sectors.

Much hinged on successfully moving forward with the Visaginas nuclear facility, seen as coming on line in 2020 (now pushed back to 2022). Once in operation, Visaginas is projected to save the country more than $1 billion annually in energy import costs; it is also promoted as a long-term job-creating project.

The government sees the country's energy future to be just as nuclear-dependent as was its past (at least since 1983 with the Ignalina start-up). The Japanese firm Hitachi-GE in March 2012 entered into a $6.7 billion agreement with Lithuania to build and operate the Visaginas plant, rated at 1,300 megawatts. Estonia and Latvia have the option to be partners; Lithuania will own just over one-third of shares in the enterprise.

Lithuanian electricity consumption in 2008 was 10.3 terawatt-hours. Production was 12.3 terawatt-hours. Since the 2004 and 2009 shutdowns of the two Ignalina reactors, Lithuania has once again turned to the once mothballed Elektrenal plant, near the capital, Vilnius. Natural gas is the chief fuel consumed at Elektrenal, which has been in operation since the 1960s. Some units at the plant, which has a total generating capacity of 1,800 megawatts, can burn oil or bitumen fuel. Prior to the start-up of Ignalina, the Elektrenal facility provided two-thirds of the country's electricity.

Lithuania produces no natural gas but consumed 3.1 billion cubic meters in 2010. Similarly, the country produces very little oil, but consumed 67,000 barrels per day in 2010. Coal is nearly absent as a factor in the economy; a small amount is imported from Poland. About 60 peat fields produce that low-grade fuel, mainly used for direct heating.

Renewables

In 2001, the entire renewables sector in Lithuania was based on wood and hydropower. As of 2008, wood and wood waste was still providing the lion's share of renewable fuels, as much as 87 percent. As early as 2002, there was interest in wind power; the Lithuanian Wind Energy Association formed that year, with goals that included private-public partnership for the construction of wind farms.

Today, the Lithuanian Wind Power Association, an investment group, reports that wind power provides 430 gigawatt-hours of electricity annually—which it calculates replaces 42.6 million cubic meters of natural gas. The country also has small, mainly decentralized production of biodiesel and geothermal power. Wind and biomass are the green sources most likely to expand in the short term, with hydropower and solar less likely. Lithuania's target for renewables by 2020, 23 percent, is above the EU standard of 20 percent. Carbon emissions in Lithuania fell from about 6 million metric tons (1.7 metric tons per capita) in 1992 to about 4 million metric tons (1.3 metric tons per capita) in 2008.

JOHN H. BARNHILL

Further Reading

BBC. "Lithuania Set for Energy Rethink." May 19, 2009. http://news.bbc.co.uk/2/hi/europe/8057526 .stm.

FORATOM. "New Lithuanian NPP Set to Ensure Energy Independence by 2020." October 8, 2010. http://www.foratom.org/e-bulletin -tout-1378/other-articles-tout-1385/767-new -lithuanian-npp-set-to-ensure-energy-indep endence-by-2020.html.

Mapsoftheworld. "Energy Sector Lithuania." http:// www.mapsofworld.com/lithuania/economy-and -business/energy-sector.html.

U.S. Energy Information Administration. "Country Analysis Brief: Lithuania." http://www.eia.gov/ countries/country-data.cfm?fips=LH.

Windfair.net. "The Lithuanian Wind Energy Association." http://www.windfair.net/lwea/ welcome.html.

World Nuclear Organization. "Nuclear Power in Lithuania." http://www.world-nuclear.org/info/ inf109.html.

See Also: Air Pollution; Belarus; Latvia; Nuclear Power; Renewable Energy Resources.

Louisiana

Category: Energy in the United States.
Summary: Louisiana is the third-largest energy producer and fourth-largest crude oil producing state in the United States. Tapping vast reserves of oil and natural gas on land and offshore in the Gulf of Mexico, the state also serves as a global center for oil refining and natural gas distribution.

Natural gas provides the largest source of electricity in Louisiana, accounting for nearly 75 percent of the state's total generating capacity. Coal-fired plants output about 13 percent, and nuclear about 8 percent, with the remaining 4 percent from a mix of oil, hydropower, and other sources including renewables. Louisiana's 10 largest power facilities include five natural gas plants, three coal plants, and two nuclear plants. Major electric utilities include Entergy Corporation, Cleco Corporation, and Southwestern Electric Power Company, which are publicly traded (Southwestern through its parent, American Electric Power). Combined, these three providers deliver more than 80 percent of retail electricity sales in Louisiana.

Energy Sources

Oil production in Louisiana began in 1901. The state reached peak production in 1969, but still ranks high among oil-producing states, trailing only Texas, Alaska, and California. Petrochemical refining is a major industry; Louisiana has the second-largest refining capacity in the nation. Louisiana is home to 17 active oil refineries, and accounts for approximately 18 percent of the United States' total crude oil refining capacity. Three of the six largest U.S. refineries are located in Louisiana: an ExxonMobil facility in Baton Rouge, a Marathon Oil facility in Garyville, and a Citgo facility in Lake Charles.

There are hundreds of offshore oil wells operating in Louisiana's section of the Gulf of Mexico. The country's first freestanding offshore platform was completed off the coast of Louisiana in 1938. Historically, offshore drilling was feasible only in shallow waters close to shore. As technology improved, producers began drilling in deeper waters. By 1998, the majority of oil extracted in the Gulf of Mexico came from 1,000 feet or more beneath the ocean surface. With greater depths came growing technical challenges.

On April 20, 2010, an explosion occurred on-board the Deepwater Horizon oil rig, owned by BP (formerly British Petroleum), which was operating 48 miles off the coast of Louisiana. The explosion killed 11 workers, sank the rig, and caused oil to begin gushing from the mangled wellhead on the sea-floor. The well continued to release oil for more than 12 weeks before it was capped. Efforts

Wikimedia

A worker cleans up oily waste after the Deepwater Horizon explosion on Elmer's Island, just west of Grand Isle, Louisiana. The explosion killed 11 people.

to stop the flow were complicated by the fact that the wellhead was 5,000 feet (nearly a mile) beneath the ocean surface. The incident proved to be the largest oil spill by volume in U.S. history to that date. The full extent of the environmental, economic, and social consequences from the spill are yet to be determined.

Natural gas is also abundant in Louisiana. The state is the fifth-largest producer of natural gas in the nation, accounting for slightly more than 7 percent of domestic marketed production. As of January 2012, Louisiana's 590 billion cubic feet of natural gas in underground storage amounted to 8 percent of the national total. Recent innovations in drilling technology have drastically reduced production costs and allowed producers to extract natural gas from underground rock formations known as shale. The two-mile-deep Haynesville Shale Formation, centered in northwestern Louisiana and eastern Texas, is an example of a field that has experienced a surge of interest and growth. Estimated to be one of the largest natural gas deposits in the world, the Haynesville Shale became the United States' most productive field in 2011, with more than 1,000 wells utilizing horizontal drilling and hydrofracturing techniques, with permits secured for nearly as many new wells.

Louisiana receives significant revenues from its oil and gas production. For each year since 2004, the state has collected mineral revenues in excess of $1 billion. In 2008, the total exceeded $2 billion. The federal government, too, receives substantial income by issuing offshore leases to oil companies for sections of the Gulf of Mexico. For each year from 2001 to 2010, federal collections ranged from $4 billion to $14 billion for leases within Louisiana's section of the Gulf of Mexico.

Transmission

An extensive network of transmission infrastructure has developed in Louisiana to accommodate shipments of energy produced within the state, offshore, and abroad. Louisiana has oil import sites in six cities. It is also home to the Louisiana Offshore Oil Port (LOOP), the only deep-draft tanker port in the country. Oil tankers that are too large to enter into coastal ports use LOOP to offload their supplies while remaining at sea. Unloaded at LOOP, the oil is transmitted through a series of hoses to land-based facilities for processing.

Louisiana's natural gas infrastructure is also extensive. There are 16 interstate natural gas pipelines passing through the state. A significant portion of natural gas consumed in the United States moves through the sprawling Henry Hub, a junction for 13 pipelines near the town of Erath. The Henry Hub also serves as the location at which the price of natural gas is traded on the New York Mercantile Exchange. Louisiana is home to three of the nation's nine import facilities for liquefied natural gas (LNG). Among them is the Sabine Pass terminal on the Louisiana-Texas border, the largest such facility in the United States. A fourth terminal, the Gulf Gateway Energy Bridge, was the world's first deepwater facility for unloading natural gas. Similar to LOOP, the port allows large tankers to offload their shipments without entering shallow water.

Two of the four sites comprising the U.S. Strategic Petroleum Reserve (SPR) are located in Louisiana. The SPR acts as an emergency stockpile of oil that can be tapped in times of supply disruptions. It was established during the 1970s in reaction to the oil crises after the Arab Oil Embargo. SPR oil is stored in massive underground salt formations and can be drawn to the surface at any time.

Offshore production can be affected by hurricanes, which enter the Gulf of Mexico periodically from June to November. These storms disrupt the flow of oil from offshore platforms and damage infrastructure. Hurricanes Katrina and Rita in 2005 destroyed more than 100 platforms and damaged a number of vessels and pipelines. Supply disruptions caused by hurricanes have led the U.S. president to authorize the tapping of SPR in the past.

This occurred several times during the administration of George W. Bush: in 2002 as a result of Hurricane Lili, in 2004 in response to Hurricane Ivan, in 2005 after Hurricane Katrina, and in 2008 in the wake of Hurricanes Gustav and Ike.

Scott Macmurdo

Further Reading

Austin, Diane, Bob Carriker, Tom McGuire, Joseph Pratt, Tyler Priest, and Allan G. Pulsipher. "History of the Offshore Oil and Gas Industry in Southern Louisiana: Interim Report." http://www.gomr .boemre.gov/PI/PDFImages/ESPIS/2/2994.pdf.

National Commission on the BP *Deepwater Horizon* Oil Spill and Offshore Drilling. "Deep Water: The Gulf Oil Disaster and the Future of Offshore Drilling." http://www.oilspillcommission.gov/.

Nussbaum, Patty. "Louisiana Electric Generation: 2007 Update." http://dnr.louisiana.gov/assets/docs/ energy/electricity/electric_generation_20071228 .pdf.

U.S. Energy Information Administration. "Louisiana." http://www.eia.doe.gov/state/state-energy-profiles. cfm?sid=LA.

See Also: BP; Energy Transmission: Gas; Gulf Oil Spill; Henry Hub; Natural Gas; Offshore Drilling; Oil Shales; Refining; Shell.

Lovins, Amory

Dates: 1947–.
Category: Biographies.
Summary: Amory Lovins believes that environmentalism is compatible with both technological innovation and capitalism, as reflected in his concepts of the "soft path" and "natural capitalism."

Amory Bloch Lovins, born on November 13, 1947, in Washington, D.C., is a physicist, environmentalist, and energy efficiency consultant to business and government. Lovins believes that environmentalism is compatible with both technological innovation and capitalism. His concepts of the "soft path" and "natural capitalism" reflect this belief.

He has worked as the British representative of Friends of the Earth International and is a cofounder of the Rocky Mountain Institute with his first wife, L. Hunter Lovins. He has also published extensively on resource conservation, natural capitalism, soft energy, and an oil-free economy. He has been the recipient of numerous awards, including the Right Livelihood Award (1983) and a MacArthur Fellowship (1993). As both an intellectual and an activist, Lovins is a central figure in the history of postwar alternative energy.

Friends of the Earth International

Lovins became the British representative for the environmental lobbying organization Friends of the Earth International (FOEI) in 1971. He became involved with FOEI when David Brower, founder of Friends of the Earth, commissioned him to publish a book of photographs of Snowdonia National Park in Wales, titled *Eryri, the Mountains of Longing* (1971, with Philip Evans). As representative, Lovins wrote policy analyses, testified on energy matters, and lobbied government agencies. During this period his interest in energy matters solidified, illustrated by his publications *World Energy Strategies: Facts, Issues, and Options* (1973) and *Non-Nuclear Futures: The Case for an Ethical Energy Strategy* (1975, with John H. Price).

The Soft Path

In October 1976, Lovins published the essay "Energy Strategy: The Road Not Taken?" in the journal *Foreign Affairs*. In the article, Lovins outlined two divergent paths for the energy future of the United States. The "hard path," which described contemporary federal policy, depended on the rapid expansion of centralized high technologies in order to increase supplies of energy, especially electricity. Lovins was particularly critical of the U.S. dependence on coal, oil, gas, and nuclear power, including the network of subsidies sustaining these industries.

By contrast, the "soft path" emphasized energy efficiency, the rapid development of renewable energy sources, and the gradual transition away from the use of fossil fuels. Lovins argued that the world's remaining fossil fuel resources should be used sparingly in order to develop and implement these energy-efficient soft path technologies.

In the article, which generated an enormous international debate over energy policy and garnered significant professional attention for Lovins, he drew attention to the impact of the United States' energy paths on international relations, economic growth, and personal values. He argued that the soft path combined environmental preservation with a political project of decentralized self-sufficiency; indeed, he believed that true systemic change would develop when individuals learned how to provide for their basic needs with simple, environmentally friendly solutions. Moreover, he argued that the soft path reflected older personal values such as thrift, simplicity, and humility.

It is useful to think of the soft path in relationship to the appropriate technology movement. Appropriate technology describes technologies that are designed to meet the specific needs of the community in which they will be used; in most cases, appropriate technologies are designed for use in rural or developing areas. Soft energy technology was Lovins's way of describing appropriate renewable energy technologies. Soft path supporters today endorse decentralized appropriate technologies, such as passive solar energy, geothermal heat, and recycled fuels. They believe that First World nations should adopt these technologies themselves and provide support for developing nations to do the same.

Rocky Mountain Institute

Lovins cofounded the Rocky Mountain Institute (RMI) with his first wife, L. Hunter Lovins, in Colorado in 1982. Originally, the organization was dedicated to advancing the soft energy path. Today it serves in an analytic and advisory capacity to governments and corporations alike, in order to facilitate the transition away from a fossil-fuel-dependent economy. The Lovinses believe that world security and sustainability, as well as economic growth, will derive from the efficient and restorative use of natural resources.

The RMI is noted for several projects and ideas. The term *negawatt* was coined by Lovins in 1989 to describe a theoretical amount of energy to be saved. He has advocated a "negawatt revolution," in which electricity would be recycled among consumers. The hypercar, developed by Lovins in the early 1990s, is an approach to building cars that combines a hybrid engine with ultralight materials to achieve 90 miles per gallon at present, with the goal of 200 miles per gallon in the future. RMI has also launched Project Get Ready, a program that assists cities in developing the infrastructure necessary for supporting electric vehicles.

Natural Capitalism

RMI has expanded its focus to encompass "natural capitalism." The concept was originally expounded in Lovins's 1999 book *Natural Capitalism: Creating the Next Industrial Revolution*, cowritten with Paul Hawkin and L. Hunter Lovins. The book asserts that industrial capitalism is wholly dependent on natural resources, which the authors refer to as natural capital. They argue that industrial capitalism is headed for a collapse, because it has failed to acknowledge this fact and use natural capital sparingly. They argue that if natural capital is properly recognized as a fundamental building block of the global economy, the next industrial revolution will bring an increased harmonization of business and environmental interests.

The practice of natural capitalism requires recognizing and conserving all forms of capital: money, goods, nature, and humans. It is based on several fundamental assumptions: radically increasing the productivity of natural resources, shifting to biologically inspired production models and materials (biomimicry), moving to a "service-and-flow" business model, and reinvesting in natural capital.

JENNIFER THOMSON

Further Reading

Kirk, Andrew. "Appropriating Technology: The Whole Earth Catalog and Counterculture Environmental Politics." *Environmental History* 6, no. 3 (July 2001).

Lovins, Amory B. "Energy Strategy: The Road Not Taken?" *Foreign Affairs* 55, no. 1 (October 1976).

"The Plowboy Interview With Amory Lovins." *Mother Earth News*, November/December 1977. http://www.motherearthnews.com/Renewable-Energy/1977-11-01-Amory-Lovins.aspx.

See Also: Alternative Energy; Electric Vehicles; Environmental Stewardship; Renewable Energy Resources; Sustainability.

Luxembourg

Official Name: Grand Duchy of Luxembourg.
Category: Geography of Energy.
Summary: Luxembourg is a very small country of just over 1,553 square miles (2,500 square kilometers), located in western Europe and bordering Germany, France, and Belgium. With few indigenous energy sources of its own, it imports oil and gas to fuel its energy sector.

Luxembourg was a founding member of the European Union (EU) in 1958, along with Belgium, France, Germany, Italy, and the Netherlands. Its capital city, also called Luxembourg, is now home to European institutions such as the European Court of Justice and the European Investment Bank. The country has one of the world's highest standards of living (second only to Switzerland) but also has the highest energy consumption and carbon emissions per capita of all 27 EU member states, at 27,000 kilograms of carbon dioxide (CO_2) per person, compared to an average of 8,000 kilograms per person for the European Union member states as a whole.

This high level of carbon emissions per capita is predominantly a result of a fossil-fuel-intensive energy sector. As a small country, Luxembourg has few natural energy resources at its disposal apart from water and timber. Consequently, it is dependent on imports of gas and oil to fuel its economy, ranking as the third-highest energy-dependent EU member state.

During the Industrial Revolution, Luxembourg was very active in the steel and iron industries, and in the 1960s this sector represented as much as 80 percent of the total value of the country's exports. These industrial processes were largely powered by coal imports. However, once the country's iron ore deposits began running out toward the 1980s, Luxembourg focused on diversifying its economy, attracting international banking and financial services by using liberal tax policies. The city of Luxembourg now houses more than 160 banks as a result.

Reducing Carbon Emissions

As the coal-intensive steel and iron industries declined, Luxembourg adapted its energy imports to meet its present energy needs, while trying to reduce its carbon emissions. As a result, it has almost completely replaced its imports of coal with natural gas since the early 1990s, and in 2002 it installed a large amount of gas-fired energy generation capacity, resulting in a 200 percent increase in overall energy supply. Although natural gas is a fossil fuel, it is much less carbon intensive than coal and now powers approximately 75 percent of the country's electricity needs. The remaining electricity is generated by pumped storage (19 percent) and renewables (6 percent), consisting of hydropower (2 percent), wind power (1 percent), and biomass energy (2 percent), as well as some solar and geothermal technologies.

With comparatively low industrial energy demands taking up 28 percent of Luxembourg's total energy needs, the transport sector is the largest energy consumer, accounting for 60 percent of total energy utilized. However, many vehicles from other countries visit Luxembourg just to refuel, taking advantage of lower value-added taxes and excise duties on Luxembourg's transport fuels compared to those of neighboring countries. This trend artificially increases the apparent proportion of energy consumed in the transport sector. Approximately 98 percent of the transport sector is fueled by petroleum products, which means that oil remains the primary source of energy for the country.

Wikimedia

There are three hydroelectric power stations on the Moselle River, including the Schengen-Apach dam, shown above. The regulation capacity of the dams is about 82 GWh for a working period of 4,800 hours; Schengen-Apach's capacity is 4.5 MW. The border between France and Luxembourg runs through the center of the Moselle river.

The remaining 2 percent is made up of a small number of electric vehicles and biofuels. Some tax exemptions exist to encourage biofuel use in powering motor vehicles, primarily in response to the European Commission's 2003 Biofuels Directive, which requires all European Union member states to increase the proportion of biofuels sold for transport to a minimum of 5.75 percent in 2010. However, Luxembourg has been criticized for being slow to respond to the directive. In 2008, only 0.8 percent of the country's transport energy came from biofuels. With such high oil dependency, Luxembourg is consequently vulnerable to oil supply disruptions, and oil importers are therefore required to store enough oil to cover a minimum of 90 days consumption.

The primary policy supporting renewable energies in Luxembourg is the 1993 Framework Law, amended in 2005, which gives preferential tariffs (also known as feed-in tariffs) to a variety of renewable energy sources for fixed periods of 10 to 20 years. Subsidies are also available for private companies that invest in renewable energy technologies such as solar, wind, biomass, and geothermal. Luxembourg also provides investment subsidy support for combined heat and power (CHP), installation of heat pumps (25 percent), and installation of solar thermal technology (40 percent).

ABIGAIL CLARE

Further Reading

Central Intelligence Agency. "Luxembourg." In *The World Factbook*. https://www.cia.gov/library/publications/the-world-factbook/geos/lu.html.

Copeland, C. "Luxembourg: World Headquarters for the Steel Industry." http://www.lehigh.edu/~incntr/publications/documents/Luxembourg.pdf.

Europe's Energy Portal. http://www.energy.eu/.

European Renewable Energy Council. "Renewable Energy Policy Review: Luxembourg." http://www.erec.org/fileadmin/erec_docs/Projcet_Documents/RES2020/LUXEMBOURG_RES_Policy_Review_09_Final.pdf.

U.S. Energy Information Administration. "Country Analysis Brief: Luxembourg." http://www.eia.gov/countries/country-data.cfm?fips=LU.

See Also: Belgium; Biodiesel; European Union; Feed-in Tariff; Germany; Industrial Revolution; Oil and Petroleum; Renewable Energy Resources.

Macedonia

Official Name: Republic of Macedonia.
Category: Geography of Energy.
Summary: Formerly part of Yugoslavia, Macedonia is a central European country that depends on hydropower and fossil fuel energy.

Macedonia is located on the central Balkan Peninsula and its estimated population slightly exceeded 2 million inhabitants in 2007. The country shares its borders with Greece, Bulgaria, Albania, Kosovo, and Serbia. Macedonia had only one hydropower storage and several small run-of-the-river and coal-burning plants prior to World War II. Its energy sector has expanded rapidly since the 1960s. However, the country remains heavily dependent on imports.

The late 1950s, 1960s, and 1970s saw the rapid development of Macedonia's hydropower sector, resulting in the construction of several dams in the western part of the country. The total installed hydropower generation capacity is about 520 megawatts, accounting for approximately 30 percent of total production. It is estimated that this represents less than a third of the total technically available installed hydropower potential.

As far as fossil fuel energy is concerned, the first of the three blocks of the Bitola thermal power plant—the backbone of the country's electricity generation network, responsible for approximately 70 percent of total production—was put into operation in 1982. Two smaller thermal electricity generation plants had already been commissioned in 1978 and 1980, the former notable for burning heavy fuel oil. A 230-megawatt gas-fired combined heat and power (CHP) plant in the city of Skopje began operation in 2010 but has yet to start feeding power into the national grid. The plant is partly owned by the same company that generates heat for the city of Skopje; the city's district heating system was built in several stages, starting in the 1960s, and currently has a capacity of 487 megawatts for generation of hot water and 26 megawatts for steam production. It should be emphasized that Macedonia also has a significant renewable energy potential in the form of geothermal, solar, biomass, and wind resources. However, this has been insufficiently exploited to date: Only 543 terajoules of heat were generated from a total potential of 220 megawatts in 2003.

The country's total primary energy consumption amounted to 115.78 terajoules in 2006, even though most of the resources necessary to meet

Author supplied photo

A newly built CHP plant (right) in the western part of Macedonia's capital of Skopje stands next to the city's main district heating plant, constructed during the 1980s.

Following the restructuring, unbundling, and partial privatization of the formerly state-owned and integrated monopoly Elektrostopanstvo na Makedonija (ESM) in 2005, three companies (the state-owned ELEM, MEPSO, and the private EVN) took charge of, respectively, electricity generation, transmission, and distribution. The OKTA Refinery, owned by Hellenic Petroleum, dominates the oil derivatives and gas production market, even though another privately owned company, Makpetrol, is the largest distributor of such products. Macedonia imports all of its gas from Russia, although the only is pipeline presently working at less than half of its capacity. The GA-MA company was established by the Macedonian government as a public enterprise for the supply, transport, and distribution of natural gas.

SASKA PETROVA
STEFAN BOUZAROVSKI

primary energy demand (49.84 percent) were imported. Services and households account for the lion's share (40 percent) of energy demand, followed by transport and industry. Although it has been estimated that primary energy consumption per capita has decreased since the early 1990s, a rise of electricity demand is projected for the future.

The main coordinator of strategic planning and legislation development within national energy policy is the Sector for Energy and Energy Efficiency (SEEE), which operates under the auspices of the Ministry of Economy. The SEEE also regulates contract licenses and agreements for energy activities and exploitation, while creating tariff systems and prices for energy products and services. In part, the SEEE implements the wide range of its activities through the State Energy Agency and the Energy Regulatory Commission. The main formal responsibilities of the institutions managing the energy policy and activities are defined by the Energy Act, which was adopted in 2006. This law also regulates key energy issues, including energy security, energy efficiency, and the usage of renewable energy resources. It is worth noting that Macedonia ratified the United Nations Framework Convention on Climate Change (UNFCCC) in 1998 and the Kyoto Protocol in 2004.

Further Reading

Bouzarovski, Stefan. "Entangled Boundaries, Scales, and Trajectories of Change: Post-Communist Energy Reforms in Critical Perspective." *European Urban and Regional Studies* 17, no. 2 (2010).

Buzar, Stefan. "Energy, Environment, and International Financial Institutions: The EBRD's Activities in the Western Balkans." *Geografiska Annaler B* 90, no. 4 (2008).

Central Intelligence Agency. "Macedonia." In *The World Factbook*. https://www.cia.gov/library/publications/the-world-factbook/geos/mk.html.

Šúri, Marcel, et al. "Potential of Solar Electricity Generation in the European Union Member States and Candidate Countries." *Solar Energy* 81, no. 10 (2007).

Ürge-Vorsatz, Diana, et al. "Energy in Transition: From the Iron Curtain to the European Union." *Energy Policy* 34, no. 15 (2006).

U.S. Energy Information Administration. "Country Analysis Brief: Macedonia." http://www.eia.gov/countries/country-data.cfm?fips=MK.

See Also: Air Pollution; District Energy; Electricity; European Union; Greece; History of Energy: Ancient Rome; Hydropower; Romania.

Madagascar

Official Name: Republic of Madagascar.
Category: Geography of Energy.
Summary: Madagascar has a limited energy production capacity, mainly through hydroelectric and diesel power plants, but is improving efforts in energy development through international partnerships.

Madagascar, the fourth-largest island nation, is situated in the Indian Ocean off the southeast coast of Africa. Since gaining independence from French colonial rule in 1960, Madagascar has faced challenges in energy and infrastructure development. The rail system and road network are in disrepair, impeding the transportation of goods and services. Chronic electricity shortages result from decades of subsides that have caused Jiro sy Rano Malagasy (JIRAMA), the state provider of water and power, to go into debt. Despite liberalization of the electricity sector in 1999, JIRAMA still retains the monopoly in transmission and distribution. JIRAMA is being privatized to better diversify energy-generation sources and provide affordable and reliable power to the public. Technological and financial foreign investments remain integral to collaborations in energy exploration and sustainable development in Madagascar.

Production and Consumption

The primary energy sources for Madagascar include burning sugarcane waste, firewood, and charcoal, which comprise 82 percent of the island's fuel. While these biomass sources are readily available for the mostly rural population of approximately 21 million people, they are acquired at a high environmental cost. Harvesting wood for fuel has caused concerns over soil erosion, deforestation, and declining habitat for Madagascar's rich biodiversity. Efforts to reduce pressure on forest resources include implementing off-grid solar technologies and planting woodlots to provide sustainable firewood sources.

Electricity makes up only 5 percent of Madagascar's total energy production, and the country's electrification rate is 25 percent. The U.S.

Energy Information Administration (EIA) reports that in 2008, Madagascar generated 910 gigawatt-hours, consumed 840 gigawatt-hours, and as a nation ranked 153rd in the world for installed capacity.

JIRAMA oversees dozens of isolated power plants, which provide approximately one-third of Madagascar's electricity. The 40-megawatt Mandroseza Station burns heavy oil and has been operating since 2007. This station was constructed to end the frequent blackouts and avoid load shedding on the grid of the capital city, Antananarivo, as well as to reduce the utility's production costs and extend the availability of electricity around the island. The 10-megawatt Ambohimanambola Station, east of Antananarivo, uses diesel oil and was built in 2000. It was Madagascar's first foreign-owned power plant and is operated by the French electrical company Hydelec.

With the rising costs of fuel needed for thermal generators and the abundance of small rivers in Madagascar, hydropower has become an environmentally and economically sound choice and generates two-thirds of the island's electricity. In 2008, the 15-megawatt Sahanivotry Hydroelectric Power Station was planned to feed the Antananarivo and Antsirabe grid and produce 10 percent of the island's electricity supply. Sahanivotry is Madagascar's first privately owned hydropower plant, also operated by Hydelec. It is the first to be built in the country since 1982, when the Andekaleta Hydroelectric Power Station, east of Antananarivo, began operation with a capacity of 58 megawatts, although there are plans for more hydropower projects from Hydelec and other operators.

Madagascar has been largely import-dependent for oil, but exploration is occurring. The EIA found that the 18,500 barrels per day consumed in Madagascar in 2008 were all imported. Oil prospecting has occurred since the early 20th century, and Madagascar's first oil refinery was established at Toamasina in 1966. U.S.-based Madagascar Oil is the sole owner and operator of oil projects and pumping in Tsimiroro and is partnered with French oil company Total to explore heavy oil reserves in Bemolanga. In 2010, these combined reserves were estimated at 3.9 billion barrels, although it is technically difficult and expensive to process heavy oil.

The development of Madagascar's extensive coal reserves, estimated at 135 million tons, has been inhibited by the poor road and rail system and costs of exploration. Madagascar Consolidated Mining (MCM), a subsidiary of the United Kingdom company Vuna Energy Limited, is the sole company on the island with a license for production in the primary coal deposit, Sakoa. MCM plans to produce 45,000 tons per year and mine 70 percent of the total coal reserves over a 25-year period, of which 10 percent will be processed into briquettes for household fuel to help replace the regular use of charcoal, which depletes wood from nearby forests. The majority of coal would be used for producing electricity and thermal energy in Madagascar and may be exported to interested trading partners in Southeast Asia.

NICOLE MENARD

Further Reading

African Development Bank. "AfDB and Climate Change." http://www.afdb.org/fileadmin/uploads/afdb/Documents/Project-and-Operations/MADAGASCAR%20anglais.pdf.
Power Plants Around the World. "Gallery." http://www.industcards.com/index.html.
U.S. Energy Information Administration. "Country Analysis Brief: Madagascar." http://www.eia.gov/countries/country-data.cfm?fips=MA.

See Also: Biomass Energy; Coal; Comoros; Electricity; Hydropower; Wind Resources.

Maine

Category: Energy in the United States.
Summary: Maine is the most northeast state in the United States. It is blanketed by forests, making wood the obvious natural energy resource. However, wood burning leads to the production of carbon dioxide.

Energy expended per person is high in Maine, and efforts to offset the carbon footprint have led to an emphasis on the promotion of energy efficiency and have ignited a search for viable alternative energy resources. The state offers financial incentives for residents who use alternative sources of energy, and projects using wind and solar energy are rapidly expanding. The governor's Wood-to-Energy Initiative draws on the state's vast forest resources to promote alternative energy sources, and the use of hydropower is being explored.

Located in the extreme northeast corner of the United States, Maine is the largest of the New England states, covering an area of 35,387 square miles. The entire eastern border of the state is the Atlantic Ocean. Maine also has ample interior water sources, with water covering 4,523 square miles. The major rivers are the Androscoggin, the Kennebec, the Penobscot, and the St. John. Moosehead and Richardson are the state's major lakes.

Maine ranks 41st in population among the 50 states, but it is one of the top-ranking states in terms of energy expended per person. Some 75 percent of all households in Maine heat their homes with fuel oil. That percentage is higher than in any other state in the United States. Much of that oil arrives in Maine as crude oil by way of the port of Portland. The oil is then piped into refineries in Quebec and Ontario. Maine generates more electricity from nonhydroelectric renewable resources than any other state in the country. Unlike the rest of New England, industry consumes the lion's share of energy in the state.

Some 17.7 million acres of Maine's land area is covered by forests. Many acres of that land are still undeveloped, and most of it is in private hands; the state controls only 6 percent of forests within its borders. Maine has the ability to generate more wood and wastewood power than any other state.

There are 17 wind projects in Maine in various stages of development. Those already in operation include Mars Hill, Stetson Ridge, Beaver Ridge, Kibby Mountain, Stetson II, and Vinalhaven. The Governor's Office of Energy Independence and Security is charged with establishing an energy plan that promotes clean, renewable energy sources and reductions in the use of fossil fuels.

Promoting the Use of Alternative Energy Sources

According to the National Renewable Energy Laboratory, in 2007 Maine generated 7.9 terawatt-hours of electricity, placing the state eighth in the nation in electricity production. Maine ranked fifth in the nation in electricity generated per capita as a percentage of the total electricity generated (49.3 percent). The state rose to fourth in the nation in the generation of nonhydroelectric renewable electricity generated (4.2 terawatt-hours) and ranked first in megawatt-hours generated per capita (3.2). Maine also ranked first (3.2 megawatt-hours) in the percentage of nonhydroelectric renewable energy generated per capita. Maine was third in the nation in the growth of hydroelectric generation (41.3 percent) between 2001 and 2007. Maine ranks 10th in the nation in energy consumption—consuming 469.3 trillion British thermal units (Btu) of electricity annually.

After Congress passed the American Recovery and Reinvestment Act in 2009, Governor John Elias Baldacci pledged to spend the share of the grant money allotted to his state, $3.1 billion, to promote energy efficiency while maintaining reasonable energy rates. New legislation was subsequently enacted to supplement existing energy laws and programs, such as the Maine Uniform Building and Energy Code Act of 2008 and the governor's Wood-to-Energy Initiative, which were designed to help free Maine from its dependence on fossil fuels. The ultimate goals of the governor's initiative were to ensure that all public buildings were converted to wood biomass heat, encourage the use of renewable energy sources in all homes, and promote the growth of alternative energy industries.

In the fall of 2010, the federal government approved $37 million in funds for 27 separate projects aimed at exploring marine and hydrokinetic energy technologies. For Maine, the $10 million allotted for the project made it possible to give the go-ahead to Portland-based Ocean Renewable Power Company, allowing that firm to build and operate a five-grid project located on the seafloor of Cobscook Bay off of Eastport.

Also in 2010, the U.S. Department of Energy handed out $30 million in competitive awards to states committed to improving energy efficiency. Maine received $4,538,571 to retrofit apartment buildings of five to 20 units in order to reduce energy consumption by at least 25 percent. By the spring of 2010, the Weatherization Assistance Program, in conjunction with MaineHousing (the state housing authority) and nongovernmental organizations had succeeded in weatherizing 1,582 low-income homes for an average energy savings of $437 annually per home. This was accomplished by installing insulation and weather stripping, sealing windows and doors, caulking cracks, and replacing ineffective heating and cooling systems. An additional $41.9 million was subsequently used to weatherize additional homes.

That same year, the governor and the state legislature worked together to pass a series of new energy bills that promoted energy infrastruc-

Wikimedia

In 2010, the governor and the state legislature worked together to pass a series of new energy bills, one of which promoted wind energy projects in the state, like the Mars Hill Wind Farm above, with 28 turbines.

ture development, created a smart-grid policy for Maine, increased efforts to make clean energy more affordable for both homes and businesses, established benefits for communities hosting wind energy projects, and implemented recommendations of the governor's Ocean Energy Task Force.

In March 2011, U.S. Secretary of Energy Steven Chu announced that the federal government had made a $102 million conditional commitment to Record Hill Wind LLC to fund the Record Hill wind project. One aspect of the project included a 50.6-megawatt wind power plant and an eight-mile transmission line located near Roxbury, Maine.

ELIZABETH RHOLETTER PURDY

Further Reading

Barnes, Roland V., ed. *Energy Crisis in America?* Huntington, NY: Nova Science, 2001.

Bird, Lori, et al. *Green Power Marketing in the United States: A Status Report.* Golden, CO: National Renewable Energy Laboratory, 2008.

Maine.gov. "Federal Department of Energy Recognizes Maine's Leadership to Weatherize Homes." http://www.maine.gov/tools/whatsnew/index.php?topic=Portal+News&id=98084&v=article-2008.

National Renewable Energy Laboratory. "NREL Uncovers Clean Energy Leaders State by State." http://www.nrel.gov/news/features/feature_detail.cfm/feature_id=1605.

U.S. Energy Information Administration. "Maine." http://www.eia.gov/state/state-energy-profiles.cfm?sid=ME.

See Also: Biomass Energy; Hydropower; United States; Wind Resources.

Malawi

Official Name: Republic of Malawi.
Category: Geography of Energy.
Summary: Malawi depends on hydropower for its electricity, importing petroleum and producing only a fifth of the country's coal

consumption. Rural areas in Malawi depend on biomass-based energy sources like firewood, agriculture restudies, and industrial wastes.

Compared to the standards of Africa, Malawi's access to energy is minute. The National Statistical Office, based in Zomba, has estimated that about 10 per 100 Malawians among a population of more than 13 million use electric energy, while the rest rely on wood fuel for daily household energy needs. Malawi's electricity is generated largely from hydropower. Thermal generators running on petroleum fuels (primarily diesel and gasoline) are used by a few commercial and industrial enterprises; photovoltaic (PV) systems are used in modular form for telecommunications, lighting, and water pumping in rural areas not connected to the grid. There is low utilization of renewable energy sources, although the potential exists for such renewables. To date, only a small fraction of wind power is used in water pumping.

Electricity supply in Malawi is dominated by a publicly owned utility company, Electricity Supply Corporation of Malawi, which was established by an act of Parliament in 1957. The company supplies 304 megawatts of electricity, of which 94 percent is generated from hydropower and the remaining 6 percent is from thermal sources. There are four hydropower plants along the Shire River and one minihydropower plant in the country. Electricity is transmitted principally through the 132-kilovolt and 66-kilovolt network and distributed at 33 kilovolts, 11 kilovolts, and 400/230 volts. Malawi produces about 825 gigawatt-hours of electricity (of which 3 percent comes from fossil fuels and 97 percent from hydropower).

There are no known oil reserves and no natural gas production in the country, and Malawi imports 97 percent of its refined petroleum products. Until 1999, the Petroleum Control Commission was the only distributor of imported petroleum. Malawi produces about 3 percent of ethanol locally, which is blended with imported petroleum. The country has a total ethanol production capacity of 18 million liters annually. It consumes about 8,000 barrels of petroleum per day. Although the existence of bituminous coal reserves was known for many years, mining did not begin until 1985. Malawi has 1 billion metric tons of coal reserves, of which 22 million tons are proven reserves of bituminous coal. By 2000, annual production was approximately 55,000 tons from two coal mines near Livingstonia, meeting only 20 percent of the country's total requirements. The remaining coal demand is supplied from imported sources.

Firewood, charcoal, and other agricultural and industrial wastes account for 97 percent of the country's total energy supply. More than a third of the biomass resources for energy come from agricultural residues. Forests provide energy for domestic consumption, including cooking and curing of tobacco, a major cash crop. Although there is good potential for other renewable energy from photovoltaic power and wind, these have not fully been utilized and currently supply only 0.2 percent of the country's energy. Biogas is yet another source of energy and is consumed in rural areas of Malawi.

BENKTESH SHARMA

Further Reading

Central Intelligence Agency. "Malawi." In *The World Factbook*. https://www.cia.gov/library/publications/the-world-factbook/geos/mi.html.

Malawi. Petaluma, CA: World Trade Press, 1993-2010.

Malawi Energy Policy, Laws and Regulation Handbook. Washington, DC: International Business Publications, 2008.

U.S. Energy Information Administration. "Country Analysis Brief: Malawi." http://www.eia.gov/countries/country-data.cfm?fips=MI.

See Also: Mozambique; Utilities; Zambia.

Malaysia

Official Name: Malaysia.
Category: Geography of Energy.
Summary: Petroleum has dominated Malaysia's energy sector and export market for more than four decades. The Malaysian government,

however, aims to decrease petroleum's share of commercial energy production by using more renewable resources.

Dominating the skyline of Malaysia's largest city and federal capital, Kuala Lumpur, are the Petronas Twin Towers built in 1998. The glittering steel, glass, and concrete buildings stand where race horses once thundered past British sahibs. They overlook the muddy waters of the river that gives Kuala Lumpur its name and overshadow the tin-mine camp that once defined the city's economy. The towers symbolize, among other things, the rise of Malaysia as an economic powerhouse both within southeast Asia and globally.

This ascent has been energized by the exploitation of large reserves of crude oil discovered during the latter 19th century, first on the island of Borneo. Most of Malaysia's reserves lie offshore, primarily on the continental shelf of peninsular Malaysia, which includes the Tapis oil field, known for its valuable light, sweet crude. Although ranked 24th among oil-producing states, the country is a net exporter of oil. It refines much of that in six oil refineries, three owned by the vertically integrated state oil company Petronas, the remainder by an international conglomerate led by Shell and Exxon.

However, the country is also looking to develop other resources, given the eventual depletion of oil. Prime Minister Dr. Mahathir Mohamad, known as the architect of modern Malaysia, recognized this when, in 1991, he set the country on a course toward sustainable industrialization by implementing Vision 2020 (Wawasan 2020 in Malay). With fewer than 4 billion barrels remaining as of 2009 within Malaysia's territorial jurisdiction—that is, 30 years of oil at current extraction rates—Malaysia's economy has taken off, fueled by petroleum and guided by visionary thinking. Modern infrastructure such as railways, highways, and port facilities are in place and expanding; foreign investment is robust; and manufacturing, particularly of electronic goods, is the alter ego of the economy. Moreover, the Petronas Towers, until recently unsurpassed in height, stand as a symbol of Malaysian vision that continues to promote sustainable growth through diversification and regulation of economic development and energy resources.

Petroleum and Petronas

Petronas, the National Petroleum Corporation of Malaysia (or in Malay Perbadanan Petroleum Nasional), was formed in 1974 through the Petroleum Development Act with a clear mandate for state ownership, control, and exclusive development rights over all of Malaysia's petroleum-based energy resources. Foreign oil companies such as Shell, BP (British Petroleum), and Exxon had up to this point been paying royalties of 8 to 12 percent for extracted crude. Petronas forced such companies to renegotiate contracts under guidelines that favored Malaysia. However, lack of technological expertise and bureaucratic red tape delayed the development of a profitable and well-managed energy sector founded on petroleum. Though once at odds, Petronas and leading international oil companies have developed a productive and mutually beneficial relationship both in Malaysia and abroad. For instance, Petronas and Shell entered into a 40–60 percent partnership set to develop an oil field in Iraq estimated to yield 1.8 million barrels of oil per day.

Two nonrenewable energy resources, petroleum and natural gas, account for most of the total commercial energy produced and consumed in Malaysia. In 2001, the burning of crude oil, its by-products, and natural gas produced more than 90 percent of Malaysia's energy. Since then, overall demand for petroleum products has increased steadily at an annual rate of about 4.5 percent because of the rapid pace of economic development. Transportation and industry utilize most of this petroenergy. Nevertheless, the other fossil fuels, including gas and coal, have replaced oil as the primary source of fuel for the production of electricity.

Natural Gas

As of 2010, Malaysia had approximately 83 trillion cubic feet of natural gas reserves, located primarily in the provinces of Sabah and Sarawak, both on the densely forested and sparsely populated island of Borneo. The country is the world's

The brightly-lit Petronas Towers in Kuala Lumpur, Malaysia, symbolize the rise of Malaysia as an economic powerhouse, both within southeast Asia and globally.

second-largest exporter of natural gas. The Peninsular Gas Utilization Project, the Trans-Thailand-Malaysia Pipeline, and the Bintulu natural gas liquefaction plant in Sarawak, the largest in the world, ensure that Malaysia will be the most important link in the Trans-ASEAN (Association of Southeast Asian Nations) Gas Pipeline Project, which aims to secure natural gas for power generation throughout the region. Natural gas has been critical to the diversification of energy resources in Malaysia, which has an extensive network of domestic pipelines. At current extraction rates, reserves will be depleted by 2050.

Coal

A global renaissance of coal production is under way as more and more countries turn to this relatively cheap and efficient thermal energy source for generating electricity. For Malaysia, the burning of coal is a major part of its energy diversification policy. Again, it is Borneo that carries the largest deposits, weighing in at an estimated 1.7 billion metric tons. There are six functional mines in Sarawak, but much of the coal is hard to reach and of low quality; therefore extraction would be economically infeasible. Malaysia's goal of satisfying more than 40 percent of its domestic electricity demand through its four coal-fired thermal power plants is largely dependent on imports from neighboring countries, particularly Australia, China, and Indonesia.

Hydroelectric Power and Other Renewable Resources

Roughly 5 percent of Malaysian electricity is derived from running water. Much of the potential hydroelectric power sits in Borneo, with its rugged mountains, abundant rainfall, and racing rivers. However, few people live in Malaysia's portion of Borneo, which is separated from mainland southeast Asia and its more populated peninsular appendage by the South China Sea. Hydroelectricity is most efficient when it is consumed locally. The Bankun Dam in Sarawak, Malaysia's first major hydropower project, has not come close to generating the expected 2,400 megawatts of electricity. The government has since restructured the agencies responsible for the development of renewable resources and so-called green technology by putting forth the National Green Technology Policy (2009), which evolved from other policy measures, such as the National Energy Policy (1979), the National Depletion Policy (1980), the Fuel Diversification Policy (1981), and the Renewable Energy as the Fifth Fuel Policy (2000), all intended to foster sustainable economic development.

Palm oil is Malaysia's newest addition to the fuel diversity policy—the fifth estate of energy that is marketed as green power, expected to resolve the country's impending energy crisis once the crude oil reserves have been depleted, perhaps by as early as 2035. Vast tracts of land are now systematically covered with row upon row of oil palm, a

species indigenous to sub-Saharan Africa, a tree so productive that its value far surpasses that of the rubber tree and tropical rain forest timber. Malaysia produces 45 percent of the world's palm oil, mostly exported to Japan. Refuse from refinement can be converted to biodiesel, a fuel the government is keenly interested in manufacturing. This green gold may soon outshine the black.

For hundreds of years, the peninsula of Malaysia has forced sea traders to travel through the Strait of Malacca, which remains at the heart of international trade. The economy of the Malaysian region once depended on the extraction and export of tin, hardwood, and rubber, thus adding to the importance of this sea lane. The commercialization of crude oil, which began in 1910 on the island of Borneo in a place called Miri, both reinforced and changed the region's economic significance. For the country of Malaysia, services and manufacturing now drive this globally competitive economy, thanks to its abundance of oil fields.

Since reserves of oil are finite, the Malaysian government is now working to ensure that the country will have secure and reliable sources of energy needed for a prosperous society. The task is somewhat urgent, since economic prosperity itself seems to have a limitless horizon that petroleum cannot reach. Fuel diversification policies should reduce petroleum's share of commercial energy production by increasing the use of other fossil fuels, such as gas and coal, and by propelling renewable energy, such as solar power, wind, and biofuel, to the fore of economic, political, and environmental sustainability.

KEN WHALEN

Further Reading

Bunnell, Tim. "Views From Above and Below: The Petronas Twin Towers and/in Contesting Visions of Development in Contemporary Malaysia." *Singapore Journal of Tropical Geography* 20, no. 1 (1999).

Chua, Shing Chyi, and Tick Hui Oh. "Review on Malaysia's National Energy Developments: Key Policies, Agencies, Programmes and International

Involvements." *Renewable and Sustainable Energy Reviews* 4 (2010).

Gale, Bruce. "Petronas: Malaysia's National Oil Corporation." *Asian Survey* 21, no. 11 (1981).

U.S. Energy Information Administration. "Country Analysis Brief: Malaysia." http://205.254.135.7/countries/country-data.cfm?fips=MY.

Zhang, Wei. *2010 International Conference on Energy, Environment and Development.* Amsterdam: Elsevier, 2011.

See Also: Air Pollution; Energy Transmission: Gas; Indonesia; Japan; Offshore Drilling; Oil and Petroleum; Shell; Singapore; Total Primary Energy Supply.

Maldives

Official Name: Republic of Maldives.
Category: Geography of Energy.
Summary: The Maldives is a small nation consisting of 1,192 islands located in the Indian Ocean, of which around 200 are inhabited by Maldivian nationals and another 100 are used as tourist resorts.

In 2009, the Maldives set the most radical renewable energy goal in the world: to become a carbon-neutral state by 2020. There are two key motivations behind the Maldives' goal of becoming carbon neutral by 2020. First, the Maldives islands constitute the lowest-lying country in the world, averaging only 5.9 feet (1.8 meters) above sea level, which makes it extremely vulnerable to sea-level rise induced by global warming. Second, the Maldives is highly dependent on oil imports for its energy needs and is therefore very vulnerable to oil price increases. The spike in oil prices in 2008 saw petroleum prices double across the country, and as a result the Maldives' fuel security and socioeconomic welfare are likely to improve as it increases its ability to generate renewable energy from indigenous natural resources.

Traditionally, Maldivian residents relied on energy from wood and biomass for cooking, and utilized wind energy to sail between islands for trade and social activities.

However, as economic development has progressed over the past 50 years, reliance on imported fossil fuels has also increased for electricity, cooking, and transport. Demand varies greatly between islands. Most islands have fewer than 1,000 people, and peak demand can be as low as 30 kilowatts. However, the energy challenge is far more acute in the densely packed capital, Malé, which hosts 30 percent of the country's total population in a space of just 2.5 miles (4 kilometers).

All islands in the Maldives now have access to electricity, although the quality of service varies and blackouts are a common experience in some outer islands. Electrical energy is delivered by diesel-powered generators, which are acknowledged by the government as inefficient, unreliable, and expensive to run. Electricity prices are consequently high, although the government subsidizes the prices to the public. Energy for cooking tends to come from liquid petroleum gas rather than local wood or biomass, resulting from a scarcity of wood resources, government restrictions on tree cutting, improved convenience, and affordability.

Tourism and Fishing

Finally, the nation's economy is based largely on two activities, tourism and fishing, both of which require high levels of motorboat transport between islands and out to sea, and each additionally fueled by oil and petroleum imports.

Thus, the Maldives is highly dependent on a resource that it does not possess and must therefore import. With such high dependence on fossil fuels, the Maldives carbon-neutral goal serves two distinct purposes. First, a concerted move toward supporting renewable energy generation could significantly boost the country's economy through reducing reliance on oil imports and increasing energy security. The islands have strong equatorial sunshine and moderate winds, making energy from solar photovoltaic (PV), solar thermal, and wind power a possibility. Research is also focused on wave, tidal, and ocean thermal technologies through a partnership with the Scottish government, and a United Nations

Development Programme project has identified renewable energy sources, such as landfill gas from biologically degradable waste and combined heat and power (CHP) from biomass, as suitable for some islands. However, installation of any renewable energy comes with high capital costs, and the Maldives will require significant international funding to achieve its goal.

The second purpose of declaring such an ambitious goal is to provide world leadership in developing a truly carbon-neutral national economy. In real terms, the Maldives carbon footprint is estimated at less than 0.01 percent of global carbon dioxide emissions; nevertheless, the nation's actions and radical stance on this issue have gained significant global attention and could catalyze other governments to set similarly ambitious goals. Famously, the Maldivian president and his cabinet staged an underwater meeting in 2009, demonstrating the grave risks faced by the country, as the climate-change-induced rise in sea level threatens to sink the nation's islands.

Whether the Maldives meets its carbon-neutral target remains to be seen. Demand for fuel and electrical services continues to rise across the islands, and current use of renewable resources is negligible, restricted to solar PV in navigation lights, outer-island telecommunication systems, and some use of solar water heaters.

ABIGAIL CLARE

Further Reading

Hekkerta, M. P. "Renewable Energy Technologies in the Maldives: Determining the Potential." *Renewable and Sustainable Energy Reviews* 11 (2007).

Lempiainen, M. "Help, My Island Is Sinking!" *International Reporting*. Paper 1 (2009). http://mediaworks.journalism.cuny.edu/ir/1.

U.S. Energy Information Administration. "Country Analysis Brief: Maldives." http://www.eia.gov/countries/country-data.cfm?fips=MV.

van der Akker, J., and M. Saleem. *Maldives: Renewable Energy Technology Development and Application Project; Mid-Term Review*. Report prepared for the United Nations Development Programme and Global Environment Facility, 2007.

See Also: Climate Neutrality; Global Warming; Nonrenewable Energy Resources; Oil and Petroleum; Renewable Energy Resources; Wood Energy.

Mali

Official Name: Republic of Mali.
Category: Geography of Energy.
Summary: Mali's agricultural status means that its energy demands are largely residential as opposed to industrial. Mali's status as a developing nation places increased importance on energy as a vital aspect to economic growth and development.

The landlocked west African republic of Mali has an estimated population of 12 million. Mali is prone to drought and desertification because of its location within the arid Sahel region, which threaten its main energy resources of wood and hydropower-generated electricity. National and international rural electrification programs are expanding access to electricity and fueling new energy demand. Mali lacks significant oil reserves and must import its fossil fuels. Biofuels produced from agricultural residue and foodstuffs have attracted international investment to Mali and show promise as a future energy resource.

Traditional energy sources such as charcoal and wood supply most of Mali's energy needs, especially in rural areas where there is limited access to electricity. Wood is the main energy resource, provided by an estimated 35.6 million acres of forests and woodland areas. Wood accounts for over 80 percent of the energy supply, largely for domestic use as a fuel source. Although the Malian government's Water and Forests Service oversees protected forest reserves and seeks to develop sustainable usage of this traditional resource, deforestation is a serious issue affecting energy as well as the environment.

Mali's energy infrastructure supplies electricity, gas, and other modern energy resources to less than one-third of the population. Fossil fuels and hydropower are the main sources used in the production of electricity, supplying approximately 43 percent and 56 percent of its electric generation respectively. Most fossil fuels are imported, as past petroleum explorations failed to locate any significant national reserves. Hydroelectric dams include the Senegal River Development Organization's dam at Manantali, operational since 1992, and another at Selingue along the Sankarani River, operational since 1982. The country's hydroelectric supply, however, faces frequent disruptions due to drought and is threatened by ongoing desertification and potential global warming. As a result of its rural, developing nation status and poor energy infrastructure, only approximately 15 percent of the Malian population had access to electricity in 2009. Access among urban residents was higher, at approximately 59 percent.

Mali's energy demand growth rate is larger than that of its gross domestic product (GDP) and is expected to climb further as increased access to electric grids fuels demand. Energy efficiency and security are also concerns as development continues. The national government has sought to increase access to electricity through the 2005 enactment of a regulatory framework for rural electrification, the creation of its rural electrification agency (AMADER), and through outreach programs. Mali also implemented a new five-year program in 2010 designed to promote energy efficiency. The plan targets energy use reductions in the residential, industrial, and transportation sectors, the development of renewable sources of electricity generation, and the reduction of carbon dioxide emissions under the clean development mechanism (CDM).

Mali has also benefited from international rural electrification programs designed as part of overall economic growth and poverty reduction strategies. Yéelen Kura SSD is a decentralized energy service company created through an international rural electrification program led by the French company EdF (Electricite de France) and the Dutch company Nuon. The company supplies electricity to several thousand rural house-

▷ *Biofuel Production*

Several nongovernmental organizations and European companies are involved in small-scale Malian projects designed to produce biofuels from agricultural residues and feedstocks. These companies then contract with local small-scale producers, providing them with technical training and other incentives such as seed purchase guarantees. Jatropha has emerged as one of the first Malian crops to be converted to biofuel. The Malian government has shown its interest in further biofuel production development through its 2009 creation of the National Agency for Biofuels Development (ANADEB). Biofuel initiatives remain at the small-scale, localized level with no major industrial-scale initiatives yet in place. The potential for large-scale biofuels production, however, is there.

Examples include projects run by the private Dutch company Mali Biocarburant SA and the joint French-Malian venture, Jatropha Mali Initiative (JMI). Efforts include research and development, training, education, and funding. Mali Biocarburant SA has produced biodiesel from jatropha to be sold within the domestic market and has tested experimental portable engines fueled either by jatropha oil or a biodiesel derivative made from jatropha. The Jatropha Mali Initiative has produced jatropha oil for both the local and domestic markets and instituted a cooperative seed collection and oil extraction program for local growers.

A leaf from a jatropha plant.

Wikimedia

holds in an agricultural area of southern Mali. Key delivery methods include the installation of solar home system photovoltaic kits and connection of households to diesel generator powered minigrids. Payment methods include fee-for-service and monthly payment options. International companies such as EdF also provide educational and technical assistance to Malian companies such as SSD Koray Kurumba.

Agricultural residues represent a key potential future source of biofuel energy production. Malian agriculture produces large amounts of residual products that have traditionally been burned off, but could be converted into usable biofuels. Examples include rice husks; millet, cotton, and sorghum stalks; groundnut, peanut, and jatropha shells; and animal dung that are little valorized into energy or other uses. Biofuels have the potential to supply all or part of Mali's energy needs, which would reduce its energy dependency while aiding economic growth. The West African Economic and Monetary Union (UEMOA) has estimated the energy potential of this largely untapped resource at 8 terawatts.

Marcella Bush Trevino

Further Reading

Banks, Douglas, Alix Clark, Katherine Steel, Chris Purcell, and Jonathan Bates. *Integrated Rural Energy Utilities: A Review of Literature and Opportunities for the Establishment of an IREU.* http://www.reeep.org/file_upload/5272_tmpphpE5UJkl.pdf.

International Institute for Environment and Development. "Biofuels in Africa: Growing Small-Scale Opportunities." http://www.iied.org/pubs/display.php?o=17059IIED.

U.S. Energy Information Administration. "Mali." http://38.96.246.204/countries/country-data.cfm?fips=ML.

See Also: Biomass Energy; Hydropower; Solar Energy.

Malta

Official Name: Republic of Malta.
Category: Geography of Energy.
Summary: The energy system of Malta has always been dependent on oil and coal. The Maltese government is trying to promote renewable energy and energy-efficiency technologies.

Malta is an archipelago, located south of Italy in the heart of the Mediterranean Sea, and is the smallest country of the European Union. Only the three largest islands, Malta, Gozo, and Comino, are inhabited. Malta's freshwater supplies are limited, and it has no domestic production of energy sources. While Malta became independent from United Kingdom in 1964, it is still totally energetically dependent on oil imports.

In 1896, the first power station in Malta began operations when the nation was still part of the British Empire. From 1905 to 1915, the power generation and the electricity system of Malta were extended to meet local demand. In 1914, World War I started, and activity in the energy sector was postponed. In 1926, a new power station was inaugurated in Gozo, but after the start of World War II in 1939, all the activities for the further development of the Maltese energy system again came to a halt. The war ended in 1945, and four years later a new power station was proposed to be constructed in Malta with the financial help of the United States.

Toward the end of the 19th century, the Maltese economy, based on the dockyard, started to decline primarily because of improvements in shipping technology and decrease in traffic at the country's docks. In 1964, Malta became independent, which opened the way for the new government to shift Malta's economy to one based on tourism and manufacturing of electronics and textiles, which led to greater independence from the British economy. To support the development of these new sectors, new power plants had to be constructed.

In 1953, a new gas turbine was installed at the Station Jesuits Hill, Marsa (an underground plant), and in 1966 another station, with two steam turbines, opened; it was expanded in March 1971. This later station helped solve one of Malta's major problems: the scarcity of freshwater. A distiller was producing freshwater in addition to limited water from underground reserves. The extension of this station in 1971 involved the installation of three more distillers. The dependence of Malta on oil was increasing during this period, and accidents in 1966 and 1972 along with a strike in 1968 highlighted the risks of this dependence.

However, these events did not immediately influence development of Malta's energy technology. Little by little, the inhabited islands of Malta, Gozo, and Comino were connected to the new energy supplies with the construction of submarine cables in 1981, 1987, and 2001.

In October 1973, the Arab Oil Embargo shocked oil-based economies worldwide, including that of Malta. The Maltese distillation plants switched off their engines, and other technologies, such as reverse osmosis, were engaged to keep the freshwater supply at a viable level for the Maltese population. In 1982, eight years after the end of the oil crisis, the first reverse osmosis plant was opened, and in 1984 a second one was added to the system.

After the oil crisis, the Maltese government tried to take the control of the country's oil supply. In 1974, it nationalized the importation of oil products, and in 1977 it set up Enemalta Corporation, which remains the main provider of energy generation and distribution, including oil and gas importation and distribution.

A Second Oil Crisis
In 1979, a second oil crisis, this time due to the Iranian Revolution, again brought into question Malta's energy policy and made the government seek alternatives. Between 1982 and 1987, four stream turbines were installed at the Marsa Power Station. This strategy could have worked if the environmental and human health impacts of the coal used at the power station had not caused the local population to protest. In 1987, construction of a new power plant, at Delimara, started; the plant was commissioned in 1994. In the meantime, the Marsa Power Station continued to be improved, with new turbines added to eliminate the use of coal. On January 12, 1995, Malta became independent of coal but consequently became fully dependent on oil.

In July 1990, Malta applied to join the European Union (EU); consequently, its energy and environmental policies had to be adjusted to meet EU requirements. In 1999, Enermalta commissioned a combined-cycle generation plant using low-sulfur gas oil. In 2011, the two power stations operating in Malta had a total nominal installed capacity of 571 megawatts.

On May 1, 2004, Malta became one of the 27 members of the EU and set some ambitious targets for use of energy from renewable sources, setting the goals of a 10 percent share of renewable energy in both final energy consumption and transport by 2020.

So far, although biofuels' penetration into the Maltese fuel mix is increasing, renewable energy technologies are not performing very well. Nevertheless, the Maltese government has subsidized the installation of photovoltaics and microwind for domestic use and has established feed-in tariffs. A big effort has been made to reduce waste of grid power. Enemalta has been installing smart meters for all its customers, and Malta aims to become the first country in the world to have a smart electricity grid across a whole nation. The Maltese have been recognized to be among the EU's biggest energy savers.

GEORGIOS SARANTAKOS

Further Reading
Central Intelligence Agency. "Malta." In *The World Factbook*. http://goo.gl/gcO0j.
Eccardt, Thomas M. *Secrets of the Seven Smallest States of Europe: Andorra, Liechtenstein, Luxembourg, Malta, Monaco, San Marino, and Vatican City*. New York: Hippocrene Books, 2005.
Enemalta. "History of Electricity." http://goo.gl/zl19K.
Environmental and Resources Unit. "Electricity Generation in Malta." http://goo.gl/khhaK.
European Commission. "Malta: Energy Mix Fact Sheet." http://goo.gl/UDKHQ.
European Renewable Energy Council. "Renewable Energy Policy Review: Malta." http://goo.gl/InUi3.
Lamendola, Michael F., and Arthur Tua. "Desalination of Seawater by Reverse Osmosis: The Malta Experience." *ACOM* 3-95. http://www.outokumpu.com/35954.epibrw.
Malta Resource Authority. "Publications." http://www.mra.org.mt/library_publications.shtml.

U.S. Energy Information Administration. "Country Analysis Brief: Malta." http://www.eia.gov/countries/country-data.cfm?fips=MT.

See Also: European Union; Feed-in Tariff; Oil and Petroleum; Photovoltaics; Rotational Energy; Smart Grids; Wind Resources.

Manufactured Gas

Category: Energy Technology.
Summary: Manufactured gas collectively refers to artificially produced gases used for lighting, heating, and cooking that were produced in Europe and North America from the early 19th until the mid-20th centuries.

The use of manufactured gas has declined as the availability and use of natural gas (methane) has become commonplace. Manufactured gas largely ceased to be produced in North America after 1960, while a few gasworks remained in operation in parts of Europe until the mid-1980s.

Manufactured gas is a flammable mixture of gases composed primarily of carbon monoxide and hydrogen, along with smaller amounts of ethylene, acetylene, propane, methane, nitrogen, oxygen, water vapor, various sulfur compounds, and ammonia. The composition and ratio of these gases varies considerably depending upon the processes used to produce manufactured gas, as well as the type of feedstocks employed. Coal was the most commonly used feedstock for manufactured gas, but other materials were also occasionally used, including wood, pine tar, oil shale, and petroleum.

Manufactured gas can be produced through a relatively simple process whereby coal or other organic feedstocks are heated in ovens in a low-oxygen environment. In the absence of oxygen, coal produces flammable gases, water vapor, and valuable by-products including coal tar and coke. The resulting flammable gas is known as coal gas or town gas. Similar processes yield slightly different mixtures of gases with varying energy values. Water gas is produced by passing steam over red-hot coal or coke; injecting a spray of petroleum produces carbureted water gas with a higher energy value, similar to coal gas. Passing air over red-hot coal or coke yields gases similar to coal gas, with a larger proportion of nitrogen. Carbureted water gas was the prevalent form of manufactured gas in the United States by the early 20th century. In some areas without abundant coal supplies, utilities turned to petroleum to produce gas. In California, several plants produced gas through the oil gas process. Similar to the production of carbureted water gas, oil gas can be created by superheating petroleum in the presence of steam.

Whichever method was employed, the resulting flammable gas was collected, metered, and piped to residential customers. Manufactured gas was not commonly used for electricity generation, since burning coal directly was cheaper and more efficient. Industrial facilities, however, often operated their own gasworks to fuel kilns or furnaces in brick and cement plants, foundries, and steel plants.

Production Effects on the Environment

The production of manufactured gas is environmentally taxing. Carbon monoxide, a major component of manufactured gas, is extremely toxic and poses serious risks of injury or death if inhaled even in low concentrations. Carbon monoxide is also a component of smog, a greenhouse gas, and a major contributor to air pollution. The production of manufactured gas required massive and unsightly gasworks close to urban areas. Larger cities might have dozens of gasworks in operation at any given time, each requiring substantial real estate (often a city block or more). The gasworks received a constant supply of coal or oil, both as a feedstock as well as an energy source for the gasworks, which produced pollution in staggering amounts. Gasworks operated around the clock, continually pumping black smoke and soot into the air. Solid by-products such as coke or coal tar could be resold, although much waste also found its way into the urban environment and watersheds, fouling groundwater, poisoning lakes and rivers, and killing fish and other creatures. In the absence of any major regulations concerning air or water pollution, manufactured gas works faced only modest local codes regulating their emissions.

Long-distance transmission of manufactured gas prior to the 1920s was not feasible due to limitations in pipeline technology. As a consequence, manufactured gas was produced in situ within or near towns and cities, exacerbating air and water pollution among other issues. It was not uncommon for large institutions such as schools, hospitals, military bases, railroads, hotels, prisons, and factories to operate their own gasworks, compounding environmental and pollution concerns on a large scale.

Origins

While burning springs and swamp gas have been known since antiquity, the production and use of manufactured gas dates back just 400 years. The first published production of manufactured gas dates to around 1609, when Belgian chemist Jean Baptiste van Helmont conducted experiments using coal. Van Helmont placed more than 60 pounds of coal in a sealed container, which he then placed in a heated furnace. The coal produced a gas that burned when exposed to flame.

In about 1683, English clergyman John Clayton excavated a burning spring near his home in Lancashire. He discovered that the source of the spring was a coal vein, which he later used to produce gas that he captured in ox bladders. To amuse his friends, Clayton would puncture one of the sealed bladders and ignite the gas with a candle, resulting in an impressive flame. Despite his innovation in capturing the gas he produced, Clayton evidently never tried to make practical use of his discovery.

The first practical application of manufactured gas came more than a century later in France. In 1785, Jean Pierre Minckelers, a professor of natural philosophy at the University of Louvain, used manufactured gas for illumination. Minckelers burned stored gas to light his classroom. For this demonstration, Minckelers is sometimes referred to as the "inventor of gas-lighting."

Another Frenchman, Philippe Lebon, received a patent in 1799 for the Thermolampe, a device that could produce manufactured gas from wood. Lebon was also the first person to recognize the commercial potential of manufactured gas. While he was unable to interest the French government in his experiments, Lebon hoped to popularize the use of manufactured gas through a public demonstration of gas lighting at the Hôtel Seignelay in Paris for several months in 1801–02. Lebon's demonstration attracted considerable attention because of its bright interior lights, heating, and an innovative outdoor water fountain illuminated by gaslights. Lebon's efforts failed to attract needed backing, and his untimely death in 1804 marked a shift to Britain as the center of manufactured gas technology and innovation.

Britain emerged as a leader in manufactured gas technology in the early 19th century for several reasons, notably its ongoing industrialization and its abundant coal reserves. A key figure in the development of Britain's manufactured gas technology was William Murdock, chief engineer for Boulton, Watt & Co., developers of the first practical steam engine. Murdock experimented widely with natural gas, leading to a number of innovations. He developed a portable gas headlight system for steam-powered horseless carriages, and experimented with methods to manufacture and transport gas. He also fitted his house with gas lighting, running more than 70 feet of copper and tin pipes to carry gas to light an interior room. In 1802, Murdock installed gas lighting at Boulton & Watt's Soho Factory in Birmingham. The experiment was a success; Murdock's gaslights proved to be less expensive, brighter, and safer than oil lamps for illuminating the factory.

Boulton & Watt soon pioneered the commercial gas-lighting business. The use of gas lighting was attractive to British cotton mills due to the danger of fire from other contemporary forms of lighting. By 1806, Murdock oversaw the installation of gas lighting at the factory of Lee and Lee, a large cotton mill. The 50 gas lamps installed by Boulton & Watt provided 2,500 candlepower of illumination. Murdock calculated the savings to the factory for using cheaper gas lighting to be some $2,266 per year.

The first demonstration of coal gas lighting in the United States came in 1802. Benjamin Henfrey of Northumberland, Pennsylvania, used a thermolampe of European design to produce gas. Henfrey's demonstration produced bright lights, but no financial backing to carry the process forward.

A more successful venture was that of Charles Willson Peale, a Revolutionary War colonel and portraitist of George Washington. Peale established a museum in Philadelphia in 1814, and to attract visitors, he installed gas lighting. Peale's museum was successful, leading one of his sons, Rembrandt Peale, to open a similar museum in Baltimore. Rembrandt Peale also used gas lighting to attract paying visitors to his establishment. The Baltimore museum featured a ring of 100 gaslights, which dazzled its patrons, leading Rembrandt Peale to explore the commercial possibilities of manufactured gas.

In 1816, Peale and a group of Baltimore investors formed the Gas Light Company of Baltimore (GLCB). The GLCB soon received a franchise from the city to construct a gas streetlight system. Within short order, GLCB service was expanded to wealthy private customers as well. The GLCB constructed a gasworks and laid out pipes underneath the major thoroughfares. The GLCB developed slowly; after five years of operation, the company only served 73 customers in and around Baltimore. Despite its slow development, manufactured gas soon spread to other cities as entrepreneurs sought larger and virgin markets for their product, and expansion gradually drove down the initial high costs of manufactured gas.

The success of manufactured gas in Baltimore soon encouraged additional ventures. Within 20 years, manufactured gas works supplied customers in New York, Boston, Louisville, New Orleans, and Philadelphia. Over the course of the next four decades, manufactured gas use gradually spread throughout the country. Gasworks were common in larger, midwestern communities by the 1850s. By the 1860s, the West Coast cities of Los Angeles and Portland were using town gas. The last major urban areas to construct manufactured gas works were in the Pacific Northwest, a region without significant natural gas reserves. Seattle built a gasworks in 1873, followed by Tacoma in 1885, and Spokane in 1887. This region was one of the last to maintain a manufactured gas infrastructure in North America.

By 1900, nearly 900 manufactured gas works were in operation across the United States. As the United States urbanized in the early 20th century, the number of gasworks increased to more than 1,000 by 1919. In 1921, an estimated 46 million individual customers in the United States used manufactured gas. The $500 million manufactured gas industry produced 450 billion cubic feet of gas annually.

Decline

A long period of decline followed the industry's heyday of the 1920s. In both North America and Europe, this decline was closely associated with the development of long-distance natural gas pipelines. Generally, when natural gas became available through discovery or pipeline construction, utilities and consumers opted for natural gas. There were several reasons for this. Natural gas was cheaper than manufactured gas, since it was extremely abundant and often discovered in conjunction with petroleum, which reduced costs further. No gasworks were required to produce natural gas, although processing plants located near the gas fields were needed to remove impurities. As a fuel, natural gas burned more cleanly than manufactured gas, produced brighter light, and was less toxic than manufactured gas.

In the United States, the manufactured gas industry declined following the discovery of massive gas fields in the southern plains region and the southwest. Between 1918 and 1922, oil wildcatters discovered several major gas fields in these areas, as well as in parts of Arkansas, Louisiana, southern California, and in the Rocky Mountain region. These discoveries totaled more than 117 trillion cubic feet of gas. Such abundance promised clean, cheap sources of energy for growing industries and cities, if the fields could successfully be exploited.

In addition to abundant supplies, advances in pipeline technology also proved crucial to developing markets for natural gas. Higher-strength rolled steel pipe introduced after World War I replaced cast-iron and other relatively brittle steel alloys previously used in pipelining. These stronger alloys could withstand the higher pressures necessary to move gas over long distances. One of most important innovations was the use of welding to join pipe segments. Various methods of welding replaced couplings and other methods of pipe fitting (such as the use of threaded pipe), which were not satisfactory even over short distances. New compressors and other related technology also made modern pipelining feasible.

The combination of large supplies of cheap gas, improved technology, and eager markets fueled a pipeline construction boom in the late 1920s and early 1930s. Snaking outward from the mid-continent fields, long-distance pipelines reached many of the larger markets of the midwest and south during this period. The rush to construct pipelines in the 1920s and early 1930s reduced the demand for manufactured gas, as natural gas reached cities including Wichita, Kansas City, Denver, Indianapolis, Chicago, Minneapolis-St. Paul, Omaha, Detroit, Dallas, Houston, and Atlanta. Utilities were quick to adopt the cheaper and cleaner fuel, shuttering manufactured gas plants in many of these markets.

The Great Depression halted the boom in long-distance natural gas pipeline construction and provided a brief respite for the manufactured gas industry. Long-distance pipeline construction ground to a halt after 1932, and only resumed during World War II. Following the war, new gas transmission companies, such as Texas Eastern and Tenneco, rushed to build new pipelines to the markets still served by manufactured gas. Texas Eastern successfully converted the war-surplus Inch Pipelines to carry natural gas from petroleum in the late 1940s, bringing new supplies of gas to Philadelphia and New York. The New England market was converted to natural gas following a contentious battle over market share in 1954. Seattle and surrounding cities received natural gas service in 1956.

As pipelines carried natural gas to more markets, the utilities that relied on manufactured gas closed their expensive gasworks. By 1947, only about 170 manufactured gas works remained in operation in the United States. With the introduction of natural gas to the Pacific Northwest and south Florida in the late 1950s, most of the remaining manufactured gas works closed. The last American town gas facilities ceased regular operation in 1966, with a few plants maintained on standby or for seasonal duty into the 1970s.

In Europe, a similar pattern of decline emerged, but only after the discovery and utilization of vast natural gas deposits in the North Sea. British utilities shifted to natural gas beginning in the 1960s. By the late 1970s, most gasworks in the United Kingdom had closed. A handful of manufactured gasworks remained in operation in Northern Ireland until the mid-1980s.

The relative stability in American wellhead gas prices, which had reigned over the market since the mid-1980s, disappeared in the 2000s. The new century saw natural gas prices spike to record levels on several occasions, prompting a renewed interest in manufactured gas. Utilities in several states, including Indiana and Illinois, proposed the construction of new synthetic gas plants in response to higher prices.

However, the future of a new American manufactured gas industry was soon called into question due to booming production of natural gas from shale and coal-bed sources, which served to once again lower prices.

DAVID RALEY

Further Reading

Accum, Friedrich Christian. *Description of the Process of Manufacturing Coal Gas.* London: T. Boys, 1819.

Castañeda, Christopher J. *Invisible Fuel: Manufactured and Natural Gas in America, 1800-2000.* New York: Twayne Publishers, 1999.

Castañeda, Christopher J. "Manufactured and Natural Gas Industry". EH.Net Encyclopedia, edited by Robert Whaples. (September 3, 2001) http://eh.net/encyclopedia/article/castaneda.gas.industry.us

Herbert, John H. *Clean Cheap Heat: The Development of Residential Markets for Natural Gas in the United States.* Westport, CT: Praeger, 1992.

Stewart, Edward George. *Town Gas; Its Manufacture and Distribution.* London: H.M. Stationery Office, 1958.

Stotz, Louis. *History of the Gas Industry.* New York: Stettiner Bros., 1938.

Tussing, Arlon R., and Bob Tippee. *The Natural Gas Industry: Evolution, Structure, and Economics.* 2nd ed. Cambridge, MA: Ballinger Publishing, 1984.

See Also: Coal; Natural Gas; Oil and Gas Pipelines; Wood Energy.

Marcellus Shale

Category: Environmentalism.
Summary: The Marcellus Shale is a geological formation that holds a vast amount of natural gas that may be a boon for U.S. energy markets. However, exploitation of this resource is mired in controversy over the safety of hydraulic fracturing.

The Marcellus Shale is a geological formation found under the Allegheny Plateau. It is rich in natural gas that can be accessed only through a controversial drilling process known as hydraulic fracturing. Supporters argue that the Marcellus Shale gas will help the United States reduce its dependence on foreign gas and bring needed jobs and revenue to rural areas; they further maintain that hydraulic fracturing is a safe and reliable process. Opponents argue that unknown environmental and human health impacts caused by drilling outweigh the short-term benefits of natural gas supply and that more study should be done to ensure the safety of drilling practices.

Description
The Marcellus Shale is sedimentary bedrock of organic-rich black shale located under the Allegheny Plateau and is about 95,000 square miles in area. The bulk of the Marcellus Shale sits under West Virginia, western and northern Pennsylvania, and southern New York, although it is also under western Virginia, western Maryland, and eastern Ohio. The Marcellus Shale is largely found deep underground, as deep as 7,000 feet or more. The shale contains pockets of natural gas that have only recently become accessible through advanced drilling techniques. It is difficult to estimate precisely how much natural gas can be extracted. Estimates also vary widely on how much natural gas the Marcellus Shale contains, ranging from 50 trillion to 500 trillion cubic feet.

Hydraulic Fracturing
Natural gas is extracted from the Marcellus Shale by a combination of horizontal drilling and hydraulic fracturing, also known simply as fracking. A horizontal well is made by drilling vertically down to the depth of the Marcellus Shale, encasing the shaft to prevent chemicals from leaking, and then drilling horizontal lines out through the rock bed. This allows the drilling of a larger area underground from one well, arguably resulting in more gas produced from a small surface footprint. A combination of water, chemicals, and sand are sent down the well at high pressure to create fractures in the shale to release the gas. Up to 5 million gallons of water may be used in the hydraulic fracturing of each well, some of which is reused and some of which is left in the ground. The process of hydraulic fracturing and the chemicals involved are at the core of the controversy.

Economic and Development Potential
The greatest potential for developing Marcellus Shale gas is in Pennsylvania. Supporters claim that natural gas development in rural communities will bring much-needed tax revenues to states, jobs to rural communities, and revenues from leasing and royalties to struggling landowners. The areas with the greatest potential for drilling extend well into regions of economic stagnation. Some landowners and farmers report that without profits from leases and royalties, they might have decided to sell their farms. Drilling companies claim that by bringing revenue to rural areas they are helping to preserve farming and rural ways of life that have been under threat.

The natural gas industry and supporters believe that the Marcellus Shale can secure the United States' energy supply by reducing reliance on imported natural gas. Natural gas is also a cleaner-burning fuel and thus has less negative environmental impact compared to other fossil fuels. It can be used to fuel electric power plants and is more efficient than coal with lower greenhouse gas emissions. The prospect of having such an abundant reserve so close to the massive energy markets of East Coast cities has attracted investment in Marcellus Shale gas development from global players, not just investment from American firms, including Indian, Japanese, and Norwegian companies that recognize the vast potential profits to be made.

Environmental Impact and Opposition

Opponents believe that hydraulic fracturing damages water quality and human health. This is of concern in rural Pennsylvania, where private wells are common and the state is one of the few states lacking any private well regulation. It is difficult to prove the source of well-water contamination. Chemicals used in hydraulic fracturing are known to be injurious to human health; some are known carcinogens. Opponents argue that such chemicals should not be injected deep into the ground, where they could find a way into drinking water sources; opponents also contest the safety of how wastewater removed from the well is processed. They lobby for the suspension of hydraulic fracturing, demand that more research be done to protect water supplies, and insist on full disclosure of chemicals being used at specific sites. Gas may also leak into water supplies; some have reported being able to set their tapwater on fire. Some rural families dependent on well water now buy and store water for all

Wikimedia

A tower used for drilling horizontally into the Marcellus Shale formation is seen from Route 118 in rural Pennsylvania. Supporters believe the Marcellus Shale can secure the United States energy supply. Opponents believe hydraulic fracturing damages water quality and jeopardizes human health.

their needs out of fear that their water is originating from contaminated wells.

In August 2010, New York passed a moratorium on issuing new well permits to allow time for a thorough environmental review. In October of that year, Pennsylvania's governor Ed Rendell issued an executive order banning new natural gas development on state forestlands in response to criticisms that unchecked industrialization was occurring on public lands and disturbing forested areas. Although this move protects the state's public lands, the vast majority of natural gas development is on private, not state, land.

SHAUNNA BARNHART

Further Reading

National Geographic. *Special Report: The Great Shale Gas Rush.* http://news.nationalgeographic.com/ news/energy/2010/10/101022-energy-marcellus -shale-gas-rush/.

Navarro, Mireya. "N.Y. Senate Approves Fracking Moratorium." *New York Times.* August 4, 2010. http://green.blogs.nytimes.com/2010/08/04/n-y -senate-approves-fracking-moratorium/.

Zeller, Tom, Jr. "Governor Bans New Gas Wells on State Land." *The New York Times.* October 26, 2010. http://green.blogs.nytimes.com/2010/10/26/ pennsylvania-governor-bans-fracking-in-state -forests/.

See Also: Fossil Fuels; Maryland; Natural Gas; Ohio; Oil and Natural Gas Drilling; Oil Shales; Pennsylvania; West Virginia.

Marshall Islands

Official Name: Republic of the Marshall Islands.
Category: Geography of Energy.
Summary: The Republic of the Marshall Islands became invested in sustainable energy relatively late. However, the measures the country has adopted over the past few years have yielded significant results.

The Republic of the Marshall Islands (RMI) is made up of two archipelagic island chains and five single islands in the northern Pacific Ocean, about halfway between Hawaii and Australia. The total population was estimated at 64,522 people in 2009. Overall, 63 percent of Marshallese households have access to electricity. Although 88 percent of urban households are electrified, the figure drops to 12 percent in rural areas.

Achieving a higher electrification rate is prevented largely by a very high reliance on expensive petroleum imports for electricity generation. In order to cope with this energy security issue, exacerbated by the 2008 fuel crisis, the RMI government devised an energy policy agreement known as the Majuro Energy Declaration. Set in January 2009, the declaration maps out the path toward greater energy efficiency and security in the Marshall Islands.

The Majuro Declaration

The Majuro Declaration materialized in September 2009 through the publication of the National Energy Policy and Energy Action Plan (NEP). The main goal set by the NEP is to achieve, by 2015, 100 percent electrification of all urban households and 95 percent electrification of rural outer atolls. (An atoll is an island or group of islands made of coral that has a lagoon at its center.) To that end, the introduction of renewable energies in the energy mix has been pursued through initiatives such as the Action for the Development of Marshall Islands Renewable Energy (ADMIRE) program, which addresses institutional capacity, policy and regulatory issues, and market development for renewables.

The aim is now to have 20 percent of the energy provision coming from indigenous renewable sources by 2020. An indigenous renewable source is a local renewable energy source, as opposed to the imported petroleum or other renewable energy sources unavailable in the Marshall Islands.

The government of RMI focuses on developing renewable energy services on outer islands, with assistance from donor agencies such as the Asian Development Bank (ADB), which supports the rural electrification of the country through solar photovoltaic (PV) systems.

In August 2010, the RMI government endorsed the RMI Climate Change Roadmap 2010 as a national framework to guarantee the coordination and coherence of efforts to address climate change issues. This framework will allow the development and implementation of fast-start finance projects, a concept established by the United Nations Framework Convention on Climate Change (UNFCCC) in 2009 as part of the Copenhagen Accord. The fast-start finance system allows developing countries to draw monies from a fund supported by a number of developed countries and use the funds for mitigation, adaptation, technology development and transfer, and capacity-building projects.

The government has two primary agencies overseeing energy-related issues. First, the Energy Planning Division of the Ministry of Resources and Development is responsible for energy policy, coordination, and implementation. One of the NEP's goals is to ensure adequate staffing and capacity of this division to manage energy planning issues. Second, the Economic Policy, Planning and Statistics Office is the key national development planning agency, closely involved in rural electrification policy.

Conservation Programs and Energy Efficiency

In 2002, the RMI government started developing and applying energy efficiency and conservation programs; for example, it endorsed the Pacific Islands Energy Policy and Strategic Action Planning project, delivered in 2002–06 and supported by the Secretariat of the Pacific Islands Applied Geoscience Commission. The subsequent successful campaign, which was supported by the Renewable Energy and Energy Efficiency Partnership, raised people's awareness of the importance of an efficient use of energy. Several energy efficiency tips were widely spread within the country through both a brochure and a weekly spot on the *Marshall Islands Journal*.

Another goal of the NEP for the development of energy services is to improve efficiency of energy use in 50 percent of households and businesses and 75 percent of government buildings by 2020. Although there are still barriers to sustainable energy, such as an inadequate institutional capacity and a lack of standards and certification components, significant progress has been made. An energy planner and an energy adviser have been appointed, and efforts are being made to establish strategies and plans.

DAPHNÉ BARBOTTE
MAAIKE GÖBEL
EVA OBERENDER

Further Reading

Central Intelligence Agency. "Marshall Islands." In *The World Factbook*. https://www.cia.gov/library/publications/the-world-factbook/geos/rm.html.

Marshalls Energy Company. "Strategic Financial Plan and Performance Audit and Review (2006)." http://www.mecrmi.net/News%20publications/DOI%20Review%20of%20MEC%20Jan%202007.pdf.

Pacific Power Association. "United States of America Insular Areas Energy Assessment Report: An Update of the 1982 Territorial Energy Assessment (2006)." http://www.doi.gov/oia/reports/iaea2006report.doc.

Republic of the Marshall Islands. "Climate Change Roadmap 2010." http://www.faststartfinance.org/sites/default/files/documents/RMI%20climate%20roadmap.pdf.

Republic of the Marshall Islands. "National Energy Policy and Energy Action Plan 2009." http://marshall.wetserver.net/livefiles/rmienergyactionplan-2009(2)_aboutdownloads_60.pdf.

Secretariat of the Pacific Regional Environment Programme. *Pacific Regional Energy Assessment 2004*. Vol. 6, *Marshall Islands National Report*. http://www.sprep.org/climate_change/documents/Vo16-MarshallIsNationalReport_000.pdf.

See Also: BP; Climate Change; Energy Poverty; International Renewable Energy Agency; Micronesia; Nauru; Nuclear Fusion; Renewable Energy Resources.

Maryland

Category: Energy in the United States.
Summary: Maryland's energy profile is connected to the Chesapeake Bay. The state receives most of its electricity from coal and plans to make solar and offshore wind a larger part of its energy mix.

Maryland's energy profile is tied to the Chesapeake Bay, which provides energy-rich food, wind for transportation, and an ideal location for trade and commerce. During the 20th century, industry in Maryland grew along with its population and total energy consumption. Today, electricity in Maryland is powered primarily by coal. The densely populated state imports electricity and is likely to see growth in either generation capacity or transmission in coming years to meet electricity demand. Although the role of the Chesapeake Bay in Maryland's energy profile has evolved over time, the connection endures. Concerns over climate change, including potential impacts on the Chesapeake Bay, have inspired citizens and government officials to transform Maryland's energy profile through use of renewable energy resources and energy efficiency investments.

Energy History

Maryland surrounds the Chesapeake Bay, the largest estuary in the United States and a source of primary energy. The Chesapeake Bay is a vast ecosystem with multiple producers and consumers interacting along the food web. Historically, Native Americans occupied the shores of the bay in part because it provided high-energy food options, including oysters and the blue crab. British and other European colonists selected the shores of the bay for settlement because it offered plentiful food. Perhaps more important, however, wind-powered ships—the only mode of intercontinental transportation in colonial America—could easily harbor in the open and protected waters of the bay.

The Chesapeake Bay's energy-laden natural resources allowed Maryland to develop as a center of trade and commerce. Baltimore, the largest city in Maryland, grew considerably during the 18th and 19th centuries. The location offered proximity to the agricultural south and an abundance of ports, which were necessary for international trade in tobacco, sugar, and flour. Maryland's economy became increasingly industrial during the late 19th and 20th centuries, with local growth in iron and steel production, metalworking, and shipbuilding. Early industrial processes were energy-intensive and required large amounts of fuel energy.

Energy Today

Today, Maryland is less industrial and agricultural. Like the United States as a whole, Maryland's economy gradually transitioned to one based on services, with the health and government sectors accounting for significant portions of the state's gross domestic product. Despite this shift away from an energy-intensive economy, Maryland's total energy consumption more than doubled in the period between 1960 and 2000 as a result of population growth and increased reliance on home appliances and personal transportation.

In 2008, Maryland consumed 1.4 quadrillion British thermal units (Btu) of energy. The transportation and electric utility sectors roughly account for one-third of total consumption each; directly consumed fuels at homes and businesses account for the remainder. Per capita energy consumption in Maryland is among the lowest in the United States, at 256 million Btu per person.

Production of fossil fuels in Maryland is minimal. Some coal and natural gas is extracted in western Maryland, which includes energy-rich portions of the Appalachian Mountains. Garrett and Allegany Counties in western Maryland lie in the Marcellus Shale geological formation, which holds significant quantities of natural gas. Extraction of shale gas in Maryland may be more common in the years ahead, depending on economic conditions and the resolution of health and environmental concerns.

The Chesapeake Bay is a critical geographic feature for energy distribution and storage in the heavily populated eastern United States. The ports of Baltimore receive oil from abroad, and the Cove Point terminal, located in the bay, receives and stores liquefied natural gas.

Wikimedia

The Sparrows Point steel mill was the world's-largest by the middle of the 20th century, covering four miles from one end to the other, with thousands of workers employed at the site.

▷ *Sparrows Point*

Sparrows Point, a peninsula near Baltimore in the Chesapeake Bay, was once home to the world's-largest steel-manufacturing plant. Steel produced at the plant was directed toward multiple end uses, including shipbuilding, which occurred at a nearby site on the Chesapeake Bay and was vital to U.S. efforts during World Wars I and II. In the early 1960s, the Sparrows Point plant produced more than 600,000 tons of steel per year, consuming roughly 27 trillion Btu of energy annually. The Sparrows Point plant remains functional today.

A fleet of more than 30 major in-state generating units supports production of electricity in Maryland. The state receives approximately 60 percent of its electricity from coal. In addition, Maryland has a large nuclear facility, Calvert Cliffs, with a maximum capacity of around 1,735 megawatts, which provides one-third of the state's electricity. Natural gas, hydropower, and other renewable resources contribute to the electricity fuel mix as well. Maryland is in a deregulated electricity market, with four investor-owned utilities that distribute electricity to 90 percent of customers in the state. In addition, the state has five municipal utilities and four rural electric cooperatives. Utilities in Maryland are subject to rate and regulatory oversight from the Maryland Public Service Commission. Currently, electricity rates for Maryland consumers are above the national average.

Maryland falls under the jurisdiction of a regional transmission organization, PJM, which serves to ensure that electricity supply meets demand over an area covering 13 states and the District of Columbia. This is relevant because Maryland currently has an insufficient supply of generating capacity to meet its demand. As a result, Maryland imports a substantial portion of its electricity from other states. Much of Maryland lies in a national interest electric transmission corridor, which means that additional transmission capacity is of central concern to the U.S. government. Maryland is expected to see expansion of its transmission capacity in the coming years.

Energy Future
Maryland, and the Chesapeake Bay in particular, are vulnerable to the impacts of climate change, including temperature increases and sea-level rise.

As a result, the state of Maryland is seeking to transform its energy profile through government policy. Maryland's energy policy considers both the quantity and quality of energy consumed.

Maryland is a member of the Regional Greenhouse Gas Initiative (RGGI), a group of 10 states in the northeastearn United States participating in a cap-and-trade market. Maryland's participation in RGGI is expected to reduce greenhouse gas (GHG) emissions from the state's electricity generators by 10 percent by 2019. Revenue from sale of GHG emissions allowances will be directed toward investment in energy efficiency. The state has also instituted a law that requires electric utilities to develop and implement energy efficiency and demand response programs. The goal of this policy, EmPower Maryland, is to reduce per capita electricity consumption by 15 percent by 2015.

Finally, Maryland has a renewable energy portfolio standard whereby 20 percent of electricity sold in the state will come from renewable resources by 2022. Of note, Maryland's renewable standard has a solar carve-out or mandate that 2 percent of all electricity sold in the state must come specifically from solar photovoltaics by 2022. Also, offshore wind development is important in the state. Maryland is a relatively small, densely populated state, which creates challenges for siting commercial-scale wind farms onshore. To meet its renewable energy portfolio standard, Maryland may install significant offshore wind capacity in the Atlantic Ocean. Maryland is coordinating with the federal government and private wind developers in the hope of constructing what would be one of the first offshore wind farms in the United States.

SEAN R. WILLIAMSON

Further Reading

Database of State Incentives for Renewables and Efficiency. "Maryland: Incentives/Policies for Renewables and Efficiency." http://www.dsireusa.org/incentives/incentive.cfm?Incentive_Code=MD05R&re=1&ee=1.

Maryland Power Plant Research Program, Maryland Department of Natural Resources. "Electricity Factbook in Maryland." http://esm.versar.com/pprp/factbook/factbook.htm.

Reutter, Mark. *Making Steel: Sparrows Point and the Rise and Ruin of American Industrial Might*. Champaign: University of Illinois Press, 2004.

Ruth, M., et al. *Economic and Energy Impacts From Maryland's Participation in the Regional Greenhouse Gas Initiative*. College Park: University of Maryland, 2007.

Thomas, William G., III. "The Chesapeake Bay." *Southern Spaces*, April 2004.

U.S. Energy Information Administration. "Maryland." http://www.eia.doe.gov/state/state-energy-profiles.cfm?sid=MD.

See Also: Carbon Tax; Energy Markets: Industrial; Evans, Oliver; Marcellus Shale; Pennsylvania; Regional Greenhouse Gas Initiative; Wind Resources.

Massachusetts

Category: Energy in the United States.
Summary: Despite a history of reliance on fossil fuels, Massachusetts has abundant renewable resources that are beginning to be developed.

Massachusetts is one of the most densely populated states in the nation. It is also one of the least energy intensive, with the transportation and residential sectors accounting for the greatest share of energy consumption. The Massachusetts Bay Transportation Authority (MBTA) is the single largest electricity user in the state, accounting for about 9 percent of the state's electricity demand. On the other hand, residential electricity use is relatively low, since most energy demand comes from heating needs that are met mostly by non-electrical sources.

Many commercial buildings and nearly two-fifths of homes in Massachusetts are heated by using distillate fuel oil. When demand rises during the cold winter months, customers become vulnerable to fuel shortages and price volatility, a problem that plagues much of the northeast.

During the winter of 2000, for example, an unexpectedly bitter winter caused shipping channels to freeze over and created high winds, which slowed the delivery of new supply and led to shortages. That summer, the federal government established the Northeast Heating Oil Reserve, which is mandated to maintain enough supply in its reserves (located in Connecticut and New Jersey) to meet consumers' needs during the length of time it takes new shipments to move from the Gulf of Mexico to Boston Harbor.

Natural Gas

The residents of Massachusetts rely heavily on natural gas for both home heating and electric power generation. Natural gas is primarily conveyed through pipelines that enter the state through New Hampshire, New York, and Rhode Island, coming from production sites in Canada and the Gulf Coast or storage areas in the Appalachian Basin. It is also imported to Massachusetts in a chilled, liquid form in tankers from South America. After the liquid natural gas (LNG) is delivered, it is warmed until it reaches the vapor stage and is then pumped into the gas line. Massachusetts is home to three natural gas import terminals that serve the greater northeast, out of 10 in all of the United States. Two are located offshore, and one is located onshore, in Everett.

Although natural gas is the leading source of electric power generation in Massachusetts, accounting for about one-half of the state's total usage, another quarter of Massachusetts's electricity supply comes from coal-fired plants that use coal mined in Kentucky and West Virginia, making Massachusetts the only New England state whose electricity mix is significantly fueled by coal. The Pilgrim Nuclear Generating Station, located in Plymouth, also contributes power to the Massachusetts grid, as do several large hydroelectric facilities.

Massachusetts has made an effort to transition to cleaner forms of energy during the late 20th and early 21st centuries. Beginning in the 1990s, petroleum-fired power plants began to be phased out in favor of natural gas, which creates fewer harmful by-products when combusted. The state leads the nation in the production of electricity from landfill methane gas and municipal solid waste. In addition, it is one of the few states to require that its motor gasoline be blended with ethanol.

Like the rest of New England, Massachusetts has abundant biomass resources. These resources consist primarily of new-growth forests, which have been replenished over the past century after a period of extensive logging and agricultural development during the 1800s. Fuelwood continues to be a principal heating source for many Massachusetts residents, and wood chips are a viable option for electricity generation in the future.

Limited Development

Massachusetts's other renewable resources are extensive. Although they have been developed only to a limited extent, the state has made renewable energy generation as well as energy efficiency a priority in statewide energy strategies and policy. In 1998, the Massachusetts legislature created a renewable energy trust (RET) fund, which as of 2010 assessed a system benefits charge to all ratepayers of investor-owned utilities in the state of around $0.29 per month. The RET is used to fund new renewable energy projects through a number of grant programs, which are administered by the Massachusetts Clean Energy Center (MassCEC) through a state mandate. In 2008, the state adopted a renewable portfolio standard (RPS) that set goals requiring the investor-owned utilities to procure 15 percent of their power from renewable sources by 2020 and 25 percent by 2030.

In addition to the investor-owned utilities, there are approximately 40 municipally owned utilities in Massachusetts, which are exempt from the same renewable energy and efficiency mandates. These municipal light departments are allowed to opt into these programs by enacting the systems benefits charge on their ratepayers as a result of the 2008 Green Communities Act, but they often choose to pursue clean energy projects on their own. For example, the largest wind project currently under construction in Massachusetts is a 15-megawatt farm owned by the Berkshire Wind Corporation, a nonprofit public power corpora-

▷ *The Massachusetts Renewable Portfolio Standard*

The Massachusetts renewable portfolio standard (RPS) requires utilities in the state to procure a certain percentage of their electricity from renewable or alternative sources. Municipally owned utilities are exempt from RPS requirements. In order to track whether or not suppliers have met their requirements, electricity generated from renewable and alternative sources is broken into two commodities: energy, which may be used on site or moved through the grid and eventually delivered to a customer, and the positive environmental attributes associated with the electricity generation. These are considered to be discrete products and are sold separately on the wholesale power market. In order to verify that RPS standards are met, rather than tracing the path of individual electrons from the generating unit to the utility to the customer, the state simply requires utilities to purchase sufficient quantities of the latter commodity, which are known as renewable energy certificates (RECs).

Every time a generating unit produces one megawatt-hour of electricity within the ISO New England control area and feeds it into the New England grid, a database known as the New England Power Pool (NEPOOL) Generation Information System (GIS) creates a serial-numbered, electronic certificate and adds it to the account of the utility that owns the generating unit. If the generating unit is certified as a renewable or alternative source, the electronic certificate will be specially coded as a renewable energy certificate (REC).

In order to meet RPS obligations, utilities must make sure they have a high enough percentage of RECs in their NEPOOL GIS account, either by producing them from their own generating units or by purchasing them from other suppliers. If they fall short of this amount, they must pay a penalty known as an alternative compliance payment (ACP) to the Massachusetts Department of Energy Resources (DOER). The ACP rate is set by DOER and serves as a price ceiling for RECs, with the goal being to incentivize the purchase of RECs that are cheaper than the ACP.

Only about 9.3 percent of the class I renewable generation certificates used to meet Massachusetts RPS requirements in 2009 were actually generated in the state. Slightly more than half came from New England, and the rest were sourced from New York and Canada. Not all RECs produced in Massachusetts are necessarily used to meet the Massachusetts RPS requirements, however. Some are sold to meet RPS requirements in other states, and others are simply retained by the generating units to show support for renewable energy.

tion whose membership consists of 14 municipal light plants across the state.

In addition to the wind resources in the Berkshire Mountains, Massachusetts's greatest wind resources are primarily located off its coasts, particularly in the southeast, off Nantucket and Cape Cod. Efforts to develop offshore wind energy projects have often been met with strong local opposition. These opponents generally live on or own property with a direct line of sight to a proposed wind energy development, and their perspective is largely driven by the "not in my back-yard" (NIMBY) phenomenon. Their arguments range from concerns that their property values will decline to anxiety over potential health issues associated with "flicker" caused by wind turbines' rotating blades to worries regarding the well-being of wildlife, such as birds and bats. The most famous example of this NIMBY response was the late Senator Ted Kennedy's opposition to Cape Wind, a 420-megawatt, 130-turbine project proposed in the Nantucket Sound. The proposed project would be located in federal waters, but the transmission lines and other infrastructure needed to connect it to land require both state and federal permits. If developed, Cape Wind would be the first offshore wind project in the United States.

Despite these challenges, Massachusetts has set a statewide goal of installing 2,000 megawatts of wind-based generating capacity by 2020, which would account for 10 percent of the state's electricity supply at that point. In 2009, the U.S. Department of Energy awarded Massachusetts a grant to build the nation's first Wind Technology Testing Center (WTTC) in Boston, which will have the capacity to test blades up to 164 feet (50 meters) long.

Solar Energy

Although Massachusetts does not receive a particularly high level of solar radiation, it is well suited for solar energy development in terms of favorable policy and markets for solar power. The administration of Governor Deval Patrick created a solar carve-out in the state RPS, mandating that a certain percentage of the renewable energy procured to meet RPS requirements come from solar-powered facilities. The renewable energy certificates (RECs) generated at solar-powered facilities are known as solar renewable energy certificates (S-RECs) and have a higher market value, which is attractive to potential developers. As of 2010, there were about 45 megawatts of solar photovoltaics (PV) installed in Massachusetts.

Massachusetts consistently ranks among the top in the nation for policies and programs that encourage the development of energy efficiency. It was ranked second only to California two years running by the American Council for an Energy-Efficient Economy. The Patrick administration declared that energy efficiency should be the state's "first fuel," and all investor-owned utilities are mandated to create three-year plans for ensuring that they secure all efficiency resources that are at or below the cost of installing new generating capacity. Massachusetts is part of the New England ISO (ISO-NE), which allows bids of efficiency and demand resources on its forward capacity market (FCM).

Helen Aki

Further Reading

An Act Relative to Green Communities. 2008. Chapter 169 in *Massachusetts General Laws*. http://www.malegislature.gov/Laws/SessionLaws/Acts/2008/Chapter169.

Berkshire Wind Power Cooperative. "The Berkshire Wind Power Project." http://www.berkshirewindcoop.org.

Cape Wind Associates. "Frequently Asked Questions." http://www.capewind.org/FAQ-Category4-Cape+Wind+Basics-Parent0-myfaq-yes.htm.

Federal Transit Administration. "ARRA Fact Sheet: MBTA Wind Energy Generation Turbines." http://www.fta.dot.gov/about_FTA_11578.html.

U.S. Energy Information Administration. "Massachusetts." http://eia.doe.gov/state/state-energy-profiles.cfm?sid=MA.

See Also: ExxonMobil; Industrial Ecology; Regional Greenhouse Gas Initiative; Renewable Energy Credits; Thompson, Benjamin (Count Rumford); Townes, Charles Hard; Vermont; Wind Technology.

Mauritania

Official Name: Islamic Republic of Mauritania.
Category: Geography of Energy.
Summary: Almost entirely dependent on imports for energy, Mauritania has in recent years accelerated its opening of onshore and offshore oil deposits through international contracts for exploration and production. Government instability has been at the root of Mauritania's halting progress in energy development.

A west African country with a 468-mile (754-kilometer) coast on the Atlantic Ocean, Mauritania shares borders with Algeria, Mali, Senegal, and the Morocco-administered Western Sahara. Large in area at more than 385,250 miles (620,000 square kilometers), Mauritania's population is approximately 3 million. Nearly all Mauritanian land is desert; less than 1 percent of the land is suitable for sustained raising of crops.

Half the population depends on livestock and agriculture for their livelihood, although droughts are forcing more farmers and herders into cities. The estimated per capita gross domestic product (GDP) in 2010 was $2,100—near the bottom of all nations—with 40 percent of the population living below the poverty line and a 30 percent unemployment rate. On measures of well-being, Mauritania's population ranks low: The country's infant mortality rate is 60.42 deaths per 1,000 live births (34th-highest in the world), life expectancy 61.14 years (184th-highest in the world), and the literacy rate is 51.2 percent.

Mauritania became independent from France in 1960 and was ruled from 1984 to 2005 by Maaouya Ould Sid'Ahmed Taya, who took power in a coup and was deposed in a bloodless coup. In 2007, Sidi Ould Cheikh Abdallahi became Mauritania's first freely elected president, but he was ousted in a military coup in 2008 by General Mohamed Ould Abdel Aziz, who was elected president in 2009. Ethnic tensions and a growing terrorism threat from al-Qaeda continue to trouble the country. This instability has hampered economic development. In 2000, most of Mauritania's foreign debt was forgiven under the heavily indebted poor countries (HIPC) initiative. In 2006 the country agreed to an International Monetary Fund three-year "poverty reduction and growth facility." This arrangement was suspended after the coup in 2008, although since the presidential election in 2009 international assistance has resumed. Mauritania is classified as a least developed country by the United Nations, along with 32 other African countries, based on its low income, low human capital status, and economic vulnerability.

China, accounting for 41 percent of Mauritania's export business in 2010, is by far the country's largest trading partner; the next largest was France, at 9 percent. The leading export goods are iron ore, gold, copper, petroleum, and fish. In 2008, 11.3 million metric tons of iron ore were mined, accounting for almost 40 percent of the country's total exports. The global financial crisis of 2008 and the resulting fall in commodity prices meant a fall in real GDP in 2009, after 4 percent growth for the years 2004–08.

Fossil Fuels

Mauritania has begun expanding exploration for and production of crude oil, an effort accelerated since the 2001 discovery of the offshore Chinguetti field, where proved reserves of at least 60 million barrels are claimed. A smaller underwater field, Tevet, was discovered in 2005. The country has produced an average of 12,000 barrels per day (bpd) in recent years. Oil consumption in 2010 was 20,000 bpd. Mauritania has one refinery, at Nouadhibou, with a 20,000-bpd capacity; it typically runs at perhaps one-quarter capacity. Mauritania has 1 billion cubic feet of proved natural gas reserves, but again this resource is not currently being exploited, and the country neither produces nor consumes natural gas.

Although Mauritania was a consumer of coal in the 1980s and 1990s (entirely imported), it no longer uses coal and has no coal reserves. In 2011, electricity generation was about 410 gigawatt-hours. Total primary energy production in 2007 was 0.033 quadrillion British thermal units (Btu), or 120th in the world; energy consumption was 0.039 quadrillion Btu, or 148th in the world; and energy intensity (Btu per dollar, using 2005 U.S. dollars) was 5,675, or 97th in the world. Mauritania's installed electric generation capacity stood at 120 megawatts as of 2007. Mauritania generates nearly 90 percent of its electricity from fossil fuels—exclusively petroleum. Most of the remainder comes from hydroelectric sources. Carbon dioxide emissions from consumption of fossil fuels totaled 2.76 million metric tons in 2008 (142nd in the world) and 2.90 million metric tons in 2009.

Current Operations

As of October 2010, the African Development Bank was involved in 14 operations in Mauritania, with 68 percent of the funding dedicated to industry and mining projects, 17 percent to water projects, 8 percent to finance projects, 4 percent to agriculture, and 3 percent to social projects. Priorities for these projects include consolidating macroeconomic stability, fostering economic growth that will benefit the poor, expanding basic services, developing human resources, and improving governance and capacity building. Priorities for infrastructure development include increasing access to clean drinking water and sanitation services, transportation, and electricity, particularly for the rural population.

Sarah Boslaugh

Further Reading

African Development Bank Group. "Mauritania: Results-Based Country Strategy. Paper (RBCSP) 2011–2015." http://www.afdb.org/fileadmin/uploads/afdb/Documents/Project-and-Operations/Mauritania-RBCSP%202011-2015x.pdf.

"Energy: Mauritania Bounces Back." *African Business*, no. 342 (2008).

Mauritania Energy Policy, Laws and Regulation Handbook. Washington, DC: International Business Publications, 2008.

See Also: Algeria; China; Energy Poverty; France; Liberia; Mali; Morocco; Senegal.

Mauritius

Official Name: Republic of Mauritius.
Category: Geography of Energy.
Summary: Mauritius, an island nation with no proven gas or coal reserves, relies heavily on fossil fuel imports, which it has reduced through an energy development program. The country also has plans to tap renewable energy sources.

Mauritius is a picturesque island and renowned tourist destination located off the southeast coast of the African continent in the Indian Ocean. Although it is fairly developed, the island has no known oil natural gas or coal reserves.

Before the 19th century, Mauritius was at different times under colonial rule of the Spanish, Dutch, and French, but it was controlled by the British from the early 19th century until independence in 1968. Before leaving, the English started a rural electrification program and established the

Central Electricity Board (CEB) of Mauritius in 1952. Responsibility for generation, transmission, distribution, and sale of electricity in Mauritius and the island of Rodrigues rests with CEB, which is a parastatal body under the Ministry of Public Utilities and owned completely by the government of Mauritius. Rodrigues, a small island located 348 miles (560 kilometers) east of Mauritius, is an autonomous region of Mauritius where all existing wind energy projects from Mauritius are located. The national rural electrification program was completed by 1981, and electricity networks reaching industries, schools, water facilities, and 153 villages and estates had commenced.

Traditionally, Mauritius has relied heavily on oil imports from the Middle East, Asia, and Europe for its entire energy requirements, including electricity. However, since the 1990s frequent fluctuations in oil prices, due to wars such as the Persian Gulf wars, and variations in global production have had an adverse impact on the country's economy, leading to large import bills and devaluation of the Mauritian rupee. To diversify its energy mix, Mauritius initiated the bagasse energy development program (BEDP) in 1991 to exploit the island's biggest natural resource: large-scale sugar plantations. After sugarcane is crushed, a fibrous residue called bagasse is obtained. Interest in utilizing bagasse as a combustion fuel increased after World War II, at a time when sugar processing was undergoing modernization.

Electricity

Since the beginning of the 21st century, Mauritius has increased coal consumption and reduced oil imports, because of comparatively lower and stable coal prices. Investment from private producers has made this possible. Electricity generated by CEB has declined by 20 percent in this period. However, the recession that began in 2007 led to record oil and coal prices, which caused considerable financial losses.

In 2009, nearly 40 percent of the island's electricity was produced by CEB from its four thermal power and eight hydroelectric plants. The remaining share, close to 60 percent, comes from sugar plantations of independent industrial producers

(IIP). Since bagasse is from natural biomass, it is considered carbon neutral, because the amount of carbon dioxide emitted during its combustion is roughly equal to that absorbed during the sugarcane's growing phase. During the crop season, bagasse is used as fuel to generate electricity. For the remaining five or six months of the year, coal imported from Mozambique and South Africa is used in thermal power plants run by IIPs. Electricity from sugar plantations is sold to CEB, and this revenue provides insurance from loss of income due to decline in sugar prices.

In 2009, generation in Mauritius was estimated at 2,577 gigawatt-hours, with 95 percent from thermal energy and the remaining 5 percent from a combination of hydropower and wind. Oil is no longer the dominant fuel input: In 2009, 48.9 percent of electricity came from coal, 26.2 percent came from oil, and 24.9 percent came from bagasse. Between 2000 and 2009, generation has gone up 45 percent.

IPPs running power projects in Mauritius include Central Thermique de Belle, Vue (CTBV), Flacq United Estates Limited (FUEL), Consolidated Energy Limited (CEL), Central Thermique de Savannah (CTSav), and Compagnie Thermique de Savannah Limitée (CTSav). These companies run cogeneration thermal power plants that use bagasse and coal for "firm production" (generation throughout the year). Their combined installed capacity is 257 megawatts. This production is supplemented by three continuous producers that produce electricity using only bagasse, during crop season.

Electricity is sold at higher prices by IIPs. To ensure affordability, units are resold to consumers at lower tariffs by CEB. The monopoly and influence of IIPs are expected to decrease with the formation of a utilities regulatory authority (URA) for the energy sector in Mauritius.

Photos.com

The island's most abundant natural resource is sugarcane, which can be used to create biofuel.

Consumption and Mix

Transport and manufacturing are the largest energy consumers. Demand for electricity will increase considerably with projects such as the Mauritius Jinfei Economic Trade and Cooperation Trade Zone project, which will bring an investment of nearly $90 million from a Chinese consortium between 2009 and 2015. Growth of the information technology and medical tourism industries will also increase energy demand in the future.

In 2009, Mauritius's total primary energy requirement was 1,347 kilotons of oil equivalent. About 55 percent, or 741 kilotons of oil equivalent, was from petroleum products such as fuel oil, diesel, aviation fuel, and gasoline. The coal requirement was 369 kilotons of oil equivalent and renewables, 236 kilotons of oil equivalent.

Renewables

Climate change and sea-level rise are major threats to this small-island developing state. Because 80 percent of greenhouse gas (GHG) emissions result from the combustion of fuels for energy, the country aims to increase its efforts to reach sustainable development goals outlined in the Maurice Île Durable vision.

As a first measure, 1 million compact fluorescent lightbulbs (CFLs) at subsidized prices were sold to residential consumers in 2008, and the resulting peak demand reduction was estimated to be 14.36 megawatts. Annual GHG reductions from this effort are about 26,253 tons of carbon dioxide. Also, 21 percent of energy demands for the year 2008 came from renewables, of which bagasse contributed about 95 percent.

The government of Mauritius outlined its long-term energy strategy in October 2009, with a comprehensive energy policy incorporating a strong focus on renewable energy. Mauritius has set a goal of supplying 35 percent of its electricity from renewable energy sources by 2025. This will be achieved by increasing bagasse utilization efficiency and exploiting 2,900 hours of annual sunlight, wind farms, and waste-to-energy facilities. For all these efforts, however, Mauritius's dependence on fuel oil and coal is likely to continue into this decade.

DINESH KAPUR
HARISH ALAGAPPA

Further Reading

Central Electricity Board. "Annual Report." 2008. http://ceb.intnet.mu/.

Hassen, S., et al. "Trends in the Power Sector in Mauritius." http://active.cput.ac.za/energy/web/icue/papers/2005/29_C_Bhurtun.pdf.

Mauritius Government. "Outline of Energy Policy 2007–2025." April 2007. http://www.gov.mu/portal/goc/mpu/file/Outline%20energy%20policy.pdf.

Ministry of Renewable Energy and Public Utilities. "Long Term Energy Strategy 2009–2025." October, 2009. http://www.gov.mu/portal/goc/mpu/file/finalLTES.pdf.

Trade Chakra. "Power Industry in Mauritius." http://www.tradechakra.com/economy/mauritius/power-industry-in-mauritius-316.php.

See Also: Biomass Energy; Cogeneration; Demand-Side Management; Maldives; Wind Resources.

Mayer, Julius Robert von

Dates: 1814–1878.
Category: Biographies.
Summary: Julius Robert von Mayer is considered one of the scholars who discovered the energy conservation law, a foundational principle of thermodynamics, by identifying the equivalency of heat and work.

Julius Robert von Mayer, a German physician, wanted to explain physiological phenomena such as body temperature, respiration, metabolism, and movement without assuming that there was a special life force or that life was directly dependent on divine action. He looked for an answer that agreed with physics.

In the early 1840s, the concept of energy did not exist. Light, electricity, magnetism, heat, and motion were considered to be different forces. Mayer decided that it was first necessary to clarify what the relationship between the different natural forces was, before he could explain the phenomena of life. He began in his first essay of 1842, "Remarks on the Forces of Inorganic Nature," with a philosophical premise: Cause is consistent with effect. Every change has a cause, and nothing can emerge from nothing—that is, without a preceding state. Applied to force, this meant that no force could be created out of nothing; every force that appeared had to have come from somewhere. Correspondingly, every force that disappeared had to have become something else. Force could not be created or destroyed, since that would contradict the philosophical causality principle. Because experiments by Michael Faraday, Hans Christian Ørsted, and other scientists had shown that there was a relationship between the disappearance of one force and the appearance of another, Mayer postulated that all forces were expressions of a single force (now called *energy*).

Although there were numerous examples of one force seeming to call forth another, such as the steam engine, batteries, and electromagnetism, scientists had no mathematical means to relate these interactions to one another. Mayer's most significant contribution to the development of thermodynamics (the study of the transfer of heat energy) was to establish a general formula that allowed scientists to compare the different forces quantitatively. He did this by making them all comparable to a determined amount of heat. This formula was called the *mechanical equivalent of heat*.

Mayer expressed the mechanical equivalent of heat through a thought experiment: He asked how far a weight would have to fall to raise the temperature of an amount of water of equal weight from 0 to 1 degree Celsius through the heat generated by its impact. This would indicate how much mechanical (lifting) work had been done to raise the weight to that height. Mayer calculated that a weight of 1 kilogram would need to be lifted, and fall from, a height of 1,197 feet (365 meters) to raise the temperature of 1 kilogram of water 1 degree Celsius. The mechanical equivalent of heat was, according to Mayer, 365 kilogram-meters.

This thought experiment quantified the relationship between motion and heat. Because every other force could also be transformed into heat, it meant that all forces could be indirectly compared with one another. The mechanical equivalent of heat was a general formula that could be used independently of a specific transformation to calculate quantitative relationships between energy transformations.

Because change in nature could be reduced to these transformations, the mechanical equivalent allowed scientists to compare very different kinds of natural processes. When Mayer returned to his original interest in living organisms in 1845, he used the mechanical equivalent of heat to estimate the relationship between the chemical energy of foodstuffs and body temperature and motion in horses and humans. He also compared the efficiency of living beings, viewed as transformation machines, with the efficiency of a steam engine, which turned the chemical energy of coal into heat and motion. Mayer later expanded his comparisons to encompass all natural processes, calculating the equivalent of the sunlight reaching the Earth into horsepower and describing the heat equivalent of the motion of a meteorite. The mechanical equivalent of heat made it theoretically possible to compare every process in the world with any other.

While Mayer was developing his ideas in Germany, the British scientist James Joule used a similar thought experiment to come to a slightly different and more accurate equivalent. As a working physician, Mayer was, during this period (the mid-19th century) a scientific outsider, and he argued from philosophy, not physics. As a result, his essays, mode of presentation, and philosophical argumentation did not conform to scientific conventions, and his writings were ignored by physicists. Joule was therefore given the credit for formulating the

mechanical equivalent of heat. In 1847, Hermann von Helmholtz abstracted from the mechanical equivalent of heat the concept of the conservation of force as a general law of physics.

Lack of recognition may have contributed to Mayer's mental breakdown in the early 1850s, but in the 1860s, his early writings were rediscovered and reassessed by some German and British scientists. They disputed the priority given to Joule as the discoverer of the mechanical equivalent of heat and fought to have Mayer's work acknowledged for its important contributions to the development of the energy conservation law. Fortunately, Mayer lived to see his accomplishments acknowledged.

Elizabeth Neswald

Further Reading

Caneva, Kenneth. *Robert Mayer and the Conservation of Energy*, Princeton, NJ: Princeton University Press, 1993.

Heimann, P. M. "Mayer's Concept of 'Force': The 'Axis' of New Science of Physics." *Historical Studies in the Physical Sciences* 7 (1976).

Turner, R. Steven. "Mayer, Julius Robert." In *Dictionary of Scientific Biography*, edited by Charles Gillispie, et al. Vol. 9. New York: Charles Scribner's Sons, 1981.

Youmanns, Edward Livingston. *The Correlation and Conservation of Forces: A Series of Expositions*. New York: Appleton, 1865.

See Also: Carnot, Sadi; Faraday, Michael; Helmholtz, Hermann von; Joule, James; Ørsted, Hans Christian; Thermodynamics.

Meitner, Lise

Dates: 1878–1968.
Category: Biographies.
Summary: Lise Meitner was one of the first successful female physicists. She worked on radioactivity and nuclear physics, discovering nuclear fission.

Wikimedia

In 1922, Meitner achieved the highest academic level a scholar can achieve, which qualified her as a professor. She was the first woman in physics to do so.

Lise Meitner was born on November 7, 1878, in Vienna. She grew up in a well educated and wealthy family. Her parents were Jewish lawyer Dr. Philipp Meitner and Hedwig Skovran Meitner. At the time, it was typical in wealthy families to bring up children incorporating Protestant traditions, and in 1908, Lise converted to Protestantism.

Professional Advances

At the start of her professional life, Meitner took the teacher's examination in French and prepared herself to take the *Matura* (the secondary school exit examination) at the Academic Gymnasium in Vienna. After graduating, she entered the University of Vienna in 1901, studying physics, mathematics, and philosophy under Ludwig Boltzmann. She obtained a doctorate degree in physics at the University of Vienna in 1906—the second woman to do so. She then applied without success in Paris to work with the legendary radiation researcher Marie Curie, and instead worked at the Institute of Theoretical Physics in Vienna.

In 1907, financially supported by her father, Meitner went to Berlin (located in what was then called Prussia) to study with Max Planck, who made an extraordinary exception by accepting a female student. It was not until 1909 that women were officially allowed to attend university in Prussia. In Berlin, Meitner also met the chemist Otto Hahn. For 30 years, they collaborated closely, combining her knowledge of physics and his knowledge of chemistry to study radioactivity. In 1909, Meitner presented two papers on beta radiation; she and Hahn developed the recoil method, enabling them to discover several new isotopes, such as protactinium 231, actinium C, and thorium D.

War, Heritage, and Exile

Meitner gained a good reputation in physics and met, among others, Albert Einstein and her idol Marie Curie. In 1912, the newly-founded Institute for Chemistry at Kaiser-Wilhelm-Institute in Berlin (today in the Hahn-Meitner Building, Freie Universität Berlin) provided laboratories for Hahn and Meitner. For another year, until 1913, she worked without pay in Hahn's department of radiochemistry. After returning from voluntary service for the Austrian army as a front-line nurse handling X-ray equipment during World War I, Meitner was given her own radiophysics division at the Kaiser-Wilhelm-Institute in 1917. Meanwhile, Hahn participated in projects led by Fritz Haber to produce lethal gas.

In 1922, Meitner achieved her habilitation, the highest academic level a scholar can achieve, which qualified her as a professor. She was the first woman in physics to do so and the first to gain the right to teach at the university level. Shortly thereafter, in 1923, she discovered the Auger effect.

The discovery of the neutron in the early 1930s allowed chemists and physicists to begin searching for and creating elements heavier than uranium. At the time, scientists believed that these investigations constituted abstract research;

none supposed their work could lead to nuclear weapons and more practical applications. When Adolf Hitler came to power as the German chancellor in 1933, Meitner was at first protected by her Austrian citizenship and was able to continue her research on radiation experiments with neutrons (with Hahn), but she soon lost her permit to teach because of her Jewish heritage. After the annexation of Austria by Germany in 1938, Meitner became a German citizen. Now, however, her Jewish heritage forced her to leave Germany; in the same year, she fled to the Netherlands, supported by Hahn and the Dutch physicists Dirk Coster and Adriaan Fokker.

Ending up in Sweden, Meitner worked at Manne Siegbahn's Nobel Institute for Physics in Stockholm, again facing prejudice against women in science. From there she continued to collaborate with Hahn and physicist Fritz Strassmann, as well as establishing a working relationship with Niels Bohr, discoverer of the structure of the atom. Meitner worked at the Swedish Defense Research Agency and the Royal Institute of Technology, participating in research on R1, Sweden's first nuclear reactor. Hahn and Strassmann continued their radiochemical experiments. Hahn wrote to Meitner, describing results that provided evidence for nuclear fission. Meeting clandestinely in Copenhagen in 1938, they proved that splitting of the uranium atom was energetically feasible.

In exile, Meitner could not publish jointly with Hahn. In 1938, Hahn and Strassmann sent their report about the detection of barium after bombarding uranium with slow neutrons to the journal *Naturwissenschaften*. In February 1939, half a year before the start of World War II, Meitner and Otto Frisch published the first physical explanation for the observations of the splitting of the uranium atom in the journal *Nature*. Frisch coined the term *nuclear fission* to describe their findings. Applying Einstein's formula, $E = mc^2$ (the mass-energy equation), Meitner identified in the conversion of mass into energy the possibility for a chain reaction of enormous explosive potential. Her report led diverse scientists to persuade Einstein to write to U.S. president Franklin D. Roosevelt a warning letter, which led to the establishment of the Manhattan Project, the program that eventually developed the atom bomb. Meitner refused an offer to work on this project.

The Nobel Prize in Physics for 1944 was awarded to Hahn for his research on nuclear fission. Meitner was ignored. After the war ended in 1945, Meitner realized the effect of German fascism. She criticized Hahn, Werner Heisenberg, and other German scientists who had collaborated with the Nazis. Nonetheless, she and Hahn remained lifelong friends.

Overdue Recognition

During a visit to the United States in 1946, Meitner was awarded the title Woman of the Year by the National Women's Press Club at a dinner with President Harry Truman. She was the recipient of many honorary doctorates and lectured at renowned universities, including Princeton and Harvard. One year later, back in Sweden, she became director of the nuclear physics department at the Institute for Physics of the University of Technology in Stockholm, with funding from the Council for Atomic Research. She obtained Swedish citizenship in 1949 and became a member of the Royal Swedish Academy of Sciences.

During her lifetime, Meitner received a number of other honors, including the Prize of the City of Vienna for Natural Sciences in 1947, the Max Planck Medal of the German Physics Society in 1949, the Otto Hahn Prize for Chemistry and Physics in 1955, and the Order Pour le Mérite for Sciences and Arts in 1957. In 1966, the Enrico Fermi Award was awarded to Hahn, Meitner, and Strassmann. In a rare honor, the element 109, the heaviest known element in the universe, was named meitnerium (Mt) in 1997.

Meitner retired to Cambridge, where she died in a nursing home October 27, 1968. During her last years, she agitated for the peaceable use of nuclear fission.

MANJA LEYK

Further Reading
Barron, Rachel. *Lise Meitner: Discoverer of Nuclear Fission*. Greensboro, NC: Morgan Reynolds, 2000.

Meitner, Lise, and Otto R. Frisch. "Disintegration of Uranium by Neutrons: A New Type of Nuclear Reaction." *Nature* 143 (February 11, 1939).

Rife, Patricia. *Lise Meitner and the Dawn of the Nuclear Age.* Boston: Birkhäuser, 1999.

Sime, Ruth Lewin. *Lise Meitner: A Life in Physics.* Berkeley: University of California Press, 1996.

See Also: Curie, Marie; Einstein, Albert; Nuclear Fission; Nuclear Power; Radiation; Uranium.

Methane

Category: Energy Resources.
Summary: Methane is a simple hydrocarbon, resulting from decomposition and fermentation of organic substances, in the form of natural gas, swamp gas, and biogas.

Methane is used as fuel for heating devices, engines, fuel cells, and gas turbines that generate electrical energy, as well as in many industrial chemical processes. It has also been regarded both as a fossil fuel and as a renewable energy source. Although it shows high potential to become an environmentally safe motor fuel, given its cleaner exhaust and abundant occurrence, it is also a potent greenhouse gas (GHG) 25 times more powerful than carbon dioxide in effecting climate change.

At room temperature, methane (CH_4) is a colorless, odorless, highly flammable, and nontoxic gas. Liquid methane does not burn unless subjected to high pressure (normally 4 to 5 atmospheres). Under certain circumstances, methane reacts explosively with oxygen or chlorine. Containers of methane should be stored in well-ventilated places, kept away from ignition sources, and protected against electrostatic charge. Usually, methane is stored liquefied in gas containers at minus 160 degrees Celsius and under high pressure of 150 bars. These conditions increase its density enormously. Upon contact with methane in this form, frostbites can occur. Methane is both the simplest alkane and the simplest hydrocarbon, soluble in benzene, diethyl ether, and ethanol but only slightly soluble in acetone and water. At the molecular level, its carbon and hydrogen bonds form a tetrahedron.

History
Etymologically, the Greek *methy* denotes wine and *hyle* means wood and refers to the distillation of methyl alcohol from wood. Medieval alchemists knew methane as a component of fermentation gas, also called swamp air. In 1667, Thomas Shirley developed it first, and Joseph Priestley observed and described the formation of methane during decomposition in 1772. A few years later, between 1776 and 1778, it was isolated by Alessandro Volta. He noticed ascending gas bubbles when studying marshes around Lake Maggiore and started experimenting, inventing the prototype of a gas lighter, called a Volta pistol, and gas lamps. In 1856, Marcellin Berthelot first synthesized methane using carbon disulfide and hydrogen sulfide. Pyrolysis, in the form of wood gasification, is another method used to produce methane. During World War II, wood gas was used to fuel automobiles.

Chemistry
Combustion of methane releases much energy as heat. An optimal energy yield results only when sufficient oxygen is available. Insufficient oxygenation causes incomplete combustion, undesirable by-products such as carbon monoxide (CO), and carbon (carbon black), also yielding less effective energy. First methane forms HCHO (or H_2CO). This formaldehyde gives a formyl radical (HCO), also forming CO. The process is called oxidative pyrolysis:

$$CH_4 + O_2 \rightarrow CO + H_2 + H_2O$$

Following oxidative pyrolysis, the H_2 oxidizes, forming H_2O and releasing heat:

$$2H_2 + O_2 \rightarrow 2H_2O$$

Finally, the CO oxidizes, forming CO_2 and releasing more heat:

$$2CO + O_2 \rightarrow 2CO_2$$

In summary, when methane burns, the products are carbon dioxide and water:

$$CH_4 + 2O_2 \rightarrow CO_2 + 2H_2O + 891 \text{ kJ/mol (at standard conditions)} \rightarrow H_R = -802 \text{ kJ/mol}$$

where kJ denotes kilojoules (J denotes Joules) and mol denotes moles.

Methane melts at minus 182.6 degrees Celsius and boils at minus 161.7 degrees Celsius. The standard molar entropy S^0 is 188 J/mol·K (kelvin), and the heat capacity C is 35.69 J/mol·K. At 90.67 K and 0.117 bar, methane has a triple point of 190.56 K and a critical pressure of 45.96 bar. The heating value H_i is about 35.89 MJ·m^{-3}.

In addition to oxygenation, methane is very reactive with all halogens, such as fluorine (F), chlorine (Cl), bromine (Br), and iodine (I), in a procedure called free-radical halogenation. The universal formula for the potential reactions is:

$$CH_4 + X_2 \rightarrow CH_3X + HX$$

where X is a halogen. For example, with chlorine, methane forms chloromethane, dichloromethane, chloroform, and carbon tetrachloride. In step 1, radical generation, the required energy comes from ultraviolet (UV) radiation, or heating. In step 2, radical exchange, the following reactions occur:

$$CH_4 + Cl· \rightarrow CH_3· + HCl + 14 \text{ kJ}$$
$$CH_3· + Cl_2 \rightarrow CH_3Cl + Cl· + 100 \text{ kJ}$$

In step 3, radical extermination, these reactions occur:

$$2 Cl· \rightarrow Cl_2 + 239 \text{ kJ}$$
$$CH_3· + Cl· \rightarrow CH_3Cl + 339 \text{ kJ}$$
$$2 CH_3· \rightarrow CH_3CH_3 + 347 \text{ kJ}$$

In addition to its widespread occurrence in nature, methane can be synthesized from carbon and hydrogen or by means of catalytic reaction from carbon monoxide and hydrogen, as follows:

$$CO + 3H_2 \rightarrow H_2O + CH_4$$

Occurrence

The major source of methane is geological deposits of natural gas known as gas fields. Gas at shallow levels (that is, at low pressure) is formed primarily by anaerobic decay of organic matter, called methanogenesis, and secondarily from reworked methane from deep beneath the Earth's surface. In general, sediments buried deeper, and therefore under higher pressures and at higher temperatures, than those that form oil generate natural gas, which often is released during volcanic eruptions. Natural gas is a mixture of gases, including 75 to 98 percent methane, depending on its source, evolving from hermetically sealed, dead biomass under high pressure. Other components of natural gas can include ethane, propane, butane, pentane, and inert gases.

Although a part of natural gas, methane is not only a fossil fuel. In fact, it is continuously produced during all organic fermentation and degradation processes, which occur in swamplands, paddy fields, landfills, and industrial livestock farms. Methane is produced by the gases of ruminants (such as cows), but also by the enteric fermentation of wild animals, during their decomposition of glucose into carbon dioxide and methane, as follows:

$$C_6H_{12}O_6 \rightarrow 3 CH_4 + 3 CO_2$$

Sources differ in estimating methane expulsion, ranging between 60 and 100 kilograms of methane per year per animal for cattle. Globally, livestock are increasing (corresponding to a growing human population) at a rate that has made methane production from ruminants a factor relevant to the climate.

The transformation of the polymer substances takes place in a multilevel process, including hydrolysis (breaking down complex organic compounds into simple sugars, amino acids, and fatty acids, similar to the beginning of human digestion), acidogenesis (resulting in carbon dioxide, hydrogen, alcohol, fatty acids, and acetic acid), acetogenesis (producing more carbon dioxide and acetic acid), and finally methanogenesis.

This last stage is performed by bacteria that produce methane and water from carbon dioxide and hydrogen ($CO_2 + 4H_2 \rightarrow CH_4 + H_2O$) or transform acetic acid into methane and carbon dioxide:

$$(CH_3COOH \rightarrow CH_4 + CO_2)$$

Biogas, as produced in biodigesters, consists of 50 to 75 percent methane, 20 to 45 percent carbon dioxide, and 5 percent hydrogen, nitrogen, sulfide, and helium. It is counted among the renewable energy sources, derived in a multilevel anaerobic bacterial decomposition of organic material, such as dung, slurry, sewage sludge, or municipal waste, at temperatures of 20 to 55 degrees Celsius.

Methane hydrates, which are icelike combinations of methane and water on the seabed formed at high pressure and low temperature, are considered a promising future source of methane. It is estimated that globally there are between 500 and 3,000 gigatons of carbon stored in methane hydrate. In comparison, the carbon content of the known coal reserves is about 900 gigatons. However, regardless of methane's high potential, drilling for methane hydrate is very risky, because the continental slopes, consisting in large part of methane clathrates, could become unstable. Also, global warming and a simultaneous warming of the oceans may cause melting and vaporization with a concomitant release of methane that could fortify and accelerate the greenhouse effect drastically. Fossil methane deposits are part of the natural methane cycle, and therefore it is necessary to keep the Earth at temperatures that allow the existence of life.

Uses

Methane is used as fuel for gas turbines or steam boilers to generate electrical power. Its heat of combustion is lower than that of other hydrocarbons, but it produces more heat per mass unit than more complex hydrocarbons, as follows:

heat of combustion = 891 kJ/mol molecular mass
= 16.0 g/mol heat per mass = 55.7 kJ/g

As part of natural gas, methane is used in private homes for domestic heating and cooking, containing energy of 39 megajoules per cubic meter, or 1,000 British thermal units (Btu) per standard cubic foot. In the chemical industry, methane is used for the production of hydrogen, methanol, acetic acid, hydrocyanic acid, carbon disulfide, and many other organic compounds.

Greenhouse Gas

In addition to carbon dioxide, methane is one of the six major greenhouse gases (GHGs), those gases responsible for increasing the greenhouse effect relevant to climate change. However, methane has an even greater potential than carbon dioxide to effect climate changes: Its density is less than that of air, which is why it rises into higher atmospheric layers. The Earth's atmospheric methane concentration has increased by about 150 percent since 1750, and it accounts for 20 percent of the total radiative forcing from all of the long-lived and globally mixed greenhouse gases. In 2010, atmospheric methane levels, at least in the Arctic, were measured at 1,850 parts per billion, the highest level in the past 400,000 years. Historically, methane concentrations in the world's atmosphere have ranged between 300 and 400 parts per billion during the glacial periods, commonly known as ice ages, and between 600 and 700 parts per billion during the warm interglacial periods.

Worldwide emissions of methane amount to 600 million tons per year, of which about 70 percent are caused by human activities. Factory farming causes about 39 percent of agricultural methane emissions. One cow emits between 150 and 250 liters of methane per day, caused by microbial decay of cellulose in the digestive organs. Paddy fields account for a 17 percent share of global methane emissions. More methane is emitted into the atmosphere through leaks in gas pipelines. Arctic methane release from thawing permafrost regions is expected to occur in response to global warming. A leaking borehole at the bottom of the North Sea releases an estimated 11 million liters of methane every hour, of which about one-third gets into the atmosphere. Forest fires release chloromethane (CH_3Cl). Additional methane occurs as a by-product of oil refinement, as well as during coking and sulfurization of coal and during steel production from blast-furnace gases.

▷ *Presence on Other Planets*

The most prevalent use of methane is as a fuel gas to produce heat, to operate engines, and as the energy source in fuel cells. In the form of compressed natural gas, it is used as a vehicle fuel and is claimed to be more environmentally friendly than other fossil fuels, such as gasoline and diesel. Research on adsorption methods of methane storage for this purpose has been conducted.

Due to its abundance in many parts of the solar system, methane is also considered a potential rocket fuel. Current methane engines produce a thrust of 7,500 pound force (lbf), or 33 kilonewtons (kN), which is far from the 7,000,000 lbf (31 mN) needed to launch the space shuttle. Methane has been found in the atmospheres of Mars, Titan, Jupiter, Saturn, Uranus, Neptune, and Pluto. It was the first organic molecule to be demonstrated on other planets.

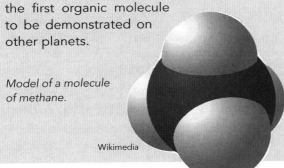

Model of a molecule of methane.

Wikimedia

Compared with carbon dioxide, methane's global warming potential is 25 times higher, according to a study by the Intergovernmental Panel on Climate Change. This means that a methane emission will have 25 times the impact on global temperature that a carbon dioxide emission of the same mass has over the following 100 years. Once in the atmosphere, methane has an average lifetime of 12 years. Photochemically produced hydroxyl radicals (OH) oxidize methane and lower its concentration in the atmosphere, as follows:

$$OH + CH_4 \rightarrow CH_3\text{-} + H_2O$$

Between 2006 and 2009, concerns arose that plants could be huge emitters of methane into the atmosphere, accounting for as much as 30 percent. By now, however, it has been shown that trees compensate for GHG emissions; their methane emissions are small in comparison with their ability to store carbon in leaves, wood, and bark, thus acting as a carbon sink.

Scientists have also measured a large amount of methane in the air above the oceans and have considered cyanobacteria as the source of these emissions. Usually cyanobacteria eat phosphate molecules, but in times when nutrients are scarce they substitute phosphonates such as methylphosphonate, and release methane. On the other hand, in the Black Sea, scientists have found sulfate-reducing bacteria that transform methane in reaction with sulfate:

$$CH_4 + SO_4^{2-} \rightarrow H_2S + CO_2$$

In waters and soils containing oxygen, methane is oxidized by *Pseudomonia methanica* bacteria to carbon dioxide and water.

Health

Methane is an asphyxiant, causing temporary symptoms such as hyperventilation, increased heart rate, low blood pressure, numbness in the limbs, drowsiness, mental disorder, and memory loss—all resulting from the oxygen deficiency upon inhalation of methane in an enclosed space.

Methane-air mixtures can therefore become hazardous. When methane reaches 5 to 12 percent by volume, due to an unperceived escape of gas, explosions can result. Miners are familiar with this dangerous phenomenon in the form of fire damps; mine gas released through coal mining amounts to about 6 percent of anthropogenic methane emissions. Efforts are under way to capture mine gas and use it to generate electrical power.

MANJA LEYK

Further Reading

Buffet, Bruce, and David Archer. "Global Inventory of Methane Clathrate: Sensitivity to Changes in the

Deep Ocean." *Earth and Planetary Science Letters* 227 (2004). http://geosci.uchicago.edu/~archer/reprints/buffett.2004.clathrates.pdf.

Demirbas, Ayhan. *Methane Gas Hydrate.* New York: Springer, 2010.

Forster, P., and P. V. Ramaswamy. "Changes in Atmospheric Constituents and in Radiative Forcing." In *Climate Change 2007: The Physical Science Basis. Contribution of Working Group I to the Fourth Assessment Report of the Intergovernmental Panel on Climate Change.* New York: Cambridge University Press, 2007. http://www.ipcc.ch/publications_and_data/publications_and_data_reports.shtml.

See Also: Anaerobic Digestion; Arctic Ocean; Biogas Digester; Flaring Gas; Gasification; Landfill Gas; Nonrenewable Energy Resources; Oil and Natural Gas Drilling; Oil and Petroleum.

Mexico

Official Name: United Mexican States.
Category: Geography of Energy.
Summary: Mexico has extensive coastlines along the Pacific Ocean and the Gulf of Mexico, which are important for the country's production of offshore oil. Mexico is the world's seventh-largest petroleum producer and a significant supplier of petroleum to the United States.

Mexico has one of the largest economies in the world, and nearly 114 million people as of July 2011. Mexico is the world's seventh-largest petroleum producer and a significant supplier of petroleum to the United States. In fact, 89 percent of Mexico's exports are destined for the United States, and nearly 75 percent of its imports are from the United States. Mexico is part of the North American Free Trade Agreement (NAFTA), which is one of the world's largest global trading partnerships.

Mexico had approximately 56 gigawatts of installed electricity-generating capacity in 2007 and produced 245 gigawatt-hours of electricity in 2008. Mexico is among the largest electricity-producing countries in all of North and South America, along with the United States, Canada, and Brazil.

The great majority of Mexico's electricity generation is fueled by conventional thermal and specifically natural gas resources. This is similar to the United States, except that the United States uses primarily coal for electricity generation. After conventional thermal resources, Mexico uses hydropower as its next-largest resource for electricity generation.

The Comisión Federal de Electricidad (CFE), which is a state-owned entity, controls approximately two-thirds of Mexico's electricity generation and has a monopoly on both electricity transmission and distribution. (Public ownership also characterizes the production of petroleum and natural gas resources.) According to the U.S. Energy Information Administration's data for 2008, in Mexico, "private generators held about 22,700 megawatts of generating capacity, mostly consisting of combined-cycle, gas-fired turbines. CFE also operates Mexico's national transmission grid, which consists of 27,000 miles of high voltage lines, 28,000 miles of medium voltage lines, and 370,000 miles of low voltage distribution lines."

Petroleum and Oil

In 2009, Mexico ranked seventh among the top 10 oil-producing nations of the world, producing more than 3 million barrels of oil per day. Mexico was the fifth-largest petroleum producer among nations not members of the Organization of Petroleum Exporting Countries (OPEC) and the third-largest petroleum producer in the Western Hemisphere. Furthermore, Mexico's relationship to the United States, which is by far the world's largest national economy, should not be understated. During November 2010, Mexico was the second-largest exporter of petroleum to the United States (at 2.5 million barrels of oil per day); only Canada exported more.

According to the *Oil and Gas Journal*, Mexico had approximately 10 billion barrels of proven oil reserves as of January 2010. The state-owned Petroleos Mexicanos (PEMEX), one of the largest oil companies in the world, holds a monopoly on oil production. PEMEX is vital to Mexico's export revnues, as well as the nation's global balance of trade and revenue for the federal government. In 2009, PEMEX's total assets were valued at 1.3 trillion pesos, or about $113 billion. It is estimated that more than 80 percent of the state-owned petroleum company PEMEX's current oil production is from the following eight projects: Ku-Maloob-Zaap, Cantarell, Crudo Ligero Marino, Ixtal-Manik, Delta del Grijalva, Chuc, Antonio J. Bermúdez, and Caan.

The majority of Mexico's oil reserves are located off its southern shores in the Gulf of Mexico and especially within the Campeche Basin. Hurricanes occasionally threaten this area and in severe seasons can disrupt oil supplies to the United States, which in turn can have an impact on global oil prices. The two main projects within the Campeche Basin, which together account for about 57 percent of Mexico's total crude oil production, are the Cantarell and Ku-Maloob-Zaap projects. According to the U.S. Energy Information Administration, "the Cantarell oil field was once one of the largest oil fields in the world, but production there has declined dramatically in the past several years. In 2009, Cantarell produced 630,000 bbl/d [barrels per day], down 38 percent from the 2008 level and down 70 percent from the peak production level of 2.12 million bbl/d in 2004." The largest oil fields are now primarily located in the Middle East, particularly Saudi Arabia's Ghawar Field.

In contrast, Mexico's onshore oil fields produce approximately 20 percent of the country's total crude oil production, with about 80 percent of such onshore production taking place in southern Mexico. Such oil fields, although producing less oil than their offshore counterparts, are not as prone to disruption by hurricanes in the Gulf of Mexico. The largest onshore oil field, which is located in Mexico's southern region, is called Puerto Ceiba; in 2009, it produced about 50,000 barrels per day. According to the U.S. Energy Information Administration, PEMEX "sees the onshore Chicontepec project, located northeast of Mexico City, as a potentially large source of future production growth. Chicontepec contains 29 distinct fields spread over an area of 2,400 square miles. ... According to PEMEX, Chicontepec contains an estimated 17.7 billion barrels of oil equivalent of possible hydrocarbon reserves."

Natural Gas

In addition to its monopoly on oil production, PEMEX also holds an exploration and production monopoly on natural gas in Mexico. The U.S. Energy Information Administration reports that the "Mexican government opened the downstream natural gas sector to private operators in 1995, though no single company may participate in more than one industry function (transportation, storage, or distribution)."

It is estimated that more than 80 percent of PEMEX's total natural gas production comes from the

NOAA

The majority of Mexico's oil reserves are located off its southern shores in the Gulf of Mexico, where this platform stands. Hurricanes occasionally threaten this area and can impact global oil prices.

following nine projects: Cantarell, Burgos, Veracruz, Crudo Ligero Marino, Delta del Grijalva, Ku-Maloob-Zaap, Antonio J. Bermúdez, Caan, and Ixtal-Manik. In addition to being the second-largest oil project, Cantarell is the largest natural gas project. Furthermore, Crudo Ligero Marino (the fourth-largest natural gas and third-largest oil producer) and Delta del Grijalva (fifth in both natural gas and oil production) are both listed among the top five projects in Mexico for both oil production and natural gas.

Because of its close proximity to the United States, Mexico has 10 natural gas import pipeline networks with the United States. In 2009, Mexico, despite its rich natural gas resources, actually imported 338 billion cubic feet of natural gas from the United States while exporting only about 28 billion cubic feet of the natural gas to the United States. Mexico also imports liquefied natural gas (LNG) from Egypt and Nigeria, along with Trinidad and Tobago.

Mexico's electricity sector is largely reliant on conventional thermal resources, particularly natural gas, and the United States imports little natural gas because it has its own extensive natural gas resources (especially in Texas, on Mexico's northern border). Approximately 41 percent of Mexico's natural gas comes from offshore reserves, particularly within the Campeche Basin's Cantarell project.

This geographic concentration of natural gas is different from that of Mexico's oil fields, which are more commonly located offshore. According to the U.S. Energy Information Administration, "while crude oil production at the Cantarell field has fallen in recent years, natural gas production has risen dramatically: natural gas production at the field increased from 262 billion cubic feet (Bcf) in 2006 to 596 Bcf in 2008." This production rate represents an increase of approximately 125 percent increase in only two years.

Approximately 59 percent of Mexico's natural gas is located onshore, with about 38 percent located in northern Mexico and about 21 percent located in southern Mexico. The Burgos Basin accounts for approximately 25 percent of Mexico's total natural gas production.

Hydropower

Hydroelectricity, which is second to conventional thermal resources, supplied about 16 percent of Mexico's electricity generation in 2008. Most of Mexico's hydroelectric sources are located in the south. The largest hydroelectric plant in Mexico is the Manuel Moreno Torres facility, located in the southern state of Chiapas.

As a signatory to the Kyoto Protocol, Mexico has hosted a few certified emission reduction hydroelectric projects under the clean development mechanism (CDM) of the United Nations Framework Convention on Climate Change (UNFCCC). Such projects include the El Gallo hydroelectric project (located in southern state of Guerrero), the Trojes hydropower project (located in southern state of Jalisco), and the Chilatán hydroelectric project (also located in Jalisco).

Energy Consumption

Nearly 90 percent of Mexico's total energy consumption was derived from either oil (55 percent) or natural gas (33 percent) resources. This is somewhat comparable to the consumption patterns of the United States, although the United States relies more on coal. In Mexico, coal served only about 5 percent of Mexico's total energy consumption in 2007. Regarding energy consumption among specific sectors, Mexico consumed approximately 200,136 gigawatt-hours of electricity and heat in 2008. More than 50 percent of this energy consumption was within the industrial sector (123 terawatt-hours), while about 25 percent (47 terawatt-hours) was consumed by the residential sector and about 10 percent (20,701 gigawatt-hours) was consumed by the commercial and public services.

A significant amount of Mexico's energy consumption serves transport. Although Mexico is the seventh-largest oil-producing nation in the world, it is actually a net importer of refined petroleum products. According to the U.S. Energy Information Administration's 2009 data, Mexico imported 519,000 barrels per day of refined petroleum products while exporting about half that amount (244,000 barrels per day). Gasoline represented about 60 percent of product imports.

Mexico's industry is concentrated mainly in and around the cities of Monterrey, Guadalajara, Tijuana, and greater Mexico City. These industries include mining, textile manufacturing, electronics, and automobiles. With 20 million residents, Mexico City is one of the world's largest cities and thus consumes a significant amount of energy.

BRIAN MCFARLAND

Further Reading

Energy Regulatory Commission of Mexico. "Mexico." November 2009. http://www.cre.gob.mx/documento/ingles.pdf.

Ibarrarán, María Eugenia, Roy Boyd, and Mario J. Molina. *Hacia el Futuro: Energy, Economics, and the Environment in 21st Century Mexico.* Dordrecht, Netherlands: Springer, 2006.

International Energy Agency. "Electricity/Heat in Mexico in 2008." http://iea.org/stats/electricitydata.asp?COUNTRY_CODE=MX.

Moroney, John R. *Energy and Sustainable Development in Mexico.* Austin: Texas A&M University Press, 2005.

U.S. Energy Information Administration. "Country Analysis Brief: Mexico." http://205.254.135.7/countries/country-data.cfm?fips=MX.

See Also: Gulf Oil Spill; International Energy Agency; International Energy Forum; Natural Gas; Natural Gas Storage; Offshore Drilling; Texas; Venezuela.

Michigan

Category: Energy in the United States.
Summary: Because of its industrial and manufacturing history, climate, and population distribution, Michigan ranks among the heaviest energy consumers in the United States, employing primarily coal but also natural gas and nuclear fuels for electric power.

Michigan has fairly significant deposits of natural gas, extracted from the state's geological formations starting in the 20th century. Many of these wells are found in and around Antrim and Otsego Counties in the northern portion of the Lower Peninsula. Other prominent sites for natural gas production include the center of the Lower Peninsula (Clare, Isabella, Osceola, and Mecosta Counties), southeast Michigan (St. Clair and Macomb Counties), and to a lesser extent in the western part of the Lower Peninsula (Allegan County). It is estimated that Michigan's natural gas production accounts for about 17 percent (or 13.7 billion cubic feet) of all natural gas consumed in the state, and production numbers have been steadily declining since the 1990s. Today, Michigan holds about 1 percent of U.S. natural gas reserves and 2 percent of all productive natural gas wells.

In areas where the natural gas has been depleted or has become too expensive to extract, utility companies have utilized the geological formations for natural gas storage. This has been of great benefit to the state, given its climate: Natural gas can be purchased more cheaply in the summer, when demand is much lower, and then released to the marketplace in colder months, when demand is high. This is an important means of stabilizing natural gas prices, especially in the event of dramatic weather, because almost 80 percent of homes in Michigan are heated with natural gas. Today, natural gas both produced in and imported into Michigan represents an important input into the generation of electric power, accounting for about 10 percent of all electricity generated.

The state possesses very little in the way of coal or liquid petroleum. There have been numerous attempts to extract oil in Michigan throughout the 20th century, focusing primarily on Midland, Bay, and Arenac Counties in the central Lower Peninsula; Kent and Ottawa Counties in the western part of the state; and Hillsdale and Calhoun Counties near the Ohio border. With that in mind, it is important to note that many oil wells have been sunk all over the state, most of them with very limited success. Today, there are a few wells with very limited production, accounting for about 559,000 barrels of oil every year (0.3 percent of the United States' total). The oil remaining in the state's geological formations is estimated to account for only 0.2 percent of all the crude oil reserves in the United States (about 33 million barrels of oil).

Michigan has no coal mines; however, coal plays a very important role in the state's energy system. Approximately 60 percent of the state's electricity is generated by burning coal, and as might be expected, all of it is imported, both from nearby states, such as West Virginia and Pennsylvania, and from more distant, western states, such as Wyoming and Montana. Nuclear power accounts for nearly 25 percent of all electricity generated in Michigan. There are three nuclear facilities in the state (all in the southern part of the Lower Peninsula) and one decommissioned nuclear facility (at Big Rock Point in the northern Lower Peninsula).

Although both energy experts and environmentalists agree that Michigan has great potential to utilize renewable resources, especially wind and wood biomass, using environmentally friendly technologies to generate electricity remains very limited in the state, accounting for less than 2 percent of all power production. In the 21st century, however, new attention is being paid to ways in which energy companies can capitalize on Michigan's long lakeshore (for wind power) and significant, if underutilized, manufacturing base for the production of new energy technologies such as solar panels, wind turbines, and batteries for electric cars.

Utilities and Transmission

In many ways, the story of electric power in Michigan is the story of the two major gas and electric utilities in the state, Consumers Energy (for most of its history called Consumers Power) and DTE Energy (for most of its history called Detroit Edison). These two companies have long been responsible for generating and supplying most of

Wikimedia

Nuclear power accounts for nearly 25 percent of all electricity generated in Michigan. Big Rock nuclear facility, in the northern Lower Peninsula, was in operation from from 1962 to 1997 before it was decommissioned.

the state's energy needs, together accounting for more than 80 percent of all electricity generated in the state today. They have also been the driving force behind the construction of most of Michigan's power plants, adopting a range of fuels from water power in the 1900s to coal, nuclear, and, today, natural gas technologies.

Rural cooperatives have also played an important role in the state, especially in areas away from major population centers. The first rural cooperatives were funded by the United States' federal government in the late 1930s. These "pioneers" brought electricity technology to the state's farms and isolated settlements, especially in the remote Upper Peninsula. Although these small organizations connected people to new technologies, they often encountered difficulties in securing supplies of electric power. This prompted many cooperatives to connect their systems together and form Generation and Transmission (G+T) cooperatives, umbrella organizations under which the costs of new power plants and transmission lines could be shared to increase efficiency. By the 1960s, most of Michigan's cooperatives were working with Consumers Power and Detroit Edison (in the Lower Peninsula) or utilities in Wisconsin (in the Upper Peninsula) to secure supplies of electricity. Today, many of Michigan's cooperatives provide more than simple electric power to their customers, with some offering cable and Internet service and others selling natural gas as well as electricity.

There are still many communities in Michigan that are served neither by the "big two" nor by a cooperative. These are municipal, or city-owned, systems. Perhaps the largest municipal system in the state serves the capital city of Lansing. The Lansing Board of Water and Light, like most municipal systems in the United States, is supported primarily by city residents, who in turn are able to vote and directly involve themselves in utility company activities and planning.

Electricity transmission lines link the state's utilities together and also tie Michigan's electricity system to those of other states in the midwest and parts of Canada (specifically Ontario, Quebec, and Manitoba) in a regional market where electricity can be bought and sold instantly. In addition to Michigan's electric power transmission system, several natural gas and liquid petroleum pipelines cross the state, importing both types of hydrocarbons from Canada and the United States' south, especially Oklahoma, Texas, and Louisiana.

JORDAN P. HOWELL

Further Reading

Howell, Jordan P. "Powering 'Progress': Regulation and the Development of Michigan's Electricity Landscape." *Annals of the Association of American Geographers* 101, no. 4 (2011).

Michigan Public Service Commission. "About Michigan's Gas Industry." http://www.dleg.state.mi.us/mpsc/gas/about1.htm.

Michigan Public Service Commission. "The Commission Had Its Historic Beginnings Over 130 Years Ago." http://www.michigan.gov/mpsc/0,1607,7-159-16400-40512—,00.html.

See Also: Cooperatives; Edison, Thomas Alva; Electricity; Green Pricing; Hydropower; Illinois; Indiana; Investor-Owned Utilities.

Microhydropower

Category: Environmentalism.
Summary: Microhydropower is a cost-effective technology that converts running water into usable energy with minimum environmental impact.

Microhydropower is a small-scale technology that converts running water into usable energy for electricity and mechanical processes, usually for immediate local use. Civilizations have used hydropower for mechanical processes for millennia. Today, microhydropower usage ranges from stand-alone systems to power remote communities around the world, such as those in the Himalayas, to systems that produce energy to feed into larger power grids, such as that in Boulder, Colorado, which generates 7 percent of the city's electricity with microhydropower.

The cost of microhydropower varies greatly based on site specifics, but the method boasts a minimal environmental impact and therefore holds promise for mitigating climate change.

Today's microhydropower technology has its roots in water mills and waterwheels, technologies that have been in use for millennia. Water-powered mills and wheels were developed for agricultural purposes, such a grinding grains into flour and hydraulically raising water into irrigation canals. The harnessed hydropower also served industrial needs, including sawmills to cut lumber, paper mills, and the textile industry. Ancient civilizations, including the Greeks, Romans, and the Han Dynasty in China, pioneered the use of water mills and wheels; the technology then spread to other regions of the world through trade and conquest.

Technology
The cost of microhydropower varies by location but is generally considered cost-effective and can last

up to 50 years with minimal maintenance. Unlike large hydropower facilities—whose dams often must entail the flooding of a large area and thus potentially the displacement of people as well as the disruption of ecosystems—microhydropower has a small environmental footprint and can generate usable energy by taking advantage of naturally occurring topography. Microhydropower systems convert falling or running water into power, typically using run-of-the-river technology that requires little or no damming or storage. Water is diverted through an intake at a human-made weir into an adjacent channel or pipe, flows through the turbine system that converts water energy into mechanical and electrical energy, and discharges into the original water body downstream. Some microhydropower systems also divert water into a storage system for controlled release.

According to the International Electrotechnical Commission (an organization that publishes international standards for electrotechnology), microhydropower is divided into three categories, based on energy produced: "Small" hydropower plants produce up to 15 megawatts, "micro" hydropower plants produce up to 500 kilowatts, and "pico" hydropower plants produce between 50 watts and 5 kilowatts. The classification of small, micro, and pico is not standardized globally, often causing confusion in comparisons of microhydropower programs across regions. For example, the United States classifies small hydropower as less than 30 megawatts; China, as less than 25 megawatts; India, as less than 15 megawatts; and the European Commission, as less than 10 megawatts.

Global Overview

Globally, microhydropower produces more than 61 gigawatts of electricity. Regionally, Asia produces 68 percent of the world's microhydropower, Europe is second with 22 percent, North America third at 6 percent, and the remaining world regions total 4 percent. China alone boasts 40 percent of the world's installed microhydropower capacity, with more to be developed. More than 80 percent of China's installed microhydropower capacity has been built since the mid-1970s. China's rural electrification and rural economic growth ambitions

rely in part on developing microhydropower in distant rural areas; around 80 million rural Chinese lack electricity.

Remote communities globally adopt microhydropower, from the Himalayas to the Andes to isolated Canadian communities. In remote communities lacking access to a national power grid, microhydropower can provide agricultural processing services by day—such as grinding and milling—and electrify villages at night. Microhydropower can also displace diesel-based energy systems in isolated off-the-grid communities. Energy generated by microhydropower in remote areas can improve the inhabitants' quality of life and contribute to local economic development.

The European Union (EU) has set specific goals to increase renewable energy production, including microhydropower, to comply with Kyoto Protocol targets. Italy leads, with 21 percent of the total EU-installed microhydropower capacity. Europe has exploited an estimated 65 percent of its microhydropower potential, with much future potential depending on updating and refurbishing existing sites, such as older water mills and wheels.

About 20 percent of the hydropower in the United States is produced by small hydropower plants of less than 30 megawatts, with 1 percent of this power coming from plants of less than 1 megawatt. An estimated additional capacity of 30,000 megawatts of hydropower is viable for development in the United States. In recent years, there has been renewed interest in microhydropower and a resurgence in building; old water mills have been converted, and new, small-scale plants have been built to feed power into existing power grids.

Environmental Connections

Microhydropower is a renewable energy resource that has been exploited for millennia. With new efficiencies in turbine technology, microhydropower can play an important role in the renewable energy technology portfolio to displace fossil fuel energy and provide energy services to remote communities that currently lack access to the modern energy sector. The European Small Hydropower Association reports that for every gigawatt of electricity produced through microhydropower, up to

220 tons of gasoline or 335 tons of coal is displaced and greenhouse gas emissions are reduced by up to 480 tons. Making full use of domestic microhydropower contributes both to states' energy security and to the mitigation of climate change while leaving a relatively small environmental footprint at the site of power generation.

SHAUNNA BARNHART

Further Reading

European Small Hydropower Association. http://www .esha.be/.

Rodríguez, Luis, and Teodoro Sanchez. *Designing and Building Mini and Micro Hydropower Schemes: A Practical Guide.* Rugby, Bourton on Dunsmore, UK: Practical Action, 2011.

U.S. Department of Energy, Energy Efficiency and Renewable Energy. *Feasibility Assessment of the Water Energy Resources of the United States for New Low Power and Small Hydro Classes of Hydroelectric Plants.* DOE-ID-11263. January 2006. http://www1.eere.energy.gov/water/pdfs/doewater -11263.pdf.

See Also: Hydropower; Renewable Energy Resources; Rural Electrification.

Micronesia

Official Name: Federated States of Micronesia.
Category: Geography of Energy.
Summary: The Federated States of Micronesia constitute a small, independent state that is dependent on imported fossil fuels and diesel generators for its energy needs. It is exploring alternative energy sources in an effort to become more self-sufficient and to reduce its carbon footprint.

Micronesia is a term that refers both to a subregion of the South Pacific consisting of thousands of small islands and to the Federated States of Micronesia (FSM), an independent nation consisting of four states: Yap, Chuuk, Pohnpei, and Kosrae. The FSM consists of more than 600 islands, although the total area of all of these islands amounts to only about 271 square miles. The FSM has a population of approximately 110,000, many of whom are employed by the government. As a small nation with a per capita income of about $2,600, the FSM is highly dependent on aid from the U.S. government. Since the FSM has no deposits of fossil fuels and few other mineral resources, the nation has a great interest in developing renewable energy sources that will both provide for its electrical needs and make employment opportunities available to its residents.

The area currently known as Micronesia was settled more than 4,000 years ago by people who lived under what was initially a decentralized, chieftain-based system of government. The Portuguese and later the Spanish arrived in the area during the 16th century, with the Spanish establishing sovereignty. Spain ceded the islands to Germany 1899. The Japanese took control of the Islands in 1914, as Germany was engaged in World War I and unable to defend them. Then Micronesia was taken over by the United States after World War II. Beginning in 1947, the United States administered the FSM pursuant to a United Nations mandate as part of the Trust Territory of the Pacific Islands. In 1979, voters in the four Trust Territory districts that currently comprise the FSM elected to approve a constitution that would permit the FSM to become an independent nation. In 1986, the United States and the FSM entered into the Compact of Free Association (along with two other nations, Palau and the Marshall Islands), which marked the FSM's emergence as an independent nation. In 2004, the Compact of Free Association was renewed.

The FSM's economy is relatively unsophisticated, as indicated by its global per capita income ranking of 116th. Economic activity in the FSM consists chiefly of fishing and subsistence farming. Although the potential for tourism exists, few adequate facilities to house or entertain tourists and the FSM's remote location make this, for now, an unrealized option. The FSM produces more than 190 gigawatt-hours of electricity per year and consumes

▷ *Solar Power Challenge*

The Federated States of Micronesia's warm and humid climate takes a toll on technology, which has made implementation of solar panels a challenge. Solar panel glass is often covered with a slime that grows if they are not cleaned regularly, and the batteries that most photovoltaic (PV) panels are designed to charge die prematurely. More promising is the possibility of harnessing ocean thermal energy. Although the FSM is in the midst of exploring how to implement ocean thermal energy conversion (OTEC) to generate electricity for its residents, these studies are only beginning. Because the FSM is ideally suited to take advantage of OTEC, however, this effort seems a worthwhile area for future development.

about 180 gigawatt-hours. Large diesel generators that feed a centralized power grid are used for this purpose. As the FSM has no petroleum deposits, imported fossil fuels are required to run these generators. Energy use and generation patterns in the FSM in many ways can be traced to the Trust Territory of the Pacific Islands era. During this era, the costs of capital equipment, maintenance, and fuel were being paid for by the U.S. government, which focused attention on issues such as the speed of installation and the logistics of supply.

Even after entering into the Compact of Free Association, the United States continued to provide subsidies that covered imported fuel. Again, this masked many of the issues associated with the FSM's lack of an energy supply and changed only after the second Compact of Free Association went into effect in 2004. For the first time, the subsidies that had made generator fuel inexpensive ended. The effects of this were significant. Prices charged for energy generated by the state-owned power companies rose precipitously. For example, the cost to consumers of a kilowatt-hour of electricity rose from 9.74 cents in September 2002 to 17.5 cents in April 2006, an increase of 80 percent. Faced with skyrocketing costs for energy, which were consuming nearly 40 percent of U.S. subsidies, the FSM government began exploring alternative sources of energy.

The FSM's widespread and decentralized geography make many conventional solutions for its energy needs irrelevant and inefficient. To that end, the FSM is investigating distributed power generation as a technologically, financially, and socially preferable solution. Microhydropower generators, which can provide energy for a few homes or a village, are thus being installed at multiple sites where feasible. Experiments have also been made producing diesel blends containing between 5 percent and 20 percent coconut oil, as this is a sustainable and locally grown option. Although the availability of coconut-oil blends is limited by available land, these might prove feasible for those who live on outlying islands, whose energy needs can be supplied by a small generator.

Stephen T. Schroth
Jason A. Helfer

Further Reading

Hanlon, D. *Remaking Micronesia: Discourses Over Development in a Pacific Territory*. Honolulu: University of Hawaii Press, 1998.

Hezel, F. X. *The New Shape of Old Island Cultures: A Half Century of Social Change in Micronesia*. Honolulu: University of Hawaii Press, 2001.

Lugg, A., and M. Hong, eds. *Energy Issues in the Asia-Pacific Region*. Pasir Panjang, Singapore: Institute of Southeast Asian Studies, 2010.

See Also: Fossil Fuels; Hydropower; Nauru; Solar Energy.

Minnesota

Category: Energy in the United States.
Summary: As of 2005, Minnesota ranked 21st among U.S. states in energy consumption per

capita, using 362 million British thermal units (Btu). Its average annual increase in total energy use of 0.7 percent ranked it eighth. Its target energy consumption per capita for 2012 was 238.2 million Btu, which would rank the state 29th.

Minnesota neither produces nor stores fossil fuels. For electric power generation, it consumes about 353 trillion British thermal units (Btu) of coal, 26.3 trillion Btu of natural gas, and 17.1 trillion Btu of petroleum. Minnesota's two nuclear power plants generate 25 percent of the state's electricity. Nuclear power provides 133.8 trillion Btu, while hydroelectric power accounts for 6.5 trillion Btu and another 30.1 trillion Btu comes from combined biomass, solar, wind, and geothermal power. As of 2005, Minnesota ranked 21st among U.S. states in energy consumption per capita, with an average annual increase in total energy use of 0.7 percent. Its target energy consumption per capita for 2012 was 238.2 million Btu, which would rank the state 29th.

Minnesota's high-voltage electricity grid is tied to the grids of the upper midwest and eastern United States. Originally intended to provide power to the Twin Cities (Minneapolis and St. Paul) and other major Minnesota cities and to tie the state's various electrical utilities together to guarantee reliable power delivery, the grid links producers, utilities, and agricultural, residential, and commercial consumers through substations and distribution systems. In 2001, Minnesota mandated that each utility with a transmission capability file transmission planning reports biennially with the Minnesota Public Utilities Commission (PUC). The reports provide data on utility planning for the state. A new rule in 2003 required that the reports include public input and required public meetings in seven zones of the state.

Annual growth of electricity consumption of 2.7 percent ranked the state 14th, and electricity production from nonhydropower renewable sources (3 gigawatt-hours) ranked the state seventh. Minnesota produced 2 percent of its electricity from wind, which it enjoys in abundance, and doubles the national average of 1 percent. As of the onset of 2008, it had 1,300 megawatts of installed wind energy. In wind energy potential it ranks ninth.

XCel Energy, the largest Minnesota utility, is a multistate provider to a combined 5 million electricity and natural gas customers, the leading user of wind and fifth leader in solar power. Still, in 2009, it depended on fossil fuels for 74 percent of its capacity. Minnesota has required Xcel to get 30 percent of its electricity from renewable sources by 2020, including at least 25 percent from wind. All utilities have a requirement of 25 percent of electricity supply from renewable energy by 2025.

Gasoline Consumption

Minnesota's 531 gallons of motor gasoline per person per year ranks the state 15th. Between 1980 and 2005, per capita gasoline consumption rose from 476 gallons to 531 gallons. Transportation uses 29 percent of Minnesota's energy, second only to industry. Minnesota is the only state that requires 10 percent ethanol in all oxygenated motor gasoline. A law of 2008 set a goal of doubling the content to 20 percent by 2015.

Minnesota's energy efficiency efforts include conservation and efficiency provisions in building codes and in industrial plants, weatherization, and education. Minnesota's renewable energy includes hydropower, biomass, and wind. Tribal projects are green as well. Furthermore, efforts are under way to promote hybrid vehicles and other green transportation. XCel has a renewable development fund. Rebates are available for grid-connected solar photovoltaic systems.

Minnesota enforces the 1995 Model Energy Code for residential buildings and the American Society of Heating, Refrigerating and Air-Conditioning Engineers' standard 90.1-1989 for commercial buildings. Four programs provide loans for energy efficiency. The Xcel Energy Renewable Development Fund collects customer user fees and uses the money to fund renewable energy projects. All state-owned buildings have to improve energy efficiency 10 percent over the 2006 baseline. New construction must consider solar and geothermal options. Finally, new buildings must exceed the state energy code by at least 30 percent.

In 2009, Minnesota began installing the smart grid in some substations in the hope of reducing demand by 20 percent, as was the case in some West Coast areas. After Xcel installed the first major smart-grid system in Boulder, Colorado, the company not only learned immediately of outages but also could repair them automatically. The data supplied by smart grids also helped both the utility and consumers to learn ways of conserving energy. Reducing demand is much cheaper than building new lines to match demand. Therefore, the federal government wanted states to require at least consideration of the smart grid before construction of large plants or lines, including CapX 2020, which involved four major power lines across the state. The PUC began drafting rules in 2008.

Wikimedia

The Rochester Public Utilities (RPU) Silver Lake Power Plant in downtown Rochester, Minnesota. To the right is the Zumbro River, which the plant derives water from for cooling. Silver Lake, which lies on the Zumbro River, operates as a heat sink and does not freeze in the winter.

Ethanol Usage

Minnesota has been the national pilot market for ethanol use since 1998. Its ethanol consumption of 276 million gallons per year makes the state first in the nation, and its 345 alternative fuel stations place it at fourth-largest. It has the largest ethanol fueling network in the United States, as well as thousands of flex-fuel vehicles and multiple ethanol production facilities.

Wind use at the county level began in 2009. In January word was that by June, Winona County, in the southeast, would become one of the first counties in the state to use wind energy. The cost was $3.5 million, with the county covering only $36,000 and state grants covering more. The project was intended to increase use of renewable energy as well as to generate revenue. The revenue was expected to be $4 million, with $3 million for investors and $1 million for the county. The county's two wind turbines were capable of producing around 1.5 megawatts, or enough to power 600 homes. The county had to find a private investor, because it lacked the legal authority to build turbines. A special law made the county effort a limited liability company (LLC) and thus eligible to partner with a private company. XCel Energy agreed to buy the energy and move it to residences.

Solar Energy

In March 2011, the St. Paul convention center's rooftop solar collectors began producing energy for local businesses and residences. The project included 144 solar collectors that provide up to 1 megawatt of thermal capacity to District Energy St. Paul, the largest hot water district heating system in the United States that heats 80 percent of downtown St. Paul from a 25 megawatt biomass combined heat and power plant. Maximum water temperature for the building is set at 160 degrees Fahrenheit, and surplus water will enter the district heating system at up to 195 degrees. The system should reduce the state's carbon footprint by 900,000 pounds per year, the equivalent of 90 vehicles. Funding came from the Department of Energy's Solar America Communities program to the tune of $1 million in American Recovery and Reinvestment Act funds. Matching funds came from District Energy St. Paul.

Wind Power

In April 2009, the CapX 2020 project got the green light from the PUC. The project required three 345-kilovolt transmission lines to cover the state. The PUC granted only one—from Brookings, South Dakota, to Hampton, Minnesota—permission to carry wind energy. CapX 2020 backers were pleased that the grid would become more reliable and that carbon emissions would drop as a result of the system's increased efficiency, although they were disappointed that there was not more wind energy capacity. Minnesota had a legal requirement to triple installed wind energy capacity to meet the renewable energy standard requiring 25 percent from renewable sources by 2025. While advocates were both disappointed and pleased, foes were disappointed that their preferences for smart-grid and localized generation technologies were not met by the approval of one wind segment. Both smart-grid and localized generation are essential, but so is a modern infrastructure capable of handling carbon-free energy to wherever it is needed. CapX generated a fairly strong opposition from environmental groups and people who felt that the eleven-utility consortium's plan for a massive array of power towers and lines was being pushed through without the mandated citizen input.

JOHN H. BARNHILL

Further Reading

Citizens Energy Task Force. "CapX2020." http://cetf.us /category/capx2020/.

Hemphill, Stephanie. "CapX 2020 Receives State of MN Approval." *Minnesota Wind Energy News*, January 11, 2009. http://www.highcountryenergy.us /mn_wind_news.

Hemphill, Stephanie. "Smart Grid Offers Energy Savings." September 30, 2008. http://minnesota .publicradio.org/display/web/2008/09/26/smart _grid/highcountryenergy.us/mn.

Minnesota Electric Transmission Planning. "Minnesota Biennial Transmission Planning." http://www.minnelectrans.com.

"SE Minnesota County Welcomes Wind Energy." *Minnesota Wind Energy News* January 11, 2009 http://www.highcountryenergy.us/mn_wind_news.

U.S. Department of Energy. "Minnesota." http://www .energy.gov/minnesota.htm.

XCelenergy.com. "About Xcel Energy." http://www .xcelenergy.com/Colorado/Company/AboutUs/ Pages/Temp.aspx.

See Also: Cooperatives; Ethanol: Corn; Geothermal Energy; Hydropower; Investor-Owned Utilities; North Dakota; United States; Waste Heat Recovery.

Mississippi

Category: Energy in the United States.
Summary: Mississippi has substantial energy resources, including oil and gas, although they have not been fully explored.

Mississippi is a southern U.S. state located along the Mississippi River. Historically dependent on its natural resources and subject to recurring ecological problems such as the flooding of the river, it is the poorest state in the union. It is also infamous for lagging behind the nation in liberal reforms: It was the last to repeal the prohibition of alcohol (in 1966), and it retained segregation-era legislation, such as the poll tax and a law against interracial marriage, until the late 1980s. Unlike most of the country, it has yet to adopt a law requiring the use of gasoline blends to reduce emissions; conventional motor vehicle gasoline is the norm in Mississippi.

Energy Resources

Mississippi does have substantial energy resources. Though its oil reserves are not as plentiful as in Louisiana or Texas, the southern half of the state does possess oil and gas fields, as well as on- and offshore oil along the Gulf Coast. Recent discoveries have been made of oil deposits in the north as well, in the Black Warrior Basin, and the general feeling of geologists is that Mississippi's oil and gas resources have yet to be fully explored.

With the decline of agriculture and the cotton industry, manufacturing is the state's largest industry, and per capita energy consumption is high: Mississippi is 16th in the country, with the industrial and transportation sectors together consuming about two-thirds of the state's energy. The punishing heat and humidity of the summers account for greater-than-average residential and business energy consumption resulting from the use of energy-intensive air-conditioning. Most homes are heated with electricity (in contrast to the national norm), but heating is not a concern for much of the year in the state's southern location, which explains the infrequency of gas and oil heaters.

Hattiesburg is home to a major propane supply hub, and liquefied petroleum gas (LPG) is used in twice as many households in Mississippi as the national average. The largest refinery in Mississippi is located in Pascagoula along the Gulf Coast; it processes crude oil brought in principally from Central and South America via tanker. The Pascagoula refinery serves markets throughout the southeast via the Colonial and Plantation Pipelines, as well as other delivery methods. The Pascagoula and two smaller refineries contribute about 2 percent of total American oil refining. Mississippi is also the site of a major strategic petroleum reserve, in Richton.

Mississippi produces little natural gas, less than 1 percent of the national output, in part because of the significant drop in production since 2003, when the state's wells began producing nonhydrocarbon gases. New wells have been drilled in response, and the natural gas processing industry has expanded to accommodate natural gas brought in by pipeline from the outer continental shelf of the Gulf Coast, an area administered by the federal government. Pascagoula is home to one of the country's largest natural gas processing plants. More than half of Mississippi's natural gas is purchased from other states, in order to meet its consumption needs, and liquefied natural gas (LNG) import terminals are under construction in Pascagoula in order to begin international imports.

The state has a single coal mine, in Choctaw County, supplying a 440-megawatt clean-coal mine-mouth power plant. The rest of the state's coal power plants use coal from other states, mainly Colorado and Kentucky. Nuclear power provides about a quarter of the electricity in the state, all of it produced by the Grand Gulf Nuclear Power Station.

Renewable Energy

At present there is little in the way of renewable energy in Mississippi, although there is one wood-firing power plant in the east, providing about 1,400 megawatts. There have been some minor movements toward sustainability and efficient energy usage, notably a plan to develop a smart grid for the University of Mississippi's campus, a joint venture between the university and Smart-Synch, a smart-grid developer based in Jackson. The university established its Office of Sustainability in 2008, and set a goal to be energy-neutral by 2050. Current programs include reusable plastic mugs, an organic campus farm, raffled-off prizes for recyclers, and the Century Park residential complex, the state's first campus residence certified by the Leadership in Energy and Environmental Design (LEED) program.

There are significant opportunities for renewable energies, however. The state could develop its ample wind and solar resources, and its agricultural resources offer significant potential for biomass energy. With seed capital, green construction and green technologies could also be job-creating opportunities for Mississippi.

BILL KTE'PI

Further Reading

Fowler, Nicholas Luke. *The Future of Energy in Mississippi: Policy and Politics*. Dissertation. Mississippi State: Mississippi State University, 2009.

McCullough, Glenn, Jr. "Copenhagen Should Look to Mississippi." *Mississippi Business Journal*, January 4, 2010. http://msbusiness.com/2010/01/copenhagen-should-look-to-mississippi/.

University of Mississippi, Sustainable Energy Resource Center. "About Us." http://www.serc.msstate.edu/about.html.

U.S. Energy Information Administration. "Country Analysis Brief: Mississippi." http://www.eia.gov/state/state-energy-profiles.cfm?sid=MS.

See Also: Alabama; Georgia (U.S. State); Gulf Oil Spill; Shell; Tennessee Valley Authority; United States; Water Pollution.

Missouri

Category: Energy in the United States.
Summary: Missouri has continued its history of traditional energy usage, resulting in a legacy of fossil fuel emissions and minimal investment in sustainable energy production.

Prior to the founding of Missouri as a U.S. state, the Louisiana Territory was recognized as a large swath of land extending from the modern state of Louisiana to North America's west coast. As a geographic entity, the Louisiana Territory had been inhabited by indigenous peoples living a hunter-gatherer lifestyle.

Although some indigenous peoples and European immigrants are known to have developed agrarian behaviors, early populations in the upper Louisiana Territory, now known as Missouri, were not dense and relied on widely available wood fuel energy for heating cabins and farmhouses as well as native tent structures. By the early 19th century, however, Missouri's population had surged, driving up demand for heating fuel. Local commerce and an explosion in the fur trade increased paddleship traffic on the Missouri and Mississippi Rivers, increasing the need for coal and wood production to fuel the boats' steam systems. Regional townships grew in population and traffic as a result of the transportation innovations that boat and train systems provided.

Growth and the Use of Coal
The growth of the burgeoning 24th state induced an appetite for more coal. By the late 1880s, Missouri's Bureau of Labor reported that more than 50 coal mines were operating or preparing to operate in the state. Expansion led the state to modernize energy resource production, driving Missouri to become the first state west of the Mississippi River to produce commercial coal from local mines.

Coal-fired power plants continue to retain their prominence in 21st-century Missouri energy delivery. In 2011, four-fifths of Missouri's electricity was generated from coal fuel, consuming more than 3 million short tons of coal per year. The long-term impacts of coal usage are still being studied; coal development demands an understanding of fly-ash storage, carbon sequestration technologies, and point-of-origin impacts. The majority of coal used in Missourian facilities originates from Wyoming mines.

Although the state's coal trend extends from its earliest days, with a future growth trajectory expanding for the next several years, alternative energy production technologies have been added to Missouri's research and development agenda, and some of this technology has even been deployed. Missouri's nuclear legacy, for instance, comprises both energy production and military readiness. In terms of electricity production, the state's singular Callaway Nuclear Generating Station, located near Fulton, northeast of Missouri's capital, Jefferson City, provides a very small portion of the state's consumed energy. Callaway produces 1,190 megawatts of power to supply its corporate owner, Ameren, which serves Illinois clients; a small portion of its energy output is designated for the Missouri side of its operation.

Energy Research
The U.S. Department of Energy provides each state a budget for energy research, in addition to supporting the United States' nuclear arsenal. The appropriation for the state of Missouri in fiscal year 2010 was more than half a million dollars, with nearly 85 percent allocated to nuclear weapons, securitization, and readiness; $5,213 was allocated to energy efficiency studies, and $13,479 was allocated to nuclear physics research, biological research, and computing research. Ethanol consumption rounds out the larger-scale alternative energy expenditures, with Missouri producing 2.5 percent of all U.S. ethanol and consuming 2 percent of U.S.-produced ethanol. Additional energy delivery occurs through the

▷ *Challenges of Being the "Gateway to the West"*

After gaining statehood in 1821, Missouri's St. Louis grew even more rapidly than in earlier centuries. The development of metropolitan St. Louis on the eastern border and later Kansas City on the western border generated new energy needs for the state of Missouri. Transportation increased, picking up steam both literally and figuratively as westward expansion and trade often found their way through Missouri's "gateway to the west."

However, from the founding of the state early in the 19th century through the birth of the 20th century, little changed for Missouri in terms of the quality of energy consumed. Kansas City grew into an important cow town and mercantile center, the Civil War was fought and ended (1861–65), three state constitutions were deliberated and voted into existence, and river traffic continued to swell local economies and populations.

The St. Louis Gateway Arch marks the western portion of the United States.

Wikimedia

burning of petroleum and natural gas, although Missouri does not enjoy large-scale, localized production of either energy source. Natural gas is used by almost three-fifths of the state's households for heating in winter months, and it arrives through pipelines from four adjacent states. Missouri also converts into electricity 26,000 barrels of oil per year.

Given the lack of natural energy reserves in the state and a production scale merely 0.2 percent of total U.S. fuel output, Missouri will be looking toward sustainable measures to supply its growing need for additional energy. In 2008, Missouri tasked investor-owned utility companies with increasing the use of renewable energy. This new energy portfolio standard requires increasing reliance on sources such as wind, solar, and geothermal power from a 2 percent increase in 2011 to a 15 percent increase by 2021. This gradual shift is presumed to allow appropriate reinvestment and adjustment in the sector.

Need for Electricity

Electricity is the end goal of most of Missouri's modern energy output. As of December 2010, the U.S. Energy Information Administration reported that Missourians paid $0.091 per kilowatt-hour for residential electricity but $0.0716 per kilowatt-hour for commercial electricity. Overall, Missouri consumes 325 billion British thermal units (Btu) of domestic energy and ranks 27th of all states in terms of energy consumption.

Compared to the rest of the United States, Missouri ranks worse than many states in terms of several emissions and energy-intensity scales. As of 2010, and using scales on which higher rank is considered better, Missouri ranked 34th in terms of carbon dioxide emissions per person, 27th in terms of energy intensity of economic output, and 41st in terms of carbon intensity of energy produced and used.

Between 1988 and 2008, Missouri has sharply increased its carbon emissions by more than 15 percent, with a 4 percent increase in carbon intensity. In 2008, the state ranked 36th in overall carbon dioxide emissions, with 140 million metric tons emitted. When factoring in industrial consumption, Missouri consumed 1,937 billion Btu to rank 31st of all U.S. states, while emitting 3.3 percent of the United States' carbon dioxide. Missouri rounds out its greenhouse gas emissions with 3.9 percent of U.S. sulfur dioxide emissions and 2.2 percent of U.S. nitrogen oxide emissions.

Curt Gilstrap

Further Reading

Chalmers, Hannah, Mathieu Lucquiaud, Jon Gibbins, and Matt Leach. "Flexible Operation of Coal Fired Power Plants With Postcombustion Capture of Carbon Dioxide." *Journal of Environmental Engineering* 135, no. 6 (2009).

Missouri Department of Natural Resources. "Missouri Fossil Fuel Use at a Glance." http://www.dnr.mo.gov /energy/utilities/Fossil%20Fuel%20Use%20at%20 a%20Glance%202008.pdf.

Snead, Mark C., and Amy A. Jones. "Are U.S. States Equally Prepared for a Carbon-Constrained World?" *Economic Review* 95, no. 4 (2010).

U.S. Energy Information Administration. "Missouri." http://www.eia.gov/cfapps/state/state_energy _profiles.cfm?sid=MO.

See Also: Carbon Sequestration; Enron; Geothermal Energy; Nuclear Power; United States; Wind Resources.

Moldova

Official Name: Republic of Moldova.
Category: Geography of Energy.
Summary: Moldova is scarce in resources and dependant on imported energy. Political instability and a slowly recovering economy in transition shape a fragile energy market.

Reduction of energy dependence is a key goal on the Moldovan energy security agenda, because more than 90 percent of the energy consumption is covered by external suppliers, dominated by Russia. Given that fossil fuels supply 99 percent of the energy for thermal and combined heat and power (CHP) plants, structural changes in energy production are a challenge to this young nation, which was shaken by civil disturbances and a severe economic depression during the 1990s.

Dependence on imports is exacerbated by the uneven distribution of energy production units in the country. With only 350 megawatts-electrical of secured installed capacity on the right bank of the Nistru River, the country's western region, including the capital city, is highly dependent on the production units located on the eastern bank of the river in the breakaway territory of Transnistria. This became obvious during the short War of Transnistria (November 1990–July 1992), fought largely through control of energy. Western regions of Moldova are still challenged to find alternative methods of domestic energy production.

Production and Consumption

As of 2009, total electricity produced amounted to 3.41 terawatt-hours, representing 21 percent of production in 1990. Electric power consumption experienced a similar decrease, dropping by 2007 to 4.83 terawatt-hours (40 percent of the consumption registered in 1990). By 1995, domestic production no longer covered demand, thus generating an average yearly deficit of up to 2 terawatt-hours. Traditionally, fossil fuels make up more than 90 percent of the primary energy supply, followed by hydropower. Moldova has traditionally exported electricity, and its power line network is directly connected to the Ukrainian, Romanian, and Bulgarian networks. In spite of its electricity system operating synchronously with that of Ukraine, strengthening links with Romania through several interconnecting overhead power lines continues to be an important issue.

Natural Gas and Oil

As of 2010, Moldova had no proven natural gas reserves, a total production of 196,850 cubic feet (60,000 cubic meters), a consumption of 10.4 billion cubic feet (3.17 billion cubic meters), and no gas exports. Russian Gazprom is the country's exclusive supplier. Private companies additionally import liquefied petroleum gas (LPG) from Ukraine, Russia, Romania, Kazakhstan, and Belarus. Fluctuating seasonal consumption and supply and a lack of gas-storage facilities have had an impact on security of supply and stocks. Among the national priorities in this area is securing natural gas supply for the capital city, Chișinău, and its suburbs. Possible solutions are a future direct link to the Nabucco Gas Pipeline and liquefied gas imports via the Giurgiulești terminal.

In 2010, Moldovans' daily oil consumption was estimated to be about 19,000 barrels. With only one oil deposit, Valenskoye field (with an annual extraction rate of 8,000 to 9,000 tons), consumption is entirely covered by imports from Russia, Ukraine, and Belarus. All refined oil products have to be imported, as there is no working refinery in Moldova.

The importance of oil as a source of energy for the country's thermal plants has been progressively decreasing. Compared to 1990, when 25 percent (4 gigawatt-hours) of the total electricity production was based on oil, in 2006 this primary source was used to produce merely 1 gigawatt-hour (0.03 percent of the nation's electricity production). The Moldovan government aims to secure consumers' supply at accessible prices by promoting competition. Several Russian and some European players are active in the market of petroleum products. In the mid- and long terms, Moldova may be included in the Euro-Asian Oil Transportation Corridor (EAOTC) project, mainly by connecting Romania to the Odessa-Brody (Ukraine) Pipeline artery. Completing the above-mentioned Giurgiuleşti terminal and building a refinery near Otaci are also among the options for enhancing security in the supply of oil products.

Renewables

According to Moldova's 2007 energy strategy, renewable energy production must increase 20 percent by 2020. From the country's total installed generating capacity of 1 gigawatt, hydropower supplies 21.5 gigawatts, compared to 60 megawatts for other types of renewable energy. There is proven technical wind potential for 1 gigawatt. Reservoirs of thermal water ranging from 30 to 45 degrees Celsius (86 to 122 degrees Fahrenheit) have also been found. Apart from proven installed solar capacity of 300 kilowatts, no other renewables are currently used for energy supply. Due to its low potential, hydropower development is limited to microhydropower and small hydropower plants.

PÉTER BAGOLY-SIMÓ

Further Reading

Encyclopedia of the Nations. "Energy and Power: Moldova." http://www.nationsencyclopedia.com/ Europe/Moldova-ENERGY-AND-POWER.html# ixzz0rMUilORE.

U.S. Energy Information Administration. "Country Analysis Brief: Moldova." http://www.eia.gov/ countries/country-data.cfm?fips=MD.

See Also: Hydropower; Renewable Energy Resources; Russia.

Monaco

Official Name: Principality of Monaco.
Category: Geography of Energy.
Summary: The Principality of Monaco is one of the smallest countries in the world and one of the first countries to make significant use of heat pumps. Its climate change and energy targets for the future are very ambitious.

The Principality of Monaco is located in southern Europe, surrounded by France and about 10 miles (16 kilometers) from Italy. With a total area of only 0.76 square mile (2 square kilometers), Monaco is one of the smallest countries of the world. However, its energy and climate change policy and achievements can be considered as good examples for other countries to follow. In the 1980s, Monaco started a waste-to-energy program.

Although waste-to-energy plants recovered energy from household waste and sludge from wastewater treatment, they were emitting a toxic soup of air pollutants, accounting for around 30 percent of total greenhouse gas (GHG) emissions generated by Monaco. A debate over the risks and opportunities of the program ensued, especially because a major plant was located in the center of the city, beside Louis II Stadium. Acknowledging the benefits of the waste-to-energy program, the government of Monaco tried to find a means of reducing emissions, especially GHGs, from the incineration of waste.

In 2005, Prince Albert II succeeded his father, Prince Rainier III, after his death in April. A new era for Monaco's environmental and consequently energy policies ensued: In May 2006, Monaco became a party to the Kyoto Protocol, with a 20/30/20 target: that is, to improve buildings' energy efficiency by 20 percent over 2007 levels, to reduce GHG emissions by 30 percent over 1990 levels, and to increase the share of renewable energies in the country's final energy mix 20 percent by 2020. Furthermore, in February 2008, Monaco committed to becoming carbon neutral by 2050.

In 2007, a preselection process was launched that allows only organic wastes to end up at the waste-to-energy plants, via collecting and recycling or reusing materials such as glass, paper, household packaging, oil, toxic household waste, batteries, and printer cartridges. From 2007 to the middle of 2008, the amount of the collected paper increased by 550 percent, and the amount of collected glass was doubled. Today, the GHG emissions due to waste incineration have been reduced, and the energy produced by waste-to-energy plants is equal to the energy consumed by the principality's public lighting and heating and cooling of one of the principal districts of the country.

Monaco's Department of the Environment noticed that another 31 percent of the overall GHG emissions of Monaco are linked to district heating. Since 2003, therefore, domestic fuel heating has been banned in new buildings, and since 2008 the state grants a 30 percent subsidy to those replacing fossil fuel heating systems with a solar heating system. However, Monaco is still dependent on its neighbors: Approximately 97.5 percent of the electricity consumed is imported from France. The government has announced several additional measures to both secure the country's energy independency and meet its climate change goals.

These measures include the energy auditing and setting of high environmental standards for buildings; promotion of the use of public transportation, carpooling, and low-carbon vehicles; the reduction of domestic energy consumption

▷ Oil Consumption Reduced by 15,000 Metric Tons

In the 1960s, Auditorium Rainier III was the first building in the country heated by a heat pump that used seawater, an innovative idea at the time. Today, 64 pumps contribute to heating in winter and air-conditioning in summer in many buildings located on the coast. In fact, heat pumps provide 74 percent of the energy produced in Monaco, or 17 percent of the energy consumed, and have led to an annual reduction in oil consumption of 15,000 metric tons.

Heat pumps like this produce 74 percent of the energy produced in Monaco.   Wikimedia

with the installation of smart meters; and subsidies for installation of solar photovoltaic and solar thermal systems.

This policy is supported by the Société Monégasque de l'Électricité et du Gaz (SMEG), which has been in charge of the distribution of electricity and natural gas in the principality for more than a century and will be at least until 2029. SMEG's shareholders include the GDF SUEZ group, the French network operator EDF, and the state of Monaco.

GEORGIOS SARANTAKOS

Further Reading

Climate Neutral Network. "Monaco." http://goo.gl/9pTKG.

Eccardt, Thomas M. *Secrets of the Seven Smallest States of Europe: Andorra, Liechtenstein,*

Luxembourg, Malta, Monaco, San Marino, and Vatican City. New York: Hippocrene Books, 2005.

"Monaco." In *Encyclopedia of Global Warming and Climate Change*, edited by S. George Philander. Thousand Oaks, CA: Sage, 2008.

Monaco Energy Policy, Laws and Regulation Handbook. Washington, DC: International Business Publications, 2008.

Principality of Monaco. "Archives Environment." http://goo.gl/3JZxZ.

See Also: France; Heat Pumps; Waste Heat Recovery; Waste Incineration.

Mongolia

Official Name: Mongolia.
Category: Geography of Energy.
Summary: Mongolia relies on domestically produced coal for energy, has an inefficient centralized energy system in Ulan Bator, and faces challenges in ensuring affordable energy access in distant provincial towns and scattered rural communities.

Mongolia's capital, Ulan Bator (also rendered as Ulaanbaatar), is home to around 50 percent of Mongolia's population. Ulan Bator is the coldest capital city in the world with average annual temperatures of minus 2 degrees Celsius and winter temperatures that dip below minus 40 degrees Celsius. Mongolia relies on its substantial coal reserves for heating and electricity. The greatest energy challenge in Ulan Bator is the efficient use of it, not the supply. The coal power plants that generate heat and electricity for the city of Ulan Bator are outdated, highly inefficient, and costly to maintain. Inefficient coal space heaters in informal settlements surrounding Ulan Bator contribute to air pollution. Securing heat and electricity in Mongolia's provincial towns and scattered rural communities is challenging, given the vast distances between sites of power generation and settlements and the limited investment for localized energy systems.

Energy Efficiency in Ulan Bator

In 1921, Mongolia became independent from China and declared itself the second communist country in the world after Russia. From 1921 until 1990, Mongolia depended on the Soviet Union for development assistance. Ulan Bator's combined coal heat and power stations were constructed with Soviet aid. These plants have high maintenance costs and high levels of inefficiency; much of the heat piped from them is lost along the pipeline. Although expensive to maintain, they would be even more costly to replace. With temperatures dipping below minus 40 degrees Celsius in winter, heating is crucial in Ulan Bator. Moreover, apartments receiving the piped heat cannot regulate the temperature; as a result, some apartments are so hot that residents must open windows in the dead of winter, whereas other apartments remain so cold that residents must bundle up to stay warm.

The government subsidizes heating costs through cheap district heating and cheap coal for space heating, resulting in reduced incentives for energy conservation and building insulation. Heat loss through poor building insulation is a widespread problem. Curbing the distribution heat leaks and improving energy efficiency through new technologies and better insulation are crucial. Straw-bale housing, with its high insulation quality, has even been piloted as a way to improve energy efficiency. Improving energy efficiency would reduce the amount of coal needed to heat the city, which in turn could reduce greenhouse gases and air pollution, thus improving air quality and halting the rising rate of respiratory illnesses among urban residents.

Half of Ulan Bator's population lives in informal ger settlements around the city, areas where people have set up traditional gers (circular tents) and often build structures around them. Such homes are poorly insulated and are heated with inefficient space-heating coal stoves that burn low-quality coal, contributing significantly to the city's air pollution and poor air quality. These informal settlements are now connected to the central grid for electricity after a multiyear project to improve electricity access and metering in Ulan Bator's ger settlements.

Energy Outside Ulan Bator

An estimated 72 percent of Mongolians have electricity access. Access to centralized heating systems is not as pervasive; about 47 percent of Ulan Bator and only 35 percent of those in provincial towns have a subsidized heat supply from the central grid. This means that about 65 percent of the rural population relies on traditional coal stoves for heating. Poor families can spend up to a third of their annual income on coal alone for heating.

Mongolia is a vast and sparsely populated territory. Thus, providing energy to all provincial towns through a central grid is not realistic. In neighboring districts, power lines extend hundreds of miles across uninhabited steppe from a central power grid in Ulan Bator. The harsh weather of the Mongolian steppe makes such long-distance power lines difficult to maintain. Closer to the western border, power is transmitted from a Russian hydroelectric facility into Mongolian towns. Other isolated regions have their own power grids, some fueled with diesel generators. Given the isolated nature of many of Mongolia's settlements, there is great potential for decentralized, clean renewable energies.

Mongolia's Energy Sources

Domestically mined coal supplies about 80 percent of Mongolia's energy. Mongolia has proven coal reserves of 12.2 billion tons, with potential reserves of up to 100 billion tons. Annual output is around 5 million tons, the majority of which is used for steam heating and electricity provision. Despite large coal deposits, limited infrastructure creates challenges in transporting coal from mines to the populated areas where it is needed. Mongolia, with assistance from South Korea, is now pursuing clean-coal technologies to improve energy efficiency and reduce pollution.

The first small hydropower dam was built in 1959 with assistance from the Soviet Union. Today there are 10 small hydropower plants around the country and two large plants under construction; more are being discussed. The existing small hydropower is for summer production only, because the water freezes in winter. Critics are concerned about the negative environmental impact on Mongolia's fragile steppe ecosystems that larger dams could create.

Large-scale solar and wind systems are being explored for remote communities, but these require a significant amount of investment. Multiple organizations have helped to install solar power systems among herder communities and remote settlements that lack other modern energy services.

Shaunna Barnhart

Further Reading

United Nations Development Programme. "Mongolia: Building Energy Efficiency." http://www.undp.mn/snrm-beep.html.

United Nations Development Programme. "Mongolia: Energy-Efficient Straw-Bale Housing." http://content.undp.org/go/cms-service/stream/asset/?asset_id=2095743.

U.S. Energy Information Administration. "Country Analysis Brief: Mongolia." http://205.254.135.7/countries/country-data.cfm?fips=MG.

World Bank. *The Next Steppe: Mongolia's Energy Future.* Documentary, 2010. http://www.worldbank.org/astae.

World Wildlife Fund. "Dams in Mongolia." http://mongolia.panda.org/en/threats/dams/.

See Also: Coal; Cogeneration; District Energy; Grid-Connected Systems; Insulation; Renewable Energy Resources.

Montana

Category: Energy in the United States.
Summary: Montana produces both coal and oil. The state also utilizes hydroelectric power and has put wind energy systems in place.

Montana produces both oil and coal for domestic and export use. Efforts to reduce its carbon footprint have led Montana to seek out sources of renewable energy. Montana is a major producer of hydroelectric power and is working to develop greater wind energy capacity. Yellowstone National Park has become a model for facilities and communities that seek to convert to clean energy and practice energy conservation.

Encompassing a total area of 147,046 miles, Montana is the fourth-largest state in the United States. Water covers 1,490 square miles of the state. The major rivers are Clark Fork, the Missouri, and the Yellowstone. The major lakes are Flathead and Fort Peck. This ready access to water sources allows Montana to use hydroelectric power at six of the 10 largest electricity-generating plants in the state, with the result that a fourth of all electricity generated in Montana is derived from hydroelectric sources. Of the coal produced in the United States, 4 percent originates in mines in Montana. The Williston Basin, which is located in eastern Montana and western North Dakota, is home to three of the 100 largest oil fields in the United States. Two of those are located within Montana's borders.

In 2009, Montana consumed a total of 343.3 trillion British thermal units (Btu) of energy and generated 27 terawatt-hours of electricity. Considerable attention has been paid to using renewable energy in Montana, and in 2007 the state generated 9,971,057 megawatt-hours of renewable electricity and ranked sixth in the United States in the percentage of renewable energy generated in relation to total electricity generated (34.5 percent).

Montana was second in the nation in renewable electricity generated per capita. Between 2001 and 2007, Montana's hydroelectricity capabilities increased by 41.6 percent. Montana has also made progress in introducing wind energy and ranked 14th in the United States in wind capacity in 2008, producing 271.5 megawatts.

Moving Toward Clean Energy

In 2009, the U.S. Congress passed the American Recovery and Reinvestment Act. In order to qualify for energy grant money, states were required to inform Congress how the money was to be spent to improve energy efficiency and enhance

efforts toward identifying renewable sources of energy. Governor Brian Schweitzer stated that Montana's share of funds was to be used to bring the state's energy, utility, and building codes up to federal standards and continue efforts toward prioritizing energy investments while improving existing energy programs and creating new ones as necessary.

The following summer, the Department of Energy earmarked $120 million in funds for innovative weatherization projects in various states. This funding allowed Montana to weatherize 989 low-income homes by May 2010 and become one of five states recognized by the Department of Energy for reaching a weatherization milestone. This success released additional American Recovery and Reinvestment Act funding and allowed Montana to weatherize additional homes, bringing the total to 2,400 homes.

Energize Montana

Through Energize Montana, the state uses various forms of assistance to teach residents about clean energy and provide financial help and tax credits to promote the practice of energy conservation and encourage the use of renewable energy sources. The Low-Income Energy Assistance Program, the Weatherization Program, and the Energy Ombudsman Program are all designed to help low-income residents.

The Energy Tax Credits Program offers incentives to any home or business that invests in energy conservation. Under the auspices of the Department of Environmental Quality (DEQ), the State Energy Program educates the public about energy conservation and alternative sources of energy, such as wind, solar, and geothermal energy. DEQ also offers information and technical assistance, through the Biomass Energy Program, on using biomass energy in homes and as a vehicle fuel.

The Alternative Energy Loan Program provides loans to homes, businesses, and nongovernmental organizations (NGOs) that install solar, wind, biomass, geothermal, and small-scale hydropower energy systems. State-owned buildings and universities may apply for loans for similar projects through the State Buildings Energy Conservation program. In 2010, one of Montana's U.S. senators, Max Baucus, introduced the Middle Class Tax Cut Act of 2010, which would have provided federal incentives to promote the use of clean energy.

During the first years of the 21st century, Montana made considerable progress in the generation of wind energy but still lagged behind neighboring states. By 2011, Montana was generating 376 megawatts of wind power. The two largest wind projects were Glacier Wind Farm (with 210 megawatts of nameplate capacity) and Judith Gap Wind Farm (with 135 megawatts of nameplate capacity).

Several others were in various stages of development, including a 24-megawatt facility that Chicago-based Invenergy was building near Great Falls and a potential facility to be erected by Xinjiang Goldwind Science and Technology Company, a Chinese wind energy company. Grasslands Renewable Energy launched the Wind Spirit Project, designed to harness, store, and transport clean energy to residents of Montana.

Wikimedia

Mammoth Hot Springs is a large complex of hot springs created over thousands of years as hot water from the spring cooled and deposited calcium carbonate.

The production of biomass energy is also a priority in Montana. An 18-megawatt plant is already in operation in St Regis and is able to transmit clean energy via NorthWestern Energy.

Montana has not fully developed solar energy, but the state has ample solar resources available, with the eastern part of the state receiving an annual average of five hours of full sunshine daily and western Montana receiving an average of 4.2 hours of full sunshine daily. Many schools and state-owned buildings have installed solar-generating equipment.

Green Energy at Yellowstone

Yellowstone National Park serves as a model for innovation in converting from fossil fuels to clean energy sources. In 2007, the park consumed 26.8 gigawatt-hours of energy at a cost of $3.1 million. The YES! Initiative was subsequently launched by the park's foundation to begin working toward reducing consumption 15 percent by 2016 as a result of employing solar and microhydropower generating systems; switching to high-efficiency appliances, equipment, lighting fixtures, and sensors; and educating employees and visitors about energy efficiency. The use of microhydropower is not new at Yellowstone. A Pelton waterwheel was installed at Mammoth Hot Springs in 1911. Although that waterwheel is no longer in operation, it proved that Yellowstone has considerable potential for generating hydropower.

In 2009, Yellowstone received $1.65 million in American Recovery and Reinvestment Act funds to install a new hydropower system with the capacity to save 900,000 kilowatt-hours of renewable energy at a cost savings of $80,000. Energy-efficient fixtures and technologies are being employed at all 1,500 buildings at Yellowstone, and the park is phasing in solar electricity and hot-water technologies with the intention of saving 450,000 kilowatt-hours of energy and cutting costs by $170,000. Gas furnaces are being replaced with electric systems to save 32,000 kilowatts of energy. Progress is monitored by electric meters.

ELIZABETH RHOLETTER PURDY

Further Reading

Barnes, Roland V., ed. *Energy Crisis in America?* Huntington, NY: Nova Science, 2001.

Bird, Lori, et al. *Green Power Marketing in the United States: A Status Report.* Golden, CO: National Renewable Energy Laboratory, 2008.

Montana Department of Environmental Quality. "Energize Montana." http://www.deq.mt.gov/energy/EEBusiness/default.mcpx.

U.S. Energy Information Administration. "Montana." http://www.eia.doe.gov/state/state-energy-profiles.cfm?sid=MT.

See Also: Bonneville Power Administration; Coal; Columbia River; Geothermal Energy; Hydropower; United States; Washington State; Wind Resources.

Morgan, J. P.

Dates: 1837–1913.
Category: Biographies.
Summary: J. P. Morgan was a leading American financier who used his bank's resources to influence the governance and organization of many leading corporations, including those involved in transportation and energy.

James Pierpont Morgan was a prominent American financier who greatly influenced corporate finance through his banking and industrial interests. Morgan greatly affected the funding and operation of many sectors of the economy, with special influence in the fields of communications, energy, steel, and transportation. A great proponent of modern and efficient management techniques, Morgan was admired by many for his philanthropy and dedication to efficiency; he was also criticized by some for the sheer power he held. Some of the companies that Morgan had a role in founding or organizing—such as the General Electric Company, United States Steel Corporation, and JPMorgan, Chase and Co.—played a leading role in the United States throughout the 20th century and continue to the present day.

History

Morgan was born on April 17, 1837, in Hartford, Connecticut. His father, Junius Spencer Morgan, was a leading banker who founded J. P. Morgan and Co. with George Peabody in 1854. After being educated at the English High School in Boston and the University of Göttingen, Morgan worked with his father's firm, taking control of the New York City office beginning in 1864. Although eligible for service during the American Civil War, Morgan paid $1,000 for a substitute to serve in his stead (a common practice during that war, for those who could afford it). During this period, Morgan was deeply involved in financing the Union's war efforts.

Railroads and Transportation

Soon after the Civil War ended, Morgan became involved in battles to acquire and control railroads throughout the United States. His first incursion into transportation involved his attempt to take control of the Albany and Susquehanna Railroad (A&S), which ran 143 miles from Albany to Binghamton, New York. While relatively small, the railroad connected four larger lines and was thus seen as a valuable asset by Jay Gould, whose Erie Railroad needed access to the A&S lines to transport coal from Pennsylvania to New England. Gould and an associate, Jim Fisk, began buying shares in the A&S in an effort to gain control of its operations.

This takeover was opposed by the A&S's president, Joseph Ramsey, and intense court battles began to ascertain who would control the railroad. Ramsey flooded the market with shares of A&S stock, and both sides engaged hired thugs to fight for control of the A&S's stations and trains. At this point, Morgan, whose firm held a $500,000 mortgage on the railroad, became involved. Morgan's firm purchased 600 shares of A&S stock and entered into a proxy battle to elect a board of directors loyal to Ramsey. Morgan, who personally supervised the voting, was elected a vice president and director of the A&S, thwarting the efforts of Gould and Fisk. After winning a court battle regarding the authenticity of the elections, Morgan entered into an agreement to lease the

A&S's lines to the Delaware and Hudson Railroad, effectively ending the controversy.

Morgan continued to finance and influence railroads, taking a leading role in the reorganization of the New York, West Shore and Buffalo Railroad, the Philadelphia and Reading Railroad, and the Chesapeake and Ohio Railroad. Morgan was also the leading financier assisting James J. Hill in his formation of the Great Northern Railway. In 1892, Morgan was the leading force in the merger of several energy and manufacturing companies that resulted in the formation of the General Electric Company (GE).

Beginning in 1890, Thomas Alva Edison had merged several of his business concerns together to form the Edison General Electric Company, which focused on the manufacture of incandescent lighting and electrical installations. Edison's major rival was Charles A. Coffin's Thomson-Houston Electric Company, which had been formed in 1883 and was a leading manufacturer of arc lamps and dynamos. The merger between Edison's and Coffin's companies permitted GE to resolve various patent disputes between the two concerns and to form a juggernaut that has continued to be a leader in lighting and power generation technology.

United States Steel Corporation

Morgan took control of his father's firm in 1890, after J. S. Morgan's death. In 1900, Morgan began negotiations with Charles M. Schwab, the president of Carnegie Company, regarding the purchases of Carnegie's steel business. Morgan was successful in his efforts, and following a $492 million payment to Carnegie, the United States Steel Corporation (U. S. Steel) was formed by merging Carnegie's concerns with several other coal, mining, shipping, and steel concerns.

Soon after its formation, U. S. Steel controlled more than 66 percent of the United States' steel market, not only producing steel but also constructing bridges, nails, rails, railroad cars, ships, and wire. U. S. Steel used economies of scale to reduce transportation and resource costs, and it attempted to expand its product lines and distribution to create an international force in the steel industry.

During the first decade of the 20th century, a financial crisis occurred that became known as the Panic of 1907. Many New York banks were on the verge of collapse, and the federal government lacked mechanisms and procedures to quell the crisis. Secretary of the Treasury George B. Cortelyou was able to allocate $35 million to be used to alleviate the panic, but he had no means of using these funds. Cortelyou turned to Morgan, who organized a meeting of bank and corporate leaders. At this meeting, it was agreed that money would be directed between banks to assuage depositors, international lines of credit were established and strengthened, and stock was purchased to shore up floundering corporations. These moves were ultimately successful and led to the formation of the Federal Reserve system in 1913.

Although he had an astonishing run of victories, not all of Morgan's investments were successful. For example, Morgan invested heavily in Nikola Tesla's Wardenclyffe Tower, an early attempt to provide commercial transatlantic broadcasting and power transmission without interconnecting wires. Although Morgan invested more than $150,000 in the Wardenclyffe Tower, Tesla's attempts to complete the project were futile. Nevertheless, Morgan's accomplishments were many and his influence great. He died on March 31, 1913, at the age of 73.

STEPHEN T. SCHROTH
CHRISTIAN D. MAHONE
JAMAL A. NELSON

Further Reading

Chernov, R. *The House of Morgan: An American Banking Dynasty and the Rise of Modern Finance.* New York: Grove Press, 2001.

Morris, C. R. *The Tycoons: How Andrew Carnegie, John D. Rockefeller, Jay Gould, and J. P. Morgan Invented the American Supereconomy.* New York: Henry Holt, 2005.

Strouse, J. *Morgan: American Financier.* New York: Random House, 1999.

See Also: Edison, Thomas Alva; Tesla, Nikola; Westinghouse, George.

Morocco

Official Name: Kingdom of Morocco.
Category: Geography of Energy.
Summary: Morocco is heavily dependent on foreign sources of energy and lacks a domestic supply of traditional energy sources. The country is diversifying its energy matrix by developing renewable sources such as solar energy, hydropower, and wind.

Morocco is the only country in north Africa that does not have substantial fossil fuel reserves. Unlike its neighbors Algeria and Mauritania, who have large oil and gas reserves, Morocco must rely on foreign imports of energy. In 2010, Morocco imported 97 percent of its energy, making it the largest energy importer in Africa and economically sensitive to energy prices of the global market. Although the country lacks traditional sources of energy, it has a large, underdeveloped potential for renewable energy. In 2008, the government enacted a new energy strategy with a focus on developing renewables as a way to continue broader development.

Morocco has an emerging economy that experienced steady growth of 4 to 5 percent between 2000 and 2010. As the economy grows, Morocco becomes more dependent on foreign sources of

Photos.com

A solar panel installed on top of a Moroccan roof. Solar photovoltaic (PV) kits were distributed to about 10 percent of the rural population by the Programme d'Electrification Rurale Global.

energy, with continual growth in imports of crude oil, petroleum products, coal, and electricity. Forecasts by the Moroccan government predict that primary energy demands could increase three to four times by 2030. This growth presents a challenge to the government because current power production is insufficient to meet demand, and Morocco must therefore rely on electricity importation through interconnections with Spain and Algeria.

Growth of Demand and Rising Costs

In Morocco, there is a large difference between the growth of energy demand and rising energy costs. Over a period from 2009 to 2010, the annual energy consumption increased 5.6 percent, while the annual cost of energy increased 38.2 percent. In order to maintain reasonable energy prices for consumers, the government subsidizes the costs of commodities such as crude oil, which levels out prices for the end consumer. However, this policy results in the government's absorbing the rising costs of energy, putting a strain on the developing country's budget.

These energy constraints and challenges have pushed the government to evaluate how the country produces and uses energy. Energy policy was restructured with a series of energy laws passed between 2007 and 2009. These laws made the mission of the Ministry of Energy, Mines, Water, and Environment to diversify energy sources, improve energy security, and lead in energy integration with European and Mediterranean markets.

Wind power, hydropower, and solar energy potentials are high in Morocco. Morocco could significantly increase its electricity-generation capacity with the appropriate policy framework, financing mechanisms, knowledge transfer, and infrastructure development. For example, a major change in Morocco's energy policy leading to more power generation is the liberalization of the electricity market. The state-owned power company, the Office National de l'Électricité (ONE), traditionally controlled the electrical sector. Although ONE continues to have sole responsibility for distribution and transmission of electricity, the generation is open for the private sector. Liberalization of the energy economy is therefore leading to

▷ *Morocco's Rural Electrification Program*

Morocco is beginning to be seen as an energy leader across the African Maghreb region because of its successful rural electrification program. In 1996, the Moroccan government implemented a social program named Programme d'Electrification Rurale Global (the Global Rural Electrification Program, or PERG), which aims to provide electricity to all Moroccans. In about a decade, Morocco increased its rural population's access to electricity from 18 percent in 1995 to 98 percent in 2007. This development has had numerous social and economic benefits, including a reduction in rural-to-urban migration, improved indoor air quality, higher productivity of rural populations, and the introduction of communication devices such as phones and radios.

In some cases, the low population densities and remoteness of villages in rural Morocco made a conventional electric distribution network uneconomical. This constraint led PERG to use distributed power generation to bring electricity to approximately 10 percent of rural Moroccans by equipping them with individual solar photovoltaic (PV) kits.

more private-sector investment and a growth in renewable energies.

Projects under development will increase the share of renewable electricity from 10 percent in 2007 to 42 percent installed capacity by 2020. This increase will come from developing solar, wind, and hydroelectricity. In 2009, Morocco announced multiple concentrated solar energy projects that, when completed in 2020, will account for 38 percent of north African–installed renewable power generation capacity and will produce 2,000 megawatts across five sites throughout Morocco. The expansion of wind farms throughout the country will also result in an additional 2,000 megawatts

by 2020. Most of Morocco has good wind potential, with many places having 32-feet-per-second (10-meter-per-second) or higher prevailing winds, making the country attractive for development.

Energy Integration

Energy integration is a high priority for Morocco, which is working on integrating the Moroccan grid with European and Mediterranean markets. As of 2010, Morocco was the only country in Africa with an electrical grid connected to Europe. The ambitious plan to develop green power will result in a surplus of renewable energies, which Morocco can sell in other markets that have less potential for the development of clean energy. Given Europe's land constraints, importing renewable energy from North Africa will be necessary if Europe is to reach the goal of having 100 percent of its electricity generated by renewable sources by 2050. Morocco is capitalizing on this and attracting foreign investment through expansion of energy integration between Morocco and Europe.

The urban market for distributed energy generation is rising in Morocco as well, with the growing adoptions of solar thermal and solar photovoltaic systems. Most thermal energy demands are met through liquefied petroleum gas (LPG), which is distributed through portable canisters given the lack of infrastructure supporting gas service lines. Morocco is poised to leapfrog across gas technologies, however, with an increasing demand in solar thermal installations on rooftops. The popularity of solar thermal power is spreading with the public's perception of this energy source as a safer and more economical alternative to more traditional sources.

M. Anwar Sounny-Slitine
Sara Bensalem

Further Reading

Central Intelligence Agency. "Morocco." In *The World Factbook*. https://www.cia.gov/library/publications/the-world-factbook/geos/mo.html.

Clery, D. "Sending African Sunlight to Europe, Special Delivery." *Science* 329, no. 5993 (August 13, 2010).

Nfaoui, H., et al. "Wind Characteristics and Wind Energy Potential in Morocco." *Solar Energy* 63, no. 1 (July 1998).

U.S. Energy Information Administration. "Country Analysis Brief: Morocco." http://205.254.135.7/countries/country-data.cfm?fips=MO.

See Also: Algeria; Energy Transmission: Electricity; Oil Shales; Saudi Arabia; Shell; Solar Concentrator; Solar Energy; Solar Thermal Systems.

Mountaintop Removal Mining

Category: Environmentalism.
Summary: Mountaintop removal mining, a type of surface coal mining, is practiced in Appalachian coalfields and has become controversial with regard to environmental and health issues.

Mountaintop removal mining (MTR) is a form of surface coal mining that was developed in the United States in the late 1960s. Today it is practiced in the Appalachian coalfields of the states of West Virginia, Kentucky, Virginia, and Tennessee. The major companies involved are Arch Coal, Massey Energy, and National Coal Corporation. Since the start of the 21st century, MTR has become a heated political issue, resulting in the delay, review, and denial of several mining permits by the U.S. Environmental Protection Agency (EPA). Central issues in this debate include the energy independence of the United States, rising greenhouse gas emissions, water and air pollution, loss of biodiversity, and damage to human health.

New Technologies After World War II
In the United States, surface coal mining increased dramatically following World War II. With the help of new technologies, particularly large steam shovels and earth-moving machin-

ery, surface mining came to be more productive and cost-effective than traditional underground mining. By 1970, strip mining (another name for surface mining) generated 40 percent of all the coal mined in the United States, and today it accounts for 60 percent. According to the World Coal Association, surface mining has outpaced underground mining because it recovers a much higher proportion of the available coal. Mountaintop removal mining is a specific type of surface coal mining.

Mountaintop removal mining was first practiced in the late 1960s in Kentucky and West Virginia. Contour strip miners began dynamiting and bulldozing the tops of mountains to reveal the coal seams beneath, then pushed the soil and rock over the side. The oil crises of 1973 and 1979 stimulated the growth of the practice. With the advent of new and more efficient technology such as the Big John dragline—which moved 65 to 75 cubic yards of earth at one time—the practice increased in popularity throughout the 1980s and 1990s, particularly in eastern Kentucky and southern West Virginia. Since the 1990s, mountaintop removal mining has begun in western Virginia and certain areas in eastern Tennessee. At present, these central Appalachian states are the second-largest providers of coal in the United States.

There are five steps to MTR. First, miners dynamite the rock and dirt overlaying the coal seams, referred to as *overburden*. Second, the top layers of the coal seam are removed, and the waste is placed in an adjacent valley, in what is known as a *valley fill*. Third, the lower layers of coal are excavated with draglines, and the waste is placed in what is termed a *spoil pile*. Fourth, regrading begins as coal excavation continues. Fifth, at the end of the extraction process, the area is regraded and revegetated. This last step is known as *remediation*.

Regulation and Opposition
At present, mountaintop removal mining is regulated by two laws: the Clean Water Act and the Surface Mining Control and Reclamation Act of 1977 (SMCRA). The Clean Water Act is used to regulate the runoff from MTR operations. SMCRA

This couple, along with 15 others, was arrested at the gates of Massey Energy-operated Goals Coal company for protesting against mountaintop removal coal mining in Appalachia.

comprises two programs: one that regulates active coal mines and a second that reclaims mine lands abandoned after 1977. These programs are pursued by the Office of Surface Mining within the Department of the Interior. The passage of SMCRA was a direct response to concerns about surface mining and the inconsistency of state regulations.

From the inception of the practice to the present day, MTR has occasioned serious protest from residents of Appalachia, environmental activists, unionized miners, and scientists. These opponents have stressed the damage that MTR causes to property values, the health of humans and ecosystems, and employment, as well as the negligence of mine operators regarding their responsibilities to rehabilitate and revegetate the land.

Opposition to mountaintop removal mining has its roots in the opposition mounted by Appalachian communities to surface-mining operations beginning in the 1960s. Grassroots responses to the destruction of local environments focused on the detrimental effect that surface mining had on property values, as well as the inefficacy of state and federal regulations. Often, these responses were confrontational and violent. In Kentucky during the 1960s, the Appalachian Group to Save the Land and People blocked

mining bulldozers with their bodies and firearms, and anonymous saboteurs blew up expensive equipment at multiple mining sites throughout Kentucky and West Virginia. Groups such as the Citizens' League to Protect Surface Rights (1970) sought adequate compensation for home owners and landowners whose property had been destroyed by mining operations.

When MTR began, the United Mine Workers of America (UMW) supported state-by-state regulation of the practice. At this early stage, the union was responsive to member concerns about the conservation of natural resources and the condition of working and living environments. The union also believed that MTR had a negative effect on coal-mining jobs. Because MTR relies heavily on large machinery, its increase has corresponded to a rise in unemployment among coal workers. The UMW became a stronger opponent of MTR in 1971, when it supported federal legislation to control coal surface mining. However, by 1976, a year prior to the passage of the Surface Mining Control and Reclamation Act, the UMW came out in support of MTR, arguing that mine workers' jobs took precedence over protecting the environment. The UMW has become a vocal opponent of the EPA's denial of permits. Despite the fact that many MTR workers are prevented from unionizing, UMW president Cecil Roberts argued in a 2008 letter to union members that the union is not interested in where or how coal is mined, but rather in the protection of mining jobs.

A wide range of national and local environmental groups currently oppose MTR, including the Rain Forest Action Network, Earthjustice, the National Resources Defense Council, Coal River Mountain Watch, Mountain Justice Summer, and the Sierra Club. These organizations have pursued a diverse range of tactics to stop MTR—from pressuring banks and universities to divest from coal companies to conducting sit-ins, organizing rallies and pickets, petitioning the EPA to ban the practice and to deny individual mining permits, and lobbying the federal government. The visibility and frequency of these protests have increased significantly.

A diverse group of scientists has criticized the negative effects of MTR on the health of humans and ecosystems. Scientific opponents share the argument of grassroots opponents that MTR operators have failed to remediate MTR sites properly. They also criticize the EPA for failing to enforce existing regulations regarding remediation. Other scientists, such as scientist James Hansen of the National Aeronautics and Space Administration, argue that MTR is facilitating the increase in greenhouse gas emissions worldwide.

A peer-reviewed study in the January 2010 issue of *Science*, which surveyed existing studies of the effects of MTR, concluded that current mitigation practices, which focus largely on erosion control rather than reforestation, do not successfully address the environmental damage caused by the practice. The study's authors argued that MTR results in the burial of biodiverse streams and the permanent loss of ecosystems. The defoliation, removal of topsoil, and soil compaction caused by MTR increase the likelihood and severity of seasonal downstream flooding. The toxic by-products of MTR, sulfate in particular, contribute to the decline of stream biodiversity. Moreover, human health is negatively impacted by the persistence of mine-related chemical runoff found in groundwater supplies, fish populations, and airborne dust. In counties where MTR is practiced, there are significantly elevated rates of adult hospitalization for chronic pulmonary disorders, hypertension, lung cancer, and chronic heart, lung, and kidney diseases, as well as clusters of children with abnormally high levels of asthma and various allergies.

Supporters

Supporters of MTR include the World Coal Association, Friends of Coal, the West Virginia Coal Association, and the National Mining Association. These organizations believe that MTR is central to the continued energy independence of the United States. Furthermore, they argue that MTR causes minimal environmental damage and that abandoned mine sites provide locations for new schools, hospitals, and shopping centers, thus promoting local economic development. Supporters have argued that the practice should be rebranded as "mountaintop development" in order to emphasize the positive effects that MTR has for local economies.

Spruce No. 1 Mine

The EPA has concluded that MTR causes a series of environmental issues, including an increase in mineral concentrations in streams, the burial of streams, the fragmentation of forests, and the interruption of native species. Under the administration of President Barack Obama, the EPA has begun to review more rigorously valley fill permit applications that have come before the Army Corps of Engineers.

In January 2011, the EPA revoked the water permit for the Arch Coal Company's Spruce No. 1 Mine in Logan County, West Virginia. The mine, which had been issued a water permit by the EPA in 2007 under the administration of President George W. Bush, would have involved blasting the tops off mountains over an area of 2,278 acres and burying more than 7 miles of stream with overburden. The EPA argued that the disposal of mining waste in area streams would cause unacceptable damage to rivers, wildlife, and communities. This decision marks the first time that the EPA has revoked a valid clean water permit for a coal mine.

The resulting furor over the EPA's decision has illustrated many of the tensions at the heart of the debate over MTR. Coal companies and lobbying organizations have insisted that the revocation of the permit will endanger jobs and economic growth, as well as shake the security of investment in coal-mining operations. Environmentalists, West Virginia residents, and many scientists have applauded the decision for embracing sound science and protecting the health of Logan County's residents and ecology.

Jennifer Thomson

Further Reading

Montrie, Chad. "Expedient Environmentalism: Opposition to Coal Surface Mining in Appalachia and the United Mine Workers of America, 1945–1975." *Environmental History* 5, no. 1 (January 2000).

Montrie, Chad. *To Save the Land and People: A History of Opposition to Surface Coal Mining in Appalachia.* Chapel Hill: University of North Carolina Press, 2003.

Palmer, M. A., et al. "Mountaintop Mining Consequences." *Science* 327, no. 5962 (January 8, 2010). http://www.sciencemag.org/content/327/5962/148.full.

U.S. Environmental Protection Agency. "Spruce No. 1 Mine: Final Determination." http://www.epa.gov/region3/mtntop/spruce1.html.

See Also: Coal; Kentucky; Tennessee; Virginia; Water Pollution; West Virginia.

Mozambique

Official Name: Republic of Mozambique.
Category: Geography of Energy.
Summary: Mozambique is an African country, rich in natural resources, that is in the process of developing, diversifying, and expanding its energy mix.

Mozambique is located on the southeastern coast of Africa and is bordered by six countries: Zambia, Malawi, Tanzania, Zimbabwe, Swaziland, and South Africa. Its population is about 21 million people, of which around 45 percent are below 15 years of age.

Mozambique became independent from Portugal in 1975, following 16 years of civil war that caused extensive damage and hampered the nation's development. Today, the country is dependent mainly on agriculture—which makes up more than 20 percent of the gross domestic product (GDP)—along with exports of commodities and merchandise. Exports include aluminum, natural gas, cotton, sugar, and tobacco. The richness of the country's natural resources, which is yet to be fully explored, and the geographi-

cal location of Mozambique are deemed to offer ample opportunities for investment. Presumably this will allow the nation to develop in both economic and social terms.

However, there are those who believe that the economy is vulnerable, in the long run, to this resource abundance, particularly if Mozambique starts to produce oil. This phenomenon is often called the "paradox of plenty" and is based on the fact that many countries rich in resources that indeed explore their natural wealth are among the poorest nations in the world. Currently, in the energy spectrum, although oil has not been extracted, Mozambique produces gas and coal. It also produces and exports electricity; in fact, Mozambique is a net energy exporter.

In Mozambique, the majority of internal energy needs are met by traditional biofuels, such as wood, charcoal, and agricultural and animal wastes, corresponding to around 80 percent of the primary energy consumption. Electricity is deemed to be crucial to improve the population's welfare and make certain investments relevant to economic growth. Mozambique has seen significant growth in the electrification rate, although as of 2010 only around 14 percent of the population had access to electricity.

Electricity Production and the Use of Renewable Sources

In Mozambique, the majority of electricity supplied from the national grid comes from hydropower, although there is also thermal production from diesel or natural gas. In 2008, about 15 gigawatt-hours of electricity was produced in Mozambique, 99 percent of which was from hydropower; that figure rose to approximately 16 gigawatt-hours in 2011.

The Cahora Bassa Dam on the Zambezi River, in the Tete Province, with an installed capacity of 2.075 megawatts, is the main source of electricity for both Mozambique and southern Africa as a whole. The erection of the Cahora Bassa Dam created one of Africa's largest artificial lakes. This dam was fully operational in 1979, although during the Mozambican Civil War (1977–92) the transmission lines to South Africa were destroyed. This dam was not transferred to Mozambique, both because of the civil war and because of unpaid debts. In 2007, however, the national government assumed control of it.

In 2008, about three-quarters of the country's electricity, nearly 13 gigawatt-hours, was exported (a number that dropped to something less than 12 gigawatt-hours in both 2010 and 2011). Imports were nearly 8 gigawatt-hours in 2008. Hence, Mozambique is a net electricity exporter. However, there are many localities with no electricity, which emphasizes the importance of both the intensification of the electricity grid and adoption of other solutions, particularly decentralized production from renewable sources. Both the government and the private sector are interested in developing use of solar, wind, and biomass energy resources. The Energy Plan of Mozambique includes guidelines for promoting the development of conversion and the use of those renewable sources. For example, photovoltaic solar technology has been gradually introduced in rural health centers, schools, and other facilities.

Oil and Oil Products

Until now, oil has not been produced in Mozambique, but surveys indicate the strong possibility of both offshore and onshore oil deposits, and the presence of this resource has been detected. However, the availability of oil reserves in quantities that justify economic exploitation is being researched. Several international companies are participating in prospecting activities.

The oil products currently used in the country—equivalent to around 650 kilotons of oil per year—are mainly for transportation and industry, and they are imported. To minimize such importation, in 2009 a policy outlining a biofuels strategy was approved by the government.

Natural Gas

Exploration for natural gas started in 2004. Mozambique has large sedimentary basins of natural gas estimated at more than 3 trillion cubic feet of proven reserves. New gas deposits have recently been discovered. Of the country's annual production (based on 2010 data) of around 135 billion cubic feet, more than 95 percent is exported to South Africa by pipeline. The remaining fraction is used in country mainly in the industry, including the electricity industry. Initiatives to promote the use of natural gas in vehicles are being implemented.

Coal

There are several large deposits of coal in the Tete Province. Coal has been produced in the region, in the Moatize mines, since 1940, but it was suspended in 1981 because of the civil war. However, operations are now being restarted in this mine, and significant production is expected. Another mine in the same region, the Benga mine, is also to start operation. The vast majority of the coal produced in Mozambique has been consumed internally, but with several new projects, Mozambique is expected to export significant amounts of coal (presumably, as much as 21.6 million tons by 2016, as opposed to about 26,000 tons in 2009).

Increased electrification through the use of decentralized electricity production, the eventual exploration for oil, renewed exploration for gas, the start-up of coal projects, and even the development of biofuel production and use of natural gas in transportation—all these are expected in Mozambique in the near future and will eventually lead to significant changes in the country extending beyond its energy sector.

Ana Penha

Further Reading

Bucuane, Aurélio, and Peter Mulder. *Exploring Natural Resources in Mozambique.* Mozambique: Direcção Nacional de Estudos e Análise de Políticas, Ministério da Planificação e Desenvolvimento, 2007.

Chambal, Hélder. *Energy Security in Mozambique.* Policy Report 3. Canada: International Institute for Sustainable Development, 2010.

International Energy Agency. "2008 Energy Balance for Mozambique." http://www.iea.org/stats/balancetable.asp?COUNTRY_CODE=MZ.

U.S. Energy Information Administration. "Country Analysis Brief: Mozambique." http://www.eia.gov/countries/country-data.cfm?fips=MZ.

Yager, Thomas. "The Mineral Industry of Mozambique." In *2009 Minerals Yearbook*. Reston, VA: U.S. Geological Survey, 2011. http://minerals.usgs.gov/minerals/pubs/country/2009/myb3-2009-mz.pdf.

See Also: Comoros; Energy Policy; Mauritius; Rural Electrification; South Africa; Utilities; Zambia; Zimbabwe.

Municipal Utilities

Category: Business of Energy.
Summary: Municipally owned utilities are one model for the provision of public services. Although originally crowded out of the market by privately owned utilities, some municipally owned utilities have begun considering public ownership of their infrastructure in recent years.

Municipal utilities are a subset of publicly owned utilities that are owned by local governments. Other types of publicly owned utilities include public utility and public power districts, state authorities, irrigation districts, and joint municipal action agencies. In contrast to investor-owned utilities, which are private companies driven by a profit incentive, publicly owned utilities are nonprofit entities charged with the provision of at-cost services to their customers. Regardless of ownership, entities that maintain the infrastructure for and provide public services such as electricity, natural gas, water, and telecommunications are referred to as public utilities. *Public utility* is a general term that can also refer to the public service provided.

According to the U.S. Energy Information Administration, there are more than 2,000 publicly owned electric utilities in the United States. Municipal electric utilities typically purchase power on the wholesale market and provide distribution and billing services to customers in their service area, although some of the larger ones also own generation and transmission resources. There are municipal utilities in each of the 50 states with the exception of Hawaii, although the highest concentration is found in the midwestern and southeastern states.

Like other publicly owned utilities, municipal utilities are tax-exempt public entities that have the ability to issue debt in the form of tax-free bonds to finance the construction of public infrastructure projects. They are financed from municipal treasuries. Most municipal utilities are overseen by a board of directors or commissioners, which is elected independently of local government.

History

Most of the existing municipal utilities were established in the United States in the late 1800s or early 1900s, when the use of electric power first became widespread. At that time, they primarily provided street lighting and trolley services. Initially, electric generating facilities had to be located near the customers they served, and electric power companies—if not municipally owned—had to obtain a franchise from the municipality in which they operated. As technology evolved and electricity could be generated in larger quantities and transmitted over longer distances, regulation of public utilities passed largely to state commissions or departments.

Private electric companies became more efficient and steadily crowded out municipal utilities from the market during the first three decades of the 20th century. By the mid-1930s, the federal government had begun to regulate private power, largely through provisions described in the Public Utility Holding Company Act of 1935 (PUHCA). During this period, the federal government also began to expand its generation and supply of power to public and cooperative utilities.

Public utilities have historically been understood to be *natural monopolies*, a term that denotes an industry in which production by multiple companies is more costly than production by a single company. This definition is based on the high cost of infrastructure required to provide the product, in this case electricity, which means a single company has decreasing average costs to serve each customer as its customer base expands. This view was perpetuated during the early growth of the utility industry, in large part by politically powerful utility managers who wanted to protect their industry from competition. This created an effectively closed system of vertically integrated utility companies with the legal right to operate as natural monopolies, also referred to as the "utility consensus," which remained unchallenged for several decades.

During the 1970s, a number of factors called into question the legitimacy of this assumption, including technological stasis in the equipment the vertically integrated monopolies used to generate power on a large-scale, centralized basis; technological advancements in small-scale power generation; and an increasing public awareness of environmental issues that called into question the fundamental assumption that utilities were responsible only for providing the most electricity at the lowest cost. The 1973 energy crisis led to public support for energy efficiency and conservation on the public side, as well as changed popular belief about how utilities should be regulated.

In 1978, Congress passed the Public Utility Regulatory Policies Act (PURPA), a piece of legislation that required the natural monopoly utilities to purchase power from other producers when it could be supplied at lower incremental cost than what it would cost the utility to produce directly. This resulted in a more competitive electric utility industry that was more conducive to the integration of distributed and renewable electric generation.

Regulation of Municipal Utilities

The activities of municipal utilities are not subject to regulation by the Federal Energy Regulatory Commission (FERC), a responsibility that falls instead to the state. Even at the state level, municipal utilities are generally subject to different laws and regulations from those that apply to private, investor-owned utilities. For example, in Massachusetts, municipal utilities are exempt from many of the clean energy mandates required of investor-owned utilities, such as the state renewable portfolio standard (RPS) or the mandate to invest in all cost-effective energy efficiency opportunities.

In many states, a public utilities commission (PUC) or department of public utilities (DPU) is responsible for oversight and regulation of the rates and services provided by privately owned utilities. These were largely established as a result of PURPA, which placed electric distribution companies under state oversight, placed transmission services under the oversight of independent system operators (ISOs), and deregulated generation services, thereby creating a competitive market for power suppliers. PUCs and DPUs represent the public interest and work to ensure safe and reliable service at reasonable rates. Their responsibilities include consumer education, policy advocacy, and market development. They are not always responsible for regulation of publicly or cooperatively owned utilities, although they do regulate rates in areas where competitive utility service is not available, regardless of ownership of the monopoly utility provider. Commissioners of PUCs or DPUs are typically chosen through gubernatorial appointment.

Where state regulation and oversight for municipal utilities are minimal, joint-action agencies often step in to serve a similar role. In Massachusetts, the Massachusetts Municipal Wholesale Electric Corporation (MMWEC) is a joint action agency with 20 municipal utility members. MMWEC provides services such as power supply planning, resource development, and support for regulatory compliance and business management. Each individual member of MMWEC is still responsible for providing services directly to their customers but benefits from participation in MMWEC's services.

The power to enable municipalities to generate and sell their own electricity is reserved by the states. Some states allow the creation of new municipal utilities, a process also referred to as *municipalization*. Others, such as Massachusetts, may not allow the creation of entire new municipal utilities but may allow municipalities to engage in *municipal aggregation*. Municipal aggregation is the process by which municipalities aggregate the load of consumers within their borders and secure contracts to serve that load, with the goal of attracting more favorable rates

▷ *Boulder, Colorado: A New Municipal Utility?*

In November 2011, the city of Boulder, Colorado, voted to establish a municipal utility that would displace the city's investor-owned utility provider, Xcel Energy. Local support for the initiative was such that voters also agreed to tax increases to cover the costs of the transition from Xcel to full municipalization of the city's electric and possibly natural gas service.

The main drivers for this vote were frustration with Xcel's high rates and local interest in creating a more renewable and sustainable power portfolio to power the city. Xcel has a primarily coal-fired power portfolio that proved politically unpopular with the residents of Boulder. However, a provision that states that the municipal utility cannot raise rates above those of Xcel could present a practical challenge if the city begins to develop more expensive renewable generation assets.

Before becoming its own municipal utility, the city must first negotiate the purchase of Xcel's "stranded assets," which is primarily distribution infrastructure located within municipal borders and currently owned by the company. Valuation of these assets ranges between $250 million and $1 billion.

There are 29 existing municipal utilities in the state of Colorado, all of which are several decades old. Boulder is one of only a handful of new municipal utilities to be created countrywide. However, growing interest in local control and the possibility of more favorable rates make Boulder a poster child for municipalization. The aftermath of the process will be closely watched by communities that have been considering taking control of some or all of the provision of their public utilities.

for their constituents. A municipal aggregator acts as an agent representing the consumers' interest to choose the most competitive supplier, but the aggregator itself does not supply power. In some cases, state agencies such as the New York Power Authority (NYPA) act as power wholesalers to municipal utilities.

Proponents of municipalization argue that municipal utilities are capable of providing a higher level of service at lower rates. This argument is made complicated by the subsidies paid to existing municipal utilities—which may overemphasize the lower cost burden perceived by customers of municipal utilities—as well as by the fact that the newly created municipal utilities enter a much different market from the one existing utilities experience. Many existing municipal utilities have been around since their municipality began using electric power and had much lower costs of acquiring infrastructure than would a community today negotiating the purchase of distribution assets from an existing private utility provider. In many cases, these early municipal utilities have been grandfathered into exemptions from new regulations, which has kept their operating costs lower than they would be otherwise. However, additional benefits, such as more responsive customer service tailored to a specific community, make municipalization a compelling prospect for many local citizen groups.

Clean Energy

In recent years, municipal utilities have begun to provide renewable energy and energy efficiency services to their customers. Some municipal utilities fund these programs by enacting a small surcharge on their customers' bills, also known as a system benefits charge (SBC). This money is put into a fund used to finance energy efficiency and renewable energy initiatives led by the utility; it may also, or alternatively, be rebated back to the customers through energy-efficient appliance and retrofit rebate programs. Another option is for municipal utilities to offer voluntary "green choice" programs, in which customers can pay a higher rate in order to purchase renewable energy. These additional funds are often used to finance distributed generation projects that are owned by the municipal utility and feed their power mix.

HELEN AKI

Further Reading

City of Boulder, Colorado. "What Is Municipalization?" http://www.bouldercolorado.gov/index.php?option =com_content&view=article&id=14247&Ite mid=4635.

Hirsh, Richard. *Power Loss: The Origins of Deregulation and Restructuring in the American Electric Utility System.* Boston: MIT Press, 1999.

Public Utility Commission of New Hampshire. "About Us." http://www.puc.nh.gov/Home/aboutus.htm.

Public Utility Commission of Ohio. "About the Commission." http://www.puco.ohio.gov/puco/ index.cfm/about-the-commission/.

Snider, Laura. "Boulder Municipalization Fact-Checking: A Look at Colorado's Municipal Utilities." October 15, 2011. http://www .dailycamera.com/ci_19121381.

Tweed, Katherine. "Boulder Fires Xcel, Wants Smart Grid on Its Own Terms." *GreenTechMedia,* November 8, 2011. http://www.greentechmedia .com/articles/read/boulder-wants-smart-grid-on -its-own-terms/.

U.S. Energy Information Administration. "Electric Power Industry Overview 2007." http://www.eia.gov /cneaf/electricity/page/prim2/toc2.html.

See Also: Arkansas; Cooperatives; Grid-Connected Systems; Idaho; Investor-Owned Utilities; Public Utility Holding Company Act of 1935; Public Utility Regulatory Policies Act of 1978.

Myanmar

Official Name: Republic of the Union of Myanmar; also known as Burma.
Category: Geography of Energy.

Summary: Given its vast natural capital and economic growth in southeast Asia, Myanmar is increasing energy trade among neighboring nations and extending its geopolitical importance.

Myanmar, formerly known as Burma, is the second-largest country by geographical size in Southeast Asia and had a population of more than 50 million as of 2009. As a country rich in natural resources, Myanmar has large reserves of offshore natural gas, petroleum, hydropower, coal, and timber. The country's natural gas reserves rank it 40th in the world, with 935 billion cubic feet (285 billion cubic meters) in 2010. The hydropower potential of Myanmar reaches more than 100,000 megawatts. Because of this energy structure, 35 percent of Myanmar's electricity supply is from natural gas, while hydropower comprises another 61 percent. In addition to natural gas and hydropower, Myanmar produces 18,880 barrels of oil per day.

Myanmar is a poor and developing country, however, and 75 percent of its population inhabit rural areas. Myanmar's rural energy consumption depends mainly on fuelwood, charcoal, and biomass. With international aid, such as that of the Technical Cooperation Among Developing Countries program, Myanmar is at the early stages of developing renewable energy sources for rural households, such as solar power, wind power, and geothermal power. The government has introduced photovoltaic systems to rural areas for generating electricity from solar energy and has reduced the consumption of fuelwoods to protect forests.

Energy Governance and Industry

As one of the world's first oil producers, Myanmar started its oil exports in 1853, under British colonial rule. During the reign of the Konbaung Dynasty, foreign oil companies such as Rangoon Oil Company and Burmah Oil Company dominated the Myanmar oil industry. With independence in 1962, the military came to power and the regime claimed ownership of Myanmar's energy industry and created the Ministry of Energy and state-owned energy enterprises. Over the past 50 years, a series of agencies have been established to oversee energy sectors: the Ministry of Electric Power, the Ministry of Mines, the Ministry of Forestry, the Ministry of Science and Technology, and the Ministry of Co-operatives. At the same time, National State Enterprises were founded to operate Myanmar's energy markets. The Myanmar Oil and Gas Enterprise was established in 1963 and is responsible for the upstream petroleum subsector. The Myanmar Petrochemical Enterprise was assigned to oversee petroleum refining and transportation, and the Myanmar Petroleum Products Enterprise takes responsibility for market distribution of petroleum products.

Myanmar's government kept foreign energy operators out until the late 1980s. Because of the liberalization of the oil and gas sector in Myanmar, in partnership with Myanmar's national energy enterprises, foreign investors have been allowed to exploit natural resources under the Union of Myanmar Foreign Investment Law developed in 1988. By 2007, nine foreign companies were involved in 16 onshore blocks to explore new areas, to enhance recovery from existing fields, to reactivate fields where production has been suspended, and to produce. These companies include Daewoo of South Korea, China National Offshore Oil Corporation, China National Petroleum Corporation, Oil and Natural Gas Corporation of India, Sun Itera Oil and Gas of Russia, Danford Equities Corporation of Australia, and Gail and Rimbunan of Malaysia.

Geopolitical Influence

Myanmar's geopolitical position and resources determine its importance in southeast Asia. Myanmar is strategically located on the western access to the Strait of Malacca, which bridges the Indian and Pacific Oceans. More than half of the oil tankers in the world travel this route from the Mideast and north Africa to several of the world's largest economies: China, Japan, South Korea, and Malaysia. Myanmar does not have good trade relations with Western countries because of economic sanctions on Myanmar's military regime. However, Myanmar is a member of the World Trade Organization, the Association of Southeast Asian Nations, and the

Bay of Bengal Initiative for Multi-Sectoral Technical and Economic Cooperation. Myanmar shares strong trade relations with its neighboring countries, especially with regard to energy and natural resources trade. With increasing economic development in this region, bordering nations are trying to improve ties with Myanmar's military junta in order to compete with Myanmar's natural capital.

China, with long-standing cultural and historical ties to Myanmar, has been providing Myanmar with development through different channels and at different levels. China's investment accounts for 11.5 percent of Myanmar's total foreign direct investment. As China's economy grows, China needs to secure its oil and gas supply, and Myanmar is an extremely important supplier. First, 80 percent of the oil shipped to China now passes through the Strait or Malacca. However, this is a region known for terrorist threats and alternative political interests. In order to cut costs and reduce threats, China is building a pipeline from the Bay of Bengal via Myanmar to Yunnan Province in China. China's state-owned companies are operating this multibillion-dollar Trans Myanmar-China Pipeline. The project is scheduled to be completed in 2013. Second, Myanmar provides China with tremendous gas and oil supplies.

Unlike China, India does not have strong ties with Myanmar, largely because of India's continuing support for the pro-democracy movement in Myanmar. However, relations have changed rapidly as India searches for energy security to support its economic development and China exerts its dominance in Myanmar. Importing gas from Myanmar has been a key priority for India.

Although Myanmar and Thailand have experienced historical border disputes, Myanmar is the largest gas supplier for Thailand. Thailand imports an estimated 60 percent of Myanmar's gas. Most important, 70 percent of electricity in Thailand is generated by natural gas, 30 percent of which is imported from Myanmar.

Myanmar and Bangladesh have maintained positive relations throughout history. However, the two countries have had a longtime dispute over a gas-rich stretch of the Bay of Bengal. In 2008, after Myanmar began exploring for gas there, Bangladesh deployed four naval ships to the disputed waters. As Bangladesh continues to experience increasing energy demands from its manufacturing sector, energy conflicts between the two countries are likely to continue.

Xiaoliang Yang

Further Reading

Central Intelligence Agency. "East and Southeast Asia: Burma." In *The World Factbook*. https://www.cia .gov/library/publications/the-world-factbook/geos/ bm.html.

"Insight: Myanmar's Power Struggle Endangers Economic Boom." Reuters (April 16, 2012). http:// in.reuters.com/article/2012/04/16/myanmar-energy- power-electricity-idINDEE83F03X20120416.

International Energy Agency. "Beyond the OECD: Myanmar." http://www.iea.org/country/ n_country.asp?COUNTRY_CODE=MM& Submit=Submit.

"A Look at Myanmar's History as an Emerging Energy Supplier." *Wall Street Journal*. http://online.wsj .com/article/SB125710430865521395.html.

Myanmar Ministry of Energy. "Energy Sector in Myanmar." http://www.energy.gov.mm/.

U.S. Energy Information Administration. "Country Analysis Brief: Burma (Myanmar)." http://www.eia.gov/countries/country-data.cfm ?fips=BM.

See Also: Bangladesh; Biomass Energy; China; Energy Poverty; India; Natural Gas; Oil and Petroleum; Photovoltaics.

Namibia

Official Name: Republic of Namibia.
Category: Geography of Energy.

Summary: Namibia imports about half of its electricity needs and all its liquid fuel, coal, and gas. The country has abundant yet undeveloped renewable energy resources and is the world's fourth-largest producer of uranium.

In the two decades following Namibia's independence in 1990, the country's energy sector has undergone significant change. Today, the White Paper on Energy Policy, the Electricity Act, and various petroleum acts shape the energy sector's policy and regulatory environment.

Namibia's Ministry of Mines and Energy is the custodian of the country's energy sector. The Electricity Control Board is the electricity sector's regulator, managing the issuance of operating licenses. Other electricity sector participants include the state-owned utility NamPower, regional electricity distributors, local authorities, municipalities, large power users such as mines, and private consumers.

The National Petroleum Corporation of Namibia and several private-sector companies are responsible for the import and distribution of petroleum products; Namibia remains entirely dependent on these imports. Uranium is mined at the world's third-largest uranium mine, Rio Tinto's Rössing uranium mine, and by Paladin Energy at Langer Heinrich mine, while the French industrial conglomerate AREVA is developing the Trekkopje mine.

Namibia's long-term national vision statement, Vision 2030, foresees the country's transformation into an industrialized nation with a natural resources-based export sector and skills-based industrial and service sectors using market-oriented production systems. Reliable, affordable, and accessible energy is a critical prerequisite to accomplish this vision.

Electricity Generation

In 2010, Namibia had three electricity-generating power stations: Ruacana is a 249-megawatt run-of-the-river hydroelectric power station on the Kunene River bordering Angola; a fourth turbine, adding 92 megawatts, was planned to begin operation in 2012. The coal-fired Van Eck Power Station on the northern outskirts of Namibia's capital, Windhoek, has a capacity of 120 megawatts. Commissioned in 1972, it is expensive to operate

Wikimedia

Since the country's independence, Namibia has made substantial progress in electrifying rural areas, yet less than one-third of the rural population have access to electricity, such as this Himba village north of Opuwo.

and used only to bridge short-term supply gaps. Similarly, the fuel-oil-fired Paratus Power Station at Walvis Bay, which has a capacity of 24 megawatts. The new Anixas diesel-powered station at Walvis Bay will add some 22 megawatts and serve as an emergency standby generation plant.

Namibia's total installed electrical generation capacity is insufficient to meet the country's demand for electrical energy. Imports, mainly from South Africa and Zimbabwe, make up the shortfall. Transmission networks link Namibia to suppliers across the border, adding a capacity of some 600 megawatts. In addition to the transmission line to South Africa, the newly built Caprivi Link provides a northern alternative for electricity imports and exports and connects Namibia with Zambia, Zimbabwe, and the eastern parts of the Southern African Power Pool.

Electricity Sector

Namibia's national electricity utility, NamPower, is responsible for generation, trading, and transmission. It also fulfills the role of system operator, balancing electricity supplies with the prevailing demand. All electricity imports and exports, as well as wheeling arrangements using Namibia's extensive transmission grid, are managed by NamPower.

Regional electricity distributors (REDs), some municipalities, and local authorities are responsible for the supply and distribution of electricity to consumers. In 2010, three REDs were established and fully operational: NORED, which has operated since 2002, serves the country's northern regions, while CENORED and ErongoRED were established in 2005 and distribute electricity to consumers in north-central and western Namibia.

There have been no new entrants into Namibia's electricity sector. Reasons include low electricity tariffs, sectorwide structural impediments, the considerable leverage that the country's monopoly generation and transmission provider has, an absence of national generation targets and incentives, and low electrical loads, with a widely dispersed population necessitating high infrastructure investments.

Since independence, Namibia has made substantial progress in electrifying rural areas, yet less than one-third of the rural population have access to electricity. Economic considerations prohibit the country's complete electrification by way of conventional grid electricity. Off-grid technologies powered by renewable energies could provide much-needed energy in areas far away from the national grid. Although sustainable rural energization models have yet to be found, the need for them may offer room for entrepreneurial action.

Namibia's electricity sector faces several challenges, which include safeguarding the security of supplies, expanding the national generation portfolio, introducing cost-reflective tariffs, attracting new sector participants, sustaining the operations of the REDs, electrifying rural areas, and developing Namibia's rich renewable energy resources. Rapid development, particularly in the country's mining sector, and ongoing southern African capacity constraints necessitate urgent investments in local electricity generation capacity.

Renewables and Uranium

In 2010, Namibia consumed some 3.7 terawatt-hours of electrical energy. The country has been meeting approximately one-half of its electrical energy requirements through imports: Also in 2010, some 12 terawatt-hours were used in the form of petroleum products, all of which were imported. An estimated 2.5 terawatt-hours of imported coal was used, while biomass contributed some 2 terawatt-hours; other renewables contributed only a few gigawatt-hours. Namibia has an abundance of renewable energy resources, including solar, biomass, and wind. In addition, there are seemingly plentiful potential indigenous energy resources, including geothermal, wave, and tidal energy. This rich natural endowment constitutes a national comparative advantage that awaits decisive development. Policy has not provided the desired impetus to stimulate much-needed advances, but fresh mind-sets and focused incentives could unlock the country's sustainable riches.

In 2010, Namibia produced some 4,500 tons of uranium, which was exported for further processing and use in nuclear power stations abroad. As the fourth-largest producer of uranium, the country exported almost 10 times the amount of energy that was consumed in that year.

DETLOF VON OERTZEN

Further Reading

"Namibia." In *Encyclopedia of Global Warming and Climate Change*, edited by S. George Philander. Thousand Oaks, CA: Sage, 2008.

Namibia Energy Policy, Laws and Regulation Handbook. Washington, DC: International Business Publications, 2008.

U.S. Energy Information Administration. "Country Analysis Brief: Namibia." http://205.254.135.7/countries/country-data.cfm?fips=WA.

See Also: Biomass Energy; Oil and Petroleum; Rural Electrification; Solar Energy; South Africa; Uranium; Utilities; Wind Resources.

Nationalization

Category: Business of Energy.
Summary: Nationalization, the act of placing assets under government ownership, is a critical issue in the energy world. Few sectors of a country's economy are seen as more strategically important, or more publicly visible, as natural energy resources and infrastructure.

Nationalization, the process of placing assets—both hard and contractual—under the majority or complete ownership of the government of a country, creates a challenge when the assets were previously owned by private-sector actors, as opposed to being recently discovered and immediately nationalized without an act of appropriation. Nationalization's purpose is often to empower elected officials and satisfy popular will, but the risk of appropriation can dissuade foreign investment, denying a country hard currency, technical know-how, technology transfer, and external market access. The threat of nationalization increases the risks that foreign investors must consider when engaging in energy projects.

The nationalization of energy resources—whether they be upstream assets, such as oil and natural gas fields, or downstream assets, such as refineries, pipelines, shipping terminals, and gas stations—inherently involve major capital assets, and frequently large sums of money, whether hard cash or future revenue streams. The contending parties sometimes settle their differences through international arbitration bodies. Varying examples of nationalization have occurred in such energy resource host countries as Mexico, Venezuela, Bolivia, Iran, and Russia.

Mexico

Mexico, a leading supplier of petroleum to the United States, originally nationalized its energy resources in the revolutionary period of 1917. Article 27 of the 1917 Mexican constitution gives the government a permanent and unalienable right to all of the nation's subsoil resources. In 1923, in the Bucareli Agreements, the United States and Mexico confirmed they would regard titles held by foreign oil companies as concessions by the Mexican government—as opposed to outright ownership claims.

On this basis, president Lázaro Cárdenas nationalized the petroleum industry in 1938, in what became celebrated as the "expropriation." As a result, Mexico forged a state monopoly in its energy sector, extending from exploration, production, and refining of its crude oil and natural gas to chemical businesses, marketing, and distribution. The international oil companies reacted with a boycott, and pressured governments to comply. In 1943, Mexico and the oil firms settled—driven in part by the overriding energy and trade needs of the Allies engulfed in fighting World War II—with a payment by Mexico of $24 million in compensation for the seized assets. Still, Mexico found itself shut off from many of the world's best technological minds, methods, and equipment—and financing—well into the 1950s.

Mexico's state-owned oil and natural gas company, PEMEX, despite having command over extensive natural resources, was plagued by inefficiencies and corruption, in part due to lack of shareholder oversight and access to foreign expertise. The problems were severe enough to stymie Mexico's broader economy; a range of successful reforms was enacted in the 1980s—and PEMEX itself was restructured in the wake of the horrific 1992 natural gas explosion in Guadalajara that killed hundreds. Over time, the Mexican government and PEMEX relaxed their control. A partial denationalization came about. In the 1990s, PEMEX divested many of its petrochemicals plants. Private investment was also permitted in parts of the downstream natural gas business.

Venezuela

Like Mexico, Venezuela is among the leading suppliers of petroleum products to the United States. In the 1990s, it allowed some private investment in its oil industry, and foreign companies were let in to form "strategic associations" to manage specific oil fields. As of 2006, approximately 23 percent of total oil production was handled in this manner.

However, in April 2006, Venezuelan president Hugo Chávez announced that Venezuela was nationalizing the oil fields that were managed by foreign companies. The government's shares in these projects, therefore, rose from 40 percent to 60 percent. This is an example of partial nationalization, as opposed to outright seizure of all privately owned assets. Nevertheless, even partial nationalization can deter future investment and hobble a host country's production.

On May 1, 2007, Chávez fully nationalized the remaining private projects in Venezuela's oil-rich Orinoco Belt. The move was estimated to have impacted $30 billion in projects and included the privatization of assets from ExxonMobil, British Petroleum (BP), and Norway's Statoil.

Venezuela's state-owned natural gas and oil company is Petróleos de Venezuela, S.A. (PDVSA). In June 2010, the U.S. oil rig firm Helmerich and Payne learned that its 11 oil rigs in Venezuela would be seized by PDVSA. The U.S. company, which had done business with Venezuela for more than 50 years, said PDVSA owed $40 million in back payments at the time of the seizure. PDVSA asserted that Helmerich and Payne had balked at renegotiating their rates when world oil prices plunged in 2009; the rigs had gone idle. In late 2011, the private company sued for breach of contract.

Bolivia

Bolivian president Evo Morales, an ally of Chávez, has nationalized a series of upstream and downstream resources since taking office in 2006. Such initiatives include seizure of natural gas fields, hydroelectric and other power generating facilities, and in 2012 the country's electric grid. These steps were a reversal of the privatization of much of this same infrastructure in Bolivia during the 1990s.

Bolivia's state-owned natural gas and oil company is Yacimientos Petrolíferos Fiscales Bolivianos (YPFB). Although it is a relatively poor, landlocked nation, Bolivia and YPFB control one of the larger natural gas resources in South America. Since major investments began in the 1990s, gas output has zoomed, to 520 billion cubic feet in 2010. More than 80 percent is exported; chief customers include Brazil and Argentina.

Iran

Nationalization of energy resources is certainly not exclusive to Latin American countries. Iran originally nationalized its oil operations in the 1950s, under the leadership of its head of state, prime minister Mohammed Mossadegh, who joined a long line of Persian political figures in denouncing the practices of the Anglo-Iranian Oil Company (a predecessor of BP) in Iran. The expropriation took place in 1951. Stung by the loss of this strategic and lucrative asset, the United Kingdom organized a boycott of Iranian oil. The resulting cutoff of much-needed hard cash hamstrung the government of Iran; a coup d'etat was precipitated in 1953, returning to power the dictator Mohammed-Reza Shah Pahlavi (who would in turn be ousted by the Iranian Islamic Revolution of 1979). In the aftermath, a new oil development consortium was established with eight oil companies participating, the National Iranian Oil Company (NIOC). Although Anglo-Iranian had hoped to regain its full mastery of Iran's industry, it settled for a 40 percent share of the restructured enterprise, the largest of any of the participants.

This is an example of a temporary nationalization scheme. The cycle turned again, however, as with the 1979 revolution all assets of NIOC were nationalized. Today, NIOC is one of the world's largest oil and gas companies. There are some private firms operating in Iran's fossil fuels sector, mainly in the downstream operations segment. Ironically, Iran has several joint ventures with BP, including a 50/50 operation in the North Sea, the Rhum field—however, production there was shut down in December 2010 in accordance with European Union sanctions against Iran.

Russia

Russia was the world's top oil producer in 2009 and is estimated to host the world's largest natural gas reserves, the second-largest coal reserves, and the eighth-largest crude oil reserves. The Russian gas titan Gazprom was created in the transformation of the Soviet Ministry of Gas Industry into a 100 percent state-owned company in 1989. Following the Soviet collapse, the structure of Gazprom was altered again; in 1993 shares were offered for sale.

In this semi-privatization, state control of shares dropped eventually to 38 percent. However, this trend was reversed through purchases—nationalization with compensation—and since 2005 Russia has owned 50.1 percent of Gazprom.

Brian McFarland

Further Reading

Alvarez, Cesar J., and Stephanie Hanson. "Venezuela's Oil-Based Economy." February 9, 2009. http://www.cfr.org/economics/venezuelas-oil-based-economy/p12089.

"Bolivia Nationalizes Four Power Companies." *The Washington Post*. http://www.washingtonpost.com/wp-dyn/content/article/2010/05/01/AR2010050102858.html.

Council on Foreign Relations. "Venezuela's Oil-Based Economy." http://www.cfr.org/economics/venezuelas-oil-based-economy/p12089.

Merrill, Tim L., and Ramon Miro, eds. *Mexico: A Country Study*. Washington, DC: U.S. Government Printing Office for the Library of Congress, 1996.

"The Nationalization of Energy Resources and Investment Incentives." *The Economist*, May 9, 2006. http://economistsview.typepad.com/economistsview/2006/05/the_nationaliza.html.

PBS NewsHour. "Venezuela Takes Control of Final Privately Run Oil Fields." http://www.pbs.org/newshour/updates/latin_america/janjune07/venezuela_05-01.html.

"Venezuela to Nationalise U.S. Oil Rigs." *Financial Times*. http://www.ft.com/cms/s/0/6a1caee4-7f49-11df-84a3-00144feabdc0.html#axzz1aPqMIRpG.

See Also: Bolivia; Iran; Mexico; Risk Management; Russia; Venezuela.

Natural Energy Flows

Category: Fundamentals of Energy.
Summary: Natural energy flows are sources of energy that do not need to be processed with additional energy but, rather, naturally flow

through the world and need only be harvested or otherwise put to work.

The term *natural energy flows* was popularized in environmentalism by the Hannover Principles, a document drafted by William McDonough and Michael Braungart in 1992, in anticipation of the Expo 2000 at Hannover, Germany. Natural energy flows are those sources of energy that are naturally flowing through the world already and need only be harvested or otherwise put to work; they include the flow of running water and the movement of the seas, the kinetic energy of wind, the solar radiation of sunshine, and the geothermal energies beneath the surface of the Earth. They are not coequal with renewable energy sources, which would include biofuel.

Constant Movement

Massive amounts of energy flow along the surface of the Earth constantly. The sun radiates some 28×10^{32} calories of energy every year, about 13×10^{23} calories of which are intercepted by the Earth. Of those intercepted calories, approximately one-third are reflected back into space. (This quantity, called the albedo, varies locally according to weather conditions and type of surface coverage; snow-covered land reflects the most energy, as much as 90 percent, while ocean surfaces reflect less than 10 percent, and cloud cover also influences albedo.) The rest of the solar energy is absorbed by the Earth or its atmosphere. Almost half is converted into heat, some of which powers the water (hydrologic) cycle of evaporation and precipitation. A small amount of sunlight, about 0.2 percent, is converted into the energy of wind, water currents, and waves. Even less than that, 0.1 percent, is used by photosynthesis. A tiny amount of the Earth's energy (tiny, that is, relative to this solar energy) comes from other sources, the geothermal heat emanating from the Earth's core and the tidal energy resulting from the gravitational interactions between the Earth and the moon. By contrast, sunlight accounts for tremendous amounts of Earth's energy and leads to most other forms. For example, photosynthesis by plants turn solar energy into chemical energy

and stores it as carbohydrates in the plant, which over a geologic timescale when buried under great pressures eventually becomes gas and petroleum deposits. Thus, even when humans are not harnessing natural energy flows, these flows are nevertheless the source of most of our energy.

McDonough was a New York City architect; Braungart, a German chemist. Together they collaborated on a sustainable design they called "cradle to cradle." The Hannover Principles articulated guidelines for the design of objects and buildings. The principles focused on interdependence with the natural world, the consequences of design decisions, waste and life-cycle assessments, the interrelationship between sustainability and human rights, and the responsible use of energy. With regard to natural energy flows, the document says, "Rely on natural energy flows. Human designs should, like the living world, derive their creative forces from perpetual solar income. Incorporate this energy efficiently and safely for responsible use."

McDonough has elaborated on this in later writing—indeed, he and Braungart have spent much of their subsequent careers refining and elaborating on the ideas in the Hannover Principles. In particular, McDonough has downplayed the idea of interpreting the directive to "rely on natural energy flows" in a quantitative way, and he does not appear to support renewable energy quotas or quantified energy efficiency goals. Instead, he and Braungart call for a fundamentally new approach to design, not simply a more efficient version of current designs. He has proposed buildings that sequester carbon, fix nitrogen, and make oxygen and distilled water while powered by solar energy; in general, the Hannover Principles seem primarily focused on solar power among the renewable energy sources.

Energy Management

The call for reliance on natural energy flows has been referred to as energy management, analogous to waste or water management. It is concerned with more than just the sustainability of its energy sources, in other words. Using natural energy flows reinforces and explicates humankind's connection to the planet by thriving from

▷ *The Benefits of Harnessing Natural Energy Flows*

The benefit of harnessing natural energy flows is that, to put it simply, they are a source of energy already present. Using them to generate electricity (or to provide for heating and other needs) neither uses them up nor diverts them from some other purpose. Harnessing wind power does not, in theory, have a significant effect on weather patterns; it does not alter the course of the wind. Using solar power does not prevent that same sunlight from warming the Earth and its inhabitants, illuminating the day, or providing energy for the photosynthesis of plants. These are not energy sources whose use requires that they be dug out of the Earth and destroyed or cause other destruction. Even biofuel requires an act of destruction, albeit of something that can be replaced, unlike fossil fuels. Relying on natural energy flows also fits into the Hannover Principles' call to eliminate waste; there is essentially no waste product in the use of wind, solar, hydro-, or geothermal power. (There is waste heat and lost energy in solar power, which can be assumed not to count.)

change and the need for proactive policies to reduce anthropogenic emissions, has also insisted that there is no known energy technology with negligible environmental impact. Windmills may harm avian life; hydropower frequently disrupts ecosystems; reservoirs and solar collectors need land to occupy; and some collection of geothermal energy is nonrenewable.

Bill Kte'pi

Further Reading

McDonough, William, and Michael Braungart. *Cradle to Cradle: Remaking the Way We Make Things*. New York: North Point Press, 2002.

McDonough, William, and Michael Braungart. *The Hannover Principles: Design for Sustainability*. New York: W. McDonough Architects, 2003.

Rogers, Elizabeth, and Thomas Kostigen. *The Green Book: The Everyday Guide to Saving the Planet One Simple Step at a Time*. Foreword by Cameron Diaz and William McDonough. New York: Three Rivers Press, 2007.

See Also: Fundamentals of Energy; Hydropower; Russia; Solar Energy; Solar Thermal Systems; Thermodynamics; Tidal Power; Wind Resources.

its already extant mechanisms, such as wind and water currents. The usual view of advocates is that natural energy flows alone—indeed, even solar power alone—are sufficient to meet humans' energy needs and that not attempting to use them to meet those needs is letting them go to waste.

There has been some suggestion that the use of natural energy flows may have environmental consequences that have not yet been made clear because their use is not yet widespread enough to understand the consequences of their use. John Holdren, one of President Bill Clinton's science advisers and Director of the Office of Science and Technology Policy under President Barack Obama, while publishing extensively on climate

Natural Gas

Category: Energy Resources.
Summary: Natural gas is largely comprised of methane and is one of the three major fossil fuels used to generate energy. Natural gas may lead to the development of economically viable and efficient alternatives to fossil fuels.

Natural gas is one of the three major fossil fuels currently used to generate energy. In 2010, it was the fastest-growing fossil fuel in use, providing approximately 25 percent of the world's energy consumption. However, uses for natural gas vary between less developed and more developed nations; the former using natural gas largely for household heating and cooking and the latter for industry, electricity production, residential uses, and a small percentage of transportation fuels.

Natural gas consists primarily of methane and other hydrocarbon compounds. It is odorless and colorless and is often found associated with other fossil fuels, such as coal or petroleum beds. However, there are nonassociated stores of natural gas in isolated beds. Like other fossil fuels, natural gas is a highly combustible substance that, with recent infrastructure developments, is relatively easy to transport and store. Its combustibility makes it a highly effective resource for generating energy and heat.

The Creation Process

It is generally believed that two processes create two types of natural gas. Biogenic gas is created when bacteria decompose organic material at shallow depths below the Earth's surface. For example, these gases can be observed when wetlands are disturbed and "swamp gas" is released. Thermogenic gas develops deep underground, resulting from compression and heat. Holes must be drilled to access thermogenic gas deposits. Once accessed, in most cases, the natural gas must then be pumped to the surface. In a few cases, however, the gas will flow freely because of natural pressure. Both thermogenic and biogenic gases are created from biomass that has been buried in anaerobic environments. There is also a third theory that nonassociated gas stores exist far below the Earth's surface, which were created during the formation of the Earth.

One of the earliest known extractions and uses of natural gas by human society occurred during the Han dynasty (200 b.c.e.). Chinese laborers drilled for natural gas with bamboo and used it to boil sea water for salt extraction. In the late 1700s, cities and towns in Britain used natural gas for lighting. In the United States, the first known intentional drilling for natural gas occurred in New York State in the 1820s. However, it was not until the invention of the Bunsen burner in 1885—allowing for more conventional uses such as cooking and heating—that natural gas became a viable option for generating energy around the world.

Nonrenewable Resource

Natural gas is considered a nonrenewable resource because recoverable reserves are being exhausted at a rate that is a tiny fraction of the amount of time needed to create them. Russia, the United States, and Canada produce 45 percent of the world's natural gas, and the United States and Russia consume nearly 38 percent. If extracted with contemporary technologies and known costs, current reserve-to-production ratio estimates (R/P ratio, measured in years) suggest there are enough conventional reserves to satisfy society's consumption needs for the next 60 years. The vast majority of these known reserves are located in Russia and the Middle East. The largest deposits are in Russia, where eight of the top 10 natural gas fields are located. The largest conventional gas field is the Urengoy Field in the Western Siberian Basin, east of the Gulf of Ob, within the Arctic Circle. The Urengoy Gas Field was discovered in the 1960s and holds an estimated total of 8 trillion cubic meters (280 trillion cubic feet).

Historically, natural gas was considered a low-value by-product found interspersed with oil and coal deposits. Until the early 20th century, natural gas was too inefficient for use as a large-scale energy resource. Because of a lack of technological development and insufficient infrastructure, producers could not get natural gas to markets in a feasible manner, and it was often burned off or allowed to vent into the air on site. Natural gas production remained slow during the industrial era, until post–World War II, when improvements in pipeline construction (and hence fuel transport) and safer infrastructure made natural gas technologically possible and economical. In 1937, after an undetected leak caused an explosion at the New London School in Texas, killing at least 300 people, minute amounts of odorants (such as mercaptan) were added to retail natural gas. This allows consumers to detect leaks in order to prevent fires or explosions.

Impact of World War II

During World War II, large pipelines were built in the United States from Texas to the northeast states to ensure energy security for the country during wartime. These pipelines were known as "Big Inch" and "Little Big Inch," and were responsible for transporting more than 350 million barrels of crude oil and refined products to the northeast before the war's end in the summer of 1945. After the end of the war, there were debates to determine if the pipelines should continue to transport oil or be converted to transport natural gas. The issue was settled in 1946, when an influential coal miner strike motivated the Senate and War Assets Administration to award the Tennessee Gas and Transmission company a lease to supply natural gas commercially. This transition made natural gas readily available to the northeastern United States, where there was a high-demand home heating market.

A Costly Endeavor

Although current techniques (such as seismology) have reduced the costs of finding, extracting, and processing the fuel, natural gas production is an uncertain, complex, and costly endeavor. Natural gas straight out of the well is often accompanied by water and liquid hydrocarbons, including benzene, toluene, ethylbenzene, and xylene (BTEX), hydrogen sulfide (H2S), and other organic compounds that must be removed. To make "pipeline quality" natural gas, it must be passed through units (called heater treaters) with chemical substances that absorb the by-product water from the gas. Once the chemical extraction solution is saturated with water, the heaters raise temperatures to boil off the water. When cool, these large volumes of by-product water are pumped to a "produced water" tank. The chemical separating fluid, which has a higher boiling point than water, cools, and is recycled into reuse. By-product oily substances that were produced with the gas and water become volatile and recondense in a separate holding tank. This "condensate water" is commonly re-injected underground or hauled offsite to waste evaporation pits. In some cases, temporary pits are constructed, which hold waste materials and drilling mud so they can be reused through the drilling process. In order to reclaim drilling pads and sites, reserve pits must be drained and covered with topsoil or a capping material within a month of drilling completion.

After natural gas is processed and impurities are removed, it is often liquefied and compressed for storage and transport. Storage is an important issue, as most gas is used for heating during winter. A refrigeration process is used to condense the gas into liquified natural gas (LNG) by cooling it to minus 260 degrees Fahrenheit. LNG is then stored in insulated tanks, specially engineered to hold a cold-temperature liquid. LNG storage tanks are typically double-walled, composed of an outer wall of thick concrete and an inner wall made of steel. Between the walls is a thick layer of insulation. Often such storage facilities are underground to increase insulation. LNG will boil off and evaporate as natural gas, no matter how efficient the storage or refrigeration. This gas is then removed from the tank and used as a fuel on site, or refrigerated again to return it to the liquid state and placed back into the storage tank. If no pipeline is available to immediately transport gas, LNG also makes natural gas easier to store and transport. When LNG is transported (by train, truck, or ocean tanker) to its destination, or when it is removed from storage, it must be regasified. Regasification is accomplished by heating LNG and allowing it to evaporate back into its gas state at typical temperature and pressure conditions. Regasification is usually done at a facility where the gas can be placed into storage or directly into a pipeline for transport.

Regasification Terminals

The two types of regasification terminals are called *liquefaction terminals* and *regasification terminals*. Liquefaction terminals, which turn natural gas into liquid, are on the export end of transactions. Regasification terminals, which turn LNG back into natural gas, are on the import side of operations. Currently, most natural gas is transported domestically within enormous infrastructure-intensive pipeline networks. Natural gas pipelines are often constructed of carbon steel to withstand the extremely high pressure of transporting compressed gas over large distances. Gas pipelines typically have small gathering systems that are composed of small diameter pipelines (2–8 inches). These "gathering lines" tap into gas fields and gather to larger "trunk lines," which

▷ *Hydraulic Fracturing ("Fracking")*

Hydraulic fracturing for natural gas—colloquially known as fracking—is an extraction technique developed in the late 1940s to access otherwise inaccessible fuel deposits locked, or interbedded, within geologic strata, such as coal or shale beds. Once costly and inefficient, the technique has experienced a resurgence, as the United States is currently undergoing the largest domestic energy boom in its history, supported in part by hydraulic fracturing for natural gas. The process involves drilling a horizontal well into shale or coal deposits and then creating a minor earthquake by injecting large volumes of water (from 1.5 million to 8 million gallons of water per "frack"), sand, proppants, and lubricants into the well. This fracturing event forces small cracks in shale deposits and forces previously inaccessible natural gas to the surface. Internationally, 80 percent of all new natural gas wells are expected to utilize some form of hydraulic fracturing.

In the United States, exploration and drilling firms are targeting the Marcellus Shale in the northeast for hydraulic fracturing. Experts suggest the Marcellus Shale is the nation's most productive natural gas stratum, estimated to contain 1.9 trillion cubic feet of gas underlying 54,000 square miles across the states of New York, Pennsylvania, Ohio, Maryland, and West Virginia. However, hydraulic fracturing technology depends heavily on the use of undisclosed types and amounts of toxic chemicals. These chemicals, as well as combustion materials and other gases, are released in the hydraulic fracturing process and could pose acute and chronic long-term health hazards to the surrounding environment and public health. Additionally, some researchers believe that these substances may endanger long-term water and air quality. Accounts of contaminated drinking water wells are emerging in the vicinity of hydraulic fracturing sites in Wyoming, Texas, and Colorado, and many residents speculate that fracturing is the culprit. However, as desires for rural economic growth and cheaper energy sources are creating strong demand for natural gas drilling, sharp tensions are developing between proponents and opponents over the impacts of hydraulic fracturing. The U.S. Environmental Protection Agency and U.S. states (such as Pennsylvania and New York) are currently reviewing policies related to hydraulic fracturing.

Detail of the Marcellus Shale drilling tower in the state of Pennsylvania.

Wikimedia

typically have a 8–48-inch diameter and are large cross-national or international transmission pipelines. Natural gas as a final product is delivered through another set of local pipelines directly to consumers. For example, the United States has natural gas gathering lines over a length of 20,000 miles, and additionally, 278,000 miles of natural gas transmission lines. The Federal Energy Regulatory Commission (FERC) regulates natural gas in the United States. Their primary responsibilities are to regulate transmission and sale, approve facility siting, render penalties for FERC energy market violations, oversee environmental matters, and administer reports.

Deregulation

Since the mid-1980s, the demand for, and production of, natural gas has risen significantly. This is largely due to deregulation, geopolitical dynamics, rising energy demands, and new technologies. In this context, natural gas is often characterized as an energy source that can potentially bridge society's current fossil fuel dependence to the development of economically viable alternatives to fossil fuels. Natural gas burns much cleaner than other fossil fuels and the development of infrastructure and technology has made it much easier to extract and transport. In the early part of the 21st century, T. Boone Pickens (an oil tycoon and prominent alternative energy promoter) advocated the development of natural gas-powered automobiles in the United States. Pickens claimed that by transitioning the transportation fleet to natural gas, U.S. society could fight the rising costs of oil with a smaller environmental impact, particularly in terms of reducing air polluting auto emissions.

Deregulation is a particularly important aspect of natural gas use. Natural gas has been regulated since the mid-1800s, when U.S. Congress passed national-scale regulations in the form of the Natural Gas Act (1938) in order to manage interstate natural gas transmission and control monopolies. By the 1970s, however, many consumer states in the midwest were experiencing shortages, despite adequate levels of supply in producer states. To remedy this, congress passed the Natural Gas Policy Act (1978), which created a single natural gas market and equalized supply and demand. This market-based approach was further embraced by FERC Orders (436 and 636), which unbundled transport, storage, and marketing, resulting in more consumer choice. As a result, prices decreased for large commercial and industrial customers but declined only slightly for residential consumers.

Traded Commodities

In the United States, a large percentage of natural gas is traded on the New York Mercantile Exchange (NYMEX) located in New York City. NYMEX is the exchange for energy products, metals, and other commodities, and transactions reflect the prices of traded commodities. Thus, U.S. gas prices are closely correlated with trading on NYMEX. Currently, the price of natural gas in the United States is significantly lower than in the rest of the world. Therefore the United States is poised to be a global exporter of natural gas, particularly for firms with access to LNG export terminals.

Global Benefits

Globally, the popularity of natural gas as a fuel around the world has initiated numerous large-scale and high-profile international natural gas pipeline projects in Asia, Europe, and North America. Today, LNG is exported from many regions where natural gas production exceeds consumption, such the Middle East and northern Africa, Russia, Trinidad and Tobago, Australia, and several southeast Asian countries. The low price of natural gas as a commodity often offsets the costs incurred when building liquefaction plants, converting the gas into LNG, and transporting the product to distant markets. Currently, the United States is the largest gas producer in the world but has almost no capacity for exporting gas. The U.S. Department of Energy is therefore promoting the construction of liquefied natural gas export terminals, and many new LNG export terminals are expected to be built in ports across the country. The larger markets for LNG include South Korea, Japan, and Taiwan. These are countries with densely-populated areas and little to no available domestic fossil fuel sources. Having access to this global LNG market has provided a relatively clean-burning fuel that can be easily distributed in pipelines.

It should be noted, however, that there are a relatively limited amount of remaining conventional deposits of natural gas and since it is a nonrenewable resource, it is not a suitable long-term substitute for oil and coal. While several large deposits of natural gas have been located throughout the world, experts believe that the majority of proven conventional reserves have been accessed. Current estimates of conventional natural gas reserves vary, but can be approximated at around 187 trillion cubic meters (Tm3). Additionally, although natural gas is considered the cleanest of the three major fossil fuels, producing it often releases methane (the main constituent of natural gas and a potent greenhouse gas) directly into the atmosphere. Further, burning natural gas emits carbon dioxide (CO_2), the most prolific greenhouse gas implicated in global climate change. Natural gas production and combustion, therefore, impact water quality, air quality, and contribute to global warming.

There are, however, several other "unconventional" deposits of natural gas located around the world that have traditionally been considered cost-prohibitive to extract. Growing demand and improved technology have increased the potential of extracting and producing unconventional natural gas deposits. The majority of these unconventional deposits are located in interbedded geologic layers such as in coalbeds and shales, mixed with heavy crude oil, as methane hydrates in cold regions, or are near the ocean floor (see sidebar: Hydraulic Fracturing ["Fracking"]). Additionally, recent research suggests that extraction of unconventional natural gas deposits inadvertently emit large amounts of methane, one of the most potent greenhouse gases. Despite concerns, unconventional natural gas resources are growing rapidly in importance. In 2000, unconventional natural gas resources contributed to only 1 percent of the U.S. natural gas supply. Today, however, they represent 20 percent and could grow to 50 percent by 2035. Therefore, much of the current speculation, investment, and technological development concerning natural gas focuses on the greater extraction, production, and consumption of what is considered, at present, unconventional natural gas resources. R/P ratio estimates for recoverable unconventional reserves could be up to one hundred times the current R/P ratio.

In the last several decades, more developed nations have taken the lead in natural gas resource development and operations. Technological advances have enabled drilling firms to drill deeper and expand the industry, tapping into formerly unrecoverable reserves with greater efficiency and reduced costs. Firms are currently expanding their pursuit of unconventional resources in several African and European countries.

MICHAEL H. FINEWOOD
LAURA J. STROUP

Further Reading

Colborn, T., C. Kwiatkowski, K. Schultz, and M. Bachran. "Natural Gas Production From a Public Health Perspective." *International Journal of Human and Ecological Risk Assessment* 17 no. 5 (2011).

Geology.com. "Marcellus Shale-Appalachian Basin Natural Gas Play." http://geology.com/articles/marcellus-shale.shtml.

National Research Council. *Hidden Costs of Energy: Unpriced Consequences of Energy Production and Use.* Washington, DC: National Academy of Sciences Press, 2009.

Palmer, Jerrell Dean, and John G. Johnson. "Big Inch and Little Big Inch." http://www.tshaonline.org/handbook/online/articles/dob08.

"A Primer." http://www.netl.doe.gov/technologies/oil-gas/publications/EPreports/Shale_Gas_Primer_2009.pdf

Rojey, A. *Natural Gas: Production Processing Transport.* Paris: Editions Technip, 1996.

Smil, Vaclav. *Energy in Nature and Society: General Energetics of Complex Systems.* Cambridge, MA

See Also: Compressed Natural Gas; Energy Transmission: Gas; Flaring Gas; Marcellus Shale; Natural Gas Storage; Nonrenewable Energy Resources; Oil and Gas Pipelines; Pickens, T. Boone.

Natural Gas Storage

Category: Energy Technology.
Summary: Natural gas is mostly methane. In the past, storage was included in the sale of natural gas by pipeline companies to distribution utilities. In 1992, the market was deregulated, opening storage to anyone rather than just pipeline companies in meeting the demand of customers.

There are about 400 natural gas storage facilities in the lower 48 states of the United States. Storage facilities are underground, commonly within reasonable distances of centers where the gas will eventually be used. The volume of U.S. storage capacity in 2000 was 3.899 trillion cubic feet.

The first successful underground storage facility was in Ontario, Canada, in 1915. The first in the United States was near Buffalo, New York, and by 1930 there were nine facilities in six states. After World War II, the industry realized that pipeline delivery was insufficient to meet seasonal demand and that technology was unavailable to create pipeline capacity sufficient for peak demand. Depleted reservoirs predominated.

Natural gas underground storage uses three types of facility, each of which has its own physical characteristics (permeability, porosity, and capacity) and economics (site preparation and maintenance, recycling speed, and delivery rate)—differences that define the purpose of the site. Before 1950, virtually all storage facilities were depleted reservoirs. A depleted reservoir is a formation that has exhausted its own recoverable gas. It is geologically suited for injection and storage and also has the extraction and distribution equipment in place from its days as a producing site. Depleted reservoir storage is cheapest and easiest to bring online and maintain. Depleted reservoirs do, however, require that 50 percent of their gas remain as cushion gas, but their unrecoverable gas is what is left over from the well. Depleted reservoirs must have high permeability and porosity; porosity determines capacity, whereas permeability determines rate of injection and withdrawal. (Depleted reservoirs were at 86 percent of capacity in 2001.)

Aquifers

Most common in the midwest, aquifers are natural underground water-containing formations that may be reconditioned for natural gas storage. Aquifers have been regulated by the Environmental Protection Agency (EPA) from the 1980s; these regulations are designed to protect freshwater from contamination by natural gas. They require extensive geological testing and the installation of infrastructure for injection, extraction, and delivery. Because reconditioning an aquifer is more expensive than using a depleted reservoir, aquifers are generally not used when depleted reservoirs are available. The aquifer is suitable once the sedimentary rock formation has an impermeable cap rock. An active water drive can improve deliverability rates for aquifers.

Salt Caverns

Salt formations allow little leakage of natural gas. They can be salt domes: salt that has leached up and created a dome perhaps a mile in diameter and 30,000 feet high. Domes typically extend 6,000 to 1,500 feet below the surface. Salt beds, by contrast, are thinner and shallower, rarely taller than 1,000 feet. They are also more likely to deteriorate and more expensive to develop than salt domes. Salt dome construction is more expensive than converting a depleted field, based on dollars per thousand cubic feet of working gas generated. The cost becomes more compatible when factoring in the ability of the dome to run several cycles per year.

Within the bed or dome, development means dissolving and extracting the salt to create an empty space, a process of cycling water through the area called salt cavern leaching. The salt cavern has the lowest cushion gas requirement, 33 percent. Most salt caverns are located along the Gulf of Mexico and in northern states. They are best for use as peak-load storage facilities, since they have only one-hundredth the acreage of the typical depleted gas reservoir. (Peak-load facilities, as described more fully below, are used to meet sudden or unforeseen needs and thus must be able to deliver gas quickly for a short period; base-load facilities, by contrast, are designed to meet ongoing and predictable demand.) At least one abandoned mine has in the past served as a reservoir, and research on the commercial viability of hard rock caverns is under way. None, however, was active as of 2004.

The daily deliverable percentages of these storage facilities break down roughly as follows: aquifers, 11 percent; salt caverns, 15 percent; depleted reservoirs, 74 percent. *Working gas* is the term for the volume that can be delivered normally. Working gas accounts for the bulk of capacity and deliverability, but salt caverns have a higher deliverability-to-capacity ratio.

Base- and Peak-Loads

Natural gas can be stored for a long time, waiting until demand justifies its movement to a point of use. Before injecting gas into the underground reservoir, regardless of type, reconditioning is necessary. Natural gas is introduced over time to build up pressure in the reservoir. Gas has to be stored at greater pressure than the wellhead so the gas will leave the chamber. Once pressure drops below the wellhead, the remaining gas is called "physically unrecoverable." Each facility has a volume of "base" or "cushion" gas, the volume needed to ensure the pressure is high enough to remove gas. Some of the base gas is extractable using special equipment.

Gas can be stored in base-load or peak-load facilities. Base-load storage helps to meet seasonal demand, and gas in this sort of facility turns over within a year. Gas enters the system in the summer (April through October) and is removed in winter for heating. Large-capacity and relatively low delivery rates characterize these reservoirs. These facilities provide a steady and reliable stream over a long term. The most common base-load facility is the depleted gas reservoir.

A peak-load facility provides a large volume of gas quickly and for the short term. The capacity is smaller, so they deplete more rapidly. They can be replenished more quickly too. Peak-load facilities can have a turnover rate of as little as a few days or weeks. The most common peak-load facility sites are salt caverns (4 percent of volume in 2001). Aquifers are also used for peak-load storage (10 percent of volume in 2001).

The principal owners and operators of natural gas storage facilities are interstate pipeline companies, independent providers, intrastate pipeline

Wikimedia

The most important type of natural gas storage is underground reservoirs, of which there are three types—depleted gas reservoirs, aquifer reservoirs, and salt cavern reservoirs. Each of these possess distinct characteristics that govern the suitability of a particular type of storage for a given application.

companies, and local distribution companies—a total of about 120 firms, all subsidiaries of 80 larger corporations. Depending on area served, the facility is governed either by the Federal Energy Regulatory Commission (FERC) or by the state. Storage facility owners, like storage rental businesses elsewhere, do not customarily own what they store. The owners determine what type of storage is used. Pipeline companies that own storage facilities use storage to manage supply and load, as well as to lease capacity to others. Local delivery companies use storage to supply ongoing customer demand and lease some capacity to other users. Deregulation of storage as well as the shift to gas-fired electricity generation has made high deliverability a strong asset, so independent storage providers, small and nimble, provide gas to marketers and generators of electricity to meet peak demand.

JOHN H. BARNHILL

Further Reading

Consumerenergyreport.com. "Natural Gas Storage and Delivery, Effect on the Environment." April 11, 2011. http://www.consumerenergyreport.com/research/natural-gas-storage-and-delivery-effect-on-the-environment/.

Naturalgas.org. "Storage of Natural Gas." http://www.naturalgas.org/naturalgas/storage.asp.

Warden, Dante. *Natural Gas: Processing, Storage andApplications.* New Delhi: World Technologies, 2011.

See Also: Compressed Natural Gas; Energy Storage; Natural Gas.

Nauru

Official Name: Republic of Nauru.
Category: Geography of Energy.
Summary: Although Nauru has had little experience with renewable energy and energy efficiency in the past, the latest projects undertaken through European Union funding have shown encouraging results.

The Republic of Nauru, formerly known as Pleasant Island, is located in the Micronesian South Pacific, south of the Marshall Islands. Nauru is the smallest independent republic and the world's smallest island nation, comprising just one island and covering 21 square kilometers. Uniquely for a small developing country, 100 percent of Nauru's 9,267 people had access to electricity as of 2010, thanks to a circular grid going around the only island.

Improving Power Supply
Nauru was once entirely dependent on fossil fuel imports for its energy needs. Even so, the island was experiencing power supply issues, as electricity services were provided only half of the day for most customers. This situation was largely caused by poor management, inadequate maintenance, low tariffs, and low revenue collection. There was therefore an urgent need to improve the system.

In order to relieve the country from its fuel dependency and improve power supply, the government of Nauru developed the National Sustainability Development Strategy, which aims at providing 50 percent of energy demand by alternative sources of energy, including renewables, by 2015. However, no government agencies are responsible for renewable energy, nor is any regulatory framework in place. The instability of the grid also makes it technically difficult to incorporate renewable energy.

The National Energy Policy Framework (NEPF) was therefore established in 2008 by the Nauru government with help from the Secretariat of the Pacific Islands Applied Geoscience Commission (SOPAC) through its Pacific Islands Energy Policy and Strategic Action Planning project. Its implementation is coordinated by the Ministry of Commerce, Industry and Resources in order to provide the island with reliable, affordable, and sustainable energy.

However, the only major renewable resource that may be exploited for the foreseeable future in Nauru is solar power. The European Union's

Support to the Energy Sector in Five ACP (African, Caribbean, and Pacific Island) Countries (REP-5) program therefore funded a 40-kilowatt-peak, grid-connected photovoltaic (PV) system, installed on the roof of Nauru College in 2008. (The kilowatt-peak is a unit that describes the peak power outputted by a solar module under full solar radiation.) In order to guarantee the permanence of the project, the Nauru Utilities Authority (NUA), as well as local contractors, were involved in the system installation and were trained in its operation and maintenance. Science teachers were also provided with a training kit to teach their students about PV technology. Since its installation in October 2008, the PV system has been generating an average of 4,500 kilowatt-hours per month, corresponding to a fuel saving of 1,325 liters per month.

Energy Efficiency Incentives

Because Nauru did not have any incentives for energy efficiency and conservation until the late 20th century and because electricity tariffs were extremely low, the island's households had the highest electricity consumption in the Pacific region. The REP-5 project therefore funded the supply and installation of prepayment meters in order to reduce energy consumption and recover generation costs. A gradually increasing electricity tariff was introduced in order to move toward a business model of cost recovery through a mix of a user-pays tariff structure and demand-side management. (Demand-side management, or energy demand management, is the modification of consumer demand for energy through various methods, such as financial incentives and education; usually, the goal of demand-side management is to encourage the consumer to use less energy or to use the energy at times of low demand.) More than 1,800 prepayment meters had been installed on residential and commercial buildings by August 1, 2009, the day the system was activated. Public reaction to the new meters has been positive, as the NUA is now providing 24-hour access power on the entire island. The rise in electricity costs does not seem to be an issue, as customers are willing to pay for the improved level of service.

Additionally, the REP-5 project undertook an energy efficiency campaign in Nauru between 2006 and 2009, focusing on an energy efficiency community awareness program launched in 2009, which was directed at the population in order to reduce fuel use for power generation. In addition to sponsoring weekly radio programs, brochures, school programs, and energy audits, the REP-5 program helped establish an the Energy Efficiency Action Plan (EEAP), implemented in 2009–10.

The combination of the solar PV project and the energy efficiency initiatives has slowly led to the changing behavior of both the general population and government officers. The growing interest in efficient appliances and renewable energy technologies is a sign of the success of those campaigns. However, such awareness campaigns must be ongoing for the message to be truly heard and implemented, as the participation of the community and stakeholders is critical to the success of the program.

Daphné Barbotte
Maaike Göbel
Eva Oberender

Further Reading

Central Intelligence Agency. "Nauru." In *The World Factbook.* https://www.cia.gov/library/publications/the-world-factbook/geos/nr.html.

Nauru Government. *Nauru Energy Efficiency Action Plan 2008–2015.* http://www.rep5.eu/files/pages/file/Nauru/EEAP%20-%20Final%20Draft%20as%20of%2006112008.pdf.

Nauru Government. *Nauru National Sustainable Development Strategy 2005–2025.* http://www.sprep.org/att/IRC/eCOPIES/Countries/Nauru/2a.pdf.

Pacific Islands Energy Policy and Strategic Action Planning. *Nauru Energy Policy Framework Consultation.* PIEPSAP Project Report 67. August 2007. http://dev.sopac.org.fj/VirLib/PI0067.pdf.

REP-5: Support to the Energy Sector in Five ACP Pacific Island Countries. "Nauru." http://www.rep5.eu/Project_Countries/Nauru.

Secretariat of the Pacific Regional Environment Programme. *Pacific Regional Energy Assessment*

2004. Vol. 7, *Nauru National Report.* http://www
.sprep.org/climate_change/documents/Vo17-
NauruNationalReport_000.pdf.

See Also: Alternative Energy; Climate Change;
Energy Poverty; International Renewable Energy
Agency; Namibia; Renewable Energy Resources.

Nebraska

Category: Energy in the United States.
Summary: Nebraska is a state rich in renewable
resources, including solar, wind, and biomass
in the form of timber. It ranks 24th among U.S.
states in energy efficiency, largely because the
state's utilities are spending about $4 million
annually to improve efficiency.

Nebraska requires all utilities in the state to offer
net metering to customers who install solar, methane, wind, biomass, hydropower, or geothermal
energy systems of less than 25 kilowatts.

The state of Nebraska has a range of natural
resources that can be used for energy generation.
Although the state has small oil reserves and no
other fossil fuel resources (importing coal for electricity generation almost exclusively from Wyoming), it has considerable potential to use wind
power. Nebraska also is one of the country's top
producers of corn-based ethanol—most of which,
however, is consumed in other states, because
Nebraska is one of the few U.S. states that allows
the use of conventional gasoline and has no state-
level mandate for blending ethanol into gasoline.
However, Nebraska has opened its first biodiesel
facility, which has the capacity to produce 5 million gallons annually.

Nebraska's total energy consumption is relatively low, commensurate with the state's population. The industrial sector leads energy demand,
and the transportation and residential sectors are
also large consumers of energy. Nonetheless, the
general trend has been a steady rise in energy consumption since the 1960s. In 1960, for example,

total energy consumption was about 308 British
thermal units (Btu). By 2007, consumption had
risen to 744 Btu, and by 2008 that consumption
was nearly 782 trillion Btu, an increase of 38 trillion Btu, or a bit more than 5 percent, over the
year and the highest since record keeping began.
Although total consumption declined to 759 Btu
in 2009, the steady increase has led Nebraska to
seek ways of both conserving energy and using
more renewables in its energy mix.

History
Nebraska and the other Great Plains states were
the last settled by American pioneers. During
much of the 1800s, the region was called the Great
American Desert and simply was bypassed. Even
after farmers began moving there after the Civil
War ended in 1865, many suffered from drought,
temperature extremes, and loneliness. For many
years, few Nebraskans had access to modern technology, including electrical power.

In the late 1960s, negotiations began that cul-
minated in the creation of the Nebraska Public
Power District in 1970. In the wake of the Arab
Oil Embargo, the energy crunch of the early 1970s
forced Nebraskans to acknowledge the prominent
role energy played in the state's economic health.
Since that time, the state of Nebraska's forward-
looking planning has addressed energy security
and economic growth in the long term.

The Nebraska Public Power District (NPPD)
is the state's largest electric utility, serving all or
parts of 91 of the state's 93 counties. It was formed
on January 1, 1970, when the Consumers Public
Power District, Platte Valley Public Power and
Irrigation District (PVPPID), and Nebraska Public Power System merged, becoming the public
agency NPPD.

In 1974, NPPD began operating the Cooper
Nuclear Station (CNS) near Brownville in southeastern Nebraska. NPPD's only nuclear reactor
used uranium fission to produce steam to turn
the plant's electrical power producing turbines.
NPPD purchased some hydroelectric power
from the Western Area Power Administration. In
the late 1980s, NPPD's major project was building a $700 million, 500,000-volt transmission line

called the MANDAN Project linking the Canadian province of Manitoba with the Dakotas and Nebraska.

In the 1990s, electric utilities across the nation faced new challenges from government deregulation. In 1992, the federal government passed a law permitting competition in purchasing wholesale electricity. Private utilities prepared to compete against public power in Nebraska. In the late 1990s, NPPD took several major steps to improve its technical and financial operations. In 1996, NPPD began a study of wind power. Monitors collected data on wind speeds, direction, and turbulence. In 1998, NPPD worked with other agencies to build its first two wind turbines, located near Springview, Nebraska. These variations on the old windmill already had operated for several years in other areas. However, deregulation and increased competition threatened investment in such alternative power sources as wind turbines, unless improved technology could bring their costs below the costs of fossil fuels, hydroelectricity, and nuclear energy—that is, those technologies already in place.

In the late 1990s, NPPD improved its customer service by consolidating its offices and using more automated technology. In the late 1990s, NPPD examined its options to offer many new electric services to its clients. Such diversification was seen as a way to prepare for deregulation and increased future competition. Although public power in Nebraska and other states had proved successful in terms of serving customers with low-cost energy, in 1999 its future appeared uncertain, in large part because of energy deregulation. Some industry leaders thought that it was time to sell publicly owned facilities and move on to a privatized system. Even if that happened, NPPD would retain its legacy as one of the nation's most significant electric power utilities.

Electricity

The United States is the world's largest energy consumer, and usage is increasing. Nebraska's electricity usage is a part of that trend. Aging generation facilities and increasing demands for electricity will require that new generating facilities be built.

Currently, electric utilities rely heavily on non-renewable fuels to produce electricity. These nonrenewable fuels include fossil fuels such as coal, oil, and natural gas. Utilization of fossil fuels draws on finite resources that cannot be replaced. Also, emissions from fossil fuel plants have been a source of discussion among environmentalists and all branches of government. Before 1930, few Nebraskans realized the state's potential for hydroelectric power, with plants in the Platte River Basin producing only 10,446 horsepower. However, successful power producers owned by Nebraska municipalities in the 1920s influenced many to favor publicly owned power over private utilities.

Nebraska generates more than two-thirds of its electricity from coal, the most inexpensive source of electricity. Nuclear power provides more than one-fourth of the state's generation. Finally, hydropower, wind power, and natural gas fuel about 3 percent of electricity production in the state.

Oil

Nebraska's few oil reserves are in the western part of the state. The Nebraska Oil and Gas Conservation Commission was created in 1959 to curb wasteful practices in oil and gas production. The director administers and enforces the Oil and Gas Conservation Act of 1959, and all rules, regulations, and orders promulgated by the commission. The director also acts as the commission's secretary and keeps its minutes and records.

When people think about countries that produce oil, the Middle East usually tops the list, but new technology is providing access to previously out-of-reach oil in the western United States. The Niobrara Chalk Basin in Wyoming, Colorado, and Nebraska shows particular promise.

Coal

About two-thirds of Nebraska's power is generated by coal (65 percent). In 2007, electric power generated in Nebraska came primarily from coal (64.2 percent), but there are no coal mines in Nebraska. Nebraska is a strong coal energy producer, however, and all 15 coal-fired generating stations in the state are owned by public utilities. The headquarters of Kiewit Mining Group, the eighth-biggest coal mining company in the United States, are located in Omaha. Also, in 1999, the Omaha-based holding company Berkshire Hathaway bought a majority share in MidAmerican Energy Holdings, which produces coal energy both independently and through its subsidiary, PacifiCorp.

By state law, Nebraska's public power entities are charged with providing the state with reliable energy at the lowest cost to consumers. For a very long time, that formula has translated into coal-fired generation. "Old coal" contracts may be relatively cheap, but costs are rising. Coal's greatest cost is rail transportation, and Nebraska is relatively close, as we reckon relative distance here on the Great Plains, to the coalfields of Wyoming.

Nuclear Energy

Nuclear energy supplies about 28 percent of Nebraska's energy needs. Cooper Nuclear Station (CNS) is a boiling-water-reactor plant located on a 1,251-acre site near Brownville, Nebraska.

It is the largest single-unit electrical generator in Nebraska. CNS is owned and operated by NPPD. In December 2007, the NPPD amended its existing contract for fuel bundle fabrication and related services to provide for long-term requirements. In March 2008, the NPPD amended its existing agreement for uranium concentrates, conversion, and enrichment to provide for short-term enriched uranium production and long-term enrichment services. These contracts do not obligate NPPD to purchase fuel components in excess of its operational needs. Nuclear fuel in the reactor is being amortized on the basis of energy produced as a percentage of total energy expected to be produced

Renewable Energy Sources

The U.S. Energy Information Administration predicts that demand for energy will grow 28 percent by the year 2035. To meet this growing electricity demand in a manner that is cost-effective and protects our air quality, the use of renewable energy sources will be necessary. Nebraska is making strides in this area. For example, work is under way on the construction of the 60-megawatt Ainsworth Wind Energy Facility, which will be the state's largest wind facility when it begins operation. Renewable resources have the potential to transform Nebraska's energy supply. Nebraska ranks near the top of the nation in its potential to generate energy from wind, cellulosic biomass, solar power, and biogas. NPPD owns and operates a wind farm near Ainsworth and purchases a percentage of the output from wind generation near Bloomfield, and about 9 percent of NPPD's annual energy generation mix comes from hydropower. In 2005, less than 3 percent of the energy consumed in the state came from renewable

Wikimedia

Nebraska City Station is a coal-fired power plant located southwest of Nebraska City. Public power entities must provide low cost resources to consumers, which has translated into coal-fired power, but costs continue to rise.

sources, but this number is certain to go up as technologies improve and more farmers find that homegrown energy is good for business.

NPPD's goal is to have new renewable energy resources comprise 10 percent of the energy supply for NPPD's native load by 2020. Clean energy investments will create opportunities for welders, sheet-metal workers, machinists, truck drivers, and others. In Nebraska, there are nearly 86,000 jobs in a representative group of job areas that could see job growth or wage increases by putting global warming solutions to work. Investing in renewable energy sources will reduce Nebraska's dependence on fossil fuels and at the same time create new green-collar jobs.

Geothermal Energy

Geothermal energy taps into reservoirs of steam and hot water beneath the Earth's surface. Most geothermal resources are concentrated in the western United States, but 2 percent of the deep geothermal energy in western Nebraska could produce the equivalent of 57 gigawatts of power. Because geothermal power does not vary based on weather or precipitation patterns, it offers an easy replacement for fossil fuel in large-scale power plants.

Nebraska has enough solar resources to produce 4,500 to 5,500 watt-hours per square meter using photovoltaic (PV) systems and 4,000 to 5,500 watt-hours per square meter using concentrating solar power systems. This means that devoting one 1 square mile in Nebraska to solar power could provide enough electricity for about 1,300 households each year.

Nebraska captures very little solar energy, but it has the potential to be ranked ninth in the country in this area. In the residential sector in 2004, only 0.02 percent of the electricity used was captured from the sun, while about 4 percent came from other renewable sources. Nebraska Renewable Energy Systems, a manufacturing and consulting firm, points out that PV solar panels can be used in tandem with a wind-energy system, as windy and sunny weather tend not to coincide. A 2003 study on a Nebraska cattle farm showed that solar energy can enhance livestock and crop manage-ment by creating free power for functions such as water pumping.

Nebraska is ranked 22nd for wind power, with 73 megawatts of existing electricity generation capacity and 81 megawatts under construction. The American Wind Energy Association ranks Nebraska sixth in terms of its future wind potential, with 99,100 megawatts of potential capacity. In 2010, more than 450 gigawatt-hours were generated by utility-scale wind energy in Nebraska. Nebraska has the potential to build an additional 7,800 megawatts by 2030, which could bring tens of thousands of new jobs.

In 2008, the state's wind turbines generated more than 200 gigawatt-hours of electricity, enough to power nearly 17,000 homes that year. Nebraska will more than double its wind production capacity when the Elkhorn Ridge Farm goes online. The power from this farm will go to NPPD, which hopes to add 800 megawatts of wind power to its portfolio through similar projects by 2020.

Nebraska has 21.8 million dry tons of biomass available each year that could be used to generate about 4,400 megawatts of electricity. Moreover, Nebraska produces 102,000 tons of methane emissions each year, making it one of the top 10 producers of methane gas in the country. In 2002, the AgSTAR program, sponsored by the U.S. Environmental Protection Agency (EPA), estimated that 148 swine farms in Nebraska were capable of using biodigesters to capture methane and produce 134 gigawatt-hours of electricity per year—enough to power more than 11,000 homes.

Nebraska has great potential to produce advanced biofuels from cellulosic biomass. In 2008, a five-year study of switchgrass grown on marginal farmland in Nebraska, South Dakota, and North Dakota, using only moderate amounts of fertilizer, yielded an average of 300 gallons of ethanol per acre, compared with 350 gallons per acre of corn in the same states. The technology that converts switchgrass and other forms of cellulosic biomass to fuel is a work in progress.

Saeid Eslamian
Rouzbeh Nazari

Further Reading

DeMeo, Edgar A. *Accelerating Wind-Power Development in Nebraska: Status, Recommendations and Perspective.* Lincoln: Nebraska Energy Office, 2003. http://www.neo.ne .gov/reports/accel_wind.htm.

Lantz, Eric. *Economic Development Benefits From Wind Power in Nebraska.* Golden, CO: National Renewable Energy Laboratory, 2009.

Nebraska Energy Office. "2010 Report." http://www .neo.ne.gov/annual_rept/NEOAnnualReport.pdf.

University of Nebraska, College of Journalism and Mass Communications. *Opportunities for Nebraska.* Vol. 2, *Energy, Climate, and Sustainability.* Lincoln: University of Nebraska, 2011.

U.S. Energy Information Administration. "Nebraska." http://www.eia.gov/state/state-energy-profiles.cfm ?sid=NE.

See Also: Biogas Digester; Dominy, Floyd E.; Ethanol: Corn; Geothermal Energy; Investor-Owned Utilities; Tennessee Valley Authority; United States.

Nepal

Official Name: Federal Democratic Republic of Nepal.
Category: Geography of Energy.
Summary: With 56 percent of Nepal's population lacking access to electricity, rural households and communities are increasingly turning to small-scale renewable energies, while cities and industries depend on large hydropower dams and diesel generators.

Nepal has one of the lowest annual average per capita energy consumption rates of all nations: 86 kilowatt-hours. It derives its energy from diverse sources, ranging from traditional biomass to large-scale hydropower to local renewable energies. Approximately 44 percent of Nepal's population has access to electricity, with stark inequalities in access between urban populations (90 percent) and rural populations (34 percent). With demand outstripping supply from the existing large hydropower dams on which cities and industries depend, load shedding is common, with power cuts up to 12 hours daily during the dry winter season. Businesses, industries, and wealthier households rely on private diesel-fueled generators or inverters to maintain power supply. Nepal's dramatic Himalayan topography and its wealth of water resources leave Nepal paradoxically wealthy in potential hydropower and yet poor in equitable distribution potential.

Hydropower

With Nepal's abundant water resources coursing through the Himalayan range, a projected 83,000 megawatts of hydropower is available, with 43,000 megawatts estimated to be economically and technically accessible. Of this, 620 megawatts is utilized through both large dams that power faraway cities and microhydropower systems that electrify small, remote communities. If Nepal harnessed the hydropower available, energy needs for private and commercial consumption could be met with excess energy to export. With Nepal's harsh typography and remote communities, microhydropower has the potential to electrify rural communities that are logistically, technically, and financially prohibitive to link to a national grid powered by a few large hydropower dams.

Microhydropower at this point provides only a small percentage of the overall hydropower, an estimated 8 megawatts in 2006. Microhydropower systems are typically less than 100 kilowatts, have a small environmental footprint, and provide both electrification and agricultural processing services (milling, grinding, and so forth) to small, often remote, communities. Microhydropower systems typically are financed by government and donors and built using the labor and additional funds of the communities that will own and operate the system.

Biomass

Although hydropower has the most potential to power Nepal, traditional biomass is the most commonly used source of energy, supplying 84 percent of energy needs. In Nepal, traditional biomass includes firewood, agricultural residue, and dung. Cooking is Nepal's most common energy demand, with firewood the most common energy source; 83 percent of rural populations and 36 percent of urban populations cook with firewood. Cooking with firewood causes indoor air pollution and disease, releases carbon dioxide, and can hamper forest conservation.

The World Health Organization estimates that in Nepal 5 adults per 1,000 and 50 children per 1,000 die from respiratory diseases caused by this indoor air pollution. Disease can develop when biomass is burned openly in an enclosed space rather than under a smoke hood or in an enclosed stove with a chimney that vents to the outdoors. Improved cookstoves have been adopted by 6 percent of households; these burn wood more efficiently, require less firewood, and reduce respiratory illness by channeling smoke away from enclosed spaces.

Biogas Digesters

More than 210,000 of the estimated 1.18 million cattle-owning households, or about 2.4 percent of the population, have built biogas digesters. Digesters are fueled by cattle dung, and seven of 10 digesters also have an attached toilet to produce methane for cooking. Cattle manure is mixed with water, released into an underground tank (from which the methane created by anaerobic digestion rises), and then, through the turning of a ball valve, is piped into the house to a gas stove for cooking. Household digesters are most commonly built in 2-, 4-, 6-, and 8-cubic-meter sizes, and the size of the digester depends on the number of cattle a household has and hence the amount of feeder material it must process. High-capacity community and institutional biogas digesters can use communal toilet waste and other organic material to create methane for lighting and cooking.

Solar and Other Schemes

With the difficulty in extending a national grid to remote villages, the Nepalese government actively promotes a variety of small-scale, place-appropriate alternative energies. More than 220,000 solar

> ### ▷ *Electric Vehicles in Nepal*
>
> In Nepal, gas stations dependent on imports frequently run short of supply, leaving motorists to wait in long lines at gasoline pumps with armed guards. In an effort to reduce dependence on imported fuels and to clean the notoriously polluted Kathmandu Valley air, Kathmandu introduced Safa Tempos in 1996. The term *safa* means "clean." These small, three-wheeled vehicles can carry 10 passengers and run on batteries charged with hydroelectricity. There are now more than 600 such vehicles in Kathmandu, serving an estimated 120,000 passengers daily, which gives Kathmandu one of the world's highest per capita rates of electric vehicles.
>
>
> *One of Nepal's three-wheeled electric vehicles.*
>
> Tsikot.com

home systems are installed in Nepal's remote communities. Solar cookers and solar dryers for agricultural processing are also used. Other renewable and alternative energies include wind, biofuels, and biobriquettes; the latter is a cleaner-burning charcoal for cooking made from waste materials.

SHAUNNA BARNHART

Further Reading

Gurung, A., A. Kumar Ghimeray, and S. H. A. Hassan. "The Prospects of Renewable Energy Technologies for Rural Electrification: A Review From Nepal." *Energy Policy* 40 (January 2012).

Nepal Government. "National Planning Commission and United Nations Country Team of Nepal. Nepal Millennium Development Goals: Progress Report 2010." http://www.undp.org.np/mdg/.

"A Social Dynamics on Launching Safa Tempos in Kathmandu Valley: A Campaign Against the Air Pollution." *Environment: A Journal of Environment* 6, no. 7 (June 5, 2001).

United Nations Development Programme. *Capacity Development for Scaling Up Decentralized Energy Access Programmes.* 2010. http://www.undp.org/energy/.

United Nations Development Programme. *The Energy Access Situation in Developing Countries.* 2009. http://www.who.int/indoorair/publications/energyaccesssituation/en/index.html.

U.S. Energy Information Administration. "Country Analysis Brief: Nepal." http://www.eia.gov/countries/country-data.cfm?fips=NP.

Zhou, K. "Himalayan Hydropower: Alternative Energy in Nepal." *Harvard International Review* 33, no. 1 (March 1, 2011).

See Also: Anaerobic Digestion; Biogas Digester; Biomass Energy; Electric Vehicles; Energy Policy; Hydropower; Microhydropower; Renewable Energy Resources.

Net Metering

Category: Environmentalism.

Summary: Net metering is a government policy in which electricity generators use a renewable energy source to provide their own electricity and are paid for any surplus electricity fed back into the grid. The objective is to encourage deployment of small-scale renewable electricity.

Net metering is one of a variety of energy policies used by jurisdictions that seek to increase the deployment of renewable energy sources. Overarching policy objectives may include decreasing dependence on traditional fossil fuels, reducing greenhouse gas (GHG) emissions, and improving the quality of the atmosphere.

Net metering is a policy whereby a grid-tied consumer enters into an agreement with its local utility to generate some of its own electricity and use a single, bidirectional meter to measure both electricity drawn from the grid and any excess electricity fed back into the grid. The meter moves forward when drawing electricity and reverses its direction when excess energy is provided to the grid. A consumer is billed for its positive "net consumption," which is defined as total consumption minus total generation during a given billing period. If a consumer generates more electricity than it consumes over a given billing period, it will be paid the difference or receive a credit toward a subsequent billing cycle.

Net-metering rules vary by country, state or province, and even utility. Programs address eligibility (consumer class, location, system size, and system ownership), whether and how long a consumer can keep banked credits, and how much the credits are worth (on the retail or wholesale market). Most programs incorporate a monthly rollover of electricity credits, a small monthly connection fee, monthly payment of deficits (that is, the normal utility bill), and annual settlement of any credit due. Some utilities allow a consumer to carry over a balance of any net extra electricity generated by the consumer's system from month to month, which is advantageous if the resource generating the electricity is seasonal.

Consumer-Based Incentive

Net metering is typically a consumer-based incentive and commonly is applied to small, renewable energy-generating facilities, such as wind and solar photovoltaic (PV) systems. However, some utilities have expanded their range of permitted technologies to include microhydropower, geothermal power, tidal energy, wave and biomass energy, cogeneration of heat and power, energy from landfill gas and municipal solid waste, fuel cells, and efficiency improvements at existing facilities. Some U.S. jurisdictions also allow net metering for generators up to 2 megawatts.

Despite being a relatively simpler approach than programs such as feed-in tariffs, net metering does raise a number of implementation issues. First, any jurisdiction that relies solely on a net-metering program to incentivize the deployment of renewable energy generation places the burden of pioneering renewable energy primarily on fragmented consumer population. In addition, it can be challenging for individuals to negotiate with large institutions to recover their net-metering credits or rebates.

Second, net metering requires technology development at two levels. From a transmission and distribution perspective, the grid must have the ability to accept electricity inflows from alternative as well as from traditional energy sources, such as large hydroelectric and nuclear power. Smart-grid systems must also incorporate bidirectional capability to integrate and to direct both traditional and alternative energy flows into and out of the grid and over transmission lines.

From a communications perspective, many net-metering programs rely on Internet communication between participating consumers and utilities. This consists of reporting on energy usage and consumption, and ultimately on electronic billings, which weigh household or business energy contributions against consumption in order to produce a final bill. Implementing such a system requires serious thought, given to the capability of utility companies' existing billing and communications infrastructure and the privacy rights of consumers.

According to the Renewable Energy Policy Network, by 2010 net-metering laws existed in at least 10 countries and 43 U.S. states. A growing number of developing countries—for instance, Tanzania and Thailand—have adopted net metering as a policy option. Net-metering programs continue to evolve, as new provisions address issues such as net excess generation, renewable energy credit ownership, and community-owned systems.

ROBERT J. WAKULAT

Further Reading

Faden, Valerie J. "Net Metering of Renewable Energy: How Traditional Electricity Suppliers Fight to Keep You in the Dark." *Widener Journal of Public Law* 109, no. 10 (2000–01).

Forsyth, T. L., M. Pedden, and T. Gagliano. *The Effects of Net Metering on the Use of Small-Scale Wind Systems in the United States.* NREL/TP-500-32471. Washington, DC: National Renewable Energy Laboratory, 2010.

Pollution Probe. "Net Metering: Getting Credit for the Electricity You Generate." http://www.pollutionprobe.org/whatwedo/greenpower/consumerguide/c2_4.htm.

Renewable Energy Policy Network for the 21st Century (REN21). *Renewables 2010 Global Status Report.* Paris: REN21 Secretariat, 2010. http://www.ren21.net/REN21Activities/Publications/GlobalStatusReport/tabid/5434/Default.aspx.

Starrs, T. *Net Metering: New Opportunities for Home Power.* Washington, DC: Renewable Energy Policy Project, 1996.

Stoutenborough, James W., and Matthew Beverlin. "Encouraging Pollution-Free Energy: The Diffusion of State Net Metering Policies." *Social Science Quarterly* 89, no. 5 (December 2008).

See Also: Electric Grids; Energy Policy; Feed-in Tariff; Green Pricing; Grid-Connected Systems; Photovoltaics; Regulation.

Netherlands

Official Name: Netherlands.
Category: Geography of Energy.
Summary: The Netherlands relies for its energy needs on a balanced mixture of domestic gas, imported coal and oil, and, to a smaller extent, nuclear energy, wind energy, solar power, and biomass energy.

The Netherlands is a highly industrialized country, situated in northwestern Europe, and a full member of the European Union (EU). Its population was 16.6 million in 2010, 80 percent of whom lived in urban areas. With 491 inhabitants per square kilometer, the country ranks among the most densely populated countries in the world. Its energy use is 4,672 kilograms of oil equivalent per capita per year, comparable to countries such as Sweden and South Korea, well below U.S. per capita consumption United States (7,075 kilograms), and significantly above that of the United Kingdom (3,195 kilograms).

Today, the Netherlands largely depends on its considerable reserves of domestic gas and imported coal and oil. It has a liberal electricity market, with several producers and a small number of transmission and distribution system operators. Several oil companies operate on the Dutch market, and gas is largely supplied by GasTerra. In the area of renewable sources, the Netherlands underperforms compared to neighboring Germany.

A Netherlands Icon: The Windmill

The icons of the Netherlands include one of its earliest energy sources: the windmill. In addition to industrial functions, such as grinding grain into flour and to a smaller degree sawing wood, traditional windmills are closely connected to another icon of Dutch culture: turning areas of water into land. Windmills driving Archimedes's screws or scoop wheels were essential to creating and managing *polders*, or areas of land in which the groundwater level is under strict control, partly situated below the "natural" water level. Additionally, a small amount of water power was used through traditional water mills, but flat as the country is, the inclination of the topography is too small for extensive use of hydropower.

Wood and Peat

For heating, preindustrial Netherlands relied on wood and peat. The wet, spongy plant material of bogs was excavated and dried into peat beginning in the early Middle Ages. The excavation of bogs led to the creation of lake areas such as the Loosdrechtse Plassen and Vinkeveense Plassen between Utrecht and Amsterdam.

In the early 20th century, peat and wood were increasingly replaced by lignite and coal, which have a higher energy content. In the southern province of Limburg, coal had been mined in shallow shafts as early as 1500, but beginning with the large-scale construction of railroads after 1900, the production of coal and lignite became a substantial industry. At its peak, Dutch coal production reached a volume of 23 million metric tons per year. However, as coal mining in the Netherlands was considerably more expensive than elsewhere, imports gradually replaced domestic production. In 1974, the last Dutch coal mine, in Eygelshoven, Limburg, was closed.

Oil is present in limited volumes. Only one oil field, in Schoonebeek (in the northern province of Drente), has been commercially exploited. Between 1947 and 1996, the field produced a grand total of 250 million barrels. It was then shut down, both because it was no longer profitable in an era when oil prices were about $10 per barrel and because the increasing viscosity of the oil made extracting it increasingly difficult. For reasons including high oil prices and advancing mining technologies, the field was considered economically viable again and reopened early in 2011. It is expected that, up to 2035, the field will yield between 100 and 120 million barrels. From the total reserve of 1 billion barrels, about 600 million are regarded as not minable, even with modern technology. In comparison to the overall consumption of oil at roughly 1 billion barrels per day, domestic production is negligible.

Natural Gas

By far the most important natural resource in the Netherlands is natural gas. The country's total reserves are estimated to be approximately 3,000 billion cubic meters. The largest gas field—below Slochteren, in the northern province of Groningen—was discovered in 1957. Until the 1980s, new gas fields were found continually at a rate that kept up with gas consumption. As a consequence, the gas reserve remained roughly constant until the 1990s. In 2011, the Slochteren field was expected to yield for another 50 years, although declining pressure was expected to impede production starting in 2020. The Netherlands is the largest gas producer and exporter in the EU and will probably be able to maintain this position until 2025. In anticipation of the depletion of gas reserves, plans are being developed to transform the Dutch gas infrastructure into a storage facility and move the country from its status as a gas producer to a role as trading hub for other suppliers, such as Norway and Russia.

▷ *Nuclear Energy Between Deliberative Democracy and Chernobyl*

The small contribution of nuclear energy to the energy mix of the Netherlands is remarkable: the strong dependence on imported oil and the consequent emissions of carbon dioxide would render nuclear energy an attractive alternative. Indeed, prompted by the promise of nuclear energy, the Netherlands purchased a load of uranium in 1938. Through cooperation with Norway and the United States, the first nuclear plant in Dodewaard (located in the central Netherlands) was delivered in 1965. Through this joint venture between government, the European atomic energy agency Euratom, and 10 Dutch electricity companies, the Netherlands hoped to secure an independent energy supply.

However, sociopolitical history decided differently. The optimism vanished rapidly after a small leak was detected at the Dodewaard plant in 1972. Even though the Netherlands faced difficulties securing its oil supply in the 1970s, the nuclear alternative was not greeted with general approval. Risks and potential military uses had been concerns as early as 1947, but an antinuclear sentiment gained broad momentum only in the early 1970s. During this period, activism emerged as a loose collection of many small organizations. In 1973, the government announced a plan of building several more nuclear plants and imposed a 3 percent tax on energy to fund some of the projects. The move served as a call to battle for the opponents of nuclear energy.

In 1978, under pressure from the antinuclear movement, the government agreed to organize a "broad societal discussion" in which every citizen could have his or her say on a democratic and rational basis. Deliberative democracy was believed to settle a complex issue. However, suspicion was raised among opponents of nuclear energy, as the government insisted that the point of departure would be the governmental plans, not open questions. Moreover, the government considered itself not bound by the outcomes of these broad-based discussions. In the end, trust in both the discussion process and the discussion content deteriorated. Nevertheless, the government proceeded largely as if the societal discussion had never taken place. In 1985, it decided to build 10 more nuclear power plants. In April 1986, the world witnessed the meltdown of the Chernobyl nuclear reactor in Ukraine. The timing of the disaster was decisive: All planned nuclear plants in the Netherlands were put on hold, and no nuclear plant has been built since.

The Netherlands' total energy consumption in 2010 amounted to 3,495 picojoules. Natural gas supplied 47 percent of energy needs, and oil accounted for 37.2 percent of energy use (though the total use of oil is roughly double this amount, half of which is exported again as oil derivatives). Another 9.1 percent came from coal and coal derivatives, and 6 percent of energy consumption was supplied by industrial surplus heat, biomass and waste, and surplus heat from nuclear power plants. About 0.7 percent of the energy used comes from (net) imported electrical power and solar, hydro-, and wind power.

Electricity

Electricity is produced primarily by gas-powered plants. In 2008, gas accounted for 59.8 percent of the electricity production, and coal and other fossil fuels for another 25.7 percent. Renewables accounted for 8.8 percent, nuclear energy yielded 3.9 percent, and another 1.8 percent came from marginal energy technologies.

The liberalization of markets in Europe has been implemented in the Netherlands as a strict separation between transmission system operators (TSOs), distribution system operators (DSOs), and energy suppliers. Both the gas network and the electricity network are built around one countrywide backbone, operated by Gas Transport Services for gas and TenneT TSO for electricity. The regional distribution is executed by eight DSOs for electricity and eleven DSOs for gas. Several DSOs are active in both the gas and the electricity markets, partly combining their services.

Electricity is supplied by more than 20 market parties, partly mere trading companies and partly trading producers. The gas supply market is dominated by GasTerra, a trading organization stemming from the earlier state-owned GasUnie, which provided comprehensive transport, distribution, and supply. GasTerra is the 100 percent shareholder of the TSO Gas Transport Services. Moreover, GasTerra is compelled by law to trade with smaller gas suppliers at economically viable rates. Its largest supplier is the Slochteren field, exploited by the Nederlandse Aardolie Maatschappij, a 50–50 joint venture of Royal Dutch Shell and ExxonMobil. The fuel market for automobility is open and has several dozen players, both trading organizations and trading producers. Because of taxation, fuel prices in the Netherlands are among the highest worldwide.

For domestic transportation, the Netherlands relies on fuel-powered road transport, its densely used network of railways (which provide predominantly electric but also diesel-powered transport), and inshore shipping for bulk cargo. Major cities have electric streetcars and subways. The country has more bicycles than inhabitants, and foreigners visiting the Netherlands are often astonished by the immense urban use of bicycles.

GOVERT VALKENBURG

Further Reading

Central Intelligence Agency. "The Netherlands." In *The World Factbook*. https://www.cia.gov/library/publications/the-world-factbook/geos/nl.html.

Energy Research Center of the Netherlands. "Working on a Sustainable Future." http://www.ecn.nl/home/.

Hagendijk, Rob, and Arjan Terpstra. "Technology, Risk, and Democracy: The Dutch Nuclear Energy Debate (1981–1984)." *STAGE (Science, Technology and Governance in Europe)*, Discussion Paper 12 (2004).

Statistics Netherlands. "Manufacturing and Energy." http://www.cbs.nl/en-GB/menu/themas/industrie-energie/nieuws/default.htm.

U.S. Energy Information Administration. "Country Analysis Brief: Netherlands." http://www.eia.gov/countries/country-data.cfm?fips=NL.

See Also: Bernoulli, Daniel; Bicycles; Ethanol: Sugar Beet; History of Energy: Medieval World; History of Energy: Renaissance; Natural Gas; Wind Resources; Wind Technology.

Nevada

Category: Energy in the United States.
Summary: The landlocked state of Nevada, in the southwestern United States, has no fossil fuel reserves but considerable hydropower, geothermal energy, and significant potential solar and wind energy.

Nevada is a landlocked state in the western U.S. sharing borders with California, Oregon, Idaho, Utah, and Arizona. It has a primarily arid climate (with an average annual rainfall of 7 inches, ranging across the state from more than 40 inches to less than 4 inches) and numerous mountain ranges. The southern third of the state is located within the Mojave Desert, and much of the northern state is located within the Great Basin. The state's land area is 110,567 square miles, and the population of 2,414,807 is highly urbanized and rapidly growing.

In the years between 1980 and 1990, Nevada's population increased by 50.1 percent; from 1990 to 2000, it increased by 66.3 percent; and between 2000 and 2009, it increased by 32.3 percent. The population of the Las Vegas metropolitan area alone increased by 38.3 percent from 2000 to 2009, with most of the increase coming from domestic migration.

Crude Oil Reserves

Nevada has no known reserves of crude oil, dry natural gas, or coal, and in 2009 production of crude oil (455,000 barrels) and natural gas (4 million cubic feet) represented less than 0.1 percent of the total U.S. production of these commodities. The state has one small crude oil refinery, which produces asphalt and diesel fuel. However, mining is a major industry in Nevada, and in 2009 the total value of all minerals produced in the state was about $5.8 billion, with $4.9 billion of that attributable to gold mining. Nevada is the leading U.S. producer of gold (producing about 75 percent of the U.S. total), barite, and lithium, and in 2009 Nevada was judged to have 65.2 million troy ounces of gold reserves, enough to sustain current levels of production for about 13 years. Also in 2009, Nevada produced 5 million troy ounces of gold, 7.3 million troy ounces of silver, 145.7 million pounds of copper, 476,000 tons of barite, 1.198 million tons of gypsum, and 303,000 pounds of molybdenum.

Wikimedia

Yucca Mountain was selected as the site for the Yucca Mountain nuclear waste repository but the proposal was fought in court and, due to scientific concerns, the project remains uncertain. The formation was created by several large volcanic eruptions.

Nevada generated 2.4 terawatt-hours of electricity in January 2011, of which the majority was generated by natural gas-fired plants (1.6 terawatt-hours), and smaller amounts were generated by coal-fired plants (471 gigawatt-hours), renewables other than hydroelectric (208 gigawatt-hours), hydroelectric (138 gigawatt-hours), and petroleum-fired plants (1 gigawatt-hour). In 2009, the electric power industry produced 18,294,514 metric tons of carbon dioxide emissions, 16,661 metric tons of nitrogen oxide emissions, and 7,186 metric tons of sulfur dioxide emissions. Two major crude oil pipelines cross Nevada—the Calnev and Kinder-Morgan—and there are three interstate natural gas pipelines, run by the Kern River Gas Transmission Company, Southwest Gas Corporation, and the Tuscarora Pipe Line Company. Nevada has 1,010 fueling stations for motor gasoline, 26 for ethanol, 37 for liquefied petroleum gas, 11 for compressed natural gas, and 16 for other alternate fuels.

On December 31, 2005, the state's largest electricity generating plant, the Mohave Generating Station, was shut down for failing to install pollution-control equipment. Located in Laughlin, Nevada, near the borders with California and Arizona, the Mojave Generating Station was supplied with coal from the Black Mesa coal mine in northeastern Arizona, delivered by means of the world's only coal slurry pipeline. The coal was pulverized and mixed with water before being transported through 275 miles of pipe. The largest power plant in Nevada is the Chuck Lenzie Generating Station, fueled by natural gas and featuring an air-cooler-condenser system and water-clarifier system which together recycle most (75 percent) of the used water and allow the plant to use only 2.2 percent of the water per megawatt of electricity generated that is required by a conventional coal power plant.

Per capita energy consumption in Nevada in 2008 was 287 million British thermal units (Btu), ranking the state 40th in the United States. Total energy consumed was 750 billion Btu, including

46.2 million barrels of petroleum. Petroleum consumption included 26.5 million barrels of motor gasoline, 12 million barrels of distillate fuel, 1.2 million barrels of liquefied petroleum gas, and 4.8 million barrels of jet fuel (primary due to demand from two air bases and the airports in Las Vegas and Reno). Cleaner-burning motor gasoline, which has low volatility and contains oxygenates, is required to be used all year in the Las Vegas Metropolitan area, while both the Reno and the Las Vegas metropolitan areas require that oxygenated motor gasoline be used during the winter. The transportation sector was the primary consumer of energy (237.081 trillion Btu) in 2008, followed by the industrial sector (198.558 trillion Btu), the residential sector (179.978 trillion Btu), and the commercial sector (124.437 trillion Btu). Home heating was most commonly produced with natural gas (56 percent), followed by electricity (36 percent). Nevada has no ethanol plants but consumed 2.104 million barrels of ethanol in 2009, and 11,029 alternatively-fueled vehicles were in use in the state.

Major Geothermal Resources

Nevada has major geothermal resources, particularly in the northern half of the state, and is second only to California as a producer of geothermal power, with 19 geothermal plants that produced 1.7 gigawatt-hours of electricity in 2009. The second-largest power plant in the state is the hydroelectric plant on the Hoover Dam, which supplies power to Arizona and California as well as Nevada. Nevada also has rich potential for producing solar energy and wind power, although these resources have been less well developed. In June 2009, Nevada passed a renewable portfolio standard (RPS) requiring that, by 2025, at least 25 percent of the state's electricity be produced by renewable sources and that, by 2016, at least 6 percent be produced by solar energy.

Although Nevada has no nuclear power facilities, since the 1980s a site in Nevada, Yucca Mountain, has been a leading candidate for construction of a repository for high-level nuclear waste (primarily spent fuel from nuclear reactors). Yucca Mountain is a volcanic ridge in southwestern Nevada, near the California border and about 100 miles northwest of Las Vegas. Nevada has fought the proposal in court and in Congress, and scientific concerns have been raised about the stability of the formation and whether the nuclear waste would pollute the water table. Questions have also been raised about the safety of transporting nuclear wastes to the repository, both in terms of ordinary accidents that might occur and the potential for terrorism. Therefore, as of 2011, the future of the Yucca Mountain project remained uncertain.

SARAH BOSLAUGH

Further Reading
Board of Eureka County Commissioners. "Lessons Learned: Summary of Findings and Recommendations for the Blue Ribbon Commission on America's Nuclear Future." March 2011. http://www.yuccamountain.org/pdf/lessons -learned_2011.pdf.
Driesner, Doug, and Alan Coyner. "Major Mines of Nevada 2009: Mineral Industries in Nevada's Economy." Nevada Bureau of Mines and Geology Special Publication P-21. http://www.nbmg.unr.edu /dox/mm/mm08.pdf.
U.S. Energy Information Agency. "State Energy Profiles: Nevada." http://www.eia.gov/state/state -energy-profiles.cfm?sid=NV.
U.S. Nuclear Regulatory Commission. "Fact Sheet on Licensing Yucca Mountain (Feb. 4, 2011)." http:// www.nrc.gov/reading-rm/doc-collections/fact -sheets/fs-yucca-license-review.html.

See Also: Arizona; Bonneville Power Administration; Columbia River; Geothermal Energy; Green Energy Certification; Hydropower; Super Power; Yucca Mountain.

New Hampshire

Category: Energy in the United States.
Summary: New Hampshire's total energy consumption and per capita consumption are

among the lowest in the country. Severe winter weather makes the state particularly vulnerable to widespread and lengthy power outages.

A northern New England state bordering Canada, New Hampshire was the first sovereign state in the Americas, and due to the large Quebecois diaspora, has the largest per capita French population, half again as large as Louisiana's. The weather observatory on the peak of Mount Washington, the tallest mountain in the northeastern United States, has long claimed to observe "the world's worst weather," and it and other mountains in the White Mountains range experience hurricane-force winds on average of more than 100 days a year. Much of the state experiences subzero temperatures in the winter, and summers have historically been mild, though since the 1990s a number of summers have seen record and near-record heat and humidity. After extreme and record-breaking winters in the 2000s, the 2011–12 winter was one of the mildest on record, not only relatively warm but extremely dry, leading to many rivers drying up, their currents falling to 3 percent of normal. The spring of 2012 saw significant wildfires impact the state, a rarity for the state, especially so early in the year.

New Hampshire's Seabrook nuclear power plant in Portsmouth is the largest nuclear reactor in New England; construction was completed in 1986 and full operation began in 1990. A second unit was planned but never completed, due to financial trouble. Seabrook's construction was viciously opposed, not only by antinuclear activists but also by Michael Dukakis, then-governor of neighboring Massachusetts, because of environmental concerns for his state. The 1986 Chernobyl disaster further invigorated the anti-Seabrook protests. Currently, the station generates 10,763 gigawatt-hours (GW-h) annually. The relicensing process, which would extend its operating license to 2050, has been delayed because of concerns about concrete degradation.

New Hampshire's electricity use is particularly low because of a lower demand for air conditioning and the fact that more than half of the state uses fuel oil rather than electricity for winter heating (wood-burning stoves and fireplaces are also com-

monly used). The state has no fossil fuel reserves and its net electricity generation is among the lowest in the country. Seabrook provided more than half of the state's electricity generation until 2003, when two natural gas power plants were added. In 2007, the state adopted a renewable energy portfolio standard, requiring 25 percent of the state's electricity to be generated from renewable sources by 2025, and a good deal of that will likely be contributed by wind farms and home windmills. At present, about 10 percent of the state's electricity is derived from renewable sources. There is one commercial wind farm in operation; the Lempster Mountain wind power project—a 24-megawatt farm near Mount Sunapee. In 2011, the Department of Energy awarded a $168.9 million loan guarantee to help subsidize the cost of constructing the $275 million Granite Reliable Power Windpark in the Phillips Brook area, operating 333-megawatt turbines in the mountains. The Granite Reliable project has been criticized as a "wind Solyndra" by the state's ultraconservative union leader, and others have alleged connections between the project's backers and U.S. Senator Jeanne Shaheen. The Connecticut and Merrimack river basins also offer considerable hydroelectric power potential, much of which remains untapped.

Severe Weather and Power Outages

New Hampshire's three most severe power outages have occurred within the same four-year period. In December 2008, the worst ice storm in decades struck New Hampshire, parts of New England, and upstate New York. (In an ice storm, freezing rain strikes surfaces of freezing or below-freezing temperatures and turns to ice, accumulating in a growing layer.) During the December 2008 storm, ice quickly accumulated in masses, resulting in snapped tree limbs, downed power and telephone lines, collapsed rooftops, and fallen trees. At least 400,000 customers in New Hampshire, about a third of the population, was left without power—five times more than in the ice storm of 1998, previously the worst power outage and devastating storm on record. Many schools and colleges ended the semester early, and some schools were turned into emergency shelters for those without power, as the outage lasted for weeks in parts of the state. While the only death caused by the storm was the result of carbon monoxide poisoning when a gas-powered generator was used indoors, the financial toll was severe. Most of those who lost power were without it for days; telephone and cell phone services were either out or spotty; and despite contractors being hired from all over the country, full power restoration to the entire state took over a month.

Second only to the 2008 ice storm was the February 2010 wind storm, during which hurricane-force gusts of wind knocked down trees and power lines, resulting in 270,000 customers without power. It took over a week to restore power to the state.

Less than two years later, the 2011–12 winter weather began with a storm many assumed would signal the character of the season: the 2011 Halloween blizzard. Snowfall and freezing rain began in North Carolina the evening of October 28th and moved steadily north. New Hampshire received 32 inches of snow and 315,000 customers lost power—again significantly more than the 1998 ice storm, and only slightly below the 2008 figure. While the key element driving the damage in 2008 had been accumulating ice, in 2011 the problem was more simple: the blizzard came too early in the season, before the trees had lost their leaves. The significantly greater surface area of the leaves resulted in more snow accumulating before breaking limbs and downing power lines. Although the remainder of the winter proved to be mild, the financial toll of the October storm was again significant. Restoring power proved a slow process, despite the utility companies' promises of improvements since 2008, and the federal funding made possible by the 2009 economic stimulus plan.

The occurrence of three widespread power outages affected more than half the state, with some customers experiencing a total of two months without power over a four year period. The result was that the state's two U.S. senators, Kelly Ayotte and Jeanne Shaheen, called for a review of National Grid and PSNH, the state's two electricity providers. Debate went back and forth between the utility companies and their critics as to whether there was an underlying problem with the electrical grid

and the utility companies' system for responding to outages, or whether these were simply three extreme weather events that exceeded the bounds of anything the utilities could be prepared for. A Lawrence Berkeley National Laboratory study had estimated that the national cost of power interruptions was about $80 billion a year—though this may have been underestimated as some costs (e.g., nonessential home repairs, repairs to outbuildings, yard clean-ups) were deferred because of the economy and others (e.g., lost school days, the use of out-of-state contractors instead of in-state employees) are difficult to quantify.

Recurring problems during these outages were grid overload and customers impacted by more than one outage event. Grid overload occurred when power was restored to a portion of the grid, causing a sudden flood of demand on that part of the grid, either because of appliances and lights that had been left on or because of a rush of customers powering up various items; this led to power re-failures. Restoration estimates were often inaccurate: a downed wire might be repaired, restoring power to a neighborhood, only to reveal that areas remained dark because of an additional problem. Because New Hampshire has so many rural areas, many of the lengthy repairs succeeded in restoring power to only a handful of homes, making restoration progress slow. Urban areas like Nashua and Manchester remained without power for over a week in some of these outages, lending support to the claim that there was a problem either with the grid itself or with restoration procedures.

BILL KTE'PI

Further Reading

Bourque, Ron. "Lessons from the Ice Storm." *New Hampshire Business Review* (February 13, 2009).

Eisenstadter, Dave. *The Weight of the Ice: The Northeast Ice Storm of 2008*. Keene, NH: Surry Cottage Books, 2010.

U.S. Energy Information Administration New Hampshire Energy Profile. http://www.eia.gov/state/state-energy-profiles.cfm?sid=NH.

See Also: Electric Grids; Massachusetts; Vermont.

New Jersey

Category: Energy in the United States.
Summary: Although home to energy-intensive industries, New Jersey's energy consumption accounts for less than 3 percent of the national total, and it contributes only 0.8 percent of the country's carbon dioxide emissions, largely because of its reliance on nuclear power.

The most densely populated state in the country with 8,791,894 people in 2010, New Jersey is also the second-wealthiest, with a median income of $70,378. New Jersey is located at the center of the Boston-Washington megalopolis, the heavily urbanized area covering the northeastern seaboard that is the financial center of the country and home to most of the Ivy League universities. New Jersey itself boasts more scientists and engineers per square mile than any other location in the world.

New Jersey's economy is fueled by energy-intensive industries: pharmaceuticals and chemicals, telecommunications, electrical equipment, publishing, and food processing (it is a leading producer of blueberries, cranberries, and spinach). Major pharmaceutical companies located in New Jersey include Johnson and Johnson, Merck,

Wikimedia

New Jersey has no fossil fuel reserves but is a major petroleum-refining state, with six oil refineries along the Delaware River and the New York Harbor. Beesley's Point Power Generating Plant north of Cape May County burns coal in two generators and fuel oil in the third.

Pfizer, Novartis, Bristol-Myers Squibb, Hoffman-LaRoche, Sanofi-Aventis, and Schering-Plough. Telecommunications giants Verizon, AT&T, and Alcatel-Lucent make their home in the state as well. Shipping is a major industry along the coast. Much of New Jersey serves as a bedroom community for either New York City or Philadelphia, and the Newark Liberty International Airport is one of the busiest in the world. Despite its dense population, half of the state is heavily wooded; the oak from the northern forests is used in New Jersey's shipbuilding industry.

In 2008, New Jersey consumed 2.6 quadrillion British thermal units (Btu) in total energy, including 201.7 million barrels of petroleum, 620,000 cubic feet of natural gas, and 2.64 million short tons of coal. A disproportionate amount of jet fuel—34.4 million barrels, 6.8 percent of the national total—was consumed because the Newark airport, the site of most of that consumption, is located in the state. Most homes, 67 percent, were heated with natural gas. The average commute time in New Jersey is the longest in the country; as a bedroom community, it consumes most of its energy for transport. New Jersey is also one of the few states that require the use of gasoline reformulated with ethanol.

New Jersey has no fossil fuel reserves but is a major petroleum-refining state, with six oil refineries along the Delaware River and the New York Harbor. Most of the oil processed in New Jersey is imported from overseas.

Nuclear Power

Despite the energy-intensiveness of its industries, New Jersey's energy consumption accounts for less than 3 percent of the national total; more significantly, it contributes only 0.8 percent of the country's carbon dioxide emissions. The latter advantage is due to New Jersey's heavy reliance on nuclear power: It draws more than half of its electricity from its three nuclear power plants.

The Oyster Creek Nuclear Generating Station is the oldest operational nuclear power plant in the United States, coming online on December 1, 1969, and licensed to continue operations until 2029. Owned and operated by the Chicago-based Exelon Corporation, the plant is located in Ocean County and gets its cooling water from the brackish estuary of Barnegat Bay. The population within 10 miles of Oyster Creek (the plume exposure pathway zone) numbers 133,000 and is growing; within 50 miles (the ingestion pathway zone) are 4.5 million people, including those who live in Atlantic City and Asbury Park.

Oyster Creek generates 619 megawatts as a boiling-water reactor. When its initial 40-year license was renewed for another 20 years, there were some concerns that the renewal process did not subject the plant to sufficient safety tests, the argument being that the prolonged operation of the plant could have led to unseen wear and tear. Exelon has since announced that the plant will close 10 years early.

General Electric supplies the Oyster Creek reactor. There have been some recent safety concerns; in May 2011, General Electric notified Oyster Creek of a mathematical error that could have resulted in the reactor fuel reaching higher temperatures than reported. In August 2009, two separate tritium (radioactive hydrogen) leaks were discovered, contaminating groundwater on site. The following May, the leak had spread to a nearby aquifer and was predicted to reach public water supplies by 2025. An Oyster Creek spokesperson announced that power plant staff were working with the state to prevent that occurrence.

The Hope Creek Nuclear Generating Station and Salem Nuclear Power Plant are both located in Lower Alloways Creek Township. Hope Creek is a single boiling-water reactor. Salem includes two pressurized-water reactors. The population within 10 miles numbers 53,000, and that within 50 miles numbers 5.5 million and includes the city of Philadelphia in Pennsylvania. Hope Creek has been operational since 1986 and is licensed to operate until 2026; Salem's reactors have been online since 1977 and 1981 and are licensed to operate until 2016 and 2020. Exelon has a 43 percent share of Salem; Public Service Enterprise Group, the largest power company in New Jersey, owns the remainder, as well as Hope Creek. General Electric supplies the Hope Creek reactor, and Westinghouse supplies both Salem reactors. The Delaware River is used for cooling water.

Two other nuclear power plants have been proposed in New Jersey in the past, without fruition. The Forked River plant, planned in the 1970s, was eventually canceled after years of construction because of financial difficulties following the accident in 1979 at the Three Mile Island facility, owned by the same parent company. The Atlantic nuclear power plant, proposed in the 1970s, would have been a floating plant on human-made islands; it was canceled in 1978 following protests.

Renewable Resources

New Jersey's renewable portfolio standard requires that by 2021, 22.5 percent of New Jersey's electricity come from renewable resources. At least 2.12 percent of the electricity must come from solar power. The state has the second-largest number of homes and businesses with installed solar panels: more than 7,500 photovoltaic systems generating 137 megawatts.

There are numerous incentives for renewable energy in New Jersey. It has one of the most favorable net-metering laws in the country: New Jersey and Colorado are the only states to allow unlimited net-metering customers (up to 2 megawatts per customer). *Net metering* refers to the practice of charging for electricity based on the net amount of electricity used and refers to the handling of customers who own renewable energy systems—such as home fuel cells, solar arrays, or wind power—and thus can often "bank" excess energy as future credit against their power bills, thus deducting the energy they generate from the energy they draw off the grid. Although U.S. energy law requires public utilities to make net metering available, quotas and other limitations are in place in most states, but New Jersey is one of the few parts of the country to actively encourage net-metering customers.

New Jersey's Clean Energy Program provides a rebate of $1.75 per watt for residential systems of less than 10 kilowatts with an energy audit, or $1.55 per watt without an energy audit. Nonresidential systems, up to 50,000 watts, receive a rebate of $1 per watt. When systems are partially manufactured or assembled in New Jersey, there is an additional rebate of $0.25 per watt.

Solar Power

Electricity suppliers must have enough solar renewable energy certificates (SRECs) to meet state targets, or they will be fined. SRECs were adopted in 2004, and the total number suppliers must have increases every year: The number was 306,000 in 2011 and will rise to more than 5 million by 2026. An SREC is generated every time a megawatt-hour is produced by a solar power system; electricity suppliers may either generate their own solar electricity or purchase SRECs from those who do. There is no mandated price for an SREC; market forces determine the price, shaped by the gap between the state's requirements and the suppliers' ability to meet those requirements and bound by the fine for noncompliance. Solar power systems must be certified by the state in order to produce SRECs. One of the benefits to electricity suppliers for purchasing SRECs is that SRECs save them the start-up costs of building their own solar farms.

Since 2009, Public Service Enterprise Group has been at work on a major solar power project, intended to install solar panels in 200,000 utility poles throughout the state. This is the largest project of its type to date, with projected completion scheduled for 2013. The company is also building solar farms in Edison, Hamilton, Linden, and Trenton.

The first tests of the PB150 PowerBuoy, a new power generation device developed by Jersey-based Ocean Power Technologies, took place in 2011. The PowerBuoy is a smart power system that responds to different wave conditions in order to use wave energy to generate power. The PB150 model has a peak-rated output of 150 kilowatts, about enough for 150 residences.

Wind power has expanded in New Jersey in 2011, with the state issuing new permits for a six-turbine wind farm off the coast of Atlantic City, with an output of about 25 megawatts. This follows the creation of the New Jersey Solar and Wind Energy Commission, which will study the feasibility of solar and wind installations on state-owned property and make its recommendations.

BILL KTE'PI

Further Reading

New Jersey Clean Energy Program. "About New Jersey's Clean Energy Program." http://www .njcleanenergy.com/.

Pruitt, Alison. "New Jersey Passes Slew of Renewable Energy Laws." http://www.energyboom.com/policy/ new-jersey-passes-slew-renewable-energy-laws.

U.S. Department of Energy. "Database of State Incentives for Renewables and Efficiency: New Jersey: Incentives/Policy for Renewables and Efficiency." http://www.dsireusa.org/incentives/ incentive.cfm?Incentive_Code=NJ05R&re= 1&ee=1.

U.S. Energy Information Administration. "New Jersey." http://www.eia.gov/state/state-energy-profiles .cfm?sid=NJ.

See Also: Edison, Thomas Alva; Energy Transmission: Electricity; Evans, Oliver; ExxonMobil; Nuclear Power; Regional Greenhouse Gas Initiative; Standard Oil Company; United States.

New Mexico

Category: Energy in the United States.
Summary: The state of New Mexico produces natural gas and oil. In renewables, the state has wind power and solar power.

Possessing a wealth of natural resources, New Mexico is a major producer of crude oil, sharing with Colorado an area that contains the largest store of proven natural gas reserves in America. Wind power is the chief source of renewable energy, but New Mexico is considered to have the second-highest potential in the nation for the development of solar energy, which is expanding rapidly. Despite its historical role as the site where the atom bomb was developed during the Manhattan Project (in Los Alamos), New Mexico has no nuclear power capability.

New Mexico, which is located in the southwestern United States, covers a land area of 121,598 square miles, making it the fifth-largest state. The Great Plains cover the eastern third of New Mexico, and only 234 square miles are covered by water. The major rivers are the Rio Grande and the Pecos. Major lakes are Elephant Butte Reservoir, Conchas Lake, and Navajo Reservoir. Thus, the use of hydropower is somewhat limited. The Navajo and Farmington dams in the San Juan Basin produce 30 megawatts, and another 50 megawatts are available from the Elephant Butte, Abiquiu, and El Vado Dams on the Rio Grande. New Mexico receives 200 megawatts from the Colorado River Project.

Largest Field of Natural Gas Reserves in the United States

New Mexico also has fossil fuel resources, including the largest field of natural gas reserves in the United States, and natural gas production provides nearly a 10th of all natural gas produced in America. The San Juan Basin, which spreads from New Mexico to Colorado, holds the largest field of proved natural gas reserves that can be found in the United States. The Blanco Hub, within this basin, serves as a transportation point for natural gas used throughout the western states. New Mexico is one of three states that contain the largest resources of coal-bed methane. The others are Colorado and Wyoming. In New Mexico, coal-bed methane accounts for a third of all natural gas produced. Three of the largest American oil fields are located in New Mexico's Permian Basin.

Wind is the primary source of renewable energy used in New Mexico, and 6.2 percent of all electricity generated in New Mexico is generated by wind projects. Total wind capacity reached 497.5 megawatts in 2008.

Reflecting its scarcity of water resources, only 0.8 percent of electricity generated in New Mexico is derived from traditional hydropower. Nevertheless, between 2006 and 2007, New Mexico reported 352 percent growth in the use of hydroelectric power, and the state ranked fifth in the United States in this area.

In 2008, New Mexico consumed 693.3 trillion British thermal units (Btu) of total energy, and the state ranked 14th in the nation in energy consumption. That same year, New Mexico consumed 22 terawatt-hours of electricity. Some 2.2 percent of total energy was generated by renewable sources.

The New Mexico Energy Conservation and Management Division serves as the entity responsible for encouraging individuals and businesses in New Mexico to reduce the state's carbon footprint and promote the use of clean energy. Spurred by the American Recovery and Reinvestment Act of 2009, Governor Bill Richardson announced in January of that year that he was establishing a new "green jobs cabinet" made up of secretaries from the Departments of Public Education, Higher Education, Work Force Solutions, Energy, Minerals and Natural Resources, and Environment and Agriculture, along with the New Mexico Investment Office. The secretary for economic development was chosen to chair the cabinet for the purpose of promoting clean energy and technology while energizing the state economy and putting people to work.

After the U.S. Congress passed the American Recovery and Reinvestment Act in 2009, state governors were required to submit letters of intent in order to qualify for grants allotted to improving energy efficiency and promoting renewable sources of energy. Governor Richardson responded with assurances that New Mexico had passed the Efficient Use of Energy Act in 1978. He noted that the Public Regulations Commission and the Regulation and Licensing Department had long been involved in promoting energy cost-effectiveness and implementing green building codes. In all, New Mexico received $612.9 million for 94 separate energy projects that included support for wind, solar, geothermal, and biofuels development. Other projects focused on cleaning up nuclear testing sites used during the Cold War. The $26.9 million allotted to New Mexico through the Weatherization Assistance Program has helped to weatherize 2,800 low-income homes and has financed training to create a green workforce. Other funds were used to finance an appliance rebate program for consumers who were replacing outdated appliances with more energy-efficient models.

Solar Power
Even though solar energy was previously not a major priority in New Mexico, in the winter of 2010

▷ Energy Conservation Projects in New Mexico

In July 2010, researchers at New Mexico's Los Alamos National Laboratory were recognized for their work on several projects that were significant in the field of energy conservation. These projects included an ultrasonic algal biofuel harvester that separated and recycled water in a single integrated system; an ultraconductor that manufactured high-tech wires and cables designed to improve the electricity conduction; and the Solution Deposition Planarization Superconductor Substrate Program, which improved the process of superconducting while yielding only negligible amounts of toxic manufacturing waste. Researchers at the Sandia National Laboratories and their partners also received honors for their work on the Micro Power Source, which served as an energy harvester.

the Department of Energy selected the state as one of several western states that were ideally situated for developing a solar energy zone. The use of solar energy subsequently accelerated. For instance, solar panels have now been installed at the Living Desert Zoo to provide an alternative source of energy and a savings of up to $10,000 annually. Dependence on wind projects has also continued. In the fall of 2003, the New Mexico Wind Energy Center became operational. The facility, which is located near Fort Sumner, contains 136 210-foot-high turbines that generate 200 megawatts of power capable of producing sufficient electricity to power 94,00 homes. New Mexico's existing wind farms are Clovis (2 megawatts), San Jon (80 megawatts), Elida (120 megawatts), House (204 megawatts), Santa Rosa (22 megawatts), Gladstone (20 megawatts), and Clayton (120 megawatts).

The search for renewable energy in New Mexico is epitomized by the Dreaming New Mexico project, which is pursing solar, wind, biofuels, and geothermal power as viable alternative sources of energy. New Mexico has been labeled as the state with the second-best potential for developing solar power. In Albuquerque, the largest city in the state, the sun shines 278 days of the year. *Scientific American* has estimated that by using an area of land 95 square miles, New Mexico could generate 1,119,000 megawatts of solar energy. This energy has the potential to slash the state's carbon footprint drastically. Proponents of green energy point out that rooftop solar power is easily affordable for most homes and businesses, and Rich Diver, a local inventor, has developed a mirror alignment device that is expected to make solar energy even more affordable and efficient. In addition to existing wind potential (1,000 megawatts), New Mexico has the potential to generate a total of 20,000 megawatts of wind power using 500 megawatts large-scale wind farms.

ELIZABETH RHOLETTER PURDY

Further Reading

Barnes, Roland V., ed. *Energy Crisis in America?* Huntington, NY: Nova Science, 2001.

Bird, Lori, et al. *Green Power Marketing in the United States: A Status Report.* Golden, CO: National Renewable Energy Laboratory, 2008.

Dreaming New Mexico. "Energy: Dreaming the Future Can Create the Future." http://www.dreaming newmexico.org/energy.

New Mexico Energy Conservation and Management Division. "Energy." http://www.emnrd.state.nm.us/ecmd.

"Richardson Rolls Out Green Jobs Cabinet." *New Mexico Business Weekly,* January 22, 2009. http://www.bizjournals.com/albuquerque/stories/2009/01/19/daily48.html.

U.S. Energy Information Administration. "New Mexico." http://www.eia.doe.gov/state/state-energy-profiles.cfm?sid=NM.

See Also: Arizona; Department of Energy, U.S.; Geothermal Energy; Hydropower; Natural Gas; Solar Energy; United States; Uranium.

New York

Category: Energy in the United States.
Summary: As the fifth-largest energy consuming state, New York is the most energy-efficient state in the continental United States on a per-capita basis.

From the installment of the world's first central generating plant in New York City in 1882 and the very early distribution of large-scale electric power to the city of Buffalo, New York is a pioneer in the history of civil use of energy. The New York energy system has evolved over the past several decades in response to a broad set of circumstances: diverse federal policies and regulations, growing demand for energy, evolution of the national and global energy market, and climate change. Energy efficiency and renewable energy have increasingly become the central concern in energy planning and implementation in New York. Accounting for 6.4 percent of the nation's population, New York accounts for 4 percent (3,795 trillion British thermal units) of the nation's total primary energy, which makes it the most energy-efficient state in the continental United States on a per-capita basis, although this is largely a result of the significant decline in the state's industrial sector. Excluding the industrial sector, New York's per capita energy use is among the highest in the nation.

New York relies on the burning of carbon-based fossil fuels for 71 percent of its energy demand, compared to 82 percent nationally. From 1995–2009, New York's consumption of coal decreased 40 percent, and nuclear energy and net electricity import increased 65 percent and 113 percent, respectively. The consumption of other energy sources during the same period had only minor changes. The residential and commercial net energy demand in New York accounts for more than 50 percent of total energy demand. Nationally, this number is only 33 percent. Another big portion of energy demand is from transportation (39 percent). Industrial net energy use accounts for only 7 percent.

Since the 1970s, New York has adapted its governance structure, issued new laws, developed new energy plans, and formulated new initiatives in response to global, national, and local challenges. In 1975, the New York State Legislature created the New York State Energy Research and Development Authority (NYSERDA), a public benefit corporation, to advance innovative energy solutions in ways that improve New York's economy and environment. Under the New York Energy Law adopted in 1976, the chief regulator for the Energy Law is the commissioner, or president, of the NYSERDA. In 1999, the New York Independent System Operator (NYISO) began its operation. It operates New York's bulk electricity grid, administers the state's wholesale electricity markets, and provides comprehensive reliability planning for the state's bulk electricity system.

Another important energy-related authority is New York Power Authority. It is America's largest state power organization, operating 17 generating facilities and more than 1,400 circuit-miles of transmission lines. Some of the major investor-owned utilities in the state include: Central Hudson Gas & Electric Corporation; Consolidated Edison Company of New York, Inc.; New York State Electric & Gas Corporation; Niagara Mohawk, a National Grid Company; Orange and Rockland Utilities, Inc.; Rochester Gas and Electric Corporation; and St. Lawrence Gas.

Demand and Supply

A decade ago, New York was facing a generation gap. Since 1996, annual electricity use in New York has grown from 146,641 gigawatt-hours to 163,505 gigawatt-hours in 2010, an increase of more than 11.5 percent. However, New York now has a surplus of over 5,200 megawatts of available resources. Since 2000, power plants with generating capacity totaling 3,510 megawatts have retired. Of that total, 3,500 megawatts were powered by fossil fuels, including 1,283 megawatts of coal-fired generation. During the same period, more than 8,600 megawatts of new generation have been built by private power producers and public authorities. Among the new power plants were numerous renewable projects. Over 80 percent of new generation has been sited in New York City, on Long Island, and in the Hudson Valley, the regions of New York State where demand is greatest. Much of the new generation developed in upstate regions is powered by wind; consequently, it was sited where wind resources are most available. Increased generation in upstate regions also resulted from upgrades in existing nuclear and hydropower plants.

In 2010, nearly 30,000 gigawatt-hours of New York's electricity was supplied by wind, hydro, and other renewable resources. Approximately 45,700 gigawatt-hours of the electricity used by New Yorkers will need to be produced by renewable resources in 2015 to achieve the 30 percent renewable goal. In addition to these efforts, to enhance efficiency of existing resources and reduce costs for power consumers, New York and Canada have developed the Broader Regional Markets initiative. The regional initiative involves Ontario's Independent Electricity System Operator, the Midwest Independent Transmission System Operator, PJM Interconnection, ISO New England, and Hydro Qubec. Due to these efforts, sulfur dioxide (SO_2) rates have seen the most dramatic decline, dropping more than 80 percent. Nitrogen oxide (NO_X) rates have dropped more than 60 percent, and carbon dioxide (CO_2) rates have dropped by 25 percent since 1999.

Transmission

In 2010, the NYISO issued a first-of-its-kind economic analysis of transmission congestion on the New York State bulk power system and the potential costs and benefits of relieving congestion. As of the close of 2010, 60 percent of New York State's power plant capacity was put into service before 1980. Similarly, 85 percent of the high-voltage transmission facilities in New York State went into service before 1980. The transmission system that will be needed in the future is essential to the continued operation of efficient and reliable wholesale power markets. The development of interstate transmission has contributed to the effort to serve New York's most power-hungry regions. Approximately 1,290 megawatts of transmission capability were added to bring more power to the downstate region from out of state. New York also invested intensively in grid-scale energy storage and Smart Grid technologies. In 2009, the NYISO became the first grid operator in the nation to implement federally approved market rules that enabled storage systems to participate in the markets as frequency regulation providers, delivering reserve capacity that helped grid operators maintain the balance between generation and load. The state is also expanding its dynamic pricing at both the wholesale and retail levels.

New York's Energy Future

After having access to plentiful and inexpensive energy supplies through much of the 1980s and 1990s, New York has experienced intermittent price increases for natural gas and petroleum products. In the meantime, there is an increasing concern both internationally and nationally on climate change. An economy that depends highly on fossil fuels cannot sustain its growth and competitiveness in the long run. In responding to this challenge, the Energy Law established the State Energy Planning Board (SEPB). The SEPB has completed State Energy Plans 2002 and 2009. The 2013 plan is still in progress. Both 2002 and 2009 state energy plans set forth a vision for a robust and innovative clean energy economy. It is the implementation of the 2002 plan that provides a baseline for the 2009 plan. Aside from the energy plan, New York put forward several initiatives in the same regard. The following initiatives will promise New York a secure and environmentally friendly energy future:

45 x 15 Clean Energy Goal (2009) challenges the state to meet 45 percent of its electricity needs by 2015 through increased energy efficiency and renewable energy. The goal calls for a 15 percent reduction in electricity end-use, primarily through expanded energy efficiency activities, while simultaneously calling for 30 percent of the state's electricity supply needs to be met through renewable resources.

Executive Order 24 (EO24, 2009) set a goal of reducing statewide greenhouse gas emissions at least 80 percent below 1990 levels by 2050. It also establishes the New York Climate Action Council (CAC) with a directive to prepare a Climate Action Plan.

Executive Order 111 (EO111): Adopted in 2001, Executive Order 111 (EO111) sets forth an energy purchasing goal that aims to meet 10 percent of the annual electricity requirement of buildings occupied by state agencies and entities through renewable technologies by 2005, and 20 percent by 2010. EO111 also sets an energy efficiency goal for 2010 of reducing the energy use of state agencies, authorities, and entities by 35 percent from 1990 levels.

Regional Greenhouse Gas Initiative (RGGI): New York is one of the 10 Northeast and Mid-Atlantic states involved in RGGI, an effort that places a cap on carbon dioxide (CO_2) emissions from electricity generators. RGGI aims to reduce greenhouse gas emissions by auctioning off a limited number of CO_2 allowances to fossil-fuel generators, the amount of which will decrease over time, and using the funds that are raised to support a variety of emissions reduction programs.

Low Carbon Fuel Standard (LCFS): The LCFS is a "greenhouse gas standard for transportation fuels" that is expected to spark research in alternatives to petroleum-based fuels while simultaneously reducing emissions.

System Benefits Charge (SBC) and Energy Efficiency Portfolio Standard (EEPS): Funding for electric and natural gas efficiency is provided through the SBC and EEPS, and both support the governor's 45 x 15 goal. NYSERDA's portfolio of programs target the residential sector, commercial and industrial customers, and governmental customers, with special attention to assisting low-income customers. The portfolio also includes research, development, and demonstration initiatives, as well as environmental and transportation program offerings.

Renewable Portfolio Standard (RPS): In a series of orders issued in late 2009 and early 2010, the New York State Public Service Commission adopted a more ambitious RPS target of having 30 percent of retail electricity sales in New York supplied by renewable resources by 2015 and authorized NYSERDA to continue administering the program.

New York State has significant natural gas resources in Marcellus Shale, a black shale formation extending deep underground from Ohio and West Virginia northeast into Pennsylvania and southern New York. Although the Marcellus Shale is exposed at the ground surface in some locations in the northern Finger Lakes area, it is as deep as 7,000 feet or more below the ground surface along the Pennsylvania border in the Delaware River valley. Geologists estimate that the entire Marcellus Shale formation may contain up to 489 trillion cubic feet of natural gas throughout its entire extent.

It is not yet known how much gas will be commercially recoverable from the Marcellus Shale in New York. New York State uses about 1.1 trillion cubic feet of natural gas a year. The New York State Department of Environmental Conservation is currently assessing issues unique to horizontal drilling and high-volume hydraulic fracturing (sometimes referred to as hydrofracking) in the Marcellus Shale and other low permeability reservoirs, which may cause contamination of local water supplies.

XIAOCHEN ZHANG

Further Reading
New York Independent System Operator. "Power Trends 2011: Energizing New York's Legacy of Leadership 2011." http://www.nyiso.com/public/webdocs/newsroom/power_trends/Power_Trends_2011.pdf

New York Independent System Operator, "Transmission Expansion in New York State: A New York ISO White Paper," November 2008. http://www.esai.com/power/09/pdfs/NYISO_Transmission_WhitePaper_1108.pdf

New York State Energy Research and Development Authority. "Patterns and Trends New York State Energy Profiles: 1995–2009," January 2011. http://www.nyserda.org/publications/1995_2009_patterns_trends_rpt.pdf

State Energy Planning Board. "State Energy Plans (2002, 2009, 2013 (in progress))," http://www.yserda.org/Energy_Information/energy_state_plan.asp

See Also: Investor-Owned Utilities; Marcellus Shale; Morgan, J. P.; Regional Greenhouse Gas Initiative; Rockefeller, John D.; Standard Oil Company.

New Zealand

Official Name: New Zealand.
Category: Geography of Energy.
Summary: Although New Zealand currently relies primarily on fossil fuel energy, it is projecting the growth of renewable sources as it aims for greater sustainability.

Energy sources used by the first inhabitants of New Zealand included wind for sailing, muscular power for transportation and agriculture, and wood and geothermal springs for cooking and warmth. When Europeans arrived by sail in the early 1800s, they employed domesticated animals for labor and transport. Wood burning provided energy for home heating and for industry. Later, the power of water was employed for the movement of timber and for gold excavation. With the coming of the Industrial Revolution, New Zealand turned increasingly to thermal energy sources. Today, about two-thirds of the nation's energy needs are supplied by fossil fuels, with imports exceeding domestic production. Overall, energy consumption is dominated by industry and transportation and is growing about 2 percent annually. Additional energy demand comes from commercial, residential, and public services, as well as from agriculture, forestry, and fishing.

Electricity

All of the nation's power stations are connected to the electrical grid, and 99 percent of the population receives electricity. Of the 44.4 terawatt-hours of electricity generated in 2010, three-fourths came from renewable resources, including hydroelectric (56 percent), gas (21 percent), geothermal (14 percent), coal (5 percent), wind (4 percent), and biomass (1 percent). (Rounding errors result in total of 101 percent.) The Rio Tinto Aluminum Smelter at Tiwai Point is the largest consumer of electricity, using 10 to 15 percent of the nation's output. Nearly all of New Zealand's electricity is produced at five power stations: Meridian Energy, Contact Energy, Genesis Power, Mighty River Power, and Trust Power. New Zealand's population of 4.3 million has an

Wikimedia

New Zealand has used geothermal facilities since the 1980s, with some power going to industry and some used to generate consumer electricity. This steam-water separator is located at the Mighty River power station.

average per capita energy consumption of 7,900 kilowatt-hours annually.

Oil Wells

The first oil well was drilled in 1866 in the Taranaki Basin. With the introduction of automobiles in the 1920s, gasoline began to be imported. In 1964, the Marsden Point refinery began processing crude oil imported from the Middle East, Australia, Malaysia, and Indonesia in order to bolster the supply of transportation fuels. Today, the Marsden plant supplies three-fourths of domestically refined oil products. However, as New Zealand's domestic crude oil is not suitable for refining at Marsden Point, most of it gets exported for processing. Price controls were removed in the late 1980s, when the oil sector was deregulated. Crude oil reserves are estimated at 200 million barrels, with the promise of undiscovered reserves in deep water. Today, the major oil companies are BP (British Petroleum), Chevron, Shell, and Mobil. Concerns for the future of oil are exacerbated by New Zealand's isolated geographical location, which makes it difficult to attract international exploration, and the possibility of future oil shocks that could hurt the $9 billion tourist industry that depends on affordable fuel for transportation.

Coal and Thermal Fuel

Coal has been used as a thermal fuel ever since the 1860s, when it overtook wood for industrial and home use. Around 1900, coal gas also came into use for lighting. Nearly all of New Zealand's coal production is either subbituminous or of the higher-quality bituminous kind, which is exported for use in steelmaking. When natural gas production began to fall in the 1980s, the state-owned Huntly power plant (with a capacity of 1,000 megawatts electric) switched to using 80 percent coal. Southland and Otago hold a vast reserve of valuable lignite that remains largely untapped. One hurdle to the economic marketing of lignite, however, is the long distance to markets.

Natural Gas

The majority of natural gas in New Zealand is used for electricity generation, petrochemical production, and industry. The gas supply comes from 16 fields in the Taranaki region that are operated primarily by Shell and Todd Energy. The vast Maui field was discovered in 1969, but its output is now in decline; newer sources include fields at Pokohura and Kupe. Spurred by the global oil shocks of 1973 and 1979, a synthetic fuel plant was built to make use of domestic natural gas; other large projects synthesize ammonia, urea, and methanol from gas.

Hydroelectric Power

Hydroelectric power on a large scale was introduced in 1888, and the industry was expanded in the 1920s. Hydroelectric plants are located at the Waitaki and Clutha Rivers on the South Island and on the Waitako River and in the Taupo region of the North Island. Measures had to be taken to reduce electricity use when New Zealand experienced severe droughts in 1992, 2001, and again in 2003. New Zealand's Electricity Commission has been set up to manage the nation's energy security.

Wood and other biomass sources provide energy for home and industrial heating. Another biomass source is methane from landfills, which is used for electricity generation as well as for liquid fuel manufacturing. Other bio-based fuels include ethanol from whey and biodiesel from tallow. Waste-to-energy plants have begun converting municipal solid waste into industrially useful process heat and power.

Geothermal Facilities

New Zealand has more than 40 years of experience with small-scale geothermal facilities. Some geothermal power goes directly to industry, and the remainder is used for electricity generation. Geothermal installations with outputs ranging from 100 to 250 megawatts-electric include the Kawerau and Nga Awa Purua stations; additional capacity use is planned for Tauhara Stage Two and the Te Mihi and Ngatamariki stations. New Zealand is one of the few countries that does not employ nuclear energy to generate electricity. Although in 1968 a national energy agenda projected a future need for nuclear energy, plans for four reactors were set aside when new fossil fuel sources were discovered. With more than 9,000 miles of coastline, New Zealand could make use of power from the ocean in the form of waves, tides, and currents.

Photovoltaic (PV) devices are used in some remote areas for the conversion of sunlight into electricity, and 2 percent of homes are equipped with solar water-heating systems. The use of wind as a renewable energy source has expanded rapidly; however, wind farm installations face some public opposition on aesthetic grounds. The Electricity Commission has also expressed concern about the intermittency of wind and its possible destabilization of the electric power grid.

New Zealand is a signatory of the Kyoto Protocol, and several national advisory agencies have been established to monitor the state of the environment. As New Zealand looks toward sustainable development, a national goal is to create 90 percent of electricity from renewable sources by the year 2025.

Margaret E. Schott

Further Reading

New Zealand Ministry of Economic Development. "Sustainable Energy: Creating a Sustainable Energy System for New Zealand," December 2005. http://www.med.govt.nz/templates/MultipageDocumentTOC____10124.aspx.

Smith, Clint. "The Next Oil Shock?" Parliamentary Research Paper, October 2010. http://www.parliament.nz/en-NZ/ParlSupport/Research Papers/4/6/a/00PLEco10041-The-next-oil -shock.htm.

U.S. Energy Information Administration. "Country Analysis Brief: New Zealand." http://www.eia.gov/countries/country-data.cfm?fips=NZ.

See Also: Alternative Energy; Biomass Energy; Climate Neutrality; International Energy Agency; Kyoto Protocol; Landfill Gas; Natural Gas; Nonpoint Source Pollution.

Nicaragua

Official Name: Republic of Nicaragua.
Category: Geography of Energy.
Summary: Nicaragua's population depends largely on wood fuel and oil imports. The country's power production and distribution system underwent a process of privatization in the 1990s.

Nicaragua has the lowest electricity generation in Central America. It is the poorest country in Central America and also has the lowest percentage of population with access to electricity. The large majority of the population, 80 percent, rely on biomass as the primary energy source, accounting for more than 50 percent of the total national energy consumption.

In 2004, the National Energy Commission (CNE) developed the National Plan for Rural Electrification (PLANER), which aimed to bring power to 70 percent of the rural population by 2005 and 90 percent of the rural population by 2012. The National Interconnected System (SIN), the Nicaraguan electricity system, covers 90 percent of the territory where the country's population lives. The other regions are covered by small generation systems. Nicaragua is very dependent on imported oil for electricity generation, with nearly all oil imports coming from Venezuela. Nicaragua has one oil refinery. The electricity sector was controlled by the state through the early 1990s. The Nicaraguan Energy Institute (INE) was created in 1979. INE was responsible for the policy making, regulation, development, and operations related to the country's energy resources. INE faced many difficulties in the 1980s. Civil war interfered with electricity generation and distribution. Furthermore, INE faced a lack of investment resources for the electricity system, currency devaluation, and a trade embargo imposed by the United States.

Reforms

In the 1990s, a series of efforts to encourage privatization was intended to promote more widespread delivery of electricity, economic efficiency, and private and foreign investment. INE was allowed to negotiate contracts with private investors beginning in 1992. The Nicaraguan Electricity Company (ENEL) was created in 1994. ENEL was a state company with the responsibility of generating, distributing, and commercializing electricity generation.

Its area of responsibility became separate from that of INE, which was to regulate and oversee the hydrocarbon and electricity sectors and apply appropriate taxation policies. In 1998, the government called for the separation of generation, distribution, and transmission assets from ENEL. The government privatized the distribution companies

of ENEL in October 2000. The Spanish company Union Fenosa bought the distribution companies.

In 1998, further reforms of INE led to the creation of CNE. CNE took over planning and policy-related responsibilities and was given special responsibility for the development of rural electrification. The Ministry of Energy and Mines (MEM) was created in 2007 and replaced CNE. Also, the hydrocarbons division of INE was transferred to MEM.

The reforms of the 1990s did not result in the more widespread and efficient system that was envisioned. The proper oversight and institutional framework did not exist during the privatization process, and years of civil war continued to deter foreign investment. The extent of rural electrification has largely remained the same, despite initial beliefs that rural electrification would improve. The privatization efforts also did little to reduce the country's dependence on fossil fuels.

In 2004, the economically viable potential of renewable energy was five times higher than the national power capacity. However, the absence of national, quantifiable renewable energy targets and a comprehensive regulatory framework have inhibited the exploitation of renewable sources. The Renewable Energy Promotion Law was adopted in 2005. It does not outline quantifiable targets, but it does assert that renewable energy is a national priority and outlines a few economic incentives, such as the exemption of renewable energy projects from import duties.

Conclusion

Currently, 11.2 percent of Nicaragua's energy comes from renewable sources: sugarcane, hydropower, and geothermal power. Solar and wind energy are not currently exploited; although good potential for solar energy generation does not exist, there is particularly good wind potential along the mountain range and along the east and southwest coasts. Nicaragua also has additional geothermal potential, particularly in the mountainous region along the east coast and the southern region of the country.

The Central American Electrical Interconnection System (SIEPAC) was first discussed as an idea in 1987. The idea behind SIEPAC was to connect the electrical grid of Central America from Panama to Guatemala. After several years of studies that demonstrated the potential benefits and opportunities of the network, planning for the SIEPAC project began in 1995. The Inter-American Development Bank was initially the primary funding source. The Spanish power company Endesa and the Central American Bank for Economic Integration (CBEI) also provided monetary support, with Central American countries providing in-kind contributions such as existing facilities and infrastructure. The SIEPAC plan includes 307 kilometers in transmission lines over Nicaragua.

SARAH ABDELRAHIM

Further Reading

Economic Commission for Latin America and the Caribbean. "Renewable Energy Sources in Latin America and the Caribbean: Situation and Policy Proposals." http://www.eclac.org/publicaciones/xml/9/14839/Lc12132i.pdf.

Martin, Jeremy. "Central America Electric Integration and the SIEPAC Project: From a Fragmented Market Toward a New Reality." Center for Hemispheric Policy, University of Miami, May 6, 2010. https://www6.miami.edu/hemispheric-policy/Martin_Central_America_Electric_Int.pdf.

U.S. Energy Information Administration. "Country Analysis Brief: Nicaragua." http://205.254.135.7/countries/country-data.cfm?fips=NU.

See Also: Biomass Energy; Geothermal Energy; Natural Gas; Oil and Gas Pipelines; Oil and Petroleum; Rural Electrification.

Niger

Official Name: Republic of Niger.
Category: Geography of Energy.
Summary: Niger is rich in natural resources such as uranium and coal but relies heavily on imported oil and domestic wood for energy production. The privatization of government-owned energy corporations and renewable energy and conservation programs are under way.

Niger's natural resources include uranium, coal, and oil, although the latter is largerly undeveloped and most petroleum is imported. Uranium mining is a major export industry. Wood is a major source of domestic energy consumption in rural areas. Most of Niger's energy infrastructure is controlled by the national government, including the Société Nigérienne d'Électricité (NIGELEC), which supplies electricity, and the Société Nigérienne de Distribution des Produits Pétroliers (SONIDEP), which controls petroleum distribution. The private corporation Société Nigérienne du Charbon (SONICHAR) powers the national mines. A privatization program begun in the late 1990s has yet to impact these companies. Niger's poor economy, growing population, and increased environmental concerns have strained its traditional energy resources, leading to the development of conservation and renewable energy programs.

Uranium

Niger is home to one of the leading global deposits of uranium, and uranium mining and exportation represent a key portion of the national economy. The Ministry of Mines and Energy oversees both uranium mining and energy production. Niger's two national mining companies are the Mining Company of Akouta (COMINAK) and the Air Mines Company (SOMAIR). AREVA, a French nuclear power company, owns controlling shares in both companies. The year 2007 witnessed a rise in the number of government mineral exploration licenses awarded to international corporations, sparked by rising uranium prices. Exelon Corporation, a U.S. public utility, is contracted to purchase 300 tons of uranium from Niger annually for a 10-year period that began that year. AREVA opened a new mine located in Imouraren in 2011.

Niger has oil deposits, but this potential energy source has yet to be fully explored or utilized. SONIDEP controls all petroleum product imports. China National Petroleum Corporation (CNPC) is developing the Agadem oil deposit north of Lake Chad, formerly explored by ExxonMobil and Petronas. CNPC is constructing a refinery in the area. Political instability and violence have periodically disrupted Niger's mining and oil exploration. For example, in 2007 disturbances were caused by rebel groups such as the Movement of Nigerians for Justice (MNJ) in the north. Peace has since been restored.

Electricity

NIGELEC provides the production, transmission, and distribution of electricity in Niger. It is a limited company in which the national government is the majority owner. The company purchases almost all of its electricity, as well as hydroelectric power and solar installations, from the National Electric Power Authority (NEPA) in Nigeria. The electricity is supplied through a 132-kilovolt interconnection constructed in 1976. NIGELEC's power plants include Niamey I and Niamey II, the Malbaza Power Station, and the Zinder and Maradi Thermal Power Station. SONICHAR, a limited corporation established in 1975, also produces electricity. SONICHAR operates coal mines to provide the source for its energy production

Wikimedia

The Sonara building in Niamey, Niger, houses Somair, a private uranium mining company. Uranium far surpasses all other commodities to be the country's top export.

and powers the two national uranium mines as well as a few nearby towns. It also sells electricity to NIGELEC. Niger joined the West African Power Pool Agreement (WAPP) in 2000. WAPP seeks to link the electrical power grids of member West African countries.

The Niger government began a privatization program in the late 1990s, with the support of the World Bank and the United Nations Development Programme, in an effort to revitalize private-sector development. Planned government divestment targets included NIGELEC and SONIDEP. The Cellule de Coordination du Programme de Privatization (CCCP) and the Inter-Ministerial Committee for Privatization oversee the program. Legislative changes have included revisions to the investment code in 1997 and 2000, revisions to the petroleum code in 1992 and 2007, and revisions to the mining code in 1993.

Environmental Damage

In 1989, Niger began a major national effort to reform the wood industry with the implementation of its Domestic Energy Strategy (DES) for forest resource planning. The use of wood as a primary domestic energy source has resulted in deforestation, desertification, and other environmental damage, as well as the development of a lucrative and often exploitative wood-gathering and distribution market in forest regions such as Gorou, Bassounga, and Faira.

The traditional lack of government regulation of this process has exacerbated its negative environmental impact. The DES now seeks to establish a locally controlled system of rural wood markets that also promote sustainable development. Rural village residents, who are most dependent on wood for energy, are the focus of the program and among the beneficiaries of the funds raised through taxes. Gasoline has been promoted as an alternative to wood, despite its source in nonrenewable fossil fuels and even more long-term environmental impact. The government, however, has made an effort to grant some forests, such as Guesselbodi, protected status.

Niger has actively begun to explore renewable energy resources in the 21st century, adopting a national strategy in 2004 that included the creation of a national renewable energy office. The government considers renewable energy an important tool in its efforts to achieve environmental sustainability and reduce poverty. Niger is currently working on the Kandadji hydroelectric power project along the Niger River, with an estimated completion date of 2012, and smaller hydroelectric projects are under consideration. Private businesses are offering renewable energy technologies such as solar power systems.

Niger is party to a number of international energy and environmental agreements in a variety of fields, including climate change, desertification, environmental modification, hazardous wastes, and ozone layer protection. The country is a signatory to the Kyoto Protocol. Niger hosted the first and second meetings of the renewable energy market in the Sahel and West Africa (MESAO). MESAO is a renewable energy forum dedicated to improving the technological and commercial viability of alternative energy sources and fostering the cooperation of the public and private sectors in the region.

MARCELLA BUSH TREVINO

Further Reading

Abdou, El Hadj Mamane. "Niger: How to Control the Exploitation of Wood; Rural Markets and Domestic Energy Strategy." http://www.unesco.org/mab/doc/ekocd/niger.html.

Emerging Minds. "Renewable Energy Market Opens in Niger Capital." May 26, 2008. http://emergingminds.org/Renewable-energy-market-opens-in-Niger-capital.html.

International Business Publications. *Niger Energy Policy, Laws and Regulation Handbook.* Washington, DC: International Business Publications, 2008.

Noppen, Dolf, Paul Kerkhof, and Ced Hesse. *Rural Fuelwood Markets in Niger: An Assessment of Danish Support to the Niger Household Energy Strategy 1989-2003.* London: IIED/Danida, 2004.

U.S. Energy Information Administration. "Country Analysis Brief: Niger." http://www.eia.gov/countries/country-data.cfm?fips=NG.

World Bank. "Privatization in Niger: Country Fact Sheet." http://www.fdi.net/documents/WorldBank/databases/plink/factsheets/niger.htm.

See Also: Deregulation; Nigeria; Petroviolence; Power and Power Plants; Public Utilities; Shell; Uranium; Wood Energy.

Nigeria

Official Name: Federal Republic of Nigeria.
Category: Geography of Energy.
Summary: Nigeria is an energy-rich nation with both fossil and renewable fuels. In conventional energy reserves, Nigeria is unsurpassed by any other country on the African continent. However, the nation is facing an energy crisis despite abundant resources.

Coal in Nigeria was first discovered in 1909, near Udi in the central-eastern portion of the country, but major exploration did not begin until 1916. At present, proven coal reserves amount to about 639 million metric tons and inferred reserves to about 2.75 billion metric tons.

The Nigerian coal industry has four existing mines: the underground mines of Okpara and Onyeama in the state of Enugu, the Aba surface mine in the state of Kogi, and the Owukpa underground mine in the state of Benue. In 1950, the Nigerian Coal Corporation (NCC) was formed and made responsible for the exploration, development, and mining of coal resources. Production rose to a peak of 905,000 tons in 1958–59, contributing more than 70 percent to commercial energy consumption in the country. The coal industry gave rise to the nation's early enterprises and industries—the Marines, the Nigerian railways, Electricity Corporation of Nigeria (now the National Electric Power Authority, NEPA), and the Nigeria Cement Company—and supplied all energy requirements up to the late 1960s.

After 1959, production decreased significantly each year, and during the period of the Nigerian Civil War (1966–70) no coal production was reported, because all the coal mines in the country were abandoned. The NCC has established several joint ventures with outside entities to mine coal, but those efforts have met with limited success. In 2001, coal's share of total commercial energy consumption was only about 0.02 percent.

Other potentially significant coal resources in Nigeria are the Inyi deposit, south of the city of Enugu, with a potential of approximately 10 million tons; the Afikpo deposit, located southeast of Inyi; and the Lafia Obi deposit, located in the northeast, with an estimated 33 million tons of metallurgical coal resources.

Oil

Nigeria is the largest oil producer in Africa and the 11th-largest producer of crude oil in the world. In January 2010, it had estimated oil reserves of 37.2 billion barrels. The primary locations of these reserves are the Niger River Delta, offshore in the Bight of Benin, the Gulf of Guinea, and the Bight of Bonny.

According to the U.S. Energy Information Administration, Nigeria's oil production capacity is around 2.9 million barrels per day; attacks on oil infrastructure have resulted in monthly crude oil production ranging between 1.6 million and 2.0 million barrels per day. Recent offshore oil developments, combined with the restart of some shut-in onshore production, boosted crude production to an average of 2.03 million barrels per day for the first quarter of 2010. Several foreign companies were operating in joint ventures or production-sharing contracts (PSCs) with the Nigerian National Petroleum Corporation (NNPC).

Nigeria has four refineries—Port Harcourt I and II, Warri, and Kaduna—with a total installed capacity of 445,000 barrels per day. As a result of poor maintenance, theft, and fire, none of these refineries has ever been fully operational. According to NNPC, a total volume of 724,479,796 barrels of crude oil was exported in 2008 to destinations all over the world, including North America, Europe, Asia, South America, Central America, and Africa. Nigeria is clearly overdependent on crude oil for its foreign exchange earnings; hence, the economy is vulnerable to the unstable nature of the international oil market.

Natural Gas

Nigeria is the eighth-largest natural gas reserve holder in the world and the largest in Africa. Prior to 1999, exploration for gas in Nigeria was limited, and much of the gas was flared. *Oil and Gas Journal* estimates that Nigeria had 185 trillion cubic feet of proven natural gas reserves as of January 2010, known to be substantially larger than its oil resources in energy terms. The majority of the natural gas reserves are located in the Niger Delta. In 2008, Nigeria consumed around 430 billion cubic feet, mostly for electricity generation; the remaining gas was either vented (140 billion cubic feet) or flared (530 billion cubic feet).

A significant portion of Nigeria's natural gas is processed into liquefied natural gas (LNG). In 2009, Nigeria exported nearly 500 billion cubic feet of LNG. Major trading partners are the United States, Spain, France, and Portugal. Nigeria's main natural gas project is the Nigeria Liquefied Natural Gas (NLNG) facility on Bonny Island. The 420-mile pipeline carries natural gas from Nigeria to Ghana via Togo and Benin. Exports in 2010 were expected to reach 170 million cubic feet per day, and plans are under way to expand capacity to as much as 450 million cubic feet per day and possibly extend the pipeline farther west to Côte d'Ivoire (Ivory Coast). Both Nigeria and Algeria are trying to construct the Trans-Saharan Gas Pipeline (TSGP), which would carry natural gas from oil fields in Nigeria's Delta region to Algeria's Beni Saf export terminal on the Mediterranean.

Renewable Energy

Renewable energy resources other than hydropower and traditional biomass have not received much consideration in Nigeria, and it is anticipated that renewables will account for only a tiny contribution to the nation's energy sector in com-

Nigeria's Energy Reserves and Potentials

Resource Type	Reserves	Reserves (BTOE)
Crude oil	36.0 billion barrels	4.896
Natural gas	185 trillion cubic feet	4.465
Coal & lignite	2.7 billion metric tons	1.882
Subtotal fossil fuels	11.243	
Hydropower, large-scale	10,000 megawatts	
Hydropower, small-scale	734 megawatts	
Solar radiation	3.5–7.0 kilowatt-hours per square meter per day	
Wind	2–4 meters per second (annual average)	

Source: Nigeria's Renewable Energy Master Plan (2006).
Note: BTOE=billion tons of oil equivalance.

ing decades. Apart from solar thermal and biogas technologies, no other renewable energy technology has been developed. According to the Energy Commission of Nigeria (ECN), utilization of renewable energy sources is minimal. As a result, investment opportunities abound.

The total technically exploitable large-scale hydropower potential of the country is estimated to be greater than 10,000 megawatts, which would be capable of producing 36,000 gigawatt-hours of electricity annually. However, only about a fifth of this potential had been developed by 2001.

Nigeria lies within latitudes that receive a great deal of sunshine, and solar radiation is fairly well distributed. Apart from traditional open-air drying, however, this solar energy has not been exploited and solar technologies are not much used. The amount of solar radiation in the country, according to 2005 estimates by the Energy Commission of Nigeria and the United Nations Development Programme, could yield about 5.5 kilowatt-hours per square meter per day, representing huge prospects for energy generation. The annual average of total solar radiation ranged from about 12.6 megajoules per square meter per day in the coastal latitudes to about 25.2 megajoules per square meter per day in the far north, according to a 2007 study by F. I. Ibitoye and A. Adenikinju.

Nigeria has also been reported to have great potential for wind energy. For instance, in areas off the coasts of several states, including Lagos, Ondo, Delta, Rivers, Bayelsa, and Akwa Ibom, there is potential to harvest energy from the strong winds that pass over lagoons and oceans throughout the year. The annual mean speed of the wind, at a height of 10 meters aboveground, ranges between 2.3 and 3.4 meters per second at such sites, and between 3.0 and3.9 meters per second in highland areas and semiarid regions; the monthly average wind power can be as high as 50.1 watts per square meter (a measure of wind-power density).

The energy sector accounts for less than 15 percent of the national gross domestic product (GDP) and Nigeria's annual energy budget is less than $6 billion. Coupled with the relatively high per-unit cost of installed capacity of renewable energy technologies, these factors make it difficult to finance renewable energy publicly. A substantial expansion in quantity, quality, and access to energy infrastructure services will be essential to rapid and sustained economic growth, employment generation, and the overall well-being of the population in a country the majority of whose 140 million people are poor.

SUMAN SINGH
MURAREE LAL MEENA

Further Reading

Energy Commission of Nigeria. *National Energy Policy.* Abuja: Energy Commission, 2002.

Energy Commission of Nigeria. *Renewable Energy Master Plan.* Abuja: United Nations Development Programme, 2006.

Ibitoye, F. I., and A. Adenikinju. "Future Demand for Electricity in Nigeria." *Applied Energy* 84 (2007).

International Business Publications. *Nigeria Energy Policy, Laws and Regulation Handbook.* Washington, DC: International Business Publications, 2008.

Ohunakin, Olayinka S. "Assessment of Wind Energy Resources for Electricity Generation Using WECS in North-Central Region." *Nigeria, Renewable and Sustainable Energy Reviews* 15, no. 40 (2011).

Shaad, Brian, Emma Wilson, and Fiona Hall. *Access to Sustainable Energy: What Role for International Oil and Gas Companies?* London: International Institute for Environment and Development, 2009.

See Also: Flaring Gas; Organization of Petroleum Exporting Countries; Petroviolence; Refuse; São Tomé and Príncipe; Shell; South Africa; Togo.

Nitrogen Oxides

Category: Environmentalism.
Summary: The term *nitrogen oxides* refers to a group of compounds denoted by the chemical shorthand NO_x. Both are gases and combine into gases. Nitrogen oxides are among the greenhouse gases, and also contribute to acid rain.

Nitrogen is a vital element for living beings as a fundamental building block of organic compounds, and it is the most abundant gas in Earth's atmosphere. Nitrogen oxides are a group of molecular compounds that combine different quantities of nitrogen and oxygen in a variety of structures. Of paramount importance in atmospheric chemistry are the two compounds nitric oxide (NO) and nitrogen dioxide (NO_2).

Nitric oxide (NO) is a colorless, odorless gas that can be isolated at room temperature and is reactive but stable. Nitrogen dioxide (NO_2) is a reddish-brown gas with a pungent odor; it also can be isolated at room temperature and is reactive but stable. Additionally, nitrous oxide (N_2O), a colorless gas with a sweet odor—known as *laughing gas* for its use as an anesthetic—reacts readily with oxygen to become NO, and is a significant source of this greenhouse gas.

Major anthropogenic releases of both NO and NO_2 include the burning of fossil fuels in automobile engines and in power plants. Automobile exhaust produces about three-quarters of such emissions. Additionally, nitrogen dioxide can be released by refineries and some manufacturing facilities in the industrial sector; and also by the residential sector from gas stoves and home heating units. The release of these nitrogen oxides stems from the oxidation of air, which is approximately 78 percent nitrogen. Indeed in nature, lightning strikes are abundant generators of nitrogen oxides, as are natural fires and biological processes in soil and water.

Harmful Effects

Specific concentrations of some nitrogen compounds, in particular NO_2, have proved toxic effects. High levels can even be fatal, while lower levels affect a range of body systems, especially lung tissue. It is also known that long-term exposure to some NO_x compounds weakens resistance to respiratory infections. For example, NO_2 increases animal susceptibility to pneumonia, influenza, and other such threats. There is little difference in human risk factors from those of other higher animals. Respiratory disease risk increase in humans is confirmed in association with chronic low-level exposures of NO_2. Specific exposures and associated human health effects include the following:

- Short-term exposure at concentrations greater than 3 parts per million (ppm) can measurably decrease lung function.
- Concentrations less than 3 ppm can irritate lungs.
- Concentrations as low as 0.1 ppm cause lung irritation and measurable decreases in lung function in asthmatics.
- Long-term low-level exposures can destroy lung tissue, leading to emphysema.
- Small levels of NO_x can cause nausea, irritation to the eyes and nose, fluid forming in lungs, and shortness of breath.
- Breathing in high levels of NO_x can lead to rapid, burning spasms, visual impairment, swelling of the throat, reduced oxygen intake, a larger buildup of fluid in lungs, and death.
- NO_x, plus other ground-level ozone, can cause other major respiratory problems at high levels.
- It can react with aerosols from aerosol cans and also cause respiratory problems.
- NO_x can cause visual impairment in areas affected by NO_x.

Nitrogen dioxide in particular is also harmful to the environment. It can damage vegetation, fade and discolor fabrics, reduce visibility, and react with surfaces and furnishings. Vegetation exposure to high levels of nitrogen dioxide can be identified by depleted foliage, decreased growth, and reduced crop yield.

The environmental effects of NO_x include the following:

- It helps form acid rain.
- It contributes to global warming.
- It hampers the growth of plants.
- It can react with other pollutants to form toxic chemicals.

Guidelines and Controls

Some studies suggest that asthmatics may experience increased airway resistance at levels as low as 0.3 ppm, but results are not conclusive. In Aus-

tralia, for example, the Queensland government's Environmental Protection (Air) Policy goal of 0.16 ppm (one-hour exposure period) is intended to protect sensitive individuals such as children and asthmatics. Exposure to levels of 0.50 ppm for one hour would be necessary before a majority of healthy people in a community were significantly affected. Typical outdoor nitrogen dioxide concentrations are well below the one-hour goal; exposure at these levels do not generally increase respiratory symptoms. The U.S. Environmental Protection Agency (EPA) has set standards for NO_x pollution on every type of motor vehicle. For power plants and factories, the EPA has set quantitative limits on coal-burning emissions (which also helps to reduce the formation of acid rain).

The EPA has standards in place specifically for upwind states as well, and since NO_x travels by wind, the states that "push" emissions are affected by such rules. With a great bulk of NO_x emissions originating in the transportation sector, the EPA established standards for installation of catalytic converters on automobiles; the rules went into effect in 1975. Catalytic converters, acting on the hot exhaust fuels prior to their release from tailpipes, also precipitate out other greenhouse gases from the exhaust mix. Even with such measures employed for several decades, however, this element of pollution has still grown by an estimated 10 percent since the first substantial attempts were made to reduce it. More needs to be done. Among the measures that individuals can take to reduce NO_x emissions and their exposure to such emissions are the following:

- Reduce the amount a person drives alone: walk, bike, or carpool.
- Support efforts to use renewable, nonpolluting power sources.
- In homes with gas stoves, smokers, or gas heaters, open up the house; fresh air helps minimize exposure to NO_x.
- Replace older gas-powered appliances such as gas stoves and heaters.
- Do not smoke cigarettes.
- Do not burn any type of gas at high temperatures.

▷ *Agricultural Sources of Nitrous Oxide Emissions*

Humankind's increasing need for food, as a result of an expanding global population, has led to steady additions in the use of synthetic fertilizers and the wider application of animal waste on agricultural soils—each of which is nitrogen-based. In many cases, use of nitrogen-based fertilizers is excessive, well beyond the effective maximum beneficial levels that aid crop yields. This leads to greater NO_x emissions, in particular N_2O. General use of animal waste as fertilizer, without effective quantitative controls, can lead to substantial emissions from agricultural soils. There is also significant leaching of agricultural nitrogen compounds into water supplies. After fertilizer application, especially when followed by precipitation, nitrogen readily leaches into irrigation ditches, ponds, rivers, bays, and ultimately the oceans.

Some of the N_2O produced in agricultural soils is thus released to the atmosphere whenever the drainage water comes in contact with the air. Still more N_2O is produced from such runoff when the leached nitrogen fertilizer in it interacts with the dissolved oxygen that naturally occurs in aquatic and estuarine sediments. There are indirect N_2O releases from agricultural soils as well; these include the volatilization of nitrogen-rich ammonia from fertilizer at one end of the cycle, and at the end of the agricultural cycle the consumption of crops and crop wastage (biomass), as well as sewage treatment processes.

Land-management strategies exist that are sophisticated enough to be applied in nearly every type of agricultural scenario. These include prescribed use of fertilizer only to the extent necessary for maximum crop yield—while holding to a minimum both the economic loss and environmental damage likely from overuse of fertilizer. Various types of nitrogen-based fertilizers can be selected with appropriate consideration of local land and water migration factors, crop types, seasonality, and wind conditions so as to limit emissions. Governments have enacted changes in policy to bring about reductions in such nitrogen leaching. For example, the United Kingdom has designated nitrate sensitive zones (NSZs) requiring particular attention.

- Do not use products from aerosol cans.
- Avoid living in a large rural area or next to industrial parts of town.
- Avoid prolonged exposure to silos that contain silage.

Again, it is largely through properly informed land-management practice and fertilization campaigns; continued application and enforcement of progressively stronger transportation sector standards; and broad efforts to shift electricity production and other industrial sector energy sources from fossil fuel to low-nitrogen renewables that NO_x emissions can primarily be controlled and reduced.

Ronju Ahammad

Further Reading

Clean Air Technology Center. *Nitrogen Oxides (NO$_x$): Why and How They Are Controlled.* Research Triangle Park, NC: Office of Air Quality Planning and Standards, et al., 1999.

Dara, S. S. *A Text Book of Environmental Chemistry and Pollution Control.* New Delhi: S. Chand, 1993.

De, Anil K. *Environmental Chemistry.* New Delhi: New Age International, 1994.

Graham, J. A. *Nitrogen Oxides.* Geneva: World Health Organization, 1997.

Hudman, R. C., et al. "Surface and Lightning Sources of Nitrogen Oxides Over the United States: Magnitudes, Chemical Evolution, and Outflow." *Journal of Geophysical Research* 112, D12S05 (2007). doi:10.1029/2006JD007912.

U.S. Environmental Protection Agency. "Nitrogen Dioxide." http://www.epa.gov/air/nitrogenoxides.

See Also: Acid Rain; Air Pollution; Energy Markets: Industrial; Energy Markets: Transport; Greenhouse Gases; Nonrenewable Energy Resources; Oil and Petroleum; Power and Power Plants.

Nonpoint Source Pollution

Category: Environmentalism.
Summary: Nonpoint source pollution is pollution that enters surface water bodies—such as rivers, streams, lakes, coastal areas, oceans, and groundwater—through diffuse pathways, primarily as a result of precipitation or atmospheric deposition.

A *nonpoint source* of pollution is generally defined as a source that does not meet the definition of *point source*. A point source is a discrete conveyance, such as a pipe, from which pollutants are discharged. Examples include discharges from industrial facilities and municipal sewage systems. Nonpoint source pollution is typically generated over land areas as precipitation produces stormwater runoff. As runoff flows from the land, pollutants are picked up, transported with the runoff, and discharged to surface water or into groundwater.

Sources and Pollutants
In the developed world, nonpoint sources can deliver a variety of pollutants. Urban stormwater runoff can contribute a number of pollutants, including nitrogen, phosphorus, sediment, toxic metals, bacteria, pesticides, and oil and grease. These pollutants are produced from the activities and actions in developed areas, including lawn care, improper disposal of pet waste, land development and construction, soil erosion, failing septic tanks, and car maintenance. In agricultural areas, sediment, nitrogen, phosphorus, bacteria, and pesticides are common nonpoint source pollutants. They are derived from agricultural practices such as crop fertilization, pesticide application, and livestock operations, as well as from soil erosion from cropland and pastures. In agricultural areas, growing pressure to increase crop and livestock yields often leads to excessive application of fertilizers and more intensive animal management. Excess nutrients from fertilizers and animal wastes increase the pollutant loads to surface and groundwater. Atmospheric deposition can also be a source of nutrients, metals, and organic contaminants.

The developing world faces exacerbated nonpoint pollution problems due to a lack of infrastructure that is present in the developed world. Often urban areas lack adequate sewer systems, and in some cases sewage and rainwater are transported, untreated, through the same systems and discharged directly to surface waters. Like developed nations, developing countries face increasing pressure to industrialize agricultural processes, and excess nutrients contaminate runoff from agricultural areas and discharge to water bodies. Deforestation can cause soil erosion and represents an important category of nonpoint source pollution in the developing world. Additionally, because of the lack of adequate emissions controls, air pollution can serve as a significant source of nonpoint source pollution, including toxics, to local streams.

Impacts From Nonpoint Source Pollution
Aquatic life can be affected by a number of pollutants. Excess nutrients, such as nitrogen and phosphorus, in surface waters can cause eutrophic and hypoxic conditions. Eutrophication is the process of excess nutrient enrichment of a water body, leading to increased growth of algae and subsequent hypoxic conditions that occur when the excess algal growth consumes oxygen through respiration and decomposition of plants after they die off.

The depletion of dissolved oxygen from excessive algal growth can result in oxygen concentrations in the water column that are insufficient to support aquatic life, such as fish and aquatic insects. Negative impacts to aquatic life can, in turn, affect humans through the decline in fisheries' populations. Examples of large hypoxic zones include the Gulf of Mexico in the United States, the Pearl River Delta in China, and the Black Sea in Eastern Europe.

Aquatic life can also be negatively affected by runoff containing toxic pollutants, oil and grease from transportation activities, and emissions from industrial processes. Toxic pollutants can originate from a number of sources, including abandoned mines and urban runoff.

Nonpoint source pollution can also negatively affect drinking water supplies and recreational waters. Nitrates, which frequently originate from agricultural activities, can contaminate surface and groundwater, making them unsuitable as sources of drinking water. Bacteria from failing septic systems, animal waste, and illicit sewage discharges can contaminate potable water supplies and cause beach closings due to violations of recreational health standards.

Nonpoint Source Pollution Control

Unlike point source pollution, which is often regulated through discharge permits, nonpoint source pollution is challenging to address, given the diverse sources and the lack of regulatory authority for controlling their discharges. Nonpoint source pollution is typically controlled through the voluntary or incentive-based implementation of best management practices (BMPs) by public and private landowners. BMPs are pollution control or treatment practices designed to reduce pollution from runoff. BMPs are generally categorized as structural or nonstructural controls and can be used separately or in combination to prevent nonpoint source pollution.

Structural BMPs are designed to retain or filter runoff in order to decrease the amount of water flow after a storm event and to remove pollutants from the runoff. For example, common structural BMPs used to reduce sediment transport from agricultural land to water bodies include the use of sediment basins that collect and store runoff to trap debris. The use of green infrastructure techniques (also referred to as low impact development) has become increasingly popular in urban areas as a way to engage the natural infiltration capabilities of vegetation to prevent nonpoint source pollution. The principle behind green infrastructure is to decrease impervious areas (including paved areas such as parking lots) and increase pervious areas that naturally filter runoff (permeable pavement, rain gardens, and constructed wetlands, for example).

Nonstructural BMPs are preventive actions that seek to increase the number of people who implement BMP practices, such as education and outreach activities and land-use policies. For instance, education programs can promote the environmental benefits or cost savings of new practices in an effort to increase the number of users.

Countries also address nonpoint source pollution through the development of watershed management plans and the regulation of pollutants. Many countries and transboundary river commissions require local governments to monitor water quality and address impaired water bodies through the development of watershed management plans that include specific management activities to decrease pollution. In the United States, the Clean Water Act requires that a total maximum daily load (TMDL) be developed for a water body that does not meet water quality standards. A TMDL is the maximum amount of pollution tolerated by a water body without causing impairment. The pollution is allocated to all the identified sources, including nonpoint sources. States and local jurisdictions then develop watershed management plans to address the required load reductions from nonpoint sources, often through the implementation of BMPs.

The regulation of pollutants is another method to address those pollutants considered particularly harmful to human health. The Canadian government, for instance, regulates the pesticide industry through the Pest Control Products Act and Pest Management Regulatory System, in order to reduce the incidence of nonpoint pesticide pollution.

Water quality trading is a relatively new approach to address nonpoint source pollution, designed to implement market-based approaches to improve water quality across a region or watershed. Trading schemes address specific water quality parameters (such as phosphorus, nitrates, and salinity) and allow those entities that have higher pollution abatement costs to trade or buy pollution reduction credits from those sources with lower pollution abatement costs. An example of a trading scheme that is focused entirely on nonpoint pollution reduction is the Lake Taupo Nitrogen Trading Program in New Zealand.

HOPE HERRON
AILEEN MOLLOY

Further Reading

American Society of Civil Engineers and U.S. Environmental Protection Agency. "International Stormwater Best Management Practices (BMP) Database." http://www.bmpdatabase.org/.

Dosi, C., and T. Tomasi, eds. "Nonpoint Source Pollution Regulation: Issues and Analysis." *Economics, Energy and Environment* 3 (2010).

U.S. Environmental Protection Agency. "What Is Nonpoint Source Pollution?" http://www.epa.gov/owow_keep/NPS/index.html.

See Also: Emissions Inventories; Ethanol: Cellulosic; Risk Assessment; Urban Sprawl; Water Pollution.

Nonrenewable Energy Resources

Category: Energy Resources.
Summary: A nonrenewable energy resource is a natural resource that cannot be produced or replaced on a scale that can sustain its consumption rate. These resources often exist in a fixed amount and are consumed much more quickly than nature can create them.

Sufficient, reliable sources of energy are a necessity for industrialized nations. Energy is used for heating, cooking, transportation, and manufacturing. Energy can generally be classified as nonrenewable and renewable. More than 85 percent of the energy used in the world is from nonrenewable supplies. A nonrenewable energy resource is a natural resource that cannot be replaced on a scale that can sustain its consumption rate. These resources often exist in a fixed amount and are consumed much more quickly than nature can create them.

The major categories of nonrenewable energy sources are the fossil fuels (oil, natural gas, and coal, including petroleum products such as gasoline, diesel fuel, and propane), and radioactive fuel (nuclear energy). Fossil fuels are continually produced by the decay of plant and animal matter, but the rate of their production is extremely slow, much slower than the rate at which we use them—thus they are nonrenewable. Nuclear energy is also considered nonrenewable in that it uses a relatively rare metal, uranium-235. Nonrenewable energy sources come out of the ground as liquids, gases, and solids. Crude oil (petroleum) is the only commercial nonrenewable fuel that is naturally in liquid form. Natural gas and propane are normally gases, but coal and uranium ore are solid.

Oil and Petroleum Products

Crude oil or liquid petroleum is a fossil fuel that is refined into many different energy products: gasoline, diesel fuel, jet fuel, and heating oil, for example. Oil forms underground in rocks, such as shale, which is rich in organic materials. After the oil forms, it migrates upward into porous reservoir rock, such as sandstone or limestone, where it can become trapped by an overlying impermeable cap rock. Wells are drilled into these oil reservoirs to remove the gas and oil. More than 70 percent of oil fields are found near tectonic plate boundaries, because the conditions there are conducive to oil formation.

More than 50 percent of the world's oil is found in the Middle East; sizable additional reserves occur in North America. Most known oil reserves are already being exploited, and oil is being used at a rate that exceeds the rate of discovery of new sources. If the consumption rate continues to increase and no significant new sources are found, oil supplies could be exhausted by about 2040.

▷ *Pros and Cons of Nonrenewable Sources*

There are both pros and cons to the use of nonrenewable sources of energy. Among the attractive aspects of nonrenewable sources is that they are cheap and easy to use. People can easily fill up their car and other motor vehicle tanks. Moreover, a small amount of nuclear energy can produce a large amount of power. Nonrenewable sources are considered cheap from the standpoint of the cost of converting their energy into forms we can use.

However, nonrenewable sources will someday be depleted, because they are being used at a rate faster than the eons of geologic time required to form them. Therefore, we must use our endangered resources carefully to create more renewable sources of energy. Moreover, the speed at which nonrewables are being used can have serious environmental changes. Nonrenewable sources undergo combustion to release their energy for use, but at the same time they release toxic gases into the air, a major cause of global warming. Finally, since these sources are going to expire soon, their cost to consumers is soaring.

Despite its limited supply, oil is a relatively inexpensive fuel source. It is preferred over coal as a fuel source because an equivalent amount of oil produces more kilowatts of energy than coal. It also burns cleaner, producing about 50 percent less sulfur dioxide. However, the burning of oil contributes significantly to environment problems and atmospheric pollution in the form of carbon dioxide, carbon monoxide, sulfur dioxide, and nitrogen oxide emissions. These greenhouse gases pollute the air and contribute to global warming.

Oil Shale and Tar Sands

One source of oil, oil shale and tar sands, is currently among the least utilized of fossil fuel sources. Oil shale is sedimentary rock with very fine pores that contain kerogen, a carbon-based, waxy substance. If shale is heated to 490 degrees Celsius, the kerogen vaporizes and can then be condensed as shale oil, a thick, viscous liquid. This shale oil is then further refined into usable oil products. Production of shale oil requires large amounts of energy, however, for mining and processing the shale. Indeed, about half a barrel of oil is required to extract every barrel of shale oil. The largest tar-sand deposit in the world is in Canada and contains enough material (about 500 billion barrels) to supply the world with oil for about 15 years. However, because of environmental concerns and high production costs, these tar sands are not being fully utilized.

Natural Gas

Natural gas production is often a by-product of oil recovery, as the two commonly share underground reservoirs. Natural gas is a mixture of gases, the most common being methane (CH_4). It also contains some ethane (C_2H_5), propane (C_3H_8), and butane (C_4H_{10}).

Natural gas is usually not contaminated with sulfur and is therefore the cleanest-burning fossil fuel. After recovery, propane and butane are removed from the natural gas and made into liquefied petroleum gas (LPG). LPG is shipped in special pressurized tanks as a fuel source for areas not directly served by natural gas pipelines (such as rural communities). The remaining natural gas is further refined to remove impurities and water vapor and is then transported in pressurized pipelines.

Natural gas is highly flammable and odorless. The characteristic smell associated with natural gas is actually that of minute quantities of a smelly sulfur compound (ethyl mercaptan) that is added during refining to allow consumers to smell the gas should it leak from pipes and thus pose a hazard.

The use of natural gas is growing rapidly. Besides being a clean-burning fuel source, natural gas is easy and inexpensive to transport, once pipelines are in place. In developed countries, natural gas is used primarily for heating, cooking, and powering vehicles. It is also used in a process for making ammonia fertilizer. The current estimate of natural gas reserves is about 100 million metric tons. At current usage levels, this supply will last an estimated 100 years. Most of the world's natural gas reserves are found in Eastern Europe and the Middle East.

Coal

Coal is the most abundant fossil fuel in the world, with estimated reserves of 1 trillion metric tons. Most of the world's coal reserves exist in Eastern Europe and Asia, but the United States also has considerable reserves. Coal formed slowly over millions of years from the buried remains of ancient swamp plants. During the formation of coal, carbonaceous matter was first compressed into a spongy material called peat, which is about 90 percent water. As the peat became more deeply buried, the increased pressure and temperature turned it into coal.

Different types of coal resulted from differences in the pressure and temperature that prevailed during formation. The softest coal (about 50 percent carbon), which also has the lowest energy output, is called lignite. Lignite has the highest water content (about 50 percent) and relatively low amounts of smog-causing sulfur. With increasing temperature and pressure, lignite is transformed into bituminous coal (about 85 percent carbon and 3 percent water). Anthracite (almost 100 percent carbon) is the hardest coal and also produces the greatest energy when burned.

Currently, the world is consuming coal at a rate of about 5 billion metric tons per year. The main use of coal is for power generation, because it is a relatively inexpensive way to produce power. Coal is used to produce more than 50 percent of the electricity in the United States. In addition to electricity production, coal is sometimes used for heating and cooking in less developed countries and in rural areas of developed countries. If consumption continues at the current rates, reserves will last for more than 200 years.

Coal mining creates several environmental problems. Coal is most cheaply mined from near-surface deposits using strip-mining techniques. Strip mining causes considerable environmental damage in the form of erosion and habitat destruc-

tion. Subsurface mining of coal is less damaging to the surface environment, but it is much more hazardous for miners because of tunnel collapses and gas explosions. The burning of coal results in significant atmospheric pollution. The sulfur contained in coal forms sulfur dioxide when burned. Harmful nitrogen oxides, heavy metals, and carbon dioxide are also released into the air during coal burning. The harmful emissions can be reduced by installing scrubbers and electrostatic precipitators in the smokestacks of power plants. The toxic ash remaining after coal burning is also an environmental concern and is usually disposed into landfills.

Radioactive Fuel

The use of nuclear technology requires a radioactive fuel. Uranium ore is present in the ground at relatively low concentrations and is mined in 19 countries. Uranium is used to create plutonium; uranium-238 is fissionable and can be transmuted into fissile plutonium-239 in a nuclear reactor. Nuclear fuel is used in nuclear power stations to create electricity. Nuclear power provides about 6 percent of the world's energy and 13–14 percent of the world's electricity. Nuclear technology is a volatile and contaminating source of fuel production, with the expense of the nuclear industry predominantly reliant on subsidies.

In most electric power plants, water is heated and converted into steam, which drives a turbine generator to produce electricity. Fossil-fueled power plants produce heat by burning coal, oil, or natural gas. In a nuclear power plant, the fission of uranium atoms in the reactor provides the heat to produce steam for generating electricity.

Originally, nuclear energy was expected to be a clean and cheap source of energy. Nuclear fission does not produce atmospheric pollution or greenhouse gases, and its proponents expected that nuclear energy would be cheaper and last longer than fossil fuels. Unfortunately, because of construction cost overruns, poor management, and numerous regulations, nuclear power has become much more expensive than predicted. The nuclear accidents at Three Mile Island in Pennsylvania (1979) and Chernobyl in the Ukraine (1986) raised concerns about the safety of nuclear power. Furthermore, the problem of safely disposing spent nuclear fuel remains unresolved.

Sustainable Development

It is our responsibility to use scarce nonrenewable energy resources judiciously and sustainably, so that we do not contribute to their fast depletion. Although today's society will remain dependent on nonrenewable energy resources for the next few decades, the development of alternative energy sources and the technology to harness them at the nascent stage should be our aim. Also, we need to have proper technology in place and devise newer methods to eliminate the negative environmental impact of fossil fuels. Overexploitation of nonrenewables will lead to excessive pollution and rising threats of global warming. The judicious use of nonrenewables can save us from an energy crisis in the immediate future until we develop alternative sources.

REZA FAZELI

Further Reading

Deffeyes, Kenneth S. *Hubbert's Peak: The Impending World Oil Shortage*. Princeton, NJ: Princeton University Press, 2008.

Heinberg, R., and D. Lerch, eds. *The Post Carbon Reader: Managing the 21st Century's Sustainability Crises*. Healdsburg, CA: Watershed Media, 2010.

Kaur, Ravnit. "Five Non-Renewable Sources." January 18, 2011. http://www.brighthub.com/environment/renewable-energy/articles/100982.aspx#ixzz1IIW0EsYG.

Maugeri, Leonardo. *Beyond the Age of Oil: The Myths, Realities, and Future of Fossil Fuels and Their Alternatives*. Westport, CT: Praeger, 2010.

University of California. "Non-Renewable Energy Sources." http://cnx.org/content/m16730/latest/.

U.S. Department of Energy. "Energy Sources: Nonrenewable." http://www.eia.doe.gov/kids/energy.cfm?page=nonrenewable_home-basics.

See Also: Coal; Fossil Fuels; Natural Gas; Nuclear Power; Oil and Petroleum; Regional Greenhouse Gas Initiative; Uranium.

North American Electric Reliability Corporation

Category: Business of Energy.
Summary: The North American Reliability Corporation provides governance and protection of the bulk power system in North America.

The electrical system in the United States and its links with Canada and Mexico have evolved from a great many small, struggling, local electrical utilities in the early history of the electric industry into a vast interconnected production and transmission system. As electrical production has grown, so has its usage. Modern society relies upon constantly available electricity for everything from operating room lighting to milking machines on farms. More broadly, the information system, financial system, security systems, and all the other innumerable interconnections of modern society are supported by reliable electrical power. Protecting the bulk power system (BPS) is vital to modern life.

A BPS is composed of the assets that generate, transmit, and control the production and delivery of bulk quantities of electrical power. The disruption of bulk power delivery can disrupt the lives and property of millions of people across vast regions. This has happened on several occasions in the past; the latest was in the northeastern United States in 2003. The most famous was in New York City in 1977. These were blackouts associated with grid overloads. However, blackouts from hurricanes, tornados, and winter storms occur more frequently. These blackouts are usually disruptions in local distribution delivery, rather than blackouts caused by BPS failures. However, BPS failures have occurred and are threatened by criminals and by terrorists. In addition, earthquakes or some accident could occur that would disrupt bulk power deliveries. To deal with these potential threats, Congress, in coordination with the electric utility industry and other parties, adopted new policies on electrical reliability.

The Energy Policy Act of 2005 (EPACT 2005) authorized the Federal Energy Regulatory Commission (FERC) to enforce regulations that affect the reliability of energy resources. FERC is an independent regulatory commission, composed of five commissioners appointed by the president of the United States with the advice and consent of the Senate. FERC is responsible for seeing that reliable, efficient, and sustainable energy services are produced and distributed at reasonable costs. The president appoints one of the FERC members as chair of the commission and as FERC's administrative head. FERC members serve five-year terms. No more than three members can be from a single political party. Also, its decisions are made before they are presented to the president or to Congress in order to avoid political pressure. FERC is funded by electrical industry fees and annual charges. Regulatory power is exercised by both regulatory rules and market tools so that the public interest is served through the delivery of safe, reliable, and efficient energy at reasonable rates. Its responsibility includes other energy sources besides electricity, such as gas and oil.

In 2006, FERC assigned the North American Electric Reliability Corporation (NERC) the responsibility for developing and enforcing reliability standards under its EPACT 2005 authority. NERC is a nonprofit corporation based in Atlanta, Georgia. It is a self-regulated organization. It was created on March 26, 2006. It replaced the North American Electric Reliability Council, which had the same acronym. The council was formed in 1968 by members of the electrical utility council in order to develop both the supplies of electricity to meet peak demand loads and the reliability of the whole bulk power system in North America. The mission of NERC is to ensure the reliability of the bulk-power system in North America. The Federal Energy Regulatory Commission has certified NERC as the electric reliability organization (ERO) for establishing and enforcing reliability standards for the bulk-power system. The authority for NERC to audit power com-

panies, and levy fines for non-compliance or for other failures, derives from its appointment by the FERC in 2007.

NERC works with the over 500 power companies in the bulk-power system in order to develop standards, monitor operations, and provide training resources. Each part of the system is accredited through its training program and thereafter recertified in order to maintain qualified and proficient personnel. The electrical utilities are organized into eight regional reliability entities covering the interconnected power system of the three power grids (east, west, and Texas) of the contiguous 48 states, along with connections to the power systems in Canada and Baja California in Mexico. It investigates and analyzes significant power system failures or disturbances in order to prevent such events in the future. System failures are basically of three types: external failures caused by storms or other events external to the system; internal failures caused by equipment malfunctions, such as an accidentally tripped switch, or by an operator error; and deliberate attacks on the system by sabotage, terrorists, criminals, or by cyber attacks using the computerized systems that direct BPS generation or transmission. Cyber attacks by foreign powers, most notably by Russia or China, are of growing concern.

Included in the mission of NERC is the development and enforcement of reliability standards. It also creates annual and decennial assessments for winter and summer forecasts. Both of these seasons are peak usage times for heating and cooling. It also monitors the training and certification of electrical industry personnel.

To prevent cyber failures, each regulated entity is responsible for meeting the NERC Reliability Stan-

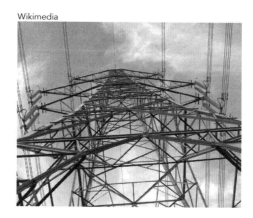
Wikimedia

In the 1960s, four interconnected transmission systems were connected to three more and formed the largest electricity grid in the world to that date.

dard IIP-002=1 Critical Cyber Asset Identification. The cyber assets to be identified are critical for maintaining reliability, regardless of catastrophic events. In a joint effort, the North American Electric Reliability Corporation (NERC), Department of Energy (DOE), and the Electric Power Research Institute (EPRI) developed a simulation tool for the electric utility industry to analyze geo-magnetically induced currents (GIC) on their systems. If a U.S. power company fails to comply with NERC reliability standards, enforcement actions can include rectification overseen by NERC. In addition, a sliding scale of fines can be levied.

ANDREW J. WASKEY

Further Reading

Kaplan, Stan Mark. *Smart Grid. Electrical Power Transmission: Background and Policy Issues.* Washington, DC: Congressional Research Service, 2009.

Mazer, A. *Electric Power Planning for Regulated and Deregulated Markets.* Hoboken, NJ: John Wiley & Sons, 2007.

Pansini, Anthony J. *Transmission Line Reliability and Security.* New York: Marcel Dekker, 2004.

U.S. Department of Energy. *High-Impact, Low-Frequency Event Risk to the North American Bulk Power System. A Jointly-Commissioned Summary Report of the North American Electric Reliability Corporation and the U.S. Department of Energy's November 2009 Workshop.* Washington, DC: North American Electric Reliability Corporation, 2010.

See Also: Electric Grids; Energy Policy Act of 2005; Risk Management.

North Carolina

Category: Energy in the United States.
Summary: North Carolina has a long history of hydroelectric and nuclear power but relies on coal-fired power plants to meet its rising energy demand, serviced by the state's leading provider of energy, Duke Energy.

The history and development of energy production in North Carolina are strongly tied to the development of the state's own Charlotte-based Duke Energy, one of the largest energy companies in the United States. Duke Energy began as Catawba Power Company in 1900 and became the Southern Power Company in 1904, led by W. Gill Wylie, James Buchanan Duke, and William States Lee in order to increase opportunities for industry in the state. The company focused on hydroelectric power stations, and its first power plant, Catawba Hydro Station, located along the Catawba River, began providing power to the Victoria Cotton Mills in Rock Hill, South Carolina, in 1904. In succeeding years, the company focused on developing hydroelectric power for the state's growing textile industry and became a very successful and influential energy company.

The rapid increase in eclectic power demand after World War II helped Duke to expand its residential market and develop its first nuclear power plant, Keowee-Toxway, in 1965. Since then, Duke Energy has increased its number of nuclear power plants in the state and also operates coal-fired plants, conventional hydroelectric plants, and natural gas turbines. In 2005, Duke Power purchased the Cincinnati-based Cinergy Corporation, expanding its customer base to the Midwest. In early 2011, Duke Energy announced a merger agreement with Raleigh-based Progress Energy. The merger will create the largest utility in the United States, with 7 million customers in six states: Duke's service area of western and central North and South Carolina, Indiana, and southwestern Ohio will combine with Progress's service area of eastern and central North and South Carolina, as well as Florida's central region and panhandle. The merged companies will retain the Duke Power name and provide 57 gigawatts of generating capacity.

Production and Consumption

North Carolina is a leading producer and consumer of electricity. The majority of the state's electric power is generated from coal-fired power plants.

▷ *Increasing Renewable Energy in North Carolina*

The Appalachian State University Energy Center created the North Carolina State Energy Plan for the North Carolina State Energy Office in 2003 with revisions in 2005. The plan specifically calls for focusing on alternative fuels from biomass and increasing uses of alternative energy sources. Biomass as a fuel includes municipal solid waste (MSW), agricultural wastes, and ethanol and biodiesel from energy crops. To increase biomass use, the plan recommends that the state invest in harvesting methane from waste from the state's leading livestock industries: swine, poultry, and dairy cows. In addition, the plan has targeted MSW sources for combustion as well as the conversion of landfill gas across the state into methane for combustion. The report describes an effective MSW direct-combustion system, which generates 7.5 megawatts of energy at the city of Wilmington, and identifies 36 potential landfills in the state under consideration for development.

The report also describes the NC Green-Power program, which enables electric utility customers to purchase electricity from renewable energy sources. This program provides a unique and affordable green pricing structure for residential customers. The plan also highlights research efforts to increase the potential for solar photovoltaic (PV) and solar thermal implementation across the state, as well as a need for increased development of micro-scale hydroelectric power systems for residential customers within range of small streams in the mountainous western part of the state. Finally, the plan calls for continued research and policy analysis for developing the state's wind resources along the coasts and in the mountain region. Research conducted at Appalachian State University's Energy Center and previous knowledge gained from a first-generation wind turbine in the town of Boone (funded by the National Aeronautics and Space Administration) have helped the university to install the largest wind turbine in the state as of 2011.

Nuclear power, natural gas, and hydropower produce the rest of the state's electricity. With three nuclear power plants, the state is a leading producer of nuclear energy. Despite its nuclear power sources and increasing renewable energy sector, North Carolina ranked 15th in sulfur dioxide and 13th in carbon dioxide emissions in 2009.

In 2009, North Carolina ranked 10th in net generation of electricity in the United States and 13th in net summer capacity. It also ranked 9th in total retail sales of energy and 13th in direct use, despite its average retail price of 8.48 cents per kilowatt-hour (29th in the United States in price). Factors contributing to the state's high energy consumption include summer air-conditioning use and the fact that more than half of North Carolinian households use electricity as the primary form of home heating.

As of 2009, the top retailer of electricity in the state was Duke Energy Carolinas, followed closely by Progress Energy Carolinas. Distant to these in production were Virginia Electric and Power, Energy United Electric Member Corporation, and Public Works of Fayetteville. These five providers produced 78 percent of energy in the state as well as 71, 81, and 87 percent of residential, commercial, and industrial demand, respectively.

Fossil Fuel Imports

Electricity generated in North Carolina comes from fossil fuel sources from other states or from foreign sources. The majority of the state's electricity is generated in power plants using coal shipped by rail from West Virginia or Kentucky. Four major pipelines bring fuel to the state: The Colonial and Plantation Pipelines bring petroleum from the Gulf Coast, the Dixie Pipeline brings propane to its terminus in Apex, and the Transcontinental Gas Pipeline brings natural gas to the state from the Gulf Coast on its route to major northeastern cities. Additional petroleum sources arrive from the ports of coastal cities Wilmington and Morehead City.

Renewables

In 2007, the state of North Carolina adopted a renewable energy and energy efficiency portfolio standard requiring utilities to meet 12.5 percent of demand through renewable energy sources or energy efficiency measures by 2021. Electric utility member corporations and municipalities selling power are also mandated to meet a 10 percent standard by 2018. As of 2008, the state's renewable net generation produced 4 percent of the state's total net electricity generation, with 2.4 percent coming from conventional hydroelectric and 1.4 percent coming from wood or wood waste. Solar, municipal solid waste and landfill gas, and other forms of biomass also contributed a very small percentage of renewable energy power. North Carolina is ranked among the highest in wind power capacity, with high capacity in its western Appalachian Mountain region and offshore along its coast. However, to date, the largest wind turbine for generating electricity is located at the Appalachian State University campus in Boone, North Carolina, within the state's mountain region.

CHRISTOPHER BADUREK

Further Reading

Duke Energy. "About Us." http://www.duke-energy.com.
NC GreenPower. "About NC GreenPower." http://www.ncgreenpower.org.
North Carolina State Energy Office. "Energy." http://www.energync.net/.
North Carolina State University. *North Carolina State Strategic Energy Management Plan*. http://issuu.com/ncsu_energy/docs/ncsu_energy_charge_v2.
U.S. Energy Information Administration. "Independent Statistics and Analysis." http://www.eia.gov/state/.

See Also: Gasification; Hydropower; Investor-Owned Utilities; Levitation; Natural Gas; Nuclear Power; Tennessee Valley Authority; United States.

North Dakota

Category: Energy in the United States.
Summary: Energy plays a major role in North Dakota's economy. The state accounts for nearly 2 percent of all crude oil production in the United States and is the number-one state for potential wind energy production.

North Dakota is a large state located in the upper Midwest of the United States, bordering Canada to the north. It is the third-least populated state in the country, with slightly more than 650,000 residents, and one of few states experiencing declines in population. The state is bordered by Minnesota to the east, South Dakota to the south, and Montana to the west. The state is formed by significant hills in the Great Plains region of the west, the Badlands to the north, the Missouri Plateau in the central part of the state, and the relatively flat Red River Valley in the eastern part of the state.

Production and Consumption

North Dakota has sizable fossil fuel reserves, with substantial surface mines in the central region of the state and crude oil and natural gas reserves in the western part. According to the U.S. Department of Energy, in 2008 North Dakota's total energy production was 884 trillion British thermal units (Btu), more than twice as much energy as it consumed, 441 trillion Btu, thanks in part to its substantial crude oil and wind energy production. The state is a major exporter of electricity.

North Dakota has a steadily growing economy, on par with the national average, and ranks among the upper half of all states for per capita income. The state economy is highly energy-intensive, and industry accounts for close to half of the state's total energy consumption. Despite having a relatively low population, North Dakota ranks as one of the highest energy consumers per capita in the nation (fourth overall), because of high energy demand in the winter. This rate is growing at more than double the average national rates.

The state regulates its market for electricity, and although the primary energy source is coal, North Dakota has already developed substantial wind energy production through the Clean Cities Coalition for the Red River Valley. North Dakota has the highest potential wind energy capacity in the United States.

Petroleum

More than 2 percent of all crude oil production in the United States comes from North Dakota, averaging 212,000 barrels per day in 2009. The state has numerous major pipelines for crude oil, petroleum products, and liquefied petroleum gas (LPG), in addition to many interstate pipelines for natural gas. With Canada at its northern border, the eastern side of the state pipes crude oil from Canada to markets in the Midwest for oil refining. Some crude oil extracted from the Williston Basin, located in the western half of the state, is refined near the capital, Bismarck, in addition to a small amount coming from Canada. Transportation fuel produced there is then distributed to the other northern Great Plains states and metropolitan areas of Minnesota.

North Dakota also has significant capacity for the production of ethanol, with six plants and a series of state-level policies and incentives for renewable energy in place. However, the state is a relatively low consumer of ethanol blended gasoline. North Dakota is one of few U.S. states to lack air quality regulations for the statewide use of nonconventional, blended motor gasoline.

Natural Gas

About 1 percent of the nation's total natural gas production comes from North Dakota, the majority of which is piped on through Minnesota and South Dakota to be consumed in other midwestern markets. North Dakota is the largest source of synthetic natural gas, thanks to the Great Plains Synfuels Plant, which produces more than 54 billion cubic feet of gas from coal annually. The majority of the state's natural gas supply is imported from western Canada and Montana, with relatively low overall consumption, most of which is accounted for by industry. While nearly 40 percent of households rely primarily on natural gas to heat their homes, the remaining households use electricity as their primary energy source.

Coal, Electricity, and Renewables

Overall electricity production and consumption are relatively low, and almost all of the state's electricity supply comes from coal-fired power plants. Several large surface coal mines are located in central North Dakota. These supply the majority of coal used in the state's coal-fueled power plants, providing nearly all of North Dakota's electricity production. This coal production is quite significant; imported coal from other states is relatively low.

All other noncoal-generated electricity is supplied by the state's hydroelectric dams. In fact, the Garrison Dam is the state's fifth-largest electricity-generating plant.

With more than 20 wind energy production sites, North Dakota is one of the nation's leading wind energy producers (11th overall) and ranks first in wind potential. In 2009, the state generated more than 4,000 megawatts of wind energy, up from just 0.5 megawatt in 2000. North Dakota also has three ethanol plants, which in 2008 produced 123 million gallons per year.

CARY HENDRICKSON

Further Reading

Dakota Gasification Company. "Great Plains Synfuels Plant." http://www.dakotagas.com/.

North Dakota State Water Commission. *A Review of Alternate Energy Sources.* Grand Forks, ND: University of North Dakota, 1974.

U.S. Energy Information Administration. "North Dakota." http://www.eia.gov/state/state-energy-profiles.cfm?sid=ND.

See Also: Coal; Gasification; Natural Gas; Nebraska; Oil and Petroleum; South Dakota; Wind Resources.

Norway

Official Name: Kingdom of Norway.
Category: Geography of Energy.
Summary: Norway has many natural resources and currently has a massive oil and gas industry, which contributes largely to its national wealth. Because it uses hydropower, it also has one of the cleanest electricity-generating industries worldwide.

Norway is well known both for its petroleum industry and for its clean electricity industry. Nevertheless, it is only since the 1970s that the energy sector has developed significantly. In 1969, Norway's oil and gas journey began when the first well was drilled in the Ekofisk field. Oil and gas production started two years later, and subsequent major discoveries launched proved immensely successful.

Creation of the Petroleum Industry

At first, exploration and drilling expertise on the Norwegian shelf was supplied only by foreign companies. However, realizing the potential of the oil and gas market for the country, the government created a state-owned oil company in 1972, Statoil. Rules were implemented to ensure that this company would be involved to a certain extent in each new project. Since then, numerous companies have been created in the petroleum industry, and the country has become an industry leader. The evolution of Norwegian economic growth has been greatly impacted, and still is, by the petroleum industry. At an international level, Norway ranked 14th among oil-producing countries in 2009 and first in Western Europe.

However, oil production is slowly declining; reserves began shrinking in 2001. Discussions on the development of new oil fields in the Barents Sea are under way, but it is an environmentally sensitive area. Currently, the petroleum industry generates a quarter of Norway's gross domestic product (GDP) and is the largest source of revenue for the Norwegian government. The country was also ranked sixth among world nations in the production of natural gas in 2009, and its gas production is expected to grow in the future. More than 90 percent of the products derived from the petroleum industry are being exported, mostly to the United Kingdom, the Netherlands, France, and the United States.

Electricity and Hydropower

Electricity is also important in Norway, representing nearly half of the energy consumed locally. The country is known for having a nearly 100 percent clean electricity generation sector, with most of it originating from the country's exceptional water reserves. Most of the hydropower infrastructure, including a number of reservoirs, was built between 1970 and 1985. Norway is the sixth-largest hydropower producer in the world, an impressive figure considering that the country is not among the hundred most populated nations. Such production covers up to 99 percent of the country's total electricity needs. The main actor in the hydropower landscape is Statkraft, a fully state-owned company. Several wind farms and thermal power plants using waste for fuel, as well as gas-fired power plants, account for the remaining 1 percent of electricity generation.

Because hydropower depends on a variable input, water, the country uses the Nordpool market to balance its needs. This electricity trading market connects Denmark, Sweden, Finland, and recently Estonia. For Norway, it means that in periods when supply cannot meet demand (for example, during dry years or harsh winter periods), Norway can import electricity from the other members of the Nordpool market. In other periods (for example, when there is an absence of wind in Denmark), Norway typically exports power through an undersea cable.

Most of Norway's energy is consumed by the transportation sector, electricity-intensive industries, and households. Roughly a fourth of the domestic energy consumption goes to the energy sector, where it is used for oil and gas extraction, for instance. Between 1990 and 2008, the total energy consumption increased 17 percent, while the population increased only 12 percent.

Carbon Neutral

Norway is pursuing the ambitious goal of becoming carbon neutral by 2030. As a result, the country is at

Norway is pursuing the goal of becoming carbon neutral by 2030. The Hywind project is the world's first offshore floating wind farm. Given the local environment and the policy scheme in Norway, it is likely that wind and small hydropower will be common sources of energy in the future.

the forefront of research, demonstration projects, and development, as new technologies regularly emerge. Among these projects are a carbon capture and sequestration (CCS) demonstration plant, an osmotic power plant, and the Hywind project, the world's first offshore floating wind farm. In addition, the government is pushing for more renewable energy capacity on its territory and therefore, in collaboration with Sweden, has created a common green certificate market. In this market, green certificates ensure that a certain amount of new capacity will be built in a cost-efficient manner.

Given the local environment and the policy scheme, it is likely that wind and small hydropower will be common sources of energy in the future. Norway's wind conditions are among the best in Europe, especially along the coastline, and the numerous streams spread around the country are well suited for power generation. Because solar radiation levels are relatively poor in this northern country, it is unlikely that solar power will contribute greatly to the electricity market in the future.

Patrick André Narbel

Further Reading

Central Intelligence Agency. "Norway." In *The World Factbook*. https://www.cia.gov/library/publications/the-world-factbook.

Nordic Council of Ministers. "Nordic Green Power Certificates." http://www.nordicenergysolutions.org/performance-policy/nordic-cooperation/nordic-green-power-certificates.

Nordpool Spot. "History." http://www.nordpoolspot.com/About-us/History.

Norwegian Ministry of Petroleum and Energy. "Electricity Generation." http://www.regjeringen.no/en/dep/oed/Subject/Energy-in-Norway/Electricity-generation.html?id=440487.

Norwegian Ministry of Petroleum and Energy. "Norway's Oil History in 5 Minutes." http://www.regjeringen.no/en/dep/oed/Subject/Oil-and-Gas/norways-oil-history-in-5-minutes.html?id=440538.

Statistics Norway. "Energy." http://www.ssb.no/energi_en.

U.S. Energy Information Administration. "Country Analysis Brief: Norway." http://www.eia.gov/countries/country-data.cfm?fips=NO.

See Also: Climate Neutrality; Denmark; International Energy Agency; Oil and Petroleum; Sweden; Tidal Power; Wind Resources; World Commission on Environment and Development.

Nuclear Fission

Category: Energy Technology.
Summary: Nuclear fission is used in electricity production and weaponry. This makes it a disputable technology that many countries, including some rogue nations, would like to master.

In 1938, Otto Hahn, Lise Meitner, Fritz Strassmann, and Otto Frisch produced smaller nuclei by bombarding uranium (U-235) with neutrons. This process is called nuclear fission because it resembles biological fission, wherein cells divide to produce new cells. Hahn, a German scientist, received the 1944 Nobel Prize in Chemistry for this work.

Neutrons have no charge and are more effective in breaking nuclei than are protons. The following is a typical nuclear fission reaction:

$$^{1}n + {}^{235}U \rightarrow {}^{236}U \rightarrow {}^{142}Ba + {}^{91}Kr + 3\ {}^{1}n.$$

Nuclei consist of neutrons and protons, commonly called nucleons. The total mass of all individual nucleons in a nucleus is more than the mass of the nucleus. This difference is the result of a loss of mass due to binding energy, which is released during the formation of the nucleus. This energy conversion of mass follows Albert Einstein's equation, $E = mc^2$, where E is the energy equivalent of mass, m, and c is the speed of light. This binding energy, if supplied to the nucleus, can break it into protons and neutrons.

In a fission process, there is an increase in the binding energy/nucleon in going from parent nuclei to daughter nuclei. This increase in binding energy is released in the form of energy and is about 200 mega-electron volts for U-235. This energy is about a million times higher than the energy from chemical reactions, such as the burning of gasoline or TNT. Currently, this enormous energy is mostly used for two purposes: in electricity generation and in weaponry.

One kilogram of U-235 has about 2.6×10^{24} nuclei. In the case of complete fission, it provides 8×10^{10} British thermal units (Btu) of energy. To supply an amount of energy comparable to 1 kilogram of U-235 using conventional energy resources would, for example, require 3,000 tons of coal or 14,000 barrels of oil to produce energy. Also, while a nuclear power plant requires the shipment of fuel once every year, a comparable coal-fired plant may require one trainload of coal every day.

Polonium and lithium are combined to produce a burst of neutrons that are employed in fission. Polonium-210 is a radioactive substance, with a half-life of 138.376 days, and serves as a source of alpha particles. Lithium reacts with alpha particles to produce neutrons.

Albert Einstein sent a letter to President Franklin D. Roosevelt on August 2, 1939, asking him to sanction a project to make a nuclear-fission bomb. He wrote: "… it may become possible to set up a nuclear chain reaction in a large mass of uranium, by which vast amounts of power and large quantities of new radium-like elements would be generated. … This new phenomenon would also lead to the construction of bombs, and it is conceivable—though much less certain—that extremely powerful bombs of a new type may thus be constructed. A single bomb of this type, carried by boat and exploded in a port, might very well destroy the whole port together with some of the surrounding territory."

The Manhattan Project and the Atom Bomb

Einstein's letter convinced President Roosevelt, eventually leading to the Manhattan Project, which resulted in the construction of the first nuclear fission (atom) bombs, detonated over Japan in the summer of 1945 and effectively ending World War II in the Pacific.

The first self-sustaining nuclear fission chain reaction was achieved in 1942 under the direction of Enrico Fermi, an immigrant Italian scientist at the University of Chicago. Fermi received the Nobel Prize in 1938 and went to Stockholm to participate in the ceremonies.

Because his wife was a Jew and anti-Semitic atrocities had already been promulgated in the lead-up to World War II, he was concerned about her safety in Italy. He therefore opted to immigrate to America after the festivities. As a result, he would contribute his expertise to those of American scientists in expediting their quest for a chain reaction. After the successful test, a secret message was sent to Washington: "The Italian navigator has landed in the New World and found the natives very friendly."

The growth of neutrons in successive fission is geometric if there is no loss of neutrons to the environment. This geometric growth of the reaction rate leads to an explosive release of energy. The first atom bomb was dropped on Hiroshima, Japan, in August 1945. This bomb used almost pure uranium, while the bomb that was dropped a few days later on Nagasaki used plutonium. Both bombs were based on the principle of nuclear fission.

The energy produced by nuclear fission would soon find multiple other uses. In 1951, electricity was first generated from a nuclear reactor, called the Experimental Breeder Reactor (EBR), in Idaho. In 1953, the nuclear-powered submarine *Nautilus* was built, launching the following January. In 1957, in Shippingport, Pennsylvania, the first commercial reactor for electricity production became operational.

The uranium ores available in nature contain only about 0.7 percent uranium-235. Most of it is in the form of U-238. To increase the probability of fission in a nuclear reactor, natural uranium must be "enriched" to increase the concentration of U-235 to a level of 2 to 4 percent, using diffusion or centrifugation. However, a concentration of about 95 percent or more of U-235 is needed for making a

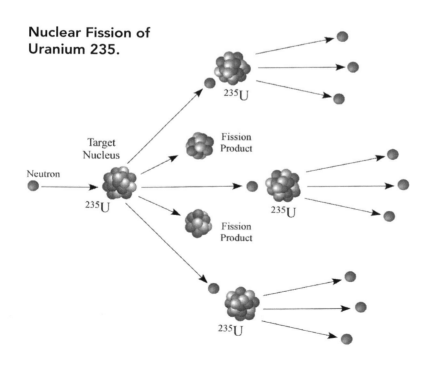

Nuclear Fission of Uranium 235.

deadly nuclear bomb. Enrichment of uranium is not an easy task, and only a handful of countries have achieved it.

It is much easier to produce plutonium, as one can separate it using chemical techniques. However, the design for nuclear fission is fairly complicated for plutonium; it requires an implosion to increase the density of plutonium before it explodes. This, too, is not an easy task. Most nuclear power plants produce plutonium because the U-238 in the fuel rods fissions into plutonium. However, most countries do not reprocess the nuclear waste to extract the plutonium. It is done to improve accountability of the radioactive materials for safety reasons.

Using neutron reflectors, one can construct a plutonium-239 bomb with only 11 pounds (5 kilograms) of material. Similarly, with only 33 pounds (15 kilograms), one can achieve a self-sustained chain reaction with uranium-235. The minimum amount of mass needed for a self-sustained reaction is called the critical mass.

The Enrichment Process

The most difficult component in achieving self-sustained fission is the acquirement of enriched uranium. While plutonium can be separated chemically, it is not possible to isolate uranium-235 from uranium-238 chemically, since both isotopes have the same chemical properties. The most common process to enrich uranium uses a gas centrifuge, which works much like a centrifuge used in a chemistry laboratory. However, a centrifuge to separate uranium isotopes spins with ultrahigh speed, comparable to the speed of sound and much faster than a classic centrifuge. Uranium hexafluoride gas is injected into the centrifuge, which spins and separates different isotopes based on weight.

Separation of isotopes using a centrifuge was accomplished for elements with small atomic numbers in 1934 by Jesse Beams of the University of Virginia. The ultrahigh speed to separate uranium isotopes was achieved with the help of Gernot Zippe, an Austrian scientist, at the University of Virginia using a magnetic field. This separation process uses a large number of centrifuges in succession. A common problem is the condensation of uranium hexa-fluoride (UF_6) on the rotor, which upsets the balance and causes the assembly to crash.

Achieving Purity

Enriching uranium is a slow and cumbersome process. However, as the concentration of U-235 increases, it becomes easier to purify it further. In other words, it is a lot more difficult to achieve 20 percent purity of U-235 from 0.7 percent purity found in uranium ore than to achieve 40 percent enrichment from a 20 percent enriched uranium sample. This fact is currently causing great concern to the world community, particularly as it attempts to monitor the enrichment process occurring in Iran. Iran claims to be enriching uranium for energy production (use in their nuclear power plants). However, some countries are concerned that further enrichment could make it possible for Iran to acquire bomb-level uranium, and some nations are concerned that Iran is deliberately seeking to achieve that goal.

A new, highly classified laser excitation technique, known as SILEX, is being used to enrich uranium. SILEX (an acronym for the separation of isotopes by laser excitation) uses a tuned laser of a particular frequency to bombard uranium ore. Lasers at this particular frequency can ionize U-235 selectively, with high precision. The ionized uranium is collected using conventional charged plates. This process is easier to achieve and consumes much less energy than the conventional gas centrifuge.

Alok Kumar

Further Reading
Frisch, O. R. "The Discovery of Fission: How It All Began." *Physics Today* 20, no. 11 (1967).
Jenkins, Brian Michael. *Will Terrorists Go Nuclear?* New York: Prometheus Books, 2008.
Muller, Richard A. *Physics for Future Presidents: The Science Behind the Headlines.* New York: W. W. Norton, 2008.
Segrè, Emilio G. "The Discovery of Nuclear Fission." *Physics Today* 42, no. 7 (1989).
Turner, Louis A. "Nuclear Fission." *Reviews of Modern Physics* 12, no. 1 (January 1940).

See Also: Curie, Marie; Einstein, Albert; Meitner, Lise; Nuclear Fusion; Nuclear Power; Radiation.

Nuclear Fusion

Category: Energy Technology.

Summary: The nuclear fusion process produces energy that is millions of times greater than the energy produced from burning fossil fuels. This has led to a powerful hydrogen bomb and may someday resolve our energy crisis by producing cheap electricity.

The process of building up larger atomic nuclei by combining smaller nuclei is called nuclear fusion. This process produces the greatest energy with the lightest nuclides, such as hydrogen and helium. In nuclear fusion, as in nuclear fission, the total mass of the resultant products is less than the original mass. This loss of mass appears in the form of released energy.

In the 1930s, Hans Bethe first recognized that stars produce energy by fusing hydrogen nuclei to form deuterium. This work led him to receive the 1967 Nobel Prize in Physics. After World War II, having learned of the power of the atom and building the atom bomb, scientists from the leading nations tried to design a nuclear fusion bomb, the so-called hydrogen bomb. They also tried to control this process in order to use it to produce electricity.

First Hydrogen Bomb

The first hydrogen bomb, code-named Ivy Mike, was detonated by the United States at Eniwetok Atoll, part of the Marshall Islands, on October 31, 1952. It had a yield of 10.4 megatons of TNT. The mastermind behind this device, Edward Teller, observed the event on a seismograph in Berkeley, California. He observed a tremor in the earth that was produced by shock waves generated thousands of miles away in the Marshall Islands by the explosion. He could not resist the temptation to inform his colleagues in Los Ala-

mos about the success and sent a coded telegram message, "It's a boy."

Deuterium (D) and tritium (T), both isotopes of hydrogen, are the two most popular raw ingredients for nuclear fusion. A deuterium nucleus contains one proton and one neutron. It is commonly found in nature in the form of heavy water. Out of 6,500 hydrogen atoms, one is in the form of deuterium. In ocean water, every liter has about 33 milligrams of deuterium. One cubic kilometer of ocean water has enough deuterium to generate energy equivalent to about 1.36 trillion barrels of oil, about the total global oil reserves.

Tritium is available in trace amounts in nature. It is usually produced by reacting neutrons with lithium. In a tokamak assembly using D-T reaction, neutrons are produced that are completely unaffected by the presence of a magnetic field. They move unobstructed and hit the surrounding wall that contains lithium and produce tritium. The following are some typical nuclear fusion reactions (MeV stands for mega-electron volts):

$$^1H + {}^2H \rightarrow {}^3He + 5.49 \text{ MeV}$$
$$^2H + {}^2H \rightarrow p + {}^3H + 3.3 \text{ MeV}$$
$$^2H + {}^3H \rightarrow {}^4He + n + 17.6 \text{ MeV}$$

A fusion reaction is about 4 million times more energetic than a chemical reaction using fossil fuels: coal, oil, or natural gas. While a 1,000-megawatt coal-fired power plant requires 2.7 million tons of coal per year, a fusion plant will only require 250 kilograms of fuel per year, half of it deuterium and half of it tritium. Although each fusion releases less energy than a fission reaction, the energy per unit mass (or per nucleon) is 3.5 times greater for D-T fusion than in uranium fission.

Distant Reality

Although a commercial reactor for electricity production was constructed in less than a decade after the discovery of nuclear fission, a commercial reactor using nuclear fusion is a distant reality. Scientists are trying to bring nuclei close enough for fusion in a controlled manner. Accelerators are not good for achieving fusion, since the scattering of nuclei due to Coulomb repulsion is more probable than fusion. Atoms are dissociated into nuclei and electrons at high temperature. This hot ionized gas, with free electrons and positively charge nuclei, is known as plasma. For the fusion of nuclei, a temperature about 10^8 kelvin (about 10 billion kelvin) must be maintained for a long enough period (for seconds) in a small, confined space for this plasma to have high density. By comparison, the sun's surface temperature is about 15.7 million kelvin. Because of the high temperature necessary for fusion, fusion devices are often called thermonuclear devices.

Such temperatures and ion density occur in the interiors of stars, where nuclear fusion reactions are common. The sun is an example: The gravitational field of the sun creates this confined space with high temperature and enables the sun to fuse 600 million tons of hydrogen into helium every second, releasing an enormous amount of energy. However, without the benefit of gravitational forces in laboratory settings, achieving fusion is a major challenge.

The plasma loses substantial energy at such a high temperature as a result of radiation (bremsstrahlung) and heat conduction to the device boundaries. It is therefore necessary to compensate for this energy loss on an ongoing basis. For sustained fusion to occur, the plasma temperature should be above 10^8 kelvin and its density should be about 10^{20} particles per cubic meter (about one-millionth of the density of air). This relationship was defined by J. D. Lawson in 1957 and is called *Lawson criterion*. This task is so complex that most nuclear reactors produce less energy than they consume.

A charged particle moving perpendicular to a magnetic field executes a circular path around the magnetic field. If the particle also has some motion (speed) along the field line, the circular path turns into a helical path. The strength of the magnetic field and mass, charge, and speed of the charged particle dictate the radius of the helical path. Thus, the charged particles get trapped in a magnetic bottle. A doughnut-shaped magnetic chamber, known as a tokamak (abbreviated from the Russian *toroid-kamera-magnit-karushka*, or toroidal chamber with magnetic coil), is commonly used to confine plasma. Two noted Russian scientists, Igor Tamm and Andrei Sakharov, contributed much to this design.

As the charged particles move, they establish current through the plasma and the charged particles collide with each other, particularly those with opposite charges that move in opposite directions. These collisions create heat, which in turn increases the resistance and decreases the current. The system reaches an equilibrium state in time. To increase the temperature further, external heating devices are used. Neutral beam injection and high-frequency electromagnetic waves are some of the techniques used to increase temperature. Recently, laser-induced fusion has been practiced, whereby hydrogen droplets are bombarded by high-energy laser beams from all sides. This compression increases the temperature of the droplet. This is a much simpler process than the tokamak process.

The Tokamak Fusion Test Reactor (TFTR) at Princeton, New Jersey, the Joint European Torus (JET) at Culham, England, and the JT-60 (JT for Japan Torus) in Naka, Japan, are the three largest new facilities. In 2010, the Japanese facility was disassembled to be upgraded to JT-60SA by using superconducting coils. This upgrading may be completed in 2016. Also, a consortium of scientists from the European Union, India, China, Japan, Korea, Russia, and the United States are trying to construct a 500-megawatt International Thermonuclear Experimental Reactor (ITER) in Cadarache, France. This reactor will fuse deuterium and tritium and requires a hot plasma of about 1.5×10^8 kelvin in a confined space. While the existing tokamaks achieve fusion for a fraction of a second, this new tokamak design in France should allow scientists to sustain the fusion reaction for extended periods. The construction of this device is expected to be completed by November 2019.

Conclusion

The technology to produce uncontrolled nuclear fusion was mastered more than a half century ago. However, the technology to control fusion reactions for extended periods still eludes scientists. The recent significant improvements in maintaining plasma temperature and confinement have nevertheless raised the prospect that one day nuclear fusion might be used for electricity production.

ALOK KUMAR

Further Reading

Hinrichs, Roger, and Merlin Kleinbach. *Energy: Its Use and the Environment.* Belmont, CA: Thomson Brooks/Cole, 2006.

Lawson, J. D. "Some Criteria for a Power Producing Thermonuclear Reactor." *Proceedings of the Physical Society B* 70, no. 1 (1957).

McCracken, G. M., and P. Stott. *Fusion: The Energy of the Universe.* New York: Academic Press, 2005.

Seife, Charles. *Sun in a Bottle: The Strange History of Fusion and the Science of Wishful Thinking.* New York: Viking, 2008.

Teller, Edward. Energy *From Heaven and Earth.* New York: W. H. Freeman, 1979.

See Also: Cold Fusion; Nuclear Fission; Nuclear Power; Potential Energy; Sakharov, Andrei.

Nuclear Power

Category: Energy Resources.
Summary: Nuclear power plants are promoted as a solution to energy problems and as a way to reduce greenhouse gas emissions. However, in the United States, the nuclear industry has not upgraded technologies or constructed new plants in 30 years.

Soon after the discovery of nuclear fission in 1938, scientists started working on producing electricity using nuclear fission. The first nuclear power station, known as APS-1 Obninsk (Atomic Power Station 1 Obninsk), was built in 1954 about 110 kilometers southwest of Moscow, Russia. The power plant had a capacity of about 6 megawatts (MW) and functioned until 2002. In the United States, the Shippingport Reactor in Pennsylvania was the first commercial nuclear power plant to become opera-tional in 1957. This reactor provided about 60 MW of energy and was located about 25 miles from Pittsburgh. It remained operational until 1982.

There are about 440 nuclear power plants located in 30 countries that are producing reliable electricity and providing 14 percent of all electricity. France and Lithuania produce over three-quarters of their electricity from nuclear power. Belgium, Bulgaria, the Czech Republic, Hungary, Slovakia, South Korea, Sweden, Switzerland, Slovenia, and Ukraine generate one-third or more of their electricity from nuclear power.

There are 104 operational nuclear power plants in the United States, providing 19 percent of the total electricity, which amounts to approximately 100,000 MW. These reactors are located in 31 states. Illinois has the largest number of nuclear power plants with 11, followed by Pennsylvania with nine, and South Carolina with seven. In contrast, in the mid-1970s, new nuclear power plants were being constructed in the United States and experts predicted that the country would have approximately 1,000 nuclear power plants in operation by 2000. The United States has not constructed any nuclear power plants in the past 30 years.

Because of the population growth in America, many old power plants are currently located in densely populated areas. The nuclear industry is at a critical juncture. To maintain about a 19 percent of electricity production share, America would need to construct hundreds of nuclear power plants by 2050 or earlier.

The U.S. Nuclear Regulatory Commission (NRC) approved licenses to construct two nuclear reactors about 170 miles east of Atlanta in 2012, the first such issuance of licenses since 1979. The Obama administration allocated $8.3 billion in federal loan guarantees to build these two reactors. This is the first loan guarantee to a nuclear power plant under the Energy Policy Act of 2005. The effort was made to promote the nuclear technologies in use in the Westinghouse AP1000 reactor, which make reactors more efficient and safer.

Nuclear Power Generation

In traditional power plants, coal, natural gas, or petroleum are commonly used to heat water.

Similarly, in the case of a nuclear power plant, the nuclear fission process is used to produce heat to boil water, and using a turbine, electricity is produced. Nuclear power is derived by splitting uranium-235 with neutrons. This reaction produces two or three neutrons that can further be used to split other uranium nuclei and produce a "self-sustaining" chain reaction. This chain reaction produces an enormous amount of energy with each fission—about 200 milli-electron volts (meV) per fission.

The first self-sustaining chain reaction was successfully carried out at the University of Chicago's Amos Alonso Stagg Field on December 2, 1942. Neutrons with an 0.4 electron volt (eV) of energy or less are most effective in the fission of U-235. Neutrons ejected during fission have energies that are comparable to millions of electron volts. These neutrons simply escape and do not produce another reaction. A medium is required to slow down the neutrons, known as a *moderator*, which dampens the energies of neutrons without absorbing them.

Graphite and water are two common moderators. The hydrogen nuclei in water play a key role in the slowing of neutrons. In a collision process, for example, when a moving tennis ball strikes another stationary tennis ball it will lose more energy than a tennis ball striking a bowling ball. It takes about 10^{-5} seconds for a 2-MeV neutron to slow down to 0.025 eV in a mere 18 collisions with hydrogen nuclei.

To maintain a steady state, it is essential that the flux of neutrons that produce fission remain constant. Since more neutrons are produced than consumed in U-235 fission reaction, it is imperative to remove some neutrons. This is accomplished by using control rods that are made of either boron or cadmium. Both elements are quite efficient in absorbing neutrons. The rate of absorption is controlled by the movement of these rods in and out of the reactor core. If the control rods do not absorb neutrons, the neutron density increases and causes a rapid release of energy. However, since nuclear fuel used in a reactor contains about 3–4 percent pure ^{235}U versus about 95 percent purity in an atom bomb, a nuclear reactor cannot explode like a bomb even in the event of a meltdown.

Types of Reactors

There is no single design to produce the fission process: approximately 82 percent of reactors in the world are light-water reactors, implying that the moderation and cooling is done by regular water; about 10 percent are moderated and cooled by heavy water; 4 percent are gas-cooled reactors; while the remaining 4 percent are moderated by graphite and water-cooled. The term *light-water* is used to distinguish it from heavy-water reactors. Water is used as a moderator, as a coolant to remove heat from the reactor, and as a source to produce steam for the turbine.

Thirty-five percent of light-water reactors are boiling-water reactors (BWRs), while 65 percent are pressurized water reactors (PWRs). In PWRs, the water in the reactor core is kept at a high pressure of about 2,200 lbs/in^2 (psi) and the reactor core water temperature is kept at about 600 degrees Fahrenheit.

Even at this high temperature, the water remains in liquid form due to high pressure. This hot water gives off its heat to the water in the steam generator through a heat exchanger. In BWRs, water in the primary core turns into steam and hits the turbine blades to produce electricity. Afterward, it is condensed and pumped back to the reactor core. Radioactivity is better contained in PWRs than in BWRs.

Both types of reactors have more or less the same efficiency rate of about 33 percent and consume the same amount of water. The remaining 67 percent of the energy is released into the environment. Most nuclear power plants use somewhere between 400 and 720 gallons of water per 1MW.h production of electricity. Thus, the water consumption of nuclear power plants is relatively high. Ocean water is usually avoided for use as a coolant due to the corrosive nature of salt water.

Heavy-water reactors use deuterium oxide rather than hydrogen oxide as a moderator. The method has several benefits: it does not absorb neutrons and it effectively slows down fast neutrons. It also can achieve a sustainable chain reaction with naturally occurring uranium. This type of reactor is common in Canada.

A new reactor design involves uranium fuel being placed inside a 2.5-inch-deep bed of pyrolytic graphite pebbles. These pebbles are covered with silicon carbide ceramic. Both materials are highly resistant to high heat and the chance of radioactive release is minimal. With this design, if a reactor becomes hotter than desired, the uranium-238 in the pebbles absorbs high-energy neutrons in a nonchain reaction and slows the fission process. Thus, this type of reactor protects the public more effectively from accidental meltdown or fires. Instead, any damage generally affects one pebble at a time. Another advantage to pebble-bed reactors is higher efficiency. Traditional nuclear power plants produce electricity at about a 35-percent efficiency rate, while pebble-bed reactors range from 40 to 50 percent efficiency.

Environmental Impact

Nuclear power plants do not generate greenhouse gases like fossil fuel plants. They do release trace amounts of radioactive gases; namely krypton, xenon, and iodine vapor. However, these power plants do indirectly cause greenhouse gas emissions. In a typical reactor, about 1.6 million tons of steel and about 14 million tons of concrete are manufactured, transported to the site, and used in construction. This process consumes millions of gallons of fossil fuel. For example, for every ton of Portland cement manufactured, about a ton of carbon dioxide is released into the atmosphere. This indirect emission is prominent only during the construction phase.

Nuclear reactors generate both high-level and low-level radioactive waste. High-level waste is waste generated in the nuclear reactor fuel cycle. Low-level waste includes gloves, clothing, tools, machine parts, and other items that may be contaminated with radioactivity. Extreme care needs to be taken in handling and storing these wastes.

A typical 1,000-MW nuclear power plant produces about 30 metric tons of high-level waste. This waste includes uranium, plutonium, cesium, strontium, and neptunium. The plutonium in this spent fuel is a major concern as it can be separated

Wikimedia

The world experienced a major global nuclear power accident at the Chernobyl reactor in Ukraine (above) on April 26, 1986. In this disaster, radioactive debris spread to the air, soil, and groundwater consumed and used for farming.

into dangerous and valuable materials using chemical techniques. Smuggling of radioactive waste is a major concern for nuclear power plants in several developing countries and in eastern Europe, where security measures may be inadequate.

In the United States, consumers end up paying about 1 cent per kilowatt-hour of electricity used toward nuclear waste management. This fee has raised billions of dollars, and yet a proper waste repository has yet to be built. Additionally, the half-life of uranium-238, uranium-235, and plutonium-239 is quite high; 24,000 years for plutonium, 713,000,000 years for uranium-235, and 4,500,000,000 for uranium-238. The half-life of strontium and cesium are 29 and 30 years, respectively. These wastes will need to be secured for extremely long periods of time.

As of 2012, the world population had faced two major nuclear power accidents: the first at the Chernobyl reactor in Ukraine (then a part of the Soviet Union) on April 26, 1986, and the second on

March 11, 2011, at the Fukushima Daiichi Nuclear Power Station in Japan after an earthquake-led tsunami. In both disasters, radioactive debris spread to the soil that produces food, groundwater used for drinking, and the air.

In the United States, the most severe nuclear accident occurred at the Three Mile Island power plant in Pennsylvania on March 28, 1979. Due to a valve malfunction, a large amount of radioactive coolant escaped. In an emergency measure, some radioactive wastewater was dumped into the Susquehanna River. The cleanup cost related to the disaster cost around $1 billion and was completed in 1993, over 14 years later.

Major Issues

In the United States, nuclear power has encountered much public opposition, turning many politicians against its proliferation. The International Atomic Energy Agency (IAEA) acknowledges the task of "achieving and retaining public confidence in nuclear power" as a challenge in many parts of the world. If nuclear power is to continue to develop, public acceptance of its importance as an energy resource needs to improve. This is true for the United States as well as for many other nations.

The IAEA acknowledges that there is a shortage of nuclear reactor design, architecture, engineering, and project management organizations internationally. Nuclear proliferation in developing countries is another major concern, where the safety of used fuel for short- or long-term storage is an issue. Since most nuclear power plants are large, producing more than 1,000 MW, proper grids for power transmission are also essential. Such grids are not widely available in many countries.

The life span of a typical nuclear reactor is about 50–60 years. Reactors need to be decommissioned and sealed for thousands of years after their use period. The decommissioning cost alone can cost $500 million or more for each reactor.

In public perception, the nuclear industry functions under a veil of secrecy. For example, the IAEA prohibited the World Health Organization from releasing information about the adverse health impacts of Chernobyl without getting prior clearance from the IAEA. For this reason, some information has never been released to the public. In Japan, the Japanese government and the Tokyo Electric Power Company (Tepco), the owner of the nuclear reactors, have admitted there was a lack of communication to the general public about the magnitude of the problem in the early stages of the disaster. As a result of the Chernobyl and Fukushima Daiichi fall-outs, German officials abandoned plans to build new nuclear power plants, and Italy became a nuclear-free country. However, China is still proceeding with the construction of about 25 new nuclear power plants.

ALOK KUMAR

Further Reading

American Nuclear Society. http://www.ans.org.

Funabashi, Yoichi, and Kay Kitazawa. "Fukushima in Review: A Complex Disaster, a Disastrous Response." *Bulletin of the Atomic Scientists* 68, no. 2 (2012).

Hinrichs, Roger, and Merlin Kleinbach. *Energy: Its Use and the Environment.* Belmont, CA: Thomson Brooks/Cole, 2006.

International Atomic Energy Agency. http://www.iaea.org.

Mittica, P. *Chernobyl: The Hidden Legacy.* London: Trolley Books, 2007.

Muller, Richard A. *Physics for Future Presidents.* New York: W. W. Norton & Co., 2008.

U.S. Department of Energy. "Nuclear Energy Research Initiative: 2009 Annual Report." http://nuclear.energy.gov/pdfFiles/neriAnnualReport2009.pdf.

Walker, J. S. *Three Mile Island: A Nuclear Crisis in Historical Perspective.* Berkeley: University of California Press, 2004.

World Nuclear Association. http://world-nuclear.org.

See Also: Chernobyl; China Syndrome; Cold Fusion; Nuclear Fission; Risk Assessment; Risk Management; Three Mile Island; Uranium.

Offshore Drilling

Category: Energy Technology.

Summary: Offshore drilling is the discovery and extraction of underwater oil and gas resources. Although drilling in lakes and inland seas is offshore drilling, in common usage the term especially applies to oil extraction from beneath the ocean floor.

More difficult than oil extraction on land, offshore drilling has become more important as the world has become more dependent on a large and reliable supply of oil, and it is at the center of an ongoing political debate over the potential environmental hazards posed by oceanic oil extraction.

Underwater drilling began quite early, with submerged oil wells in Grand Lake St. Marys, Ohio, in 1891. Five years later, piers were built extending into the Santa Barbara Channel off California, from which to drill submerged oil wells, and soon thereafter offshore drilling commenced in Lake Erie and the tidal zones of the Gulf of Mexico. As offshore drilling shifted to deeper waters in the mid-20th century, new methods needed to be developed and new equipment built. First came fixed-platform rigs for depths up to 100 feet, then jack-up rigs for depths up to 400 feet, as in the Gulf of Mexico.

A jack-up rig is a mobile platform with supporting legs (usually three) that rest on the seafloor. The platform is towed into position or propelled under its own power, at which point the legs are jacked down onto the seafloor until the rig is at rest. Ballast water added to the weight of the platform drives the legs into the sea bottom so that the weight of operations will not push them down further, and the platform is then jacked up above the level of the water so that an air gap prevents waves, currents, and tides from exerting force on the hull. Today, jack-up rigs are the most common type of mobile offshore drilling rig. They are also used for specialized platforms that act as a base for maintenance work, typically on drilling platforms but also on bridges and offshore wind turbines.

Another type of drilling platform is the semisubmersible, a specialized marine vessel designed for enhanced stability. Semisubmersibles are typically used for drilling in depths greater than 400 feet, where they excel at resisting the pitch and yaw of the forces of large waves. The hull structure can be submerged, and the operating deck is kept well above sea level, connected by structural columns to ballasted pontoons far below.

Keeping so much of the structure below the water helps keep it stable, but the vessel is never entirely underwater. Removing ballast water from the hub makes the structure float back up to the surface, a method used by heavy-lift semisubmersibles to submerge most of their structure below the water, position themselves underneath another floating vessel, and then deballast in order to pick the floating vessel up as cargo.

The construction of semisubmersibles has occurred in phases, or generations, because it tends to occur in boom periods, with designs being improved and advanced somewhat each time. There have been six such generations. The first generation of semisubmersibles, built in the 1960s, could be used to depths of 600 feet. Subsequent generations date to 1969–74 (1,000 feet), the 1980s (1,500 feet), the 1990s (3,000 feet), 1998–2004 (7,500 feet), and the current and sixth generation, beginning around 2005, which can be used at depths of up to 10,000 feet. The greatest gains in semisubmersible construction have been realized in the back-to-back boom periods since the 1990s, an indication of the significant financial interest in offshore drilling. Today, major semisubmersibles are in use for offshore drilling in the British North Sea, off the coast of Brazil, in the Norwegian Sea, in the South China Sea, in the Gulf of Mexico, in the Indian Ocean, and off Malaysia.

Drillships

Drillships are ships that have been fitted with an apparatus for oil and gas drilling; they can also be used as a platform from which to perform well maintenance. When not purpose-built to an oil company's specifications, a drillship is often converted from tanker hulls and equipped with dynamic positioning systems, which helps it maintain position over the oil well. Drillships can handle greater depths than most semisubmersibles—in excess of 8,000 feet—and drillship production accelerated in the 2010s, with a worldwide fleet of 80 ships expected by 2013, compared to fewer than 40 in 2009.

Drillships drill by lowering a drilling riser (a specially equipped thick, low-pressure tube) with a subsea blowout preventer and connecting the apparatus to the wellhead. Because of their independence, size, and speed, drillships make exploratory drilling—the drilling of wells to gather information and establish the presence and extent of oil reserves—a faster process.

Dangers of Deepwater Drilling

Deepwater drilling is offshore drilling at depths of more than 500 feet, the drilling conducted by semisubmersibles and drillships. One reason for the sudden rise in those technologies is that, until recently, deepwater drilling was considered economically impractical compared to the shallow-water drilling of jack-up rigs and other platforms. Rising oil prices and fears of the depletion of existing wells finally led to extensive investment in deepwater drilling during the late 20th century, although during the Deepwater Horizon oil spill of April 20 to July 15, 2010, the United States' secretary of the interior placed a moratorium on offshore drilling on the outer continental shelf for six months beginning on May 30, 2010. The Deepwater Horizon spill occurred when a wellhead blew out, resulting in 11 deaths, 17 injuries, and approximately 200 million gallons of crude oil (some estimates are higher) released into the Gulf of Mexico. The spill persisted for nearly three months and was not fully sealed until September 19. The full extent of the damage and the length of time until recovery are not yet known; in 2011, oil was found on the seafloor that showed no signs of degradation, and environmental concerns have been raised about the cleaning methods used to deal with the spill.

The 2010 moratorium was itself a return to a norm established by executive order of President George H. W. Bush in 1990. That executive order was not lifted until 2008, when his son, President George W. Bush, called for expanding American oil exploration, both through offshore drilling and by drilling in the Arctic National Wildlife Refuge. Bush's successor, President Barack Obama, also called for the expansion of offshore drilling on March 31, 2010, only three weeks before the Deepwater Horizon disaster.

The most persuasive argument in favor of offshore drilling in the United States is the expected impact on oil prices and the resultant stability in fuel sources, particularly for the American consumer. Oil consumption has gone steadily up since the energy crises of the 1970s. Food and other goods are transported further and consume much more fuel energy in their production than they did 30 years ago. Commuting distances have increased, more students attend college (and more of those who do, do far from home), more households have two or more cars, and the rise of e-commerce has made fuel costs, reflected in shipping charges, a significant factor in the cost of the typical consumer's purchases. All these factors tie the country's economic health to fuel costs, even more closely than in the 1970s. Although alternatives to fossil fuels are one solution, they are a long-term solution that requires time to develop; in all likelihood, even an earnest attempt to develop alternative energy sources will require multiple generations before demand can be met sufficiently to shield the economy from oil price spikes and shortages. In the meantime, increasing the supply of American oil offers a greater degree of energy security.

Energy Security Versus Environmental Concerns

Energy security is important not simply for economic reasons but for political ones. Dependence on foreign oil has deep impact on American foreign policy. It encourages diplomatic relations with countries toward which the United States might otherwise be more aloof. It motivates wars in the Middle East in which the country would

U.S. Coast Guard

Fire boat response crews battle the blazing remnants of the oil rig Deepwater Horizon on April 21, 2010. Coast Guard helicopters, planes, and cutters responded to attempt to rescue the 126-person crew. The spill occurred when a wellhead blew out, which resulted in 11 deaths and 17 injuries and environmental damage to the surrounding area.

otherwise have little interest. It encourages taking sides in internal disputes in oil-producing countries, which contributed to the energy crises of the 1970s, when oil-producing countries in the Middle East were unhappy with the nature of Western intervention in the politics of their region.

The environmental concerns, however, are considerable. The Gulf of Mexico and the Atlantic Ocean are vulnerable to hurricanes, and the aftermath of 2005's Hurricane Katrina, for instance, included 8 million gallons of oil spilled from coastal facilities.

Oil spills harm seabirds and marine mammals, which become coated in the oil, making them less buoyant in the water, less able to insulate themselves, more vulnerable to hypothermia and temperature fluctuations, and more likely to become unable to fly. Attempts to clean themselves result in ingestion of crude oil, damaging their organs, throwing their metabolism and other functions out of balance, and contributing to dehydration. Marine plants and phytoplankton suffer when oil spills cover the water and prevent sunlight from passing through the surface, and oil-consuming bacteria crowd other bacteria out of the ecosystem, a condition that is incredibly difficult to remedy.

There are no perfect methods of oil clean-up. Physical collection, such as skimming, is limited by environmental circumstances; not all of the oil may be on the surface, and calm waters are required for skimming to be effective. Controlled burning can be done only during conditions of low or no wind, and it results in air pollution and harm to local wildlife. Dispersants and other chemical remedies may degrade the oil more quickly but can also simply transfer the oil to other parts of the ecosystem; for example, dispersed oil droplets are able to penetrate deep waters and can kill off coral. The chemical remedies themselves may have harmful effects, many of which are poorly understood. Centrifuge systems, in which oil-tainted water is sucked up, mostly cleansed, and dumped back into the sea, are limited by laws limiting the amount of oil that can be returned to the sea in such a manner, making them feasible only for small spills. The best solution may be chemi-cal solidifiers, which change the oil from a liquid into a rubberlike material that floats on the water and will not be dissolved into it, allowing it to be skimmed fairly easily and efficiently. Solidifiers proved useful in dealing with the *Deepwater Horizon* spill. Nevertheless, it is possible that there are ecological consequences to the use of solidifiers that are not yet known; if nothing else, their use raises the question of what to do with all the solidified oil.

BILL KTE'PI

Further Reading

Deffeyes, Kenneth S. *Hubbert's Peak: The Impending World Oil Shortage.* Princeton, NJ: Princeton University Press, 2008.

Downey, Morgan. *Oil 101.* New York: Wooden Table Press, 2009.

Haerens, Margaret. *Offshore Drilling.* Detroit: Greenhaven Press, 2010.

Leffler, William L., Richard Pattarozzi, and Gordon Sterling. *Deepwater Petroleum Exploration and Production: A Nontechnical Guide.* Tulsa, OK: PennWell, 2003.

U.S. National Commission on the BP *Deepwater Horizon* Oil Spill and Offshore Drilling. *Deep Water: The Gulf Oil Disaster and the Future of Offshore Drilling; Report to the President.* Washington, DC: National Commission on the BP Deepwater Horizon Oil Spill and Offshore Drilling, 2011.

See Also: BP; Energy Policy; Gulf Oil Spill; Louisiana; Oil and Gas Pipelines; Oil and Natural Gas Drilling; Oil and Petroleum; Oil Market and Price.

Ohio

Category: Energy in the United States.
Summary: Ohio is a relatively large and heavily industrialized state, located in the American Midwest; by population, it is the seventh-largest U.S. state. Ohio is a coal-producing state.

The state of Ohio has significant coal reserves and is a moderate producer of coal. As a result, the state still obtains over 85 percent of its electrical energy from coal, making it the nation's second leading emitter of greenhouse gases. However, in 2008 the state legislature adopted a clean energy law that mandates that 12.5 percent of the state's electricity must come from renewable sources by the year 2025.

Ohio has long been at the center of energy development. It was the birthplace of Thomas Alva Edison (America's leading pioneer in the development of electrical applications and transmission), as well as the incubator for the wind and oil-refining industries as they emerged during the 19th century. With its significant coal reserves, it relies on coal-fueled electricity. However, it is seeking to develop renewable sources as mandated by its legislature in 2008.

History

In 1862, John D. Rockefeller established the Rockefeller and Andrews Oil Company (later called the Standard Oil Company) in Cleveland, Ohio. By 1880, Standard Oil controlled more than 90 percent of America's oil refining capacity.

Charles F. Brush, also of Cleveland, designed and built one of world's earliest electricity-generating windmills. His engineering company built the windmill dynamo, which operated from 1886 until 1900. Mounted on a 60-foot tower with a 144-blade 56-foot rotor, this early wind turbine was only rated at 12 kilowatts.

Another early energy pioneer, Arthur Compton (a Nobel laureate from Wooster, Ohio), is credited with inventing the fluorescent light tube and was instrumental in the early development of nuclear energy.

Ohio also played a prominent role in the early development of the U.S. oil and gas industry, and these energy sectors continue to influence the state's economy. The first oil well drilled in North America can still be found in Caldwell, Ohio. Dug in 1814 by two pioneers looking for salt, it yielded crude oil that they sold as a digestive elixir. Since that first well, the state has drilled more than 273,000 additional wells, ranking it fourth in oil exploration behind Texas, Oklahoma, and Pennsylvania. Ohio was the country's leading producer of oil between 1895 and 1903. At its peak of production in 1896, the state produced 24 million barrels of oil. By 2009, production had dropped to only slightly more than 5 million barrels per year.

Natural gas was first discovered in 1887 in Clinton County. By 2008, the state produced nearly 85 billion cubic feet of natural gas, almost 100 percent of this production consumed within the state. Much of the eastern half of the state lies above the Marcellus and Devonian shale formations, thought to contain vast and largely untapped amounts of natural gas. Industry experts estimate the amount of natural gas in the Marcellus Shale at between 363 and 1,307 trillion cubic feet of recoverable resource, which would be enough to supply U.S. consumption for 14 years at the low end of the estimate and for as long as 42 years at current rates of consumption. However, recovery of this resource relies on a technique known as hydraulic fracturing, which has raised considerable environmental concerns as well as resulting in significant groundwater contamination.

Electricity Generation

Ohio has a deregulated competitive electric power market. Four investor-owned electrical utilities provide more than 90 percent of the electricity consumed within the state. The remaining electricity is provided by various municipal electrical systems (not-for-profit, government-subsidized utilities that provide electricity largely within defined municipal limits) and rural electric cooperatives (consumer-owned cooperatives formed to ensure access to electricity for Ohio's rural consumers). The investor-owned electrical utilities (in order of size) include FirstEnergy, American Electric Power (AEP), Duke Energy, and Dayton Power and Light (DP&L).

In 2010, fuel sources for Ohio's electrical generation consisted of coal, at 1,373 trillion British thermal units, or Btu (86 percent); nuclear power, at 154.3 trillion Btu (10 percent); petroleum, at 30.6 trillion Btu (2 percent); and natural gas, at 28.8 trillion Btu (2 percent). Hydropower, at 5.2 trillion Btu, and renewable energy sources, at 1.2 trillion

Btu, account for a negligible amount of the state's electricity. Clearly, the vast majority of electrical power is from coal, much of it mined within the state, but more than 60 percent of Ohio's power-plant fuel is imported from out of state, at a cost of more than $1.5 billion annually.

The energy generated from nuclear sources comes from two power plants located in northern Ohio. The Perry Nuclear Power Plant began operations in 1987. A boiling-water reactor, it produces 1,258 megawatts of electricity, enough to power about 750,000 homes. Built at a cost of $6 billion, it is one of the most expensive power plants ever built. The second nuclear power plant operating in Ohio is the Davis-Besse Nuclear Power Station. It began generating power in 1978.

Energy Consumption

Electricity consumption in Ohio is growing at a rate of 1.4 percent per year, even though the state's population growth is only 0.2 percent per year. Energy consumption in Ohio's industrial sector ranks among the highest in the nation.

Although Ohio is ranked seventh among U.S. states in population, it ranks third in consumption of coal (1,438.4 trillion Btu), seventh in consumption of natural gas (824 trillion Btu), ninth in consumption of petroleum (1,299.7 trillion Btu), and fourth in retail electricity sales (543.8 trillion Btu). However, Ohio ranks 24th in total energy consumption per capita, at 345.9 million Btu (based on 2008 figures).

State Senate Bill 221

In 2008, the Ohio legislature passed the Clean Energy Law (Senate Bill 221). The law outlines four separate clean energy requirements for the state's investor-owned utilities; municipal systems and electrical cooperatives are not subject to the law's provisions. These requirements include a reduction in consumption of electricity (net sales) of 22 percent by 2025 through electrical efficiency measures and programs; a reduction in peak electrical demand by 1 percent in 2009 and by 0.75 percent each year during the 2010–18 period; and a mandate to provide 12.5 percent of all electrical sales from renewable energy sources by 2025.

Also by 2025, 0.5 percent of all electrical energy must come from solar power sources; however, a study by the Environment Ohio Research and Policy Center found that none of the investor-owned utilities had met the law's solar energy benchmarks during 2009.

Renewable Energy Potential

Ohio has made a significant investment in the development of its renewable resources. The state has more than 2,100 companies—the fourth-highest number in the nation—in industries related to the manufacture of components for renewable energy systems.

While ranked 36th among the states in wind energy potential, Ohio currently ranks 27th in wind power production. Estimated to have a potential capacity of at least 415 megawatts, this resource is located primarily along Lake Erie and the plains in the northwestern part of the state.

Although Ohio is a significant producer of solar panels, with 63 companies working to develop solar power components as of 2011, the state has been slow to install systems within its borders. There are a number of significant installations in various stages of completion, but Ohio currently ranks 43rd among the 50 states generating solar power, according to statistics provided by the U.S. Energy Information Administration.

Ohio also possesses significant biomass resources. The state currently produces more than 7 million dry tons of biomass each year from urban wood waste, crop residues, and forest residues, an amount that ranks it seventh-highest among U.S. states. The Oak Ridge National Laboratory estimates that biomass could generate 7.5 percent of Ohio's electricity needs by 2020.

JAY WARMKE

Further Reading

Environment Ohio Research and Policy Center. "Ohio's Clean Energy Report Card: How Wind, Solar, and Energy Efficiency Are Repowering the Buckeye State Environment Ohio Research and Policy Center." March 2011. http://www.morpc.org/calendarfiles01/OHCleanEnergyRepCard.pdf.

Green Energy Ohio. "About GEO." http://www
.greenenergyohio.org/page.cfm?pageID=292.

National Resources Defense Council. "Ohio." http://
www.nrdc.org/energy/renewables/ohio.asp.

Office of the Ohio Consumers' Counsel. "Renewable
Energy Sources: Solar Power." http://www.pickocc
.org/publications/renewable_energy/Solar_Power
.pdf.

Ohio Air Quality Development Authority. "Ohio:
Energy Summary Fact Sheet." http://apps1.eere
.energy.gov/states/energy_summary_print.cfm
?state=OH.

Ohio Electric Utility Institute. "Electric Restructuring
in Ohio: The Big Picture." 1999. http://www.oeui
.org/ElectricRe.htm.

U.S. Energy Information Administration. "Ohio."
http://www.eia.gov/state/state-energy-profiles.cfm
?sid=OH.

See Also: Biomass Energy; Photovoltaics; Rockefeller, John D.; Standard Oil Company; Tennessee Valley Authority; United States; Wind Resources.

Oil and Gas Pipelines

Category: Technology.

Summary: Oil and gas pipelines are continuous pipe conduits for transporting oil and natural and/or supplemental gas from one point to another. Pipelines provide one of the safest, most efficient, and economical solutions for transporting oil and gas resources.

Pipeline networks are composed of several types of equipment: valves, pumps/compressor stations, communications systems, and meters. The flow of oil is kept in motion by pumps, while natural gas pipelines require special compressors. Both pumps and compressors are installed along the pipeline to maintain the flow of products.

Oil pipelines are made from steel or plastic tubes. Oil pipeline networks usually include crude oil and refined products pipelines. For crude oil, its pipelines can be subdivided into "gathering lines" and "trunk lines." Gathering lines are small diameter pipelines (2–8 inches) tapping into the oil fields to gather the sources to the trunk lines, which have a larger diameter (8–48 inches) and serve the purpose of delivering crude oil to refineries. Pipelines that deliver refined petroleum products also vary in size (8–42 inches). The end point of the refined products pipeline is not end users but rather large fuel terminals where products are loaded onto tanker trucks and delivered to retail points, such as gas stations.

Natural gas pipelines are usually constructed of carbon steel to withstand the higher pressure of compressed gas. Gas pipeline networks also have small gathering systems and large cross- or inter-country transmission pipelines. Another difference between gas and oil refined product pipelines is that the former is delivered directly to end users through local distribution lines.

The Largest Network in the World

Currently, the United States has the most extensive oil and gas pipeline network in the world, more than 10 times larger than that of Europe as a whole. There are an estimated 55,000 miles of crude oil trunk lines, 30,000 to 40,000 miles of small gathering oil pipelines, and 95,000 miles of refined products pipelines in the United States. The United States also has about 20,000 miles of natural gas gathering lines and approximately 278,000 miles of natural gas transmission lines. The U.S. government ordered the construction of two of its most well-known pipelines, named the Big Inch and Little Big Inch, from 1942–43 to avoid the dangers tankers would face from German submarines during World War II. The Big Inch was 24 inches in diameter and transported crude oil, while the Little Big Inch was 20 inches in diameter and transported refined products. The two pipelines ran from east Texas to the northeastern United States. After the war ended in 1945, the Big Inch was converted to natural gas and leased and later sold to a private corporation.

Although pipeline companies prefer to operate their systems as close to full capacity as possible to maximize their revenues, the average utilization rate (flow rate/design capacity) seldom reaches 100

Wikimedia

At Getty Terminal in Providence, Rhode Island, oil pipelines run from the unloading docks to huge storage tanks. The oil is then loaded onto trucks for delivery.

percent. Several factors contribute to this outcome: scheduled or unscheduled maintenance, temporary decreases in market demand, and weather-related limitations to operations.

Pipeline Safety Issues and Technological Solutions

The flammability of oil and gas raises special concerns for pipeline safety. There are many historical records of oil and gas pipeline exploration accidents. Leakage accidents are usually attributed to pipeline aging and corrosion. Numerous technological solutions to avoid leakage and enhance sur-veillance have been developed. The most economical method to avoid corrosion is to use pipeline coatings and pipeline monitoring technologies. Some monitoring technologies require walking along the line to detect potential leakage; others use remote satellite surveillance systems. Computation pipeline monitoring systems (CPMs) are the most commonly used technology to monitor pipeline safety. CPMs bring on-field information such as pressures, flows, and temperatures back to control rooms.

The control rooms use a supervisory control and data acquisition (SCADA) system to analyze and control the sensor–based data in order to esti-mate the status of the pipelines. The estimation is then compared to the baseline scenario to detect anomalies and leaks, as well as plan for preventive maintenance. Sometimes, a video pipeline moni-toring system that provides visual assistance to the human operator to facilitate problem attribution and decision making is also incorporated into the CPM. Although a growing number of monitoring technologies have emerged to meet the safety demands, many are not ready for commercialization because of the high costs to install such technologies. Besides monitoring, some pipeline systems suffer from severe aging problems and require replacement.

On-Going Global Oil and Gas Pipeline Expansions

Currently, there are 15 strategically important oil and gas pipelines that are newly operational or under construction in the world: the TAPI Pipeline (starts from Turkmenistan and delivers gas to India through Afghanistan and Pakistan); the Denali Natural Gas Pipeline (delivering from Alaska to Alberta, Canada, then onto the American midwest); the Keystone Pipeline (delivering oil from Alberta, Canada, to Illinois and Oklahoma); the IGI Poseidon Off-Shore Gas Pipeline (connecting Greek and Italian gas transportation systems, expected completion in 2012); the Mozdok Gas Pipeline (which reaches from Azerbaijan to North Ossetia); the Altai Gas Pipeline (which starts from Russia and delivers Gazprom natural gas to China, expected completion in

2011–15); the South Stream Pipeline (delivering gas from Russia to Austria through southeastern Europe, expected completion in 2015); the Nord Stream gas pipeline (delivers from Russia to Germany, expected completion in 2011); the Trans-Caspian Natural Gas Pipeline (which reaches from Turkmenistan to Azerbaijan); the White Stream Pipelines (which deliver gas from Georgia to Romania and then on to western Europe); the Nabucco Pipeline (which links Turkey's gas supply to southeastern Europe and eventually Austria, expected completion in 2015); the ESPO pipeline (expected to deliver oil from Russia to China and potentially Japan in 2014); the Pars Pipeline (delivers gas from Iran to Turkey); and the Iran–Pakistan–India Pipeline (that delivers gas from Iran to India and Pakistan, expected completion in 2015).

MARCELLA BUSH TREVINO

Further Reading

Goodland, Robert, et al. *Oil and Gas Pipelines Social and Environmental Impact Assessment: State of Art.* Fargo, ND: International Association of Impact Assessment Conference, 2005.

Herberg, Mikkal E., et al. *Pipeline Politics in Asia: The Intersection of Demand, Energy Markets, and Supply Routes.* Seattle, WA: National Bureau of Asian Research, 2010.

White, Gregory. "The 15 Oil and Gas Pipelines That Are Changing the World's Strategic Map." http://www.businessinsider.com/the-15-oil-and-gas-pipelines-changing-the-worlds-strategic-map-2010-3.

U.S. Energy Information Administration. "International Energy Outlook 2010: Natural Gas." http://www.eia.doe.gov/oiaf/ieo/nat_gas.html.

U.S. Energy Information Administration. "Natural Gas Pipeline Capacity & Utilization," http://www.eia.doe.gov/pub/oil_gas/natural_gas/analysis_publications/ngpipeline/usage.html.

See Also: Energy Transmission: Liquid Fluids; Henry Hub; Natural Gas; Natural Gas Storage; Oil and Natural Gas Drilling; Oil and Petroleum; Oil Sands; Oil Shales.

Oil and Natural Gas Drilling

Category: Energy Technology.
Summary: The biophysical characteristics of oil and natural gas define the ways in which these fossil fuels are extracted, as well as how they are distributed and commodified.

Petroleum and natural gas are hydrocarbons, organic compounds that consist entirely of hydrogen and carbon in various combinations. Like coal and many other substances, these hydrocarbons are extracted from the earth following a series of physical and chemical transformations that continues in their commodification process. In his work on the global production network of oil, Gavin Bridge conceptualizes this processes as a linear production chain (consisting of exploration, extraction/production, refining, and distribution) with materials transformation and product flow at the center of analysis. These sequential processes are better known as the hydrocarbon commodity chain.

The process starts by determining the location, quantity, and condition of oil and natural gas in order to extract them from the environment. This initial phase is known as the upstream phase; it includes exploration, production, and extraction processes. After extraction, oil and natural gas enter the midstream stage, which is characterized by the processing and transportation of these resources in a petrochemical facility. Once in the petrochemical industry, oil and natural gas undergo their downstream transformations into a wide variety of refined final products, such as fertilizers, plastics, lubricants, and textiles, which are incorporated into the global economy.

Two key characteristics make hydrocarbons extremely important to our civilization, throughout many industries, and to countries at every range of industrial development, across the globe. First, hydrocarbons contain immense amounts of stored energy. Second, hydrocarbons can take on many different forms. However, hydrocarbons in their crude form have limited uses. In order to be refined into functional products such as gasoline, heating gas, and petrochemical feedstock, both oil and gas must be manipulated and transformed physically and chemically. One problem with crude oil is that it contains hundreds of different types of hydrocarbons all mixed together. That is one of the reasons petroleum needs to be refined: to separate the different types of hydrocarbons, each with different molecular structures, characteristics, and uses. Unraveling the geographical complexities of the hydrocarbon sector in the context of local and global economies has pivotal concerns in different disciplines. Many scholars, engineers, and economists have studied the geographic, social, economic, and environmental impacts associated with the extraction of oil and natural gas.

Oil Exploration and Drilling

In the early stages of oil exploration and extraction, oil companies invest time and capital in exploration tours to find where the major oil deposits are located. Once the geologists in charge of exploration activities find a prospective oil strike, oil companies begin perforation activities after legal issues are settled. Oil companies need to secure concessions, lease agreements, titles, and rights of way before drilling the land. For offshore sites, legal jurisdiction must be determined. Oil drilling is an extremely energy-intensive activity. It requires specialized knowledge and highly specialized equipment to drill through the rock strata and connect the reservoir to the oil platform.

Today, the majority of wells are drilled using rotary drilling rigs. In his book on petroleum geology, Norman Hyne describes this system as follows: "The rotary drilling rig rotates a long length of steel pipe with a bit on the end of it to cut the hole called the wellbore. The rotary rig consists of four major systems. These include the power, hoisting, rotating, and circulating systems." The drilling rig goes through a casing, a large-diameter concrete pipe that lines the drill hole, preventing it from collapsing, and allowing mud to circulate. A circulation system pumps drilling fluids through the casing, generally a mixture of water, clay, weighting material, and salt (sodium hydroxide or sodium bromide) that lifts rock cuttings from the drill bit to the surface under pressure. Caus-

tic soda is used in alkaline flooding of oil and gas fields to enhance the recovery of these fossil fuels, and to prevent widening of boreholes in rock-salt strata, which in turn inhibits fermentation and increases mud density.

Another drilling function applies muriatic acid, an aqueous solution of hydrogen chloride, in a process known as stimulation. This removes rust, scale, and undesirable carbonate deposits in oil wells in order to encourage the flow of crude oil or natural gas to the well. Stimulation is used in carbonate or limestone formations, whereby hydrochloric acid is injected into the formation to dissolve a portion of the rock, creating a larger pore structure in the formation. This process increases the permeability and the flow of oil and natural gas in the well, which in turn maximizes the recovery of these fossil fuels.

A combination of increasing demand pressures and continual technological advances has made the successful tapping of more and more remote oil deposits practical, from a financial viewpoint, and made it possible, from a technical standpoint. For example, in the 1960s, nautical drilling rigs first came into their own. The North Sea and the Gulf of Mexico were among the handful of geographic backdrops to the early evolution of offshore hydrocarbon capture on an industrial scale. New international legal measures were adopted in the 1960s, clarifying ownership rights and claims to many of the known continental shelf hydrocarbon deposits and spurring the methodical search for new such fields by a variety of bodies, whether individual private corporations, national ministries, or international consortia of companies and government agencies.

The Arab Oil Embargo of 1973 and the Iranian Revolution-ignited 1979 oil price crisis together drove an acceleration of the technology, the know-how, and the willingness of capital sources to fund new offshore ventures around the world. This gave fresh impetus to exploring and drilling into ever deeper offshore fields. The infrastructure value of the whole installed deepwater drilling segment of the industry was estimated at $145 billion worldwide in 2011. Deepwater drilling as a component of the offshore industry has now advanced to where it is feasible for a wellhead to be emplaced as much as a mile or more below the ocean surface, and with its wellbore extending as much as another mile or more beneath the seafloor itself. Wells of this type are referred to in the industry and by regulatory bodies as "ultra deepwater" rigs.

Several decades later, some of the world's largest and most reliable onshore and offshore producing fields have been depleted past the point where hydrocarbon recovery is relatively easily profitable. However, there are numerous cases where such depleted reservoirs are regenerated or revived to a practical degree of economic feasibility by the use of enhanced oil recovery (EOR) technologies. One such EOR extraction technique is water injection. Whether using seawater, aquifer sources, or river sources, the water medium must be de-oxygenated, it must be filtered, and it must be pumped at high pressure into the heart of the oil or gas field over a considerable stretch of time in order for optimum results. Careful economic modeling must be done prior to such an investment, especially in desert environments or other locations where additional equipment must be built and to connect the hydrocarbon to a sizable and useful source of water.

Other types of EOR include chemical injection and gas injection—which is the form in broadest use. Ironically, the greenhouse gases methane and carbon dioxide are among the most widely used gases for this process. The application of EOR techniques can raise recovery of hydrocarbons from reservoirs from the usual 25 percent to 40 percent of a deposit to a range of 30 percent to 55 percent or more of the deposit.

Once oil (and natural gas) is extracted, it is transported to refineries or petrochemical facilities. At this stage, refineries produce pure chemicals, called feedstock, from crude oil or natural gas, which is sold to petrochemical industries. This moment in the material flow of oil and natural gas is referred to as the downstream stage of the hydrocarbon commodity chain.

Natural Gas Production

The normal production of petroleum by extraction brings with it a certain amount of natural gas per oil well in the process. The gas is found entrapped in the Earth's crust at varying depths beneath rigid strata, such as limestone. When raw natural gas is found together with oil deposits, it often contains water vapor, hydrogen sulfide, carbon dioxide, helium, and nitrogen, among other components, and it is referred to as "wet" gas or associated gas. Like oil, natural gas needs to be processed and refined. These processes consist of separating all of the existent hydrocarbons and fluids from the pure natural gas to produce pipeline-quality "dry" natural gas that can be marketed as a commodity.

In the past, the appropriate infrastructure to take gas to a market did not exist; natural gas was initially considered an undesirable by-product of oil production. Unwanted natural gas thereby became a disposal problem at the well site. On one hand, if there were no market for natural gas closer to the wellhead it would need to be piped to the end user, decreasing its exchange value closer to the well site. On the other hand, much of the gas produced as a by-product of oil extraction became unwanted, or stranded, gas, and it was either burned off ("flared") at the extraction site or pumped back into the reservoir with an injection well for disposal because of the difficulties of handling it on site. As a result, immense amounts of capital were invested in research and technology allowing industries to maximize the production of natural gas. The use of gas injection became widespread, and the appreciation of the versatility and importance of natural gas, both as a source of energy and as a petrochemical feedstock, increased. This, in turn, reduced the wasteful practice of flaring.

Natural gas needs a different set of processes and technologies to be extracted and transported in comparison to those of oil. The biophysical characteristics of natural gas makes it extremely difficult to extract, commodify, and transport. In an editorial piece on natural gas, Bridge argued that producing gas as a commodity, as a substance to be exchanged on the market, takes a considerable amount of work; in particular, the expansive and unstable characteristics of natural gas require its chemical and physical transformation in order to be commodified. This metamorphic process involves the reconfiguration of space and technology when extracting its exchange value. However,

▷ *Finding, Extracting, and Transporting Product*

The markets for natural gas can be divided into three main categories: the generation of electricity, industrial processes, and domestic/commercial activities. The three main components of bringing natural gas to market are production, transportation, and distribution. The first of these components includes finding the gas that will then be processed and refined to remove undesirable constituents, as well as to achieve a uniform quality that is characterized by the absence of heavier hydrocarbons.

Whether found mixed together with oil or in deposits by itself, natural gas is always located under major pressure. Therefore, the use of a pipe driven down into the deposit will cause the gas to leave the deposit under major pressure. Pressure therefore plays an important role in the extraction of natural gas, and keeping that pressure constant is key to its transportation. The transportation phase involves moving gas from producing to consuming areas by large-diameter, high-pressure pipelines. However, as the gas flows out of its deposit, the pressure decreases. On one hand, if the gas is to be used only a short distance from the extraction site, a decrease in pressure may not be of great importance. During the extraction phase, almost all of the gas will have left the deposit before the pressure falls far enough to prevent the gas from being captured and routed to the end user without the use of compression technology. On the other hand, when natural gas needs to flow long distances, the decrease in pressure needs to be controlled using compression stations. Sometimes compressors are not needed at first, but as gas covers more geographical area, compressors are installed as pressure drops at different points along the pipeline or when the demand for gas increases.

the challenge with natural gas is not its availability, since it is most typically greater than the absorption capacity of local markets. Instead, the problem lies in its distribution to downstream and foreign markets in its original form.

Conclusion

Both oil and natural gas are transported through extensive pipeline systems. However, oil has a geographical advantage over natural gas. This advantage is defined by biophysical differences of the two commodities. In this sense, it is easier and cheaper to move oil in a pipeline than to transport gas by pipeline. In his work on the political economy of natural gas, Ferdinand Banks argues that one of the reasons oil is generally called the highest-quality source of energy is the relative ease with which it can be transported. In this context, the distribution of natural gas through pipelines has a geographical limitation. That is, the pressure of gas decreases with distance, which requires investment in larger-diameter pipelines to allow the passage of larger quantities of gas and the installation of multiple compression stations along the way. This approach solves the problem when gas is transported at continental distances.

Extraction, commodification, and transportation of natural gas is challenging, and it can also be dangerous and volatile. To that extent, natural gas requires a multiscalar geographical reconfiguration of space, economy, and technology. The expansive characteristic of natural gas defines the technology needed for its extraction, refining, and distribution, thus creating a set of social and institutional organizations to accommodate those needs.

Oil and natural gas, therefore, have proven to be significant and contested fuels, both reconstituting nature during extraction activities and transforming local and global economies in their commodification processes. Even though the physical and chemical manipulations of these commodities happen at the molecular level, the effects of these transformations have a multiscalar impact beyond the commodities themselves, reconfiguring social, economic, and geographic spaces.

ELVIN E. DELGADO

Further Reading

Banks, Ferdinand. *The Political Economy of Natural Gas.* New York: Croom Helm, 1987.

Bridge, Gavin. "Editorial: Gas and How to Get It." *Geoforum* 35 (2004).

Bridge, Gavin. "Global Production Networks and the Extractive Sector: Governing Resource Based Development." *Journal of Economic Geography* 8 (2008).

Hyne, Norman. *Dictionary of Petroleum Exploration, Drilling and Production.* Tulsa, OK: PennWell, 1991.

Hyne, Norman. *Nontechnical Guide to Petroleum Geology, Exploration, Drilling, and Production.* 2nd ed. Tulsa, OK: PennWell, 2001.

Langenkamp, R. D. *Handbook of Oil Industry Terms and Phrases.* 5th ed. Tulsa, OK: PennWell, 1994.

Laszlo, Pierre. *Salt: Grain of Life.* New York: Columbia University Press, 2001.

PVC Organization. "What Is PVC?" http://www.pvc.org/What-is-PVC.

Salt Institute. "Industrial Uses of Salt." http://www.saltinstitute.org/Uses-benefits/Salt-in-industry/Other-industrial-uses.

See Also: Natural Gas; Natural Gas Storage; Offshore Drilling; Oil and Gas Pipelines; Oil and Petroleum; Oil Market and Price; Refining.

Oil and Petroleum

Category: Energy Resources.
Summary: Oil and petroleum are nonrenewable combustible liquids that can be refined into gasoline or petrol, diesel fuel, motor oil, and many other compounds.

Crude oil, a naturally occurring, flammable fossil fuel, is a mixture of various hydrocarbons and other chemical compounds. Today, crude oil, also called petroleum, is one of the world's most important energy sources, producing gasoline, kerosene, and heating fuel, among other products. However, there is increasing debate on how long the production of crude oil can continue and whether it will be able to meet market demand.

Unrefined Petroleum

Crude oil—that is, unrefined petroleum—is a flammable fossil fuel in a mixture of up to 17,000 substances in variable compounds, including diverse hydrocarbons, such as alkanes (paraffins), cycloalkanes (naphthenes), aromatic hydrocarbons, and asphaltenes, which bind nitrogen, oxygen, and sulfur and form compounds such as thioether, alcohols, and resins. Also, metals, such as iron, copper, vanadium, and nickel, may be found in crude oil. Not only does the chemical composition of crude oil vary; so do its physical properties, including color and viscosity, from transparent, light yellow and thin fluid to deep black and viscous, depending on its source. Its density ranges from 0.82 to 0.94 gram per cubic centimeter. Crude oil containing only little sulfur is referred to as "sweet," while crude oil relatively rich in sulfur is called "sour." The latter has an unpleasant odor. Low density refers to light oil, and high density refers to heavy oil. Crude oil is not soluble in water or ethanol, but it is soluble in ether, benzene, and tetrachloromethane.

Currently, crude oil is the most important fuel of modern industrialized societies. More than 80 percent of global oil production goes into fuels. The remaining oil is used in industrial chemical processes to produce pharmaceuticals, fertilizers, foods, plastics, paints, textiles, and construction materials. Industrially developed countries are highly dependent on petroleum. Most chemical products can be synthesized from about 300 bulk chemicals based on natural gas and petroleum, including ethane (or ethylene), propene, benzene, toluol, and xylol. About 6–7 percent of the global petroleum production is used to synthesize bulk chemicals, avoiding expensive alternative methods. The biggest part is burned as fuel in power plants and engines. Between 2000 and 2009, about 242 billion barrels of crude oil were produced worldwide. (One barrel equals about 159 liters.)

Global processes of exploration, extraction, refining, and transporting (by means of both supertankers and pipelines), and marketing of petroleum products are major areas of the oil industry. Until 1985, global oil prices followed a pricing system administered by the Organization of Petroleum Exporting Countries (OPEC). After this system collapsed, oil-exporting countries adopted a market-linked pricing mechanism for international crude oil trade. Currently, the benchmarks for pricing are the Brent, WTI, and Dubai/Oman markers.

Like with all fossil fuels, petroleum fuels, when combusted, pose environmental risks, mainly with respect to exhaust products. Too little oxygen during combustion yields carbon monoxide. Exhaust gases from car engines include nitrogen oxides, which cause photochemical smog.

History

In a technical sense, *petroleum* refers only to crude oil, but in a broader sense it describes all liquid, gaseous, and solid hydrocarbons. *Petroleum* means literally "rock oil" (from the Latin *oleum petrae*). Its density is lower than that of water, so it wells up to the Earth's surface through vugs (cavities) in sediments of shale, sand, or carbonate. Crude oil at the Earth's surface, mostly in the form of bitumen due to a reaction with oxygen, was known 12,000 years ago in Mesopotamia.

The ancient Babylonians used bitumen to pave for roads, seal ship planks, and impregnate textiles. Naphtha can be traced back to the Babylonian word *naptu*, which means "to glow." The first known public regulation of oil respective of bitumen was written by Hammurabi, first king of the Babylonian Empire, in 1875 B.C.E. The Roman army probably used crude oil as lubricant for axes and wheels. In early medieval Byzantium, bitumen was used for flamethrowers during battles, and in the Renaissance so-called St. Quirin oil was sold by German monks as a medicine. The Pechelbronn oil field in Alsace was the site of the first European oil well, productive from 1498 until 1970.

In 1854, the Canadian physician and geologist Abraham P. Gesner obtained his first U.S. patent for the synthesis of kerosene from coal and petroleum, providing the impetus initial for the oil industry. The development of kerosene was motivated by the search for a reasonable alternative to train oil

(from whales), at that time the common lamp fuel. Only a few years later, in 1859, Colonel Edwin L. Drake drilled for oil in Pennsylvania and found a big deposit only 70 feet (21.2 meters) underground. In the same year, the first oil refinery was established, soon followed by many others. After the introduction of electric lighting, oil lost its attraction for a while, only to return in the form of benzine, or petroleum ether. Henry Ford considered ethanol as fuel for his automobiles, but John D. Rockefeller, founder of Standard Oil Company, used benzine as motor fuel. It was Standard Oil of California that discovered the first oil deposit in Saudi Arabia close to Dammam in 1938. Since then, giant amounts of crude oil have been used as motor fuels.

Geophysical Prospection

Precise maps provide fundamental information prior to geophysical prospection (or geophysical surveys), a systematic search for oil in place. In certain areas, such as Iran, deposits can be identified by means of aerial photographs. In cases where there are rocks at the surface that are typical for oil in place, samples are taken.

During prospection, physical properties, such as magnetism, density, sonic speed, electrical resistance, and radioactivity, are measured. The most often applied method is seismic reflection. To receive computable data, a controlled seismic source, such as an artificially induced dynamite explosion, an air gun, or a seismic vibrator, is required; these methods produce acoustic waves that propagate in the Earth's crust. The waves need different times to pass different rock formations, and reflect at the border of two formations. Reflected waves are received by sensitive geophones or hydrophones and are logged in a seismogram. The result is an image of the underground, providing information about existent trap structures.

Based on seismic data, sample drills are done. In a next step, three-dimensional measurements are taken in selected areas. In combination with geophysical measures at the borehole, a quantitative model of oil or natural gas deposits, as well as plans for further boreholes and production, can be prepared.

▷ *Petroleum's Origins*

To date, petroleum's origins are still not entirely explained. Global crude oil deposits have been dated to the following prehistoric ages: About 12 percent originate from the Paleozoic era (about 542 to 251 million years ago), 13 percent from the Jurassic period (about 200 to 145 million years ago), and 17 percent from the Cretaceous period (about 145 to 65 million years ago). About 200 million to 65 million years ago, during the Jurassic and Cretaceous periods of the Mesozoic era, dead marine organisms sank to the floors of shallow seas and offshore waters. Conditions that were particularly favorable to the formation of petroleum were present in warm, nutrient-rich environments—for example, in the Gulf of Mexico and the ancient Tethys Sea, where large amounts of organic matter accumulated. High salt concentrations retarded common putrefaction. Over millennia, many sediment layers settled on top, causing high pressure and high temperature and allowing anaerobic bacteria to transubstiantiate the oxygen-deficient sapropel. Insoluble, long-chain hydrocarbons, so-called kerogens, were split into gaseous and liquid hydrocarbon chains in a process called catagenesis. (This process, in industrial terms, is also known as cracking.)

Hydrocarbons are able to migrate inside rocks and concentrate in reservoir rocks or source rocks, which are impenetrable sediment layers, also called traps, that provide the basic conditions for the formation of a natural oil deposit. In oil fields, saline water and natural gas are often also present, the latter forming a so-called gas cap. Geologists believe that crude oil occurs from the surface of the Earth down to depths of about 13,123 feet (4,000 meters).

Only natural gas is likely to be found at lower depths. The optimal conditions for the formation of petroleum are given at the passive shelf edges of continents, at grabens, and close to underground salt deposits. In the course of further diagenesis, kerogens often become viscous (heavy and thick), leading to high costs of production and at a certain point making deposits economically uninteresting. On the other hand, increasing costs of extracting and processing crude oil could make the production of heavy oil profitable. Sediments that include high concentrations of biogenic carbon are called crude oil parent rocks, such as oil shale. Near-surface, sandy sediments are called oil sands.

Wikimedia

A fossilzed Acanthoceras rhotomagense, an extinct mollusk from the Cretaceous period.

Production

When oil occurs subaerially (at or near the Earth's surface), it can be recovered by means of open-cast mining. For deeper deposits, boreholes are drilled to recover the oil. Deposits under the sea are recovered by means of offshore drilling. At a water depth of up to 328 feet (100 meters), the oil platforms stand on stilts. Another type of drilling platform is called semisubmersible floating platform, carrying heavy ballast weights to stabilize the platform. The deepest successful offshore wells have been drilled at depths of several thousand feet below sea level. Drillships can even drill in depths of up to 12,000 feet (more than 3,600 meters). The deepest oil platform as of 2011 was Shell's *Perdido*, at 9,627 feet (nearly 3,000 meters). The installation of a permanent drilling platform costs several billion dollars. However, offshore drilling has made enormous additional oil reservoirs available, in the United States accounting for 5 percent of total reserves.

Most drilling in the United States is done using the rotary drilling technique. Steel drilling rods hang at the oil derrick and are attached at the rotary table at the bottom of the derrick. Scavenging pumps flush water into the borehole, forcing the drilling cuttings through the hollow spaces between rods and borehole to the surface. The mixture of water and cuttings covers the borehole wall, preventing it from collapsing and thus making extremely deep boreholes possible. Once the drill reaches the oil reservoir, pressure can be so high that the oil rockets upwards like a fountain.

Commonly the recovery of conventional crude oil takes place in three stages. The natural reservoir pressure is exploited for the primary oil recovery. Natural gas in the reservoir enables an eruptive recovery of about 10 to 30 percent of the oil available in that reservoir. For the second oil recovery phase, two primary methods are used to boost production: the water flood method, which is the injection of water into the reservoir to increase pressure, and the thermal flood method, which is injection of steam (primarily used to give very viscous oil a lower viscosity and thus force the oil to the borehole). Because water is denser than oil, it sinks beneath it, filling up the reservoir from the bottom without mixing with the oil. More specialized methods include the injection of solvents via the chemical flood technique. These methods enable the recovery of 10 to 30 percent more oil, so that altogether 20 to 60 percent of the available oil can be recovered.

In the final, third stage of recovery, complex substances such as polymeres, carbon dioxide, and mircoorganisms are injected to increase the capacity of the well again. High prices and global market dynamics are expected to intensify efforts at this tertiary stage of oil recovery, not only at currently producing reservoirs but also at old reservoirs. Usually, the cost of recovering oil increases as the amount available at the well decreases until production becomes too expensive and the borehole is shut down. However, as world reserves decline and the price of oil rises, the economics of oil recovery may change to encourage more recovery at later stages.

When crude oil is found in semisolid form mixed with sand and water, it is also called crude bitumen, or oil sand. There are abundant reservoirs known in Canada, the Athabasca oil sands, and in Venezuela, the Orinoco oil sands. Together these deposits are estimated to be able to yield 3.6 trillion barrels of crude heavy oil, which is much more than prospected global reserves of conventional oil. These sands are considered unconventional oil sources, because the oil cannot be recovered by means of traditional drilling methods. In addition, oil shales represent an indirect source of oil. These rocks contain the waxy, high-carbon substance called kerogen. Using heat and high pressure, the process that leads to the geological formation of crude oil can be simulated, converting the trapped kerogen into oil. This method it not a modern discovery but has been known for centuries. It was even patented in 1694 under British Crown Patent No. 330.

Factors for the classification of crude oil, conducted by the oil industry, are the geographic location of its source, the API gravity (a measure, devised by the American Petroleum Institute, of the density of a petroleum liquid compared to water), and the sulfur content. The geographic location determines transportation costs to the refinery. Lighter grades of crude oil are more eligible than heavier grades, because upon refining they produce more gasoline. Also, sweet oil is traded at higher prices than sour oil because it causes less environmental problems. Refineries have to meet strict sulfur standards, just as fuels for consumption must. The specific molecular characteristics of the different crude oil grades are listed in crude oil assay analysis, used in petroleum laboratories.

Processing

First the recovered crude oil is separated into oil, natural gas, and saltwater by means of a gas separator. When the gas is completely escaped, oil and saltwater can be separated by density separation.

Petroleum refineries then decompose crude oil into light and heavy components, such as heating oil, kerosene, jet fuel, and gasoline, by means of distillation columns, called fractional distillation or rectification. Because of these distillates' different boiling points, they can be fractionated into boiling ranges. During this first distillation, fractioned gases, such as methane, ethane, propane, and butane, are important heating fuels. Light and heavy petrols (with boiling points of 30–180 degrees Celsius) are used as gasoline for cars. The medium distillate (180–250 degrees Celsius) is used as lamp oil or is processed into jet fuel. In a subsequent vacuum distillation of the residue, additional important petroleum products are produced, such as lubricants, used to grease engines, and bitumen, used to pave roads. The heavy fuel oil fuels power plants and ship's engines. Special refineries recycle waste oil.

The amounts of naphtha produced directly from crude oil per fractional distillation are not sufficient to cover the market. However, a process that takes place at high temperatures, called catalytic cracking, cracks long-chain alkanes into short-chain alkanes. With this method, petrol can be produced from paraffin oil. For example, decane cracks up into propene and heptane. A trap inside the reactor separates the cracking products from the spent catalyst. Again, the cracked hydrocarbons become fractionated in a subsequent distillation. At the surface, the catalyst segregates carbon, making the catalyst ineffective. Upon mixing with hot air, the carbons burn up, regenerating the catalyst. This process is also used to crack heavy crude oil, because it often contains too much carbon and too little hydrogen.

Gasoline (Petrol) Production

The compression and heat in the cylinders of a gasoline engine may cause untimely spontaneous combustion of the gasoline-air mixture, resulting in engine knocking. Unramified hydrocarbons tend toward untimely ignitions, while unsaturated, ramified hydrocarbons are relatively knockproof. The antiknock rating is indicated by an octane number. The higher the octane number is, the more knockproof the gasoline is. Pure isooctane would have an octane number 100, while pure n-heptane would have an octane number of 0. Common octane numbers for gasoline are 87, 95, and 98, and the higher the antiknock rating of

the gasoline used, the longer the life of an engine. Therefore, naphtha is converted into gasoline with high antiknock ratings by means of a platinum catalyst in a process called platinum reforming. By-products of this process are hydrogen and gaseous alkanes. Prior to reforming, the naphtha needs to be desulfurized, releasing hydrogen sulfide, because sulfur would destroy the catalyst.

Desulfurization, Hydrofining, and the Claus Method

After fractional distillation, heating fuel and lubricants still contain much sulfur, leading to toxic sulfur dioxide exhaust upon combustion; these emissions lead to environmental degradation in the form of acid rain and forest decline. In a process called hydrofining, the oil is mixed with hydrogen and heated. Then the hydrogen in the hot mixture reacts in a catalytic reaction with the contained sulfur to form hydrogen sulfide. Subsequently, the hydrogen sulfide is burned in the Claus desulfurization process, forming sulfur and water, as follows:

$$6H_2S + 3O_2 \rightarrow 6S + 6H_2OH = -664 \text{ kJ/mol}$$

Synthesis Gas

Other residues from fractional distillation are used to produce synthesis gas. That is a mixture of carbon monoxide and hydrogen, used to produce many other, organic compounds, such as ammonia and methanol. Synthesis gas production from methane occurs as follows:

$$CH_4 + H_2O \rightarrow CO + 3H_2 \text{ (endothermic)}$$
$$2CH_4 + O_2 + 4N_2 \rightarrow 2CO + 4N_2 + 4H_2$$
$$\text{(exothermic)}$$

The carbon monoxide can be converted with water vapor into hydrogen and carbon dioxide, which can be washed out with water. The carbonized water is sold to the soft-drink industry. The pure gases nitrogen and hydrogen are left over as chemical precursors for other products.

Another refining process is called pyrolysis, used to crack light gasoline at very high temperatures into ethene, acetylene, and propene. A mixture of methane and oxygen is heated to 2,500 degrees Celsius. When the light gasoline is conveyed into this mixture, it cracks. For example, pyrolysis for n-heptane occurs as follows:

$$\text{n-heptane} \rightarrow \text{ethene} + \text{acetylene} + \text{propene} + \text{hydrogen}$$

Ethene and propene are important key precursors for the production of plastics. Compared to catalytic cracking, pyrolysis takes place at much higher temperatures and without a catalyst.

Oil Spill Disasters

In 2010, the largest marine oil spill disaster in the history of the petroleum industry occurred in the Gulf of Mexico, known as the Deepwater Horizon oil spill or BP oil spill. After the explosion of the offshore platform Deepwater Horizon, which drilled in the BP-operated Macondo Prospect, on April 20, 2010, oil from a leak at a seafloor oil gusher flowed for three months into the sea. Although the gushing wellhead was capped on July 15, it took until September 19 to complete the process; by then, the leaking well was effectively dead. Official estimates state that about 4.9 million barrels, or 205.8 million gallons, of crude oil spilled into the Gulf; some estimates are higher.

Generally, transport of oil via oil tanker is not only very expensive but also hazardous with regard to environmental and ecological issues. Supertankers carry up to 300,000 tons of oil. About 100,000 tons of crude oil leak every year into the ocean as a result of tanker accidents. An especially drastic accident happened in 1989, when the *Exxon Valdez* lost an estimated 11 million barrels of crude oil off Alaska's coast. After the accident occurred, immediate efforts to use dispersants to clean it up failed because of a storm that rendered the dispersants ineffective, and booms were used to collect oil and burn it. Nevertheless, the oil slick spread and contaminated about 1,300 miles of coastline, killing wildlife. Catastrophic ecological consequences led to broad public discussions about risks and dangers of maritime oil transports. Eventually this incident resulted in more regulations for oil tankers and an investigation of how to avoid such disasters.

▷ *Radioactive Waste*

Millions of tons of radioactive wastes result every year from the production of crude oil and natural gas, and often these are improperly disposed. Sludge and wastewater, pumped to the Earth's surface during oil production, include naturally occurring radioactive materials, such as toxic radium 226 and polonium 210. The radioactivity of such wastes has been measured at between 0.1 and 15,000 becquerels (Bq) per gram. There is no independent monitoring of these contaminated residues. The results have been disastrous for the environment; for example, in Kazakhstan there are large contaminated regions. Great Britain even disposes of radioactive residues in the North Sea. In the United States, repeated problems have occurred; for example, in Martha, a community in Kentucky, the company Ashland Inc. sold contaminated conveying tubes to farmers and schools without informing anybody about the contamination. A preschool and some residential buildings had to be evacuated immediately.

Global Resources, Production, and Consumption

The question of how long global oil resources will be able to cover the world's consumption is debated. Key publications, such as the International Energy Agency's annual *World Energy Outlook*, present a scenario that assumes a global oil peak between 2010 and 2020. Furthermore, by around 2030 only 75 percent of the global demand will be met by oil deposits known today. At the same time, global economic growth is leading to increases, not decreases, in consumption. Other sources, such as Abdullah S. Jum'ah, president of Saudi Aramco from 1995 through 2008, assert that with today's technology, prospected areas, and consumption, Earth's oil resources will cover the world's consumption for at least another century; this prediction assumes that only 10 percent of all liquid oil resources have been recovered. In fact, many scientists agree that peak of oil discoveries was reached in 1965, and since 1980 oil consumption has exceeded oil discoveries every year.

The most important producing countries are Russia, Saudi Arabia, and the United States, followed by Iran, Iraq, China, and Venezuela. The main exporting countries are Saudi Arabia, the Russian Federation, and Iran. The United States, China, Japan, and Germany were the main consumers in 2008. However, world consumption has been increasing by 2 percent per year. The annual per capita consumption in the United States in 2003 was about 26 barrels, 11.7 barrels in Germany, 1.7 barrels in China, 0.8 barrel in India, and in 0.2 barrel in Bangladesh. Although during the 1970s, private Western oil companies controlled almost 50 percent of global oil production, this figure had declined to less than 15 percent by 2008.

Worldwide Oil Prices

It is not certain yet if oil prices worldwide are increasing as a result of reaching peak oil. However, the immediate problem is not yet a decrease in production but an increase in demand and the resulting coverage deficit. The only corrective right now is the price, as shown in a peak of almost $150 per barrel in 2008. In the past, price increases have been followed by significant increases in production. However, in 2008, for the first time, capacity did not expand in reaction to high prices.

Currently, the most important reference oils are West Texas Intermediate (WTI), considered a high-quality, sweet, light oil from Cushing, Oklahoma, used as a reference for North American oil; Brent Blend, which integrates 15 fields in the East Shetland Basins of the North Sea and is used to price oil produced in Europe, Africa, and the Middle East flowing west; Dubai/Oman, used as a benchmark for Middle East sour crude oil flowing toward the Pacific; Tapis, from Malaysia, for light Far East oil; Minas, from Indonesia, for heavy Far East oil; Midway Sunset Heavy, for heavy oil in California; and the "reference basket" of the Organization of Petroleum Exporting Countries (OPEC), a weighted average of oil blends from various OPEC countries.

After the world reaches peak oil, global production will decrease. Potentially, at this point in time there is still enough oil available to cover daily consumption, even at the current increasing rates, but oil cannot be produced quickly enough to sustain this, so there is a de facto deficit. In other words, it is clear—long before the deposits have been emptied—that crude oil is a finite resource. According to Aramco, Saudi Arabia's state-owned oil company, a total of about 1.1 trillion barrels of crude oil have been produced. Most deposits were discovered in the 1960s. Since the early 1980s, annual production has been higher than the capacity of the discovered sources, so since that time the available resources have been decreasing. For instance, England, a former export country, has had to import petroleum since 2006. Critical analyses conducted by the British government, the U.S. Department of Energy, and the central analytical service of the U.S. armed forces, the U.S. Joint Forces Command, have predicted the possibility of short-term deficit scenarios.

MANJA LEYK

Further Reading

Deffeyes, Kenneth S. *Hubbert's Peak: The Impending World Oil Shortage.* Princeton, NJ: Princeton University Press, 2008.

Glasby, G. P. "Abiogenic Origin of Hydrocarbons: An Historical Overview." *Resource Geology* 56, no. 1 (2006).

Glover, Peter. "Aramco Chief Debunks Peak Oil." *Energy Tribune*, January 17, 2008. http://www.energytribune.com/articles.cfm?aid=764.

International Energy Agency. "Oil Market Updates." http://www.iea.org.

Kolesnikov, Anton, et al. "Methane-Derived Hydrocarbons Produced Under Upper-Mantle Conditions." *Nature Geoscience* 2 (2009).

Maugeri, Leonardo. *Beyond the Age of Oil.* Westport, CT: Praeger, 2010.

Ruppert, Michael C. *Confronting Collapse: The Crisis of Energy and Money in a Post Peak Oil World.* White River Junction, VT: Chelsea Green, 2009.

Speight, James G. *The Chemistry and Technology of Petroleum.* New York: Marcel Dekker, 1999.

See Also: Aramco; ExxonMobil; Gulf Oil Spill; Oil and Gas Pipelines; Oil Sands; Oil Shales; Oil Spills; Organization of Petroleum Exporting Countries.

Oil Market and Price

Category: Business of Energy.
Summary: Oil prices are formed on oil markets. Although markets have diminished the threat of physical supply shortages, they are accompanied by worries about rising and more volatile oil prices.

Today, the price of oil is probably the most cited, commented upon, and observed price in the world. However, while reference to the "oil price" suggests a homogeneous price and a single market, neither of these actually exists: There are a variety of different crude oils and there are several ways of trading oil—for example, by making long-term contracts on the global oil market. In the oil trade, these global markets have gained great importance over the past decades. Today, there are spot, forward, and future markets. Oil markets have eased worries about energy security in the Western world. They provide the opportunity to obtain petroleum in a flexible and timely manner. On the other hand, the growing importance of oil markets has led to new vulnerabilities; the risks of rising and volatile prices have, to a great extent, replaced the risk of physical shortages.

Instead of only one oil price, there are many prices in the oil trade. The term *crude oil* refers to a variety of fossil, mineral liquid hydrocarbons. According to the Energy Charter Secretariat (based on the 1991 Energy Charter Agreement, which established a multilateral framework for energy trade), there are 130 crude grades worldwide. When traded, the prices of these oils are usually strongly related to the prices of particular benchmark crudes. Since the 1980s, three major benchmarks have emerged: Brent for North Sea oil, West Texas Intermediate (WTI) in North America, and Dubai crude in the Middle East.

Given the functional similarity of different crudes, price differences between crudes appear to be relatively small compared to their shared overall price developments. Despite the great variety of crude oils in practice, it might therefore be legitimate to talk about the "oil price" not as a concrete price but as a broad category.

It took several decades of international oil trade before this market emerged. The initial years of international oil trade were dominated by the North American and European oil companies that started to develop and exploit petroleum resources in various regions of the world. These major companies, often referred to as the Seven Sisters, dominated oil trade until the producing states began to nationalize domestic production sites and determine the conditions of oil sales, particularly during the early 1970s. With nationalization, pricing power shifted from the companies toward producing countries. In 1973, Middle Eastern oil producers raised the oil prices unilaterally for the first time. During 1970s, crude oil from the Organization of Petroleum Exporting Countries (OPEC) was then sold at an official price determined by OPEC. Under both the dominance of the Western companies as well as producing states, oil was commonly sold on the basis of long-term contracts.

The spot market for oil emerged slowly. Before the events of the early 1970s, less than 5 percent of global oil was traded on this market. However, in response to the first oil crisis of 1973, Western oil companies started to develop oil resources in countries that were not OPEC members. Most of that oil was subsequently traded on the spot market, and by the mid-1970s up to 15 percent of global oil trade was processed on that market. The price pressure from this additional oil forced OPEC to cut production levels significantly to sustain its selling price. Saudi Arabia alone cut production volumes from 10 million to only 3.5 million barrels per day. In 1986, Saudi Arabia suspended production restrictions and introduced the netback pricing system to sell its crude oil. This system determined the price of crude oil by considering the spot price of refined products and subtracting a fixed refining margin and transportation costs. As a consequence, oil prices plunged, and the OPEC pricing system collapsed. In 1988, OPEC stopped determining prices and introduced a more refined system of contracts.

Today, roughly 30 to 50 percent of all oil is traded on this market. Most of the remaining volume, particularly crude from the Middle East, is traded in the form of long-term contracts. However, contracts no longer involve a fixed price but instead contain a mathematical formula to determine the actual selling price of oil. This formula is normally closely tied to the spot price of one or several crude oils. Therefore, spot prices determine the value of crude oil far beyond the actual market volume.

The oil market is by no means a perfect market. OPEC is still a production cartel and a powerful player on the market. According to the International Energy Agency (IEA), about 44 percent of today's global crude oil supply comes from OPEC countries. The IEA predicts this share will rise 52 percent between 2010 and 2030. The pricing power held by OPEC tends to be greatest in times of tight markets. Nevertheless, it is mostly unclear how great this power actually is. A defense against potential OPEC ambitions to cut the amount of oil available to specific consumers was organized by IEA members after the first oil crisis in the early 1970s. These states committed themselves to establish strategic petroleum reserves and facilitate a coordinated response to oil crises through the IEA. These reserves amount to at least 90 days of the state's net oil imports. Moreover, OPEC states themselves have long been interested in a stable oil market.

The global oil market has substantially lessened the risk of serious physical supply shortages. If a producer—whether intentionally or as a consequence of natural disasters, accidents, or a terrorist attack—cuts production, customers can avoid physical shortfalls by turning to other producers. Instead of a physical shortage, the shifting balance between (constant) demand and (decreasing) supply would then lead to rising oil prices, which would in turn reduce demand and thus lead to a new market equilibrium. This way, physical shortages are translated into rising prices, the consequences of which are borne by all consumers on the market. To hedge against the resulting price risks, future and forward oil markets have coevolved with spot markets. On these markets, consumers can buy options or future contracts to sell or buy oil at a time in the future at a price fixed when the contract is made.

The current energy security challenges on the oil market are therefore related to high, volatile, and erratically fluctuating prices. The issue of price stability has drawn much attention in recent years, as oil prices at one point shot up to more than $140 per barrel and then plunged to less than $40 per barrel. Uncertainty about future prices negatively affects investment decisions and thereby impedes economic growth. Moreover, uncertain future prospects about oil prices negatively affect investment into oil exploration and production itself. This might lead to even greater future price hikes due to insufficient supply. There are two major positions regarding the causes of price volatility. Some experts hold market fundamentals, such as a rapidly growing demand and a lack of spare production capacity, responsible. Others point to increasing speculation in the oil markets; financial investors, they argue, exacerbate or even cause fluctuating prices. The first of these analyses calls for investing more in production infrastructure; the latter calls for stricter regulations of investors in oil markets. Internationally, these issues are continuously addressed in the context of the International Energy Forum, an international group of energy ministers from 87 of the world's largest oil- and gas-producing nations.

Jörn Richert

Further Reading

Energy Charter Secretariat. *Putting a Price on Energy: International Pricing Mechanisms for Oil and Gas.* Brussels: Energy Charter Secretariat, 2007.

Fattouh, Bassam. "OPEC Pricing Power: The Need for a New Perspective." In *The New Energy Paradigm*, edited by Dieter Helm. New York: Oxford University Press, 2007.

International Energy Agency. *World Energy Outlook 2011.* Paris: International Energy Agency, 2011.

See Also: Energy Markets: Commercial; Energy Markets: Industrial; Energy Markets: Residential; Energy Markets: Transport; Internal Energy Market; International Energy Agency; Organization of Petroleum Exporting Countries.

Oil Sands

Category: Energy Resources.
Summary: Oil sands are an unconventional petroleum resource that contains a viscous type of crude oil known as bitumen, which is refined into crude oil and fuels. Canada is home to the world's largest oil sands reserves, as well as the only large-scale commercial production.

Oil sands are a naturally occuring fossil fuel composed of sand, clay, various minerals, water, and bitumen. Bitumen is a type of crude oil or petroleum known for its heavy viscosity. Oil sands are sometimes mistakenly referred to as tar sands, a synthetic substance similar in appearance, but with different uses. Tar sands do not have potential as usable fuel sources. Oil sands represent much of the global supply of oil deposits, although not all of it can be profitably recovered at present. The World Energy Council (WEC) lists oil sands and natural bitumen reserves in over 20 countries; the largest are found in Canada, Venezuela, Russia, Kazakhstan, the Middle East, and the U.S. state of Utah.

Utilization of natural bitumen dates back to ancient times, but the first recorded oil sands mining operation dates to 1745. Canadian scientist Dr. Karl A. Clark patented the hot-water-based extraction process underlying modern oil sands recovery technology. Canada is the global leader in the oil sands industry. Canada holds the world's largest recoverable deposits, estimated at approximately 170 billion barrels. The largest deposits are found along the Athabasca River, while smaller deposits are found in Cold Lake and along the Peace River. Recent acknowledgement of oil sands as global oil reserves moved Canada to second behind Saudi Arabia in terms of proven reserves. Smaller scale production occurs in Venezuela.

The growth of the oil sands industry has been limited by the difficulty, expense, and environmental concerns of extraction. Oil is more difficult to extract from oil sands and is recovered through mining or in situ production methods. Recovered bitumen then requires additional treatment to make it transportable via pipeline and to refine it into crude oil and from crude oil into fuels. Rising conventional oil prices may make oil sands production more economical in the future. Environmental concerns linked to the oil sands industry include greenhouse gas emissions, land use impacts, pollution, loss of habitat, and threats to animal and human health.

Oil extraction from oil sands requires more complex recovery operations than oil extractions from more conventional oil deposits, as it cannot simply be pumped from the ground. Oil sands deposits that lay near the surface are extracted through strip or open-pit mining techniques. Heated water is used to separate out the bitumen, with the water and other residual materials such as sand and clay discharged into tailings ponds. Materials left after extraction, such as sand, are returned, allowing for later mine reclamation.

Over 80 percent of global oil sands deposits cannot be profitably extracted through mining using current technology.

Deposits lying too far below the surface to be mined are extracted instead through various in situ drillable production methods based largely on steam or solvent injection methods or firefloods. Examples of more developed techniques

Wikimedia

The Athabasca Tar Sands in Alberta, Canada, c. 1900–1930. Currently, Canada is producing oil from sands at a large scale.

include cyclic steam simulation (CSS), steam assisted gravity drainage (SAGD), and cold heavy oil production with sand (CHOPS); while vapor extraction process (VAPEX), toe to heel air injection (THAI), and combustion overhead gravity drainage (COGD) are newer, more experimental methods. The injection of steam, solvents, or heated air allows the bitumen to flow into oil wells by reducing its viscosity.

Bitumen is diluted with hydrocarbons or chemically split to ensure flow through pipelines to production facilities. Next, the bitumen is separated and processed into heavy crude oil, using a hot water process similar to mining production to remove water, sand, and minerals. The bitumen recovery rate is approximately 75 percent. Finally, it is refined into fuels such as gasoline or diesel. The technological difficulty of extracting and processing oil sands means that approximately two tons of oil sands are required to produce just one barrel of oil. Rising environmental concerns have also made the oil sands industry vulnerable to environmental controversy and legislative requirements governing such issues as greenhouse gas emissions and land reclamation.

Sites must be cleared of forest and vegetative growth, as well as the top layer of peat and soil, prior to extraction. Those in favor of oil sands production note that the disturbed land in places such as Canada is only a small portion of total land and that much of that land will be reclaimed after extraction. Habitat concerns center on reports of deaths and deformities among nearby animal and aquatic life, while human health concerns center on toxic by-products and potential cancers or other ailments. Greenhouse gas emissions associated with bitumen and synthetic crude oil production are higher than those for more conventional types of fossil fuel production. Oil sands also require large amounts of water and steam, some of which can be recycled.

Marcella Bush Trevino

Further Reading

Government of Alberta Energy. "What Is Oil Sands?" http://www.energy.gov.ab.ca/oilsands/793.asp.

Kunzig, Robert. "The Canadian Oil Boom." *National Geographic* (2012). http://ngm.nationalgeographic.com/2009/03/canadian-oil-sands/kunzig-text.

Maugeri, Leonardo. *The Age of Oil: The Mythology, History, and Future of the World's Most Controversial Resource.* Westport, CT: Praeger, 2006.

Oil Sands Developers Group and the Alberta Chamber of Resources. "Oil Sands Facts" (February 2011). http://www.oilsandsdevelopers.ca/wp-content/uploads/2011/03/FINAL-OSDG-2011-Canadian.pdf.

See Also: Flaring Gas; Nonrenewable Energy Resources; Oil and Natural Gas Drilling; Oil and Petroleum; Oil Shales; Refining; Uganda; Water Pollution.

Oil Shales

Category: Energy Resources.
Summary: Oil shales are sedimentary rocks embedded with kerogen, which has not matured into petroleum, or crude oil, due to insufficient heat, pressure, depth, or time. These kerogens can be used to produce synthetic oil and gas.

Oil shales form from organic material that accumulates in sedimentary rock layers and becomes kerogen, a dense mixture of organic chemical compounds. Under sufficient conditions of heat, pressure, and time, kerogen can develop into crude oil and natural gas. Particular oil shales vary in the richness of their organic matter and composition, including the organic matter that forms the kerogen as well as other compounds and minerals found in the deposit. These variations are due to both the particularities of the organic material that forms the kerogen and the specific composition of the sedimentary rock where it is deposited. Oil shales can be categorized as terrestrial, lacustrine, or marine oil shales, based on the kerogen content. Terrestrial oil shales comprise organic material from land plants and animals. Lacustrine oil shales contain remains of freshwater or brackish water algae. Marine oil shales derive from mostly saltwater algae and plankton.

Oil shales can also be categorized by sedimentary deposition, including siliceous shales and carbonate-rich shales. Siliceous shales are predominantly silica-based shales and tend to have higher moisture content, whereas carbonate-rich shales are more likely to crumble through extraction and handling. The origins of the oil shale have an impact on its quality, method of extraction, and use. Oil shales tend to be found within 0.5 mile (900 meters) of the Earth's surface, closer than petroleum deposits, which require geologic zones at greater depth and temperature to form. Oil shales are distinct from oil sands in that the latter result from the biodegradation of crude oil reserves. Oil shales, in contrast, are kerogen deposits that have not undergone sufficient conditions to become crude oil and thus remain in an immature state.

Extraction and Processing

Oil shale can be used by humans as solid fuel, since it can be ignited without processing. It is most commonly obtained through surface mining procedures, such as open-pit mining and strip mining, when the oil shale deposit is near the surface. If the oil shale resource is farther from the surface, it is extracted via the room-and-pillar method, similar to the underground mining of coal and iron. Once the oil shale has been extracted, it is processed to remove sulfuric and nitrogenous impurities.

Subjected to sufficiently high temperatures, the kerogen derived from oil shales can be distilled by retorting the kerogen through pyrolysis to produce shale oil and oil-shale gas. Pyrolysis is the process of inducing decomposition in organic materials by applying high heat without oxygen. Char, a solid residue that can be used as fuel, may result from pyrolysis. Shale oil is a kind of synthetic unconventional oil, a petroleum product that can be used like conventional oil but extracted or generated through different means from those used to obtain traditional crude oil. Oil-shale gas, which is different from the natural gas produced from shale, called shale gas, can be used in place of natural gas.

By-Products and Environmental Impact

The by-products of converting oil shale into shale oil and oil-shale gas include sulfur, ammonia, asphalt, and waxes. Because its composition is different from that of crude oil, shale oil is not directly substituted for crude oil for all uses. However, some conventional fuels, such as kerosene and diesel fuel, can be produced effectively from shale oil. Additionally, it can be used to fuel power plants and to manufacture carbon materials, resins, glues, tanning agents, cements, fertilizers, and glass.

Much of the environmental concern surrounding oil shale centers on its mining, processing, and use. Like other surface mining activities, oil shale mining results in increased erosion, particulate and acid pollution of surface water and groundwater, and sulfur gas emissions. Particulate air pollution is perhaps the most significant concern during processing. Moreover, during its use as fuel, which requires combustion, oil shale and its derivative products release carbon dioxide, a greenhouse gas, into the atmosphere.

Locations

Unlike petroleum deposits, which are concentrated in certain geographic regions, oil shales are widely distributed throughout the world. As of 2010, the countries with the 10 largest known deposits of oil shale resources were the United States, Russia, the Democratic Republic of the Congo, Brazil, Italy, Morocco, Jordan, Australia, Estonia, and China. The United States contains more than half of the world's known oil shale reserves. There are many deposits around the world, however, although little is known about either the quality or the extent of these oil shale resources.

By the late 1830s, modern commercial mining of oil shale reserves was under way in Autun, France. The United States began promoting shale oil as a replacement for wood as fuel in the 1850s, establishing the oil shale industry as a key factor in the U.S. economy until the discovery and adoption of crude oil by 1859; it was then found that the processing of oil shales to produce shale oil was costlier than obtaining crude oil. Similarly, from 1850 to 1864, Scotland had a stable shale oil industry until imported crude oil became a cheaper alternative. After a brief revival of interest in shale oil in the 1920s, the United States did not show serious interest in oil shale production until the 1970s and the 1980s, as a result of the Arab Oil Embargo, and then the interest was only temporary.

The early 21st century, however, has seen renewed interest in developing an oil shale industry in the United States, a consequence of unstable and high costs for natural gas and petroleum products. Currently, oil shale resources are commercially exploited by Brazil, Australia, Estonia, and China, among other nations.

JOSEF NGUYEN

Further Reading

Bartis, James T., Tom LaTourrette, Lloyd Dixon, D. J. Peterson, and Gary Cecchine. *Oil Shale Development in the United States: Prospects and Policy Issues*. Santa Monica, CA: RAND, 2005.

Hyne, Normal J. *Nontechnical Guide to Petroleum Geology, Exploration, Drilling and Production*. Tulsa, OK: Pennwell Books, 2001.

Lee, Sunggyu. "Shale Oil From Oil Shale." In *Handbook of Alternative Fuel Technologies*, by Sunggyu Lee, James G. Speight, and Sudarshan K. Loyalka. Boca Raton, FL: CRC Press, 2007.

Loucks, Robert Alden. *Shale Oil: Tapping the Treasure*. Philadelphia: Xlibris, 2002.

Ogunsola, Olayinka I., Arthur M. Hartstein, and Olubunmi Ogunsola. *Oil Shale: A Solution to the Liquid Fuel Dilemma*. Washington, DC: American Chemical Society, 2010.

See Also: Canada; Colorado; Hubbert's Peak; Israel; Jordan; Marcellus Shale; Oil and Petroleum; Oil Sands.

Oil Spills

Category: Environmentalism.
Summary: An oil spill is the accidental release of liquid petroleum into the environment as a result of human activity. This definition excludes natural oil seeps, in which liquid petroleum leaks out of the ground or through the ocean floor.

Oil spills can occur on either land or at sea, but because spills on land are usually smaller and more easily contained, much more attention has been focused on marine and coastal spills.

Oil spills can result in extreme environmental damage to the environment, whether on land or at sea. Because most large oil spills at sea have been more difficult to contain than those on land, they are especially damaging, polluting the ocean and nearby shoreline as well as the plant and animal communities living nearby. These spills can also have significant negative economic effects on communities. For instance, fishing and shrimping in the area affected by the spill may be banned for an extended period because of pollution from the spill, and tourists may avoid visiting the area because of either the actual or the perceived effects of the spill. Extensive cleanup and restoration efforts may be required over a period of years to restore the natural and human communities affected by a large oil spill to their status before the spill.

History and Incidence

Somewhat surprisingly, oil spills are a fairly common occurrence. The International Tanker Owners Pollution Federation (ITOPF), a not-for-profit organization established by ship owners and insurers, maintains a database of information on almost 10,000 accidental oil spills from tankers, combined carriers, and barges that have occurred since 1970. This database actually underestimates the problem of oil spills, because it does not include those resulting from acts of war or from drilling operations, such as the 2010 *Deepwater Horizon* spill in the Gulf of Mexico; it also omits spills on land. ITOPF classifies these spills by size, in terms of the amount of oil spilled, as small (less than 7 tons), intermediate (7 to 700 tons), and large (more than 700 tons).

Media Attention Given to Large Spills

One reason oil spills may appear to the general public to be a rare event is that, according to

ITOPF's records, most of them (81 percent) fall into the small category. This type of spill, although common, may receive little media attention, whereas the rarer large spills may be featured in news reports for an extended period of time. In addition, the damage created from a single large spill may be substantially greater than that from numerous small spills, and thus large spills are naturally accorded more media attention.

Finally, according to the ITOPF, most spills occur in port or at oil terminals during routine operations, such as loading or discharging, which explains why small spills are fairly common and not considered particularly newsworthy (although they may also result in environmental damage). Large spills are more commonly caused by accidents, such as grounding or collisions; 88 percent of spills of more than 700 tons are associated with such causes, which are themselves newsworthy.

Decreasing Over Time

A historical analysis of large oil spills, based on the ITOPF database, shows that the number of large oil spills has decreased in every decade from the 1970s forward, with the greatest drop occurring between the 1970s and the 1980s. In the years from 1970 to 1979, there were 253 large spills (55 percent of all spills); in 1980–89, 93 large spills (20 percent of all spills); in 1990–99, 78 large spills (17 percent of all spills); and in 2000–09, 33 large spills (7 percent of all spills).

The amount of oil spilled has also decreased over the decades, with the greatest change coming between the 1990s and the 2000s. In the years 1970–79, 3.174 million tons of oil was spilled into the environment; 1.77 million tons were spilled in the 1980s; 1.137 million tons were spilled in the 1990s; and 212,000 tons were spilled in the years 2000–09. Notably, the amount of oil transported in the seaborne oil trade has shown a general increase since the recession of the early 1980s, while oil spills have decreased over that time.

Response and Environmental Consequences

A number of methods for containing and cleaning up an oil spill are available, and those charged with oil spill cleanup may combine several different approaches simultaneously or in succession. Natural processes—including evaporation, oxidation, and biodegredation of the oil—may also aid in the cleanup effort. Examples of cleanup techniques available include the use of mechanical means such as booms and skimmers to collect and remove the oil; burning oil in situ (for instance, an oil slick on the surface of the water); using chemicals, called dispersants, to accelerate the degradation of the oil and to hasten dispersion from the surface of the water; and using biological agents (such as nutrients, enzymes, and microorganisms) to hasten oil degradation. If spilled oil reaches a shoreline, other types of intervention may be required, including wiping down surfaces with absorbent materials, pressure washing (rinsing shorelines and rocks with water streams), and raking or bulldozing sand to increase evaporation. However, all these interventions also have environmental consequences or may yield imperfect results. For instance, some argue that the use of dispersants may make an oil spill look smaller by decreasing the size of the slick, while actually perpetuating worse environmental damage.

The environmental consequences of any marine oil spill depend on a number of factors, including the particular type of oil, the quantity spilled, the location of the spill, the local weather and environmental conditions, and the rapidity and effectiveness of the cleanup response. Most oils are lighter than water and will spread horizontally in a slick on the surface of water. The amount of spread depends on several factors, including the surface tension, specific gravity, and viscosity of the oil as well as the effects of natural actions, including weathering, evaporation, oxidation, biodegradation, and emulsification. Although it is common to focus on the visible extent of an oil slick as a measure of the severity of the spill, in fact if oil becomes emulsified (mixed with water in small droplets), the appearance of the slick may be reduced (because emulsions are heavier than water and sink) but the cleanup could be hampered, because emulsions can persist in the environment for months or years.

Aquatic and shoreline habitats are sensitive environments whose health depends on a complex web of relationships among plants, animals, and the physical environment. These relationships are easily disrupted by the presence of spilled oil, as harm suffered by one species may impact others and throw the entire ecosystem out of balance. Birds and mammals may be hurt by physical contamination with the oil; for instance, fur or feathers contaminated with oil no longer serve as good insulation, and the mammal or bird may freeze to death. Birds may also lose the ability to fly or to float on the water if the structure of their feathers is damaged by the oil. Moreover, oil contains toxins that may harm birds and mammals if ingested or inhaled. Destruction of habitation poses a risk for all organisms and may disrupt the ecosystem beyond those organisms directly affected by the oil. For instance, contamination of species lower on the food chain may spread to those above them, as predators consume oil-damaged prey. In addition, the loss of a usual source of food may bring about the destruction of a species that has had no direct contact with the oil. In the case of birds, oil may be transferred from feathers to eggs, smothering the chicks inside by sealing pores in the eggs, and long-term reproductive problems have also been noted in animals exposed to oil spills.

Coral reefs and the organisms that live in and around them are sensitive to smothering from the oil as well as harm from the toxic substances contained within it. Tidal flats, which generally contain rich communities of birds, plants and animals, may be harmed immediately by the spill and also suffer long-term damage as oil seeps into the muddy bottoms of the flats. Sheltered beaches and salt marshes are prone to oil accumulation, as they have little wave action to aid in dispersion. If not removed

Wikimedia

Shoreline habitats are sensitive environments whose health depends on a complex web of relationships. Harm suffered by one species due to an oil spill may impact others and throw the entire ecosystem out of balance.

by a cleanup effort, the oil may remain in the environment indefinitely. The root systems of plants, including those growing in marshes and swamps, are easily damaged by oil; in the case of species such as mangroves, it may takes years for new plants to replace those that have been damaged.

Sarah Boslaugh

Further Reading

Burger, Joanna. *Oil Spills*. New Brunswick, NJ: Rutgers University Press, 1997.

Fingas, Mervin F., and Jennifer Charles. *The Basics of Oil Spill Cleanup*. 2nd ed. Boca Raton, FL: Lewis, 2001.

International Tanker Owners Pollution Federation Limited. "What We Do." http://www.itopf.com/about/what-we-do.html.

Juhasz, Antonia. *Black Tide: The Devastating Impact of the Gulf Oil Spill*. New York: John Wiley, 2011.

National Oceanic and Atmospheric Administration, Office of Response and Restoration. "Emergency

Response: Responding to Oil Spills." http://
response.restoration.noaa.gov/topic_subtopic
.php?RECORD_KEY%28subtopics%29=subtopic
_id&subtopic_id(subtopics)=8.

U.S. Environmental Protection Agency. "Emergency
Management: Response to Oil Spills." http://www
.epa.gov/emergencies/content/learning/response
.htm.

U.S. Environmental Protection Agency, Office of
Emergency and Remedial Response. *Understanding
Oil Spills and Oil Spills and Oil Spill Response.*
Washington, DC: Environmental Protection
Agency, 1999. http://www.epa.gov/osweroe1/
content/learning/pdfbook.htm.

See Also: Arctic National Wildlife Refuge; BP; *Exxon Valdez* Oil Spill; Gulf Oil Spill; Offshore Drilling; Oil and Petroleum; Public Relations; Shell.

Oklahoma

Category: Energy in the United States.
Summary: The history of Oklahoma epitomizes the close relationship between society and energy resources. Much of Oklahoma's social and economic organization focused on energy extraction from oil, natural gas, and wind.

The biophysical environment within the boundaries of the state of Oklahoma offers varied and plentiful energy sources. Over the past 110 years, much of the social and economic organization of the state has been focused on energy extraction from oil, natural gas, and wind. Providing energy for the industrialized world has created fortunes, created jobs, generated tax revenues, and spawned legal systems for wealth distribution. The abundance of energy sources has fostered the development of residential living in suburban and rural locations dispersed over wide geographic areas. Accessible energy has an impact on all aspects of human activity, from agriculture to social activities to migrations of populations. The supply and demand for energy has accordingly shaped the historic social and economic character of Oklahoma and will continue to do so in the future.

The energy resources of Oklahoma historically have been among the most abundant and accessible in the United States. In this regard, Oklahoma is best known for its petroleum reservoirs; the state overlies vast geological formations that still contain large volumes of natural gas and oil.

Oil

The indigenous inhabitants of the Oklahoma lands were aware of seeps of oil but did not use the crude oil as an energy source. These peoples valued oil for various purposes, including medical treatment. In 1859, a resident in the northwestern part of the state drilled for saltwater but instead found unexpected oil. During this time, small amounts of oil were typically sold for household purposes, such as lamp fuel. As oil uses and value expanded, a resident in what is now known as Rogers County drilled a well in 1889 to find oil for topical application on cattle for parasite control. A successful venture, this resulted in a well said to produce a half of barrel per day. A few years later, in 1897, a major oil find in Washington County started a century of extensive oil exploration, production, and processing. Within the following decade, Oklahoma became the largest oil-producing region in the world, providing energy that fueled early 20th-century industrialization.

Opportunities created by the boom spurred inmigration. By 1927, producers in the state reached a peak of 278 million barrels of oil. To process the crude oil, investors built refineries throughout the state. During this time, Oklahoma established its place in the history of energy. Petroleum became the fuel of war, industrialization, and automobile-based lifestyles. This inexpensive fuel powered mechanized agriculture. While not recognized at the time, oil also fueled unsustainable farming practices that resulted in the 1930s Dust Bowl. Today, with much of its petroleum reserves depleted, Oklahoma accounts for a mere 3.3 percent of the crude oil production in the United States.

Natural Gas

One by-product of oil extraction is natural gas. Natural gas is a form of hydrocarbon energy that can be isolated and found alone, but it is also a constituent of oil and saltwater found in geological formations throughout Oklahoma. In the early days of oil exploration, the industry considered gas a waste product, and it was burned off at the well site. Gas is now recognized as a valuable product, with producers going to great lengths to extract it. The deepest producing well in the world is in Oklahoma, located in Beckham County in the southwestern part of the state, at a depth of 31,411 feet. The peak production was in 1990, with extractions of nearly 2.3 trillion cubic feet of gas. By 2009, the figure was 1.3 trillion cubic feet of gas, with approximately 43,600 gas wells in the state of varying depths. Overall, geological formations in Oklahoma contain approximately 8.5 percent of the estimated reserves of natural gas in the United States.

Electricity

Oklahoma's electrical energy comes from a variety of sources, and because of its local abundance, natural gas is a primary fuel source for electricity. With the electrification of the United States in the early 20th century, electrical power became available in large urban areas. Because of the wide dispersion of customers, the distribution of electrical power to rural areas was not profitable. As a result, much of rural Oklahoma was without electricity until the 1930s. As part of the federal government's response to rural needs, the Rural Electrification Administration was created in 1935 and made loans to customer-owned electric cooperatives. Cooperatives formed across the state and supported the erection of electrical facilities serving rural areas. Oklahoma's state legislature created the Grand River Dam Authority (GRDA), which used federal money to build a hydroelectric dam in far northeastern Oklahoma. To this day, this agency is one of the few electrical power providers in the United States owned by a state government. Today, the GRDA operates electrical generation facilities fueled by coal, gas, and hydropower with a capacity of more than 1,536 megawatts.

Federally built reservoirs were constructed from the 1940s through the 1960s and now provide relatively cheap hydroelectric energy for publicly owned utilities. Coal fuels about 27 percent of the electrical generation capacity in Oklahoma. Both for-profit and public-owned utilities have coal-fired electrical generation facilities in the state. Coal is railed into the state from large deposits in the northwestern part of the United States (primarily Wyoming). Although coal is still mined within state boundaries, little is used because of its large sulfur content and associated air quality issues. Oklahoma generating stations produce about 2.1 percent of the total electrical energy in the United States.

Folklorists, songwriters, and meteorologists have long recognized the Oklahoma wind. Situated on the eastern edge of the U.S. Great Plains, Oklahoma experiences an ever-present wind. In the early 20th century, Oklahomans used wind to pump groundwater for irrigation and watering livestock. In areas off the early electrical power grid, homesteaders used small wind-powered generators to produce electricity for domestic use and for agriculture. At the beginning of the 21st century, demand for renewable and less polluting sources of energy increased dramatically. Between the late 1970s and the turn of the century, the unit cost of producing wind energy dropped eightfold, making wind commercially viable on a large scale. Supported by state and federal government incentives, private investors found profit in the construction and operation of large wind farms in western Oklahoma. The term *wind farm* refers to dedicated land with a concentration of anywhere from 20 to 84 turbine towers equipped with three 250-foot-long blades designed to capture wind energy. By 2009, Oklahoma wind farms had the capacity to generate 1,031 megawatts of power, accounting for about 5 percent of the electrical power generation in the state.

Agriculture, Biomass, and Organic Energy

As part of the search for alternative fuels, government entities and private investors turned their focus to the use of agricultural products and byproducts for viable sources of energy. With abundant productive farmland, the state's agricultural sector is an expanding part of meeting energy demands. Society has long used grains to produce ethanol for various uses, including as fuel. Corn, which grows well in Oklahoma, is a source of biomass for ethanol production. Biomass, the organic by-products of agricultural and forestry products, is also a potential source for other organically based fuels. Although biofuels are not currently a primary energy source in the state, they are expected to play an increasingly important role in the future to meet the state's fuel demands.

Energy Consumption and Prospects

With a population of 3.7 million people, Oklahoma ranks 28th among the 50 states. Located in the southwestern part of the continental United States, Oklahoma sustains hot summers that create a high demand for electricity to power air-conditioning. The availability of land and inexpensive gasoline has fostered urban sprawl and a private-automobile-based demand for gasoline. Petroleum refining and processing, electrical power generation, and manufacturing create the primary industrial demand for energy in Oklahoma. Oklahomans rank 23rd in the United States in energy consumption: 1,603 trillion British thermal units (Btu) in 2008, out of the total 99,383 trillion Btu consumed in the United States.

As in other parts of the United States, demand for energy will continue to increase. Population growth, innovation and proliferation of energy-consuming products, and continued urban sprawl will generate more demand for all sources of energy.

In the future, the various sources of energy in Oklahoma will be a factor in meeting demands for power in the United States. The production of petroleum, coal, hydropower, wind power, fossil-fuel-generated electricity, and biofuels will continue to be an essential part of the state's economic and social organization. The depletion of sources of energy and environmental consequences of using them will create new challenges not only for the people within the state but also for people globally. Just as the historic production of energy was the genesis of what Oklahoma is today, future production will determine the economic and social character of the state.

EDWIN J. ROSSMAN

Further Reading

Oklahoma Corporation Commission, Oil and Gas Division. "Annual Reports." http://www.occeweb .com/og/annualreports.htm.

Oklahoma Department of Commerce. "Oklahoma Biofuels." http://www.okcommerce.gov/Commerce/ About/rc/Oklahoma-Biofuels.

Oklahoma Wind Power Initiative. *Community Wind Guidebook.* http://www.okcommerce.gov/Libraries/ Documents/Oklahoma_Community_Wind _Guidebook_2008072238.pdf.

U.S. Energy Information Administration. "Oklahoma." http://www.eia.doe.gov/state/state_energy_profiles .cfm?sid=OK.

See Also: Cushing Trading Hub; Investor-Owned Utilities; Oil and Petroleum; Pickens, T. Boone; Texas; United States.

Oman

Official Name: Sultanate of Oman.
Category: Geography of Energy.
Summary: Oman, located at the southeastern edge of the Arabian Peninsula and bordered by the United Arab Emirates, Saudi Arabia, Yemen, the Arabian Sea, and the Gulf of Oman, is one of the most developed and stable nations in the Arab world.

In 2000, Oman produced 60 Mtoe (million metric tons of oil equivalent), or the equivalent of 427,000 barrels of oil, three times the energy it did in 1980. Total domestic energy consumption of 8.469 Mtoe provided 3,000 metric tons equivalent per capita, an increase of 21 percent in a decade. All domestic energy came from fossil fuels oil and natural gas, with no use of coal or renewable energy. Fossil fuels (oil and natural gas) provided 9.5 million metric tons, and renewable sources and coal provided nothing. Consumption in 2009 was 115,000 barrels per day of petroleum, more than double the 52,000 barrels per day in 2000. Industrialization and a growing petrochemical sector are major reasons for this increase, as are more roadways and more vehicles.

Oil and Natural Gas

Oman currently uses its own natural gas to produce energy in gas-turbine-fired generators, which are highly efficient and can be started and stopped quickly. They are also much cheaper to build than coal plants of comparable size. The Omani plants can also combine with desalinization plants. Although Oman has additional gas reserves, they are underdeveloped because of the difficulty of accessing them. Oman imports gas from Qatar to satisfy internal demand, which is so great in summer that there is a shortage of electricity. The result is that economic development is hampered. Oman's diversification efforts rely on oil and gas as feedstocks, so diversification hinges on success in the sectors from which it seeks alternatives.

Oman has the largest oil reserves of any Middle Eastern country not a member of the Organization of Petroleum Exporting Countries (OPEC), estimated in January 2011 at 5.5 billion barrels, located primarily in the north and central offshore areas. It also has significant natural gas reserves, leading the region in exports of gas. Oman's proven natural gas reserves were estimated at 30 trillion cubic feet as of January 2011.

Oman produced 860,000 barrels of oil per day in 2010, up from 714,000 in 2007. It was the world's eighth-largest exporter of liquid natural gas (LNG) and the 19th-largest oil exporter. By OPEC standards, the output is relatively small.

The Sohar refinery, northwest of Muscat, opened in 2006 with a capability of processing 116,000 barrels per day. The other Omani refinery is the 106,000-barrel-per-day Mina al-Fahal facility, near Muscat, which refines all exported oil. The government owns 75 percent of the Oman Refineries and Petrochemicals Company, which runs the refineries, with the Oman Oil Company, which owns the rest.

The government owns 60 percent of the primary oil production company, Petroleum Development Oman, which has 90 percent of the oil reserves and operates 1,000 miles (1,609 kilometers) of pipeline. Oman produced about 82 billion cubic feet (25 bil-

lion cubic meters) of gas in 2009, the 27th-largest production in the world. However, domestic use has risen markedly, and only 37.7 billion cubic feet (11.5 billion cubic meters) were exported in 2009. The Gulf Cooperation Council is building a regional grid that will give Oman the option of importing electricity from neighbors, particularly the United Arab Emirates, which is planning to build a nuclear energy capability to come on line in 2017.

Prospects for Renewable Energy

In 2008, the Authority for Electricity Regulation received a report from a team of international consultants about the potential of renewable energy for Oman. The report indicated that Oman has one of the highest densities of solar energy of any area of the world. Technical difficulties with renewables include the unreliability of wind and the cost-effectiveness of storing solar power for use during times of darkness. If developed properly, solar power could meet all of Oman's domestic needs and provide electricity for export. Especially high densities are in the desert areas, while the southern coastal areas have the lowest densities; by world standards, however, all regions have high solar density.

Wind is a good potential source of renewable energy in the mountains north of Salalah and in the southern coastal region. Those areas record wind

Wikimedia

The rugged terrain of Oman in the mountains north of Salalah provides good potential for wind and solar power as renewable energy sources.

speeds comparable to those at inland wind turbine sites in Europe. Moreover, wind energy peaks in the summer, the period of highest electricity demand in Oman. A theoretical subsidy for renewable sources through carbon trading has not yet been put into place by the Omani government. The amount of money involved, according to the Kyoto Protocol, is $20 per ton of carbon dioxide saved. That could generate a cost reduction of the "gas price equivalent" by more than $1.20 per thousand cubic feet.

Landscape Drawbacks

Geology makes Oman's oil production costs among the highest in the region. Examination of the feasibility of enhanced oil recovery (EOR) began in 2002, and Oman now is dependent on EOR of various types, depending on geology. As the country moves increasingly to secondary and tertiary extraction methods, its costs will rise even more, but so far EOR has managed to stem and reverse the decline in production it has endured for nearly a decade. Production in 2010 was 863,000 barrels of petroleum liquids, 860,000 of that crude oil. Production has risen by better than 20 percent over three years from the 714,000 barrels the country produced in 2007. The government wants to increase gas reserves by a trillion cubic feet per year for 20 years because of growing demand for domestic consumption, exports, and reinjection. The country is short of feedstock at peak electricity generation periods, and the result is service interruptions that hamper industrialization and diversification and overall economic growth.

Although oil and gas are becoming inadequate, Oman remains slow to develop renewable energy. One problem is that wind and solar have to compete with the current fossil fuel electricity-generating infrastructure. The government provides a significant subsidy for electricity, which is sold well below the real cost of production. The subsidy is between 120 million and 250 million Omani rials (between $46 and $100 million) per year. Moreover, the situation is politically sensitive. Batinah coast energy, for example, is subsidized by 38 percent, with customers paying 16 baisa (4 cents) per kilowatt-hour for energy that really costs 25 baisa (6.25 cents) to produce. Remote areas are even more heavily subsidized, with customers paying 14 baisa (3.5 cents) for energy that costs 82 baisa (20.5 cents)—an 80 percent subsidy. A second problem slowing development of renewable energy is that the cost of generating energy is currently low, based on gas at $1.50 per million British thermal units (Btu), roughly 1,000 cubic feet of gas. The price is triple the $0.50 that the government pays to produce the gas but is well below the spot price at LNG plants, around $4.00 per million Btu and well below the European and American prices.

Eventually alternative fuels will be competitively priced, and eventually state supports for fossil fuels will become unpopular—or too expensive, as the cost of production rises. At that point, Oman will have no choice but to transition from fossil to renewable energy.

John H. Barnhill

Further Reading

Fineren, Daniel, and Simon Webb. "Factbox: Oman's Energy Export Facilities." February 28, 2011. http://uk.reuters.com/article/2011/02/28/oman-energy-idUKLDE71R1ZB20110228?pageNumber=2.

Undercover Dragon. "It's Time for Renewable Energy in Oman!" June 25, 2008. http://muscatconfidential.blogspot.com/2008/06/its-time-for-renewable-energy-in-oman.html.

U.S. Energy Information Administration. "Country Analysis Brief: Oman." http://www.eia.doe.gov/cabs/Oman/pdf.pdf.

WRI Earthtrends. "Country Profile: Oman, Energy, and Resources." http://earthtrends.wri.org/text/energy-resources/country-profile-139.html.

See Also: Bahrain; Natural Gas; Oil and Petroleum; Qatar; Renewable Energy Resources; Saudi Arabia.

Oregon

Category: Energy in the United States.
Summary: Oregon has historically relied on hydroelectric power for its energy but is working

to develop renewable resources, including solar and wind power.

Oregon is a state in the Pacific Northwest, one of the largest states in area but with a total population of only 3,831,074, making it only the 39th most densely populated. The 26th-wealthiest state by gross domestic product (GDP), it is smack in the middle, with the timber industry historically central to the state's economy but declining significantly in recent decades, offset somewhat by the rise of the Oregon technology sector and the so-called Silicon Forest of the Portland metropolitan area. The largest corporations headquartered in the state include Nike, Precision Castparts, FLIR Systems, StanCorp, and Schnitzer Steel. The dot-com bust at the beginning of the 21st century hit the state's technology sector hard, but it has become a popular site for data centers because of its cool climate and the low cost of electricity. Amazon, Google, and Facebook, for example, all operate important data centers in Oregon.

Diversification

In general, Oregon has attempted to diversify its economy and no longer relies as heavily on natural resources as its three historically primary sectors—timber, salmon, and agriculture—have done. The emphasis on the technology sector has aided Portland and brought many new residents to an area that has developed a reputation as a liberal white-collar mecca, but this industry has left the rural parts of Oregon out, and the benefits brought by the construction industry boom did not survive the collapse of that boom with the worldwide financial crisis that began in 2007. In 2010, Oregonian unemployment exceeded 10 percent; it was 14th-highest in the country.

One of the draws for the technology sector has been the low cost of energy in Oregon. Because of its longtime reliance on hydroelectric power, which provides about two-thirds of the state's energy, Oregon ranks third in renewable-energy-producing states. Coal is the second-largest energy source, either via Wisconsin or from the Boardman Coal Plant, Oregon's single coal power plant. The Boardman plant has been targeted by the Sierra Club and other organizations, which have called on the state or Portland General Electric to close it down, because as the only remaining coal plant in the state it is the single largest source of greenhouse gas emissions. Although it produces only about 15 percent of the state's electricity, it is responsible for 65 percent of its stationary sulfur dioxide (SO_2) emissions and 7 percent of its carbon dioxide (CO_2) emissions. Portland General Electric has announced a plan to close the plant in 2020.

Oregon also has significant geothermal resources, with a large geothermal district heating system in Klamath Falls. For a brief period, Oregon had a single nuclear power plant, the Trojan Nuclear Power Plant, a pressurized-water reactor plant southeast of Rainier. From its commissioning in 1976 until Portland General Electric decommissioned it in 1993, it contributed about 12 percent of the state's electricity. Environmentalists opposed it from the start, and protests in its first year of operation led to nearly 100 arrests (though no convictions). Its early decommissioning was prompted by the discovery of a steam generator tube leak only a week after Portland General Electric had spent $4.5 million to defeat ballot measures that would have forced the plant to close; documents leaked from the Nuclear Regulatory Commission revealed that some staff scientists were unconvinced that the plant could be made safe again. The decommissioning and detonation of the plant took 13 years. There have been no serious attempts since to commission a commercial nuclear power plant in the state.

Wind Power

The wind energy resources in Oregon are considerable but underdeveloped. The Oregon legislature has twice encouraged the development of these resources, first by passing a net-metering law in 1999 that encouraged consumer wind power systems as a way for households to reduce their energy bills and their carbon footprint, and later in 2007 by requiring that, by 2025, 25 percent of an electrical suppliers' electricity must be generated by renewable sources. The largest wind turbine manufacturer in the world, the Danish company Vestas, has located its U.S. headquarters in Portland.

A 2010 study by the National Renewable Energy Laboratory claimed that Oregon has the potential for more than 27,000 megawatts of onshore wind power, vastly in excess of the previous estimate of 5,000 megawatts touted by wind power advocates. Over the course of the 2000s, wind power increased considerably in the state, accounting for 7 percent of the electricity generated in Oregon at the end of the decade, although the total capacity was still less than 2,000 megawatts, significantly short of the state's full potential. Portland General Electric was awarded a contract in 2009 to develop the largest wind farm in Oregon, using more than 300 turbines across 30 square miles to generate 845 megawatts—a major leap forward for the state's wind sector, once it is completed.

Solar power has grown in the 21st century, again thanks in part to the net-metering law and the requirement placed on electricity producers. A 2007 law also required that public entities spend 1.5 percent of their construction budgets for new or renovated buildings and on-site solar technology, which helped affirm the state's commitment to developing solar power resources. Tax credits are available for both residences and businesses, and long-term fixed-rate loans are available in amounts up to $20 million for renewable energy investments.

Oregon is the first state to install solar panels on the state capitol building (although President Jimmy Carter installed solar panels on the White House roof, soon removed by his successor), in 2002. In 2008, the first solar highway in the United States was completed by the Oregon Department of Transportation, which oversaw the installation of solar panels along the interchange of Interstate 5 and Interstate 205; expansions and further solar highways are planned, including a 3-megawatt solar highway in West Linn, which will be the largest solar highway in the world.

Bill Kte'pi

Further Reading

Condon, Patrick M. *Seven Rules for Sustainable Communities*. Washington, DC: Island Press, 2010.

"Oregon." In *Encyclopedia of Global Warming and Climate Change*, edited by S. George Philander. Thousand Oaks, CA: Sage, 2008.

Oregon Department of Energy. *2011–2013 State of Oregon Energy Plan*. http://www.oregon.gov/ENERGY/docs/reports/legislature/2011/energy_plan_2011-13.pdf.

See Also: Geothermal Energy; Hydropower; Idaho; Nevada; Texas; United States; Washington State; Wind Resources.

Organization of Petroleum Exporting Countries

Category: Business of Energy.
Summary: The Organization of Petroleum Exporting Countries (OPEC) is an organization consisting of 14 oil-producing nations that are major exporters of oil.

The Organization of Petroleum Exporting Countries (OPEC), founded in 1960 at the Baghdad Conference, is an intergovernmental organization whose main goal, expressed in its statute, is to coordinate and unify the petroleum policies of its members and determine "the best means for safeguarding their interests, individually and collectively." The member countries of OPEC as of 2011 were Algeria, Angola, Ecuador, Gabon, Indonesia, Iran, Iraq, Kuwait, Libya, Nigeria, Qatar, Saudi Arabia, the United Arab Emirates, and Venezuela. OPEC is based in Vienna, Austria.

At the beginning of the 20th century, multinational oil companies began to look for oil in many countries in Africa, the Middle East, and Latin America. In some of these countries, they found important oil reserves and began to exploit them under concessions issued by host countries. At the time, the political reality of these nations was very heterogeneous: While Latin American countries had already been independent for 100

▷ *The Oil Rent*

On one hand, rent is the right of landowners to impose a payment on tenants if they want to have access to natural resources; this is called *absolute rent* by economists. On the other hand, rent can also result from the productivity difference of natural resources. According to the English economist David Ricardo (1772–1823), prices in the market are set according to the least productive lands or mines for the whole production, and for that reason more productive natural resources receive the so-called differential (or Ricardian) rent, since their production costs are lower.

The absolute rent exists because the owner demands a payment to make property available for the production process; its level depends on the owner's bargaining power vis-à-vis the tenant. Differential rents, on the other hand, are a function of productivity or location. When oil fields come into production, they can be more productive because of better natural conditions than the oil fields previously in production or because of investments that improve the natural conditions. In such cases, they need fewer resources to be exploited, therefore yielding a profit in excess. This excess is known as differential, or Ricardian, rent. This kind of rent does not influence the product's end price, because the price is determined by the lowest-quality oil field. That is, oil coming from a lower-quality oil field needs a higher price to be sold; consequently, a barrel of oil coming from a higher-quality oil field sold at a higher price receives an extra profit (or a differential rent).

In most oil countries, the appropriation of the absolute oil rent (also known as a royalty) was almost settled from the beginning of oil exploitation, because in most of them the subsoil is a public property and governments could negotiate the amount of royalty to be paid by producing companies, if the companies wanted to have access to the oil fields. However, the appropriation of differential rent is not as simple as the appropriation of absolute rent. Costs for producing oil in developing countries are lower than in the United States or the North Sea, but the United States and European markets determine prices worldwide, consequently originating a differential rent. The question of who owns this differential rent was a core issue when the Organization of Oil Exporting Countries (OPEC) was founded in 1960. At the beginning of the 1970s, oil-producing countries managed to impose their own terms and achieved the complete appropriation of differential rent.

years, Middle Eastern countries were European "protectorates," and African countries were still colonies. In none of these countries was either the local government or the population aware of the strategic importance of oil; thus, multinational oil companies could negotiate oil concessions under extremely favorable conditions.

Taking Control of Oil

The first attempts to change this situation were taken by Venezuela. During the 1940s, the Venezuelan congress passed the Law of Hydrocarbons and the first income tax law, which allowed the nation simultaneously to increase the royalties and government share in the differential rent. By 1945, royalties were at 16.67 percent of the oil production value, and the profit was split at 50–50 between the government and the companies.

In 1949, oil production in the Middle East, where both royalties and rent share was lower, for the first time surpassed that of Venezuela, and the government feared that competitive pressure would eventually harm what the country had achieved. Thus, it sent a delegation to Saudi Arabia, Egypt, Iraq, Iran, and Kuwait to give details of what Venezuela had accomplished in the previous years and encourage them to take a similar path. Afterward, but not without reluctance, the oil concessionaires established similar agreements of profit-sharing in those countries, which by 1954 was common to all other oil-producing countries of the time. Nevertheless, there was one slight but significant difference in the way oil countries achieved 50–50 profit sharing: While in Venezuela it was a sovereign decision expressed in laws enacted by its congress and was therefore exempt from any possible negotiation in the Middle Eastern countries, in the Middle East it was a result of negotiations between the companies and the governments, and any disagreement would go to international arbitration and not to the respective national courts.

In December 1958, Venezuela—still the first-oil exporting country worldwide—unilaterally decided to increase its share of profits by 64 percent. Shortly thereafter, the U.S. government imposed quotas on imported oil to protect domestic production, and the multinational oil companies decided to lower their posted prices (or, as Shukri M. Ganem puts it, "the price … oil companies [used to] transfer the crude and refined product to their affiliates"); posted prices were not necessarily equal to market prices (the realized prices), but they were the key variable when calculating profit sharing and taxes. These actions eventually prompted the Venezuelan government to seek support from Middle Eastern oil exporters, also worried about price lowering; the chance came in April 1959, when a Venezuelan delegation was invited as an observer, alongside with Iran, at the First Arab Petroleum Congress, held at Cairo, Egypt. There, in a secret meeting outside Cairo, the Venezuelan minister of mines and hydrocarbons, Juan Pablo Pérez Alfonzo, and the Saudi minister of petroleum and mineral resources, Abdullah al-Tariki, managed to persuade the other delegations to sign the first common document of the oil-producing countries in the

Photos.com

OPEC is an intergovernmental organization whose main goal is to coordinate and unify the petroleum policies of its members and determine the best means to safeguard their interests.

form of a "gentlemen's agreement"—that is, a nonbinding agreement—to set up the new Venezuelan profit sharing as a guideline for all other oil-producing countries present at the meeting. Moreover, it was proposed to create an oil consultative committee in order to discuss further oil policies, such as tax policy, buildup of domestic refining capacity, and the creation of national oil companies. This agreement was the first step toward the foundation of the Organization of Petroleum Exporting Countries (OPEC).

The Foundation of OPEC

More than one year later, after the multinational oil companies decided to lower their posted prices once again, Saudi Arabia, Iraq, Iran, Kuwait, and Venezuela (which jointly produced about 40 percent of the world's oil, exported 55 percent, and had about 70 percent of the world's proven oil reserves) met in Baghdad from September 10 to 14, 1960, and created OPEC in order to coordinate and unify their oil policies and find the best way to defend their collective and individual interests. OPEC's most immediate goal was to stabilize posted prices worldwide and at the same time find a mechanism to avoid fluctuations in state revenues of the producing countries, guarantee efficient and regular supply to the oil-consuming nations, and secure fair profits for the multinational oil companies. The creation of OPEC was an extraordinary statement of self-confidence from the founding nations—all of them developing countries, which, for the first time in their history, had united to exercise their sovereignty and defend their interests. The organization was not exactly in the position of achieving little more than common declarations, however.

After OPEC's foundation, endless disputes among Middle Eastern members prevented the newly created organization from taking any effective common action beyond freezing posted prices. Between 1960 and 1968, OPEC succeeded only in getting from the multinational companies the promise of not cutting them again, which, nevertheless, was an important achievement, since oil market prices were falling during the 1960s due to overproduction worldwide. Thus, rent sharing was slowly moving toward a 70–30 split in favor of the oil-producing nations, yet this success was sustained on the companies' promise of stabilizing posted prices and not on an active collective policy from producing countries. Moreover, since OPEC was not able to gain control over oil production, oil companies could still punish one country that was not "behaving" well with less production—which meant less income for that country—while companies could increase production anywhere else, as they controlled production almost everywhere in the world.

This was to change starting in 1969. On one hand, during the 1960s, another five oil-exporting countries joined OPEC: Qatar in 1961, Indonesia and Libya in 1962, Abu Dhabi (today, the United Arab Emirates) in 1967, and Algeria in 1969. On the other hand, after 1968, posted prices, frozen since 1960, became tax reference prices, that is, prices upon which taxes or any other payment due to the government would be based, and these were to be negotiated between the governments and the companies and not unilaterally set by the latter. Moreover, the tax reference prices were valid only for a determined period. Additionally, the member countries agreed to seek control over production by gradually raising governments' equity participation in the concessionaires' companies, that is, joint ownership with concession holders. In summary, OPEC's target was, on one hand, to increase rent sharing per barrel and, on the other, to slowly gain control over production.

Thus, in 1970, Libya—taking advantage of the closure of the Suez Canal and an ever-increasing oil demand that had drained the overproduction seen throughout the 1960s—nationalized retailers of refined products, demanding and achieving a reduction of oil production and an increase in tax reference prices of 30–40 percent, plus a 5 percent increase in the income tax rate. These measures catalyzed further actions from all other OPEC nations: During the Caracas Conference, held in December 1970, it was unilaterally decided to scrap any discount on tax reference prices, starting in January 1971; additionally, the organization decided that one month later negotiations would be held in Tehran with all multinational oil companies in order to increase income tax rates to at least 55 percent and uniformly raise tax reference prices in all member countries. OPEC's members also decided to take these actions unilaterally, without any other consultation, if negotiations did not succeed by February 15, 1971. On February 14, the oil companies gave in: The price of oil (tax reference price) increased by about 35 cents per barrel, and the minimum income tax rate to 55 percent, as OPEC had determined. The Tehran Agreement was supposed to last for five years. In April 1971, the Libyan government succeeded in negotiating, with OPEC's support, a raise in tax reference prices from $2.23 to $2.53 per barrel immediately, plus an additional annual increase of 2 cents per barrel until 1975. Furthermore, the income tax rate was also increased to 55 percent.

Oil Shocks

Between 1971 and January 1973, different member countries either nationalized several oil concessions (Algeria, Libya, Iraq, and Iran) or raised their equity participation to 25 percent in all concessions (Iraq, Kuwait, Qatar, Saudi Arabia, and the United Arab Emirates). However, during 1973, oil demand was steadily increasing, and OPEC demanded new negotiations to increase tax reference prices, which were falling behind market prices for the first time in two decades. Negotiations were scheduled for October 8 in Vienna, but two days before the round of negotiations began, the fourth Arab-Israeli War broke out. Nevertheless, negotiations proceeded as scheduled with no results; on October 16, the Persian Gulf members, five Arab countries and Iran, met in Kuwait City and unilaterally decided to raise tax reference prices by 70 percent, to $5.11 per barrel; from then on, tax reference prices would never again be negotiated with oil companies.

As for production, one day later, on October 17, some Arab countries decided to apply a selective embargo on oil exports to those countries that were supporting Israel in the war: the United States and the Netherlands and then Portugal, South Africa, and Rhodesia. They also decided to apply monthly production cutbacks of 5 percent. In the context of an increasing oil demand, the decision of selectively restricting oil supply for some countries was initially, by itself, not of sufficient scope to cause an oil shortage and could easily have been evaded by affected nations. However, the embargo prompted a series of issues in the U.S. domestic oil market that broke the balance between demand and supply: On one hand, the Nixon administration had imposed price controls on oil products in 1971, which stimulated demand further; on the other, as domestic production peaked in 1971, import quotas were abolished and the United States began to compete with other industrial nations on an international oil market where supply and demand were tightly balanced.

In December 1973, as Arab oil production cutbacks amounted to 14 percent of traded oil worldwide and market prices were soaring, OPEC decided to raise tax reference prices once more, to $11.651 per barrel—almost four times the price of two months earlier. OPEC members had definitely reached control over their own production (it is important to bear in mind that OPEC members could only set tax reference prices; market prices have been under their control, if ever, only partially). Since 1974, OPEC has been able to make some decisions regarding oil production and how, and at which price, to tax it without consulting the multinational oil companies. Between 1974 and 1978, market prices remained relatively stable, ranging between $12.21 and $13.55 per barrel. However, in February 1979, the Iranian monarchy was overthrown by a revolution; more than a year later, Iraq invaded Iran, initiating a war that was to last until 1988. Both events, the Iranian Revolution and the Iran–Iraq War, caused a combined oil production fall of 6.5 million barrels per day, or 10 percent of world oil production, which in turn led to a price increase of more than 100 percent, from $14 per barrel in 1978 to $35 per barrel in 1981.

Increasing oil prices in 1973 and 1981 gave impetus to improved energy use in industrial countries

and allowed alternative sources (coal, production from new oil fields, and renewable energies) to enter the market; it also caused a global economic recession, which reduced demand for oil. Meanwhile, oil supply outside OPEC was increasing again: Between 1980 and 1986, non-OPEC production rose by 10 million barrels per day and prices began to fall.

From Production Quotas to Price Bands

In order to keep oil prices stable, OPEC cut production and set production quotas for all members in 1982. Nevertheless, the system did not work as expected, as various members did not respect their quotas; only Saudi Arabia respected its quota, until, in 1985, it decided to increase production again from 2 million barrels per day to 5 million in a few months. By mid-1986, oil prices were less than $10 per barrel. Since these extremely low prices were undermining the state revenues of most OPEC members, in December 1986 OPEC members decided to observe their quotas more strictly and set an average price of $18 per barrel as a target for 1987. However, prices remained under that target, partly because certain members produced beyond their assigned quotas and partly because of higher non-OPEC production levels—until 1990, when the Gulf War broke out.

From 1990 to 1997, oil prices oscillated between $18 and $25 per barrel, world consumption increased by 6.2 million barrels per day, and production increased by 12 million barrels per day, 7 million of them outside OPEC. In 1998, OPEC decided to increase its production by 10 percent, just as the Asian Pacific economies were entering a recession and their oil consumption was declining for the first time since 1982. Higher OPEC production, combined with the recession in the Asian Pacific countries, caused the oil price to plummet below the $10 per barrel, as in 1986. Thus, OPEC decided to cut production again, and in 2000 it introduced a price band mechanism: Production would be regulated to maintain prices in the target range of $22 to $28. Moreover, OPEC negotiated a joint production cut with non-OPEC producers Mexico, Norway, and Russia.

From 2000 to 2005, oil prices ranged between $18 per barrel (December 2001) and $62 (September 2005), and OPEC adjusted its production accordingly to maintain prices in the target range. Nevertheless, events such as an oil strike in Venezuela (from December 2002 to February 2003), the Iraq War (beginning in 2003), and demand recovery led to a lowering in excess production capacity from 6 million barrels per day to less than 1 million barrels per day. Additionally, a weak U.S. dollar, natural catastrophes such as hurricanes, bottlenecks in U.S. refineries, and the booming Asian economies caused oil prices to skyrocket after 2005, reaching a record of $147.27 on the New York Mercantile Exchange on July 11, 2008.

In 2009, OPEC countries produced about 29 million barrels oil daily (41.6 percent of world production). However, as non-OPEC production was reaching a plateau at about 70 million barrels of oil per day and OPEC owned 80 percent of world proven oil reserves, it became clear that OPEC's importance in world oil production would only increase over the following years.

GERMÁN MASSABIÉ

Further Reading

Ghanem, Shukri M. *OPEC: The Rise and Fall of an Exclusive Club*. London: KPI, 1986.

Mommer, Bernard. *Global Oil and the Nation State*. New York: Oxford University Press, 2002.

Organization of Petroleum Exporting Countries. "OPEC Statute." http://www.opec.org/opec_web/static_files_project/media/downloads/publications/OS.pdf.

Seymour, Ian. *OPEC, Instrument of Change*. London: Macmillan, 1980.

WTRG Economics. "Oil Price History and Analysis." http://www.wtrg.com/prices.htm.

Yergin, Daniel. *The Prize: The Epic Quest for Oil, Money, and Power*. New York: Simon & Schuster, 1991.

See Also: Fossil Fuels; Oil and Gas Pipelines; Oil and Natural Gas Drilling; Oil and Petroleum; Oil Market and Price; Qatar.

Ørsted, Hans Christian

Dates: 1777–1851.
Category: Biographies.
Summary: Hans Christian Ørsted was a Danish physicist and Kantian philosopher. Ørsted contributed to the discovery of electromagnetism and research on the compressibility of fluids and gases.

Hans Christian Øersted was born August 14, 1777, the son of Soren Christian Øersted and Karen Hermansen. His father was a practicing apothecary in the small town of Rudkjobing, on the island of Langeland, Denmark. His brother Anders was born the next year. Local individuals at Rudkjobing taught Hans and Anders how to read and write (the barber's wife), arithmetic (his father), mathematics (a local surveyor), basic German (the barber), rudimentary French (the burgomaster), art (the baker), and other subjects. Hans, at age 12, began helping his father with the apothecary business, which introduced him to elementary chemistry. The boys also avidly read the books they could get, which inclined them toward literature.

In 1794, Hans and Anders went to Copenhagen University, having passed the state examination. They shared a room and many studies. In 1797, Hans completed the pharmacy degree. Hans was also drawn to literature and philosophy, winning the university prize, a gold medal, in 1797, for an essay, "On the Limits of Poetry and Prose." In 1799, he won a prize for work in metaphysics, showing the influence on his views of Friedrich Wilhelm Joseph von Schelling (1775–1854) and Immanuel Kant (1724–1804).

In 1799, Øersted received a doctorate in pharmacy with a dissertation ("The Architectonicks of Natural Metaphysics") that covered a new theory of alkalies. He was able to remain at the university as a lecturer in pharmacy. He also worked at the Loeveapotheket (Lion Apothecaries) in Copenhagen, which was owned by Professor J. G. L. Manthey (1769–1842). In 1800, Manthey began a scientific tour of Europe, leaving Øersted in charge of the Loeveapotheket and with permission to use his collection of scientific equipment, since the university was poorly equipped.

In 1800, Alessandro Volta (1745–1827) introduced the Volta pile (a set of individual Galvanic cells placed in series), which was a landmark in the shift from static electricity to electrical current and its properties. In 1801, Ørsted was also experimenting with a voltaic battery. In 1803, he discovered that acids increase the strength of a battery, as did Humphry Davy (1778–1829) at about the same time. Ørsted wanted to pursue this line of inquiry into "galvanizing," but he was only able to experiment on Sunday afternoons because of his pharmacy and teaching responsibilities. In 1801, he won the university prize money, the *stipendium cappelianum*, which gave him the funds to do a scientific tour of Europe. After Manthey returned, Ørsted left for Germany, where he found theory prevailing; and then to France, where he found an experimenter's paradise.

In 1803, Ørsted traveled home via Brussels, Leiden, Haarlem, and Amsterdam, having made numerous contacts and friends in all places. In 1802–03, he had translated into French Johann Wilhelm Ritter's (1776–1810) paper on the Ladungsaule (secondary cell), which was an electrochemical battery that he had used to decompose water into hydrogen and oxygen. The paper was then submitted for a prize to the French Institute in natural science. When Ørsted returned to Copenhagen, his application for the university chair in physics was denied. Undaunted, he continued his experiments, lecturing on physics, and publishing the results of his experiments in German and Danish. In 1806, he published an analysis of Ernst Florens Friedrich Chladni's (1756–1827) acoustic figures (tone-figures). This so impressed the university authorities that he was given the position of professor *extraordinarius* (associate) of physics in 1806. His full professorship (*ordinarius*) was not awarded until 1817.

In 1808, Ørsted published a book on mechanics. He also gave public lectures and demonstrations seeking to raise the level of scientific education and knowledge in Denmark. He taught at the military school and at times gave lectures to the general staff, with the king of Denmark occasionally in attendance. In 1809, he published a textbook on mechanical physics. Between 1813 and 1814, Ørsted took another scientific tour of Germany and France. While in Berlin, he published in German "Researches on the Identity of Chemical and Electrical Forces," which had been previously published in French. Returning to Copenhagen in 1814, Ørsted married Inger Birgitte Ballum (1789–1875), from the island of Moer, the daughter of a Lutheran minister. Their home was happy, blessed with children, and eventually visits by the young Hans Christian Andersen. In 1815, Ørsted was appointed secretary of the Royal Society of Sciences of Copenhagen. He was also knighted by King Frederick VI to the Order of Daneborg that year.

The day of Ørsted's great electromagnetic discovery came in 1820. He set up the experiment, but was unable to conduct it because he was due to lecture. After teaching, he invited those who wished to remain to see what would happen. The flowing current deflected the magnetized compass needle. After conducting more experiments, Oersted wrote a description of his discovery in Latin, *Experimenta circa effectum conflictus electrici in acum magneticam* ("Experiments about the Effects of an Electrical Conflict [Current] on the Magnetic Needle"). The findings were announced July 21, 1820, and sent to the various societies and academies of Europe. Highly praised, he was awarded the Copley Medal in London by the Royal Society, and a 3,000 gold franc prize by the Institut de France. In 1822, Ørsted published a scientific work on the compressibility of water. In 1825, he isolated aluminum. He promoted the founding of the Royal Polytechnic Institute in 1829, of which he became the director. He thereafter promoted scientific education in Denmark. He died at Copenhagen on March 9, 1851.

ANDREW J. WASKEY

Further Reading

Appleyard, Rollo. *Pioneers of Electrical Communication*. [1930]. Freeport, NY: Books for Libraries Press, 1968.

Jones, Bessie Zaban, ed. *The Golden Age of Science*. New York: Simon & Schuster, 1966.

Meyer, Kirstine B. *Scientific Life and Works of H. C. Ørsted*. Copenhagen, Denmark: A. F. Høst, 1920.

Verschuur, Gerrit L. *Hidden Attraction: The History and Mystery of Magnetism*. New York: Oxford University Press, 1993.

See Also: Compressed Air; Compressed Natural Gas; Denmark; Mayer, Julius Robert von; Radiation.

Otto, Nikolaus

Dates: 1832–1891.

Category: Biographies.

Summary: German engineer Nikolaus Otto designed the Otto-cycle engine, the first practical four-stroke, gasoline-powered internal combustion engine, which today powers most automobiles as well as other motors.

German engineer Nikolaus August Otto achieved renown in the field of engine design despite a limited education and lack of formal training. He and partner Eugen Langen founded what became Gasmotoren-Frabrik Deutz AG, known simply as Deutz AG since 1997. Working alongside fellow designers Gottlieb Daimler and Wilhelm Maybach, Otto designed the first practical four-stroke, gasoline-powered internal combustion engine, which became popularly known as the Otto, or Otto-cycle, engine. His design was a revolutionary advance in the field of energy that led to the replacement of steam power and the introduction of the automobile.

Otto was born in Holzhausen, Germany, on June 14, 1832. His father's early death and Germany's political and economic instability led him to drop out of high school and become a clerk in a Frankfurt grocery store. His brother Wilhelm soon found him work as a traveling salesman. Although he lacked formal training, he decided to pursue his interest in the mechanical design of engines. He married Anna Katherina Gossi-Rouply in 1886. Otto's letters to Anna during their courtship would later become a key source of information on his early experiments. The couple had one son, Gustav.

Otto's interest in engine design was sparked by his belief in the potential future of internal combustion engines and his desire to improve upon the two-stroke, gas-powered internal combustion engine designed by Étienne Lenoir. Otto experimented with the development of a liquid gasoline-fueled engine through models built by Cologne manufacturer Michael Zons. He introduced the first gasoline-powered engine in 1861, filing for a patent alongside his brother in that same year.

Otto was able to demonstrate that internal combustion engines fueled by liquid gasoline were more efficient than that of Lenoir, which used a system of natural gas and air. Otto's early successes gained him the support of businessman Eugen Langen in 1864, who supplied the capital and business knowledge necessary to form the N. A. Otto and Cie company to manufacture internal combustion engines based on Otto's designs. Otto and Langen's fuel-saving atmospheric gas engine received a gold medal at the 1867 Paris World Exhibition, and the partners quickly moved to patent their design.

Otto and Langen were soon overwhelmed with the demand for their new engine. Their company expanded with the addition of German businessman and investor Ludwig August Roosen-Runge in 1869, and the company came to be known as Langen, Otto, and Roosen; in 1872, it reincorporated as Gasmotoren-Frabrik Deutz AG. Otto, who had no financial stake in the company, was not a stockholder. He instead signed a long-term employment contract. New designers were also added, notably Daimler and Maybach. Otto's most significant contribution would come as the direct result of one of the projects he and Maybach undertook, the design of an internal combustion engine capable of powering road vehicles, first known as horseless carriages and later as automobiles.

Otto designed a four-stroke-cycle internal combustion engine in 1876 alongside Daimler and Maybach. He first used the engine to power a motorcycle. Otto created the model engine, while Maybach made the necessary alterations for mass production. It became popularly known as the Otto engine, or Otto-cycle engine. The Otto cycle is a four-stroke piston cycle consisting of intake, compression, power, and exhaust. The Otto-cycle engine was the first practical gasoline-powered internal combustion engine, offering an alternative to steam power and introducing an energy and transportation revolution. It incorporated the main components of the modern four-stroke engine and paved the way for Karl Benz's 1879 two-stroke engine.

Otto continued to experiment and improve on his engine design throughout the remainder of his career, culminating in his 1884 design for a practical low-voltage magnetic ignition system for the four-stroke engine. Otto also continued to pursue his interest in stratified-charge theory, or shockless combustion. He believed that a stratified-charge engine would run more smoothly and cleanly. Although this belief was never widely accepted, the Japanese automobile corporation Honda would introduce such an engine in the 1970s.

Otto would lose his German patent rights in 1886 after the emergence of a French patent granted to French engineer Alphonse Beau de Rochas for his pamphlet detailing the concept of the Otto cycle, even though Rochas had failed to pay the required publication fees and had never built a working model engine based on his design. The Otto engine was still patented in Britain, where Francis and William Crossley held the license for its production. Despite the overturning of Otto's German patents in 1886, the terms *Otto engine* and *Otto cycle* still enjoy widespread usage.

Gasmotoren-Frabrik Deutz AG emerged as a European leader in engine manufacturing through

Wikimedia

A German stamp in Nikolaus Otto's honor stating "75 Years of Otto Motor."

its licensing agreements and subsidiary arrangements with other companies. It has been known as Deutz AG since 1997. Daimler and Maybach left to form their own company in 1882, and Daimler's name lent itself to one of the first automobiles ever produced, based on the four-stroke Otto-cycle engine. Nikolaus Otto died in Cologne, Germany, on January 26, 1891 at the age of 59. His son, Gustav, followed in his footsteps, helping found the Bayerische Motoren Werke AG, commonly known as BMW. The four-stroke engine remains one of the most common of all engine designs and is found in most modern automobiles and trucks.

MARCELLA BUSH TREVINO

Further Reading

Eckermann, Erik. *World History of the Automobile.* Warrendale, PA: Society of Automotive Engineers International, 2001.

Pulkrabek, Willard W. *Engineering Fundamentals of the Internal Combustion Engine.* Upper Saddle River, NJ: Pearson Prentice Hall, 2004.

"The Steering Column. Nikolaus Otto and His Remarkable Compression Stroke." *Car and Driver* 39, no. 8 (February 1994): 7.

Van Basshuysen, Richard, and Fred Schafer. *Internal Combustion Engine Handbook: Basics, Components, Systems, and Perspectives.* Warrendale, PA: Society of Automotive Engineers International, 2004.

See Also: Automobiles; External Combustion Engine; Internal Combustion Engine.

Pakistan

Official Name: Islamic Republic of Pakistan.
Category: Geography of Energy.

Summary: The installed capacity per capita of electricity is low in Pakistan, and the electrification rate is only 59 percent, which is at the bottom end in comparison with other countries and implies that almost 40 percent of the population does not have access to electricity.

Pakistan's power system has come under increased stress because of inadequate attention over the years to augmentation and upgrading of the system and the lack of commitment to undertaking necessary institutional reforms. In 2007, there was an expected shortage of more than 1,500 megawatts of electricity in the country, and the demand and supply gap for power is expected to grow in the coming years. The system experiences high technical and commercial losses, transmission constraints, and unreliable service, and it is hampered by an irrational tariff structure. This has left a fragile cash- and investment-starved energy sector mired with governance problems. A key constraint in the energy sector is a serious lack of integrated energy planning to analyze and implement a consolidated plan to address the country's energy needs in the short, medium, and long terms.

Energy Trends

Pakistan's energy requirements are huge. Already the world's sixth-largest nation with more than 160 million people, Pakistan's population is projected to grow at an annual rate of slightly less than 2 percent and is expected to exceed 190 million by 2015. At the same time, the country's pace of economic development is accelerating: The gross domestic product (GDP) grew on average 7 percent between 2005 and 2010, and the size of the national economy and per capita incomes doubled in less than a decade.

These trends translate into rapidly escalating energy demand: Primary energy supply in Pakistan has been increasing at 5.4 percent per annum since 2004. Over the same period, electricity consumption in the country has risen at an average annual rate of 6.8 percent, natural gas by 10.4 percent, liquefied petroleum gas (LPG) by 17.6 percent, and coal by 22.8 percent. Only oil consumption leveled off temporarily because of large-scale fuel switching in the power and cement industry, displaced by natural gas and coal, respectively, and transportation, because of increased use of compressed

An electrical worker in Pakistan. Electricity use in Pakistan is growing robustly across all sectors—industry, agriculture, domestic, and commercial. The country thus faced serious peak electricity supply shortfalls, necessitating significant load shedding, or forced outages that adversely affected aconomic activity and social services.

natural gas (CNG) in vehicles. Nevertheless, oil imports in 2004–05 increased by 4.7 percent over the preceding year, at a 44.5 percent higher cost due to international crude price escalation.

Electricity use, in particular, is growing robustly across all sectors—industry, agriculture, domestic, and commercial—recording a 10.2 percent overall jump in 2005–06, with generation increase lagging behind, at 9.3 percent during the same period. The country thus faced serious peak electricity supply shortfalls, in the range of 1,500–2,000 megawatts, during the summer of 2007, necessitating significant load shedding, or forced outages that adversely affected economic activity and social services. Despite a steady improvement in recent years, systemwide transmission and distribution losses remain high, on the order of 24 to 25 percent of dispatched power.

The installed electricity generation capacity in Pakistan in 2006 was 19,505 megawatts, for which the primary energy sources utilized were natural gas (about 55 percent), hydropower (about 29 per-

cent), oil (about 13 percent), nuclear power (less than 3 percent), and coal (less than 1 percent).

The Water and Power Development Authority (WAPDA) system, including independent power producers in its service territory, represented 89 percent of the total installed capacity; the Karachi Electric Supply Corporation (KESC) system made up the remaining 11 percent. Countrywide shortfall in power supply is a daily reality, with regular peak load deficits.

Increase in Energy Consumption

Pakistan's *Medium Term Development Framework for 2005–2010* (MTDF) established a challenging program with the hope of achieving an average annual growth in gross domestic product (GDP) of 8 percent. The associated increase in energy consumption was forecast at 12 percent per annum, more than double the rate witnessed between 2000 and 2006. This would increasingly strain Pakistan's primary energy supply sources. Rising oil consumption and flat domestic production would once again trigger rapidly increasing oil imports, while declining domestic natural gas reserves—in the absence of substantial new discoveries—were expected to see the country importing gas for the first time in its history, both through pipelines and through shipments of liquefied natural gas (LNG).

Electricity consumption, slated to grow on average at 8 percent per annum to 2015 (although recent experience suggests even higher demand growth), will similarly require large increases in the capacity to generate power. Electricity imports from Iran have been in effect for several years for the Balochistan coastal grid, and larger power imports from Central Asian states to the national grid, although logistically challenging, are under active consideration. Higher energy demand and imports will also require massive investments in associated port terminals, storage facilities, refining capacity, pipeline and transmission networks, and surface fuel transport infrastructure. There is increasing recognition of the need to expedite exploitation of all indigenously available energy resources, especially the significant Thar coal deposits as well as renewable resources, such as small hydropower, wind power, solar power, and biomass energy. Simultaneously, it will be necessary to undertake large hydroelectric projects on the country's main rivers. Success in efforts to enhance Pakistan's energy supplies is subject to a host of technical, financial, institutional, and political constraints being addressed in a timely manner; to energy market reforms and a smooth privatization of state-controlled institutions,; and to the efficiency with which available supplies are harnessed and used.

About 45 percent of Pakistan's population, located mostly in rural areas, does not have access to grid-supplied electricity. The government of Pakistan had committed to electrify all remaining villages in the country by the end of 2007, either through grid extension or via alternative dispersed generation. This target was not achieved on time, but it underscores an aggressive rural electrification program that will eventually increase electricity access significantly across the country.

JOANTA GREEN

Further Reading

Hydrocarbon Development Institute of Pakistan. *Pakistan Energy Yearbook 2006*. Islamabad: Hydrocarbon Development Institute of Pakistan, 2006.

Masood, Asif. *Gap Analysis on Energy Efficiency Institutional Arrangements in Pakistan*. October 20, 2010. United Nations Economic and Social Commission for Asia and the Pacific. http://eeasia.unescap.org/PDFs/Gap-Analysis-Pakistan.pdf.

Pakistan Government, Planning Commission. *Medium Term Development Framework 2005–2010*. Islamabad: Planning Commission, 2005.

U.S. Energy Information Administration. *International Energy Outlook 2006*. Report DOE/EIA-0484(2006). Washington, DC: Energy Information Administration, 2006.

See Also: Afghanistan; Compressed Natural Gas; Electric Grids; Energy Poverty; Grid-Connected Systems; Oil Shales; Saudi Arabia; Turkmenistan.

Palau

Official Name: Republic of Palau.
Category: Geography of Energy.
Summary: Although its national energy security is threatened by its dependence on imported fossil fuels, Palau has been able to take a number of steps forward, achieving promising results in the renewable energy and energy-efficiency sectors.

The Republic of Palau is an island nation in the Pacific Ocean, some 497 miles (800 kilometers) east of the Philippines and 1,864 miles (3,000 kilometers) south of Japan. Palau consists of six island groups comprising more than 300 islands. In 2010, the population was around 20,800 people, of which as many as 97 percent had access to electricity.

However, Palau completely relies on fossil fuels for its energy consumption, since less than 0.1 percent of the country's energy use comes from local renewable energy (RE) sources. As a consequence, the Palau government launched the development of a National Energy Policy (NEP), submitted for endorsement in October 2009, covering both RE and the energy efficiency (EE) and conservation sectors, in order to relieve the economy from its fuel dependency. Funded by the European Union's Support to the Energy Sector in Five ACP (African, Caribbean, and Pacific Island) Countries (REP-5) program, the draft NEP also covers energy sector management, fossil fuel management, and electric power. The targets set for 2020 are to achieve a 20 percent electricity generation from RE, as well as to meet a 30 percent reduction in overall energy consumption.

Solar Photovoltaic Systems

The National Development Bank of Palau (NDBP) constitutes a major actor in both the RE and EE fields. NDBP launched an innovative loan program in 2010, directed at households and businesses, to install solar photovoltaic (PV) systems in order to minimize the impact of rising tariffs on their future energy costs. By providing loans to install solar PV panels as a source of electricity as well as solar water heating (SWH) systems, the NDBP's Renewable Energy Fund Window (REFW) provides home and business owners the opportunity to reduce their dependency on power generation from the Palau Public Utility Corporation (PPUC). It also allows home owners living off the grid to have their own independent sources of energy. The contribution of power generated by the solar PV arrays is small, but through a net-metering arrangement with PPUC it is demonstrating the value of such energy sources.

This solar PV program builds on experience that NDBP has gained in implementing an EE project for households, funded by the International Union for Conservation of Nature (IUCN). The Energy Efficiency Subsidy Program (EESP), launched in January 2009, has already helped numerous home owners improve the quality and value of their homes while reducing their demand for electricity. It is expected that the total electricity consumption will be lowered by an estimated 15 percent in new homes and that a local market

for EE products and services will be developed. The next step would then be to expand those EE measures in existing homes. In early May 2010, NDBP was awarded a plaque of merit by the Association of Development Financing Institutions in Asia and the Pacific (ADFIAP), based on the innovative financing and environmental value of the EESP project.

Palau's energy security was put under further strain in 2007 upon completion of a new capitol building. Dubbed the Little White House, it consumed 234,000 kilowatt-hours of electricity in January 2007, costing $78,000. An energy audit was therefore conducted, recommending a series of behavioral and equipment changes and leading to the EE Action Plan (EEAP) in 2008. Drafted by the Energy Office with funding from REP-5, it contains short- and medium-term EE actions to be implemented in government buildings. Additionally, the REP-5 program funded a 100-kilowatt grid-connected solar-PV system installed at the capitol building at the end of 2008. It was expected to produce 120,000 kilowatt-hours per annum, which translated into electricity savings of $40,000 per year.

Thanks to these various measures, the capitol's energy consumption was lowered to 61,200 kilowatt-hours in May 2010. Nevertheless, the building's electricity bills still constituted a significant part of the national budget, threatening the country's economic and energy stability. This example underlines the energy security implications that a decision made at the highest level can have.

Although Palau is in the early stages of implementing RE and EE projects, there has been limited domestic capacity to ensure their effective execution. This is being addressed through external support for NDBP's projects; local technical skills are being upgraded, small contractors trained and supported, and the importation and sale of preapproved equipment undertaken by local retailers. Attention is also being focused on removing subsidies of the electricity tariffs, in order to reflect the true cost of energy in the country. While this is politically unpopular, it is working to encourage the uptake of renewable alternatives, such as solar PV, SWH, and the general improvement in the energy efficiency of homes and small commercial businesses. The pressure of energy costs on hotels, particularly for water heating, has seen many install large SWH arrays. However, there still remains the need for the government to provide clear and consistent policies to drive an effective national energy conservation strategy.

DAPHNÉ BARBOTTE
MAAIKE GÖBEL
EVA OBERENDER

Further Reading

Palau Energy Office. *Palau Draft National Energy Policy*. 2009. http://www.rep5.eu/files/pages/file/Palau/Energy%20Policy%20Final%20Draft.pdf.

REP-5: Support to the Energy Sector in Five ACP Pacific Island Countries. "Palau." http://www.rep5.eu/Project_Countries/Palau.

Republic of Palau. "Energy Efficiency Action Plan." February 2008. http://www.rep5.eu/files/pages/file/Palau/Palau%20Energy%20Efficiency%20Action%20Plan.pdf.

Secretariat of the Pacific Regional Environment Programme. *Pacific Regional Energy Assessment 2004*. Vol. 9, *Palau National Report*. http://www.sprep.org/climate_change/documents/Vol9-PalauNationalReport_000.pdf.

See Also: Alternative Energy; Climate Change; Energy Poverty; International Renewable Energy Agency; Micronesia; Photovoltaics; Renewable Energy Resources.

Palestine

Official Name: Palestinian territories (generic for Palestinian-occupied West Bank and Gaza Strip); Occupied Palestinian Territories (used by the United Nations), State of Palestine (proclaimed in exile, 1988).
Category: Geography of Energy.
Summary: Energy is a key factor for the economic growth of Palestine and could increase tensions with neighboring countries, especially Israel, on which the Palestinian National Authority is wholly dependent for its energy needs.

Unlike several countries in the Middle East, Palestine has been unable to exploit any local natural resources to produce energy, and the region's increasing energy demands, especially in the electricity sector, have to be met with a growing dependence on costly fossil fuels. As a developing nation, Palestine needs energy to sustain its economic growth, and the supply of energy at sensible prices is one of the least addressed reasons of conflict with Israel. Conversely, an effective peace process should take this matter into serious account. As Palestine has one of the fastest-growing populations in the world, the Palestinian National Authority has predicted that the West Bank and the Gaza Strip will witness a fourfold increase in electricity demands by 2020, along with a significant rise in demand for motor fuel and liquefied petroleum gas (LPG). Nevertheless, Palestinians remain among the most energy-impoverished populations in the world. The average electricity consumption is 854 kilowatt-hours per capita per year, a figure that makes Palestine the 127th country in the world, just after Egypt. In the Gaza Strip, this average decreases to 654 kilowatt-hours per capita per year, which ranks at 136th in the world. The total installed electric generation capacity is 140 megawatts.

The Gaza Strip Power Plant was another important project. The only electric power plant on Palestinian ground, the plant was commenced in 1999, when the Palestinian National Authority formed a partnership with the Greek company CCC and Enron. A key goal of the plant was to provide energy for the process of water desalinization, a particularly critical issue for the inhabitants of the Gaza Strip. The construction of the plant, however, ran into several obstacles, including Enron's bankruptcy and the violent events linked to the second Intifada. The plant started to be commercially operative in 2004. While its rated output is estimated at 140 megawatts, the plant is currently working at about half this capacity, for lack of an adequate transmission infrastructure. In addition, although the plant was conceived

▷ *Independence Issues*

Although most Palestinian people have access to electricity, the region is constrained by its dependence on Israel for energy. Not only does Israel supply almost all of Palestine's energy; it also determines the condition and quantity of the energy imported. Therefore, the Palestinian National Authority is forced to comply with Israeli regulations and is not allowed to buy electricity and petroleum products from other countries. This means that Israel can impose noncompetitive prices for its exports and threaten to suspend power supplies to influence Palestinian political decisions.

This complete reliance could be broken by the development of the Gaza gas field. Discovered in 1999, the field is said to contain at least 1.4 trillion cubic feet of gas. Further explorations of offshore drilling in Palestinian waters could lead to more discoveries of natural gas reserves. However, the commercial development of the Gaza field has been repeatedly halted and, in spite of its location on Palestinian land, the Israeli government has prohibited the construction of a pipeline that would carry the gas ashore to then be sold to Israeli power plants. This incident shows how the energy independence of Palestine is closely linked to its political independence.

is highly exposed to solar radiation, and solar power is already used domestically for water heating. However, the high costs involved in the production of photovoltaic energy have always been considered a great obstacle to the full commercial development of this renewable source. As oil prices rise and reducing the country's reliance on Israel is becoming a priority, the commercial feasibility of renewable energy has been reconsidered as a possible solution for Palestinian energy needs.

LUCA PRONO

Further Reading

Bryce, Robert. "Oil, Peace, and Palestine: Energy Key to Holy Land's Past, Future." *World Energy Monthly Review* 1, no. 4 (July 2005).

Ibrik, Imad. "Energy Profile and the Potential of Renewable Energy Sources in Palestine." In *Renewable Energy in the Middle East: Enhancing Security Through Regional Cooperation*, edited by Michael Mason and Amit More. New York: Springer, 2009.

Shabbaneh, R., and A. Hasan. "Wind Energy Potential in Palestine." *Renewable Energy* 11, no. 4 (1997).

Smith, Dan. *The State of the Middle East: An Atlas of Conflict and Resolution*. Berkeley: University of California Press, 2008.

See Also: Aramco; History of Energy: Ancient Egypt; Israel; Natural Gas; Photovoltaics; Saudi Arabia; Solar Thermal Systems.

to exploit gas, the Palestinians have so far been unable to use the Gaza gas field to operate the plant. The desalinization programs, therefore, remain largely unrealized.

Other possible strategies to reduce Palestinian reliance on Israeli energy supply point to a reduction in wasteful energy consumption through the modernization of industries and campaigns for a more careful domestic use of electricity. In addition, the Palestinian National Authority is considering the use of renewable energy resources, such as solar thermal and solar photovoltaic. The region

Panama

Official Name: Republic of Panama.
Category: Geography of Energy.
Summary: Panama is largely dependent on oil imports, although hydroelectricity has become a popular alternative.

The primary source of energy in Panama is oil, making up to 68 percent of the country's energy portfolio. The majority of the country's energy is imported, including virtually all its oil. One of the largest commodities (in tonnage) shipped through the Panama Canal is petroleum. The country has one oil refinery, near the port city of Colón. The country does not produce or consume natural gas.

Demand

Biomass accounted for more than 50 percent of energy consumption in Panama through the 1950s. This figure rapidly began to decline in response to fears associated with deforestation. However, even today, approximately a quarter of Panamanian homes still lack connection to the national power grid, according to the National Institute of Statistics and the Census. Overall energy demand doubled in percentage growth from 2008 to 2009. The increase in demand is largely related to growth in population and gross domestic product (GDP). With the rising demand, new energy projects and investments are actively being encouraged.

Hydroelectricity and Other Renewables

The country slowly began to substitute some of its fossil fuel use with hydroelectric power generation in the 1970s and has continued to do so ever since. The majority of electricity generation comes from hydroelectric power plants and thermal electric power plants. Much of the electricity that is generated is provided by the Panama Canal. The Panama Canal Authority (ACP) operates a thermoelectric plant and two hydroelectric plants. The ACP has an energy division to oversee the reliability and pricing of the canal's power supply.

Solar and geothermal energy sources have not been largely exploited, but approximately 12 percent of the energy portfolio comes from other renewable sources, namely sugarcane and hydropower. Ethanol production based on sugarcane is becoming more prevalent, and other alternatives, such as palm oil, are showing promise. In 2010, Panama's Energy and Environmental Engineering Corporation announced the construction of two wind farms; plans were to begin construction in 2012 and finish by 2013. While geothermal energy does not currently make up part of the power generation portfolio, it is believed to have enormous potential.

Government Reforms

In 1998, the Panamanian government separated generation, distribution, and transmission assets from the state-owned Hydraulic Resources and Electricity Institute (IRHE) and privatized several IRHE power plants. The state still kept its monopoly on energy transmission. The privatization was part of broader sectoral reforms. The state-owned Electric Transmission Service (ETESA) still has the primary responsibility for energy transmission. The reforms also resulted in the creation of the Energy Policy Commission (COPE) in 1997. COPE was established to guide energy policy. COPE shares this authority with the National Environmental Authority (ANAM), which is charged with examining the impact of policies on the environment. In 2012, the National Secretary of Energy was created, which set an energy strategy that included improved access to energy, taking advantage of the country's renewable energy potential, and improved energy efficiency.

Energy Transport

The Central American Electrical Interconnection System (SIEPAC) has a mission of interconnecting the electric grid of Central America. The electric transmission line system runs from Panama to Guatemala. The concept of SIEPAC was first brought forth in 1987, with studies subsequently demonstrating the potential benefits and opportunities that such a network would provide. By 1995, planning for the SIEPAC project had begun. The Inter-American Development Bank provided a large part of the initial funding. The Spanish power company Endesa and the Central American Bank for Economic Integration (CBEI) also provided monetary support, with Central American countries providing in-kind contributions, such as existing facilities and infrastructure. Panama will have a 94-mile (151-kilometer) segment of the system, the shortest segment of the planned system.

The Trans-Panama Pipeline is an 81-mile (130-kilometer) oil pipeline built in 1982 to facilitate oil transport, as many crude oil carriers were too large to cross the Panama Canal. The pipeline was originally built to transport crude oil shipments from Alaska to refineries in the Caribbean and the U.S. Gulf Coast. Oil companies, however, began shipping Alaskan crude oil using other mechanisms, and the pipeline was shut down in 1996.

The pipeline was reopened in 2003 for the transport of Ecuadorian crude oil to the U.S. Gulf Coast. In 2005, Venezuela began talks regarding the reversal of the pipeline for shipments to China. British Petroleum (BP) signed an agreement in 2008, after which the pipeline was modernized and reversed. Construction on the Trans-Caribbean Pipeline began in 2006 and was completed in 2007. The first stage of the Trans-Caribbean Pipeline transports gas from Colombia to Venezuela. The second stage is expected to be completed in 2012, which will reverse the flow of natural gas from Venezuela to Colombia and will extend it to Panama.

SARAH ABDELRAHIM

Further Reading

Economic Commission for Latin America and the Caribbean (ECLAC). "Renewable Energy Sources in Latin America and the Caribbean: Situation and Policy Proposals." http://www.eclac.org/publicaciones/xml/9/14839/Lc12132i.pdf.

Global Energy Network Institute. "Renewable Energy Potential of Latin America." http://www.geni.org/globalenergy/research/renewable-energy-potential-of-latin-america/Potential%20of%20Renewables%20in%20latin%20America-edited-12-16%20_Letter_.pdf.

Martin, Jeremy. "Central America Electric Integration and the SIEPAC Project: From a Fragmented Market Toward a New Reality." Center for Hemispheric Policy, University of Miami, May 6, 2010. https://www6.miami.edu/hemispheric-policy/Martin_Central_America_Electric_Int.pdf.

U.S. Energy Information Administration. "Country Analysis Brief: Panama." http://www.eia.gov/countries/country-data.cfm?fips=PM.

See Also: Biomass Energy; Guatemala; Hydropower; Natural Gas; Nicaragua; Oil and Gas Pipelines; Oil and Petroleum; Wind Resources.

Papua New Guinea

Official Name: Independent State of Papua New Guinea.
Category: Geography of Energy.
Summary: Papua New Guinea is highly dependent on fossil fuels for its energy production and consumption. Discoveries of petroleum and natural gas reserves in the 1990s boosted the country's economy.

Papua New Guinea's growth of gross domestic product (GDP) is driven mainly by mineral and petroleum mining. The country initiated its oil and gas production in 1991 at Kutubu oil fields. Realizing how important those resources were for the economic growth of the country, the government pushed for increased exports, which accounted for 79 percent in 2001. The institutional body responsible for energy policies and plans is the Energy Division of the Department of Petroleum and Energy (DPE). PNG Power is the national electricity utility, responsible for most of the power sector planning, from production to transmission.

Energy in the country is predominantly used for electricity generation and transportation, and the national energy mix is dominated by fossil fuel sources consisting of crude oil and natural gas, which are responsible for approximately 65 percent of the energy production in the country. The country also has significant renewable energy resources, largely unexploited, in the form of geothermal and biomass, as well as well-developed hydropower. Renewable energy sources, mainly in the form of hydropower, form around 35 percent of total electricity production.

The energy production from fossil fuels for 2009 came to 2.3 terawatt-hours; however, this did not meet consumption, which was 3.2 terawatt-hours. As Papua New Guinea has developed economically, its electricity consumption has rapidly increased, mainly because of a shift in consumption from primarily industrial to both industrial and household use. In 2001, estimates were that only around 10 percent of the population was electrified. In the same year, industry was responsible for around 60 percent of total energy consumption, transport for 17 percent, and the residential sector for 23 percent. By 2009, per capita consumption was 530 kilowatt-hours.

Nonrenewable Energy

Papua New Guinea is heavily dependent on fossil fuels. Oil supply is estimated to be declining; in 2010, for example, it was down by 30 percent from 2006 levels. At the same time, consumption is increasing. With reserves of 0.088 billion barrels of crude oil left (2010, national consumption will have to be satisfied with costly oil imports.

Natural gas is also playing an important role in the country, but mainly in exports to Australia through the pipeline to northern Queensland. The first gas field, the Pandora field, was discovered in 1988, and in 1992 another field was discovered, confirming the presence of more gas reserves. Gas reserves were estimated to be 8 trillion cubic feet as of 2011.

Renewable Energy Resources

Papua New Guinea has a great potential for renewable energy. However, these resources are often located in remote areas, making them difficult to exploit. Moreover, there is little awareness among the population of renewable resources and their importance, and therefore they are not in high demand. The most commonly exploited renewable energy sources in the country are hydropower, which forms 69.3 percent of the renewable electricity generation mix, followed by geothermal energy, at 28.6 percent. Biomass is underexploited, generating only 2.1 percent to the mix.

Hydropower, however, has ceased its development in recent years, with a growth of only 0.6 percent since 1999; its installed capacity in 2009 came to 867 gigawatt-hours, a quarter of total electricity production. It has been estimated, however, that large-scale hydropower has a high technical potential of roughly 14,000 megawatts and 122,600 gigawatt-hours per year. In addition to large-scale hydropower, about 100 potential small hydropower plants have been assessed.

The other renewable sources on the island include geothermal energy, which was discovered in 2007 at New Ireland Island and has rap-

idly developed, reaching 358 gigawatt-hours of installed capacity, or 10.1 percent of total electricity generation.

Until mid-1980, Papua New Guinea was a leader in the region for biomass energy. The country still has dense forests, and its biomass is underexploited in comparison with other renewable sources. Papua New Guinea is also rich in plant oils, such as palm and coconut oil, which can be used as fuel and have been produced mainly for export, which has offered the greatest economic returns. Biomass is typically used for heating and cooking, but some of it is converted to electricity; 26 gigawatt-hours of electricity was generated from biomass in 2009.

As Papua New Guinea continues to face the potential threats posed by the depletion of fossil fuel reserves and high-priced imported fuels, renewables are gaining greater attention.

LILI ENCHEVA ILIEVA

Further Reading

Energiesrenouvelables.org. "Renewable Origin Electricity Production: Papua New Guinea, 2010." http://www.energies-renouvelables.org/observ-er/html/inventaire/pdf/12e-inventaire-Chap03-3.13.3-Papouasie.pdf.

Secretariat of the Pacific Regional Environment Programme. *Pacific Regional Energy Assessment 2004.* Vol. 10, *Papua New Guinea National Report.* http://www.sprep.org/climate_change/documents/Vol10-PapuaNewGuineaNationalReport_000.pdf.

U.S. Energy Information Administration. "Papua New Guinea." http://205.254.135.7/countries/country-data.cfm?fips=PP.

See Also: Australia; Oil and Petroleum; Solomon Islands.

Paraguay

Official Name: Republic of Paraguay.
Category: Geography of Energy.

Summary: Paraguay is a unique case in the world of energy in two ways: First, total primary energy supply comes completely from renewable sources (hydropower and biomass); second, most generated electricity is not domestically consumed but is exported to the neighboring countries of Argentina and Brazil.

Situated in the heart of South America, at the confluence of large, mighty rivers, Paraguay has enormous hydroelectric potential. The country has no coal, oil, or natural gas reserves, though there are signs of modest oil and natural gas reserves in the region bordering with Bolivia and Argentina.

Throughout the 19th and most of the 20th centuries, Paraguay's main primary energy source was biomass in the form of firewood; that biomass still accounted for 64 percent of total energy consumption in the mid-1980s. Compared to its neighbors, electrification began in Paraguay relatively late. In 1910, the first power plant was installed in Asunción, the country's capital city, to supply electricity for public illumination and streetcars. Power supply to industries and households began a few years later through concessions granted to private investors. In 1947, the Paraguayan government decreed the nationalization of the main power utility, the Compañía Americana de Luz y Tracción (CALT), until then in hands of Swiss and Argentinean investors; one year later, the Administración Nacional de Energía (ANDE) was created as an independent state entity with its own legal identity. In 1964, ANDE was reorganized as an autonomous, decentralized public utility, which has monopolized the Paraguayan electricity sector since then.

Serious efforts at electrification beyond major cities began during the 1960s. The first major hydroelectric power plant in Paraguay, the 190-megawatt Aracay plant, was put in service in 1969. The Aracay plant allowed the country to break its dependence on oil for power generation; for almost 15 years, it was Paraguay's main power supply. In 1977, the 103-megawatt Yguazú hydroelectric plant entered into service, increasing hydro-generation capacity by a third.

However, the most important hydroelectric project in Paraguay is the 14-gigawatts Itaupú power plant on the Paraná River, which is on the border between Brazil and Paraguay. The Itaupu Hydroelectric Power Plant is operated by Itaupu Binacional, a joint consortium between the Paraguayan ANDE and the Brazilian Furnas Centrais Elétricas S.A. Negotiations between both countries for exploiting the enormous hydroelectric potential of the Paraná River began in the 1960s. In 1970, feasibility studies were conducted, and construction began three years later. Operations started on May 5, 1984, with three generation units; additional units were installed over the next seven years, bringing the total to 18 with a total installed capacity of 12.6 gigawatts by 1991. At that point, Itaupu surpassed the Venezuelan 10-gigawatts Guri Power Plant as the world's largest power plant.

In 2006 and 2007, two additional units were put in operation at Itaupu, increasing installed capacity to 14 gigawatts. In 2006, Itaupu was displaced as the largest power dam in the world, based on installed capacity, by China's Three Gorges Power Plant, although Itaipu remained the first in terms

Wikimedia

Negotiations between Brazil and Paraguay for exploiting the enormous hydroelectric potential of the Paraná River began in the 1960s

of electricity-generating power; it generated 91,652 gigawatt-hours in 2009. The same year, a storm caused damage to three transmission lines that transported electricity from Itaupu to consumption centers, causing a blackout in 10 Brazilian states and Paraguay. At present, Itaupu's generated electricity covers more than 90 percent of electricity consumption in Paraguay and about 20 percent of Brazilian electricity consumption.

Downstream from Itaupu, also at the Paraná River, is the Paraguayan-Argentinean Yacyretá Power Plant, with an installed capacity of 3.2 gigawatts. In 1973, Argentina and Paraguay signed an agreement for jointly completing the project; building began in 1983 and commercial operations in 1998. Yacyretá is operated by the Entidad Binacional Yacyretá (EBY), a consortium equally owned by ANDE and the Argentinean Energéticos Binacionales S.A, or EBISA (formerly Agua y Energía Eléctrica). The Yacyretá Dam has been plagued by corruption scandals, and several EBY employees have been convicted for corruption; the company itself has been taken to the Inter-American Court of Human Rights for violation of the human rights of settlers from the region where the power plant is located.

There are plans to build another Argentinean-Paraguayan hydroelectric power plant, situated between Itaupu and Yacyretá, the Corpus Christi Power Plant. Corpus Christi would have an installed capacity of 2,880 megawatts; however, the plan has encountered strong resistance among inhabitants of the region where the plant would be built, and its construction has been delayed for two decades.

In 2008, total generated electricity in Paraguay amounted to 55,454 gigawatt-hours. Domestic demand amounted to 9,162 gigawatt-hours. The difference between generated and consumed electricity, 46,292 gigawatt-hours or 83 percent of generated power, was exported to Argentina and Brazil. Domestic primary energy supply in Paraguay is provided only by renewable sources: hydroelectricity, 70 percent, and biomass (firewood, farm and forest waste, and other biomass), 30 percent. On the other hand, final energy consumption is up to 40 percent satisfied by imported oil derivatives (diesel, motor gasoline, jet fuel, and fuel oil), used almost exclusively for transport, and liquefied gas; electricity, charcoal, and alcohol account for the other 60 percent. Import of all fossil fuels and its distribution in the retail market are exclusively in the hands of the state-owned Petróleos Paraguayos (PETROPAR). Since 1989, PETROPAR has distilled ethanol from sugarcane, which since 2005 has gained importance in the domestic market as a result of higher oil prices. Since 2005, a law has regulated the introduction of biofuels such as ethanol and biodiesel.

The government is also studying the introduction of other renewable energy sources for rural electrification, as 40 percent of the Paraguayan population lives in rural areas. These sources would mainly involve minihydroelectric plants, solar photovoltaics, and wind energy.

GERMÁN MASSABIÉ

Further Reading

CNN. "Dam Failure Triggers Huge Blackout in Brazil." http://edition.cnn.com/2009/WORLD/americas/11/10/brazil.blackout/index.html.

Itaupu Binacional. "The World's Largest Generator of Renewable Clean Energy." http://www.itaipu.gov.py/en.

U.S. Energy Information Administration. "Country Analysis Brief: Paraguay." http://www.eia.gov/countries/country-data.cfm?fips=PA.

World Bank. "Paraguay: Issues and Options in the Energy Sector." Report 5145-PA. October 1984. http://www-wds.worldbank.org/external/default/WDSContentServer/WDSP/IB/1999/09/17/000009265_3970904163241/Rendered/PDF/multi_page.pdf.

See Also: Argentina; Bolivia; Brazil; Hydropower.

Parsons, Charles

Dates: 1854–1931.
Category: Biographies.
Summary: English mechanical engineer Charles Algernon Parsons invented the steam turbine

in 1884, a breakthrough in marine engineering because it made high-speed ocean liners possible. This turbine was later used to generate electricity aimed at driving an alternator.

Born on June 13, 1854, at 13 Connaught Place, Hyde Park, London, Charles Algernon Parsons was the youngest of the six sons of the famous astronomer and president of the Royal Society William Parsons, the third earl of Rosse, who was known for his construction of the great 72-inch (6-foot) reflecting telescope. Mary, countess of Rosse, was his mother, a pioneering photographer. Parsons was married to Katherine Bethell in 1883.

Parsons was intellectually precocious from a young age, often fueled by his father's encouragement to innovate and develop practical skills. In his childhood, Parsons received his tuition from the famous astronomer Sir Robert Hall. In 1871, he began his career at Trinity College, Dublin, and after graduation he attended St. John's College at the University of Cambridge, studying mathematics as well as applied mechanics under Professor James Stuart. In 1877, Parsons became an apprentice at the Newcastle-upon-Tyne engineering firm of W. G. Armstrong, a move that began his long and outstanding association with the north of England. In 1881, he met Sir James Kitson, the famous locomotive manufacturer, at Leeds, where Parsons worked on rocket-powered torpedoes. However, after two years he returned to Newcastle to join the Gateshead firm of Clarke Chapman and Company as a junior partner in the department of electrical equipment development.

During that time, it was difficult to generate large amounts of power. Moreover, existent steam engines were very large and annoyingly noisy. For instance, the power station in Manchester had to be closed down as a result of increasing objections to noise pollution. Parsons understood that he needed an ingenious solution to this problem, the need for a rotating machine or turbine to transform the power of steam directly into electricity. For this, he founded the firm C. A. Parsons and Company and developed a multistage reaction turbine in 1884 for driving an electrical generator. In an experiment, Parsons placed multiple blades

▷ Around the World With the Parsons Turbine

Modern steam and nuclear power plants still use multistage turbines to turn on their generators. In 1997, Jock Wishart of Thames Rowing Club, along with the boat designer Nigel Irens, redesigned Charles Parsons's *Turbina* with the application of technology and materials not available in Parsons's time and adapted it to their ship to form the basis of the 115-foot stabilized monohull *Cable and Wireless Adventurer*, the first powered 21st-century vessel, when Wishart and his team made an attempt to circumnavigate the living planet in fewer than 80 days. The journey remains a success story in the history of British navigation and marine engineering. It was also the first boat trip around the world to beat the 80-day target of Jules Verne's classic novel.

on a single shaft (rotor) and was successful in driving high-velocity steam through a fixed casing and vanes (stator), through which he achieved rotor speeds in excess of 15,000 revolutions per minute. In his 1911 Rede lecture, Parsons described how he took financial risks, spending £24,000 to develop a compound steam turbine that was designed to be more reliable and to perform better than the existing steam turbine, developed by Gustav de Laval.

Revolutionizing an Era

In 1885, Parsons embarked on the design of complementary dynamos, commencing with a unipolar machine to be driven directly by his turbines. Gradually, Parsons's process of inexpensive electricity generation revolutionized the era, not only for electricity generation on land but also for marine transport and naval warfare. By the year 1888, 200 combined sets of steam turbine and turboelectric generators were in use in marine service. In 1895, radial flow generators were installed in Cambridge Power Station, which was then used to power the first electric streetlights in the city of Cambridge. In addition, Parsons's 100-foot, 44-ton demonstration vessel, the *Turbina*, which attained a speed of more than 34 knots, was labeled as the fastest vessel when it successfully gatecrashed Queen Victoria's 1897 Diamond Jubilee Naval Review of the Fleet at Spithead. This development led to a revolution in ship propulsion: A number of ships adopted Parsons's turbine engines, including the naval ships *Viper* and *Cobra* (1899), the passenger ships *Clyde Steamer* and TS *King Edward* (1901) and *Mauretania* (1906), the transatlantic liners RMS *Victorian* and *Virginian* (1905), and the battleship HMS *Dreadnought* (1906). Today, *Turbina* is housed at the Discovery Museum in Newcastle-upon-Tyne.

Parsons was a multitasking experimentalist. Altogether, he held more than 300 patents. Some of his other important inventions include a powered model helicopter; a monoplane and a three-wheeled go-cart, which he used to entertain his children; and the Auxetophone, a mechanical amplifier for stringed musical instruments. In addition, Parsons designed searchlights. He also aimed at transforming the British optical industry and therefore designed optical instruments and developed methods for the production of optical glasses. In 1925, Parsons acquired and revitalized the Grubb Telescope Company, which produced large telescopes for the world's great observatories; there, he designed a 74-inch reflector for Toronto, the longest instrument ever made in Europe, which also surpassed his father's record. At the same time, however—despite a robust and strenuous attempt—he failed to synthesize diamonds using high pressures and temperatures. Nevertheless, in recognition of his other great achievements, in June 1898, Parsons was elected as Fellow of the Royal Society. He was knighted in 1911, and in 1927 he was made a member of the Order of Merit. He received numerous other honors as well—including the Rumford Medal (1902) and the Copley Medal (1928)—and he delivered the Bakerian Lecture of 1918.

Parsons Turbine Company is still in operation in the Heaton area of Newcastle and is now part of Siemens, a German company. Parsons had two children: a son and a daughter. His son was killed during World War I, but his daughter, Rachel, became a naval architect. Parsons died aboard a ship at Kingston, Jamaica, on February 11, 1931.

RITUPARNA BHATTACHARYYA

Further Reading

Clarke, J. F. *An Almost Unknown Great Man: Charles Parsons and the Significance of the Patents of 1884.* Newcastle upon Tyne: Newcastle upon Tyne Polytechnic, 1984.

Institute of Mechanical Engineers. "Biographies: Charles Parsons." http://heritage.imeche.org/mecheng/Parsons.

Parsons, C. A. *The Steam Turbine. The Rede Lecture.* Cambridge: Cambridge University Press, 1911. http://www.history.rochester.edu/steam/parsons/.

Parsons, R. H. *The Steam Turbine and Other Inventions of Sir Charles Parsons, O.M.* London: Longmans, Green, 1948. http://www.houseofdavid.ca/parsons.htm.

Scaife, Garrett. *From Galaxies to Turbines: Science, Technology, and the Parsons Family.* Philadelphia: Institute of Physics, 2000.

U.S. Patent Office. "Charles Algernon Parsons, of Ryton, England: Steam Turbine." October 29, 1895. http://www.google.co.uk/patents?hl=en&lr=&vid=USPAT549010&id=VEhCAAAAEBAJ&oi=fnd&dq=Charles+Algernon+Parsons&printsec=abstract#v=onepage&q&f=false.

See Also: Electricity; Rotational Energy; Ships.

Peat

Category: Energy Resources.
Summary: Peat has a long history as an energy resource, although its use has declined in modern times. Peat fuel is cheaper to produce and has a lower environmental impact than other

fossil fuels, but has lower burning capacity and produces more smoke.

Peat is a soft, wood-like organic material formed from the long-term accumulation of layers of decaying plant matter in an oxygen-deprived environment. The types of peat fuel are sod peat, milled peat, and peat briquettes. Peat also contains various minerals and over 90 percent water. Peat deposits are found throughout the world in both temperate and tropical climates. According to the International Peat Society, countries with notable peatlands are: Argentina, Belarus, Brazil, Burundi, Canada, China, Denmark, Estonia, Finland, Germany, Greece, Iceland, Indonesia, Italy, Latvia, Lithuania, Norway, Poland, Romania, the Russian Federation, Sweden, Ukraine, the United Kingdom, and the United States. A variety of local conditions must be considered in determining the potential of peat as an energy source. Europe is one of the leading regions in terms of peat usage as an energy source.

The history of peat as an energy resource dates back thousands of years, most notably in Europe's

Briquettes extracted from a natural peat moor in Frasne, France. In the right conditions, peat is formed by compressed and decaying marshland trees, grass, and insect and animal matter.

temperate regions. Peat, like wood, was primarily used for domestic cooking and heating. Peat was later utilized to fuel electric generation power plants. Mechanization of peat production was introduced in the mid-19th century, although hand cutting remains in local areas. Fossil fuels such as coal, natural gas, and oil became more economical by the late 19th century and had largely eclipsed peat, although its use as fuel continued. International Peat Congresses were held in Dublin, Ireland (1954), Leningrad, Soviet Union (1963), and Quebec, Canada (1968), resulting in the formation of the International Peat Society in 1968.

Peat reemerged as a viable energy resource in Europe in the 1970s due to a global oil crisis and rising prices of both oil and natural gas. Ireland, England, the Netherlands, Germany, Sweden, Poland, Finland, and the Russian Federation are significant consumers of peat as an energy source. Most peat energy is produced for local use, although small-scale exportation occurs. Coal, oil, and natural gas are widely available and are the predominant fuel sources in the United States and Canada. Peat emerged as an alternative energy resource for developing countries such as Burundi, Indonesia, and Malaysia in the late-20th and early-21st centuries.

A multitude of factors affect the choice of peat as an energy source. Chief among these considerations are the availability and viability of alternative fuels; costs; climate; scale; transportation; legal regulations; social, economic, and environmental impacts; and other potential land uses. Analysis of the peat must consider the decomposition stage of plant remains; particle size; ease of drainage; and wood, ash, carbon, and hydrogen contents. The main alternative uses for peatlands are agriculture, forestry, horticulture, and preservation.

The extraction and production of peat into energy has a lengthy history in temperate climates, but is a newer, emerging industry in tropical climates. Preparation for extraction involves clearing of surface vegetation and tree stumps followed by ditching and drainage, a process that takes years to complete because peatlands are over 90 percent water. Peat extraction may follow a wet or dry sod production method. Fuel peat may take several forms: Sod peat slabs and compressed peat briquettes mainly serve as local domestic fuel, while milled peat either fuels power plants or is processed into briquettes.

Milled peat is loose peat extracted from peatlands through large-scale mechanized production and is laid out to dry naturally. Both sod peat and peat briquettes are generally produced on a much smaller scale than milled peat, either by hand, mechanized production, or both. Sod peat is extracted, air dried, compressed, and cut into blocks of varying shapes and sizes. Peat briquettes are mechanically extracted, dried, compressed, and uniformly shaped and are the easiest and most economical form to transport. Milled peat has the highest moisture content and lowest calorific value, followed by sod peat and peat briquettes. Problems of peat storage include location, moisture content maintenance, internal heating, and spontaneous combustion.

Peat extraction and fuel use raise many of the same environmental issues as fossil fuels such as coal, oil, and natural gas, resulting in grassroots campaigns against peat fuel in many countries. Environmental sustainability within the peat industry centers on maintaining a balance between peat extraction and peat formation and regeneration, reducing greenhouse gas emissions such as sulfur dioxide, nitrogen oxides, and carbon dioxide related to peat extraction and fuel use, and reducing water pollution associated with peatlands drainage. Methods include chemical or other forms of water purification, planting forests on reclaimed peatlands, and allowing natural peat regeneration. The major uses of peatlands after extraction are agriculture, forestry, peat regeneration for future use, and natural preservation.

The peat industry must abide by a growing number of local, national, and international regulations, such as legislation regarding greenhouse gas emissions, water, and mining, and the legal protection of some peatlands. Peat is classified as a fossil fuel under the International Panel for Climate Change (IPCC). Peat use supporters note that unlike other classified fossil fuels, peatlands can be reused in environmentally sustainable ways and that its regulation as a fossil fuel does not account for the carbon sink properties of remaining and regenerating peatlands. Peat also has a significantly lower climate impact than other fossil fuels. Proponents claim that peat is better classified as a biomass fuel and a slowly renewable natural resource.

MARCELLA BUSH TREVINO

Further Reading

Andriesse, J. P. "Energy Use of Peat." Food and Agriculture Organization of the United Nations (1988). http://www.fao.org/docrep/x5872e/x5872e0b.htm.

Howes, R., and A. Fainberg, eds. *The Energy Sourcebook*. New York: American Institute of Physics, 1991.

Sopo, Raimo. "Peat as an Energy Resource." International Peat Society. http://www.peatsociety.org/peatlands-and-peat/peat-energy-resource.

See Also: Biomass Energy; Carbon Emissions Factors; Fossil Fuels; History of Energy: Medieval World; History of Energy: Renaissance; History of Energy: 1800–1850.

Pennsylvania

Category: Energy in the United States.
Summary: Pennsylvania coal mines supply a number of eastern and midwestern states, and the state leads the northeast in petroleum refining. Pennsylvania is second in the nation in the generation of nuclear energy.

The birthplace of the Declaration of Independence and the U.S. Constitution, Pennsylvania has long held a significant role in American political history. Pennsylvania has also played a significant role in the history of energy production. In 1859,

Edwin L. Drake discovered oil in Titusville, creating the first oil boom in the world and launching the modern petroleum industry. Almost a century later, the first nuclear power plant became operational in Shippingport. The Keystone State spans an area of 46,058 square miles, and water covers 1,239 square miles of that area. The major rivers are the Allegheny, the Susquehanna, the Delaware, and the Ohio. The only major lake is Lake Erie, the fourth-largest of the Great Lakes. Pennsylvania is in a unique position to share energy resources, because it has common borders with six other states: New York, West Virginia, Maryland, Delaware, New Jersey, and Ohio. Pennsylvania leads the Northeast in petroleum refining and ranks second in its capacity for generating nuclear energy. Some 35 percent of electricity generated in Pennsylvania is derived from nuclear power. Coal mining has always been a major activity; Pennsylvania is one of the top coal-mining states. Around 50 percent of all coal produced in Pennsylvania is transported to other states on the East Coast and in the Midwest. In order to reduce its carbon footprint, Pennsylvania is an active participant in regional efforts to improve carbon sequestration technologies, and the pursuit of alternative and renewable sources of energy has taken center stage.

The Office of Energy and Technology Deployment, under the state's Department of Environmental Protection (DEP), has the chief responsibility for energy policies and for assessment and promotion of related technologies. The DEP team consists of the Bureau of Energy Innovations and Technology Deployment, the Governor's Green Government Council, the Office of Energy and Technology, the Pennsylvania Energy Development Authority, and the Small Business Ombudsman's Office. Pennsylvania offers various incentives for promoting energy conservation and the use of

Wikimedia

The Bear Creek Wind Power Project is located in Kingston, Pennsylvania. The Appalachian and Allegheny Mountains in Pennsylvania are great sources for wind power. Wind energy used in the generation of electricity supplies 26 percent of all electricity generated in the state.

renewable energy, including grants for those who use electric vehicles and a biodiesel production incentive program. Public benefit funds have been set aside to allow low-income homes to practice energy conservation, and Pennsylvania is the only American state to mandate universal service and energy conservation by law. The Pennsylvania Low-Income Renewables Pilot Program has made cutting-edge energy technology available to a range of households. Additionally, Pennsylvania participates in the U.S. Department of Energy's (DOE) Energy Weatherization Assistance Program, which makes low-income homes more energy efficient.

The Path to Alternative and Renewable Energy Sources

With the sixth-largest population in the United States and a healthy industrial sector, Pennsylvania has a carbon score of 23, with residents emitting a yearly average of 22 tons of carbon dioxide each. Although most electricity (56.8 percent) is still generated from coal, the state has made considerable progress in the pursuit of alternative and renewable sources of energy. By 2007, the state was generating 2.0 terawatt-hours of electricity from biomass sources.

Pennsylvania possesses minor reserves of crude oil and natural gas. The Susquehanna River and several smaller river basins are ideal for generating hydropower. Between 2001 and 2007, the generation of hydroelectricity rose by 35.5 percent, accounting for 17.8 percent of all electricity generated in the state. The Appalachian and Allegheny Mountains are great sources for wind power, and high winds can be found onshore and offshore around Lake Erie. Thus, the use of wind energy used in the generation of electricity also expanded during that same period, increasing by 30.2 percent and supplying 26 percent of all electricity generated. In 2008, wind capacity reached 360.7 megawatts, and Pennsylvania ranked 16th in the United States in this field. Pennsylvania has 10 wind farms with a total capacity of 293.5 megawatts, and planned capacity will reach 5,120 megawatts. The two largest wind farms are Allegheny Ridge (80 megawatts) and Waymart Wind Farm (64.5 megawatts). In 2007, Montgomery County became the first county in the United States to operate completely on wind energy.

Pennsylvania has five nuclear power plants: Susquehanna, Three Mile Island, Beaver Valley, Peach Bottom, and Limerick. These plants generate 34.5 percent of the state's supply of electricity.

Pennsylvania installed its first solar hot water heaters in the 1970s, but the solar energy sector has taken on new life in the 21st century. The state Alternative Energy Portfolio Standard requires that by 2020, 0.5 percent of all electricity generated in the state will be derived from solar energy. DOE has identified Pittsburgh as one of 13 cities to be classified as a Solar American City, and the city received $200,000 to implement solar energy systems and infrastructures.

Other sources of renewable energy are concentrated on biomass fuels, cellulosic ethanol, and biogas. The potential for producing ethanol is considerable; studies have predicted that the state has the capacity to grow 825,000 acres of switchgrass, resulting in 250 million to one billion gallons of ethanol.

In 2004, the Pennsylvania legislature passed the Alternative Energy Portfolio Standards Act, stipulating that 8 percent of all electricity sold within the state must derive from renewable sources such as wind, biomass, and biogas energy, 5 percent from solar energy, and 10 percent from alternative sources such as waste-to-energy and waste coal. Subsequent legislation increased the emphasis on renewable sources of energy. In 2007, the legislature enacted the Pennsylvania Biodiesel Incentive and In-State Production Act to offer incentives for using cellulosic ethanol and biodiesel. The following year, the Alternative Energy Act set aside $650 million in grants, loans, and tax credits to promote clean energy by helping homes and businesses to engage in energy conservation and encourage business investment in alternative energy generation.

In response to the passage of the American Recovery and Reinvestment Act of 2009, all states were required to inform the DOE of their agendas for spending federal funds designated for promoting energy efficiency and affordability and pursuing alternative sources of energy. Governor Edward G. Rendell responded that the focus of Pennsylvania's energy efforts was on five cornerstone projects designed to assist low-income families in becoming more energy efficient, promote the growth of business within the energy sector, reduce greenhouse gases, slash energy consumption, and decrease dependence on foreign oil. Pennsylvania received funding for a number of research-based grants under the Recovery Act, including $1 million grants to Dynalene, Inc., for work on a nanoparticle-based fuel cell coolant, and to Strategic Polymer Sciences, Inc., for research into high temperature direct-current (DC) bus capacitors for electric vehicles; Electron Energy Corporation received a $3,000,000 grant to work on high-performance magnets for advanced motors.

ELIZABETH RHOLETTER PURDY

Further Reading

Barnes, Roland V., ed. *Energy Crisis in America?* Huntington, NY: Nova Science, 2001.

Bird, Lori, et al. *Green Power Marketing in the United States: A Status Report.* Golden, CO: National Renewable Energy Laboratory, 2008.

National Renewable Energy Laboratory. "State of the States 2009: Renewable Energy Development and the Role of Policy." NREL/TP-6A2-46667. October 2009. http://www.nrel.gov/docs/fy10osti/46667.pdf.

U.S. Energy Information Administration. "Pennsylvania." http://www.eia.doe.gov/state/state -energy-profiles.cfm?sid=PA.

See Also: Giant Power; Marcellus Shale; Nonrenewable Energy Resources; Nuclear Power; Oil and Petroleum; Refining; Solar Energy; Standard Oil Company.

Peru

Official Name: Republic of Peru.
Category: Geography of Energy.
Summary: Peru has experienced rapid economic growth, which has led to an increased demand for energy. The country has significant untapped petroleum resources. More than half its electricity generation derives from fossil fuels, and more than a quarter is from hydropower.

Peru is a country in northwestern South America with a long Pacific coastline of 1,499 miles (2,414 kilometers). It shares borders with Bolivia, Brazil, Chile, Colombia, and Ecuador. Peru's area is 798,596 square miles (1,285,216 square kilometers), and the country has several types of climate and terrain, including a coastal plain, lowland jungles, and the Andes Mountains. Only 2.88 percent of the land is arable, but Peru is rich in mineral resources, including copper, silver, gold, iron ore, and petroleum, as well as hydropower, wind, and solar resources. The population as of July 2001 was estimated to be 29,248,943, with 77 percent living in urban areas. The per capita gross domestic product (GDP) in 2010 was $9,200, with 34.8 percent of the population living below the poverty line and a Gini Index rating of 49.6, reflecting the country's high income inequality and ranking it 25th in the world.

Economic Growth

Peru has experienced rapid economic growth, which has led to an increased demand for energy, a trend that is expected to continue, since energy consumption is predicted to rise by more than one-third by 2020 with the country's further economic development and population growth. Although Peru has the potential to be a major producer of petroleum and natural gas, lack of investment has left its reserves largely untapped, and it is a net importer of both crude oil and refined petroleum products. In 2008, Peru consumed 0.7 quadrillion British thermal units (Btu) of energy. Fifty percent was produced from oil, followed by 27 percent from hydroelectric, 17 percent from natural gas, 5 percent from coal, and 1 percent from renewable other than hydroelectric.

Most electricity in Peru is generated by hydropower, with the remainder generated by coal or natural gas. Recently there has been interest in exploring the possibility of creating more small hydropower facilities (with capacities of less than 20 megawatts) to supply isolated communities with electricity; only 35 percent of citizens in rural areas have access to electricity. Peru also has numerous areas suitable for production of solar and wind energy, and solar energy has already been used to bring power to some remote areas off the national grid.

Peru has 533 million barrels of crude oil reserves, according to *Oil and Gas Journal*; the Peruvian government claims that as many as 6 million barrels may in fact be recoverable. Peru produced 158,328 barrels of oil per day in 2010, a substantial increase from the production of 99,565 barrels per day in 2000. Peru lacks the capacity to refine heavy crude oil, which constitutes most of its production, and hence it exports much of the oil it produces while importing more than half of the oil it consumes: Of 181,000 barrels per day of oil consumed in Peru in 2009, 99,500 were imported, mostly from Ecuador. Most onshore oil fields are in the Amazon region, and because of environmental concerns over drilling construction and oil spills, in 2009 Peru's highest court placed a moratorium on exploration in this region.

The state-owned company Petroperu oversees all oil exploration and production contracts, but the actual production of oil is run by foreign consortia. Peru has one crude oil pipeline with two branches, which run from the export terminal of Bayovar on the Pacific coast to the Ucayali and Maranon Basins in the northeastern jungle region of the country. Petroperu owns this pipeline, which has a maximum capacity of 250,000 barrels per day, and is adding loops in order to facilitate transporting oil from more distant Amazon regions. Peru has six oil refineries that jointly can distill 198,950 barrels per day.

Natural Gas Reserves

Peru has proven natural gas reserves of 12.2 trillion cubic feet, according to *Oil and Gas Journal*, giving it the sixth-largest reserves in South America after Venezuela, Bolivia, Trinidad and Tobago, Argentina, and Brazil. In 2010, Peru produced 255.6 billion cubic feet of dry natural gas, most of which was exported. In June 2010, Peru opened the first natural gas liquefaction plant in South America, at Pampa Melchorita; this plant is capable of processing 215 billion cubic feet of gas per year. Natural gas consumption has increased rapidly in Peru, from 56 billion cubic feet in 2005 to 123 billion cubic feet in 2009, driven largely by the demand for fuel to be used in the gas-fired power plants, which account for two-thirds of Peru's natural gas consumption. Peru's main gas reserve is the Camisea project, where production began in 2004 and output has increased by an average of 37 percent per year since then. Explorations are under way at another gas field, Madre de Dios, which some believe could be as large as Camisea, and natural gas is also produced from the Talara Basin in northwestern Peru. Two pipelines carry natural gas from the Camisea gas fields in southeastern Peru; one terminates at the Paracas National Reservation and passes through the Malvinas plant, where propane and heavier liquids are separated from natural gas. The second pipeline runs from Malvinas to Lima and Callao for distribution within the capital city.

Electricity consumption has almost doubled in the 10-year period from 1998 to 2008: from 15.8 terawatt-hours to 29.3 terawatt-hours. Most (85 percent) of the electricity in Peru is delivered by the national grid, the Sistema Electrico Interconectado National (SEIN), and in 2009 85.7 percent of the population had access to electricity. The Peruvian government plans to invest $2.2 billion to connect an addition 8 million citizens to the grid by 2018.

In 2008, Peru had 7.2 gigawatts of electricity-generating capacity, with about 45 percent from hydroelectric generators. A transmission line between Peru and Ecuador was built in 2003 but has rarely been used, as the companies could not settle on a price for electricity. As of 2010, Peru had signed an energy integration agreement with Brazil and was expecting to begin exporting 6 gigawatts of electricity to Brazil annually. Plans to build six new hydroelectric dams on the Maranon River have met with local resistance, while plans to export electricity to Chile have met with nationalist resistance.

Sarah Boslaugh

Further Reading

Latin American Energy Organization. "Peru." http://www.olade.org.ec/en/node/390.

Meier, Peter, Eduardo H. Zolezzi, Susan V. Bogach, Terence Muir, and Karen Bazex. *Peru Opportunities and Challenges of Small Hydropower Development.* Energy Sector Management Assistance Program Formal Report 340/11, March 2011. http://www.esmap.org/esmap/node/1238.

U.S. Department of Energy. *An Energy Overview of Peru.* Oak Ridge, TN: U.S. Department of Energy, Office of Scientific and Technical Information, 2003.

U.S. Energy Information Administration. "Country Analysis Brief: Peru." http://www.eia.doe.gov/countries.ab.cfm?fips=PE.

See Also: Carbon Sequestration; Climate and Weather; Enron; Hydropower; Natural Gas; Oil and Petroleum; Renewable Energy Resources; Trevithick, Richard.

Petroviolence

Category: Environmentalism.
Summary: *Petroviolence* refers to behavior intending to damage property, or hurt or kill persons, as a response to transnational extraction of crude oil from developing countries.

In the term *petroviolence*, the prefix petro means "rock" and is also an abbreviation for petroleum (from the Latin for "rock oil"). This liquefied hydrocarbon embedded in Earth's crust is viscous, highly flammable, and can be refined into gasoline, kerosene, jet fuel, and other thermal energy resources; it is also manufactured into such useful commodities as asphalt, plastics, and lubricants. Petroleum is thus critical to the industrialized nations.

The world distribution of this nonrenewable fossil fuel is uneven and generally does not match the spatial patterns of its consumption. During the 20th century, petroleum became the most vital strategic energy source for the United States and for other developed countries, generating unprecedented mass prosperity and geopolitical dominance. Since much of the production of crude oil takes place outside these regions, there is a need for indirect and direct coercion to gain and maintain suitable levels of control of the resource.

Indeed, some researchers argue that violence flows from the culture of petroleum, harming both human beings and their environments at various ecological scales. For instance, scientific evidence supports the theory that the burning of fossil fuels such as petroleum and its by-products causes rapid global warming that could lead to large-scale extinctions among terrestrial flora and fauna. On a lesser scale, although no less significant, are the health risks related to the use of petroleum products such as plastics—the scourge of the Holocene (our current geologic era), as some would say. However, petroviolence stands for something more specific: the violent conflict, corruption, and criminality that can erupt in developing countries whose economies are overly dependent on oil revenues that can materialize only from foreign investment and the imported technologies owned by the "supermajor" oil companies and their state sponsors.

Geographer Michael Watts was perhaps the first to use the term, in an article entitled "Petro-Violence: Community, Extraction, and Political Ecology of a Mythic Commodity" published in an edited volume titled *Violent Environments*. Since its publication in 2001, others have applied the concept to petroleum-dependent states other than Nigeria, the country that has been the particular focus of Watts's work even before the inception of the term *petroviolence*. He has spent more than a decade tracing the political economy of oil and has uncovered a suite of social ills that consistently affect oil-rich developing countries where Western neoliberal governments, oil companies, and Third World autocrats and dictators collude to service their appetites for wealth, influence, and power. As Watts has documented, such collusion can spawn corruption, disregard for local traditions, internecine fighting and conflict, ecological degradation, and loss of national sovereignty to foreign oil companies holding the technological know-how to bring oil to the Earth's surface.

The interests of the few but mighty in such cases are backed by amorphous, oblique threats emanating from the core states of "hydrocarbon capitalism" and toward the resource-full periphery. Sometimes push literally comes to shove, as it did when the United States invaded Iraq in 1991 and again in 2001 to maintain access to some of the largest oil reserves in the world—so surmises the thesis of petroviolence.

Nigeria, Shell, and Chevron

One significant event that has perhaps most influenced the development of this framework of interpretation is the execution of the Nigerian author and human rights activist Ken Saro-Wiwa in 1995 by a military dictatorship that has in one form or another governed Nigeria for most of its postcolonial span, beginning with independence from British rule in 1960. Saro-Wiwa's peaceful movement for political justice and economic development for the people of the Niger River Delta stemmed from resistance to the exploitation of the people and places caught in the middle of this asymmetric oil development scenario.

▷ Petroviolence in Developing Countries

Petroviolence has been proven endemic to developing countries where transnational extraction of crude oil cycles petrodollars through political, economic, and cultural institutions, leaving behind change that can tend toward social instability and violent unrest—for example, in certain countries in South America that have modest reserves of crude oil. For decades, U.S. foreign policy assumed guardianship over a region where economic activities such as resource extraction and agriculture have been closely tied to the U.S. economy. The element of petroleum has given the United States impetus to deepen its involvement so that supermajors can gain access to unexplored areas where new deposits might be discovered and drilling rights then granted.

Plan Colombia, a U.S. policy venture, has been the target of criticism by those studying petroviolence. They claim that the so-called war on drugs, which involves the annual transfer of billions of dollars worth of military hardware and training to Colombian forces, is a pretext opening the jungle to foreign ownership of what lies beneath: likely more than a billion barrels of oil. Civil war has ravaged the country for more than 30 years, and it can be argued the primary cause is not North America's insatiable hunger for cocaine and cannabis but the threat of sovereignty denied. Militants in Colombia, as well as Ecuador, are in some cases fighting a centuries-old struggle against major landowners—and now perhaps hydrocarbon developers as well.

Although Africa contains only 9.3 percent of the world's known oil reserves and produces only 10 percent of world output, it is concentrated. Fully 85 percent of the continent's oil flows from just four African countries: Algeria, Angola, Libya, and Nigeria, the latter handling half of total output by using the infrastructure built by the Royal Dutch Shell and Chevron oil corporations. Nigeria has over 30 billion barrels on reserve and pumps 2.2 million barrels per day, which together with its gas production and refined products generates sufficient revenue—$59 billion in 2010, for example—that the average Nigerian citizen could have a modest standard of living. This is not and has not been the case.

Of the hundreds of billions worth of hydrocarbon exports since 1970, at least $100 billion has gone completely missing. Much of the rest has gone to 1 percent of the population, those most closely connected to the military and the oil companies. Per capita income has actually dropped, from $250 in 1965 to $212 in 2004. In 1970, 36 percent of the population subsisted on a $1 per day; by the turn of the 21st century, that figure had risen to 70 percent.

Saro-Wiwa's movement originated in the Niger River and Delta regions, where today thousands of oil wells sit atop 250 of Nigeria's 300 oil fields, feeding export terminals and refineries through thousands of kilometers of pipelines. Nevertheless, the people of these regions suffer demeaning hardship due to the uneven distribution of oil revenues, which rarely make it back for reinvestment in the development of physical and social infrastructures such as schools and hospitals. The oil states of Nigeria average only one doctor per 150,000 citizens. Oil ponds, well seepage, and deforestation create a climate that contributes to the erosion of tribal customs and the rearing of black-market petroleum, whereby local syndicates vie for "buckets" of oil that fuel criminality, degeneracy, and general lawlessness. Saro-Wiwa resisted the impact hydrocarbon capitalism had on his community, but in 1995 was hanged for his resistance by the military government of Sani Abacha.

After his death, the Delta slipped into a low-intensity warfare of demonstrations, blockades, occupations, lawsuits, and strikes, which next transmogrified into kidnappings, shootings, sabotage, and small-scale but widespread and persistent oil piracy. An estimated 1,000 people die annually from this petroviolence, most from black-market lawlessness. The rebels of the Delta are no match for the oil companies' well-equipped and heavily armed security forces, trained in U.S. and British military science. The western coast of Africa, from Nigeria to Angola, has become militarized to protect the lifeblood of the world's most developed countries.

Conclusion

Violence pervades the history of natural resource extraction, be it the violence of governance, criminality, warfare, or ecological degradation. Petroviolence is a particular type of resource violence tied to the extraction of petroleum from developing countries. A poignant depiction of petroviolence infecting the hearts and minds of individuals is the critically acclaimed Hollywood movie *There Will Be Blood* (2007), which tells the story of the Southern California oil boom of the late 19th and early 20th centuries. At the time, the United States was in many ways a developing country, but the focus of the film is at the family scale, where positive American values of independence and perseverance combine with deceit, greed, and cruelty to rend apart community. With oil a fundamental building block of 20th-century industrial capitalism, it often seems violence is its keystone.

KEN WHALEN

Further Reading

Achebe, Chinua. "Nigeria's Promise, Africa's Hope." *New York Times* (January 15, 2011). http://www .nytimes.com/2011/01/16/opinion /16achebe.html.

Chijioke, Evoh J. "Green Crimes, Petroviolence and the Tragedy of Oil: The Case of the Niger Delta in Nigeria." *In-Spire Journal of Law, Politics and Society* 4, no. 1 (2009).

Dunning, Thad, and Leslie Wirpsa. *Oil Rigged: There's Something Slippery About the U.S. Drug War in Colombia.* http://www.cyberclass.net/oilrigged .htm.

Watts, Michael J. "Petro-Violence: Community, Extraction, and Political Ecology of a Mythic Commodity." In *Violent Environments*, edited by N. Peluso and M. Watts. Ithaca: Cornell University Press, 2001.

See Also: BP; Nationalization; Nigeria; Oil and Petroleum; Shell; Venezuela.

Philippines

Official Name: Republic of the Philippines.
Category: Geography of Energy.
Summary: The Republic of the Philippines appears as a regional leader in renewable energy and energy efficiency policy developments in southeast Asia. Its regulatory enforcement is, however, insufficient at this time and may threaten its permanence as a model.

The Philippine archipelago is located to the south of Taiwan and the north of Indonesia and consists of 7,107 islands, of which 2,880 are inhabited. Around 33 percent of its population of 99 million (as of July 2010) lived below the poverty line. According to the International Energy Agency, in 2008, 65 percent of its people had access to electricity. The government, however, considers the country fully electrified, as all the neighborhoods, or *barangays* (districts or wards—the smallest administrative division in the Philippines), have access to electricity. This reckoning, however, includes all partially electrified communities, as well as those with limited services.

Imported Energy Sources

Because of its relatively small exploitation of indigenous energy, the Philippines relies on imported energy sources. Imported coal and crude oil accounted for 50 percent of the total energy supply in 2007. However, the country owns rich renewable energy (RE) resources, including robust wind energy sites, ideal solar conditions, and an abundance of geothermal and biomass resources.

The fuel crisis that erupted in 2008 compelled the Department of Energy (DOE), responsible for overall policy goals in the energy industry, to devise the 2008 Renewable Energy Act. Its aim is to promote the development of RE resources and their commercialization by providing fiscal and nonfiscal incentives to institutions that invest in the sector. These incentives have been well received, as testified by the 200 RE projects contracted between the DOE and the private sector in 2009. However, difficulties remain with the implementation of these projects, such as the high risk involved with RE investments and the difficulty in securing funding.

At the consumer level, the Renewable Energy Act encourages the consumption of RE through a green energy option allowing end users to choose RE power sources. The act also promotes net metering to enable end users to generate their own RE power and sell it to the grid. Finally, it encourages RE power that is free of value-added tax (VAT, similar to U.S. sales tax). Moreover, all savings from the reduced corporate tax rate are passed through to end users via cheaper electricity rates.

The final goal of the act is to achieve greater energy independence, by making the country 60 percent energy self-sufficient.

In 2010, electricity generated from renewables represented 33 percent of the Philippines' energy mix. The government aims to bring that figure to 40 percent by 2020. Moreover, under the DOE's medium-term RE policy framework, the government aims to achieve a 100 percent increase in renewable energy power capacity by 2013, compared to the 2002 level. More than 4 gigawatts of additional RE capacity are thus to be developed by 2013, some 1.2 gigawatts of which are planned to come from geothermal sources, to reach a total capacity of 9 gigawatts.

The First Steps

In February 2011, the DOE took the first steps toward the creation of the Philippines' first RE market, creating a steering committee to formulate and oversee the establishment of the RE market. Its missions are to issue, trade, and monitor RE certificates, in compliance with the renewable portfolio standard (RPS) introduced by the Renewable Energy Act.

As a market-based policy, the RPS requires electricity suppliers to provide a certain amount of their energy supply through RE sources. Under the new proposed rules, priority connections to the grid will be given to electricity generated from RE resources. To that extent, the RPS is a major contributor to the growth of the RE portion of the national energy mix.

Considering energy efficiency (EE), recent studies (including the *South East Asia Energy Efficiency Financing Market Feasibility Report*, conducted by ReEx Capital Asia in 2010) show that the Philippines is one of the four Southeast Asian countries that have the best paybacks for EE projects.

In 2004, a National Energy Efficiency and Conservation Programme (NEECP) was launched by the Energy Efficiency and Conservation Division, and its implementation is overseen by the DOE. The NEECP is a plan aiming to implement measures to improve EE and energy conservation in all sectors of the Philippine economy by 2014. All government agencies thus have to reduce their energy consumption by 10 percent annually. The NEECP is an essential strategy in rationalizing the country's demand for petroleum and eventually reducing the impact of rising fuel prices on the economy. However, there are no penalties for failure to meet the target, thus limiting the effectiveness of the program.

The DOE has also been actively promoting EE to the public and private sectors and directly to end users, through the Philippines Energy Efficiency Project (PEEP). Supported by the Asian Development Bank, this project includes initiatives such as the retrofitting of lighting in selected government buildings, the provision of 13 million compact fluorescent lamps (CFLs, or energy-saving lights) to consumers, the implementation of energy-efficient public lighting programs, and the implementation of a certification scheme for energy-efficient buildings. In the long term, the project will allow a large-scale implementation of EE programs while reducing expenditures and health risks, as well as enhancing community livelihoods.

However, due to its complexity, EE is pursued mainly by more advanced economies and thus remains a low priority among Philippine policy makers. The policies currently in place do not have strong enough mechanisms to guarantee their effectiveness and permanence. The need for a committed national push toward EE or a legal framework supporting EE developments is therefore very high.

Internationally, the Philippines is an eligible recipient country for fast-start finance projects. Established by the United Nations Framework Convention on Climate Change (UNFCCC) in 2009, as part of the Copenhagen Accord, the fast-start finance system allows developing countries to draw monies from a fund supported by a number of developed countries. Those funds can then be used for mitigation, adaptation, technology development and transfer, and capacity-building projects.

Major Energy-Related Changes

In summary, the Philippines seems ready to undertake major energy-related changes to move toward more sustainable and cleaner energy services. However, various barriers remain and limit the uptake of RE and EE. It is necessary to overcome those obstacles through a range of strong policy measures providing information on available technologies that raise awareness, that support technical training and capacity building, and, most important, that enforce these regulations. The government adopting an integrated approach will foster stronger participation of the private sector, mainly in project development and implementation. Without regulatory enforcement, the question of the actual effectiveness of the RE and EE targets set by the Philippine government will continue to linger.

Daphné Barbotte
Maaike Göbel
Eva Oberender

Further Reading

Asia-Pacific Economic Cooperation. "APEC CEO Summit 2010—Benigno S. Aquino, President of the Philippines." November 13, 2010. http://www.apec.org/Press/Videos/2010/2010_1013_aquino.aspx.

Asian Development Bank. "ADB, Philippines Mark New Clean Energy Investment on Copenhagen Sidelines." December 18, 2009. http://www.adb.org/news/adb-philippines-mark-new-clean-energy-investment-copenhagen-sidelines.

Norton Rose. *Renewable Energy in Asia Pacific.* 2010. http://www.nortonrose.com/knowledge/publications/pdf/file29339.pdf?lang=en-gb.

Philippine National Energy Efficiency and Conservation Program. "About Us." http://www.doe.gov.ph/neecp/aboutus.htm.

"Philippines Renewable Energy Act, 2008." http://www.reeep.org/file_upload/6119_tmpphp8YpUel.pdf.

ReEx Capital Asia. *South East Asia Energy Efficiency Financing Market Feasibility Report.* 2010. http://www.reexasia.com/.

Renewable Energy and Energy Efficiency Partnership. "The Philippine Renewable Energy Market." http://www.reeep.org/index.php?assetType=news&assetId=499.

U.S. Department of Energy. *New and Renewable Energy Resource Development.* 2005. http://www.doe.gov.ph/NRE/default.htm.

U.S. Energy Information Administration. "Country Analysis Brief: Philippines." http://www.eia.gov/countries/country-data.cfm?fips=RP.

See Also: Energy Poverty; Geothermal Energy; Indonesia; International Renewable Energy Agency; Japan; Palau; Renewable Energy Resources; Tidal Power.

Photovoltaics

Category: Energy Technology.

Summary: Solar cells, semiconductor devices that convert sunlight into direct-current electricity, are called photovoltaics. Groups of these cells can be used to charge batteries and power electrical loads to operate appliances and even return power to the electrical utility grid.

Photovoltaics (PV), or solar cells, are semiconductor devices that convert sunlight into direct-current (DC) electricity. Groups of PV cells are electrically configured into modules and arrays, which can be used to charge batteries or power a variety of electrical loads. With the appropriate power conversion equipment, PV systems can produce alternating current (AC) compatible with conventional appliances and can operate in parallel to, and interconnected with, the electrical utility grid. This has made PV technology a strongly promoted renewable energy option across the world.

History

The origin of the word *photovoltaic* consists of two roots: *photo* and *volta*. The former comes from the Greek word *phos*, meaning "light," while the latter means "producing electric current" and originates from the name of the Italian physicist Alessandro Volta (1745–1827), who was a pioneer in the field of electricity.

The *photovoltaic effect* is the basic physical process through which a solar cell converts sunlight into electricity. The term refers to photons of light knocking electrons into a higher state of energy to create electricity. French physicist Alexandre-Edmond Becquerel (1820–91) first recognized the photovoltaic effect in 1839.

Credit for building the first solar cell is given to American inventor Charles Edgar Fritts (b. 1850). In 1883, Fritts coated the semiconductor selenium with a very thin layer of gold, thus creating a device that was about 1 percent efficient. Five years later, Russian physicist and Moscow University professor Aleksandr Grigorievich Stoletov (1839–96) built the first cell based on the outer photoelectric effect discovered by Heinrich Hertz (1857–94). The photoelectric effect occurs under the right circumstances when light is used to push electrons, freeing them from the surface of a solid. Albert Einstein (1879–1955) finally explained the photoelectric effect in 1905 and received the Nobel Prize in Physics for that work in 1921. Russell Ohl (1898–1987) patented the modern solar cell in 1946, which he discovered while working on a series of advances that would lead to the transistor.

The modern age of solar photovoltaic (PV) technology arrived in 1954, when Bell Laboratories discovered that silicon doped with certain impurities was very sensitive to light. This first solar PV module was mostly a curiosity, since it was too expensive to be given widespread application. The first practical use for PVs was in the space industry. The Soviets employed a solar array as early as May 15, 1957, when they launched the Sputnik 3 satellite. Throughout the 1960s, the technology was employed to power other orbiting satellites and spacecraft.

Through space programs, PV technology advanced, its reliability was established, and costs began to decline. During the energy crisis in the 1970s, PV technology gained recognition as a source of power for nonspace applications. Improvements in manufacturing, performance, and quality of PV modules helped open up a number of opportunities for powering remote terrestrial applications, including battery charging for navigational aids, signals, telecommunications equipment, and other critical, low-power needs.

The Basics

Electricity is a stream of moving electrons—tiny charged particles that orbit the nucleus of an atom. A basic PV cell allows for the direct

Wikimedia

In order to produce more power, PV cells are electrically interconnected and mounted in a support structure to form a panel or module. A number of modules can be wired together to form an array. Some arrays follow the sun, capturing the most sunlight possible.

conversion of solar radiation into electricity at the atomic level. The photons in sunlight hit the semiconductor materials in a panel and are reflected, are absorbed, or pass right through. The absorbed photons knock free the electrons from their atoms. One or more electric fields act to force the freed electrons to flow in a certain direction. This flow of electrons is an electrical current that can be drawn off for external use, such as a providing light.

PV systems may employ a variety of materials in their construction, displaying different efficiencies. The most prevalent materials are derived from crystalline silicon and include monocrystalline silicon, polycrystalline silicon, and amorphous silicon. Monocrystalline cells produce the most electricity per unit area and amorphous cells the least. However, amorphous silicon is part of a group of other materials (including copper indium diselenide, cadmium telluride, and gallium arsenide) that is contributing to major developments in thin-film PV technology.

Thin-film PV modules offer the promise of reducing material requirements and manufacturing costs of PV modules and systems. This increases the attractiveness of thin film's usage in building-integrated PV (BIPV) products, where the PV system essentially becomes an integral part of a building envelope. BIPV may be embedded as roofing tiles, building walls, or façades. The advantage over traditional PV is that thin film is lightweight, not subject to wind lifting, and capable of being walked upon. The comparable disadvantages are increased cost and reduced efficiency, as commercial thin-film efficiency ranges from 7 to 10 percent, whereas traditional crystalline efficiency ranges from 12 to 18 percent. Future generations of PV technology will be able to capture and convert a greater percentage of sunlight.

A traditional PV cell typically produces a small amount of power. In order to produce more power, PV cells are electrically interconnected and mounted in an environmentally protective support structure to form a panel or module. Modules are designed to supply electricity ranging in output from 10 to 300 watts. A number of modules can be wired together to form an array. Another way to increase power output is to move from a fixed-angle array (oriented and inclined according to its latitudinal location) to one that is mounted on a single- or dual-axis tracking device. These types of arrays follow the sun, capturing the most sunlight possible throughout the day.

Today's PV modules are a safe, reliable, low-maintenance source of electricity that produces no on-site pollution or emissions. They boast minimal failure rates and projected service lifetimes of 20 to 30 years. Most major manufacturers offer warranties of 20-plus years for maintaining a relatively high percentage of the initial rated power output (up to 80 percent).

Renewable Energy Generation

The 1970s energy crisis prompted the development of PV systems designed for residential and commercial usage. These systems operate interconnected with or independent of the utility grid, and they can be connected with other energy sources and energy storage systems. A grid-tied PV array may be deployed as an electricity generator in a variety of ways. Two of the more prevalent options are rooftop and ground-mounted systems, although BIPV products are increasing in popularity. Rooftop PV systems are particularly ideal in urban settings (though they may also prove useful in some rural areas), whereas ground-mounted systems are favored by rural generators.

Grid-tied systems are primarily connected with one of two different types of metering arrangements, depending on the local utility. Net metering is a program through which a utility charges a consumer for its net consumption of electricity. If the consumer produces a net surplus of electricity over the course of a given billing cycle, the utility will either pay that amount back or credit the consumer's next utility bill.

Consumers contracting into feed-in tariff programs use the second option. In this arrangement, a separate utility meter measures the electricity generated by the PV system. The utility pays the consumer for electricity that is generated at a different rate (a tariff) from that used for what is taken from the grid. For example, in 2009, the Canadian province of Ontario started offering 20-year fixed-price contracts paying rooftop PV generators $0.802 (Canadian) for every kilowatt-hour produced from rooftop systems smaller than 10 kilowatts.

The PV Market

Today, the majority of PV installations supply grid-tied power generation. As of 2010, solar PV generated electricity in more than 100 countries and was the fastest-growing power-generation technology in the world. Between 2004 and 2009, grid-tied PV capacity increased at an annual average rate of 60 percent, leading to approximately 21 gigawatts of installed capacity. The rapidly growing global market share of thin-film PVs has it contributing up to 25 percent of the annual total.

Off-grid PV generation is a smaller market, accounting for an additional 3 to 4 gigawatts, and is used for remote homes, boats, recreational vehicles, electric cars, telecommunications, and remote sensing and monitoring. In 2009, solar PV accounted for about 16 percent of all new electric generation capacity in Europe.

Driven by advances in technology and increases in manufacturing scale and sophistication, the cost of PVs has declined steadily since the first solar cells were manufactured. Some estimates cite annual manufacturing cost reductions of 3 to 5 percent. In recent years, the total installed costs for solar PV were estimated at $7 (U.S.) per watt, although a reasonable estimate for 2009 was probably $6 per watt. Government- and utility-backed incentive programs, such as net metering and feed-in tariffs targeting solar-generated electricity, have also supported the deployment of solar PV installations in many countries. Global leaders include Spain, Germany, Japan, the United States, and China.

Germany is the primary global driver of PV installations, having added 3.8 gigawatts in 2009. This surpassed Spain's prior record-breaking addition of 2.4 gigawatts in 2008 and brought total German capacity to 9.8 gigawatts by year's end. The German market accounted for 47 percent of existing global PV capacity. However, other countries are experiencing increased demand and will likely reduce the industry's reliance on a single market.

PV technology is also experiencing growing demand in the developing countries of Africa, Asia, and Latin America as they purchase very small-scale, off-grid systems. Sales and total capacity of off-grid systems have increased steadily since the early 1980s. In many cases, these systems are already at price parity with fossil fuels.

ROBERT J. WAKULAT

Further Reading

Canadian Mortgage and Housing Corporation. "Photovoltaic Systems: Photovoltaic System Overview." http://www.cmhc-schl.gc.ca/en/co/maho/enefcosa/enefcosa_003.cfm.

International Energy Agency. *Technology Roadmap: Solar Photovoltaic Energy*. Paris: International Energy Agency, 2010. http://www.iea.org/papers/2010/pv_roadmap.pdf.

Knier, Gil. "How Do Photovoltaics Work?" *NASA Science News*. http://science.nasa.gov/science-news/science-at-nasa/2002/solarcells/.

Renewable Energy Policy Network for the 21st Century (REN21). *Renewables 2010 Global Status Report*. Paris: REN21 Secretariat, 2010. http://www.ren21.net/REN21Activities/Publications/GlobalStatusReport/tabid/5434/Default.aspx.

See Also: Alternative Energy; Solar Energy; Solar Thermal Systems.

Pickens, T. Boone

Dates: 1928– .
Category: Biographies.
Summary: T. Boone Pickens is an oilman-turned-financier who has become a strong proponent of wind power for electricity and natural gas as a transportation fuel.

Thomas Boone Pickens Jr. is an oil tycoon, the chairman of BP Capital Management (no relation to British Petroleum), a well-known billionaire, and a strong proponent of wind power and natural gas. Pickens began his career in the oil industry and has since diversified as a financier with a wide range of

▷ *The Pickens Plan*

In 2008, Pickens invested $62 million in promoting the Pickens Plan, an energy strategy focused on expanding the use of wind power in the United States and reducing dependence on foreign oil via the use of natural gas as a transportation fuel. At the same time, Pickens founded Mesa Power, a company to oversee the installation of a 4,000-megawatt wind power project in Texas (sufficient to power 1.3 million homes). Pickens has thus played a significant role in bringing the discussion of alternative energy possibilities to the forefront of debate and legislation in the United States. Pickens says on his autobiographical Website, "I've been an oilman my whole life, but this is one emergency we can't drill our way out of."

Such statements have earned unlikely allies for the Pickens Plan. In legislative circles, both Republicans and Democrats have agreed with Pickens that a national energy plan to transition the United States to clean fuels and renewable energy sources is necessary for the future prosperity and energy security of the country. However, tight credit markets and transmission line problems forced Pickens to cancel his 2007 plan for the world's largest wind farm. In the wake of this setback, Pickens focused more heavily on developing and expanding natural gas production and use.

energy and resource interests. Pickens holds interests in Clean Energy Fuels Corporation, a natural gas distribution company with outlets throughout the United States; Mesa Water, which controls 200,000 acres of groundwater rights in Texas; and Mesa Power, which is focused on the production and installation of wind power. Despite his background in oil, Pickens has spoken publicly about the decline of oil production and the need for sustainable energy solutions. Concerned with both the security implications of U.S. dependence on foreign oil imports and the need to pursue a sustainable energy future for environmental reasons, Pickens has become an advocate of alternative fuels and electrical generation methods. The Pickens Plan, an energy policy proposal, promotes the reduction of dependence on foreign oil via the use of natural gas as a transportation fuel and the installation of wind farms for electricity in the United States

Career

After earning his degree in geology from Oklahoma A&M (now Oklahoma State University) in 1951, Pickens worked for Phillips Petroleum for three years. Pickens formed his own oil company in 1956, Mesa Petroleum, which would later grow into one of the largest independent oil production and exploration companies in the world. After a series of corporate takeovers throughout the energy sector, Pickens divested himself from Mesa Petroleum and founded BP Capital Management in 1997 (BP stands for "Boone Pickens" and has no relation to the company British Petroleum). During the same year, Pickens also formed Pickens Fuel Corporation, now reincorporated as Clean Energy Fuels Corporation, a natural gas distribution company. BP Capital Management focuses on investment in the energy sector, through such companies as Halliburton, Schlumberger, Occidental Petroleum, and ExxonMobil. Pickens's other interests include subsurface water rights in Texas, under the umbrella of Mesa Water; wind power, through his Mesa Power LP company; and the distribution of natural gas for transportation, through Clean Energy Fuels Corporation. In 2010, *Forbes* listed Pickens as the 290th-richest man in the United States and the 880th-richest man in the world. Pickens had an estimated net worth of $1.4 billion in 2010.

Aubrey Wigner
Jason Delborne

Further Reading

Pickens, T. Boone. *The First Billion Is the Hardest: Reflections on a Life of Comebacks and America's Energy Future.* New York: Crown, 2008.
Pickens, T. Boone. "PickensPlan." http://www.pickensplan.com.

Pickens, T. Boone. "T. Boone Pickens: His Life. His Legacy." http://www.boonepickens.com.

Smil, Vaclav. "A Reality Check on the Pickens Energy Plan." *Yale Environment* 360 (August 25, 2008). http://e360.yale.edu/feature/a_reality_check_on_the_pickens_energy_plan/2058/.

See Also: Natural Gas; Oil and Petroleum; Transportation; Wind Resources; Wind Technology.

Pinchot, Gifford

Dates: 1865–1946.
Category: Biographies.
Summary: Gifford Pinchot was the founder of forestry conservation practices in the United States. Pinchot believed that forests could be continuously harvested while generating a profit.

The formation of the U.S. Forest Service hinged on Gifford Pinchot's political will to fight prevailing ideas about forestry in the United States. At the time, the general population felt the forest resources of the United States were limitless and should be exploited as fast as possible, with little if any concern for related environments and enterprises. Forestry conservation involves the scientific management of a forest tract through the harvesting of mature trees while preserving the smaller, younger trees in order to generate continuous profits over the long term. Pinchot believed in the management of forests for multiple uses and that the greatest good for the greatest number of people would be achieved through the wise use of all natural resources. The Hetch-Hetchy and Ballinger-Pinchot controversies found Pinchot engaged in political struggles at the national level to realize the twin goals of conservation and profitability.

With the support and foresight of his father, Pinchot was introduced to the idea of forestry as an occupation. As a student at Yale University, Pinchot was advised against a career in forestry by academics and government administrators. However, he successfully sought out mentors that fostered his interests. His lifelong mentor Sir Dietrich Brandis guided Pinchot toward enrolling in 1889 at the French National Forestry School, where Pinchot studied forests around Europe. Upon returning to the United States, Pinchot ventured for the first time beyond the eastern seaboard, where he witnessed the devastation of rapid deforestation. Determined to demonstrate the viability and desirability of forestry conservation, Pinchot sought out the means to realize this goal. In 1898, Pinchot began the management of a private forest owned by the Vanderbilt family at Biltmore Estate, ultimately bringing modern forestry practices to the United States.

Scientific Management of Forests
During the late 19th and early 20th centuries, the dominant ideology was that the natural resources of the United States were inexhaustible. Pinchot fought the use of clear-cutting practices, which denuded landscapes, leading to soil erosion and silted-up waterways, which posed problems for hydropower dams, fisheries, and agriculture. Pinchot brought European methods of forest management to the United States, adapting those practices for the U.S. situation and developing forestry in the United States with the support of President Grover Cleveland and later President Theodore Roosevelt. The scientific management of forests through selective cutting, coupled with planting trees after forest harvests, would conserve the ecology of the land (and waters) and benefit the economy in the long term. The federal administration of forestry began as a decentralized institution and eventually moved toward a centralized administration through Pinchot's political work.

Pinchot became the first head of the U.S. Forest Service when it was created in 1905, with the mission of managing forests for the public good. Conservation enabled the continuous use of natural resources without taking land out of circulation or locking it into specific uses. Pinchot had a particular interest in maintaining forests and the resources on and below forestlands, such as timber, water, pasture, minerals, and hydrocarbon energy, for the benefit of the public. He was staunchly against private monopolistic control over publicly owned natural resources and saw monopolies as destructive of the environment while profiting at the public's expense. Private enterprises could access Forest Service lands by obtaining permits. Any financial gains were in turn used to maintain a labor force on reserve lands. Pinchot established a federal administration that enabled as much exploitation of forest resources for profit without compromising the sustainability of the land.

Hetch-Hetchy Debate with John Muir

The limits of conservation were still being drawn at the turn of the century. While Pinchot saw conservation of forests as related to other aspects of the environment, he equally promoted the full use of natural resources for profitability. The Hetch-Hetchy debate found Pinchot in the center of a controversy over whether to dam the waters of the Colorado River in the Hetch-Hetchy Valley, a wilderness area in Yosemite National Park, in order to provide the city of San Francisco with a permanent source of potable water. On one side of the debate was preservationist John Muir, who argued against the dam and saw the proposal as negatively impacting the public by endowing special interest groups with political power and unfair profits and degrading the valley's natural beauty. Opposing Muir was Pinchot, who believed that a dam would facilitate the best use of the valley and would benefit the public welfare. While in other aspects of his career Pinchot sought to spend time with local people learning about the local landscape, he had never ventured into the Hetch-Hetchy Valley to learn about the landscape and what it offered to visitors and users. In a sense, Pinchot's rising political status had pitted him against his original stance against monopolized

water power and land-grabbing special interests. Ultimately the dam project would proceed.

Pinchot's tumultuous political career continued in 1909 with the Ballinger-Pinchot controversy, which resulted in Achilles Ballinger's dismissal and Pinchot's dismissal from the Forest Service, ending Pinchot's federal political career. The controversy arose after Ballinger became secretary of the interior and reopened 3 million acres of public land to private use. Pinchot, as head of the Forest Service, thought this would have a detrimental impact on the public and environment, as private initiatives would exploit the land as much and as quickly as possible, with little regard for sustainability. Development interests that were involved sought to exploit coal deposits and obtain sites for waterpower development.

Later, as Pennsylvania's governor from 1923 to 1927, Pinchot was active in attempts at early regulation of electricity as a public utility and commissioned the Giant Power Survey, which promoted large power plants built at the mouths of coal mines to allow electric generation near the mine sites and thus avoid the need to transport the coal. According to Pinchot, energy was the new economic revolution. Committed to equi-

Left: U.S. Geological Survey; right: Wikimedia

The Hetch-Hetchy Valley in Yosemite National Park, California, before and after completion of the controversial dam of the Colorado River. Gifford Pinchot faced opposition from preservationist John Muir over the dam.

table distribution of power at fair prices, Pinchot felt private regulation was unlikely and would lead to monopolies. At the time, the federal government was dominated by business elites and special interests. Pinchot advocated in the public interest when it came to public utilities and natural resources, seeking fair distribution and prices for all. In taking such stands, he engendered political turmoil, which ultimately led to his failure to be reelected as state governor.

American Conservation Movement

Pinchot played a pivotal role in the American conservation movement through a dedication to forestry, which blossomed into a political career focused on advocating conservation in the name of economic prosperity and public welfare. The U.S. Forest Service was founded on Pinchot's personal devotion to forestry and conservation. Scientific management of natural resources would bring long-term economic prosperity when coupled with sustainable practices. Public interest guided Pinchot's political agenda. The Hetch-Hetchy debate marked Pinchot as a conservative advocate of the American public, while the Ballinger-Pinchot Affair found Pinchot ostracized and ousted from the federal government. These outcomes of these debates formed the foundation upon which the U.S. approach to conservation and natural resources was based. Pinchot's legacy from his involvement with the Giant Power plan is mixed. His proposal that electric generation, transmission, and distribution should be under separate ownership finally came to fruition with electricity utility deregulation in many states, while his promotion of large coal-fired power plants was a major cause of air pollution and especially acid rain, which seriously damaged his beloved forests.

SAMANTHA FOX

Further Reading
Miller, Char. *Gifford Pinchot and the Making of Modern Environmentalism*. Washington, DC: Island Press, 2001.
Pinchot, Gifford. *Breaking New Ground*. Washington, DC: Island Press, 1998.
Pinchot, Gifford. *The Conservation Diaries of Gifford Pinchot*, edited by Harold K Steen. Durham, NC: Forest History Society, 2001.
Pinchot, Gifford. *The Fight for Conservation*. Seattle: University of Washington Press, 1967.

See Also: Conservation; Giant Power; History of Energy: 1900–1950; Pennsylvania; Super Power; Sustainable Development.

Plug-in Hybrid Vehicles

Category: Environmentalism
Summary: A plug-in hybrid electric vehicle, like all hybrid-electric vehicles, can run on liquid fuel as well as electricity from a battery. The vehicle's battery can be recharged by plugging it into a wall socket or other source of electricity.

Plug-in hybrid electric vehicles (PHEVs) generally have a larger-capacity battery than hybrid-electric vehicles (HEVs), increasing their potential to displace liquid fuel use with electrical power, and provide the advantage that the car can be plugged in at night to recharge for the next day's driving. Currently available or slated to be introduced PHEVs include the Chevy Volt, the Fisker Karma, the BYD F3DM (from BYD Auto in China), the Toyota Prius Plug-In Hybrid, the Volvo V70 Plug-in Hybrid, and the Ford Escape Plug-in Hybrid.

At the start of a trip, a PHEV runs entirely on battery power, as if it were an entirely electric vehicle. When the battery power runs down to a minimum level, known as the *minimum state of charge*, it begins to operate on a mixture of conventional fuel (e.g., gasoline) and battery power, similar to a HEV. Some PHEVs can also be engineered to run in a "blended mode," during which an onboard computer determines the most efficient blend of conventional and battery power. There are currently two competing technologies for PHEV batteries: nickel metal hydride and lithium ion. Nickel metal hydride batteries are cheaper to produce and have a known safety record, but are heavy. Lithium ion batteries are lighter and can store more electricity but have an unproven safety record. However, most experts think that lithium ion battery technology will improve and ultimately be the battery of choice for PHEVs.

The distance that a PHEV can be driven on a single charge is generally in the 10–60 mile range, with 40 being an average value. This coincides well with the driving habits of many American motorists because most automobile trips are relatively short, and on most days people drive a relatively small number of miles commuting to work or school or running errands. According to the U.S. Bureau of Transportation Statistics, on weekdays, 10 percent of Americans report 5 or fewer vehicle miles of travel daily, 23 percent report 10 miles or less, 44 percent report 20 miles or less, 60 percent report 30 miles or less, and 71 percent report 40 miles or less. For weekend travel, 22 percent of Americans report 5 miles or less of vehicle travel per day, 42 percent 10 miles or less, 69 percent 20 miles or less, 77 percent 30 miles or less, and 82 percent 40 miles or less.

PHEVs offer most of the advantages of both HEVs and all-electric vehicles while mitigating some of their disadvantages. Because they can run on conventional fuels like gasoline if necessary, a PHEV driver is not limited by the range of the battery, nor does their use require a new infrastructure (electrical charging stations). Instead, they can operate on ordinary gasoline, while the battery can be recharged from any outlet attached to the electrical grid. PHEV batteries are generally smaller than those used in all-electric vehicles, reducing the cost of the battery and the time required to fully charge it. Like HEVs and all-electric vehicles, PHEVs have the potential to lower the costs of driving: one estimate is that the electricity necessary to replace one gallon of gas would cost on average about $0.75 in the United States.

The use of electricity to do the work formerly performed by gasoline reduces petroleum dependence and the corresponding influence that the need for petroleum plays in geopolitics. According to the U.S. Department of Energy (DOE), PHEVs in all-battery mode are more efficient than

A RAM 1500 plug-in hybrid pickup truck exhibited at the 2011 Washington Auto Show. The truck was part of a three-year demonstration program that was developed from a partnership between the Chrysler Group and the U.S. Department of Energy.

HEVs running in combined mode. The DOE estimates the fuel efficiency of a PHEV at 105 miles per gallon in charge-depleting mode (running entirely by battery) and 42 miles per gallon in charge-sustaining mode (using both conventional fuel and the battery). PHEVs also have significant potential to reduce pollution, particularly in densely-travelled areas, such as cities. The success of HEVs in the United States and elsewhere suggests that there is limited consumer resistance to the idea of a hybrid vehicle.

The primary barriers to rapid adoption of PHEVs are the size and cost of the battery required, and the possibility that the battery may need replacement one or more times over the life of the vehicle, further increasing cost. Another issue that must be addressed is the development of a network of charging receptacles similar to the current network of gas stations, thus overcoming the issue of limited driving ranges. Creating an efficient network will require adoption of common standards so that any vehicle's battery can be recharged in any charging station. Even matters as simple as the design of the plug have proven contentious in Europe, while in the United States, manufacturers have agreed on a common standard.

Of course, reduced fuel costs can compensate for the increased upfront cost, but estimates of fuel cost savings depend on the all-electric range of the PHEV and price of gasoline. In 2007, the U.S. Energy Information Administration estimated reduced fuel costs (comparing a PHEV with a conventionally-fuelled car) ranging from $1,381.83 annually, based on a gas price of $3.00 a gallon, and an all-electric range of 10 miles, to $6,474.59 annually, based on gasoline costs of $6.00 a gallon and an all-electric range of 60 miles. Similarly, estimating the number of years of reduced operating costs required to compensate for the initial higher cost of a PHEV as compared to a conventional vehicle depend on variables, including cost of gasoline and electricity, and an individual's driving habits. Andrew Simpson estimates that, based on gasoline costing $5.00 a gallon and the vehicle being driven 15,000 miles annually, a PHEV could achieve lower total costs (purchase plus operation) than a conventional vehicle after 12 years of ownership.

SARAH BOSLAUGH

Further Reading

"Electric Car Makers Fight Over Plug Standard." EurActiv (April 11, 2011). http://www.euractiv .com/innovation-enterprise/electric-car-makers -fight-plug-standard-news-503854.

Fletcher, Seth. *Bottled Lightning: Superbatteries, Electric Cars and the New Lithium Economy.* New York: Hill and Wang, 2001.

Simpson, Andrew. "Cost-Benefit Analysis of Plug-In Hybrid Electric Vehicle Technology." Conference Paper presented at the 22nd International Battery, Hybrid and Fuel Cell Electric Vehicle Symposium and Exhibition, Yokohama, Japan, October 23–28, 2006. NREL/CP-540-40484. http://www.nrel.gov/ docs/fy07osti/40485.pdf.

U.S. Energy Information Administration. "Economics of Plug-in Hybrid Vehicles" (2009). http://www.eia.gov/oiaf/aeo/otheranalysis/ aeo_2009analysispapers/ephev.html.

See Also: Automobiles; Batteries as an Energy Source; Electric Motors; Electric Vehicles; Flex-Fuel Vehicles; Hybrid Vehicles.

Poland

Official Name: Republic of Poland.
Category: Geography of Energy.
Summary: Poland has significant coal resources and is highly reliant on them. Since Poland's market reformation in the 1980s, the energy sector has undergone privatization, but the energy mix has remained largely unchanged, with a small increase in alternative energy sources.

During the 1970s, Poland's energy production and consumption increased along with the expansion of the economy and rise in industrial output. Energy utilization, however, sharply decreased in 1981, when martial law was imposed in Poland. During this period, the political situation worsened and economic productivity deteriorated as energy-intensive industries' output declined. In the late 1980s and early 1990s, Poland began its transformation from a centrally planned economy to a liberalized market economy. As a result, industrial output gradually began to recover. The World Bank financed some sector reforms during the 1990s, helping to establish energy laws, the Energy Regulatory Office (URE), and the electricity exchange market. The government lifted pricing controls as a part of its economic "shock therapy" in an attempt to increase prices in the energy sector gradually; however, this led to rapid price increases instead.

Industry and commercial buildings responded to the rise in energy prices by increasing energy efficiency. Consequently, energy production began to decrease as economic output declined. State industries suffered as a result of increased competition and cuts in state subsidies. To make the economic situation worse, trade relations with eastern European countries and the Soviet Union deteriorated, cutting off a supply of cheap, raw materials and export markets. Since Poland's energy sector was tied to that of the Soviet Union, the Polish were reliant on Soviet oil imports and Soviet markets for coal exports. Eventually, Poland's economy began to recover as the private sector developed. However, energy production has declined since the 1980s, compared to the

1970s, primarily because of a reduction in energy intensity and consumption in industries.

Poland's historically energy-intensive economy and strong reliance on coal led to serious environmental degradation, particularly from emissions. According to the International Energy Agency (IEA), in the late 1980s Poland's electricity generation accounted for 52 percent of sulfur dioxide (SO_2) and 32 percent of nitrogen oxide (NO_x) emissions. Other environmental issues include large quantities of ash disposal, large volumes of waste from electricity generation, and waste discharges from coal mining. Major rivers, such as the Vistula and the Oder, were polluted by discharges of saline water from coal mines in the resource-rich Silesia region of Poland. Additionally, groundwater extraction near the mining areas resulted in water shortages, and open-pit (surface) lignite mining reduced the land available for agricultural use. In 1990, the government enacted a framework regulation based on the "polluter pays" principle for environmental protection. The regulation established emission limits (mainly for SO_2 and NO_x) for each unit of fuel consumed.

In 1997, the Energy Act was established as the overarching energy framework, covering areas such as energy security and efficiency, promoting competition and consumer choice, and environmental issues. The act appointed the Ministry of Economic Affairs to oversee the Polish energy sector and outlined the obligations of the Energy Regulation Office (URE), the government executive body created in 1997. The URE's role was to ensure regulatory compliance and to protect consumers' rights. This was to be achieved by overseeing energy production licensing, trade, transmission, pricing, and third-party access to the energy market. The Energy Act was revised in 2005, establishing a green certificate system and a renewable energy source (RES) quota for renewable energy, as well as tax exemptions, particularly for biofuels. The RES quota required energy suppliers to reach a minimum 4.8 percent share of renewable energy by 2007 and 7.5 percent by 2010, according to the European Union (EU) accession treaty. In 2007, the Energy Act was once again amended

to increase the share of renewable energy from 9 percent to 10.4 percent from 2010 to 2014.

By 2004, all consumers, excluding households, were free to choose their suppliers, and in 2007, the market expanded to include household consumers. Furthermore, accession to the EU in 2004 required Poland to modify all national energy laws to adhere to EU regulations. Energy reforms in the Energy Act led to the first privatization of the energy sector, in 1998, when EDF, the French energy company, purchased Elektrociepłownia, Krakow's largest heat and electricity supplier. In 2000, the Council of Ministers in Poland adopted a long-term approach to energy policy in the Assumptions for Poland's Energy Policy Until 2020, which focused on energy safety and security, market competitiveness, and environmental protection. In 2005, another plan, Poland's Energy Policy Until 2025, was created to address the development of renewable energy sources. The 2005 Energy Policy was superseded in 2008 by the new Energy Policy, effective until 2030.

Market reforms in Poland led to limited vertical integration, with most energy firms operating in one of three areas: generation, transmission, and distribution. Additionally, the market is highly fragmented, with low horizontal integration. The four major power generators that have been partially or fully privatized are Polaniec, Rybnik, Skawina, and PAK. Transmission activities are run by the state-owned transmission system operator Polskie Sieci Elektroenergetyczne (PSE), and distribution companies are also primarily dominated by state-owned companies and two private companies, Vattenfall and RWE.

Electricity Generation by Fuel Type

According to Eurostat, Poland's primary energy consumption ranked sixth in the EU-27, making up 5.4 percent of the total EU gross consumption of primary energy in 2004. Because of its high reliance on locally sourced coal, Poland has a relatively strong energy independency rate and is ranked as the eighth most energy-independent nation in the EU-27. According to the IEA, in 2008 coal accounted for 91.8 percent of Poland's electricity generation and 89.3 percent of heat generation. Gas and oil make up the next-largest share of electricity and heat generation, while hydropower and biomass together form the largest renewable energy share in the overall mix.

Electricity Generation

Electricity generation in Poland is dominated by coal and lignite. Coal reserves, located primarily in the Upper Silesian region and in the Lublin basins, contain 10.3 billion tons of coal equivalent (tce). Additionally, 573 million tce of known lignite reserves are located in the central and southwest regions of the country. From 1972 to 1979, Poland was Europe's largest coal producer, with 150.7 million tce, and the second-largest coal producer in the world until 1979 (according to Euracoal, the European association for coal and lignite). Coal production decreased in 2002, to 102.1 million tce, and in 2007 it decreased further, to 87.4 million tce. The demand for Polish coal began to decrease both because of domestic economic reforms and the availability of competing fuels on the international market. Nevertheless, coal continues to play a vital role in Poland's economy, employing around 116,000 people.

In 2000, Poland began a gradual diversification of its energy mix with renewable energy sources. Hydropower has the largest share of Poland's renewable energy, while biomass, wind, and biogas form the next-largest percentage of renewable energy sources. The potential for bioenergy is large but remains mostly untapped, with around 13 megatons of municipal solid waste (MSW) produced each year and about 97 percent disposed in more than 900 landfills. Despite the potential, methane was recovered in only 28 landfill sites in 2005. Wind power is gaining momentum in Poland, producing around 250 gigawatt-hours of electricity between 2001 and 2006. In 2005 alone, wind power generated 4.9 percent of the total renewable energy in Poland but amounted to only 0.1 percent of total electricity consumption. Although renewable energy development has been limited, the implementation of the renewable energy quota obligations and the certificate of origins are expected to propel the growth of renewable energy, particularly the wind power sector.

Aside from renewable energy sources, Poland has a relatively large district heating sector in which nearly 64 percent of its sources are derived from recycled heat or the indirect use of renewables. By recycling surplus heat from electricity generation, as well as industrial and fuel refinement processes, district heating could contribute to decreasing carbon emissions and to meeting EU targets of reducing primary energy consumption by 20 percent by 2020. Additionally, district heating provides affordable heating for around 50 percent of the population, primarily in the residential sector. It is an expanding sector that connected 64,000 new households in 2009 and employed more than 40,000 people, according to Euroheat and Power.

Future potential energy sources include nuclear power and anticipated natural gas deposits. Although Poland does not currently have nuclear power stations, there are future plans to build plants after 2015, which would help to reduce carbon emissions from energy-generating facilities. In 2010, there were predictions that Poland might have between 4.9 and 9.8 trillion cubic feet (1.5 and 3 trillion cubic meters) of shale gas in the northern region, equivalent to Iraq's deposits. However, further test wells must be drilled and further research conducted to determine the true potential of Poland's shale gas. If the discovery materializes, the country may once again become a major world energy player in fossil fuels and gain considerable wealth within the next 10 to 15 years.

JENNY LIEU

Further Reading

Euroheat and Power. "District Heating and Cooling: 2009 Statistics." http://www.euroheat.org.

European Association for Coal and Lignite. "Poland." http://www.euracoal.be/pages/layout1sp.php?idpage=76.

International Energy Agency. "Electricity/Heat in Poland in 2008." http://www.iea.org/stats/electricitydata.asp?COUNTRY_CODE=PL.

International Energy Agency. *Energy Policies of IEA Countries: Poland, 2011.* Paris: International Energy Agency, 2011.

Jouret, Laurent. "Electricity Market in Poland: Changes in the Horizon." ING Bank, April 2006. http://custody.ingbank.pl/_itemserver/wholesale/raporty/ING_Raport_Energetyczny_eng.pdf.

Nilsson, Lars J., Marcin Pisarek, Jerzy Buriak, Anna Oniszk-Poplawska, Pawel Bucko, Karin Ericsson, and Lukasz Jaworsk. "Energy Policy and the Role of Bioenergy in Poland." *Energy Policy* 34 (2006).

Paskaa, J., et al. "Current Status and Perspectives of Renewable Energy Sources in Poland." *Renewable and Sustainable Energy Reviews* 13 (2009).

Polish National Energy Conservation Agency. "District Heating Sector National Report." http://www.opet-chp.net/download/wp1/PolandKAPENationalDHReport.pdf.

See Also: Clausius, Rudolf; Curie, Marie; Ethanol: Sugar Beet; International Energy Agency; Natural Gas; Russia; Slovakia; War; Waste Heat Recovery.

Portugal

Official Name: Portuguese Republic.
Category: Geography of Energy.
Summary: Portugal has developed a significant renewable electric power generation capacity—largely based on wind and hydropower—which will improve the share of electricity produced by renewable energy to as much as 60 percent in 2020.

Portugal is a member of the European Union (EU). In 2002, Portugal had a relatively low nominal per capita gross domestic product (GDP) compared to its neighbors. However, since it joined the EU (in 1986, when the EU was the European Economic Community), the country's economy has been expanding robustly. Funds from the European Commission have been used to invest in Portugal's infrastructure.

Energy Production and Consumption
The vast bulk of Portugal's energy requirements are met through imports, predominantly of oil and gas. The country made a strategic shift in introducing natural gas in 1997. While oil use by volume is almost the same today as 1997 levels, and coal consumption has dropped to zero, natural gas use in Portugal has zoomed from zero in 1997 to 182 billion cubic feet in 2010—100 percent of it imported.

Energy consumption in Portugal has roughly doubled in the two decades since 1990. The increase has taken place across the transport, industrial, and commercial sectors. Total consumption was 18.5 million tons of oil equivalent (Mtoe) in 2008. Transport is the largest energy-consuming sector in the country, accounting for a 36 percent share in 2008, or approximately 6.7 Mtoe. The EU average for transport as a fraction of total energy consumption is 31 percent. Pronounced increase in tourism as well as daily commutes by employees in the rapidly developing industrial and commercial sectors were the key factors. Industry accounted for 29 percent of total energy consumption in 2008; residential use accounted for 17 percent; services 12 percent—having tripled since 1990—and agriculture 2 percent.

In terms of fuels used in the various sectors, petroleum products in 2008 amounted to approximately 9.6 Mtoe, representing 52 percent of fuel consumption, easily the dominant share. However, this actually represents a dramatic reduction in proportional dependence on oil; as recently as 1998 this fuel represented more than 60 percent of total energy consumption. Electricity, still growing in share, was the second-largest fuel in 2008, at about 3.8 Mtoe. Renewables were quite significant, at 1.5 Mtoe. The still expanding natural gas contribution was 1.3 Mtoe, much of it fueling industrial uses; the remainder was from direct heat sources at 1.1 Mtoe.

Renewable Energy Sources
The contribution that renewable sources—mainly hydroelectricity and wind—make to total energy supply was almost 22 percent in 2009, significantly higher than the EU average of 11 percent. Domestic production of energy, which has increased by 50 percent since 1990, is exclusively based on renewable energy sources, mainly hydro, wind, and biomass energy.

Wikimedia

This thermal power station is located in Setúbal, Portugal, on the northern bank of the Sado River. It provides heating for buildings, swimming pools, and greenhouses.

According to the statistical convention of Eurostat, Portugal is among the leading countries in Europe in terms of its contribution of renewable energy to the national energy balance. According to statistics from Direcção-Geral de Energia e Geologia (DGEG), the share of renewable energy (excluding large hydropower) in total primary energy consumption increased from 10.3 percent in 1999 to 19.9 percent in 2009.

The development of small hydropower in Portugal is a good case study in how to remove non-technical barriers to private investment in the power sector. In 1988, Decree Law 189/88 came into force, defining the rules for the independent production of electricity from renewables. This regulation was the main reason for the small-hydro market boom in the early 1990s. According

to DGEG data, there is an installed capacity of 600 megawatts from small-hydro plants, which generated about 2,000 gigawatt-hours in 2010.

There has also been a huge improvement in wind-farm-installed capacity since 1999. In that year, about 64.5 megawatts of electricity-generating wind turbines were operating in Portugal: 57.5 megawatts in mainland Portugal and 6.9 in the island regions of Madeira and the Azores. According to DGEG, in 2010 the installed capacity exceeded 4,000 megawatts, which generated about 9,000 gigawatt-hours. The plan is to install more wind turbines in order to reach the target of 8,500 megawatts of installed capacity in 2020.

Among the country's latest initiatives in this area is the development of pumped storage hydropower. The technology is seen as an ideal, low-emission tie-in to wind turbine power, as the pumped storage reservoirs can be called into action in periods of low winds, thus smoothing out the wind-based power supply.

Low-temperature geothermal resources are exploited mostly on mainland Portugal, with high-temperature resources restricted to the Azores. These sites provide heating for buildings, swimming pools, and greenhouses, in certain cases associated with thermal spas. Current installed capacity is about 30 megawatts, producing about 190 gigawatt-hours in 2009.

The photovoltaic (PV) total installed capacity exceeded 128 megawatts in 2010, and the power generated was about 210 gigawatt-hours. Most PV sites are stand-alone systems that provide electricity for homes in remote locations (73 percent) and service applications (21 percent), mainly telecommunications repeaters.

After the originally successful solar market development in the 1970s, solar equipment sales crashed in the mid-1980s because of sinking oil prices, solar companies' lack of credit access, and the poor quality of the installed systems. The market was stagnant, with spurts of activity depending on available subsidies. However, market conditions and improved solar industry standards seem to indicate a sector poised for expansion. According to the European Solar Thermal Industry Federation (ESTIF), the total area of solar collectors in operation was estimated at almost 500,000 square meters in 2009, a year of impressive growth in new installations—driven by an aggressive financial incentive program launched in March 2009.

Emissions

According to the Agência Portuguesa do Ambiente, in 2006, Portuguese greenhouse gas (GHG) emissions represented 82.7 million tons of carbon dioxide equivalent. This value has been relatively stable since 1999 but is well above the target, 75.1 million tons of carbon dioxide equivalent, defined for Portugal in the burden-sharing agreement that has allocated emission reduction efforts among 15 EU countries.

Among Portugal's main energy policy goals are the European climate and energy targets to be met by 2020, known as the 20-20-20 targets. These represent a reduction in EU GHG emissions of at least 20 percent below 1990 levels, with 20 percent of EU energy consumption to come from renewable resources, and a 20 percent reduction in primary energy use compared with projected levels, to be achieved by improving energy efficiency. To fulfill this plan, Portugal would have to increase its electricity production from renewables to more than half of the total electricity produced. To this end, the country has set goals for energy energy use reduction on the order of almost 10 percent of final energy consumption.

REZA FAZELI
GUSTAVO B. HAYDT DE SOUZA

Further Reading

European Energy Agency. "Climate Change Mitigation: Drivers and Pressures (Portugal)." http://www.eea.europa.eu/soer/countries/pt/climate-change-mitigation-drivers-and.

European Renewable Energy Council. "Portugal: Renewable Energy Policy Review." http://www.erec.org/fileadmin/erec_docs/Projcet_Documents/RES2020/PORTUGAL_RES_Policy_Review_09_Final.pdf.

Royal Institution of Chartered Surveyors. "Energy Factsheet: Portugal." February 2008. http://www.rics.org/site/download_feed.aspx?fileID=3074&fileExtension=PDF.

U.S. Energy Information Administration. "Country Analysis Brief: Portugal." http://205.254.135.7/countries/country-data.cfm?fips=PO.

See Also: Hydropower; International Energy Agency; Mozambique; Nigeria; Organization of Petroleum Exporting Countries; São Tomé and Príncipe; Wind Resources.

Potential Energy

Category: Fundamentals of Energy.
Summary: Energy exists in several forms, but most scientists agree that the two basic forms of energy are potential energy and kinetic energy.

Potential energy is energy that is stored rather than used and can exist in many subforms, including chemical, mechanical, and atomic energy. Kinetic energy is energy that is being used; most kinetic energy is associated with some form of motion.

To convert energy to work, it is advantageous to have stored energy in a form that can be converted to both kinetic energy and work in a controlled and metered fashion. *Potential energy* is the scientific name for energy that is in a stable, stored form (as opposed to *kinetic energy*, which is energy that is in use). Potential energy in sources that are stable and available in abundance are needed so it can be converted for the generation of electricity to power homes, run machinery, provide lighting, and meet myriad other energy needs.

Gravitational Potential Energy

The most common or recognizable form of potential energy is the energy stored when an object that has mass is moved from a lower, stable energy state to a second stable position higher in energy and physical elevation than the original state. This is called gravitational potential energy and is expressed mathematically as $E = mgh$, where E is the potential energy, m is

▷ *Chemical Potential Energy*

Chemical potential energy is another common form of potential energy. The binding energy that holds molecules together is the source of chemical energy, and if this binding force is stable and can be contained, it is a source of potential energy. Chemical reactions initiated as activation energy can form or break these chemical bonds and release the potential energy stored in the bonds.

A good example of chemical potential energy occurs with lead (Pb) and sulfuric acid (H_2SO_4) batteries. This type battery has a lead peroxide (PbO_2) anode (positive terminal) and a lead (Pb) cathode (negative terminal) in a jar where both are submersed in sulfuric acid. The chemical bonds of these compounds store a good bit of potential energy that can be released when the anode and cathode are connected to something with electric resistance, such as a lightbulb. The battery is stable and holds its energy as potential energy until the lightbulb is connected and the connection destabilizes the sulfuric acid. A chemical reaction occurs in which the sulfuric acid's molecular bonds are broken and free diatomic hydrogen (H_2) and free sulfate (SO_4) are formed. The lead peroxide's bonds are also broken, and some of the anode turns in free lead and free diatomic oxygen (O_2). When the electrons released by this reaction flow through the lightbulb, the potential chemical energy is converted to heat and light. The free diatomic hydrogen combines molecularly with the free diatomic oxygen to form water (H_2O), and the free lead molecularly combines with the free sulfate to form lead sulfate ($PbSO_4$), which is a white powder in the battery's acid jar that collects on both the anode and the cathode. As soon as the load is removed, the reaction is stopped, and the battery will still hold potential energy, although not as much as when all of the solution is sulfuric acid. If an electric source puts electrons back (charging) into the battery, the reaction occurs in reverse, and the full potential chemical energy state can be restored if the entire lead sulfate content is reacted back to its original form.

The carbon and hydrogen stored in coal, oil, gas, and other fossil fuels are also forms of chemical potential energy. Fossil fuels' potential energy is released by the chemical exothermic reaction of rapid oxidation, commonly called *burning*.

mass, g is the gravitational constant, and h is height. An easy visualized example of this type of potential energy is demonstrated by a person picking up a round, large rock at the bottom of a hill and carrying it to the top of the hill. The round rock is then set down on a stable ledge, where it can rest without further restraint. The person carrying the round rock provided the kinetic energy to lift it to a higher elevation and transferred this kinetic energy at some efficiency to the rock as a new, higher potential energy state. The potential energy in the rock could be released and returned to kinetic energy if the person pushed the rock off the ledge on which it is now sitting and letting the rock roll down the hill. The force of gravity would compel the rock to release its potential energy as the kinetic energy of motion, when a small amount of destabilizing energy was added by pushing the rock off its ledge. The push is the energy required to destabilize the potential energy state and cause it to transform to kinetic energy. If the destabilizing energy were not added, the rock would have sat on top of the hill indefinitely with more potential energy than it had before it was carried up the hill.

The formal name of the energy used to destabilize the potential energy state is *activation energy*. One very common practical use of stored potential energy is in the construction of dams to store water at an elevated height above the normal water level. Most of the water in rivers and streams originates from rain, which is at an elevated height. If a container can be constructed to capture this water before gravity pulls it to the normal water level, the water will retain potential energy due to its elevated height.

This is exactly what dams can do; dam reservoirs are really large containers that capture water. The elevated water level in the dam's reservoir represents potential energy; if the water is allowed to fall to normal water level, through a controlled opening, the mass and velocity of the falling water can be used to turn a waterwheel or water turbine. The waterwheel or water turbine's rotating energy can be used to run machinery or generate electricity.

Electricity is very hard to store at large power levels, and one of the few practical ways to do so is to pump water up to an elevated level for storage using electricity-driven pumps. Some hydroelectric generating plants have water turbines that do not just let falling water turn the turbines to generate electricity but have the ability to allow the generator to function as a motor and take power off the electric grid, then pump the water back up into the dam's reservoir. These generating stations are called *pumped-storage units*, and they convert electric energy back into potential energy by using electricity to push water to a higher elevation, where it can be stable.

Springs, Accumulators, and Flywheels

Mechanical springs and hydraulic accumulators are good sources of stored potential energy as well. These devices are often used on hydraulic systems to provide stored energy to be turned into kinetic energy on demand. The most common use is to store energy to take a valve or other device to a safe position upon failure of the device's primary drive. The potential energy device, such as a spring, is thus a secondary source of energy used when the primary source of energy is unavailable due to failure.

Springs and accumulators can also store energy from a primary movement to be used to assist in returning to an original position. Large flywheels are also sources of mechanical potential energy, and these devices can be used to store energy and even out load on variable demand energy sources.

Nuclear Energy

Nuclear energy, another a form of potential energy, is similar to chemical potential energy but with the source of the stored energy in the bonds between atomic particles of the molecular forces or bonds that unite the atoms of one element to atoms of the same or another element. Breaking or joining atomic nuclear bonds releases the stored potential energy in these bonds.

Some very large atoms have a nucleus whose bonds can be broken by the bombardment of free neutrons in what is called nuclear fission. For example, when the nucleus of an atom of uranium-235 is exposed to bombardment by neutrons traveling at a sufficiently high velocity, the nuclear bonds will break apart, releasing more neutrons, daughter nuclear products, radiation, and potential energy.

If the uranium is arranged in the right geometry with the right amount of uranium, the neutrons released will break the bonds of other uranium atoms close by in a self-sustaining chain reaction. If the amount and speed of these neutrons can be controlled by a moderator in which the uranium is immersed, the reaction can be controlled and used to heat fluids, and those fluids can then power Rankin-cycle power plants used to generate electricity.

Potential energy can also be released from nuclear fusion, during which atoms with small nuclei, such as hydrogen (whose nucleus consists of a single proton), are forced to bond together to form helium. This form of nuclear energy, called fusion energy, is not yet practical; the extremely high pressures and temperatures needed to make the reaction occur also make it difficult to control. Stars, however, have large reserves of potential fusion energy in hydrogen reserves, and it is theorized that some stars have enough stored potential energy to keep fusing hydrogen for billions of years.

The heavier elements are thought to have been formed (and continue to be formed) when stars explode using large amounts of stored energy at once to make elements heavier than helium.

DAMON ERIC WOODSON

Further Reading

Chopey, Nicholas P. *Handbook of Chemical Engineering Calculations.* New York: McGraw-Hill, 1984.

Kenward, Michael. *Potential Energy: An Analysis of World Energy Technology.* New York: Cambridge University Press, 1976.

PowerStream Technology. "Chemical Changes in the Battery." http://www.powerstream.com/1922/battery_1922_WITTE/batteryfiles/chapter04.htm.

U.S. Energy Information Administration. "Energy Explained: Your Guide to Understanding Energy." http://www.eia.doe.gov/energyexplained/index.cfm.

Viegas, Jennnifer. *Kinetic and Potential Energy: Understanding Changes Within Physical Systems.* New York: Rosen, 2005.

World Nuclear Association. "What Is Uranium? How Does It Work?" http://www.world-nuclear.org/education/uran.htm.

See Also: Entropy; Fundamentals of Energy; Hydropower; Kinetic Energy; Renewable Energy Resources; War; Wind Resources; Work and Energy.

Power and Power Plants

Category: Energy Technology.
Summary: Modern power plants typically convert energy inputs into rotational energy to spin an electric generator and create electricity. Leading fuel inputs include coal, natural gas, nuclear fission, and hydropower.

Electricity is a versatile energy source used to power much of modern life. However, this form of energy is difficult and expensive to store in large quantities. As a result, most electricity must be generated as it is needed. This puts a premium on understanding the power plants used to generate the electricity we use.

Modern power plants tend to produce electricity using the same components: a fuel source to generate heat, a boiler or similar component to generate steam or to direct combusted gas, a tur-bine that converts that steam or gas into rotational energy, and an electrical generator that converts the rotational energy into electricity. Fully 82.6 percent of global electricity produced in 2008 was generated this way. The major sources of heat include coal, natural gas, and nuclear fission. An additional 16.2 percent of electricity in 2008 was generated using hydropower as the energy source, replacing the thermal energy source with falling or running water. Less frequently used sources of energy include oil, biomass, waste, and geothermal sources.

Electric Generators

The basic form of an electric generator is a loop of wire between two stationary magnets. When the wire rotates, the electric field generates voltage. Since the movement of the wire coil is in different directions relative to each of the two magnets, the voltage generated is an alternating current (AC), meaning that the direction of the flow of electrons in the system changes. The frequency of AC is measured in hertz, or cycles per second. In the United States, electricity from the electric grid has a frequency of 60 hertz, meaning that it alternates 60 times every second. In Europe, for example, electricity from the grid alternates at 50 hertz. In addition to AC, there is direct current (DC), which comes from batteries. The main difference between power plants tends to be the way in which the electric generator is made to spin: Thermal power plants boil water to make steam to spin a turbine, which is connected to the generator; gas turbines burn gas to accomplish the same result; other plants use a different mechanical force, such as moving water or wind, to turn the generator directly. A small portion of the world's electricity, less than 1 percent, comes from other forms of generation, such as solar photovoltaic (PV) or certain forms of wave energy.

Measuring Output and Efficiency

The electric output of power plants is measured in units of energy called watts, equal to 1 joule per second. One kilowatt is equal to 1,000 watts and is very roughly equal to the amount of energy used by a typical household in the United States at any given moment. That means that over the course of one hour, such a household would have used 1 kilowatt-hour of electricity.

The maximum amount of electricity that a power plant can produce at one time is referred to as the plant's capacity. The potential capacity of power plants connected to the electric grid is typically measured in megawatts; 1 megawatt is equal to 1 million watts. A typical large coal, nuclear, natural gas, or hydroelectric power plant may have a capacity of anywhere from a few hundred megawatts to more than 1,000 megawatts.

One important measure of a power plant is its operating efficiency. The efficiency of a modern thermal electric generator is measured as a percentage of the energy content of the fuel that is converted into electricity or other usable outputs. Efficiency generally increases as plant temperature and pressure increase. Although typical thermal power plants may have efficiencies of between 20 and 45 percent, plants that effectively utilize waste heat can achieve operating efficiencies of 60 percent or greater.

The availability factor of a power plant is how often the plant is available to produce electricity, as opposed to being off line for a mechanical failure or maintenance. Availability factors are rarely below 70 percent and can be above 98 percent for some nuclear or gas plants or wind turbines. A related measure is a power plant's capacity factor, or how much electricity the power plant produces over a period of time compared to how much it could have produced if it had been running at full capacity for that entire period. Typical capacity factors can be very high, above 90 percent, for nuclear or coal plants that run nearly constantly. Capacity factors can also be much lower, in the range of 20 to 45 percent, for wind farms, and even lower for solar plants.

Coal-Fired Power Plants

Along with wood-fired and hydroelectric power, coal-fired power plants are one of the original sources of energy used in power plants to generate electricity. Coal-fired power plants remain a leading source of electricity in the world. In 2008, 40.8 percent of the world's electricity was produced from coal. In the United States, that percentage was even higher, 48.2 percent. In the decade from 1998 to 2008, the absolute amount of coal-fired electricity generated in the United States increased about 6 percent, but coal-fired generation as a percentage of all electricity generated fell from 51.8 percent to 48.2 percent as other sources grew more quickly. In 2009, the percentage of electricity generated from coal in the United States fell further, to 44.4 percent.

Originally, coal-fired boilers were fed directly with coal. Over time, a number of ways to improve the efficiency of the system were devised. By pulverizing coal before feeding it into a boiler, its surface area is increased and the boiler can be operated at a hotter temperature and higher efficiency. Other technological improvements have allowed development to move from so-called subcritical coal plants, in which steam temperature may be about 1,000 degrees Fahrenheit and steam pressure of 2,400 pounds per square inch, to "critical," "supercritical," and "ultrasupercritical" coal power plants, in which steam temperatures may be above 1,100 degrees Fahrenheit with pressures of 4,500 pounds per square inch. The efficiency of coal plants increases from about 35 percent to 42 percent or more (an increase in efficiency of 20 percent or more) along this continuum from subcritical to ultrasupercritical.

Coal-fired power plants tend to be moderately expensive to build, with a cost of $3,000 to $5,000 per kilowatt of capacity. However, they tend to be cheap to operate because of the low price of coal per unit of energy. Coal is a common choice for new power plants in developing countries, whose economies require large increases in electricity generation to be developed as cheaply as possible. In developed countries, where electricity demand tends to grow more slowly and more of a premium is placed on the environment, new coal power plants are built less frequently. Note that in coal-fired power plants, as with most technologies, expertise is highest and costs lowest where the most new development is occurring. Currently, China leads the world in building new coal-fired power plants. As a result, while China has many relatively inefficient plants, new coal plants in China are often some of the most efficient ultrasupercritical plants in existence. By comparison, most coal plants proposed in the United States in recent years have been supercritical plants, and most existing coal plants in the United States are subcritical.

Burning coal can produce emissions of sulfur dioxide, nitrogen dioxide, particulate matter, mercury, and carbon dioxide. Many developed countries place environmental restrictions on coal generators to reduce the impact of some or all of these emissions. For example, regulations to limit the emissions of sulfur dioxide in the United States, including portions of the Clean Air Act, have led many coal plant operators to install "scrubbers" to capture the sulfur dioxide before it is released into the air. Scrubbers force the exhaust from the plant through a mixture including lime or limestone, which binds with the sulfur.

Natural Gas–Fired Power Plants

There are three basic types of natural gas power plants: steam turbines, simple-cycle combustion turbines, and combined-cycle gas combustion turbines. Combustion turbines are more commonly used with natural gas today. These power plants are cheap to build, about $700 to $1,000 per kilowatt of capacity, but can have high and variable operating costs due to the fluctuating price of natural gas.

Simple-cycle gas turbines create a mixture of air, fed through a compressor at hundreds of miles an hour, and natural gas. The air-gas mixture is burned at temperatures above 2,000 degrees Fahrenheit. This stream of hot gas hits the turbine, which causes it to spin and run an electric generator and drive the compressor. Because of this simple design, basically that of a jet engine, a gas turbine is quick to start up. However, efficiencies range from only 20 to 35 percent. These units are typically used only for peak periods of demand, when an additional amount of electricity must be generated quickly and the cost of that generation is less important.

A combined-cycle gas turbine begins with the simple cycle, then passes the waste gas turbine exhaust through a heat-recovery steam generator to create steam to run a steam turbine. This process can increase efficiency to between 50 and 60

percent. With higher efficiencies, such units can be run regularly.

In 2008, 21.2 percent of the world's electricity was produced from natural gas, according to the International Energy Agency. In the United States, that percentage was 21.4 percent, according to the U.S. Energy Information Administration. Between 1998 and 2009, the growth in electricity production from natural gas was greater than the growth in electricity generation; natural gas production grew from 14.7 to 23.3 percent of electricity generation in the United States.

Natural gas–fired electricity generation produces almost no sulfur dioxide or mercury emissions, about one-quarter the amount of nitrogen oxides, and about half as much carbon dioxide as coal-fired generation.

Hydroelectric Power Plants

Using falling or running water for power is an ancient technique. Because hydropower was understood prior to the development of electric power in the late 19th century, hydroelectric power plants were quick to develop. As a result, the best places for large dams in most developed countries were quickly used. Since the best locations for hydroelectric power plants tended to be chosen first, and because environmental concerns around hydropower have increased, few new hydropower plants have been built over time, and hydropower has contributed a smaller portion of total electricity generation in the United States and most developed countries. However, some developing countries, such as China and Brazil, have recently built or are considering building large hydroelectric power plants. Today, this technology encompasses dams, run-of-the-river units, and pumped storage.

Typical hydroelectric power plants with dams may cost about $3,000 per kilowatt of capacity, but they have essentially zero operating costs. These units can provide base-load electricity generation, because operators control gates that hold water back and choose when and how much electricity to produce. This is not the case with pure run-of-the-river hydroelectric power plants, which do not have those options. Also, uniquely among

The Robert Moses Power Plant on the Niagara River below Niagara Falls is on the United States side of the border (there is a Canadian plant on the other side of the river). In combination, these two plants generate more power than is produced from any other single location in the world.

large sources of power, hydroelectric power has the ability to store energy at a reasonable cost, through the use of pumped storage. Storage is a little more expensive, between $5,000 and $6,000 per kilowatt of capacity, but because water is pumped into a reservoir when electricity prices are low, the energy in that water can be stored until needed, when prices are higher.

Hydroelectric power plants generated 16.2 percent of global electricity in 2008, but with significant variability across countries. For example, in the United States that percentage was just 6.9 percent.

Nuclear Power Plants

Nuclear power plants differ from other thermal power plants in that the heat source is not a fossil fuel but refined uranium, U-235. Rods enriched to contain about 3.5 percent U-235 (compared to just 0.7 percent natural enrichment) are placed near each other in a pool of water. When a U-235 atom is hit by a neutron, it splits and throws off two or three additional neutrons. If those neutrons hit other U-235 atoms, a chain reaction of fission can

occur, creating a large amount of heat. This heat is used to heat the water, making steam to turn a turbine.

The fission process, once started, cannot be easily ratcheted up or down. As a result, nuclear power plants are typically run at a high capacity, as often as possible. If needed, the fission reaction can be slowed or stopped under normal conditions by inserting control rods made of a neutron-absorbing substance such as boron, often encased in stainless steel, or by moving the fuel rods farther apart to slow the interaction between them.

Opponents of nuclear power point out the risks of radiation in case of accidents and the difficulties of storing nuclear waste. Nuclear supporters tout low operating costs and the fact that the operation of a nuclear power plant creates zero emissions.

At the beginning of 2011, there were 442 nuclear reactors in operation around the world and 65 under construction. In 2008, 13.5 percent of the world's electricity was produced from nuclear power plants, according to the International Energy Agency. This percentage varies greatly across countries. In some countries, such as France, the vast majority of electricity is generated from nuclear power. As a result, France enjoys low electricity prices and is able to export large amounts of electricity. Alternatively, some countries, especially many developing countries, have no nuclear power. In the United States, nuclear power supplied 19.6 percent of electricity in 2008, according to the U.S. Energy Information Administration. Between 1998 and 2009, the generation of electricity from nuclear power plants grew by 20 percent in the United States, although no new nuclear plants were constructed. This growth in generation was due solely to the improved operations and reduced downtimes of existing nuclear power plants.

Oil-Fired Power Plants

Oil can be used to make electricity in the same ways that natural gas is used: via steam turbines, simple-cycle combustion turbines, and combined-cycle combustion turbines. In 2008, oil-fired power plants were responsible for generating 5.5 percent of global electricity. Much of this generation is focused in oil-producing countries, where the cost of oil is low. In the United States, electricity from oil-fueled power plants has fallen sharply in recent years, from 3.0 percent in 2005 to only 1.1 percent and 1.0 percent in 2008 and 2009, respectively. The quantity of oil-fueled electricity generation can be volatile, because many plants that are powered by oil can switch fuels to take advantage of fuel price fluctuations. Emissions from fueling a power plant with oil are slightly less than those from coal-fired plants.

Nonhydro Renewable Power Generation

Generation from fuel sources in the category of nonhydro renewable generation include wind, biomass, waste, geothermal, solar photovoltaic, solar thermal, and tidal energy. These sources amounted to about 2.8 percent of electricity generation globally in 2008, according to the International Energy Agency. In the United States, these categories of renewable resources were responsible for 3.2 percent of electricity generation in 2008 and 3.7 percent in 2009. This is a large percentage increase from 2.0 percent of electricity generation in 2003 and 2.7 percent in 2007.

Of these resources, wind is the largest and fastest-growing source, both in the world and in the United States. Recent growth in the percentage of electricity generated by nonhydro renewables is nearly entirely due to the construction of new wind farms. Wind generation increased from 0.3 percent of electricity generation in the United States in 2003 to 0.9 percent in 2007 and 1.9 percent in 2009. Onshore wind farms have experienced growth because the cost of construction, about $2,500 per kilowatt, is competitive with other resources and wind farms have almost no operating costs.

Wind turbines generate electricity at the hub, where the rotors connect to the tower. The spinning blades turn an electrical generator. This hub can sit 328 feet (100 meters) or more aboveground, and blades for larger units can measure between 196 and 328 feet (60 and 100 meters) in diameter. Most utility-scale onshore wind turbines have the capability to generate about 1.5 to 3 megawatts of electricity each. Offshore wind farms, which have been developed in Europe but have only been proposed elsewhere, often are made of slightly larger turbines, and proposed turbines would be capable of generating as much as 7 megawatts. Either onshore or offshore, wind turbines can be placed individually or in a large array of dozens or hundreds.

However, wind power—as well as solar and tidal power—suffers from an inability to choose when power will be generated. This situation is referred to as intermittency. Intermittency limits the usability of these renewable energies because they cannot be increased or decreased to follow changes in electricity demand; rather, they are subject to the availability of the resource, whether wind, sunshine, or appropriately strong tides. Intermittency also reduces these resources' capacity factor, or average amount of electricity generated compared to how much can be generated. The capacity factor of wind farms may be 20 to 40 percent, while solar photovoltaic (PV) cells, which produce electricity when photons of light hit a surface of silicon or other material and create a flow of electrons, have capacity factors of about 10 to 20 percent.

ANDREW GISSELQUIST

Further Reading

European Nuclear Society. "Nuclear Power Plants, World-Wide." http://www.euronuclear.org/info/encyclopedia/n/nuclear-power-plant-world-wide.htm.

International Energy Agency. "Electricity/Heat in World in 2008." http://iea.org/stats/electricitydata.asp?COUNTRY_CODE=29.

Klein, Maury. *The Power Makers*. New York: Bloomsbury Press, 2008.

National Association of Regulatory Utility
Commissions. "Clean Coal Generation
Technologies for New Power Plants." March
2008. http://www.naruc.org/Publications/
CoalGenerationTechnologies.pdf.

Shell. "History of Energy." http://www.shell.us/home/
content/usa/environment_society/education/
student/energy_timeline/.

U.S. Department of Energy. "How Gas Turbine Power
Plants Work." http://fossil.energy.gov/programs/
powersystems/turbines/turbines_howitworks.html.

U.S. Energy Information Administration.
"International Energy Statistics." http://www.eia.gov
/cfapps/ipdbproject/IEDIndex3.cfm.

See Also: Best Management Practices; Cogeneration;
Demand-Side Management; District Energy; Energy
Transmission: Electricity; Grid-Connected Systems;
Hydropower; Municipal Utilities; Nuclear Power.

Public Relations

Category: Business of Energy.
Summary: Public relations is the planned actions
of a business, trade association, or an opposing
group to put forth its message to the public
through the media. The object is to be viewed
favorably by the public and often to sway opinion
to generate change.

Public opinion is a factor determining the fate
of the energy industry. Public relations therefore
plays a critical role for both energy companies
and environmental organizations. As one of the
first industries to use public relations services,
the energy industry is now very skillful in pub-
licity techniques. Environmental organizations,
watchdogs over energy companies, are proficient
in using framing as a public relations tool and conducting their own public relations campaigns with
Websites and newsletters.

Today, more than 80 percent of Americans
report that they are environmentalists. There are
approximately 150 nationwide environmental

organizations and more than 12,000 grassroots
groups concerned with environmental issues. The
high environmental awareness poses a challenge
for the energy industry, which is seen by many of
these groups as a major polluter.

If the energy industry or one of its sectors ignores
public relations, the results can be disastrous,
as demonstrated by the rapid demise of nuclear
power in the 1970s and 1980s and the moratorium
on offshore oil drilling in the 1990s. Until the late
1970s, a majority of Americans supported nuclear
power. However, the 1979 accident at Three Mile
Island dramatically lowered the public support,
which dropped from 50 percent in January 1979
to only 39 percent in April of that year. Congress
and state governments then imposed increasingly
costly regulations and licensing hurdles on nuclear
power plants. Despite its wealth and power, the
nuclear industry began to die. In the 1980s and
1990s, as oil prices fell, Americans began to want
to preseve the nation's coastal beauty and turned
against offshore oil drilling. The oil industry has
gained little access to offshore oil fields since then.

Public relations professionals, who use their
expertise to influence and maintain public opinions and attitudes, thus play a critical role in the
energy industry.

Evolution of the Energy Industry's Public Relations
The energy industry was one of the first industries
to use public relations services. When intensive
muckraking journalism attacked the Rockefeller
family, its business, and the "tainted money" the
oil industry was making, raising public aversion
toward the family, the Rockefellers decided to
abandon their traditional policy of silence. In
1907, they hired Joseph I. C. Clarke, a former
journalist and arguably the second public relations man in American history, to be the public
agent of their company, Standard Oil. Clarke had
complete access to the company's files and execu-
tives. When a newspaper attacked Standard Oil,
Clarke collected related facts, wrote a story from
the company's perspective, and then requested
the same paper to publish his story. The strategy was very successful, and the public image of

the Rockefeller family and Standard Oil greatly improved. Clarke also arranged to publish stories on John D. Rockefeller's philosophy of philanthropy. In 1909, Rockefeller published *Random Reminiscences of Men and Events*, a memoir that enhanced his public image.

The Ludlow strike brought another public relations man to Standard Oil, Ivy Lee. On April 20, 1914, a fight between striking workers of Colorado Fuel and Iron, a subdivision of Standard Oil, and the national guide sent by the Colorado governor, as well as company guides, took place. Two women and eleven children died in burned tents during the fight, and dozens of other people died afterward or were injured. The incident was finally ended when President Woodrow Wilson sent the army to quell the uprising, but the Rockefeller family inevitably became the target of the public's protests and repugnance. The Rockefellers hired Lee in May. He restored the Rockefeller family's image and that of the company by publishing bulletins about the strike and publicizing the entire Rockefeller holdings in the company. He also convinced the Rockefellers to develop a comprehensive plan to address workers' grievances. They posted placards all over the mines to inform the workers that the company wanted to listen to them and treat them fairly. They met with the workers, danced with their wives, and established an industrial relations counselors' network to provide advice on labor issues for the Rockefeller companies and other companies, which thereafter became very popular.

Lee believed that "crowds are led by symbols and phrases." He designed some public relations projects for John D. Rockefeller, including establishing huge foundations and giving coins to people he met (nickels for children and dimes for adults). It is estimated that Rockefeller handed out 30,000 shiny new dimes to people in his late life. Lee never announced Rockefeller's philanthropic endorsements; instead, he arranged for the recipients of the donations to announce their appreciation. During World War I, Lee worked hard to associate the Rockefellers with patriotism and support for the war effort, planting in newspapers stories about John D. Rockefeller Jr. knitting scarves in his free time for the doughboys overseas. Lee greatly changed Americans' impressions about the Rockefeller family.

Environmental Risk

In cases of environmental risk, research shows that merely publicizing facts is not enough. Emotional aspects need to be addressed. For example, it is factually true to say that properly trained and equipped workers are safer when working in an asbestos-contained environment than when they are smoking, but it is impossible for the workers' spouses and the general public to believe that smoking is more dangerous than working with asbestos—at least from sources that have a vested interest in working with asbestos. Meanwhile, attempts to minimize the importance or degree of risk from an accident always fail or backfire. Instead, showing that the company is committed to the implementation and operation of systems designed to control or reduce the risks is likely to make the public more accepting of the information the company is sharing. In any situation, building up public trust is the key to successful public relations efforts.

Management of community relationships, as Frank Friedman notes, is also critical for companies generally viewed as polluters, such as energy companies. He points out that early community opposition to a project with environmental impacts is usually based, not on ideology, but on economic or personal concerns, such as fears that the project may lower real estate or home values. Such opposition needs to be addressed as early as possible, as long as solid data about the project are available. This timely confrontation of the issues will mitigate the intensity of possible litigation, if not reduce it. Friedman also recommends that a company's public relations professionals and environment managers should coordinate closely to uniformly and clearly enunciate the company's position to all media, all the time. Some companies limit media access to their public relations departments to help them avoid public relations disasters. A reasonable public relations goal is also important. For companies generally viewed as polluters by the public, no matter how well the companies and their public relations staff work, it

▷ *Exxon Valdez Oil Spill*

The handling of the *Exxon Valdez* oil spill is probably the most classic example of how vital public relations can be for any energy business. On March 24, 1989, the supertanker ran aground on Goose Island in Prince William Sound. Within 56 days, crude oil had spread across 470 miles along the pristine Alaskan coast. It was the largest oil spill in U.S. history at the time.

Although Exxon immediately fired the ship's captain (who was reportedly under the influence of alcohol at the time of the accident), the company mounted no cleanup effort for the first three days following the oil spill. Exxon was not ready for the crisis, and the ship's crew was busy saving what remaining crude oil it could in order to minimize the company's loss. By contrast, local fishermen started their cleanup immediately.

Exxon also complained of government regulations that delayed their cleanup initiatives, which was later rebutted by the critics. The company limited their public updates to a spokesman in Valdez, Alaska, a location inconveniently located for access by national reporters, particularly television journalists and photographers, who had to transport heavy television equipment to the site.

Exxon's spokesman insisted that the company did not expect any environmental damage. Higher-ranking company officials showed no concern about the incident, until one week later, when the media climate turned hostile. When Exxon chairman Lawrence Rawl had to appear on television, he had no information to convey concerning Exxon's cleanup plan, blamed the press for overblown concern, and tried to minimize the long-term impact of the accident to zero.

Researchers generally agree that almost everything Exxon did in dealing with the crisis goes against the principles of public relations and crisis communications.

is impossible for them to be loved by the public. If those companies can be sensitive to environmental issues and generate a substantial number of jobs, however, they can at least achieve a reputation as socially responsible companies within a polluting industry.

As the overall public relations industry becomes more profit-driven, public relations for the energy industry follows a trend. For instance, since 1995, Shell has been transforming its public relations department. Under a new president, Phil Carroll, the company adopted a new governing model that emphasized the independence of business units. Shell was formed into four independently operated companies, each run by its own chief executive officer. Tax, legal, planning, finance, human resources, and public relations organizations were restructured into four professional firms, providing services to the corporate center, to the four principal companies, and to each other. Being part of one of the four professional firms, Shell's public relations department was told to add value to other units and compete with outside public relations services to survive in the new Shell. In the traditional model, the value of Shell public relations was measured by the amount of media coverage or column inches garnered to tout the company's accomplishments. In the new model, the value is measured by how much the public relations service helps the companies and the professional firms to meet their business objectives, usually in terms of financial value. The model worked well even after Carroll retired. Public relations professionals no longer sit idly waiting for unsolicited assignments; they now know their partners' public relations needs better than their partners themselves.

Many new communications formats and technologies, such as podcasting, wikis, and blogs, have been introduced in energy public relations practices. During the 2010 Deepwater Horizon oil spill in the Gulf of Mexico, for example, BP was reported to use advanced public relations techniques, such as search-engine optimization, to mitigate negative public opinion, which saw the oil spill as a major environmental disaster and was angry with the U.S. government for not doing enough to handle the crisis and regulate BP.

Framing and the Environmental Organizations' Public Relations

Environmental organizations, usually strong watchdogs of energy companies, are one of the forces that drive energy companies to polish their public relations skills. At the same time, those environmental organizations are also effective in using public relations techniques to achieve their activist goals. Newsletters and Websites, which can reach their members, media outlets, and the general public, are the major public relations tools that they use. Frames are often used in those newsletters and Websites to persuade the audience.

For example, a study of the Sierra Club's newsletters from spring 2001 to spring 2002 and its Website found that the Sierra Club often framed oil drilling in the Arctic National Wildlife Refuge as a threat to one of the America's greatest natural wilderness treasures—and to traditional American ways of life and wilderness values. The message was that drilling would not serve America's energy needs and a comprehensive energy plan based on conservation, alternative sources of energy, and improved efficiency standards should be established. Coal-fired power plants were generally framed as causing environmental problems and climate change, from which future generations needed to be protected. The Sierra Club also advanced a message that new technology needs to be developed and used to lessen the impacts of those coal-fired power plants, and that cleaner fossil fuels could be found to replace coal-fired power.

Although environmental organizations also mention some pro-development frames in their Websites and newsletters, they often present two-sided messages. Research shows that environmental organizations are generally effective in influencing national and regional newspapers with pro-environmental frames but have no influence with pro-development frames. Researchers have also found that national and regional newspapers have no influence on each other within presented environmental frames: Both news sources take their pro-environment frames mainly from the environmental organizations' publications.

Public relations messages from environmental organizations often contain three types of framing: diagnostic framing, identifying the parties that have caused the problems and thus can be blamed; prognostic framing, which proposes a solution to the problems stated in the messages; and motivational framing, which calls for action from supporters. A study by Lynn Zoch and her associates analyzed 16 environmental organizations' Web pages and found that the most commonly used framing device among those Web pages was general description—that is, the use of sensory language to create an impression. Sensory language may include statistics (numbers), real examples, testimonials, and organization as a solution (clearly proposing a solution on the Website). In this study, it was surprising that only a few visuals (drawings and animations) and no videos were used as framing devices on those Websites. The researchers called upon environmental organizations to use more powerful framing devices to achieve the full potential of their Websites as public relations tools.

QINGJIANG YAO
C. S. EIGENMANN

Further Reading
Bushell, Sharon, and Stan Jones. *The Spill: Personal Stories From the* Exxon Valdez *Disaster.* Kenmore, WA: Epicenter Press, 2009.

Coombs, Timothy, and Sherry Holladay, eds. *The Handbook of Crisis Communication.* Malden, MA: Wiley-Blackwell, 2010.

Friedman, Frank. *Practical Guide to Environmental Management.* 9th ed. Washington, DC: Environmental Law Institute, 2003.

Hutchins, H. R. "A New Order for Public Relations: Goodbye Cost Center, Hello Profit Center." In *Handbook of Public Relations*, edited by R. L. Heath. Thousands Oaks, CA: Sage, 2001.

Wilson, Albert R. *Environmental Risk: Identification and Management.* Boca Raton, FL: CRC Press, 1991.

Yao, Qingjiang. "An Evidence of Frame Building: Analyze the Correlations Among the Frames in Sierra Club Newsletters, National Newspapers, and Regional Newspapers." *Public Relations Review* 35, no. 1 (2009).

Zoch, Lynn, Erik L. Collins, Hilary Fussell Sisco, and Dustin H. Supa. "Empowering the Activist: Using Framing Devices on Activist Organizations' Websites." *Public Relations Review* 34, no. (2008).

See Also: Advertising and Marketing; BP; China Syndrome; Communication; *Exxon Valdez* Oil Spill; Gulf Oil Spill; Shell; Standard Oil Company.

Public Transportation

Category: Environmentalism.
Summary: Public transportation is becoming increasingly important to economies, energy policies, and the environment, promising a better quality of life.

In England, bus and rail are popular methods of public transportation. Pictured is the Manchester metrolink, one of Great Britain's most successful light rail systems, with over 20 million passengers annually.

Transportation technologies in the 21st century have pros and cons: On one side, transportation critically supports the mobility needs of passengers and the movement of freight, ranging from urban areas to international trade across the globe. On the other side, transport activities have resulted in growing motorization and traffic congestion, and consequently the increased use of fossil fuels, particularly to drive internal combustion engines used for transportation, as well. A large portion of the population in every developed and developing nation travels daily for work, shopping, and many other social purposes.

The direct causal relationship to environmental damage and negative effects is clear; in fact many assess the level of carbon load, atmospheric pollution, and related social health impacts as having reached a critical point. With transportation needs a priority for continued economic growth as well as the development of better living conditions for global societies, the environmental impacts in particular must be addressed. It is generally agreed that transportation outputs upwards of 20 percent of carbon emissions worldwide. What is more, transportation-sourced greenhouse gas (GHG) emission levels seem to be growing faster than all other sectors of the energy economy.

Public transportation, however, is still an underused component of the overall transport sector. It offers positive options to several of the major drawbacks of individual, private transportation: Public transportation's expansion can be seen as both a benefit and a necessity. Public transportation can be defined as a shared passenger transportation service, available for use by all facets of the general public in a given political jurisdiction. In contrast to private taxicabs or cars, public systems can accommodate the largest numbers of passengers. Public transport systems include buses, trolleys, trains and trams, rapid transit (variously called metros, subways, and undergrounds), ferries, shuttles, and related modes. Rail and bus lines dominate the intercity portion of public transport; the advantages of rail in fuel efficiency, carrying capacity, and urban center penetration of stations make it one of the chief options under study or construction in many countries and interconnected urban areas.

Public transportation can give large numbers of people broader and wider geographic access—even while it contributes strongly to environmental and economic sustainability. Many developed countries have adopted public transportation as an important tool for reducing their over-reliance on foreign fuels and also for protecting the environment. Some countries have done an excellent job of developing, implementing, and maintaining high-quality public transport, notably Sweden, Japan, and Singapore.

Reducing Carbon Footprint

Mass transit transport saves energy compared to personal vehicle use, and can significantly reduce a nation's or state's carbon footprint. Public transportation in the United States, for example, requires less than half of the fuel used by private vehicles. According to the Center for Transportation Excellence, private transport emits about 95 percent more carbon monoxide, 92 percent more volatile organic compounds, and twice as much carbon dioxide (CO_2) and nitrogen oxides as does public transport, based on passenger miles traveled. Taking as example a 20-mile round trip, if a single person were to replace transportation by private car with public transportation, the result would be a net CO_2 emissions reduction of 4,800 pounds per year.

Public transportation provides still other benefits: savings in energy costs, avoiding traffic congestion, and efficient land use in urban areas. With pressure mounting on urban lands for housing and transport, public transportation offers an important alternative.

Analysis of the London public transportation system reveals that, between 2006 and 2007, the total energy cost of all passenger train service in the metropolitan area equated to 15 kilowatt-hours (kWh) per 100 kilometers—or about five times the energy efficiency of personal cars in the same metropolitan area. Using like calculations for bus travel in London, the energy used was approximately 32 kWh per 100 kilometers, or about 2.5 times more efficient than personal cars. It should be noted that these calculations even take into account the ancillary costs of providing lighting at public stations and depots.

Fuel Alternatives

Public transportation provides opportunities to test so-called green vehicles, which are environ-mentally friendly in terms of their use of alternatives to fossil fuels. Among the technologies now employed are electric trains, trams, and buses. Such green vehicles emit less pollution than equivalent standard vehicles (even accounting for the emissions output from generating the electricity they use). Public transport based on electric technology has the potential to reduce transport sector CO_2 emissions, to a degree that depends on the ultimate source of the electricity in question. Hybrid vehicles, those using an internal combustion engine combined with an electric engine under one hood to achieve better fuel efficiency than a regular combustion engine, are already becoming somewhat common. Natural gas is also being used as a transport fuel in urban buses.

Biofuels in public transport are a less common and qualitatively less promising energy source. Brazil, as a leading example in biofuel development and testing, derived more than 15 percent of its transportation fuel needs from ethanol in 2007. Sweden has tested biofuels for its public bus network to some extent. However, the Organisation for Economic Co-operation and Development (OECD) pointed out that Brazil must be seen as a special case. Brazil, the world's largest ethanol producer and exporter, provides a full range of government subsidies of the industry—from sugarcane production to high taxes on gasoline—and few if any other countries will have the motivation or ability to reproduce the success of its program. Biofuels are destined to make some impact on global GHG emissions, but unlikely a large one.

Conclusion

Public transportation is critical for the world's future. It promotes an environment-friendly and sustainable economy across a full range of local to international scales. It stimulates commerce and can create new, green jobs. Public transport saves families money and can increase sales for businesses in urban centers and near outlying transit hubs. It can reduce dependence on imported, expensive fuels while helping extend mobility to the full citizenry. With strong contributions to reducing GHG emissions and improving air quality, public transportation will always be a responsible and sustainable choice. Committing to its expansion, improvement, and maintenance is not always the easiest decision for cash-strapped governments. But the long term economic, social, and environmental benefits are becoming too plentiful to ignore.

RONJU AHAMMAD

Further Reading

Feitelson, Eran, and E. T. Verhoef. *Transport and Environment: In Search of Sustainable Solutions.* Northampton, MA: Edward Elgar, 2001.

Iles, Richard. *Public Transport in Developing Countries.* San Diego, CA: Elsevier, 2005.

International Energy Agency. *Bus Systems for the Future: Achieving Sustainable Transport Worldwide.* Paris: International Energy Agency, 2002.

Jones, David W. *Mass Motorization + Mass Transit: An American History and Policy Analysis.* Bloomington: Indiana University Press, 2008.

Newman, Peter, and Jeffrey R. Kenworthy. *Sustainability and Cities: Overcoming Automobile Dependence.* Washington, DC: Island Press, 1999.

Post, Robert C. *Urban Mass Transit: The Life Story of a Technology.* Westport, CT: Greenwood Press, 2007.

Rodrigue, Jean-Paul. *The Geography of Transport Systems.* http://people.hofstra.edu/geotrans/index.html.

Tolley, Rodney. *Sustainable Transport.* Boca Raton, FL: CRC Press, 2003.

Vigar, Geoff. *The Politics of Mobility: Transport, the Environment, and Public Policy.* New York: Spon Press, 2002.

White, Peter. *Public Transport: Its Planning, Management, and Operation.* London: UCL Press, 1995.

World Bank. *Sustainable Transport: Priorities for Policy Reform.* Washington, DC: World Bank, 1996.

See Also: Automobiles; Aviation; Carbon Footprint and Neutrality; Energy Markets: Transport; Energy Policy; History of Energy: 1850–1900; Levitation; Trains; Transportation.

Public Utilities

Category: Business of Energy.
Summary: Public utilities are essential services provided by the government to citizens, either directly through the public sector or indirectly by financing private provision of services subject to regulation.

The term *utility* usually means a company that maintains the infrastructure for a public service, often providing a service using that infrastructure. Opinions differ as to the characteristics that an industry must possess to merit classification as a public utility, since all industries in a sense serve the public.

Originally, the concept of a public utility originated in the United States as a means of providing the government and social controls required to prevent abuse of private market power by firms supplying essential services in energy, water, the environment, sanitation, health, education, transportation, infrastructure, information, and knowledge.

Public utilities can include economic infrastructures, such as those supporting telecommunications, electricity, gas, water, postal services, and transportation (roads, railways, buses, ports, airports, and so forth), and social infrastructures, such as education and health. These utilities satisfy the vital needs of large populations, and their absence would negatively affect public health and welfare. They are therefore "public goods," resources that are collectively owned or shared between or among populations; hence, they are affected by "externalities."

These essential services provided by government are "institutional commons" and belong to the larger category of "commons," which include biodiversity, physical or environmental commons, and the knowledge commons. The commons are fundamental for the sustainable development of a community, in terms of endurance, independence, and identity. Because of the intrinsic nature of these essential services, Adam Smith's well-known metaphor of the invisible hand, arguing for the free markets, does not work well.

Public Control and Regulation

The existence of commons requires that people operate on a collective rather than an individual basis, as magnificently highlighted by Garrett Hardin in his 1968 essay "The Tragedy of the Commons." This pioneer study demonstrated the dilemma underlying the concept of commons, arising from the situation in which multiple individuals, acting independently and rationally and consulting their own self-interest, will ultimately deplete a shared limited resource, even when it is clear that it is not in anyone's long-term interest for this to happen. As a result, public utilities are usually subject to forms of public control and regulation, ranging from local community-based groups to statewide government monopolies. The first typology includes cooperatives, usually found in rural areas. Cooperative utilities are owned by the customers they serve.

Publicly owned utilities are often government monopolies, because it is very expensive to build and maintain the infrastructure required to produce and deliver these services. As such, public utilities are not prevented by competing companies from charging exorbitant prices. These utilities usually operate under a license or franchise whereby they enjoy special privileges, such as the right of eminent domain.

Investor-Owned Utilities

Private utilities, or "investor-owned utilities," are owned by investors. Unlike public companies, private utilities may be listed on stock exchanges. *Private*, in this context, means not owned by the public or the government.

In most European nations, utilities have often been owned by the state, although many have been privatized in recent years. In addition, the network infrastructure used to distribute most utility products and services has remained largely monopolistic. In the United States, however, many public utilities are privately owned. If privately owned, the sectors are specially regulated by public utilities commissions, such as the Federal Energy Commission, the Nuclear Regulatory Commission, the Federal Communications Commission, and the Securities and Exchange Commission.

A concern about public ownership is the governments' lack of economic orientation. Governments demonstrate paternalistic or political behaviors insofar as they seek to protect employment. In some countries, government or state provision of utility services has therefore resulted in inefficiency and poor service quality. It is well known that public ownership generates inefficiencies, because it encourages governments to subsidize money-losing firms. Since less efficient firms are allowed to rely on government funding, they lack the financial discipline required for efficient management. By hardening the firm's budget constraints, privatization helps restore investment incentives. The transfer of public to private ownership is therefore often advocated as a remedy for the poor economic performance of public enterprises.

Deregulation and Privatization

In the 1990s, state regulators began to end utilities' monopolies by permitting business and residential consumers to select utilities (primarily electricity and gas suppliers) based on rates and services. However, such deregulatory efforts have not always resulted in lower rates. Privatization of public utilities from traditional government monopolies has also started to take place as a consequence of recent developments in technology of services, such as electricity generation, electricity retailing, and telecommunication. As a result, new services and lower prices were often introduced. Increased competition among investor-owned utilities also has led to mergers and acquisitions and a concentration of ownership.

Privatization brings well-known economic costs when industries are characterized by strong economies of scale. Infrastructure and utility owners benefit from market power. By giving up the direct control of firms' operations, governments lose control over prices, to the disadvantage of consumers.

Rates are subject to review by the courts, which have held that they must provide a "fair" return on a "fair" valuation of investment. The commission holds public hearings to help decide whether the proposed schedule is fair. That a utility may not earn excessive profits is an established principle of regulation. The means of regulation include supervision of accounting and control of security issues. The commission may also require increased levels of service from the utility to meet public demand.

Government plays an important role in ensuring safe operation, reasonable rates, and service on equal terms to all customers. Many politicians and economists argue that the marketplace, not government regulation, should determine utility prices. Many consumers also seek lower prices through deregulation. The real debate today is about finding the right balance between the market and government (including the third "sector," nongovernmental nonprofit organizations).

The privatization decision depends on the value of opportunity costs of public funds and on profitability in the market segment where the firm operates. Since the opportunity cost of public funds is higher in developing countries than in developed countries, optimal privatization policies are likely to differ between those countries. In poorer developing countries, public utilities are often limited to wealthier parts of major cities, but in some developing countries utilities do provide services to a large share of the urban population. In countries such as those of Latin America, liberalization, competition, and regulatory policies are very recent developments. The empirical evidence is limited and case studies offer the only scientific approach available. Although the economic theory relevant for developing countries is still very vague, some general considerations can be provided, as follows:

- A public firm is the natural option in a low-density area, typically secondary road or electrification projects. This market segment can have a such low profitability that no private firm is able or willing to cover it.
- Privatization with price liberalization dominates regulation if the opportunity cost of public funds is large enough. Examples can be found in Africa, where urban dwellers (the middle class and the poor) rely on private providers for water service. In the telecommunications

industry in Africa and in Latin America, privatization combined with an independent regulation does yield improvements.
- Privatization of profitable public utilities, such as fixed lines or international telecommunications services, is not efficient in very poor countries, which are plagued with financial problems and welcome the potential revenues that can be extracted from a public firm.
- Privatization with price liberalization is not optimal when the market is so profitable that a second firm is able to enter the market.

PATRIZIA LOMBARDI

Further Reading

Auriol, Emmanuelle, and Pierre M. Picard. *Infrastructure and Public Utilities Privatization in Developing Countries.* Policy Research Working Paper Series 3950. Washington, DC: World Bank, 2006. http://idei.fr/doc/by/auriol/developing.pdf.

Beato, Paulina, and Jean-Jacques Laffont. "Competition in Public Utilities in Developing Countries." Inter-American Developing Bank, Sustainable Developing Department Technical Papers Series, Washington, DC, February 2002. http://cdi.mecon.gov.ar/biblio/docelec/MU2007.pdf.

Bijoy, C. R. "Beyond Resistance and Cooption." January 2, 2009. http://www.countercurrents.org/bijoy020109.htm.

Hardin, Garrett. "The Tragedy of the Commons." *Science* 162, no. 3859 (December 13, 1968).

Lai, Loi Lei. *Power System Restructuring and Deregulation.* Hoboken, NJ: Wiley, 2001.

Miller, E. S. "Is the Public Utility Concept Obsolete?" *Land Economics* 71, no. 3 (2009).

Warkentin, Denise. *Electric Power Industry in Nontechnical Language.* Tulsa, OK: PennWell, 1998.

See Also: Deregulation; Energy Policy Act of 2005; Federal Energy Regulatory Commission; Municipal Utilities; Nationalization; Public Utility Holding Company Act of 1935; Public Utility Regulatory Policies Act of 1978; Regulation.

Public Utility Holding Company Act of 1935

Category: Business of Energy.
Summary: The Public Utility Holding Company Act of 1935 allowed states to regulate financial transactions from utility companies operating across states. Previously, control of the electric and gas markets was in the hands of a few companies and pricing was uncontrolled.

By the late 1800s into the mid-1900s, utility companies began to operate across scores of states; these multistate corporations could shift expenses and revenues across states, making it difficult for states to receive their just share of utility revenues. In addition, these same companies oftentimes were purchased and sold into other companies, creating massive holding companies whose principal reporting requirements were to the Securities and Exchange Commission.

The Securities and Exchange Commission (SEC) was responsible for overseeing these holding companies in the electric and gas utility industries, primarily because of the stock, investor, and public financial transactions involved in these businesses. The SEC was challenged in its ability to regulate these issues adequately, and these issues were the basis for the creation of the Public Utilities Holding Company Act of 1935 (PUHCA 1935).

In particular, Samuel Insull was an innovator and major driver in the use of holding companies in developing the electric industry infrastructure within the United States. Insull rose to the position of vice president of Edison General Electric. By 1907, Insull controlled and then merged several electric companies. He then created the Commonwealth Edison Electric Company. In later years, Insull switched his support within the industry from direct-current electricity production to alternating-current electricity production. This occurred as the debate involving the generic use of alternating current (invented by Nikola Tesla) as opposed to direct current (invented by Thomas Alva Edison) was coming to a close. The principle mechanism that Insull used to push the electricity industry forward was creating holding companies, through which he was able to leverage much power and money over many different infrastructure entities. Insull left the United States in a cloud after the collapse of his multibillion-dollar energy empire. Insulls actions were one of the driving industrial events that led to the creation of the creation of the PUHCA 1935.

Need for Regulation

From 1900 to 1920, the number of private electric systems grew from approximately 2,800 to 6,500. As many as 10 layers separated the top and bottom of some holding companies. By the early 1930s, approximately 47 percent of all electricity, either generated or investor-owned, was controlled by three groups. This was in deference to the fact that a majority of states had public utility commissions.

By the 1920s, approximately 66 percent of all states had public utility commissions. The Public utility commissions were incapable of controlling transactions of these multistate holding companies. Prior to the enactment of the PUHCA 1935, utilities had historically been driven by company self-interest. The result of this behavior was poor or unreliable service and excessive cost to the consumer. Utilities that were holding companies were able to charge their subsidiary companies exorbitant fees for services, and excessive fees were passed on to consumers as higher rates. A company could finance new construction or repairs and pass these charges along to consumers along with any additional handling charges they incurred.

The stock market crash of 1929 revealed that many utility holding companies had serious financial problems, and investors lost millions. During the seven-year period between 1929 and 1936, 53 holding companies with combined securities of $1.7 billion went into bankruptcy or receivership. In 1928, the Federal Trade Commission issued a report detailing the abusive practices of holding companies. It concluded that the holding company structure was unsound and "frequently a menace to the investor or the consumer or both." The Public Utility Holding Company Act of 1935 and the Federal Power Act were established at the same time and were intended to work in tandem. It was determined that with federal regulatory control of interstate public utility holding companies, unfair and abusive practices of utility companies could be controlled and eliminated. Utilities were given proprietary territory choices, and in exchange, the firms had to provide reliable and consistent power to consumers at an affordable or regulated rate. The PUHCA eliminated holding companies that were more than two levels removed from the subsidiaries they owned. On August 8, 2005, the Energy Policy Act of 2005 was signed into law, effectively replacing and repealing the PUHCA, effective as of February 8, 2006.

Positive Results

There were several problems eliminated by the introduction of the PUHCA 1935. Investors were better able to understand the financial positions and earnings powers of issuers. Securities issued by companies are now issued with consent of the states in which they are issued. Securities are also issued based upon sound asset value and not fictitious values, and are not based upon intercompany transactions. The PUHCA eliminated or restricted the ability of utilities to charge excessive charges for services, or arms-length transactions where market competition is absent or restricted. The PUHCA helped control accounting practices, rates, dividends, and other policies so that states could more effectively regulate utilities and the industry within their jurisdiction. The PUHCA also aided the economics of fund-raising and capital structure evolution.

The main goal of the PUHCA was to regulate holding companies that had electric utility companies subsidiaries or that engaged in the retail distribution of natural gas or manufactured gas. The statute defined a holding company as (1) a company that controls 10 percent or more of the outstanding voting securities of a public utility company (or of another holding company); or (2) a person whom the SEC determines to be exercising a controlling influence over the management of policies of any public utility or holding company, so as to make it necessary or appropriate in the public interest to

subject that person to the requirements of the statute. The PUHCA was, for its time, a response to the need to protect consumers and states from the predatory business practices instituted by a small number of power trust companies in the early part of the 20th century.

RICHARD BRENT

Further Reading

Abel, Amy. "RS20015: Electricity Restructuring Background: Public Utility Holding Company Act of 1935 (PUHCA)." CRS Report for Congress, 1999. https://wiki.umn.edu/pub/ESPM3241W/S11TopicSummaryTeamTwentyfour/CRS_Report__RS20015_-_Electricity_Restructuring_Background__Public_Utility_H.pdf.

Cudahay, Richard D. "From Insull to Enron: Corporate (Re)Regulation." *Energy Law Journal* 26, no. 1 (January 2005).

U.S. Department of Energy. "A Primer on Electric Utilities, Deregulation, and Restructuring of U.S. Electricity Markets" (2002). http://www1.eere.energy.gov/femp/pdfs/primer.pdf.

See Also: Electric Grids; Energy Policy; Energy Policy Act of 2005; Holding Companies; Insull, Samuel; Investor-Owned Utilities; Municipal Utilities; Public Utility Regulatory Policies Act of 1978.

Public Utility Regulatory Policies Act of 1978

Category: Business of Energy.
Summary: PURPA was passed to promote renewable energy generation in 1978 and obliged utilities to purchase electricity from all qualifying facilities.

The global energy crises in the mid-1970s contributed to reshaping the United States' energy policy. In 1973, the Organization of Petroleum Exporting Countries (OPEC) placed an oil embargo on the United States, lasting until the following year, which contributed to rising energy prices. As a nation dependent on oil imports, the United States and its energy security were threatened by rising oil prices, and consequently the Public Utility Regulatory Policies Act (PURPA) was enacted in 1978. PURPA supported the development of alternative energy sources, such as renewable energy, as well as the diversification of the energy mix, by opening up the energy market, allowing nonutility electricity generators, or qualifying facilities (QFs), to participate.

In particular, renewable energy generators benefited from the new legislation, which classified nonutility, small-power producers, and cogeneration facilities as QFs. Small-scale power producers were defined as having less than 80 megawatts of generating capacity, whereas eligible facilities that produced power from wind, solar geothermal, hydroelectric, or municipal waste power that met the requirements set forth in the Federal Power Act did not have capacity limitations.

The inclusion of QFs in the power generation market enabled small-scale self-generating plants to connect to the grid. PURPA clearly stated, in Section 111, that "each electric utility shall make available, upon request, interconnection service to any electric consumer that the electric utility serves." Previously, utilities could refuse grid connection. Thus, self-generating plants were obliged to supply their own power at all times in addition to their redundant backup power systems. PURPA increased energy efficiency, since qualifying facilities were able to sell excess electricity to the utility during times when their supply exceeded demand.

In Section 201, PURPA stipulated that the utilities were obligated to purchase electricity from QFs at a just and reasonable price, equivalent to the avoided cost, defined as "the cost to the electric utility of the electric energy which but for the purchase from such cogenerator or small power producer, such utility would generate or purchase itself from another source." In other words, the utilities compensated QFs according to the avoided cost for electricity generation rather than according to the actual cost of generation, leading to a favorable

price for the new energy generators. The measures set in PURPA initially predicted that 12,000 megawatts of nonhydropower renewable energy would be developed. By 1991, 32,000 megawatts produced by QFs had been added online.

Although PURPA was one of the most effective laws in supporting renewable energy development, it has been marred by several issues. The price determined by the avoided cost was excessively high, since prices were based on forecasts of increasing fuel prices. While fuel prices did not reach the forecasts, utilities were still required to honor the 15- to 20-year fixed contracts, passing on the increased power costs to consumers. QFs artificially increased the electricity price, but contracts persisted for some time, given the utilities' purchase obligation. Additionally, inefficiencies have arisen, since utilities were forced to purchase electricity from QFs despite having adequate power suppliers through their own facilities or through external sources. At times the QFs offered 10 to 20 times more than the utility's capacity; thus, competitive bidding was used in the mid-1980s to choose QFs for long-term contracts.

Mandatory grid connection, open access to transmission lines, and the creation of a competitive generation market led to the revision of some measures in PURPA in the Energy Policy Act of 2005 (EPACT 2005). A utility was exempted from purchasing QF-generated power on condition that it was able to prove that QF electricity could be sold in the competitive wholesale market. Not all utilities were able to demonstrate the requirement, and therefore several states were required to continue purchasing from QFs at the avoided costs. EPACT 2005 also encouraged greater development in renewable energy by promoting the continuous assessment of renewable energy resources and stimulated demand by obliging the government to purchase a fixed amount of electricity from renewable energy sources. EPACT also included a clause promoting alternative energy sources, including renewable energy.

Utilities were given two years, until August 8, 2007, to begin considering the additional standards and three years to finalize the consideration to implement or reject the new standards. If the standards were declined, a public statement had to be made in writing. Each state commission and utility was required to make an independent evaluation of the new PURPA standards and was allowed to modify, set standards, and adopt some or all of the standards and set more or less rigorous standards in accordance with the state law. Since each state had varying laws and procedures or may have adopted equivalent standards, the *Reference Manual and Procedures for Implementation of the PURPA Standards in the Energy Policy Act of 2005* was created as an information and procedural guide to help with the evaluation process.

The evolution of PURPA since 1978 illustrates that development in renewable energy was stimulated by strong policies, which were not without their shortcomings. Over time, the policies were revised in an attempt to address the issues of artificially high, avoided costs and to streamline the implementation of policies across a diverse range of states.

JENNY LIEU

Further Reading

Graves, Frank C., James A. Read, and Joseph B. Wharton. "Resource Planning and Procurement in Evolving Electricity Markets." January 31, 2004. http://www.brattle.com/Publications/ReportsPresentations.asp?PublicationID=923.

International Energy Agency. "The Public Utility Regulatory Policies Act (PURPA) Review." 2007. http://www.iea.org/textbase/pm/?mode=weo&id=1060&action=detail.

McNerney, Rebecca A. "The Federal Statutory Background of the Electric Power Industry." In *The Changing Structure of the Electric Power Industry 2000: An Update*. Washington, DC: U.S. Department of Energy, Energy Information Administration, 2000.

Masters, G. M. *Renewable and Efficient Electric Power Systems*. Hoboken, NJ: John Wiley & Sons, 2004.

Rose, Kenneth, and Karl Meeusen. "2006 Performance Review of Electric Power Markets." August 27, 2006. http://www.kenrose.us/sitebuildercontent/sitebuilderfiles/2006_Performance_Review.pdf.

U.S. Senate Committee on Energy and Natural Resources. "Energy Policy Act of 2005." August 8, 2005. http://energy.senate.gov/public/index.cfm?FuseAction=EnergyBill.Home.

See Also: Energy Policy; Energy Policy Act of 2005; Feed-in Tariff; Municipal Utilities; Public Utility Holding Company Act of 1935; Renewable Energy Credits; United States; Vertical Integration.

Qatar

Official Name: State of Qatar.
Category: Geography of Energy.
Summary: Despite its small size, Qatar's strategic location near natural gas and oil reserves has propelled major economic growth. Located on the Arabian Peninsula on the Persian Gulf, Qatar's natural resources supply both domestic and global demand.

The emirate of Qatar's sustained political and economic development coincided with the mid-20th-century discovery of oil in the Persian Gulf. In the wake of World War I, Qatar signed a treaty of suzerainty with Britain wherein the emirate relinquished control over its external affairs in exchange for military protection. The British had maintained a strong economic interest in the Middle East since the discovery of oil in Iran in 1908. In that year, the British established the Anglo-Persian Oil Company, which would later become the British Petroleum Company. An increasingly lucrative British asset in the region, the Anglo-Persian Oil Company exacted a concession regarding oil rights from Qatar in 1935, before oil was discovered there.

Despite the 1939 discovery of oil in Qatar, exports and bids for offshore drilling did not begin until after World War II, in 1949. The British then established themselves in local governance and remained there until Qatar's independence in 1971. Britain's control led to a period of gradual political, economic, and infrastructural development funded by oil revenue. After Britain's departure from the gulf, Qatar's government nationalized the remnants of the Anglo-Persian Oil Company's subsidiary Petroleum Development (Qatar) Limited and created the Qatar Petroleum Company. The energy sector in Qatar remains nationalized, with the Qatar Petroleum Company acting as the dominant force in both the oil and the natural gas sectors. Oil and natural gas revenues comprise 60 percent of Qatar's gross domestic product (GDP). Natural gas provides 79 percent of the energy used in Qatar, while 21 percent comes from oil.

Qatar maintains memberships in several energy-related international organizations, chief among them the Organization of Petroleum Exporting Countries (OPEC) and the Cooperation Council for the Arab States of the Gulf, also called the Gulf Cooperation Council (GCC). Qatar is among the original 12 member states that founded OPEC in 1960. OPEC's members control approximately 79 percent of global oil reserves and 44 percent of global production. The GCC is a regional entity ratified in 1981 by Bahrain, Kuwait, Oman, Qatar, Saudi Arabia, and the United Arab Emirates. Although the members do not have a unified energy policy, the GCC seeks to foster technological and economic growth in energy-related sectors through an open exchange and trade system.

Qatar is situated near major offshore oil deposits, namely, the Dukhan 1, Idd Al-Shargi, Al-Shaheen, Maydan Mahzam, and Bul Hanine oil fields. According to the U.S. Energy Information Administration, Qatar produced 1.1 million barrels of oil daily in 2006 and maintains 15.2 billion barrels of oil reserves, which, according to the Central Intelligence Agency's *World Factbook*, should allow sustained production for 37 years at this level. In 2008, Qatar was the 15th-largest crude oil exporter. The sector, while still growing, has shown signs of maturity, and the Qatari government is exploring enhanced oil-recovery projects to mitigate projected declines in productivity.

Since 1995, Qatar has significantly expanded its production and exports of natural gas. With 83.5 trillion cubic feet of natural gas reserves, Qatar increased annual production of natural gas from 44.3 billion cubic feet in 1995 to 252.5 billion cubic feet in 2008, according to the Energy Information Administration. The majority of Qatar's natural gas reserves are offshore in the North Field. Qatar's natural gas pipelines are connected with those of Oman and the United Arab Emirates via the Dolphin Project, the first transborder natural gas venture undertaken by the GCC states. The Qatari government has also devoted significant resources to the development of liquid natural gas exports, and the country ranks first among global suppliers of liquid natural gas.

With a rapidly growing population and economy, Qatar's rate of energy consumption has increased substantially. In order to increase the country's electricity generation capacity, the Qatari government's Ministry of Electricity and Water reallocated assets to the semipublic Qatar Electricity and Water Company. The government still maintains control over the distribution of electricity through the state-run Qatar General Electricity and Water Corporation. In 2007, Qatar produced 15.11 terawatt-hours and consumed 13.73 terawatt-hours.

Qatar faces several environmental consequences related to its energy consumption. In 2005, Qatar had the highest carbon dioxide emissions per capita. This level is due in part to the high energy needs of air-conditioning, water desalination, electricity generation, and natural gas processing. Additionally, the continued growth of Qatar's economy and infrastructure has put strain on the country's ability to maintain water reserves. Water is necessary for the production of natural gas and oil as well as the generation of electricity. Increased energy consumption in conjunction with Qatar's natural water scarcity puts mounting stress on its water resources.

ALLISON HARTNETT

Further Reading

Central Intelligence Agency. "Qatar." In *The World Factbook*. https://www.cia.gov/library/publications/the-world-factbook/geos/qa.html.

Cleveland, William. *A History of the Modern Middle East,* 3rd edition. Boulder, CO: Westview Press, 2004.

Dargin, J. "Qatar's Natural Gas: The Foreign-Policy Driver." *Middle East Policy* 14, no. 3 (Fall 2007).

Dowding, Heather. "Energy Profile of Qatar." In *The Encyclopedia of Earth*, edited by Cutler J. Cleveland. Washington, DC: National Council for Science and the Environment. http://www.eoearth.org/article/Energy_profile_of_Qatar.

U.S. Energy Information Administration. "Country Analysis Brief: Qatar." http://www.eia.gov/countries/country-data.cfm?fips=QA.

See Also: Bahrain; Energy Transmission: Gas; Flaring Gas; Natural Gas; Oil and Petroleum; Oman; Organization of Petroleum Exporting Countries; Saudi Arabia.

Radiation

Category: Environmentalism.
Summary: Radiation, as a physical, electrodynamic process, comprises the propagation of energetic particles or electromagnetic waves within a space or a medium.

There are two distinct types of radiation: ionizing and nonionizing. Many phenomena occur as a result of distinct forms of radiation, including light, heat, and radioactivity. The physical unit used to measure all types of radiation is the joule.

Electromagnetic radiation (EMR) is characterized by both electric and magnetic fields, oscillating perpendicular to each other. All kinds of electromagnetic radiation are based on photons. The electromagnetic spectrum has been divided into certain ranges of frequencies that classify the associated radiation (from longer-wavelength, lower-frequency to shorter-wavelength, higher-frequency) as radio waves, microwaves, terahertz radiation, infrared radiation, visible light, ultraviolet radiation, X-rays, and gamma rays. The human eye is capable of seeing EMR in only a small range of frequencies, called the visible light spectrum.

Radiation with sufficiently high energy, such as alpha particles, beta particles, gamma rays, and X-rays, can ionize atoms and molecules and thus fall into the category of ionizing radiation. Other forms of radiation, such as radio waves, microwaves, and light waves, are not energetic enough and thus are categorized as nonionizing forms of radiation. All forms of radiation, ionizing and nonionizing, can be harmful to organisms and the natural environment. Nonetheless, medicine has found various forms of radiation and radioactive substances to have many useful applications. For instance the imaging technologies produce X-rays and magnetic resonance images enable doctors to diagnose conditions and illnesses, and radionuclides can be used not only diagnostically but also therapeutically, to treat disease, as well as in research. Since radiation disturbs cell division, radiotherapy is a way to treat cancer and prevent tumors from growing. In the geological sciences, radiocarbon dating is used to determine the age of organic materials. Tracer atoms help to identify the pathways taken by pollutants through the environment.

Nonionizing Radiation

Although by definition nonionizing radiation is relatively low energy, it can modify the rotational, vibrational, or electronic valence configurations of molecules and atoms.

Visible light falls into the range of EMR with wavelengths between about 380 and 760 nanometers, with a frequency range of about 405 terahertz (THz) to 790 THz. Its speed, about 186,411 miles (300,000,000 meters) per second in a vacuum, is one of the fundamental constants of nature.

Infrared (IR) radiation is EMR with a longer wavelength than light, between 0.7 and 300 micrometers, and frequencies between approximately 1 and 430 THz. Thermal radiation, synonymous for infrared red, occurs from the movement of charged particles within atoms converting into electromagnetic radiation and then radiated from the surface of an object as heat. Corresponding physical laws are Wien's law (giving the most likely frequency of the emitted radiation) and the Stefan-Boltzmann law (giving the heat intensity).

Microwaves are electromagnetic waves longer than infrared light, with frequencies between 300 megahertz (0.3 gigahertz) and 300 gigahertz, and wavelengths between 1 meter and 1 millimeter.

Radio waves occur naturally, from lightning, and are emitted from bodies in space. Artificially generated radio waves are used for communications systems, including telecommunications and cell phones, broadcasting, radar, satellite communication, and Wi-Fi networks. Nikola Tesla invented a prototype of wireless telephone by tuning a transmitter and a receiver to the same frequency.

Ionizing Radiation

When highly energetic electromagnetic waves or subatomic particles detach electrons from atoms, they become ionized.

Alpha (a) particles are emitted during the decay of large nuclei. Consisting of two neutrons and two protons, they have a doubly positive charge, high atomic mass, and propagate slowly. Alpha particles can be stopped with a sheet of paper. They are unable to penetrate human skin, thus causing no external hazardous effects, but they may be dangerous upon ingestion.

Beta (b) radiation in the form of energetic electrons is called beta-minus (b-) radiation and requires

Schematic of a Light Wave

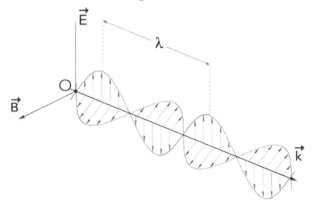

Note: The Greek letter lambda, λ, denotes one full wavelength (from peak to peak). B refers to magnetic field, E to electric field, and O the direction of radiation.
Source: Manja Leyk, 2011.

a few centimeters of metal to be stopped. Beta-plus (b+) radiation is the emission of positrons. Because these are antimatter particles, they annihilate any matter nearby, releasing gamma photons.

Gamma (g) photons have a frequency higher than 10^{19} hertz. During atomic decay, gamma photons follow alpha particles and beta radiation, to release so-called excess energy. Different from alpha and beta particles, photons have neither mass nor electric charge. Gamma radiation penetrates deeply through matter, stopped only by lead or depleted uranium shields.

The smaller the wavelength, the higher the energy, according to the equation $E = h \times c/l$. Wavelengths smaller than 10 nanometers describe the range of X-rays. X-ray photons are absorbed by atoms, because of energy differences between orbital electrons.

Neutrons, from spontaneous or induced nuclear fission or fusion, are categorized according to their speed. They require hydrogen-rich shielding, such as concrete or water, as used in nuclear reactors, to block them. Neutrons do not ionize atoms, because they have no charge, but they do create unstable isotopes; thus they induce radioactivity in a previously nonradioactive material.

The physical unit of radioactive decay (from the SI, or International System, of units) is the becquerel (formerly curie): 1 Bq = 1 decay per second. The sievert (formerly rem) is the unit of the dose for biological effects of ionizing radiation: 1 Sv = 1 J/kg. Another unit used to measure the dose of radiation absorbed by matter is the gray: 1 Gy = 1 Sv. Non-SI units are the rad (radiation absorbed dose; 1 rad = 0.01 Gy) and the rem (roentgen equivalent mammal/man; 1 rem = 0.01 Sv).

Health Concerns

Infrared and ultraviolet radiation may cause burns. Air travel exposes passengers to increased radiation from cosmic rays. For passengers, the recommendation from the International Commission on Radiological Protection (ICRP) is no more than 1 mSv per year.

Exposure to radiation causes changes in the chemical composition of gases and liquids, mainly as a result of radiolysis, and leads to the formation of free radicals. Water subjected to ionizing radiation forms free radicals of hydrogen and hydroxyl. This leads to oxydative stress in the cells of living organisms, because they are composed primarily of water. Excessive exposure to ionizing radiation results in poisoning, which is called acute radiation syndrome (ARS). A chronic radiation syndrome typically appeared in workers in early uranium and radium mines. Potential hazards include the development of cancer, tumors, and DNA damage.

Typical symptoms of radiation poisoning are nausea, bloody vomiting, bloody stools, headache, weakness, high fever, (permanent) hair loss, skin damage (called cutaneous radiation syndrome), and poor wound healing. Intense irradiation of the whole body causes immunodeficiency resulting from destruction of bone marrow.

To avoid radiation damage, the amount of energy deposited in sensitive material should be reduced by shielding or distance from the source. Some materials can be modified to be less sensitive to radiation damage by adding antioxidants or stabilizers.

MANJA LEYK

Further Reading

Dunning, F. B. *Electromagnetic Radiation.* San Diego, CA: Academic Press 1997.

Gaskell, D. C. *Electromagnetic Radiation.* London: Longman, 1973.

Heald, Mark A. *Classical Electromagnetic Radiation.* Fort Worth, TX: Saunders, 1995.

International Occupational Safety and Health Information Centre. *Electromagnetic Radiation.* Geneva, Switzerland: International Occupational Safety and Health Information Centre, International Labour Office, 1981.

Marion, Jerry B. *Classical Electromagnetic Radiation.* New York: Academic Press, 1965.

Read, Franck Henry. *Electromagnetic Radiation.* New York: John Wiley, 1980.

See Also: Chernobyl; Curie, Marie; Meitner, Lise; Nuclear Fission; Nuclear Fusion; Photovoltaics; Radiative Forcing; Uranium.

Radiative Forcing

Category: Environmentalism.
Summary: Radiative forcing is an atmospheric measure of the imbalance in the Earth's energy budget, resulting from human activities or natural phenomena.

Radiative forcing occurs when the balance between the energy reaching Earth through the atmosphere and the amount of energy radiating away from the planet is altered. The word radiative refers to the energy flow that takes place through incoming solar radiation and outgoing infrared rays. The term forcing implies that the imbalance is forced, or caused by external influences, on the atmospheric and climatic systems of our planet. Any changes in the Earth's energy balance resulting from changes in the internal dynamics of the atmosphere are not considered a part of radiative forcing. The phenomenon is measured between two layers of the atmosphere, the troposphere and stratosphere.

▷ *The Intergovernmental Panel on Climate Change*

The World Meteorological Organization (WMO) and the United Nations Environment Programme (UNEP) constituted the Intergovernmental Panel on Climate Change (IPCC) in 1988. The IPCC is a scientific body. It reviews and assesses the most recent scientific, technical, and socioeconomic information produced worldwide relevant to the understanding of climate change. It does not conduct any research, nor does it monitor climate-related data or parameters. Scientists contribute voluntary research to the IPCC, which is reviewed and assessed. Membership in the IPCC is open to all members of the WMO and UNEP. The IPCC's First Assessment Report was published in 1990 and the Fifth Assessment Report is expected in 2014. Among other things, the reports provide detailed information on the linkages between observed climatic changes, causes of climate change, near- and long-term impacts, and adaptation and mitigation strategies to combat climate change.

In 2007, the Nobel Committee decided to award the 2007 Nobel Peace Prize, in two equal parts, to the IPCC and former U.S. vice president Albert Arnold (Al) Gore for their efforts to build up and disseminate greater knowledge about anthropogenic (human-related) climate change and to lay the foundation for measures that are needed to counteract such change. The Nobel Committee applauded IPCC's efforts over a span of two decades to provide informed consensus on the relationship between climate change and anthropogenic activities.

Radiative forcing is measured in the units of net energy incident per unit area of the planet's surface, generally watts per square meter. A positive value for radiative forcing is associated with an increase, or warming, of surface temperatures. Substances that absorb the solar radiation or trap infrared radiation are responsible for positive forcing. These substances include gases with high global warming potential (GWP). Negative radiative forcing, by contrast, is a cooling effect and is associated with substances that reflect incident radiation. If the rate of incoming energy is equal to the rate at which energy is lost, then the value of radiative forcing will be zero and the planet's temperature will remain in equilibrium.

Gases and Other Factors

Some of the major factors that have an impact on the value of radiative forcing are changes in the concentration of greenhouse gases (GHGs) in the atmosphere, changes in the area of the planet's surface covered by forest, the presence of aerosols in the atmosphere, variation in the sun's radiation output, and volcanic output. Estimating the value of radiative forcing allows us to understand, as well as compare the climatic impacts of, anthropogenic activities and natural phenomena.

The Intergovernmental Panel on Climate Change (IPCC) first used the term *radiative forcing* in its reports. According to the Fourth Assessment Report (2007), the largest contribution to positive forcing comes from well-mixed GHGs, which include carbon dioxide (CO_2), methane (CH_4), nitrous oxide (N_2O), chlorofluorocarbons (CFCs), and hydrochlorofluorocarbons (HCFCs). GHG molecules tend to be extremely persistent generating cumulative effects. And they circulate well; a "well-mixed" gas is distributed at a given concentration fairly evenly throughout the atmosphere, as by definition its concentration is not temperature–dependent.

The contribution of aerosols, however, is difficult to determine. Certain types have a cooling effect, while aerosols such as black carbon increase the absorption of incoming radiation. The effect of clouds on radiative forcing is also uncertain. Clouds can reflect radiation, but their water vapor absorbs infrared rays. Volcanic eruptions have been observed to cause a cooling effect in the atmosphere; the particles released tend to reflect radiation flowing from the sun.

Human Inputs

Radiative forcing has increased since the beginning of the Industrial Revolution, as a result of the emission of GHGs. For the sake of calculations, scientific studies consider the era between the 18th and the 19th centuries as the base period. This is the period before the beginning of industrialization, for which the value of radiative forcing is considered as zero; the year 1750 correlates to this start point. According to the Fourth Assessment Report, since 1750 a radiative forcing (RF) contribution of plus 2.4 watts per square meter is attributed to the increase in the concentration of well-mixed GHGs such as CO_2, CH_4, N_2O, CFCs, HCFCs, and fluorinated gases.

Of that amount, plus 1.6 watts per square meter—about two thirds of the total— is due to the increase in atmospheric CO_2 alone. The direct cooling impact of aerosols is estimated to be minus 0.5 watt per square meter. Human land use patterns taken as a whole have had a minor cooling effect. The values of radiative forcing for each factor have a corresponding uncertainty. For example, the uncertainty in radiative forcing due to linear contrails is minimal, whereas great uncertainty occurs in the RF value due to aerosols.

The Annual Greenhouse Gas Index (AGGI) also tracks changes in RF value due to the concentration of GHGs. The United States National Oceanic and Atmospheric Administration maintains this index. According to the AGGI, RF from GHGs increased by 21.5 percent between 1990 and 2006.

The combined RF due to human activities since 1750, ranging from deforestation to industrial and transportation sector emissions, is pegged at 1.6 watts per square meter. This implies that human existence has resulted in a net warming, and hence stimulated changes in the planet's climate system.

While RF is intrinsically linked to the phenomenon of climate change, the value of radiative forcing cannot be used on a simple, one-to-one basis to quantify the extent of climate change. However, an increase in concentration of GHGs will cause an increase in radiative forcing, which

▷ *The Montreal Protocol*

The Montreal Protocol is hailed as one of the most successful international agreements and an example of exceptional international cooperation. The Montreal Protocol was a treaty that was outlined in September 1987 in the city of Montreal, Canada. It was enforced in the subsequent years with the aim of arresting the depletion of the ozone layer and drastically reducing the emission of certain gases with high global warming potential (GWP).

The treaty specifically targets halogenated hydrocarbons, such as chlorofluorocarbons (CFCs) and hydrochlorofluorocarbons (HCFCs). These gases are nontoxic and chemically inert when released in the troposphere. These properties made CFCs a popular choice for a variety of purposes, including refrigerants, deodorants, spray paints, and asthma inhalers. However, in the 1970s scientists Frank Sherwood Rowland and Mario Molina discovered that these gases had long lifetimes and were destroying the protective ozone layer in the upper atmosphere. These gases also have extremely high GWP— that is, positive radiative forcing (RF): One molecule of a CFC leads to 4,600 to 14,000 times the RF due to one molecule of carbon dioxide.

The clearly demonstrated harmful effects of these gases led to widespread acceptance of the Montreal Protocol. Since the enforcement of the Montreal Protocol, the atmospheric concentration of these gases has remained constant and has begun to decrease. CFCs have been replaced by transitional HCFCs. The signatories to the protocol plan to freeze consumption and production of HCFCs sometime before 2015. The restoration of the ozone layer is expected in the next few years.

in turn will accelerate climate change and magnify its impacts.

Dinesh Kapur

Further Reading

Chandler, David L. "Explained: Radiative Forcing." Massachusetts Institute of Technology. March 10, 2010. http://web.mit.edu/newsoffice/2010/explained-radforce-0309.html

Dawson, B., and M. Spannagle. *The Complete Guide to Climate Change.* New York: Routledge, 2009.

Intergovernmental Panel on Climate Change. *Changes in Atmospheric Constituents and in Radiative Forcing: Contribution of Working Group I to the Fourth Assessment Report of the IPCC.* Geneva: Intergovernmental Panel on Climate Change, 2007.

National Research Council. *Radiative Forcing of Climate Change: Expanding the Concept and Addressing Uncertainties.* Washington, DC: National Academies Press, 2005.

See Also: Air Pollution; Aviation; Climate Change; Greenhouse Gases; Intergovernmental Panel on Climate Change; Methane.

Rankine, William

Dates: 1820–1872.
Category: Biographies.
Summary: One of the originators of the laws of therodynamics, William Rankine is best known for his complete theory of heat engines.

William John Macquorn Rankine was a Scottish engineer and physicist who, along with Rudolf Clausius and Lord Kelvin (William Thomson), was one of the fathers of thermodynamics. Rankine's best-known work was his complete theory of heat engines, and his engineering manuals continued to be used for most of the 19th century.

Initially educated at home, Rankine later attended the High School of Glasgow, the Military and Naval Academy, and the University of Edinburgh, which he began attending at age 16, working under James David Forbes, who was also mentor to physicist and mathematician James Clerk Maxwell.

During Rankine's time, there was a continual problem in railway engineering in putting down curved rails, and Rankine's method was significantly more accurate and efficient than preceding methodologies, making use of the recently developed theodolite, a precision surveying instrument used for measuring angles in vertical and horizontal planes. From early in his career, Rankine was interested in representing heat mathematically, but in his university years, he suffered from the dearth of experimental data from which to extrapolate. His interest in heat soon turned into an interest in heat engine mechanics, the mechanics of any engine that converts thermal energy into mechanical work, which in Rankine's time included the steam engine and today also includes the internal combustion engine, among many

Wikimedia

William Rankine's academic career included awards for his work on the wave theory of light. He also made advances in analyzing gases, vapors, and steam for use in heat engines and identified what is now known as metal fatigue.

other types. In 1849, Rankine successfully deter-mined the relationship between temperature and saturated vapor pressure. He soon moved on to establish relationships between the temperature, pressure, and density of gases, and he predicted the counterintuitive conclusion that saturated steam has a negative apparent specific heat.

Soon Rankine had succeeded at calculating the efficiency of heat engines, and he extrapolated from his experimental data that the maximum efficiency of such an engine is a function of the temperatures between which it operates (the thermodynamic function). These results were reformulated and rephrased several times and were used to support an energy-centric formulation of dynamics, which described dynamics in terms of energy and energy transformations rather than motion and force: the science of energetics. For a time, Rankine was a vocal critic of James Clerk Maxwell's theories of heat, because they were incompatible with some of his own models, but in 1869 he eventually admit-ted the validity of Maxwell's equations.

Rankine's best successes were in working toward practical results, analyzing properties of gases, vapors, and steam to achieve more effi-cient heat engines. He was also among the first to understand the fatigue failure of railway axles; he was able to show how they developed from brit-tle cracks and described the process now called metal fatigue.

BILL KTE'PI

Further Reading

Karwatka, Dennis. "William Rankine and Engineering Education." *Tech Directions* 69, no. 3 (October 2009).

Lewis, Christopher J. T. *Heat and Thermodynamics.* Westport, CT: Greenwood, 2007.

Liszka, John. "Are You Sure, Mr. Carnot? A Re-examination of the Thermodynamic Principles as Formulated by Nicolas Carnot and William Rankine Over One Hundred Years Ago Might Lead to Greater Efficiency in Electrical Power Generating Stations, Together With Reduced Emissions." *Engineering Digest* 38, no. 3 (June 1992).

Muller, Ingo. *A History of Thermodynamics.* New York: Springer, 2010.

Raman, V. V. "William John Macquorn Rankine (1820–1872)." *Journal of Chemical Education* 50, no. 4 (1973).

Sutherland, H. B. "Professor William John Macquorn Rankine." *Proceedings of the Institution of Civil Engineers Civil Engineering* 132, no. 4 (1999).

See Also: Austria; Enthalpy; Thermodynamics; Waste Heat Recovery.

Recycling

Category: Environmentalism
Summary: Recycling is the reuse of materials that would otherwise be discarded. Recycling reduces the energy costs associated with the production, distribution, and disposal of consumer and industrial products.

Recycling on a larger scale emerged in the late 20th century as a response to the growth of waste production, especially in developed industrial-ized countries and urban areas. Products can be recycled in whole or in component parts. Con-sumers recycle household materials and pur-chase items made from recycled materials as part of an overall strategy of environmentally sustain-able living. Commonly recycled household items include aluminum cans, glass containers, news-papers and magazines, and cardboard. Com-monly recycled commercial and industrial items include aluminum, steel, and copper, among other industrial waste products. Energy itself can be produced through recycling agricultural wastes into biofuels or through recycling waste heat into electricity or steam by cogeneration or waste heat recovery methods.

Traditional waste disposal methods such as securing waste in landfills or containers and incin-eration began to come into question due to their expense as well as rising environmental concerns as to their sustainability. Landfills began to reach capacity, leaving communities to seek new disposal locations. Environmental contamination concerns, rising land prices, and grassroots neighborhood movements against nearby planned landfills and incinerators made securing new locations difficult. Many countries began to seek alternate waste depositories overseas, leading to rising shipping costs. Countries such as India and China began to accept international toxic and hazardous waste such as electronic or e-waste.

The growing field of waste management sought a variety of solutions to the waste disposal problem. Recycling had been practiced on a small scale for centuries, notably among people or communities suffering through economic hardships. Lack of finances or resource scarcity made recycling of individual items a necessity. The late 20th-century growth of the environmental movement brought recycling to the forefront of more sustainable waste management initiatives as traditional waste disposal methods became linked to climate change and global warming. Grassroots movements, increased environmental regulation at all levels of government, pollution and greenhouse gas emissions reductions, and cost effectiveness made recycling an increasingly popular alternative.

Recycling became an important component in the growing adoption of a sustainable lifestyle,

alongside the purchase of energy-efficient appliances, compact fluorescent light bulbs, and hybrid and fuel-efficient cars and attempts to use less energy more efficiently. Other motivations for recycling included potential earnings from the resale of collected items such as bottles and cans or from the theft and resale of valuable recyclables such as copper wiring and pipes. Recycling has emerged as part of the informal economy among the poor in developing nations such as India.

Recycling and other environmental strategies lag behind in countries with lax environmental regulations and oversight or limited green culture movement penetration. Recycling is also vulnerable to price changes for recyclable materials and problems caused by contamination of separable groups of recyclables, which can result in unusable items or additional sorting costs. Projects to expand recycling rates are popular among both environmentalists and governments. Common examples include promotional campaigns and items, the use of recycling bins, and payments such as can or bottle return deposits. Recycling is expected to become a larger part of waste management as recycling participation rates, strategies, and methods improve.

Photos.com

While movements toward expanding recycling are popular among both environmentalists and governments, these projects often face a number of challenges, including price fluctuations for recyclable materials like these bales of used cardboard awaiting processing at a recycling center. Other problems may occur when contamination among the different types of recyclables adds to sorting costs or results in some materials becoming unusable.

Energy Benefits

Recycling goods has energy-saving as well as environmental benefits. All goods utilize energy in their production, distribution, and disposal. Energy costs involved in product production can include the acquisition of needed raw materials and the manufacture and assembly of product components. Energy costs of distribution include transportation to markets. Indirect energy costs can include the power needed to light, heat, or air condition manufacturing plants and retail stores. Energy is also used in the disposal of items that are discarded. These energy costs include waste collection, transportation to disposal sites, and the power needed to run incinerators.

Environmentalists calculate the energy costs associated with goods throughout the course of their production and lifetime, from source material collection through manufacture and distribution to use and disposal. Recycling reduces these energy costs and their associated environmental impacts, as does the purchase of products made from recycled materials. Although recycling represents overall energy savings, it includes higher initial energy costs of the product's original manufacture and distribution. Recycling is thus considered as one component of overall energy savings and environmental sustainability initiatives, alongside reduction and reuse. Recycling also saves energy by reducing the amount of waste that must be transported to landfills or incinerated.

The higher the energy intensity of original production, the greater the energy savings provided by recycling. Recycling metals such as aluminum, steel, and copper for reuse in manufacturing represents large energy savings over the use of newly mined ore or manufactured metals. Recycling also creates energy savings when waste is recycled into new energy resources. The recycling of agricultural waste that is traditionally burned off in the fields or otherwise disposed of into biofuels is a small but growing sector of the energy market. Such waste includes the husks, shells, or stalks of various plants.

Energy itself can also be recycled. Both cogeneration (combined heat and power, or CHP) and waste heat recovery are methods that capture waste heat and recycle it into clean, carbon-free electricity or steam. Both offer an alternative method of reducing fossil fuel use and related environmental damage. Cogeneration produces recycled energy by capturing the waste heat generated through traditional power generation. Waste heat recovery captures and recycles waste heat that is already emitted through industrial manufacturing processes. The increased efficiency of recycling energy also represents cost savings. Since waste heat cannot travel far before cooling off, cogeneration or waste heat recovery needs to occur close to the source of waste heat generation. Power plants that generate electricity are prime targets for energy recycling as they traditionally operate at very low energy efficiency levels, releasing waste heat generated as a by-product into the atmosphere. Examples of industrial plants that can benefit from waste heat recovery include those that produce various metals, glass, pulp, paper, and silicon. Industrial plants have used waste heat recovery to generate new energy for in-house use or have partnered with other companies who use the recovered energy. Countries such as Denmark have emerged as global leaders in the adoption of cogeneration technology while lack of knowledge and interest and the hindrance of governmental regulations have slowed its adoption in other countries such as the United States.

MARCELLA BUSH TREVINO

Further Reading

Ayres, Robert U., and Ed Ayres. "Bridge to the Renewable Energy Future." *World Watch* 22, no. 5.

Border, Rosemary. *Recycling.* New York: Oxford University Press, 1996.

"Materials: A Report of the Interagency Workgroup on Industrial Ecology, Material, and Energy Flows." http://www.umich.edu/~indecol/materials.pdf.

Recycling Energy Council. "Recycling Energy. It's Time." http://www.recyclingenergy.org/.

Young, Mitchell. *Garbage and Recycling.* Detroit: Greenhaven, 2007.

See Also: Battery Disposal; Chlorofluorocarbons; Environmentally Preferable Purchasing; Green Energy Certification; Industrial Ecology; Landfill Gas; Life-Cycle Analysis; Refuse.

Refining

Category: Energy Technology.

Summary: The refining of crude oil and natural gas is essential for the production of high-value hydrocarbons, which find use as fuels, lubricants, and chemical feedstocks for manufacturing.

Modern civilization is overwhelmingly fossil-fueled. This use of fossil fuels requires refining. A refinery is a large industrial plant that processes crude oil into more useful products, such as fuels, lubricants, and chemical feedstocks for plastics manufacturing. Refined products also end up in everyday items: cosmetics, clothing, furniture, aspirin, compact discs, crayons, and lighter fluid, to name a few. Refining is a mature and highly internationalized industry that employs engineers, scientists, laboratory testing staff, operators, and computer technicians.

Even though two-thirds of the crude oil refined in the United States is imported, 95 percent of the total refined products consumed domestically are also refined domestically. However, because of its huge demand for gasoline—some 9 million barrels per day in 2009—the United States relies partly on imports from refineries in Canada, Venezuela, Europe, and the Caribbean.

The refining of fossil fuels dates back thousands of years, as evidenced by the use of semirefined asphalt for waterproofing in ancient Mesopotamia. Modern refining began in the 1850s, when Benjamin Silliman worked out a method for distilling petroleum based on the difference in boiling points of the various hydrocarbon components. During the 1860s, the first fully operational refinery began production of kerosene in Pennsylvania, and shortly thereafter the Standard Oil Company entered the refining business.

With the introduction of the gasoline-powered internal combustion engine and the founding of the Ford Motor Company, petroleum-based locomotion expanded quickly and soon came to include planes and military vehicles. During and after World War I and World War II, refining capacity continued to grow as new uses were found for motor fuels. Global refining capacity saw a tenfold increase between 1938 and 1981. More recently, in response to environmental regulations such as the Clean Air Act of 1990 and later mandates requiring the use of reformulated gasoline (RFG) and low-sulfur fuels, refiners have had to perform costly upgrades to their facilities in order to reduce industrial plant emissions, as well as manufacture cleaner-burning and more efficient fuels.

Crude oil is a complex mixture that can be separated into simpler classes of components by fractional distillation, the universal first step in oil refining. When crude oil is heated, the lightest hydrocarbons begin to vaporize and boil off. Vapors coming off a distillation tower within a similar boiling range can be recondensed and collected as subgroups of hydrocarbon compounds called fractions. The lowest boiling fraction contains the C_1–C_4 gases, namely methane, ethane, propane, and butane.

The second major fraction, called light straight naphtha, contains the C_5–C_9 alkanes, which are used for gasoline blending. The next fraction is called naphtha and contains alkanes and cycloalkanes up to around C_{12}. This fraction usually goes on to a catalytic reforming unit for the production of motor fuel and solvents. Together, these three low-boiling fractions are referred to as light distillates.

The kerosene fraction, which consists of C_{10}–C_{18} alkanes and aromatics, is used as fuel for jet engines and tractors. Gas oil, also called diesel distillate, boils off next, as a mixture of C_{12}–C_{18} hydrocarbons, and is used as diesel fuel or home heating oil. Kerosene and gas oil are referred to as middle distillates. Still higher-boiling is the lubricating oil fraction (C_{20}–C_{50}), which is suitable for use as motor oil, grease, and lubricants. The final distilled fraction is heavy gas oil (C_{20}–C_{70}), which is used for industrial fuel.

The leftover, tarlike stuff resulting from fractional distillation is called heavy residue, residuum, or "the bottom of the barrel." When the residuum is heat-treated in a coking unit, it turns into petroleum coke, which can be used for industrial heating and for making graphite products. Alternatively, if the leftovers are further processed by vacuum distillation, waxy hydrocarbons such as petrolatum and paraffin wax can be obtained. Asphalt is another product derived from residuum.

The simplest refineries stop after distillation, while more elaborate refineries carry out chemical processing steps on the heaviest hydrocarbon fractions in order to make more of the lighter, higher-value products. These steps are referred to as downstream processes because they are closer to the refinery gate and consumers. Downstream processing generates a specific "demand slate" of lighter, higher-value products. Because of variations in oil characteristics, refinery operators try to start with an optimal mixture of crude oils to produce the desired demand slate.

The major processing steps include cracking, alkylation, isomerization, and reforming. Cracking involves the treating of high boiling fractions (greater than C_{10}) with a catalyst and high temperature (about 1,000 degrees Fahrenheit) in order to "crack," or break down, large hydrocarbons into smaller ones. For instance, when gas oil is cracked, it yields diesel fuel. Cracking is also used to produce high-octane gasoline. A related process, called hydrocracking, adds hydrogen gas to produce lighter products. Visbreaking is the name given to a cracking step that reduces the viscosity of heavy residual oils.

In alkylation, isobutane (C_4) is heated together with smaller alkenes (C_3–C_6) in the presence of acid to form higher-octane branched alkanes for gasoline blending. Isomerization converts straight-chain (linear) hydrocarbons into branched ones by altering their molecular structure. This process uses heat plus a catalyst to make isobutane feedstock for the alkylation step, or else to improve the octane rating of straight-run gasoline. Reforming involves heating a lower-octane fraction with a special catalyst that converts the components into a mixture of aromatics called reformate.

Refinery process streams are also treated to remove contaminants such as water, dissolved salts, trace metals, and sulfur-containing compounds. For example, the hydrotreater unit removes sulfur by treating diesel distillate and naphtha with hydrogen gas. Additional processing occurs in the amine gas, Claus, and tail gas treatment units. Petrochemical plants, which carry out finer solvent fractioning and plastics manufacturing, are often located at or near a refinery to minimize transport. Double-bond-containing hydrocarbons, such as ethylene and propylene, are particularly useful as petrochemical feedstocks.

Like crude oil, natural gas must be processed before use. Raw natural gas contains a mixture of light hydrocarbons (C_1–C_8) plus a number of impurities, such as hydrogen sulfide, nitrogen, helium, water, and sometimes mercury and radon. Contaminant removal not only adds value to the product gases but also helps protect processing equipment. Various specialized absorbents called molecular sieves are employed for soaking up contaminants from the gas process stream. Condensate from a gas field behaves like an ultralight crude oil and is easily refined into gasoline, or it

Photos.com

Within a refinery, many processes operate simultaneously, and arrays of piping carry streams between process units. Some refineries are capable of processing hundreds of thousands of barrels of crude oil per day.

can be transported to an oil refinery for recovery of the valuable natural gas liquids (NGLs).

Gas-processing plants are usually located near sites of gas production. After purification, pipeline-quality dry natural gas (mainly methane) is transported through underground pipes to regional storage reservoirs called hubs, or else is stored in pressurized tanks. The gas is then delivered by pipeline for use in industrial and residential heating and electric power generation. Several criteria are used to judge its quality, including caloric value and hydrocarbon dew point.

Additional facilities common to all refineries include utilities and on-sites. Utilities provide the operational infrastructure to keep all of the processes running smoothly: boilers to supply steam, electric power, cooling towers, fuel supplies, and instrument air stations for pneumatic operation of control valves. Some of the low-boiling gases that result from refining are used to fuel on-site heaters and boilers.

Energy Creates Energy

Refining is one of the world's most energy-intensive industries. On-sites typically include a flare station for safe disposal of gas in case of an operational upset, liquid and solid waste management systems, and emergency response stations. A laboratory for testing samples is another standard refinery feature. Construction and upgrading of refineries is carried out by contractors such as Bechtel and Lummus, and Honeywell's subsidiary UOP serves the refining industry by developing high-performance catalysts, adsorbents, and separation membranes.

Large storage tanks for crude and finished products are usually located near a refinery. Tanks are either cylindrical for liquid storage or spherical or bullet-shaped for pressurized gas storage. The so-called tank farms employ earthen berms for spill control. Provision must also be made for the storage of oxygenates and gasoline blending components. In selecting a storage site, engineers must take into account a range of factors, such as weather, temperature swings, and seismic activity in the area. Transport of refined liquid fuels in the United States relies on an extensive distribution network to move these products to wholesalers, distributors, and retailers, such as gasoline stations. Pipelines and barges move refined products from one region to another at speeds of a few miles per hour. Additional transportation capacity is supplied by rail tank car, tank trucks, and U.S. flagships, which move products between ports.

International Network of Companies

Globally, the refining industry consists of a complex network of integrated international companies and subsidiaries. Some members of the Organization of Petroleum Exporting Countries (OPEC) operate state-run energy companies that have invested in U.S. downstream processing since the 1990s. One example is Venezuela's PDVSA, which acquired Citgo Petroleum in 1991. Another example is the massive joint venture between Dow Chemical and Saudi Aramco called Sadara, slated for completion in 2016 in Jubail Industrial City.

Dominating the refining industry in the United States are the integrated international oil companies BP Amoco, ExxonMobil, and ChevronTexaco. The term *integrated* is applied when a company conducts both upstream oil production and downstream refining operations. Independent companies such as Marathon, Ashland, and Tosco, on the other hand, depend on the purchase of crude oil to use as their refinery feed. As a consequence of oil price instability and increasingly stringent environmental regulations, there has been an overall movement toward consolidation among refining companies. In 2010, there were just 148 refineries owned by 58 companies with a combined crude distillation capacity of 17.7 million barrels per day. Many of the largest domestic refineries are located along the coasts of Texas, Louisiana, and California; others are located in the Northeast and Midwest. Overall, the United States has one-fourth of the global distillation capacity and the largest downstream refining capacity, which churned out 7 billion barrels of finished product in 2010.

Refinery operation is not without its safety and environmental concerns. Traditionally, refineries have been responsible for air pollution, odors, noise, groundwater contamination, and occasional explosions. These concerns have led to strong pressure to prevent new refinery construction; in fact, no major refineries have been built since 1976 in the United States.

Recent policy commitments, if implemented, could have an impact on the refining industry. An example is the 2009 Copenhagen Accord, which seeks to limit global warming to 2 degrees Celsius above preindustrial times. The dominance of refined oil products in the transportation sector will be difficult to replace, however, especially as developing economies, such as China's, increase their use of personal transportation. Continued worldwide demand for fossil-fuel-based energy has prompted new exploration and extraction of non-traditional sources, including Venezuelan extra-heavy oil, Canadian oil sands, shale gas, and coal-bed methane, all of which will need refining. Some experts think that natural gas may be a bridge to the next, more sustainable, energy economy.

MARGARET E. SCHOTT

Further Reading

Armaroli, Nicola, and Vincenzo Balzani. "Oil Refining." In *Energy for a Sustainable World: From the Oil Age to a Sun-Powered Future*. Weinheim, Germany: Wiley-VCH, 2011.

MIT Energy Initiative. "The Future of Natural Gas: An Interdisciplinary MIT Study." http://web.mit .edu/mitei/research/studies/naturalgas.html.

National Energy Technology Laboratory. "Transmission, Distribution, and Refining." http:// www.netl.doe.gov/technologies/oil-gas/.

National Petrochemical and Refiners Association. "Refinery Facts." http://www.npra.org/ourIndustry/ refineryfacts/.

"Oil Refining." *Oil and Energy Trends* 36 (2011).

Pearce, Lynn M., ed. "Petroleum Refining and Related Industries." In *Encyclopedia of American Industries*. Vol. 1. 6th ed. Detroit: Gale Cengage Learning, 2011.

U.S. Energy Information Administration. "Refining." ftp://ftp.eia.doe.gov/pub/oil_gas/petroleum/ analysis_publications/oil_market_basics/refining_ text.htm.

See Also: Aramco; BP; ExxonMobil; Fossil Fuels; Gasification; Natural Gas; Oil and Petroleum.

Refuse

Category: Energy Resources.
Summary: Integrated waste management is emerging as the preferred approach to address the growing problem of refuse generated as the result of human consumption patterns.

Refuse is defined as anything that is worthless or unsuitable for further use and is often referred to as garbage, trash, or municipal solid waste (MSW). In addition to garbage, human activity produces sewage sludge, clinical and industrial waste, used tires, construction and demolition debris, electronic waste, and old appliances. Refuse is a growing problem as the world's population continues to rise, megacities grow larger, and places for disposal diminish. Many developing nations lack an infrastructure for effective waste management, and refuse often goes uncollected or is illegally disposed of at open dumps or along roadways. In contrast, when economies start to grow, countries move toward the use of sanitary landfills, recycling, and landfill gas recovery for electric power generation, along with stricter environmental regulations.

The total amount of MSW generated globally in 2010 was around 1.7 billion tons, with 1 billon tons disposed of in landfills. The United States, with less than 5 percent of the world's population, leads in MSW generation, followed by Japan and Western Europe. The total amount of MSW in the United States in 2009 was 243 million tons, which translates to 4.3 pounds per person per day. Data for the United States from its Environmental Protection Agency indicates that more than one-fourth of MSW consists of paper and paperboard; other items include food scraps, yard trimmings, plastics, metals, rubber, leather and textiles, wood, and glass.

Whereas the municipal waste stream in the industrialized West consists mainly of discarded manufactured goods, the waste stream in poorer nations has a larger percentage of putrescent (biodegradable) material, reflecting a higher proportion of food in their consumption patterns. For example, urban areas of India generate mostly putrescent material, along with ceramics, ash, and stones; goods such as leather, paper, rubber, glass, and metals either are rare or are scavenged for profit value.

Concepts about managing refuse have been changing over time and vary among cultures. Industrialized nations are now moving beyond the three *R*s—reduce, reuse, recycle—to embrace energy-saving and energy-recovering technologies. The cradle-to-grave concept, in which materials are created, used, and discarded, is beginning to yield to a more sustainable cradle-to-cradle approach that aims for the maximum reuse of materials in order to reduce consumption of resources as well as the energy that goes into the mining, processing, and manufacturing of new goods.

Recent decades have witnessed the creation of the integrated waste management strategy, a comprehensive system of waste disposal that emphasizes four main options: source reduction and product reuse, recycling and composting, landfill disposal, and burning with energy recovery. Source reduction, also called waste prevention, entails the reuse of goods and the onsite use of materials such as grass clippings. The scientific fields of industrial ecology and green chemistry are significant contributors to this approach.

Recycling serves to minimize the use of virgin raw materials while reducing fossil fuel combustion and greenhouse gas emissions that result from mining, transportation, and materials processing; landfill costs are also reduced. The recycling of 1 ton of aluminum cans, for example, saves the energy equivalent of more than 1,600 gallons of gasoline. Composting is the microbial process in which organic nutrients in biomass are allowed to decay and then are returned to the soil. Composting can be carried out either on a small scale, in yards at residences, or on a larger scale, at community-based facilities. Many U.S. municipalities have banned yard clippings from trash pickups in order to reduce the volume of compostable refuse going to landfills.

Biologically derived organic matter in landfills can also serve as a source of energy. In one common approach, the methane produced during the bacterially aided decomposition of carbon-rich material such as food waste is collected for use as a combustible fuel. One disadvantage of landfill disposal practices, however, is the energy-intensive nature and escalating cost of collecting and transporting waste to distant locations. To address this concern, the European Union (EU) has set up environmental laws that severely restrict new landfill creation and limit landfill disposal to non-biodegradable and nonrecyclable inert materials, such as construction debris.

One of these regulations is called the European Landfill Directive, which diverts the biodegradable waste stream for other uses. In the future, many landfills will likely employ microbial bioreactor technology to accelerate waste decomposition. Currently, the United States has more than 500 landfill gas-to-energy projects out of 1,800 operational municipal landfills.

Waste incineration, or the controlled burning of organic-rich MSW in specially designed combustion chambers, can provide heat as well as steam-generated electric power. Incineration with or without energy production typically reduces refuse to just 10 percent of its original volume. Although the heat content of individual components varies widely, on average the heat content of MSW is around 4,300 British thermal units (Btu) per pound, or one-third the heat content of high-quality coal.

Waste-to-Energy

Waste-to-energy (WtE) plants became popular in the 1980s as a response to the alarming increase in volume of municipal refuse and shrinking landfill space in many industrialized areas. In 2009, there were 90 such plants in the United States, generating a combined total of 2,500 megawatts of electricity.

Europe is the global leader in WtE technology, with 900 operational plants in several countries. Most of these plants utilize thermal technologies to generate heat and electric power for use by local communities. Out in front are Denmark, Germany, Belgium, Sweden, Norway, France, Italy, and the Netherlands—all members of the Confederation of European Waste-to-Energy Plants. Many European countries have established regulations with the threefold aim of restricting new landfill creation, promoting recycling, and banning the

A Cradle-to-Cradle Approach

The following articulation of the cradle-to-cradle approach to refuse management is from *The State of the World 2010*, based on concepts found in *Cradle to Cradle: Remaking the Way We Make Things*, by William McDonough and Michael Braungart (North Point Press, 2002):

"Imagine buildings, neighborhoods, transportations systems, factories, and parks all designed to enhance economic, environmental, and social health. To help realize this vision, production can be based on three key operating principles of the natural world.

Waste equals food. In nature, the processes of every organism contribute to the health of the whole. One organism's waste becomes food for another, and nutrients flow perpetually in regenerative, cradle-to-cradle cycles of birth, death, decay, and rebirth. Design modeled on these virtuous cycles eliminates the very concept of waste: products and materials can be designed of components that return either to soil as a nutrient or to industry for remanufacture.

Use current solar income. Nature's cradle-to-cradle cycles are powered by the energy of the sun. Trees and plants manufacture food from sunlight—an elegant, effective system that uses Earth's only perpetual source of energy income. The wind, a thermal flow fueled by sunlight, can be tapped along with direct solar collection to generate enough power to meet the energy needs of entire cities, regions, and nations.

Celebrate diversity. Healthy ecosystems are complex communities of living things, each of which has developed a unique response to its surroundings that works in concert with other organisms to sustain the system. Abundant diversity is the source of an ecosystem's strength and resilience. Businesses can celebrate the diversity of regional landscapes and cultures and grow ever more effective as they do so. Food and materials grown in the countryside, using implements and technology created in the city, are absorbed by the urban body and returned to their source as a form of waste that can replenish the system. Thus, human settlements and the natural world flourish side by side."

---

incineration of waste without energy recovery. Because the operation of high-efficiency incinerators equipped with modern emission controls is a costly endeavor, some countries offer construction subsidies along with tax exemptions for electricity production. Since new WtE plants must meet strict emission standards, newly built incinerators are far cleaner than conventional ones. The European regulation limiting toxic emissions is called the Waste Incineration Directive.

Recent improvements in WtE technology have significantly reduced the amount of toxic materials entering the environment. Heavy-duty baghouse air filters collect solid particulates, and scrubbers remove gaseous and aerosolized air pollutants. Another key environmental benefit of processing refuse into energy—as compared with conventional landfill disposal—is a reduction in greenhouse gas emissions. For example, for every ton of waste burned in a WtE plant, between 0.5 and 1 ton of greenhouse gases is prevented from entering the atmosphere.

Japan and Taiwan stand out in the Asia-Pacific region in employing WtE. For instance, 75 percent of Japan's MSW is incinerated for energy, while recycled plastics are used in place of coke to fuel steel mill blast furnaces. This part of the world is expected to surpass Europe in the coming decades with respect to new investments in WtE technology, especially as China and India—with their growing populations—catch up. Japan also practices "urban mining," the extraction of combustible and recyclable and precious materials from landfill mountains. Australia has government regulations aimed at landfill reduction but practices far less incineration of waste.

As the WtE industry matures, advanced thermal methods such as plasma-arc gasification and pyrolysis are being developed to produce synthetic gas (often called syngas) for use in fuel cells or for making combustible fuels and electricity. Additionally, advanced biological methods are widely employed. One of these methods is anaerobic digestion, which produces biogas (a mixture of methane and carbon dioxide) and biosolids, primarily from wet wastes. Denmark, Germany, and Belgium all generate biogas for use in process heating and on-site electrical generation using this technology. A second method, called mechanical biological treatment (MBT), involves the sorting and shredding of mixed waste, followed by either aerobic composting or anaerobic digestion. MBT is carried out on a large scale across Asia and Europe, especially in Germany, Austria, and Italy.

Wikimedia

Wood energy is used by millions and has great potential as a sustainable resource. This former petroleum station in the United Kingdom has replaced its old gas pumps with piles of firewood for sale.

Integrated MSW-processing facilities can be engineered to accept a range of biomass inputs, such as wood, wood pulp, and even construction debris. The United Kingdom is one of several countries that convert biomass consisting of household waste and agricultural residues into second-generation alcohol-type biofuels. (First-generation biofuels are made from sugar-containing food crops such as corn, sugarcane, sugar beets, and wheat; second-generation biofuels are based on nonfood crops.)

In 2010, the Canadian municipality of Edmonton, Alberta, began construction of the world's first industrial-scale municipal waste-to-biofuels facility, with a goal of 90 percent landfill diversion. The steps involve sorting to remove recyclable items, shredding, and finally conversion into refuse-derived fuel by a process involving gasification, cleaning and conditioning of the syngas (a mixture of carbon monoxide and hydrogen), and ultimately the transformation of this gas mixture into methanol or ethanol. The overall process is accelerated by the use of heat, pressure, and advanced catalysts.

Animal manure and human sewage represent another source of energy. Using modern biological treatment methods, such waste can be converted into fuels such as methane and ethanol. Methane is produced when manure and sewage decompose in an anaerobic (oxygen-free) environment. Alternatively, sewage sludge can be turned into fuel ethanol by fermenting its carbohydrate components.

Hazardous Waste

Another category of energy-containing refuse is hazardous waste. Liquids and solids are often generated as hazardous by-products from the petroleum, chemical, electronics, and coal industries; households and vehicles also contribute a share. Until the 1950s, half of all hazardous waste was dumped indiscriminately on land or in rivers and oceans in a practice called "dilute and disperse." Nowadays, industries often employ material-recovery techniques to capture solvents and acids for reuse after the contaminants are separated out. Hazardous wastes containing organic materials can be incinerated with the twin aims of waste destruction and volume reduction, or else they can be transformed into liquid fuels and synthesis gas for use in energy production.

E-Waste

The proliferation of used consumer electronics represents another potential source of recoverable materials as well as energy. Discarded items such as televisions, printers, and cell phones, often called electronic waste or e-waste, contain two major types of materials: engineered plastic housings and heavy metals. The recycling of 1 million cell phones, for example, would yield more than 35,000 pounds of metals, including copper (a major component), gold, silver, and palladium. To address the glowing e-waste crisis, the EU has introduced a program called Extended Producer Responsibility, whereby electronic equipment manufacturers take charge of recovery and recycling. Some states in the United States, such as Maine and California, have adopted similar guidelines. Nevertheless, e-waste is often shipped overseas to countries such as China and Nigeria, where components are disassembled, often by hand, for raw materials that can be sold for profit.

As one component of an integrated waste management strategy, WtE technologies have the potential to contribute to a nation's energy security and diversification. A number of global forces are expected to drive the maturation of this energy technology: increasing population, urbanization, rising standards of living, and individual consumption patterns. All these factors promote greater waste generation as well as a seemingly limitless demand for power. The global waste management services industry is growing, thanks to enhanced environmental awareness, newer treatment technologies, and the institution of regulatory policies. Significant challenges must be overcome, however, before these technologies will become more widely used. These challenges include enhancing the energy efficiency of WtE plants, lowering initial construction costs, and designing better infrastructures for local heat distribution and access to the power grid.

Margaret E. Schott

Further Reading

Confederation of European Waste-to-Energy Plants. "Heating and Lighting the Way to a Sustainable Future." http://www.cewep.eu/news/arts/index.html.

Edmonton Waste-to-Biofuels Project. "Project Description: Overview of the Edmonton Waste-to-Biofuels Project." http://www.enerkem.com.

LaGrega, Michael D., Phillip L. Buckingham, and Jeffrey C. Evans. *Hazardous Waste Management.* 2nd ed. Long Grove, IL: Waveland Press, 2010.

McDonough, William, and Michael Braungart. *Cradle to Cradle: Remaking the Way We Make Things.* New York: North Point Press, 2002.

U.S. International Trade Commission. *Solid and Hazardous Waste Services: An Examination of U.S. and Foreign Markets.* Publication 3679. Washington, DC: U.S. International Trade Commission, 2004. http://www.usitc.gov/publications/332/pub3679.pdf.

Waste Management, Inc. "From Waste to Resources." Waste Management Sustainability Report, 2010. http://www.wastemanagement.com.

See Also: Agricultural Wastes; Battery Disposal; Biomass Energy; Industrial Ecology; Landfill Gas; Recycling; Waste Heat Recovery; Waste Incineration.

Regional Greenhouse Gas Initiative

Category: Environmentalism.
Summary: The Regional Greenhouse Gas Initiative (RGGI) is an agreement between states in the northeast and mid-atlantic areas of the United States to reduce greenhouse gas emissions from power plants.

Through the Regional Greenhouse Gas Initiative, participating states from the mid-atlantic and northeast of the United States have committed to reducing the amount of carbon dioxide that is emitted from identified power plants as a means of limiting the region's contribution to greenhouse gases (GHGs). Although it is in the early stages of development, this regional cap-and-trade program provides a model for other regional and national GHG reduction initiatives.

The Regional Greenhouse Gas Initiative (RGGI) agreement was signed by the governors of 10 states in 2008 as a commitment to reduce regional greenhouse gas (GHG) emissions, the leading cause of climate change. RGGI is a regional cap-and-trade program in which participating states identify a regional emissions budget, are provided allowances (equivalent to 1 ton of carbon dioxide), and trade allowances in auction. A limited number of offsets—projects that reduce emissions—can also be used to meet compliance objections. RGGI was the first auction of carbon dioxide (CO_2) allowances in the United States and is one of three regional GHG reduction initiatives in the United States; the others include the Midwestern Greenhouse Gas Reduction Accord and the Western Climate Initiative.

RGGI was initiated in 2003 when the governors of seven states discussed developing a regional cap-and-trade program. The objective was to limit, and eventually reduce, CO_2 emissions from regional power plants. An agreement outlining the framework was signed in 2005, and the original signatory states included Connecticut, Delaware, Maine, New Hampshire, New Jersey, New York, and Vermont. Massachusetts, Rhode Island, and Maryland signed on to the agreement in 2007. Following completion of individual states' rule-making processes, the first three-year compliance period began in 2009 and continued through December 2011. In May 2011, New Jersey governor Chris Christie announced the state's withdrawal from the agreement, based on the belief that it is an ineffective way to regulate CO_2 emissions and perceived costs to ratepayers.

Regional collaboration intends to reduce the leading GHG contributing to climate change—carbon dioxide—while developing high-quality offsets in a regulatory GHG cap-and-trade program. Participating states have various emissions reduction and offset opportunities, allowing for greater flexibility and reducing costs of the cap-and-trade program. Lower costs reduce the impact on consumers and allow for pursuit of more aggressive emissions reduction targets. Proposed benefits of regional collaboration include increased program transparency, an objective project review process, reduced project transaction costs, reduced financial risk for project developers, reduced market uncertainty, and a more streamlined project regulatory review process.

RGGI collaborators have agreed on standards for the emission auctions and offset programs. For the auction, emission allowances are available for sale on a quarterly basis. The initial auctions were flexible in order to identify the most appropriate format, with the ultimate format being a multiple-round, ascending auction able to adjust to evolving market conditions. All participating states are eligible to engage in the auctions; notification must be made to the public, and a total limit of the number of allowances an entity may purchase in a single auction, as well as the price of the allowance, is predetermined. If allowances are unsold, they can be used in the next auction. States are required to retain an independent market monitor to evaluate auctions and market activities, observe conduct of the auction, and provide reports on whether auctions are in accordance with the agreement. Results of auctions, including price and amount of allowances sold, are made public.

Greenhouse Gas Offset Criteria

Participating states have also agreed on offset criteria. GHG offsets are project-based emissions reduction or removal that occurs outside the cap-and-trade program. For every ton of carbon dioxide equivalent (CO_2e) of emissions reduced or carbon sequestered (carbon captured through, for example, tree planting), a credit or allowance is awarded that can be used by a capped emission source to emit a CO_2e ton of GHG. Offset projects include capturing methane from landfills, improved efficiency of natural gas or heating oil, and avoiding emissions from animal waste. The compliance unit must represent 1 ton of CO_2e emissions reduction or removal and must be specifically intended to compensate for emissions elsewhere, in that the project would not have occurred in the absence of the offset program. In addition, offsets must be permanent, not reversible. Offset programs are subject to enforcement mechanisms to ensure compliance with program requirements, and penalties are imposed on those found noncompliant. The programs undergo regular review and adjustments to allow them to respond to changes in science, technology, regulations, market conditions, and other relevant factors.

The emissions cap will decrease by 2.5 percent each year starting in 2015, with a 10 percent reduction expected by 2018. According to independent reports released in January 2012, the program is successful, with participating states exceeding emission reduction targets at lower costs than expected. Consumers have benefited though lower electricity costs, fewer fossil fuel imports, and more jobs. Auction proceeds have been reinvested in local energy efficiency and renewable energy programs. RGGI has proven a strong model for the rest of the country, demonstrating significant environmental, consumer, and economic benefits, including reduced emissions, lower electric bills, and new jobs.

STACY VYNNE

Further Reading

Environmental Northwest. "Offsets Summary: The Regional Greenhouse Gas Initiative." Summer 2008. http://www.env-ne.org/public/resources/pdf/ENE _RGGI_offset-design.pdf.

Regional Greenhouse Gas Initiative, Midwestern Accord, and Western Climate Initiative. "Ensuring Offset Quality: Design and Implementation Criteria for a High Quality Offset Program: Joint Offset Quality White Paper." May 19, 2010. http://www .rggi.org/docs/3_Regions_Offsets_Announcement _05_17_10.pdf.

Resources for the Future. "Auction Design for Selling Carbon Dioxide Emission Allowances Under the Regional Greenhouse Gas Initiative." Final Report. October 2007. http://www.rff.org/rff/News/ Features/upload/31127_1.pdf.

See Also: Carbon Trading and Offsetting; Climate Change; Emissions Trading; Maryland; United States.

Regulation

Category: Business of Energy.
Summary: Regulation is the act of government intervention in a market intended to influence the behavior of firms and other market players toward a more socially desirable outcome.

Regulation is one of the main tools governments have to implement their energy policies, along with taxation. Regulation of energy markets is meant to address the failure of markets to deliver desired results, whether they are economic, social, or environmental. Firms participating in energy markets usually are subject to environmental, safety, inspection, and labor regulations, although the focus here is on the economic regulation of the electricity sector and the closely related gas sector. This includes the regulation of price tariffs, market access, investment levels, and service quality.

The level and form of regulation vary greatly by the energy industry's structure, which can vary in terms of competition level, degree of integration, whether ownership is public or private, and whether the system is fully developed or if access is limited. Any of the four activities within the electricity industry—generation, transmission, distribution, and retail sales—can be undertaken by a private or a government-owned company, and the regulation to which those activities are subject can vary in terms of flexibility. Policy makers decide what form the regulation will take. Usually an independent, specialized regulator is responsible for the regulation of the energy industry, but other entities may be responsible for some regulatory elements, including departments in national governments, local authorities, competition regulators, and environmental agencies.

Role

Although regulatory models vary by energy market structure, the role of regulation is broadly the same in most areas. Regulation is intended primarily to address market failures and is considered necessary to protect consumers in industries with the characteristics of natural monopolies. Electricity and often gas are important inputs in a well-functioning economy, which lacks straightforward substitutes for these power sources in the short term, so demand for them does not drop significantly when prices increase. A firm that benefits from natural monopoly status could charge very high prices in the short run, because it competes with no one on its delivery. Mitigation of such market power is introduced either through competition, where possible, or through regulation.

Maintaining low prices is not the only aim of energy regulation. Because there is little market incentive for firms to reduce their level of environmental damage, policy makers create regulation aimed at reducing emissions, protecting water resources, minimizing land contamination, and reducing noise pollution. In many developing economies, where scarcity of supply is an issue, regulations are often designed to meet the goal of universal supply of electricity or heating fuels. Many policy makers are now introducing regulation aimed at incentivizing the use of alternative energy and enhancing security of energy supply.

Nonliberalized Versus Liberalized Markets
Some markets are characterized by a single vertically integrated supplier who generates, transmits, and delivers energy services to all users in an area. If this monopolistic firm is owned by the government, it often operates with a government mandate to supply consumers with the energy they demand for a set price. If the monopolistic firm is privately owned, it is often subject to command and control regulation—that is, legislation that articulates what an industry legally can and cannot do—to ensure that the firm does not abuse its market power and acts in the interests of the people or government. The level of regulation is usually a direct political decision. The regulator or government agency usually sets prices and outlines investment requirements, which often are written into legislation. If firms do not comply, legal action can be taken.

Since the 1980s, most developed economies have liberalized their energy markets, meaning that they have restructured and deregulated those markets and have introduced competition where possible. The vertically integrated energy sup-

plier has been unbundled and its activities divided between different companies, often private. Generation of electricity and retail sales to end users have been regarded as particularly suitable to introduce competition as the main tool in maintaining low prices to consumers.

However, even the most liberalized energy market is subject to some regulation, largely because some activities within energy delivery systems are considered natural monopolies and are noncompetitive in nature, such as transmission and the operation of gas pipelines. For these activities, the economies of scale are so great that it is economically inefficient to have more than one firm operating in an area, and so these activities must be regulated. In liberalized markets, an independent regulator aims to set guidelines that create conditions under which prices are similar to what they would be under perfect competition.

Command and Control Versus Incentive-Based Regulation
There are some clear benefits to command and control (CAC) regulation. Clear targets and limits can be outlined, and standards can be imposed quickly. However, neoliberal economists can provide ample criticism of nonliberalized energy systems, and experience of CAC regulation has shown multiple problems. CAC is the least desirable form of regulation from the point of view of the private sector, as it does not allow firms any flexibility in their decision making. There is no inherent incentive to improve efficiency or innovation within the system, and cost increases are usually passed on to the consumer through tariffs or taxes. The involvement of politicians creates a risk that regulation is set with short-term political interests in mind as opposed to long-term economic or environmental interests. CAC regulation has not always been successful in setting standards, such as acceptable levels of pollution or realistic operational targets for electricity delivery systems, and has largely been abandoned in developed economies.

Incentive-based regulation is meant to incentivize firms to stop undesirable behavior through imposing taxes or granting subsidies. In economic

Wikimedia

Few proposed energy regulations are without controversy. Critics of carbon trading schemes claim that they will only lead to the commodification of pollution rights, forests, water, soils, agriculture, and biodiversity, putting a market price on resources that should belong to the global commons. The photograph shows Chicago Climate Justice activists, who oppose any privatization of public resources, gathered to protest cap-and-trade legislation in November 2008.

terms, an incentive seeks to modify firms' available choices by changing the marginal costs or marginal benefits associated with that choice. This type of regulation reduces the possibility for regulatory discretion and therefore regulatory capture. Companies often favor this type of regulation, since it allows the firm to choose whether to follow the rule or accept the consequence. It is the preferred type of regulation in liberalized energy markets, although CAC mechanisms may be imposed in crisis situations. Regardless of the regulatory structure applied to an electricity or natural gas market, regulation has its costs, including the cost of operating a regulatory agency, the social costs of ineffective regulation, and the costs imposed on firms by the regulator.

Regulation in Liberalized Energy Systems

Within the last several decades of energy system liberalization, government oversight was largely abandoned and independent regulatory agencies established. The regulatory agency, or regulator, acts to protect the interests of consumers by ensuring economic efficiency in a market.

The belief that effective competition is the best regulator and leads to the most economically efficient solution is commonly held among economists. Because the introduction of competition reduces the need for regulation in the competitive aspects of energy delivery, the role of the regulator is to provide guidelines that should be applied only where the benefits of regulation reduce costs to a greater extent than if the regulation were not in place. However, regulation is often designed to prevent market abuse or anticompetitive behavior, ensure effective competition is maintained, and prevent the growth of a dominant group.

The role of economic regulation of noncompetitive activities in liberalized electricity markets and their closely related natural gas markets is twofold: to ensure that enough investment is made in the long term to meet demand and to ensure that investors receive a reasonable rate of return on their investments. In natural monopoly industries, dominant firms can charge prices so low that competitors are forced out of the market. Once competition has been eliminated, the dominant firm can charge monopoly prices and reduce social welfare. Transmission and distribution have strong natural monopoly characteristics and are regulated in liberalized energy systems. However, generation and retail sales are generally considered competitive activities and are usually not subject to economic regulation.

There are several policy components for which a regulator can outline incentives or requirements in order to improve economic efficiency. Tariffs can be regulated, or the rate structure defined. Investment levels can be incentivized to ensure adequate investments that will protect long-term prices. Access rules can be outlined with regard to entry into the market, access to the transmission network for generators, and access to the distribution network for customers. Because private firms act to maximize their profit, there is, for example, strong incentive in place to focus on customers to whom it is cheaper to supply electricity than customers in rural areas. The regulator can also make requirements as to the quality of service with regard to reliability.

In the short run, the regulator aims to set a tariff structure that allows the firm to meet its costs and be recompensed for its investments. To do so, the regulator must determine the firm's total revenues and its required revenues, or the amount needed by the firm to maintain the level of service customers require. In the long run, the regulator aims to encourage the electricity supplier to build enough infrastructure to meet long-term demand. This is usually done by ensuring a reasonable return on investment for shareholders. If the firm's rate of return on investment is too high, the regulator may be creating incentive for the firm to build more capacity than is necessary. That is why there is usually a license requirement on new capacity for which firms must apply to the regulator. In the United States, the regulator is often involved in integrated resource planning (IRP), a process whereby the regulator determines

if the system being proposed will ultimately lead to the lowest possible cost to customers.

A regulator can usually outline access rules, where competition has been introduced, that clarify the system's entry and exit rules. Because new competitors reduce the market power of dominant firms, generally regulators want as many generators as possible to have access to the regulated transmission and distribution grids and therefore gain entry into the market. This may involve costs to the regulated industry that it would not assume unless expressly told to do so by the regulator. Exit rules usually apply to the regulated firm's abandonment of high-cost customers, such as those living in rural areas. Although this does not usually occur, there is a tendency for regulated industries to better serve their low-cost customers. In such cases, the regulator must introduce some sort of incentive or rule to improve capacity in high-cost regions.

Usually regulators are charged with seeing that firms maintain a quality of service that guarantees reliability, minimizes disturbances, and ensures that customers are satisfied.

Price Regulation of Natural Monopolies

Because competition cannot be introduced to transmission and distribution, these activities need regulatory incentives to reduce costs and prices. In areas where competition has not been introduced to generation activities, they too are usually subject to price regulation. The regulator limits how much profit the regulated firm can make from efficiency improvements through price regulation. There are two commonly used methods for price regulation.

Rate-of-return regulation, also known as cost-of-service regulation, requires the regulator to determine a rate level based on allowed costs and investments and an appropriate rate of return. The goal for regulators is to determine levels so that economic profits are zero, although investors receive an approved rate of return on their investments. This type of price regulation is costly and time-consuming for regulators, although it can be highly precise. It usually involves a very close relationship between firms and their regulators, and it creates a risk for regulatory capture, whereby the regulator starts to become overly concerned with the interests of the firm and overlooks the interests of consumers. The most controversial issues in rate-of-return regulation are often determining required investment levels and determining an acceptable rate of return on equity investment.

Performance-based ratemaking (PBR) occurs when the regulator sets a particular rate and then allows the firm to keep any cost savings as profit. As a result, investors receive higher profits and a better return on their investment. Consumers benefit from lower prices and improved service levels. This method of regulation is less costly and time-consuming for the regulator. It is the method of choice in most U.S. electricity markets and has several variations, including sliding scales, revenue caps, and price caps. All of the variations provide incentives for performance and cost reduction. Proponents of PBR say it helps improve efficiency, reduce operation and maintenance costs, and improve reliability. It gives firms flexibility on how to respond. PBR's main regulatory risk is that it may cause firms to cut operational and maintenance costs too much, resulting in reduced service in the long run. Although PBR aims to provide economic benefit to both consumers and firms, if targets are wrong, unfair benefit can be provided to either firms or consumers.

Other Market-Based Mechanisms

To influence the activities of both competitive and monopolistic firms, policy makers may use any of the wide range of market-based mechanisms designed to provide cost-effective incentives with minimal involvement of the regulator. A few of these mechanisms are described below.

Competition laws, designed to prohibiting predatory pricing and other anticompetitive behavior by firms, can be a less expensive way to regulate, as disputes are settled by courts instead of a regulatory agency. Their application to the electricity and gas sectors is often criticized, however, because they generally outline broad rules and the judicial system often lacks the specialized knowledge to apply them to energy systems. They are, however, sometimes applied to fuel providers such as oil companies.

Cap-and-trade legislation has been introduced in the European Union and in other areas as a market-based mechanism for limiting greenhouse gas emissions from energy production. The government or regulator decides an appropriate level of emissions and then divides allowances among firms. Firms can then choose to reduce their emissions and sell off their surpluses or buy allowances from other firms so as to emit more than their allowances specified. From the firms' perspective, this is preferable to CAC regulation and results in the most economically efficient solution. From an environmental perspective, the success of the scheme is dependent on the emissions levels a government is willing to set.

Disclosure regulation has been passed in some economies where competition has been introduced to retail sales. Such regulation requires suppliers to specify the source of their electricity or heat and allows consumers to switch providers based on the sources from which they supply. Experience in these markets, including the United Kingdom and the Netherlands, has shown that consumers sometimes choose to pay a higher rate for their electricity if they know it is generated from alternative sustainable sources of energy, therefore increasing demand for alternative energy production.

The Successful Regulator

In order to achieve economic efficiency, the regulator must have access to good information about the costs, quality of service, and performance of the firms providing the regulated services. The regulator must have the authority to enforce the requirements and an expert staff able to make sound decisions on effective regulatory requirements. The independence of the regulatory agency must be protected, and a judicial process must be available for regulatory disputes.

In the United States, state regulatory agencies oversee the price and delivery to end users, while the Federal Energy Regulatory Commission regulates the wholesale or generation market. In the European Union, the independent national regulatory agencies, which are all subject to the laws of the unified European energy market, coordinate their policies through an advisory council made up of individual independent regulators.

Although broad-issue stances should rightfully be determined by policy makers as opposed to regulators, the regulator is often left with the responsibility of making determinations when it comes to individual cases. Moreover, regulators often play an advisory role to policy makers, because of their experience in the practical implementation and monitoring of energy regulation. Consequently, they are often valued participants in the energy debate and can have major influence on the developments of policies.

Contradictions in Regulatory Aims

There are some regulatory aims that may not always be compatible. A nation's energy policy goals may focus on energy supply, improving the performance of energy markets, reducing poverty, improving energy access, and promoting the use of alternative energy. These goals are often in contradiction to the traditional short-term goal of energy regulation: keeping prices low and improving economic efficiency.

Since the ratification of the Kyoto Protocol, regulation has often been introduced to promote the use of electricity from alternative energy or alternative fuel use. Alternative energy is most often more expensive to produce than traditional forms of energy, and promoting it through regulation seems to work against one of the main roles of the regulator: to keep prices to consumers as low as possible.

Alternative energy projects are often smaller and farther away from the grid than conventional generation facilities, making marginal costs higher for the monopolistic delivery firm. Ensuring access to transmission and distribution networks for alternative energy producers is the responsibility of the regulator in economies where policy makers have designed legislation to promote the use of alternative energy. Government-owned systems have a distinct advantage when it comes to the speed at which electricity and heat from alternative energy sources can be delivered to customers. In liberalized energy systems, economic regulation must be introduced to incentivize investment in alternative energy with its accompanying time lags.

The introduction of incentives, such as subsidies and tax credits meant to increase generation from alternative technologies or increase energy efficiency, may be more expensive to consumers in the short run, but policy makers must take into account the longer-term effects of such policies. In the long run, new technologies become cheaper, the learning effect increases, and depletable resources become more expensive.

Increasing access to electricity in developing areas usually indicates upward pressure on prices for consumers in the short run. In the long run, improved access is often accompanied by poverty reduction through the increased economic development that improved access brings. Energy systems that are still developing have an advantage in promoting the use of alternative energy. Their systems are not mature and are often in a better position to add small-scale alternative electricity generation to rural areas with limited access. These conditions also allow developing economies to leap-frog conventional polluting energy sources and use modern, clean technology.

One of the main goals of most countries' energy policies is ensuring security of supply. There is increasing criticism that deregulated systems have underinvested in capacity and relied on the asset-sweating of capacity built before deregulation and privatization. This can be combated through increasing investment requirements in electricity capacity, implementing storage requirements for gas suppliers, and outlining regulation for interconnections with neighboring regions' energy delivery systems. Increasing interconnections is costly but is often considered vital in minimizing any potential effects of delivery disruptions. Having unused capacity on the system is inefficient in the strictest economic terms but may be desirable where there is political uncertainty of supply or delivery disruptions have occurred.

Decreasing demand is often named as one of the most effective ways of both decreasing greenhouse gas emissions and ensuring security of supply. There is little incentive for energy suppliers to decrease demand, because they usually sell power or heat by a metered amount. One way of decreasing demand is making demand-side programs available, such as those provided by energy service companies. The energy service company offers to provide consumers with a certain level of heat or electricity services and often installs energy savings measures in a customer's home or business in exchange.

There is no standard method of regulation that is successful in every situation; individual situations, with regard to access, price, and the environment, have to be considered and weighed carefully by policy makers in choosing the most successful regulatory regime for the desired energy policy outcomes. In most developed economies, the regulatory regime is under continual review and reform as situations and policy goals change.

Nanna Baldvinsdóttir

Further Reading

European Energy Regulators. "About the European Energy Regulators." http://www.energy-regulators .eu/portal/page/portal/EER_HOME/EER_ABOUT.

Pollitt, Michael G. "The Future of Electricity (and Gas) Regulation in a Low-carbon Policy World." *Energy Policy* 29, no. 2 (2008).

Rothwell, G., and T. Gomez. *Electricity Economics: Regulation and Deregulation*. Hoboken, NJ: John Wiley, 2003.

Stigler, George J. "The Theory of Economic Regulation." *Bell Journal of Economics and Management Science* 2, no. 1 (1971).

Ter-Martirosyan, Anna, and J. Kwoka. "Incentive Regulation, Service Quality, and Standards in U.S. Electricity Distribution." *Journal of Regulatory Economics* 38, no. 3 (2010).

United Nations Industrial Development Organization. *Introduction to Energy Regulation*. http://www .unido.org/fileadmin/media/documents/pdf/ Module3.pdf.

See Also: Deregulation; Energy Independence and Security Act of 2007; Energy Policy; Energy Policy Act of 2005; Federal Energy Regulatory Commission; Public Utility Holding Company Act of 1935; Public Utility Regulatory Policies Act of 1978; Taxation.

Renewable Energy Credits

Category: Environmentalism.
Summary: Renewable energy credits are certificates for electricity generated from a renewable energy source distributed by government agencies to power companies.

Renewable energy credits (RECs)—also referred to as renewable energy certificates, green tags, or tradable renewable certificates—may be sold or traded on the open market separate from physical electricity and have become a flexible currency in the renewable energy market because they impose no geographic or physical transmission limitations. They provide incentives to companies that produce green power and support customers that hope to reduce their emissions. While RECs face a number of challenges, such as financing of projects and verification of environmental claims, they meet the demand for renewable, or green, energy from customers and support utilities' compliance with renewable energy regulations.

How RECs Work

RECs are issued by participating state government agencies to utilities generating renewable energy. Another party sells the energy generated to obtain the REC, and the consumer receives the certificate. RECs were first proposed during the U.S. energy-restructuring debate in the mid-1990s as part of a discussion for designing renewable portfolio standards (RPS), a requirement that utility providers generate a specified amount of electricity from renewable sources. While a federal RPS was not passed, RECs were adopted by states in defining their own RPS policies and by states initiating voluntary green-power markets.

Typically, for every thousand kilowatt-hours (1 megawatt-hour) of renewable energy generated, one credit is given. Qualifying sources of renewable energy include solar, wind, geothermal, biomass, biodiesel, some fuel cells, and low-impact hydropower. Each credit is given a distinct number to allow for tracking and to ensure no double counting. The power is fed into the electrical grid, at which time the company can offer the credit for sale or trade. REC markets are verified by a certified third party to ensure legal compliance.

RECs typically contain the following data for identification and tracking: the type of renewable resource producing the electricity, the date the REC was created, the date the renewable generator was built, the generator's location, eligibility for certification or renewable portfolio compliance, and the greenhouse gas (GHG) emissions associated with the renewable generation. RECs are sold at different prices in different markets, depending on the region, resource type, and volume. The price is expected to reflect the difference in costs for generating electricity from renewable resources compared to the market price for conventional energy. Examples of prices in 2008 (according to the Environmental Protection Agency) included $0.70 per megawatt-hour for existing renewables and $49 per megawatt-hour for new renewable energy sources. Some states also issue solar renewable energy certificates (SRECs), which also vary in price depending on the market.

Compliance market prices are generally higher than voluntary markets. Compliance markets exist in states with RPS's, requiring electric companies to supply a certain percentage of electricity from renewables by a specified date. Currently, 30 states and the District of Columbia have RPS's. In voluntary markets, customers (corporate and household) drive the market for renewables. Utilities that generate renewable energy outside compliance states (those with RPS's) can sell RECs at a cheaper price in the voluntary market.

Challenges and Benefits

RECs face a number of challenges, particularly in voluntary markets and because of a lack of federal regulation. Some of these challenges include financing for new projects, communicating purpose and value, verifying integrity and tracking, specifying ownership, identifying emerging markets, presenting and verifying environmental claims, and developing a consistent definition across states. In addition, many consumers may not find RECs acceptable for meeting their renewable energy demand, given that they are essentially a piece of paper and do not provide a visible renewable energy generation resource. In addition, some critics also claim that RECs do not provide *additionality*, meaning that the project or energy generation would exist in the absence of the REC, and no new renewable energy is brought onto the electricity grid.

RECs are also proving to be beneficial for meeting consumer demand and promoting renewable energy generation. Because RECs can be traded and sold on the open market, there is an incentive for companies to produce renewable power. Buying and selling of credits also provides renewable energy access to companies and consumers who do not have direct access to these sources through their utility providers. RECs provide more choices for consumers at competitive prices because they are not constrained by where energy is created or by transmission-related expenses and bottlenecks. Generators of renewable energy benefit from the program, as many cannot compete with subsidized nonrenewable energy sources and RECs serve as an investment in their products. As consumers demonstrate demand for renewable energy through voluntary markets, the companies can invest in more plants or increase production with the funds raised through selling RECs.

Federal, state, and local governments are increasingly using RECs as a means to meet renewable energy generation goals and regulations. Moreover, all utility customers currently have access to buying RECs.

Stacy Vynne

Further Reading

Berry, David. "The Market for Tradable Renewable Energy Credits." *Ecological Economics* 42, no. 3 (2002).

Database for State Incentives for Renewables and Efficiency. "Federal Incentives." http://www.dsireusa.org/.

Hold, Ed, and Lori Bird. *Emerging Markets for Renewable Energy Certificates: Opportunities and Challenges.* NREL/TP-620-37388. Golden, CO: National Renewable Energy Laboratory,

2005. http://apps3.eere.energy.gov/greenpower/
resources/pdfs/37388.pdf.

U.S. Department of Energy. "Green Power Network."
http://apps3.eere.energy.gov/greenpower/.

U.S. Environmental Protection Agency. "EPAs Green
Power Partnership: Renewable Energy Certificates."
2008. http://www.epa.gov/greenpower/gpmarket/
rec.htm.

See Also: Green Energy Certification; Net Metering;
Renewable Energy Portfolio.

Renewable Energy Portfolio

Category: Environmentalism.

Summary: The renewable energy portfolio is
a quota-based system that specifies a target
percentage of energy to be supplied by renewable
sources.

Photos.com

*The photo shows a wind turbine under construction off the
coast of Norfolk, England. The United Kingdom did not
meet its 2003 quota of 3 percent renewable energy and
may also miss the EU-wide 15-percent target for 2020.*

The renewable energy portfolio, referred to as the
green certificate system in Europe or renewable
portfolio standards (RPS) in the United States,
is a quantity-based system that specifies a target
percentage of energy to be supplied by renewable
sources. The government establishes the quantity
of renewable energy produced, while the market
sets the price of the electricity produced. Often,
renewable energy operators will individually negotiate the sale electricity price to the grid operator.
Renewable energy electricity generators receive
a certificate of origin for every unit of electricity
produced, which then can be sold in the market to
offset the premium required to generate electricity
from renewable sources. The demand for the certificate is artificially created by the state through
setting a fixed quota. As the demand for certificates increases, the price of the certificate will subsequently increase. Under the system, retail electricity suppliers must supply a certain amount of
electricity from renewable energy sources to end
users. Utilities can comply either by purchasing
exchangeable certificates or by owning a renewable energy electricity generation facility and its
generated output. Failure to comply often results
in financial penalties.

There are a growing number of countries implementing quota systems—at least 49 countries or
regional localities. The RPS in the United States is
among the most commonly cited renewable energy
portfolio policies. Although there is currently no
comprehensive mandatory national RPS enacted
in the United States, many states have voluntarily
pushed RPS targets forward. Iowa was the first state
to adopt the RPS, in 1983. The implementation process and criteria for RPS differ in each state. As of

October 2010, 26 states had established a variation of the RPS, four with an "alternative portfolio standard" and four with a "renewable and alternative energy goal." The alternative portfolio standard is similar to the RPS but includes alternative energy forms such as nuclear energy. State RPS goals range between 10 and 14 percent, and compliance dates fall between 2013 and 2025. Some states have also set "carve-out" targets, which establish requirements within the RPS for certain renewable energy sources, particularly solar power.

The success of RPS policies depends on the details and the method of execution. Well-designed policies have contributed to increasing the share of renewable energy in the electricity mix at minimal cost to electricity end users. Some key factors for successful policy design include establishing a long-term quota to provide a clear signal to the market regarding the commitment level toward renewables. Furthermore, the structure must be well planned and precisely implemented, even more than the feed-in tariff system. The quota system should place mandatory obligations on the utilities, and a transparent method for accounting renewable energy production is required, either through energy production (in megawatt-hours) or through installed capacity (in megawatts). The quota targets and time line must be clearly announced, and there should be a flexible compliance structure to account for factors such as a shortage of renewable energy electricity generation. Providing incentives, such as credits for early compliance, can encourage earlier adoption of renewable energy.

One of the challenges of the quota system is that it favors large renewable energy generators and low-cost technologies. Since prices are generally fixed for electricity generation, additional compensation often occurs through the sales of certificates. The certificate prices do not differentiate the cost of electricity generation; thus, naturally, the most economical renewable energy technology would be developed first in the highest resource locations. As a result, larger players, often consisting of multinational firms, invest in large-scale projects such as wind farms and biomass generation plants. This trend can push out smaller market participants, since they cannot benefit from the economies of scale. The number of renewable energy generators is limited, and there is little space in the market for small-scale household electricity generation from renewable sources.

Additionally, because of the limited number of participants in the renewable energy markets, there is lower pressure for homegrown innovation and competition; as a result, technologies are often purchased from abroad. Other technologies in earlier phases of development, including solar photovoltaic (PV) and geothermal systems, are often neglected given their higher generation costs. Furthermore, the prices of certificates are dependent on the market, which fluctuates according to supply and demand. This lack of long-term security may dampen the investment enthusiasm for the renewable energy market. Compared to the feed-in tariff structure, designing and managing a quota system may be more difficult for policy makers, and generators may have to deal with more complex development procedures and contract agreements.

The United Kingdom's implementation of the quota system has been disappointing; the country missed its moderate 3 percent renewable energy target in 2003 by 1.2 percent. According to the country's Renewables Advisory Board, the United Kingdom is unlikely to meet its 15 percent European Union-wide target by 2020. In spite of the drawbacks in the quota system, more countries are adapting this policy instrument and revising the structure to help address some of its weaknesses. One means of dealing with the technology price variations is setting a quota system that has several resource tiers and requirements. A tier can be established for more mature and economical technologies, while another tier can be set for less mature and less expensive technologies. Overall, the quota system is a preferred mechanism applied in countries that favor lower government involvement and wish to leave renewable energy price setting to market forces.

JENNY LIEU

Further Reading

Adam, David. "Britain Set to Miss EU Renewable Energy Target." *The Guardian*, June 19, 2008. http://

www.guardian.co.uk/environment/2008/jun/19/
renewableenergy.alternativeenergy.

European Renewable Energy Council. "Renewable
Energy Target 20 Percent for 2020." 2007. http://
www.erec.org/fileadmin/erec_docs/Documents/
Publications/EREC_Targets_2020_def.pdf.

Pew Center on Global Climate Change. *Renewable
and Alternative Energy Portfolio Standards.* July 29,
2009. http://www.pewclimate.org/what_s_being
_done/in_the_states/rps.cfm.

Renewable Energy Policy Network for the 21st
Century (REN21). *Renewables 2010 Global Status
Report.* Paris: REN21 Secretariat, 2010. http://
www.ren21.net/REN21Activities/Publications/
GlobalStatusReport/tabid/5434/Default.aspx.

Solar Energy Industry Association. "Renewable
Portfolio Standards." *Solar Energy Industry
Association.* 2009. http://www.seia.org/cs/federal
_issues/renewable_portfolio_standards.

U.S. Environmental Protection Agency. "Renewable
Portfolio Standards: An Effective Policy to Support
Clean Energy Supply." April 2009. http://www.epa
.gov/chp/state-policy/renewable_fs.html.

van der Linden, N. H., et al. "Review of International
Experience With Renewable Energy Obligation
Support Mechanisms." *Energy Analysis
Department.* Energy Research Centre of the
Netherlands ECN. May 2005. http://eetd.lbl.gov/ea/
ems/reports/57666.pdf.

See Also: China; Energy Policy; Feed-in Tariff;
Maryland; Renewable Energy Credits; Renewable
Energy Resources; Tennessee; United Kingdom;
United States.

Renewable Energy Resources

Category: Environmentalism.
Summary: Renewable energy is the type of
energy that comes from regenerative resources,
namely: biomass, hydro, solar, wind and
geothermal power.

Renewable energy is energy derived from regenerative resources. These resources can be fully replenished in a short time period. Renewable energy is generated from elements found in nature and include the use of biomass in fuels such as ethanol, biodiesel, charcoal, and biogas; the use of water or hydropower by means of waterwheels, water mills, run-of-the-river hydroelectricity facilities, hydroelectric dams, tidal power, and wave power; the use of solar energy in solar heating, photovoltaic (PV) systems, and concentrating solar power; the use of wind to drive turbines via windmills; and the use of geothermal energy, the heat energy that emanates from deep inside the Earth. These renewable energy resources, if well explored and developed, can be inexhaustible.

By contrast, nonrenewable energy resources, such as fossil fuels and nuclear power, are limited, and their use leads to the depletion of those reserves. For much of human history, the kind of energy used to power societies came from renewable resources; however, with the rise of the Industrial Revolution and its use of coal and later oil, nonrenewable fossil fuels became predominant. The foundation of our energy systems on these fossil fuels has made us dependent on a resource that will soon be depleted.

Historical Aspects

Until the 19th century, civilization survived using essentially renewable energy resources, based on firewood and biomass burning for cooking, heating, and building materials. Nowadays, least developed countries are still using essentially these kinds of energy resources.

The use of fossil fuels became dominant in the 20th century and it is still increasing at the beginning of the 21st century. During the Industrial Revolution, the demand for energy increased drastically, and the high use of coal, petroleum, and natural gas led to the large-scale generation of electricity, heat, and fuel. Today, fossil fuels account for more than three-fourths of the energy used in the world. Fossil fuels have higher energy density when compared to the raw biomass. They are easy to extract because huge amounts of these materials are found in a single place, which make them relatively low-cost raw materials. The use of fossil fuels has had a large impact on civilization's industrial development. However, the reduction of fossil fuel usage is an important issue today, mainly for two reasons: The first is related to the depletion of reserves, cost instability, and irregular distribution of these resources around the world, conditions that have led to many conflicts and wars; the second reason is related to the climate change that is resulting from the emission of greenhouse gases from the burning of these fuels for energy.

World Energy Scenario

The *2009 Renewable Energy Data Book*, issued by the U. S. Department of Energy, notes that, worldwide, 19 percent of energy consumed comes from renewable sources and 81 percent from nonrenewable resources, of which 78.2 percent are based on fossil fuels and the remaining 2.8 percent on nuclear energy. The renewable sources are divided among traditional biomass (13 percent), hydropower (3.2 percent), and new renewable sources (2.8 percent), such as small hydropower plants and wind, solar, and geothermal energy. In 2009, during the worldwide economic recession, there was a boom in renewable energy. In mid-2010, more than 100 countries focused their energy production on renewable sources, an increase of almost 100 percent compared with 2005.

There has thus been a major shift in the global energy scenario with regard to renewable fuels, with more than half of the efforts to cultivate renewable sources concentrated in developing countries. In 2009, wind power and solar photovoltaic (PV) power had record growth in both Europe and the United States: Renewable energy accounted for more than half of new installations in that year. For the second straight year, more money was invested in new renewable energy sources than in new sources of fossil fuels. Globally, Brazil leads the production of sugar-derived ethanol and has also been adding new sources of biomass to its energy matrix. Other countries, such as Argentina, Uruguay, Costa Rica, Egypt, Indonesia, Kenya, Tanzania, Thailand, and Tunisia, are rapidly increasing their market share of renewables. Developing countries already account for half of all countries with some sort of policy to promote renewable energy.

In 1990, wind power was used in only a few countries, but now it plays a role in the energy sources of more than 80 countries. In 2009, China produced 30 percent of the world's wind turbines and 77 percent of the world solar collectors for hot water. Argentina, Brazil, Colombia, Ecuador, and Peru have become Latin America's major biofuel producers, and other renewable technologies are being expanded as well. At least 20 countries in the Middle East, North Africa, and sub-Saharan Africa have active markets for renewable energy. In addition to Europe and the United States, other developed countries, including Australia, Canada, and Japan, are diversifying their renewable technologies. All these changes in the world energy scenario have helped to increase confidence in renewable energy. By the year 2009, the United States had 12 percent of total installed capacity and more than 10 percent of total generation focused on renewable sources.

Biomass

The first application of biomass as a source of energy occurred in the early days of humankind, when people learned to use fire to produce heat and cook food. The first evidence that humans cooked food over controlled fires, based on the evolution of human molars, dates to 1.9 million years ago.

Biomass is organic raw material derived, directly or indirectly, from plants as a result of photosynthesis and includes crop residues for cogeneration, forest residues, animal wastes, municipal solid waste, and energy crops such as sugarcane, switchgrass, jatropha, and corn. Photosynthesis is the chemical process plants use to convert energy from sunlight, carbon dioxide, and water into oxygen and organic compounds, especially sugars (stored energy). The use of biomass to generate energy, as a substitute for fossil fuels, mitigates the greenhouse effect, because even though the carbon present in the biomass will be emitted when used as fuel, it comes from plants that previously removed the carbon (as carbon dioxide) from the atmosphere; hence, the "carbon sink" role of the

Wikimedia

Following an uprating project from 1986 to 1993, the total gross power rating for the Hoover Dam power plant increased to a maximum capacity of 2080 megawatts.

plant has balanced the later combustion of the fuel and emissions from the plant.

Biomass can provide raw material for multiple fuel uses, for the production of heat, electricity, and both liquid and gaseous fuels for transport. We can extract the energy from these various sources of biomass through biochemical processes, chemical reactions, and mechanical technologies to convert biomass into liquid or gaseous fuel. However, a considerable disadvantage of biomass is related to its low energy density when compared with that of fossil fuels. The processing of biomass can require significant energy inputs, which should be minimized to maximize the conversion of biomass and energy recovery.

There are three basic uses of biomass as fuel. These include biofuels, biogas, and thermochemical energy.

Biodiesel and bioethanol are the best-known biofuels available for use in automobiles and other motor vehicles. Biodiesel is produced by transesterification, which is a reversible chemical reaction of vegetable oils or animal fats with alcohols, producing esters (biodiesel) and glycerin. Currently in the world, the most commonly used raw materials to produce biodiesel are canola and sunflower oils. Biodiesel can be mixed with traditional diesel fuel and used in compression-ignition engines without engine adaptations. Sugarcane, maize, wheat, sugar beets, and sweet sorghum can be used as raw materials for the production of bioethanol. These products are rich in sugars or starches, which are converted to alcohol by means of fermentation. Bioethanol production using sugarcane fermentation techniques has been commercially undertaken in Brazil since the 1980s.

Biogas can be produced from any kind of biomass by means of anaerobic microbes (bacteria that live in the absence of oxygen). Pigs, cattle, and chickens reared in confined areas produce a considerable concentration of organic waste matter with high moisture content, which can be use for biogas production. Biogas contains mainly methane and carbon dioxide, along with small amounts of other gases, such as hydrogen sulfide, ammonia, hydrogen, and carbon monoxide, giving it a very bad smell. The wet biomass is fed into an enclosed digestion tank together with a source containing anaerobic microbes; in the tank, anaerobic reactions occur. The remaining solid and liquid residues can be used as fertilizers. The period of time that biomass should remain in the digestion tank can range from a single day to several months. In 1630, it was discovered that decomposing organic matter is capable of producing a flammable gas, and in 1808 it was discovered that the gas contained methane. Biogas can be used as a low-cost fuel for heating and cooking; it can also be converted to electricity and heat or purified and compressed, much like natural gas, to create fuel to power motor vehicles.

Finally gasification and pyrolysis are thermochemical processes in which organic matter is degraded by thermal reactions in the presence of limited amounts of air or oxygen. The major products are biochar (charcoal), bio-oil, or a gaseous product, which can also be burned as fuel. The amount of each of the three products formed is dependent on the type and nature of the biomass input, the type of facility used, and the particular process adopted. Pyrolysis aims to obtain solid and liquid products, whereas gasification produces a gaseous product, composed mostly of hydrogen, carbon monoxide, methane, carbon dioxide, and water vapor.

Hydropower

Hydropower refers to the energy generated through the use of flowing water. From millennia, hydropower has been used for irrigation; notable engineering of water channels has been found in the ancient remains of Egyptian and Mayan civilizations, and the engineering feats of the Roman civilization are well documented. There are many ways to harness the potential and kinetic energy of water to perform work; some examples include the use of waterwheels, water mills, run-of-the-river hydropower plants, hydroelectric dams, tidal power, and wave power.

Hydroelectric power is the electricity generated when water flows through a turbine to a lower level. These turbines, which are flow controlling blades mounted on rotating shafts, are usually located within the dams. The potential energy is stored by dams as a volume of water located behind the dam. As long as water is being released through the dam, it rotates the turbines, which are coupled to generators that then supply electricity to transmission lines. Hydropower plants play a major role in the world's capacity to generate electricity. For example, the Three Gorges Dam in China—the greatest hydropower plant in the world—has more than twice the capacity of the Kashiwazaki-Kariwa Nuclear Power Plant in Japan, which is the nuclear plant with greatest capacity in the world.

Tidal power is the energy that can be extracted from the rise and fall of ocean tides. Extraction of tidal power is simple in theory. The tidal dam, termed a *barrage*, is built across an estuary and creates an enclosed basin for storage of water at high tide. Turbines in the barrage are used to convert the potential energy, resulting from the difference in water levels, into electrical energy.

▷ Renewable Versus Environmentally Friendly

Renewable energy generation and use are not by definition environmentally or ecologically friendly. The terms *renewable* and *environmentally friendly* are related to different issues. *Renewable* energy refers to energy generated from regenerative resources. However, the generation of renewable energy can affect the environment and various life forms. Hydropower, for example, is an important type of renewable energy, originating in the motion of water in rivers and the oceans. This water is periodically supplied by rain, and then, via evaporation, is returned to the Earth's atmosphere in a process called the hydrologic cycle. The water from rain therefore is virtually inexhaustible, and it makes hydropower renewable. However, hydroelectric power plants require huge water reservoirs for their operation. The building of dams and the associated flooding of large land areas can cause several environmental impacts. The damming of rivers results in the submersion of extensive areas upstream of the dams, destroying biologically rich lowlands. Aquatic riverine ecosystems change drastically, both upstream and downstream of the dam site. Damming can also have a negative influence on the migration of fish, although this can be mitigated in some cases by installing appropriate fish ladders. Ultimately, however, the alteration of natural ecosystems to make use of renewable hydropower will have an environmental impact that needs to be weighed against the benefits of harnessing renewable energy.

Less common types of hydroelectricity are wave power, run-of-the-river hydropower, and marine (or ocean) current power.

Solar Energy

Most of the energy used on Earth has its origin from the electromagnetic radiation from the sun, including biomass, hydropower, and wind power. However, the term *solar power* in the context of energy generation is used to refer to the direct conversion of solar radiation to a useful form of energy. Forms of solar power include photovoltaic electricity, solar power tower plants, and solar thermal heating, among other forms.

Although only a very small fraction of the radiation from the sun reaches the Earth, sunlight represents a tremendous source of renewable, greenhouse-gas-free energy. Passage through the atmosphere splits the radiation reaching the surface into direct and diffuse components, reducing the total energy through selective absorption by dry air, water molecules, dust, and cloud layers, while heavy cloud coverage eliminates all the direct radiation. Sunlight is intermittent; it varies diurnally from day to night over a 24-hour period as the Earth rotates. Thus, storage of the energy is a very important factor if it is to be used efficiently and economically.

A typical procedure is to use a solar collector to absorb the solar energy and convert it to thermal energy, which is transferred by heat pipes carrying pumped fluids for low-temperature (less than 100 degrees Celsius) heating or storage. Therefore, the collector should be made of materials with high thermal conductivity and low thermal capacity, such as metals (copper, steel, and aluminum) and some thermal-conducting plastics. The most common collectors are flat, blackened plates, since they convert both direct and diffuse (cloud-mitigated) radiation into heat.

Direct solar radiation can also be focused by a range of concentrating solar power technologies and collected to provide medium- to high-temperature heating. These technologies for concentrating solar power are of three types: parabolic troughs, power towers, and heat engines. The heat generated by the radiation is then used to operate a conventional power cycle, generally by steam-generating techniques similar to those used in conventional power plants. Solar thermal power plants designed to use direct sunlight must be sited in regions with high direct solar radiation.

Another way to use solar power is by means of photovoltaic (PV) conversion. The PV effect is the production of electric potential and current when a system is exposed to light. A solar cell is the PV device, and the light source is the sun. A solar PV cell consists in a semiconductor electrical junction device, which absorbs and converts the radiant energy of sunlight directly into electrical energy. Solar cells may be connected in series and/or parallel to obtain the required values of current and voltage for electric power generation needs. Most solar cells are made from single crystal silicon and have been expensive for generating electricity, but they have found applications. Research has emphasized lowering solar cell cost by improving performance and by reducing the costs of materials and manufacturing. Besides their low efficiency (relative to the percentage of the incident sunlight that is converted into electrical output power) and high costs, solar cells' power generation is limited by the presence or absence of solar radiation. For some applications, the electricity can be stored (in batteries, for example) to supply electricity on cloudy days and during the night.

Wind Power

Windmills have been used to pump water and perform other kinds of mechanical work for centuries, but they were not used to produce electric power until the late 1800s. A wind power station consists of rotating blades attached to a generator, which is connected to transmission lines.

Wind power does not emit polluting emissions and does not produce unwanted substances that require careful disposal. There appear to be minor environmental impacts associated with the installation of wind turbines, aside from the possible disturbance of wildlife habitat and farming, which for some include the visual impact of a large, multiturbine wind farm on the natural beauty of an area. Wind turbines are not considered to be noisy machines; however, some noise is generated in their operation, and this has led to negative reactions of the public in some areas. Another issue is the coincident location of wind turbines in areas along the migration routes of birds; there have been reports of birds dying after colliding with the rotating blades of wind turbines. However, perhaps the greatest obstacles to wind farms have been that the areas where there is wind are often heavily populated and that the kind of equipment wind farms require is still too expensive.

Geothermal Power

Geothermal energy is heat energy from the depths of the Earth. It originates from the Earth's molten interior and from the radioactive decay of isotopes in underground rocks. The heat is brought near the surface by crustal plate movements, by deep circulation of groundwater, and by intrusion of molten magma, originating from a great depth, into the Earth's crust. In some places, the heat rises to the surface in natural streams of steam or hot water, which have been used since prehistoric times for bathing and cooking. Wells can be drilled to trap this heat to supply pools, greenhouses, and power plants. The reservoirs developed to harness geothermal energy to generate electricity are termed *hydrothermal convection systems* and are characterized by circulation of water to depth. The driving force is the convection, via the density difference between cold, downward-moving recharge water and heated, upward-moving thermal water. Hot water from a reservoir is flashed partly to steam at the surface, and this steam is used to drive a conventional turbine-generator set.

Geothermal energy tends to be relatively diffuse, which makes it difficult to trap. If it were not for the fact that the Earth itself concentrates geothermal heat in certain regions—typically regions associated with the boundaries of tectonic plates—geothermal energy would be essentially useless.

Geothermal resources are renewable within the limits of equilibrium between off take of reservoir water and natural or artificial recharge. Within this equilibrium, the energy source is renewable for a long period of time. Although geothermal energy may not be technically "renew-able," the global geothermal potential represents a practically inexhaustible energy resource. The issue is not the finite size of the resource but the availability of technologies able to trap this kind of energy.

ANNA LETICIA MONTENEGRO
TURTELLI PIGHINELLI
LEONARDO FONSECA VALADARES

Further Reading

Boyle, Godfrey. *Renewable Energy*. New York: Oxford University Press in Association with the Open University, 2004.

Klass, Donald L. *Biomass for Renewable Energy, Fuels, and Chemicals*. San Diego, CA: Academic Press, 1998.

Renewable Energy Policy Network for the 21st Century (REN21). *Renewables 2010 Global Status Report*. Paris: REN21 Secretariat, 2010. http://www.ren21.net/REN21Activities/Publications/GlobalStatusReport/tabid/5434/Default.aspx.

Sørensen, Bent. *Renewable Energy: Physics, Engineering, Environmental Impacts, Economics, and Planning*. Burlington, MA: Academic Press, 2011.

Spellman, Frank R., and Revonna M. Bieber. *The Science of Renewable Energy*. Boca Raton, FL: CRC Press, 2011.

U.S. Department of Energy. "2009 Renewable Energy Data Book, August 2010." http://www1.eere.energy.gov/maps_data/pdfs/eere_databook.pdf.

See Also: Biomass Energy; Hydropower; International Renewable Energy Agency; Microhydropower; Renewable Energy Credits; Renewable Energy Portfolio; Tidal Power.

Rhode Island

Category: Energy in the United States.
Summary: A densely populated small state, Rhode Island uses less energy per person than any other state in the United States. Most

electricity generated in Rhode Island is derived from natural gas (89 percent).

Rhode Island is committed to energy efficiency and reduction of its carbon footprint and has made significant progress in this area since the beginning of the 21st century. Existing and potential sources of renewable energy for Rhode Island include biodiesel, wind, solar, and hydropower.

Covering an area of 1,545 miles, Rhode Island is only 40 miles long and 30 miles wide, making it the smallest of any American state. Water covers 500 square miles of Rhode Island, and its southern border runs for 400 miles along the Atlantic Ocean. The only major river is the Sakonnet, and the only major lake is Scituate Reservoir. Therefore, the use of hydroelectricity is negligible. Rhode Island's land area is densely populated, and there is significant industrialization throughout the state.

Of all the 50 states, Rhode Island uses the least energy per capita. The state used 220.1 trillion British thermal units (Btu) of energy in 2008 and ranked second after Vermont in the least amount of carbon dioxide generated (11.35 million tons). Natural gas is the most commonly used source of energy, and Rhode Island is one of the few American states that mandates the use of reformulated motor gasoline blended with ethanol. As early as 2006, Rhode Island began actively pursuing the feasibility of deriving energy from wind sources. The RIWINDS program set out with a goal of ensuring that Rhode Island would be receiving a fifth of all of its renewable energy from wind power by 2011. Rhode Island has also formed a partnership with neighboring Massachusetts to examine the feasibility of using renewable biodiesel fuel for home heating purposes. Following the release of a 2007 study that estimated that the state could meet 15 percent of its electricity demand from offshore wind energy, efforts to promote the use of wind energy accelerated more rapidly.

Most residents of Rhode Island receive their electricity from ISO-New England, and gas is supplied by Algonquin Gas Transmission as part of a regional transmission system. Petroleum, heating oils, transportation fuels, and liquid natural gas are channeled through the Port of Providence. In 2005, Rhode Island consumed 8,049 kilowatt-hours of electricity per capita, less than any other state except Vermont. Rhode Island used only 0.2 percent of the total amount of electricity consumed by Americans during that period. Electricity consumption in Rhode Island increased by only 1.7 percent during that period, as compared to 2.2 percent for the United States as a whole. Commerce consumes the lion's share of electricity in Rhode Island (45 percent), followed by homes (39 percent) and industry (16 percent).

Policies and Funding

At the end of the 20th century, Rhode Island, like most American states, was heavily dependent on fossil fuels. The 21st century brought a new commitment to converting to renewable forms of energy. Rhode Island offers state residents financial incentives to convert to renewable forms of energy. By state law, renewable energy products are not subject to sales tax. Residents may also apply for a 25 percent residential renewable energy system tax credit on items such as solar hot water systems, solar space-heating systems, and wind, geothermal, and photovoltaic energy systems. This credit is in addition to a 30 percent tax credit on solar energy products available from the federal government.

The Rhode Island Office of Energy Resources provides funding for exploration of alternative sources of energy and grants low-interest loans for completion of such projects. An effort has been made to coordinate the efforts of grassroots groups working to promote wind energy under the Rhode Island Wind Alliance. The Rhode Island Renewable Energy Fund, which operates under the auspices of the Rhode Island Economic Development Corporation, has approved a number of projects designed to harness wind and wave energy. One such project was the first utility-scale wind turbine built in the state. Portsmouth Abbey Wind Turbine was erected at the Portsmouth Abbey School overlooking Narragansett Bay. The turbine provides 40 percent of the school's need for electricity. In 2003, the Rhode Island Renewable Fund began participating in a partnership with the Australian-based Oceanlinx with the intention of building a moored system at Point Judith Harbor of Refuge, which is capable of generating 225 kilowatts of energy annually and has a 750-kilowatt maximum capacity. Rhode Island is also pursuing the use of solar energy with funding from the Renewable Energy Fund and the Office of Energy Resources. The Solar on Schools Initiative, for instance, furnishes schools with solar photovoltaic equipment, a Web-based data-collecting system, teacher training, and course materials.

In 2009, the U.S. Congress passed the American Recovery and Reinvestment Act and asked each state to submit to the federal government information on how energy grant money would be spent. Governor Donald L. Carcieri assured Secretary of Energy Steven Chu that Rhode Island was prioritizing energy investments, improving building codes, and enacting new legislation. Rhode Island benefited from the August 2010 announcement that the Department of Energy was releasing some $120 million to be used for advancing innovative weatherization projects in the various states.

In October 2010, the Department of Energy, the National Oceanic and Atmospheric Administration, and other relevant federal agencies announced the release of approximately $5 million to be used to promote research on renewable ocean energy, including the construction of offshore wind energy facilities and the possibility of generating energy from waves, tides, currents, and thermal gradients. The University of Rhode Island was selected to conduct research on the use of the Atlantic Ocean to generate renewable energy. The following month, Secretary Chu announced that roughly $21 million was to be distributed for funding state technical assistance projects designed to improve energy efficiency in commercial sectors. This funding was instrumental in paving the way for pressurized-water reactor development in North Kingstown, Rhode Island.

ELIZABETH RHOLETTER PURDY

Further Reading

Barnes, Roland V., ed. *Energy Crisis in America?* Huntington, NY: Nova Science, 2001.

Bird, Lori, et al. *Green Power Marketing in the United States: A Status Report.* Golden, CO: National Renewable Energy Laboratory, 2008.

"Massachusetts, Rhode Island Join Forces to Explore Offshore Wind Energy." *Boston Herald*, July 26, 2010.

Rhode Island Office of Energy Resources. "State Energy Plan." http://www.energy.ri.gov/documents/RI_State_Energy_Plan.pdf.

U.S. Department of Energy. "Rhode Island Energy Summary." http://apps1.eere.energy.gov/states/energy_summary.cfm/state=RI.

U.S. Energy Information Administration. "Rhode Island." http://www.eia.doe.gov/state/state-energy-profiles.cfm?sid=RI.

See Also: Connecticut; Hydropower; Massachusetts; Regional Greenhouse Gas Initiative; Solar Energy; United States; Vermont; Wind Resources.

Risk Assessment

Category: Environmentalism.
Summary: The growth of alternative energy technologies is both fed by the findings of, and has complicated the process of, risk assessment in the energy sector. Risk assessment is the study of the presence, probability, outcome, and remedy of risks attached to the use of a given energy source.

Risk assessment is one of the key elements of risk management; it is the determination of risk in a specific scenario, whether actual or hypothesized, including a reasonable projection of potential negative outcomes and their impact in both quantitative and qualitative terms. Risk assessment is the science of painting the most realistic picture of the risk scenario with the information available (and consequently of knowing which information is relevant, and in some cases of generating such information). It is not sufficient to know that a risk of failure or disaster exists: Risk assessment determines exactly which risks exist; what their probability of occurrence is or which behaviors, decisions, or events will impact their probability; and what outcomes the realization of those risks will yield. The informed decision making of risk management requires being well versed in the risks pertinent to the scenario, which includes acknowledgement of those areas where the risks or their probabilities are unknown.

A new solar energy company cannot accurately predict whether its product or service will catch on, for instance, but it can assess the cost of its entrance into the market and the possibility of factors, including possible future government subsidies or other incentives, consumer interest in sustainable products, consumer spending patterns and projected economic behavior, and the performance of similar business ventures. Implicit in this hypothetical company's plans, though, is awareness of another risk: the risk posed by conventional energy sources such as fossil fuels to climate change and public health; and perhaps also the political and economic risks of continued reliance on fossil fuels. The environmental, political, and social risks faced by various sources of energy are increasingly addressed in the energy sector. While the solar energy company seems to represent a less risky alternative to fossil fuel energy, it could still assess environmental factors such as the effects on the local environment of the use of its technology, or the environmental impact of the life cycle of its product (including manufacture, transportation, warehousing, and disposal).

Financial risks and environmental risks are not necessarily separate. When the environmental movement first gained steam in the 1960s and 1970s, its early targets included companies dumping raw sewage into waterways, industrial plants with heavy emissions, strip mining, and other visible, obvious examples of polluting activity. The cost of changing behaviors or cleaning up environmental damage was in many cases greater than the cost would have been of avoiding that damage, particularly when the impact on public opinion was considered. But that, in turn, drove the types of environmentally friendly behaviors companies were most likely to practice. The most obvious pollutants, those that caused visible smog or noticeable smells, or had an obvious effect on water quality, were more likely to be avoided than less obvious pollutants that could still have detrimental environmental or health effects.

The consumer can also make informal or formal risk assessments of possible choices, whether that consumer is a private household, business, or government (in which case the "consumption" may be literal, or in the form of regulation over an industry). Risk assessment is the best framework in which to compare two or more energy source possibilities, weighing the advantages, disadvantages, and worst possible outcomes of conventional energy sources, alternative energy providers, and do-it-yourself alternative energy solutions. The process of making such an assessment begs answers to these questions: How does one weigh the low probability of a massive nuclear power disaster against the certain ongoing pollution caused by fossil fuels? Across what timescale should risk be assessed: the short term and immediate future, the period of use of the energy solution, the lifetime of the consumer, or the entirety of the foreseeable future? Is a high risk of eventual disaster more acceptable than the low risk of an immediate disaster? Ideally, a risk assessment will take into account the entire energy cycle and the life span of all relevant materials; later stages of the risk management process may choose to consider only the risks posed in the immediate future, but are at least informed by a complete picture.

There is a large body of studies on the comparative risk of conventional energy sources such as coal, oil, nuclear power, and natural gas. Biomass, ocean thermal power, wave power, geothermal power, solar, wind, and other energy sources have less data available for risk assessments, especially in the cases of energy sources that either haven't yet been developed commercially, or have only been used for a brief period of time or in a limited region. In such cases, there is simply less hard data about the probability of negative events and the cost of addressing them. Similarly, there is less data available pertaining to hybrid solutions, not simply the hybrid vehicles which have become popular in the 21st century, but energy solutions that employ multiple energy sources.

BILL KTE'PI

Further Reading

Dahlgren, R. "Risk Assessment in Energy Trading." *Power Systems* 18, no. 2 (May 2003).

Ebinger, Jane, Walter Vergara, and Irene Leino. *Climate Impacts on Energy Systems*. New York: World Bank Publications, 2011.

Eydeland, Alexander, and Krzysztof Wolyniec. *Energy and Power Risk Management*. New York: Wiley, 2003.

Inhaber, Herbert. *Energy Risk Assessment*. New York: Routledge, 1982.

Ramanathan, R. "Comparative Risk Assessment of Energy Supply Technologies: A Data Envelopment Analysis Approach." *Energy* 26, no. 2 (February 2001).

Rasmussen, N. C. "The Application of Probabilistic Risk Assessment Techniques to Energy Technologies." *Annual Review of Energy* 6 (1981).

See Also: Communication; Energy Policy; Gulf Oil Spill; Life-Cycle Analysis; Risk Management.

Risk Management

Category: Business of Energy.

Summary: Risk management is a growing field focused on the identification, analysis, and application of mitigating measures for any factor that can generate undesired consequences for individuals or organizations.

Reducing the impact of both anticipated and unexpected events is the goal of risk management; most risk management activities are involved in business administration and political arenas. Energy is a rich field for risk management, due to the broad scope and diversity of its operating environments, dynamic markets, and strategic tie-ins to major corporate and government bodies.

Definition and Application

The increasing presence of risk factors in complex modern society has led to an expansion of its analysis, with the goal of its minimization and management through different branches of scientific knowledge including economics, agriculture, chemistry, engineering, finance, and many other disciplines. Today, one can find diverse and complementary approaches to this topic. According to Douglas Hubbard, a preeminent expert in the field, risk management is defined as "the identification, assessment, and prioritization of risk followed by coordinated and economical application of resources to minimize, monitor, and control the probability and/or impact of unfortunate events." From an economic point of view, risk is presented as the chance that the final output of a project will not be sufficient to recover all the costs encountered in its completion. Risk, for example, must be calculated in any analysis of the anticipated costs and desired profits involved in oil and gas field exploration and development.

However, this definition can also be explained from an alternative point of view, wherein public image, company brands, and other intangible values are the indicators to be considered. The economic approach to risk management can thus be seen to complement other approaches. As a result, risk has turned into a business for a wide array of companies that specialize in its management, from the first steps of prevention to the last steps of mitigating the impact of negative outcomes on organizations and individuals. This holistic approach to risk management attempts to integrate the whole range of potential impacts of risk.

Since the 1990s, universities have established programs to qualify people for specialized tasks in risk assessment and management. There are potential risks to an employee's health and safety at work, for example; these can vary greatly, depending on the environment in which the work takes place. Thus, health and safety measures have been approached not only as good practices but also as legal mandates addressed by laws and regulations on the one hand and company policies on the other. A good risk assessment and management policy is vital in order to apply these rules intelligently and consistently, as well as to improve a company's external image and provide better participation by the individuals working for the organization. International associations

▷ *Crisis Communication*

The management of crises has turned into a common event for many business and social organizations. The growing visibility of any action in today's media society, in which news and information are broadcast 24 hours a day, has changed the way public relations are planned. As a consequence, an organization's reputation has been given a high priority, turning into one of the most valuable assets of any company.

Public relations firms have dedicated departments to crisis management in order to mitigate the impact on the reputations of the organizations that hire these firms; many large corporations, by the same token, have even dedicated internal personnel and divisions to this effort. Control of the internal and the external communications of any individual or company is the best way either to contain a crisis or to handle a potential scandal. The final goal is always to increase the prestige and the public value of the company's brand, so previous preparation makes a big difference for actors dealing with risky situations and circumstances.

The creation of specialized departments devoted to public relations and crisis communication strategies has also led to the introduction of risk management in the daily life of organizations, because public relations communication strategies must be accompanied by the elaboration of clear, preventive protocols to avoid crises in the first place. This precautionary principle rules in most risk management departments, linking the adoption of actions and policies, available scientific knowledge, potential risks of harm to society or the environment, and political responsibility. As a consequence, all decision makers are forced to anticipate potential damage before crises occur by means of a solid scientific approach. Decision makers are increasingly aware that any kind of choice bears potential consequences. This principle applies to activities in the energy sector, particularly since such events as the Earth Summit in 1992 have heightened the public awareness of energy policy issues.

such as the International Community on Information Systems for Crisis Response and Management (ISCRAM), the Institute of Risk Management (IRM), the Risk and Insurance Management Society (RIMS), and the International Organization for Standardization (ISO) have focused on the study of these processes

In general, systems for responding to crises currently seem better developed than efforts to identify and work beforehand against those threats. However, the best way to manage any risk is to avoid the negative consequence in the first place. Mitigating disasters requires risk managers to envision diverse scenarios, ranging from worst-case to best-case possibilities and advancing the expected outcomes of a variety of potential situations. Plans to respond to all these potential outcomes must be completed well before a crisis occurs, if its impact is to be reduced.

Two Sources of Risk

Risk situations have diverse origins and require various management processes, although all of them can be seen to derive from one of two main sources that point to varying causes, consequences, and responses.

First, natural circumstances can create unexpected events, forcing managers to act and reduce the impact of nature. Earthquakes, tsunamis, hurricanes, and tornados are good examples of risks that are not directly caused by human activity (although some natural events are increasingly seen as the indirect consequence of human activity, such as greenhouse gas emissions and their climate impact). These unexpected natural events immediately break the normal flow of life in their locality, and directly challenge the risk management strategies designed by local governmental or corporate authorities.

Second, the actions of humans and societies—anthropogenic activity—constitutes another powerful source of risks. The pace of social evolution has accelerated in recent decades, underpinned by a faith in scientific and technological advancements as the measure of collective progress—and as a bulwark against risk. While human society has undeniably advanced technologically, however, this evolution has also led to whole new arrays of risks. Nuclear power plants and petrochemical production and transport have occasioned some of the more visible examples, resulting in accidents with notoriously severe consequences for the health of humans and other living organisms, the economy, and political ramifications.

Both types of risk—natural and anthropogenic—can be linked, as the occurrence of a natural disaster can have an effect on the normal functioning of human activities, making some of them potentially more dangerous. A good example occurred in March 2011 in Japan, when a strong earthquake (a natural event) damaged the Fukushima nuclear power plant (a human enterprise), threatening the lives and health of the surrounding population, environment, and economy with radioactive pollution. Accidents like this demonstrate the inherent fragility of some of the most technologically advanced human activities on Earth, and they also have revealed the inadequacies of some current risk management principles. In the case of Fukushima, a lack of redundant networks to bring offsite electrical power to the reactor site in case of emergency was a factor in the delayed effectiveness of what was otherwise a bold response by engineering personnel.

The Risks Ahead

The quantity and diversity of risks faced are constantly growing. New risks emerge, while known risks do not disappear. A key issue in risk management concerns the short-term and often short-sighted strategies that organizations engage to prevent, control, and minimize ongoing risks. Thinking about long-term strategies is one of the main challenges both in research and in professional development. As researchers Bryan Richardson and Peter Gerzon put it, emerging risks are "those that have not yet occurred but are at an early

Wikimedia/Jorge Rodriquez

A reactor at the Fukushima I nuclear plant in December 2011. The covering on the top of the structure was mostly blown off by a hydrogen explosion after the March 11, 2011, earthquake and tsunami.

stage of becoming known and/or coming into being and expected to grow greatly in significance." Most emerging risks are associated with human activity.

For example, one emerging issue for the near future is the risk that the energy required to produce the world's goods and services, particularly the necessities of life such as food and drinking water, will be insufficient to meet demand. Natural and economic resources are finite; populations and national economies are growing. Priority should be given to the full range of risk management options: opening doors across industry, academia, and government to analyze and consider strategic political decisions, economic interests, technological factors, and conflicting social trends.

MIGUEL VICENTE-MARIÑO

Further Reading

Beck, Ulrich. *Risk Society: Towards a New Modernity.* London: Sage, 1992.

Coombs, Timothy, and Sherry Holladay, eds. *The Handbook of Crisis Communication.* Malden, MA: Wiley-Blackwell, 2010.

Heath, Robert, and Dan O'Hair, eds. *Handbook of Risk and Crisis Communication*. New York: Routledge, 2009.

Hubbard, Douglas. *The Failure of Risk Management: Why It's Broken and How to Fix It*. Hoboken, NJ: John Wiley and Sons, 2009.

Hubbard, Douglas. *How to Measure Anything: Finding the Values of Intangibles in Business*. Hoboken, NJ: John Wiley and Sons, 2007.

Richardson, Bryan, and Peter Gerzon. "Emergent Risks." Institute of Risk Management. http://www.theirm.org/publications/documents/irm_emergent_risks.pdf.

See Also: Best Management Practices; BP; Communication; Gulf Oil Spill; Public Relations; Risk Assessment.

Rockefeller, John D.

Dates: 1839–1937.
Category: Biographies.
Summary: John D. Rockefeller, an American oil titan and philanthropist, defined the shape of the modern petroleum industry.

John Davison Rockefeller was born on July 8, 1839, in Richford, New York. He was the second of six children of William Avery Rockefeller, a traveling salesman, and Eliza Davison. Between 1852 and 1855, Rockefeller attended Owego Academy in Owego, New York; he also attended Cleveland Central High School and Folsom's Business College in Cleveland, Ohio. In his education, he excelled in arithmetic and business-related subjects, such as single- and double-entry bookkeeping, banking, and exchange.

After graduating, Rockefeller began working as an assistant bookkeeper with the commission merchants and shippers Hewitt and Tuttle, where he earned a reputation for diligence, precision, and resolve. By 1859, having learned the particulars of the trade, Rockefeller formed a partnership with his neighbor Maurice Clark. They operated as commission merchants in grain, hay, meats, and miscellaneous goods. The firm Clark and Rockefeller rapidly became profitable and expanded with rising commodity prices during the early years of the Civil War.

In 1863, suspecting that railroad expansion would limit the growth of their business in Cleveland, a port city, Rockefeller persuaded Clark to explore the opportunities offered by the emerging oil-refining business. With the newly established firm Andrews, Clark and Company, the partners built an oil refinery in Cleveland's industrial area. Shortly thereafter, in 1865, Rockefeller bought out the Clark brothers and gained control of the business, renaming the firm Rockefeller and Andrews.

A highly efficient, integrated approach to oil refining allowed the company to take full advantage of postwar prosperity, the expansion of railroads, and the growing demand for oil. In a critically important decision, Rockefeller chose to borrow heavily in order to expand his business, reinvesting profits and streamlining refinery operations. In 1866, he and his brother William built a second refinery in Cleveland, Standard Works, and opened a marketing office in New York City. Joined by Henry M. Flagler as a third partner in 1867, Rockefeller, Andrews and Flagler rapidly became the largest refinery in the world.

On January 10, 1870, Rockefeller, his brother William, Flagler, Andrews, Stephen Harkness, and O. B. Jennings established the Standard Oil Company of Ohio. Low entry costs for oil drilling and refining had resulted in a surfeit of small companies, resulting in excess capacity and price-cutting practices. In 1871, Rockefeller therefore elaborated a plan to consolidate competing oil refineries with backing from lending institutions. Following a short setback caused by the failed attempt to pool railroads and refineries in the so-called Southern Improvement Scheme, Standard Oil began acquiring competitors in Cleveland and surrounding areas, increasing its capitalization and using company stock for the transactions.

Standard Oil improved its nationwide distribution system both by acquiring existing and by building new pipelines, which Rockefeller eventually organized under the name United Pipe Lines;

he also negotiated advantageous carriage terms with railroads and obtained access to important terminal facilities in major cities. At its peak, this elaborate distribution network reached nearly 80 percent of U.S. towns, with Standard Oil carts delivering fuels and lubricants directly to businesses and households. By 1879, Standard Oil was refining in excess of 90 percent of the oil produced in the United States, enabling Rockefeller to exert substantial negotiating power for aggressive and increasingly controversial tactics against competing oil companies, railroads, and consumers.

Public sentiment turned against Rockefeller and his business empire when, in an attempt to improve management of the various corporations established in different U.S. states, he formed the Standard Oil Trust in 1882. Ida Tarbell's *The History of the Standard Oil Company* (1904) highlighted the secretive, heavy-handed, and often ethically questionable practices that resulted in the growth of Standard Oil and dramatically increased public scrutiny and media attention. Following congressional passage of the Sherman Antitrust Act in 1890, the U.S. Supreme Court had a legal basis to break up the Standard Oil Trust, which it did in 1911, ruling that the trust had originated in illegal monopolistic practices.

In the wake of this decision, the trust was broken into 34 new companies, including the predecessors of several major oil and gas companies still operating today, such as Chevron and ExxonMobil. Rockefeller himself, while losing some degree of control over the oil market that he once had sought to own in its entirety, nonetheless went on to become one of the wealthiest individuals in human history, as well as one of the most generous. Among the beneficiaries of his many charitable efforts are the University of Chicago, Spelman College, and Rockefeller University. His Rockefeller Foundation continues to make charitable grants.

An avid donor throughout his career, John D. Rockefeller defined modern philanthropy through his systematic approach to charitable giving.

In his private life, Rockefeller had married Laura Celestia Spelman in 1864, with whom he went on to have four daughters and one son. Several of his descendants have had highly successful careers in the philanthropic, commercial, and political worlds, including several state governors and a vice president of the United States. Rockefeller's strategy, applied to creating one of the largest and most powerful commercial entities to date, remains an influential case study and has had lasting implications for the shape of contemporary corporate culture as well as for the oil and gas industry and its markets.

MICHAEL MEHLING

Further Reading

Chernow, Ron. *Titan: The Life of John D. Rockefeller, Sr.* 2nd ed. New York: Warner Books, 2004.

Collier, Peter, and David Horowitz. *The Rockefellers: An American Dynasty.* New York: Holt, Rinehart and Winston, 1976.

Hawke, David F. *John D: The Founding Father of the Rockefellers.* New York: Harper & Row, 1980.

Morris, Charles R. *The Tycoons: How Andrew Carnegie, John D. Rockefeller, Jay Gould, and J. P. Morgan Invented the American Supereconomy.* New York: Owl Books, 2006.

Nevins, Allan. *Study in Power: John D. Rockefeller, Industrialist and Philanthropist.* 2 vols. New York: Charles Scribner's Sons, 1953.

Tarbell, Ida M. *The History of the Standard Oil Company.* 2 vols. Gloucester, MA: Peter Smith, 1963.

See Also: Aramco; ExxonMobil; History of Energy: 1850–1900; Holding Companies; Ohio; Oil and

Petroleum; Oil Market and Price; Standard Oil Company; Tarbell, Ida.

Romania

Official Name: Romania.
Category: Geography of Energy.
Summary: Romanian domestic production covers a large percentage of the country's energy demand. Renewables and electricity generation position Romania above the European Union average but still show high energy intensity.

In the 1950s and 1960s, the communist government of Romania began a 10-year electrification plan. Electric power generation experienced a spectacular increase between 1950 (2.1 terawatt-hours) and 1968 (75.5 terawatt-hours). This ambitious plan was in service of the nation's forced industrialization, and the country often experienced power shortages and strict energy rationing for private consumers. During this period, the country's dependence on coal and oil imports from the Soviet Union was gradually mitigated by the development of domestic hydropower. The construction of a nuclear power plant with five reactors started in the late 1980s. Two functional units, using Canada Deuterium Uranium (CANDU) reactor technology from Atomic Energy of Canada Limited (AECL), produce 1,412 megawatts of electricity. The slowly liberalizing postsocialist Romanian energy market still carries the fingerprints of a path-dependent development.

Production and Consumption

With average carbon dioxide emissions per capita of 4.8 metric tons, Romania is among the lower carbon producers of the European Union (EU) member states. Early development plans based on renewables still compensate for slowly growing industry and a shift in lifestyle. As of 2009, electricity production reached 15.81 terawatt-hours, exceeding the national consumption by 2.29 terawatt-hours. In the same year, exported electricity reached 2.94 terawatt-hours, while imported electricity (0.651 terawatt-hour) dropped to half of its 2007 value. Oil and natural gas made up more than 60 percent of the energy supply, followed by coal, hydropower, biomass, and nuclear energy.

Natural Gas

As of 2010, proven natural gas reserves of 206 billion cubic feet (63 billion cubic meters) ranked Romania 40th in the world and first among southeastern European states. In 2008, 72 percent of the natural gas consumption was met by domestic sources. Compared to 82 percent in 1992, this might suggest a higher dependency on natural gas imports.

In reality, Romania's natural gas consumption has been gradually decreasing, from 85.49 billion cubic feet (26.06 billion cubic meters) in 1992 to 50.88 billion cubic feet (15.51 billion cubic meters) in 2009. Both domestic production and imports halved during this interval. Apart from slight fluctuations during the mid-1990s, Romanian households consumed 2.67 billion cubic meters of natural gas in 2009, less natural gas than in 1990 (8.89 billion cubic feet or 2.71 billion cubic meters). These numbers primarily reflect structural changes from the country's raw-material-intensive socialist economy after the dissolution of the Soviet Union in 1991.

Political decisions of the early 2000s opened the Romanian energy market to foreign investors. The German multinational company E.ON Ruhrgas invested 304 million euros, in June 2005 taking over the distribution of natural gas in 20 northern counties of the country. As of 2006, 10.1 billion cubic feet (3.1 billion cubic meters) of gas were distributed through 11,000 miles of pipeline (more than half of the national network).

Imports of natural gas are mainly from Russian supplies via the main gas pipeline, Progress, which crosses Romania in the southeast. The proposed route of the Nabucco gas pipeline (also referred to as the Turkey-Austria pipeline) would connect Bulgaria to Hungary by complementing the national network of pipelines.

Photos.com

This experimental wind energy plant in Sfantu Gheorghe, Romania, was constructed in the late 20th century; however, hydropower and biomass remain the country's primary renewable energy sources.

Oil

Proven reserves of 600 million barrels and production of 117,000 barrels per day position Romania 43rd in the world and first in southeastern Europe. Domestic production experienced a decrease of 34 percent between 1992 and 2009; during that period, oil consumption decreased more than 15 percent, from 102.2 billion barrels to 86.57 billion barrels. Fluctuations induced by growing demand between 1990 and 1995 and 2003 and 2008 were covered by oil imports (46–59 percent of general consumption), mainly from the Russian Federation and Kazakhstan. The important players in Romania's oil market are currently Kazakh and Austrian companies. After the liberalization of the energy market, Romanian investors took over the company Rompetrol (founded in 1974) and

expanded it to become a major player in southeastern Europe (with sister companies in Ukraine, Georgia, and Albania) and in France (by owning the chain Dyneff). In 2007, Rompetrol became controlled through subsidies by the Kazakh company KazMunaiGaz after a transaction of 2.7 billion euros. In 2004, the Austrian company OMV took over the country's largest gas station network, along with the majority of the refineries, formerly owned by Petrom, for 1.53 billion euros.

Romania's oil pipeline network has been recently included in several regional plans of Europe-wide importance. As an alternative to the Burgas-Alexandroupolis and the Albania-Macedonia-Bulgaria line (AMBA), the Constanta-Omišalj-Trieste line could unite several refineries and have a dramatic impact on the region's energy market. Two major disadvantages of the project are its projected cost and the lack of a global power as its patron.

Renewables

Renewable energy made up 16 percent of domestic production in 2004, with hydropower and biomass as major resources. Compared to the EU-27 average, 12 percent of Romania's gross domestic consumption in 2004 was met by renewable energy. At least 20 percent of the electricity is produced in hydroelectric plants.

PÉTER BAGOLY-SIMÓ

Further Reading

Central Intelligence Agency. "Romania." In *The World Factbook*. https://www.cia.gov/library/publications/the-world-factbook/geos/ro.html.

Encyclopedia of the Nations. "Romania: Energy and Power." http://www.nationsencyclopedia.com/Europe/Romania-ENERGY-AND-POWER.html.

European Commission. "EU Energy and Transport in Figures." http://ec.europa.eu/energy/publications/statistics/doc/2010_energy_transport_figures.pdf.

European Commission. "Romania: Energy Mix Fact Sheet." http://ec.europa.eu/energy/energy_policy/doc/factsheets/mix/mix_ro_en.pdf.

U.S. Energy Information Administration. "Country Analysis Brief: Romania." http://www.eia.gov/countries/country-data.cfm?fips=RO.

See Also: Georgia (Nation); Hungary; Hydropower; Macedonia; Moldova; Natural Gas; Oil and Petroleum; Renewable Energy Resources.

Rotational Energy

Category: Energy Technology.
Summary: Rotation has long been used to generate energy and transfer forces, from the treadwheels of the ancient world to some types of internal combustion engines today.

As far back as 3,000 years ago, early machines used wheels pulled or pushed by animals or humans in order to move heavy weights, grind grain, or raise water. They were a frequent feature in Greek and Roman engineering and were spread particularly by the Romans through the ancient world. The Greeks also developed toothed gearing and waterwheels, the main components of water mills, which use a waterwheel to transfer the force of moving water to the mechanical components of the mill in order to power it. Water mills are built along a body of running water or an artificial water body such as a millpond.

The flow of the water could be controlled or maintained by various means; often there was at least a channel or a pipe directing the water to the waterwheel. The force of the water striking the wheel turned the wheel, rotating the axle to which the wheel was attached and in turn driving whatever gears were also attached to the axle. In this manner, early rotational motion was harnessed to produce energy.

Water and Rotational Power

The earliest known waterwheel is the Perachora wheel, on the periphery of Peloponesse, in the 3rd century B.C.E. Written references to such wheels date to the same century, especially in the technical manuals of Philo of Byzantium (280–220 B.C.E.), a Greek engineer. Both horizontal and vertical wheels were in use. Waterwheels became more sophisticated over time, connected to gearing mechanisms, aqueducts, sluices, and dams to adjust the speed of the water or the rotation of the wheel.

Water-powered sawmills operated saws that sliced not only through lumber but also through stone. Later, the Muslim agricultural revolution of the 9th to 13th centuries was driven in large part by the golden age of Muslim mathematics and science—and the ingenuity of Arab engineers in finding numerous applications for hydropower, mechanizing many farm tasks.

Both Arabs and Europeans also experimented with tide mills, which were powered by tidal flow instead of running water. In such a mill, gates trap rising water during high tide and then drain it through sluice gates at low tide, so that the force of the draining water drives the waterwheel—a technique useful in many coastal locations but especially efficient in places where there is a particularly great difference between high and low tides.

In some parts of the world, the advantages of waterwheels were so great that the spread of their use required laws, such as those of 8th-century China, which restricted their usage in order to prevent them from blocking the passage of ships on the waterways.

Gearing could also translate vertical rotation into horizontal rotation and vice versa. The water mills used for grinding kernels of grain in Britain and the United States leading up to and during the Industrial Revolution used a vertical waterwheel (and therefore a horizontal axle, creating horizontal rotation), which drove a horizontal shaft mounted to another wheel, which linked with a "wallower" on a vertical shaft in order to drive a spur wheel at the other end of the shaft, turning a small wheel called a stone nut, which was attached to the stones that ground the kernels. The same waterwheel could in this manner be connected to several stone nuts, grinding a great deal of grain in a short time. This gearing arrangement also allowed wheels to be rotated at a speed greater than the speed of the water driving the waterwheel, rather than being limited by it, as early Greek and Roman water mills had been.

Until the introduction of the steam engine, the water mill was the keystone of industry throughout Europe and the United States. Mills were used to cut timber and stone, to grind not only grains for food but also bark for use in leather tanning, to manufacture gunpowder, to spin yarn, to smelt lead, to make paper, to crush mined ore, to slit iron in order to make nails, and to shape metal by passing it through heavy rollers. Water mills were even used to power blast furnaces, and even after the steam engine was introduced, cotton mills used this rotational energy first to increase the water flow to the waterwheel, only later adopting steam as the principal motive power.

Wind and Rotational Power

Only slightly younger than the waterwheel is the windmill, which similarly uses the force of the wind to drive vanes that rotate an axle (usually vertical vanes and a horizontal axle, although other designs were common in antiquity). Early examples of wind-driven wheels are found in 1st-century Greece and 4th-century Tibet, and the technology became more common in medieval Europe. The earliest European mills were used to grind grain, with later industrial applications developing. The gears inside the windmill transfer the energy of the rotary motion of the vanes to mechanisms similar to those of the water mills. Never quite as popular as the water mill, there were about 200,000 windmills in Europe at the peak of their popularity, compared to half a million water mills.

Still in common use in dry agricultural regions—such as the American Southwest and Great Plains, South Africa and Namibia, and Australia—are wind pumps, which convert the rotary motion of the vanes to power a pump cylinder that either draws water up from wells or drains low-lying land. Windmills have been used for this purpose since the 9th century in the Middle East and China, but the modern wind pump dates to an 1854 design by Vermont engineer Daniel Halladay. In the United States alone, there are some 60,000 wind pumps, drawing water usually for agricultural purposes but sometimes for drinking water.

From the 19th century on, windmills have been built that generate electricity via a wind turbine. These have enjoyed a resurgence in the 21st century as concerns over the costs and effects of fossil fuels have motivated serious investment in other energy sources. Wind turbines that generate electricity instead of simply turning the wind's kinetic energy into mechanical energy are sometimes called wind generators for clarity's sake. High-efficiency windmills, typically with three-vaned rotors, are arranged in large numbers on wind farms. The gearbox of the turbine converts the slow rotation of the vanes into a faster rotation of wheels generating electricity.

The conventional electricity-generating windmill has a horizontal axis design, but in places with highly variable wind direction, vertical-axis wind turbines are sometimes used. This also eliminates the need for a tower and allows the generator and gearbox to be near the ground, making maintenance easier. Vertical-axis wind turbines do best when mounted on rooftops, to avoid the turbulent airflow at ground level. One common type of vertical-axis turbine is the "eggbeater" turbine, designed by French engineer Georges Darrieus, which is efficient but unreliable. Shaped like an eggbeater whisk, this wind turbine has vanes curve from the top to the bottom of a vertical shaft. There have been many attempts to develop airborne wind turbines with no mount, but none has yet succeeded in producing useful amounts of electricity.

Steam and Rotational Power

The steam turbine was a sophisticated steam engine introduced in 1884, developed by English engineer Charles Parsons. It quickly replaced the extant reciprocating piston steam engine, which was heavier and less efficient. The steam turbine continues to be used today as an electricity generator; most of the world's electricity is in fact generated this way, with coal or petroleum serving as the fuel to generate the steam. Parsons's steam turbine was instrumental in making electricity affordable throughout the world; it brought about the 20th century, the age of power lines and electric lighting.

Condensing turbines are the most common in power plants, and they exhaust partially condensed steam. Reheat turbines, instead of exhausting the steam, cause the steam to flow from a high-pressure section of the turbine back to the boiler, where it is heated again and cycles through the system repeatedly.

Steam is expanded as it travels through the turbine, in order to maximize efficiency by generating work. Two types of turbine can accomplish this, referred to as impulse turbines and reaction turbines—even though in practice, most power plant turbines will operate as both an impulse turbine and a reaction turbine, at different stages of their operation. In the impulse-turbine stage, fixed nozzles direct the steam into high-speed jets. The turbine's rotor blades convert the kinetic energy of those jets into rotational speed. The pressure drop as the steam flows through the nozzle causes the steam to expand, contributing to its velocity. In the reaction-turbine stage, the turbine's rotors themselves form nozzles.

Gas turbines are a type of internal combustion engine, in which—as in the steam turbine—a stream of high-velocity gas is directed by a

Wikimedia

Modern steam turbines range from mechanical drives of less than one horsepower to large power plants of more than 2,000,000 horsepower.

nozzle over the turbine blades in order to spin them and generate energy or mechanical output. "Air-breathing" jet engines use gas turbines that produce thrust from exhaust gases; when most of their thrust is so produced, they are referred to as turbojets, whereas those that produce thrust by connecting ducted fans to the gas turbines are turbofans. Gas turbines can also be incorporated into liquid propellant rockets. While gas turbines are sometimes used on ships and locomotives, the use of them in automobiles and buses has been in the experimental stage since the 1940s, with intended applications including luxury cars (Jaguar is a major funder of gas turbine automobile research) and hybrid electric cars. A small number of hybrid buses, such as the HEV-1, developed by AVS of Chattanooga, Tennessee, in 1999, use gas turbines.

The Wankel Engine
Another internal combustion engine using rotating motion instead of reciprocating pistons is the Wankel engine, named for German engineer Felix Wankel (1902–88). The terms *rotary engine* and *Wankel engine* are sometimes used interchangeably, although the Wankel engine is only the best-known rotary internal combustion engine. Its innovation was its compact size, and it was refined shortly after Wankel's invention of it by the Japanese car company Mazda, which continues to be the most extensive user of it in automobiles. However, the design is also used in chainsaws, single-passenger watercraft (such as Jet Skis), go-karts, and other applications where a compact engine is needed.

BILL KTE'PI

Further Reading
Boyce, Meherwan P. *Gas Turbine Engineering Handbook*. New York: Gulf Professional, 2006.

Burton, Tony, David Sharpe, Nick Jenkins, and Ervin Bossanyi. *Wind Energy Handbook*. New York: Wiley, 2001.

Hau, Erich. *Wind Turbines: Fundamentals, Technologies, Application, Economics*. New York: Springer, 2006.

Saravanamuttoo, H. I. H., G. F. C. Rogers, H. Cohen, and P. V. Straznicky. *Gas Turbine Theory*. New York: Pearson Prentice Hall, 2008.

Shlyakhin, P. *Steam Turbines: Theory and Design*. Honolulu: University Press of the Pacific, 2005.

See Also: Electric Motors; Hydropower; Natural Energy Flows; Power and Power Plants; Wind Technology.

Rural Electrification

Category: Business of Energy.
Summary: Rural electrification brings electricity to rural communities and customers, an effort that began in the 1930s in the United States.

Rural electrification is the process of making electrical power available to rural areas and customers. It is most strongly associated with the Rural Electrification Administration (REA) established by the New Deal in 1936, which greatly accelerated the electrification of the rural United States.

At the time, the process of electrification that had been so rapid in the 19th century had slowed to a crawl: Cities had been electrified, those suburbs that existed had been electrified, and 90 percent of city residents had electricity. But only 10 percent of rural Americans did, and getting power to them was not considered economically feasible. While bringing electricity to the country would benefit the American economy by increasing agricultural production, creating new customers for electricity (even the sale of new electric lights was a significant economic gain), and making rural commercial interests more competitive, those economic gains would not be seen directly by the companies responsible for laying the wire and setting up the equipment to electrify the region. Those companies that did provide electricity to the countryside charged as much as four times as much per kilowatt-hour as they did in the city, in order to maintain their profit margin; further, in some cases they required payment in advance of installation, by farmers or groups of farmers, in order to finance construction of the grid.

The Rural Electrification Act provided federal loans—later extended to telephone companies in a 1949 amendment—for the purpose of installing electrical distribution grids in the rural United States. The Rural Electrification Administration, later renamed the Rural Utilities Service, oversaw the installations by over 400 rural electric cooperatives run by farmers and other local consumers, many of which still exist today. Many opposed this as one of the most alarming examples, in their eyes, of New Deal legislation that positioned the government as a competitor with the private sector; many lawsuits were filed, and the conservative coalition in Congress was invigorated by the perception of anti-business activities on the part of Franklin D. Roosevelt's Democratic Party.

Further, the existing utility companies that had previously opted not to install electricity distribution in rural areas, or had done so only for punitive fees, often interfered with the work of the rural electric cooperatives, trying to prevent them from forming, or installing "spite lines" (power lines installed for the sake of staking a claim to an area, just to spite the cooperatives). Without such opposition, rural America would have been electrified more rapidly. But the gains were clear. By 1942, nearly half of American farms were electrified; by 1952, nearly all of them were.

The REA promoted electrical appliances to help rural customers make the best use of their electricity, as did other federal agencies. The Tennessee Valley Authority (TVA), a federally owned corporation created in 1933 to assist in specific areas of economic development in the Tennessee Valley, was one such agency. Walk-in coolers, for instance, were built by the TVA and made available for $650. They were refrigeration units big enough for 10 families to use, not only for household use but also to store farm goods like meat, eggs, and dairy products before sale. This was an even bigger gain than it may at first appear to be: While modern Americans are generally aware of the existence of the pre-electric icebox, it was never as omnipresent in the American household as the electric refrigerator has become, and the cost of ice delivery was prohibitively expensive for many families, especially in hot climates.

The gains of electrification were not just economic; they significantly raised standards of living and increased leisure time without reducing productivity, while also freeing up more time for housewives and young family members who, once concerned principally with chores or housework, could now consider educational or social options, or work outside of the home. The flight of Americans from rural areas to urban and suburban ones continued, however, as did the decline of family farms in favor of large commercial operations.

Developing World

The basic issues facing the United States in the area of rural electrification in the 1930s are found throughout the world, but especially the developing world, where increased standards of living could rescue many from poverty. Further, climate control (air conditioning and heating), electric pump-driven wells (which reduce the spread of water-borne disease), and refrigeration are significant boons to public health, which is widely taken for granted in developed countries like the United States.

A 2009 estimate by the International Energy Agency stated that 83 percent of the 1.5 billion people worldwide without electricity live in rural areas. Initiatives to electrify rural areas exist in three of the rapidly developing "BRIC" (Brazil, Russia, India, and China) nations—India, China, and Brazil—as well as the European Union. Widespread need for electrification also exists in sub-Saharan Africa, including South Africa, and parts of the Middle East. While current trends will result in that number falling, in some parts of the world the number of people without electricity is actually growing, due to higher population growth rates in the rural parts of these countries.

One of the concerns with rural electrification efforts is that when developing countries have no assistance or are provided with no motive to make other choices, their electrification efforts will naturally gravitate toward the cheapest solu-

A farmer in the early 1940s stands beside refrigeration equipment for his dairy business that the U.S. Rural Electrification Administration helped bring to isolated American farming communities.

tions, which are also the most highly polluting. While renewable energy can theoretically be made cheaply available, only recently has serious work gone into developing renewable energy technologies for markets other than commercial niches and well-off Westerners. In recent years, small solar energy systems have become more widely available; in India and Bangladesh they are distributed by Grameen Shakti, and financed with a microfinance system.

While diesel generators are popular throughout the rural world, they are not only noisy, dirty, and inefficient, they require fuel, which can be expensive and in some cases may be difficult to find. On the other hand, they provide more power than solar systems usually do; the solar energy systems distributed by Grameen provide only enough power for lighting and small appliances, not enough to electrify a whole house or run most small businesses.

Planning

Important considerations in rural electrification initiatives include creating or acquiring sound statistical data on the populations to be served. While the REA had decades of census work to rely on, this is rarely the case in the parts of the developing world most in need of electrification today, and resource allocation, end-use considerations, and funding depend on having a clear idea of the demographics, geographical distribution, and energy needs of the population. Initiatives also need to be independent from political agendas and entities that could divert resources, either to other purposes or nepotistically.

The establishment of a strong infrastructure is required in order to make electrification "stick," which is one problem with generators and other portable systems: A permanent grid supported by investors is one for which there is a profit motive for repair if something goes wrong in the future after the initiative's work is complete. Stand-alone systems, though, are in turn immune to grid-related problems, and are a faster route to electrification in circumstances where serious infrastructure work is needed in order to build and maintain a grid—the equivalent of feeding people meals while helping them plant their gardens. Key to attracting the investment and ongoing support of the private sector is the creation of electricity customers, though this is an area where some initiatives face criticism for failing to understand or internalize the effects of severe poverty on the consumption potential of the population.

The most common end use of rural electrification is light, followed by television and radio. While they may at first seem like luxuries, TV and radio provide valuable information in rural areas in the developing world, in addition to entertainment. Even so, the popularity of television is sometimes highlighted as a symptom of a problem with rural electrification initiatives that concern themselves mainly with infrastructure and not with end use. The situation faced by such initiatives differs relevantly from the 1930s Rural Electrification Administration's: While a gap between haves and have-nots existed in the 1930s, the post–World War II boom in labor-saving devices and the late 20th century boom in microchip-driven consumer technologies have made the gap much bigger and more complicated. The world of the 1930s "haves" was one in which some things were electrified and most things weren't; that of the 21st century is one in which a typical living room may contain a dozen different electrical devices and appliances, with more in the average person's pocket or purse. It is often things such as televisions, DVD players, and music players that drive much of the demand for electricity in the developing world, where people are accustomed to a work life without electricity but have no nonelectrical alternatives to television and recorded music.

In India, one of the obstacles to electrification is not a lack of distribution, but trouble with utility company practices. About 400 million Indians (one-third of the world's powerless) have no electricity, in part because electricity is so frequently stolen by those with access to the grid but no money to pay for it that the utility companies impose high tariffs (above and beyond the value of the stolen electricity) on legitimate customers. This in turn drives customers away. As counterintuitive as it seems, most of the large electric companies in India subsist on serving mainly large institutional and commercial customers, not residences or small businesses. Recent legislation has compelled the installation of biomass-powered generators in villages under arrangements whereby the cost, billing system, and fuel source can be controlled by village leadership according to what is the most sensible and desirable for the community; it is too early to say how successful this initiative will be, and many have expressed doubt at the adequate distribution of technical expertise in order to operate and maintain the generators.

In 2012 the government of Namibia announced a five-year plan to electrify all rural schools. Rural electrification has been a concern of Namibia's since becoming independent of South Africa, but the new plan interrupts the broad-based electrification plan—which included household electrification—in order to focus on the largest priorities: schools, government buildings, and public institutions such as hospitals. The government promised that household, farm, and business electrification would resume in 2018 after the completion of the plan.

BILL KTE'PI

Further Reading

Bhattacharyya, Subhes. "Energy Access Problem of the Poor in India." *Energy Policy* 34, no. 18 (December 2006).

Chakrabarti, Snigdha, and Subhendu Chakrabarti. "Rural Electrification Programme With Solar Energy in Remote Region—A Case Study in an Island." *Energy Policy* 30, no. 1 (January 2002).

Foley, Gerald. "Rural Electrification in the Developing World." *Energy Policy* 20, no. 2 (February 1992).

See Also: Electric Grids; Electricity; Energy Poverty; Energy Transmission: Electricity; Giant Power; India; Microhydropower.

Russia

Official Name: Russian Federation.
Category: Geography of Energy.
Summary: Russia is the world's largest oil producer and holds the world's largest natural gas reserves. It constitutes an ideal supplier to Asia because of its important unexploited gas and oil fields in its east Siberia and far eastern regions.

After the dissolution of the Soviet Union in 1991, the "shock therapy" of privatization, and the ensuing financial crash of 1998, the Russian economy, including its energy industry, was deeply affected. The nation has recovered, however, and its newly found economic health is mainly attributable to the rising price of crude oil, which began to inject considerable cash into the Russian economy in 2007. The economic recovery has also been characterized by a new trend in Russia's foreign policy behavior, especially regarding energy issues.

Russia is a major player in the world energy markets. According to BP (British Petroleum), it accounts for 12.9 percent of global oil production. Russia is the world's largest oil producer (outshining Saudi Arabia), with roughly 10 million barrels per day in 2009. For that same year, Russia consumed 2.7 million and exported 7 million barrels per day. According to the U.S. Energy Information Administration (EIA), Russia's proven oil reserves are estimated at around 60 billion barrels. Russia's oil production could reach up to 11.2 million barrels per day by 2025. In terms of downstream activities, Russia has 40 oil refineries, which can process close to 5.4 million barrels per day. The majority of Russia's oil production comes from its fields in western Siberia. Among the main actors responsible for oil exploration and production (E&P) in that region are the state-run companies Rosneft and Transneft and the privately owned companies Lukoil and TNK-BP.

Russia holds the world's largest natural gas reserves, evaluated at 1,680 trillion cubic feet. According to BP, Russia accounts for 17.6 percent of global gas production, placing it second to the United States, with 1,730 trillion cubic feet (527.5 billion cubic meters) in 2009. It is also the world's largest exporter, exporting 7.3 trillion cubic feet in 2009. The EIA estimates that Russian production could reach up to 31.3 trillion cubic feet by 2030. The largest fields of gas production are located in Siberia, nearly all of which are controlled by Russia's state-run natural gas monopoly Gazprom, which accounts for 83 percent of gas production in Russia.

According to the EIA, Russia's total electricity consumption was 983 terawatt-hours in 2008. The main segment in the Russian power sector is "thermal power" (comprising fossil fuels), which currently accounts for 68 percent of Russia's electricity generation. Other segments include hydropower and nuclear power, each accounting for 16 percent of total electricity generation. The electricity sector is divided in eight regional systems. Among these systems are Urals, Western Siberia, Eastern Siberia, and the Far East.

Regaining Control Over the Energy Sector

The retaking of the energy sector is an essential component of Russia's resurgence on the international scene. To better understand how controlling energy resources and extraterritorial activities line up behind Russia's statecraft, one must look at some political "coups" orchestrated by the Kremlin. In 2003, Mikhail Khodorkovsky, former chief executive officer of Yukos, once the largest Russian private oil firm, expressed a desire to build private pipelines (one to China and another to the United States through Murmansk in the northwest of Russia) without obtaining the approval of the state-run company Transneft, which is responsible for oil pipeline routes. In parallel, Khodorkovsky intensified negotiations with American majors ExxonMobil and ChevronTexaco in order to sell 40 percent of the shares (a $25 billion value) of a company that was supposed to be created by the fusion between Yukos and Sibneft, the fifth-largest Russian firm.

For the Kremlin, it was inconceivable to see a strategic asset such as oil being controlled by foreign interests. Accused of fraud and tax evasion, Khodorkovsky was arrested in October 2003, and 44 percent of Yukos's capital was seized. In April 2004, the Russian state announced the freezing of Yukos's assets. Later that year, the company was ordered to pay $13 billion in tax arrears in addition to the $6.8 billion already requested by the Russian Federal Tax Service. According to expert Philippe Sébille-Lopez, this was the beginning of the "informal" dismantling of Yuganskneftegaz, the main subsidiary of Yukos, which alone accounted for $11.63 billion barrels of crude—more than 17 percent of Russian reserves. Yuganskneftegaz was later acquired by Rosneft, which became the leader of the oil industry in Russia. In 2004, Rosneft was also instrumental in the Kremlin's refusal to let Chevron and ExxonMobil participate in the development of the Sakhalin-3 project.

In December 2006, Gazprom retook the E&P rights from Royal Dutch Shell in Russia's far eastern Sakhalin Island. According to the Russian Petroleum

Research and Exploration Institute, the reserves of this region amount to 3.4 billion tons of oil and 10 trillion cubic feet (3 trillion cubic meters) of gas. By playing the "environmentalist" card, the Kremlin wanted to renegotiate the terms of the contract with Shell to make them more advantageous for Russia. As Jeronim Perović and Robert Orttung noted, Shell was indirectly forced to sell half of its shares in the Sakhalin-2 project (with reserves totaling 155 million tons of oil and 1,607 billion cubic feet or 490 billion cubic meters of gas) to Gazprom for $7.45 billion or risk losing its E&P license on the grounds that the project was vio-

Wikimedia

A pipeline segment intended for a portion of the Nord Stream in the Baltic Sea off of Sweden being loaded onto a ship in July 2011. At 1,220 kilometers, the Nord Stream will be the longest undersea pipeline in the world.

lating Russian environmental law. Finally, in 2007, the Russian state took control over the Kovytka field (with reserves of 6.98 trillion cubic feet or 2.13 trillion cubic meters of gas and 108 million tons of oil) by "strongly urging" the joint venture TNK-BP to sell the entirety of its shares in a project whose value was estimated at $20 billion.

These political moves were part of the Kremlin's efforts to regain control over its energy sector in response to an imminent threat to its domestic regulatory authority and Russia's market power in global energy markets.

European Projects

Most of Russia's energy resources are located in western Siberia. Close to 80 percent of these resources are destined for European markets, particularly Germany. In fact, because of Europe's precarious energy situation, Russia is its most important supplier. According to specialist Jeffrey Mankoff, in 2007, the European Union (EU) imported nearly 30 percent of its oil and 50 percent of its gas from Russia. Helped by effective and persuasive "pipeline diplomacy," Russia seeks to control the energy flows from outside the EU to secure its western borders by building pipelines in partnership with European energy firms and offering special business and energy security to EU members, which benefit from a strategic hub position for Russia's energy exports. To that end, several projects are envisaged to achieve these goals.

In the north, Russia is cofinancing with Germany the Nord Stream project, a 758-mile (1,220-kilometer) gas pipeline that will run from Vyborg in Russia to Greifswald in Germany via the Baltic Sea, thereby circumventing the Baltic states and the Yamal-Europe Pipeline, which currently traverses Poland.

The first portion of the line went up at the beginning of November 2011 and, when the second portion is completed, the pipeline will be the longest undersea pipeline in the world, with a capacity of 180 billion cubic feet or 55 billion cubic meters per annum (although complications between Moscow and Berlin over price issues may retard its operationalization).

Gazprom also launched the Yamal Megaproject in late 2008, which provides for the exploitation of the Yamal Peninsula and its adjacent offshore areas in northern Russia. Based on Gazprom's figures, these areas are believed to hold 52 trillion cubic feet (16 trillion cubic meters) of explored gas reserves and 72 trillion cubic feet (22 trillion cubic meters) of forecast gas reserves. In the south, Russia has convinced many European countries to support the construction of the South Stream project, a 559-mile (900-kilometer) pipeline with a capacity of 206 billion cubic feet (63 billion cubic meters) per annum that will run from the Russian Black Sea coast to Austria and Italy via Bulgaria, Serbia, Hungary, Croatia, and Slovenia, as well as by Bulgaria and Greece. The project's completion is scheduled for 2015.

Northeast Asia

While energy resources coming from western Siberia and the Russian Caspian Sea sector will continue to flow toward Europe, the Russian energy complex is increasingly sliding toward northeastern Asian markets. Russia has an enormous potential for energy development in the regions of eastern Siberia and the Far East. According to the Geological Institute for Oil and Gas (part of the Siberian Branch of the Russian Academy of Sciences), extractable energy resources (underground and subsea) in those regions are estimated at 85–90 billion tons of hydrocarbon: 20–22 billion tons of oil, 196–206 trillion cubic feet (60–63 trillion cubic meters of gas), and 3–5 billion tons of "condensed" gas. Annual oil and gas production is estimated to reach 67 billion tons and 110.2 billion cubic meters, respectively, by 2015.

Based on data collected by Paradorn Rangsimaporn, by 2015 annual exports of crude oil and gas (mostly destined for East Asia) are estimated at 40 billion tons and 142 billion cubic feet (43.4 billion cubic meters), respectively. According to estimates provided by the Japanese Economic Research Institute for Northeast Asia, the region of eastern Siberia might hold more than 18 percent of Russia's oil and 29 percent of its natural gas. However, it should be noted that, thus far, only 5–6 percent of the resource-rich areas have been explored.

Upon the completion of the exploration, TNK-BP believes these areas could be holding close to 75 billion barrels of oil reserves, more than a quarter of Saudi Arabia's reserves.

Russia's energy power depends largely on western Siberia. The production in eastern Siberia and the far east remain minimal. According to the EIA, only 12 percent of Russia's oil exports currently go to Asia. That is why, in 2007, the Russian government adopted the Eastern Gas Program. According to this program, gas production in these regions is projected to reach 492 billion cubic feet (150 billion cubic meters) per annum by 2020 and 531 billion cubic feet (162 billion cubic meters) by 2030. The program provides for gas exports of around 82–164 billion cubic feet (25–50 billion cubic meters) per annum, while exports of liquefied natural gas (LNG)—based on the production of Sakhalin—are projected at 68 billion cubic feet (21 billion cubic meters) per annum by 2020 and 92 billion cubic feet (28 billion cubic meters) by 2030. That said, the volumes destined for China remain uncertain.

Based on the data gathered by specialist Hongchan Chun, the eastern Siberia and far east regions should produce between 71 and 106 million tons of oil by 2020, which constitutes an augmentation of roughly 700 percent compared to 2000 levels. According to the Russian Ministry of Industry and Trade, gas exports to Asia via pipeline should reach 164 billion cubic feet (50 billion cubic meters) by 2020, while gas exports via LNG carriers are projected to reach 68 billion cubic feet (21 billion cubic meters) by that same year.

However, the development of reserves in the east poses many problems, including a lack of modern infrastructure, high production costs, uncertainty surrounding Russia's reserves and the Asian demand, and a lack of technological investments required for the exploitation and export of the resources in question. That explains why attracting foreign direct investments for the development and construction of a state-of-the-art energy network in these regions is a top priority for the Kremlin.

Several projects are planned to achieve these objectives, such as the construction of the Eastern Siberia-Pacific Ocean (ESPO) Pipeline, which will directly link Russia to northeast Asia. Once completed, this pipeline, whose cost is estimated at $30 billion, will be the world's longest (3,017 miles or 4,857 kilometers), with an estimated capacity of more than 1.6 million barrels per day or 80 million tons per annum.

The ESPO is expected to stretch from Taishet in eastern Siberia to the Bay of Kozmino, south of Vladivostok, on the Russian Pacific coast. The project is divided into two parts. The first part, 1,674 miles (2,694 kilometers) from Taishet to Skovorodino, has been operational since December 2009. The second part, which should be operational in 2014, will stretch over 1,242 miles (2,000 kilometers) from Skovorodino to the Pacific coast.

There are also plans to link Skovorodino to Daqing in China with a section 656 miles (1,056 kilometers) long. Once that section is completed, oil exports to China could reach 15 million tons per annum. As regards gas, plans are being considered to build a gas pipeline parallel to the ESPO. In October 2009, a new agreement was signed between Gazprom and the China National Petroleum Corporation providing for deliveries of about 229 billion cubic feet (70 billion cubic meters) of natural gas per annum by 2014, but a price has yet to be fixed.

Russia's New Energy Strategy

The *Energy Strategy of Russia for the Period up to 2030* was approved by the Russian government in November 2009 and published in 2010, but its implementation is still under way. Therefore, it is too soon to know whether Russia will effectively succeed in realizing all of its objectives. The outcome is likely to be influenced by domestic dynamics within Russia's energy sector, geopolitical and geoeconomic developments in Eurasia, and the alignment of Russia's foreign policy. One thing is certain, however: Russia will remain a major actor in the global energy system and is not likely to loosen control over energy production and exports or end its strategic interactions with its energy firms and its assertive pipeline diplomacy. Indeed, its strategy emphasizes that the "[d]evelopment and implementation of the foreign energy policy is based on the principle of ... synchronized activity of the state and energy companies, mechanisms of control and monitoring, [and] determination to achieve the shared result."

According to the latest data provided by the strategy statement, Russia should produce up to 535 million tons of oil and 3,084 billion cubic feet (940 billion cubic meters) of gas by 2030. The strategy plans for exports of 330 million tons of oil (an increase of 86 million tons compared to 2008) and 1,207 billion cubic feet (368 billion cubic meters) of gas (an increase of 636 billion cubic feet or 194 billion cubic meters compared to 2008) by 2030.

Furthermore, as noted by Alexei Gromov, the deputy director of Russia's Institute of Energy Strategy, an important point of the strategy is to "support the Russian gas companies" in the E&P of gas fields as well as "building gas-transport infrastructure abroad" and widening the "integrated gas-transporting system between Europe and Asia" so as to give Moscow the upper hand in the management of energy flows. On this point the strategy is clear: "Russian pipeline infrastructure will become an integral part of the 'power bridge' between Europe and Asia, and Russia will become the key center of its management."

According to Gromov, the strategy aims at shifting from a "resource-based and export-oriented" economy to an "innovative economy" further integrated into the global energy system. The strategy aims at reducing the share of the energy sector in the structure of gross domestic product from 30 percent to 18 percent by 2030.

To this end, Russia's new strategy is based on three critical stages: (1) the "engine" stage (2009–13), with economic recovery and investment to create a "backlog" of massive construction and renovation of Russia's energy production assets and infrastructure; (2) the "innovative designer" stage (2015–20), entailing investment in "capital-intensive projects" to modernize the material and technical base of the Russian fuel and energy complex; and (3) the "innovative development" stage (2022–30), during which energy development will be based on new technologies, modern equipment, and new "operating principals," as well as the development of alternative energy sources.

The strategy also seems to recognize the need to increase investment in the energy complex. Indeed, during the three stages, the strategy provides for investments of about $1.8 trillion to $2.2 trillion, of which $609 billion to $625 billion will be for the oil industry, $565 billion to $590 billion for the gas industry, and $483 billion for energy transportation and production infrastructure. That said, the share of foreign direct investment accounts for only 12 percent of the entire investment structure provided in the strategy.

GUILLAUME MASCOTTO

Further Reading

Chun, Hongchan. "Russia's Energy Diplomacy Toward Europe and Northeast Asia: A Comparative Study." *Asia Europe Journal* 7, no. 2 (June 2009).

Goldman, Marshall. *Petrostate: Putin, Power and the New Russia*. New York: Oxford University Press. 2008.

Ministry of Energy of the Russian Federation. *Energy Strategy of Russia for the Period up to 2030*. Moscow: Institute of Energy Strategy, 2010. http://www.energystrategy.ru/projects/docs/ES-2030_(Eng).pdf.

Perović, Jeronim, et al, eds. *Russian Energy Power and Foreign Relations: Implications for Conflict and Cooperation*. New York: Routledge, 2009.

Perović, Jeronim, et al. "Russia's Role for Global Energy Security." In *Energy and the Transformation of International Relations*, edited by Andreas Wenger, Robert Orttung, and Jeronim Perović. New York: Oxford University Press, 2009.

Russian Federal State Statistics Service. *Russia's Regions: Socio-Economic Indicators in 2007*. Moscow: Rosstat, 2007. http://www.gks.ru/bgd/regl/b07_14p/IssWWW.exe/Stg/d02/13-15.htm.

U.S. Energy Information Administration. "Country Analysis Brief: Russia." http://www.eia.doe.gov/cabs/russia/pdf.pdf.

See Also: Chernobyl; Georgia (Nation); International Energy Agency; Nationalization; Natural Gas; Oil and Gas Pipelines; Oil and Petroleum; Sakharov, Andrei.

Rwanda

Official Name: Republic of Rwanda.
Category: Geography of Energy.
Summary: Rwanda faces a number of energy challenges, including widespread deforestation due to uncontrolled fuelwood consumption, dependence on imported energy sources, and unreliable electricity generation and distribution.

Rwanda's population density is one of the highest in sub-Saharan Africa, with an annual growth rate of 2.8 percent as of 2008. Much of the population lives in rural communities and relies on localized energy sources, such as wood. There is low reliance on the national grid; only 4 or 5 percent of the population has access. For those who are connected, per capita consumption is estimated at 720 kilowatt-hours per person per year.

Installed electricity generation capacity was approximately 72 megawatts as of 2009. The gap in demand is filled through imports from the Democratic Republic of the Congo and Uganda. In-country energy production comes primarily from wood and biomass (80–86 percent), hydrocarbon (petroleum), hydropower, and renewables. Because of major gaps in supply and demand, electricity supply is commonly shut off, resulting in a number of individuals, as well as companies, using diesel-powered generators.

Biomass, in the form of firewood, charcoal, or agricultural residues, is used mostly for cooking in Rwandan households, as well as by some industries. Use of firewood is not only common in rural areas, where it is consumed by 90 percent of households, but there are also high consumption rates in urban areas (40 percent) and the capital of Kigali (25 percent), according to Developing Renewables (2011).

Almost all of the firewood (80 percent) used is foraged and therefore does not contribute to a market economy. While consumers may not be open to alternatives that have associated costs, creating a market will encourage efforts to develop environmentally friendly alternatives and reduce the time spent by households for collecting firewood. Fuelwood consumption is expected to increase in the near term, yet the country is already seeing major deficits as well as impacts from deforestation. The government aims to nearly eliminate fuelwood consumption by 2020 and to reforest areas that have been depleted. Efforts are also under way to improve efficiency of the cookstoves in order to reduce demand for firewood.

Rwanda does not have its own petroleum supply and instead depends on imported products from neighboring countries. Petroleum products are used to power diesel generators (which make up 42 percent of the electricity produced by the county) and are also used by the transportation sector. While natural gas is currently not produced or consumed by the country, there are proven natural gas reserves, and several projects are under way to expand this sector.

Management and Development

From 1973 to 2008, Electrogaz (which previously existed under a different name) was responsible for Rwanda's electricity production and supply. In 2008, the company was split into the Rwanda Energy Corporation and the Rwanda Water and Sanitation Corporation. In 2010, the two merged to form the Energy, Water and Sanitation Corporation (EWSC). EWSC is involved in coordination of all activities involving exploitation of energy resources, sanitation, management of electricity infrastructure, and waste management.

Rwanda has a number of undeveloped renewable reserves. Peat is estimated at 155 million tons and could replace wood, charcoal, and fuel oil. Lake Kivu also provides a geothermal resource, with potential power generation estimated at 170 to 320 megawatts. Wind and solar potential are also being explored through support from international investors and governments. Although the country of Rwanda has faced a number of political and economic challenges, it has begun to attract foreign investment in the energy sector.

With assistance from the World Bank and other international financial lending institutions, efforts are under way to deregulate the power sector, conduct feasibility studies on energy alternatives, and

▷ *Alternative Energy Sources*

Rwanda has a number of alternative and renewable energy sources that are in development. Lake Kivu is expected to be a major contributor to the electric grid through extraction of methane gas. The estimated reserves are 40 million tons of oil equivalent, or 900 megawatts generated annually over a 55-year period. While construction and operating costs are expected to be low, this resource has not yet been fully utilized, given political and economic problems in Rwanda and other countries bordering the lake. There are also concerns regarding environmental impacts, should leakage occur during extraction.

Ntaruka and Mukungwa hydropower stations, located in the Northern Province and supplied by Lakes Burera and Ruhondo, are major contributors to Rwanda's electricity grid. With falling lake-water levels since the mid-2000s, production has dropped significantly. The two stations collectively had the potential for 23.5 megawatts of power, but they produce only about one-quarter of this amount, which has had a significant impact on Rwanda's energy supply. Rwanda also generates hydroelectric energy through shared operations with Burundi and the Democratic Republic of the Congo. Additional agreements to connect with Uganda and Tanzania would increase supply and distribution. It is estimated that Rwanda has a hydroelectric potential of 100 megawatts through the use of small hydroelectric stations and micro-hydroelectric stations.

World Bank/Arne Hoel

A methane gas extraction plant on Lake Kivu in Gisenyi, Rwanda. The site's estimated methane gas reserves are the equivalent of 40 million tons of oil, or 900 megawatts generated annually for more than 55 years.

increase production and distribution across the country.

STACY VYNNE

Further Reading

Developing Renewables. "Country Energy Information: Rwanda." http://www.energyrecipes .org/reports/genericData/Africa/061129%20 RECIPES%20country%20info%20 Rwanda.pdf.

Energy, Water and Sanitation Corporation. "Our History." http://www.ewsa.rw/overview.html.

Kironde, E. G., ed. *Rwanda Environment Management Authority.* http://www.rema.gov.rw/soe/full.pdf.

Sustainable Energy Africa. *Poverty-Environment-Energy Linkages in Rwanda.* http://www.unpei.org /PDF/Rwanda-Pov-env-energy-linkages.pdf.

U.S. Energy Information Administration. "Country Analysis Brief: Rwanda." http://www.eia.gov/ countries/country-data.cfm?fips=RW.

See Also: Biomass Energy; Burundi; Congo, Democratic Republic of the; Hydropower; Methane; Natural Gas; Peat; War.